CULTURAL AND HISTORICAL GROUNDING FOR HISPANIC AND LUSO-BRAZILIAN FEMINIST LITERARY CRITICISM

Hernán Vidal
Editor

SERIES
LITERATURE AND HUMAN RIGHTS Nº4

INSTITUTE FOR THE STUDY OF IDEOLOGIES AND LITERATURE
MINNEAPOLIS MINNESOTA

This volume is Nº4 of the series
Literature and Human Rights.
Published by
the Institute for the Study of Ideologies and Literature
3840 Sheridan Ave. So.
Minneapolis, MN 55410

Editor-in-chief
Hernán Vidal
Associate Editors
José Cerna-Bazán & Gustavo Remedi

Cover and logo design by Studio 87501, Santa Fe, New Mexico

The editors gratefully acknowledge the contribution from
the Program for Cultural Cooperation between Spain's Ministry of
Culture and United States Universities and
the Office of the Deans, College of Liberal Arts, University of
Minnesota towards this edition.

ISBN 1-877660-01-9
ISSN 0893-9438 Series Literature and Human Rights

Library of Congress Cataloging-in-Publication Data

Cultural and historical grounding for Hispanic and Luso-Brazilian
    feminist literary criticism / Hernán Vidal, editor. —1st ed.
    p. cm.   — (Literature and human rights, ISSN 0893-9438 ; no. 4)
    English and Spanish.
    "Trabajos presentados en la conferencia internacional realizada
en la Universidad de Minnesota entre el 31 de marzo y el 2 de abril,
1988, bajo el título de Cultural and Historical Grounding for Hispanic
and Luso-Brazilian Feminist Literary Criticism/Bases Culturales e
Históricas para la Crítica Literaria Feminista Hispánica y Luso-
Brasileira"—Introd.
    Bibliography: p.
    ISBN 1-877660-01-9 : $14.95
    1. Latin American literature—History and criticism—Congresses.
2. Spanish literature—History and criticism—Congresses.
3. Feminist literary criticism—Congresses. 4. Feminism and
literature—Congresses.   I. Vidal, Hernán. II. Series.
    PQ7081.A1C85 1989
    860.9'98—dc20   89-11192
                                                  CIP

TABLE OF CONTENTS

INTRODUCCION

Hernán Vidal

University of Minnesota, Minneapolis

Esta edición reune la mayoría de los trabajos presentados en la conferencia internacional realizada en la Universidad de Minnesota entre el 31 de marzo y el 2 de abril, 1988, bajo el título de *Cultural and Historical Grounding for Hispanic and Luso-Brazilian Feminist Literary Criticism/Bases Culturales e Históricas para la Crítica Literaria Feminista Hispánica y Luso-Brasilera.* Casi todos fueron discutidos en las sesiones; un pequeño número fue solicitado como reacción a las problemáticas planteadas.

Como estrategia de presentación de estos estudios sería cómodo sintetizar globalmente sus proposiciones. Sin embargo, pienso que esto equivale a prejuiciar la aproximación del lector, a quien, por lo demás, lo asiste su propio criterio informado. No deseo caer en tal arbitrariedad. Por tanto, estimo menos redundante y mucho más productivo dar una perspectiva sobre la dinámica de la discusión, tanto durante los preparativos para la conferencia como en las sesiones de trabajo, pues ello puede contribuir al entendimiento de una instancia de creación de crítica literaria feminista.

Los preparativos para toda conferencia necesitan del perfilamiento de un foco de discusión que plantee un número de problemáticas relevantes y que oriente las conversaciones convocadas hacia un fin provechoso para el campo de investigación implicado. El enfoque propuesto para la reunión de Minnesota correspondió a las preocupaciones del Institute for the Study of Ideologies and Literature a través de los años: la promoción de aproximaciones socio-históricas al estudio de las literaturas hispánicas y lusófonas en que el crítico literario demuestre una conciencia de su propia postura ante el sentido histórico de la producción cultural.

Específicamente, se planteó a las participantes en esta conferencia una preocupación por el predominio de aproximaciones positivistas en la crítica literaria feminista en nuestro campo. Esta problemática surgió en el período de preparación de la conferencia, durante el cual se consultó la opinión de colegas involucrado/as en la evaluación de manuscritos para publicaciones profesionales. El aspecto más sobresaliente surgido de estas conversaciones preliminares fue que, en la experiencia y a juicio de nuestros consultores, circula una gran cantidad de material cuya asunción del feminismo y criterios analíticos e interpretativos se reduce a la mera aplicación instrumental de teorías ya consagradas en la crítica feminista francesa y anglosajona a una obra específica, sin que se trasluzcan las pautas culturales que motivaron al estudioso para la selección del texto estudiado ni la posible contribución de tal ejercicio a la causa feminista. Dado este tratamiento, con frecuencia este tipo de material deja la impresión de querer convertir a esas intelectuales feministas francesas y anglosajonas en monumentos a quienes debe rendirse un homenaje, más bien que la de un trabajo en que el crítico mismo elabora una concepción propia del feminismo en la cultura y en la historia como fundamento de un plan de investigación a largo plazo, del cual se desprende conscientemente la selección de las obras que deben merecer atención especial. En particular esto afecta a la crítica literaria hispanoamericana, en que se acumulan trabajos inspirados solamente por la popularidad ocasional de una autora o de una obra. En general, esto también afecta los intentos de producir antologías de autores femeninos, en que se los agrupa a través del tiempo como si representaran una comunidad indivisible, sin que se enmarque su obra en una teoría que dé cuenta de su diversidad social, étnica e histórica, creándose la imagen de una mujer arquetípica y ahistórica. Se convino en que tal problemática tenía la envergadura necesaria como para hacerla foco para las discusiones de la conferencia.

Considerando, además, que críticos de diverso origen nacional comparten un mismo campo de estudio, se sugirió a las participantes que quizás ese positivismo "monumentalista" incidiera en dos cuestiones de importancia en cuanto a la necesidad de mantener una perspectiva en lo transcultural. La primera es la continua reiteración de ciertas temáticas investigativas que, aunque de extraordinaria importancia, quizás resultaran limitadas para las preocupaciones sociales generadas por la realidad de los países hispanos y lusófonos: el silenciamiento de la voz femenina en la institucionalización de la literatura; la representación literaria de los roles mutilantes en que se socializa a las mujeres; las consecuencias de la instrumentalización de la imagen femenina para la legitimación del poder político; la exploración de un discurso literario esencialmente femenino. Segunda, dado que el gran auge de la crítica literaria feminista está relacionado con el desarrollo de los programas de estudio de la mujer en los Estados Unidos, quizás sea necesaria una meditación sobre las temáticas y teorías que desde allí se proyectan sobre la producción literaria de otras culturas. Incluso se sugirió al comité organizativo que, para mejor perfilar estas problemáticas de transferencia cultural, quizás el formato más apropiado para la discusión sería el de organizar los paneles según el origen nacional de las participantes. Esta sugerencia fue vehementemente rechazada por las participantes invitadas, aduciéndose que de algún modo introducía un divisionismo entre feministas que entienden su movimiento como una unidad. En atención a este sentimiento, las sesiones de trabajo fueron organizadas en torno a ejes temáticos comunes que integraron indiferenciadamente a peninsularistas y latinoamericanistas.

Las participantes, investigadoras de reconocida contribución a la crítica literaria feminista, fueron invitadas a la conferencia con la expectativa de que no sólo se dirigieran a la posibilidad de expandir las temáticas de la investigación literaria feminista, a la proposición de áreas de investigación a largo plazo y al comentario y evaluación de la actual teoría feminista frente a las necesidades culturales hispánicas y lusófonas, sino a que, desde su experiencia personal, también superaran los parámetros de discusión propuestos por los organizadores de la conferencia, entendiéndose que estos parámetros eran nada más que un foco de discusión amplio, flexible, que de ningún modo intentaba interpretar el estado actual de la crítica literaria feminista de las literaturas hispánicas y lusófonas.

El mérito que las participantes atribuyeron a la conferencia fue el de haber congregado por primera vez a críticas hispanistas y luso-brasileristas a compartir preocupaciones especialmente teóricas, hecho que, a su juicio, anteriormente no se había dado. En las reuniones profesionales prevalecen los trabajos de análisis textual específico. Por ello es que varias participantes dieron a la reunión la categoría de un "state of the arts"/una muestra representativa del estado actual de las capacidades, posibilidades y preocupaciones de la crítica feminista de las literaturas hispánicas y lusófonas.

Otro aspecto de consideración es que colegas que se conocían solamente a través de sus publicaciones tuvieron, finalmente, un encuentro personal. Más allá de las sesiones mismas, este contacto llevó a compartir impresiones, preocupaciones y proyectos futuros. Surgió la idea de programar conferencias anuales para dar continuidad a estos logros iniciales. Se discutió la forma de influir sobre las empresas editoriales para llevarlas a la publicación de material de utilidad para los estudios feministas hispanos y lusófonos; también se habló de la opción de iniciar una editorial especializada.

En atención a que esos proyectos nacientes pueden llegar a ser de gran importancia, me parece que, al introducir los estudios de esta edición, un aporte positivo sería el de reflexionar sobre la experiencia de la reunión de Minnesota, señalando puntos que quizás sea útil considerar en conferencias futuras. Con este propósito, en las observaciones siguientes resaltaré dos puntos que estimo centrales. En ello reuno mi propia experiencia de la conferencia y la de aquellas participantes que me entregaron sus apreciaciones.

ESTRATEGIAS DE DISCUSION COLECTIVA

La dinámica de la conferencia hace pensar que quizás haya un desfase entre la retórica de unidad del movimiento feminista y la práctica concreta de las diversas ten-

dencias teóricas presentes en ella. Esto pudo notarse en el
formato de las sesiones: por una parte se insistió en que
no se debía proceder con la "tradicional" diferenciación
entre peninsularistas, hispanoamericanistas y luso-brasileristas en sesiones separadas, tanto porque los estudios
feministas son esencialmente interdisciplinarios como
por el hecho de que, en las reuniones profesionales, son
escasas las demostraciones globales, en sesiones conjuntas,
de las problemáticas que motivan a cada área. Sin embargo, las discusiones evidenciaron una mayor preocupación política entre las latinoamericanistas, lo cual las lleva
a la búsqueda de un mayor discernimiento teórico en
cuanto a las implicaciones sociales del feminismo y de su
teoría en el contexto socio-histórico que les incumbe. Por
su parte, el trabajo y la discusión de las peninsularistas se
caracterizó por una tendencia mucho más pragmática, en
que se privilegia la investigación práctica en períodos específicos, el Siglo de Oro, por ejemplo y, muy particularmente, el siglo XIX. En éste se produjeron espontáneas
convergencias investigativas de gran interés. Pero, en especial, esa disparidad y ese desfase se revelaron en las dificultades que hubo para generar una discusión general sobre política feminista en torno al trabajo de Gabriela Mora,
lleno de ricas sugerencias para el debate, centrado, no obstante, en el medio latinoamericano.

Por otra parte, hubo evidencia de que la retórica indispensable para la configuración de la identidad y de la unidad feminista y su rechazo de las jerarquizaciones puede
entrabar el intercambio abierto y productivo entre posiciones teóricas discrepantes o la exploración más intensa
del significado profundo precisamente de esa retórica. Así
fue como un interesante debate suscitado por el trabajo de
Teresa Vilarós, entre su posición freudianista e interpela-
ciones historicistas que se le dirigieron, fue efectivamente
difuminado y terminado por una intervención que hizo
un emotivo llamado a no olvidar que el problema central
que concierne a las feministas es la opresión de la mujer y
que, frente a ello, es preciso salvaguardar tanto la unidad
como la pluralidad de las diversas posiciones feministas
de fuertes divergencias internas. Esta intervención recibió

un caluroso aplauso, pero así se clausuró la ocasión para un mejor intercambio de ideas al respecto.

Asimismo se podría señalar que la radical propuesta de Amy Kaminsky sobre el imperativo de integrar el lesbianismo a la crítica literaria latinoamericanista fue desaprovechada en aras de una discusión sobre la validez de su interpretación de la película que integró a su estudio. En una situación similar, la amplitud de la propuesta para la investigación a largo plazo hecha por Susan Kirkpatrick se diluyó en una discusión excesivamente larga del símbolo de la aguja como significación retórico-existencial para la mujer, longura que hizo que un tema de importancia se extraviara finalmente en la nimiedad. Si mi observación es correcta, no se trataría simplemente de instancias de mala fortuna en la elección de las moderadoras de paneles, quienes debieron haber ejercido la autoridad que se les delegara para recentrar la discusión, volviéndola a su cauce principal, sino que la gravitación del aspecto retórico y su imperativo de evitar el conflicto para proteger una imagen de unidad feminista no jerarquizante crean las condiciones para que todo un grupo de participantes permita tales desviaciones y se sume a ellas.

¿Cómo diseñar mejores formatos y protocolos de reunión que permitan una unidad que a la vez dé cabida aun a las más fuertes discrepancias? Al respecto sería de importancia considerar las observaciones de Susan Kirkpatrick en cuanto a que aun las más fuertes divergencias e inseguridades teóricas y políticas en el trabajo de la crítica literaria feminista pueden constelarse en un todo productivo, si es que se fijan tareas consensual y claramente delimitadas, tareas a las que cada perspectiva puede hacer una contribución sin difuminar ni tergiversar su identidad específica. Si esta apreciación es recogida, la mejor estrategia de investigación y discusión futura podría gestarse en torno a temas y áreas consensualmente designadas y especificadas de antemano, dispositivo ya practicado por grupos feministas regionales. Generalizar esta práctica promovería la investigación programática, a largo plazo, con mayor conciencia de las necesidades del movimiento, con un cierto grado de organicidad de coordinación que cree la atmósfera de cordialidad básica necesaria para airear y escuchar aun las más fuertes discrepancias, sin que se cuestione que hacerlo implica una falta contra la unidad en una causa. Esto es difícil de lograr en el medio académico, que más bien promueve el trabajo aislado, con ocasionales contactos en congresos profesionales. En cuanto a esto, es sugerente que un buen número de participantes sólo se conociera a través de sus publicaciones.

LA CONCIENCIA INTERDISCIPLINARIA

En particular se me sugirió que esta introducción debía dedicar cierto espacio a la discusión ocurrida en torno al término castellano "género" en la crítica literaria feminista hispánica como traducción de la palabra inglesa "gender", que hace una diferenciación social con respecto a la categoría biológica "sex". La participante que promovió la discusión manifestó incomodidad con el término castellano, puesto que, al contrario del inglés, su enorme variedad de significados lo hace ambiguo. Frente a este problema, propuso la necesidad de crear un nuevo término para reemplazarlo. En el debate se manejaron términos aclaratorios como "género social", "género cultural", "sistema genérico", sin que se llegara a ningún acuerdo.

La audacia de la propuesta responde a la lógica de las argumentaciones académicas del feminismo, entre cuyas tareas se incluye el cuestionamiento de las categorías epistemológicas que consciente o inconscientemente sostienen el orden social patriarcalista. No obstante, a mi parecer, la discusión no prosperó porque se la ubicó puramente a nivel léxico —la "incomodidad" con el significado difuso de una palabra—, sin ninguna referencia a su horizonte semántico, que, sin duda, está en su elaboración por las ciencias sociales y no en la lexicografía ni en la crítica literaria. De hecho, ninguna de las participantes adujo a la discusión los antecedentes de su uso en la sociología y en la antropología como para calibrar la posibilidad, la necesidad y la validez reales de crear un nuevo término de reemplazo.

Como ocurre con frecuencia en una disciplina de aspiraciones científicas, callejones sin salida como este debate inconcluso tienen la ventaja de servir de síntoma iluminador de una problemática subyacente que es necesario traer a la superficie para crear una conciencia más ajustada y real de las opciones de investigación futura. En este caso particular, creo que la carencia de una perspectiva proveniente de las ciencias sociales en el debate y su reducción meramente a un nivel lexicográfico apunta a dos órdenes de problemas. El primero sólo quiero mencionarlo de paso, porque no tiene prioridad en una ocasión como esta. Me refiero a la frecuente práctica de muchas críticas literarias feministas de discutir las categorías sociales que conciernen a la condición de la mujer de modo mediatizado, echando mano de la forma en que las han adoptado pensadoras feministas francesas y anglosajonas de prestigio ya establecido —quienes las utilizaron para reaccionar a la situación muy acotada de su sociedad—, sin también compulsarlas directamente con sus fuentes en la filosofía social. Aunque esta mediatización pueda ser provechosa en cuanto a solidificar la identidad diferencial de la investigación feminista, se corre el peligro de entender el radicalismo epistemológico como un mero juego lexicográfico de creación de nuevos términos.

El segundo orden tiene que ver con el sentido que pueda tener el trabajo interdisciplinario para las crítica literaria, meta anunciada de los estudios feministas. ¿Qué entendemos, realmente, por estudios interdisciplinarios? Una definición de lo que se puede entender por investigación interdisciplinaria es cuestión resbaladiza en extremo. Se podría argüir que, en realidad, hay tres grandes concepciones al respecto: quizás la más genuina es la constitución de un equipo de trabajo, en que quedan representadas diferentes disciplinas de las ciencias sociales y de las humanidades, con alto grado de acuerdo doctrinario, de conciencia y de perspectiva social, equipo que, por tanto, puede fijarse a sí mismo un programa de trabajo que responda a objetivos estrechamente conectados con esa perspectiva y conciencia social. Sobre la base de ese acuerdo, la solución de las agendas colectivas planteadas permite al equipo un intenso intercambio de conocimiento que, en el transcurso de las tareas, lleva a una interpenetración de las diferentes lógicas de cada una de las disciplinas participantes, hasta un grado tal en que se puede afirmar que no sólo los estudios producidos forman un caleidoscopio de diferentes perspectivas sobre un mismo objeto, profundamente unidas por un núcleo de concepciones teóricas homogéneas, sino que, además, cada uno de los miembros del equipo ha alcanzado una organicidad totalizadora de su visión de mundo.

No es esta la definición de interdisciplinariedad que predomina en un medio académico como el nuestro, en que, por las características de su institucionalización de las humanidades, cultiva, más bien, un trabajo individualista orientado por el juicio subjetivo del investigador, desenfatizándose, a la vez, cualquiera homogenización de criterios en aras del libre mercado de las ideas. En estas condiciones, generalmente se entiende por interdisciplinariedad la ocasional reunión de expertos en diferentes ciencias para dar su opinión sobre un tópico designado, sin que medie un trabajo colectivo en que la lógica de cada una de las disciplinas llegue a interpenetrarse en una visión orgánica de conjunto. Si es que se busca realmente esta organicidad interdisciplinaria, ello ocurre por el interés de investigadores aislados, que inician programas de lecturas en otras disciplinas, con el propósito de explorar modos de trasladar sus categorías epistemológicas y discursivas a la disciplina propia, a menudo exponiéndose no sólo a cargos de diletantismo y de positivismo, sino también al fracaso rotundo en sus intentos interpretativos. Sectores importantes de la crítica literaria hispanista y luso-brasilerista han buscado evitar estos cargos abandonando toda aspiración interdisciplinaria, cualquiera sea su definición, para concentrarse únicamente en los parámetros de su disciplina.

Frente al dilema esbozado, ¿qué podría significar el debate inconcluso al que me refiero? Al respecto surgen cuestiones de orden organizativo e intelectual, en estrecha relación mutua. Dada la ausencia de la perspectiva más amplia de las ciencias sociales en la discusión, se podría argüir que las participantes en la conferencia no han tomado una resolución clara en cuanto al modo en que entenderán el sentido de los estudios interdisciplinarios, lo cual, sin duda, afectará los trabajos futuros del grupo. Si es así, en futuras reuniones de críticas literarias hispanistas y luso-brasileristas como la ocurrida en la Universidad de Minnesota se debería presupuestar tiempo y paneles para determinar la definición de interdisciplinariedad a seguir, quizás con la asesoría de feministas en las ciencias sociales que ayuden a establecer una discusión de lecturas teóricas comunes, paralelamente con los trabajos prácticos programados en la disciplina propia.

Lo anterior de nuevo trae al tapete de la discusión las apreciaciones de Susan Kirkpatrick y los trabajos de grupos feministas regionales en cuanto a la búsqueda de una cierta organicidad en las tareas comunes. Pero, a la vez, esto también vuelve a llamar la atención sobre las estrategias prioritarias para la investigación en un medio académico que más bien tiende, según decía con anterioridad, a un alto grado de dispersión de esfuerzos en aras del libre mercado de las ideas. Y es que, en justicia, ¿hasta qué punto estamos preparados a abandonar la concreción inmediata de nuestra investigación individual para sumarnos a proyectos de investigación interdisciplinaria colectiva todavía no bien definidos? Me parece que aquí yace el desafío central que deben enfrentar las participantes en reuniones futuras.

LA DISPOSICION TEXTUAL DE LOS TRABAJOS RECOLECTADOS

La relevancia de estas apreciaciones generales y, en particular, las del acápite anterior, quedan validadas en el agrupamiento mismo de los estudios contenidos en esta edición. Este sigue, en buena medida, el sentido temático de los paneles organizados para la conferencia. Aunque, en general, todos los trabajos son producto de investigaciones individuales, se podrá comprobar, que la sección primera, titulada *Perspectivas y Cuestionamientos*, reune un conjunto abigarrado que, a mi juicio, claramente expone la dispersión de esfuerzos que caracteriza al mercado liberal de las ideas. Por el contrario, la sección segunda — *El Siglo XIX Peninsular y Latinoamericano*— demuestra un apreciable grado de organicidad temática y también de orientación teórica y tácticas investigativas basadas en una preocupación por la cotidianidad de la mujer y en el desvelamiento ideológico del uso de la figura femenina como ícono para la legitimación del poder social hegemónico. En parte esta organicidad se debe a que un pequeño núcleo de estas investigadoras mantiene relaciones de origen académico y de amistad personal que parecen haber cimentado preocupaciones intelectuales similares. Pero la organicidad de este pequeño grupo debe ser puesta en la perpectiva mayor y más importante de la convergencia espontánea de interés y tácticas mostradas por el resto de los contribuyentes a esta sección, quienes no han tenido tales lazos. Digo que tal perpectiva mayor es de más importancia porque, a mi juicio, la organicidad espontánea de esta sección evidencia la búsqueda inconsciente y la viabilidad factible de un proyecto intelectual colectivo. ¿Qué tendencia primará en reuniones futuras para el perfilamiento más intenso de una identidad más diferenciada para una crítica literaria feminista de las literaturas hispánicas y lusófonas?, ¿la dispersión de esfuerzos que por sobre todo valora el pluralismo ideológico, o la concertación de esfuerzos que por sobre las diferenciaciones ideológicas consensualmente establezca tareas comunes bien delimitadas?

Los colegas interesados en participar en las reuniones de crítica literaria feminista que se programan para el futuro en la Universidad de Minnesota deben dirigirse a:

Prof. Joanna O'Connell
Dept. of Spanish & Portuguese
5C Folwell Hall
University of Minnesota
Minneapolis, Minnesota 55455
(612)-625-0110

PRIMERA PARTE

PERSPECTIVAS Y CUESTIONAMIENTOS

Feminist Criticism of Hispanic and Lusophone Literatures: Bibliographic Notes and Considerations

Naomi Lindstrom
University of Texas, Austin

The first part of this paper will be a historical review of the routes by which feminist criticism made its way into the academic study of Latin American, including Luso-Brazilian, and Spanish literatures. The criticism of Chicano writing and Portuguese and less-studied Lusophone literatures will also be cited; though there are fewer studies in these latter categories, they also illustrate the tendencies under discussion. The emphasis is on those associations, events, and publications that first brought feminism into literary discussion and hence gave it the image and the forms it most typically assumed. Attention also goes to the ways in which these early-established conduits of intellectual exchange have evolved, especially as they cease to be isolated, pioneering efforts and become specialized outlets of discussion in an environment where feminism has gained a measure of mainstream presence. The paper then presents a listing of significant feminist criticism of these literatures that appeared in book form or published in mainstream journals, once commentary of this type had attained access to these outlets. Finally, it offers evaluative comments on the directions this criticism has taken and those it might most productively explore in its search for a historical and cultural grounding as well as for stimulating and intellectually worthwhile forms of literary discussion.

Feminist criticism has, in recent years, increased so greatly in prominence that it is easy to forget that there is a long history of debate over sex roles, considerations of the real and ideal images of women, and applications of such forms of discussion to the study of literary works. The history of feminist criticism up to the current-day movement toward women's studies would, in itself, provide the sub-

ject matter of a lengthy survey. Here, however, only the
modern variants of feminist thought in literary criticism
receive attention; the works cited are from the 1970s and
1980s, some reflecting research underway in the 1960s.
While it is certainly not ideal to separate of recent feminism from its historical roots, in compiling these notes it
has been necessary to keep the survey of manageable extension. Perhaps on another occasion it will be possible to
place currently prevalent forms of literary feminism and
feminist criticism in the historical perspective in which
they ought to be seen.

With the decade of the 1970s, there arises a deliberate
and widespread attempt to extend feminist principles, then
enjoying widespread circulation in the general climate of
social thought, to the discussion of literary texts. From its
inception, feminist criticism faces certain fundamental
questions of orientation. How much importance should be
given to the male or female authorship of a text, or to
"feminine" qualities that may be perceived in writing?
Should feminist criticism seek to distinguish itself from
other forms of literary commentary by developing its own
unique extensions of theory, or should it be understood as
a set of issues that may be explored through existing forms
of theory and criticism? In the case of literatures outside
Western Europe and the United States, what measures are
necessary to avoid a misapplication of feminist thought as
elaborated largely in French-, English-, and German-lan-
guage literary cultures? Certainly it is true of English-lan-
guage literary cultures that feminist criticism made its initial impact through denunciatory treatments of works by
male authors, who were held responsible for the statements their texts generated concerning men and women.
Kate Millett's 1970 *Sexual Politics* (Garden City: Doubleday)
provided the still-rough model on which subsequent feminists would work refinements. This type of critical writing, though, was not the point of entry for feminist
thought as it began to affect the Spanish- and Portuguese-
language literary worlds. The validity of applying the Millett model directly to Hispanic studies came in for questioning in a polemic in *Journal of Spanish Studies: Twentieth Century*. Patricia O'Connor's Millett-patterned

"Francisco García Pavón's Sexual Politics in the Plinio Novels," 1.1 (1973): 65-81, drew a rebuttal from Birgitta Vance in the latter's "The Great Clash: Feminist Literary Criticism Meets Up with Spanish Reality," 2.2 (1974): 109-114. Vance argued that García Pavón's representation of female characters, while it might strike U.S. readers as narrow-mindedly stereotypical, in large part simply reflected the tighter constraints on women's behavior and expression already present in Spanish society. An ensuing exchange appears in 2.3 (1974): 193-96.

Despite the limitations inherent in this negative criticism, intelligent critics have on occasion used allegations of sexism as the point of departure for comments with wider implications. For instance, Martha Paley Francescato, "The New Man (But Not the New Woman)," *Books Abroad* 50.3 (1976): 589-95, rptd. Jaime Alazraki and Ivar Ivask, eds., *The Final Island: The Fiction of Julio Cortázar* (Norman: U of Oklahoma P, 1976): 134-39. Paley Francescato, in pointing out disparities in Julio Cortázar's treatment of male and female characters, suggests that these contradictions betray a lack of principled system in the author's vigorously-proclaimed progressive social thought and a split between announced ideal and novelistic practice.

A more extensive example is Walnice Nogueira Galão, "Amado: respeitoso, respeitável," collected in her *Saco de gatos: ensaios críticos* (São Paulo: Livraria Duas Cidades, 1976) 13-22. The identification of crudely biased characterizations leads to considerations of why an author displaying such an outlook should continue to enjoy an image as a progressive writer. The essay not only looks at unjust literary representations of women but also at the mechanisms that allow such features of literature to go unperceived and uncommented upon, and constitutes well as a meditation on the social responsibility of writers and their commentators.

Instead of a search for the literary perpetuation of sexism, feminist criticism made itself known in Spanish- and Portuguese-speaking countries primarily through a renewed interest in and promotion of texts written by women. The principal wrong that literary feminism first set out to correct was not the unjust depiction of women characters or women's culture, but the lack of attention or esteem accorded women's writing. Various activities have sought to bring to women's texts new readers, both general reading publics and those based in colleges and universities. The first Congreso Internacional de Escritoras Latinoamericanas was held at Carnegie-Mellon University in 1975 (Yvette Miller, organizer); the proceedings were issued by the Latin American Literary Review Press as *Latin American Women Writers: Yesterday and Today* (1978). The Congreso has since met at irregular intervals and given rise to other similar events. The proceedings volumes to emerge from these meetings are, among other things, telling historical evidence of the issues that most engaged feminist critics at a given moment. For example, while the 1975 volume emphasizes women's awareness of their situation in society, the 1982 *La sartén por el mango: actas del Congreso de Escritoras Latinoamericanas* (San Juan, P.R.: Huracán, 1983), edited by Patricia González and Eliana Ortega, shows feminist critics struggling to determine whether women's writing has textual characteristics that distinguish it from the work of male authors. An emphasis on hypothesizing distinctive features of women's expression also characterizes a conference that has come into being in the second half of the 1980s: Creación Femenina en el Mundo Hispánico. These sessions, held at the Mayagüez and Río Piedras campuses of the Universidad de Puerto Rico, involve creative artists displaying or performing their work, as well as commentators.

An alternative type of project, typically resulting in more focused critical texts than the often dispersed proceedings volumes, has been to bring together critics who agree upon a common approach and produce papers on a given topic. An early example of such an enterprise is Vicente Cicchitti et al., *La mujer, símbolo del mundo nuevo* (Buenos Aires: Fernando García Cambeiro, 1976), which evaluates the portrayal of women and womanly qualities without concern for the sex of the author. The essays are all aligned with an attempt to create a hermeneutical, Peronist criticism following a pattern set by Leopoldo Marechal, together with theoretical infusions from archetypal studies, Third World thought, and other sources. Whatever one may make of this extremely interpretive system with its heavy load of religious and political doctrine, it does make the volume unusually coherent in a field where critical unanimity is rare.

Thematically specialized journals and newsletters also began to appear in response to the resurgence of interest in women's writing and women's representation in literature. The Asociación de Literatura Femenina publishes the journal *Letras Femeninas*. This organization, as it was run by Victoria Urbano until her death in 1984, sponsored a variety of activities: publications of critical studies and creative works, and special discussion sessions and readings at conferences of learned associations.

The Asociación and *Letras Femeninas*, now under the guidance of Adelaida López Martínez, have moved toward more thematically specific events and journal issues. Especially deserving of mention is the I Simposio Internacional de la Asociación de Literatura Femenina Hispánica in New Orleans (April 1984), distinguished by its focus on a single figure, Sor Juana Inés de la Cruz. The conference resulted in the special double issue of *Letras Femeninas* 11.1-2 (1985), *Sor Juana Inés de la Cruz. México 1651-1695*. Also characteristic of the new tendency is the thematic issue 12.4 1-2 (1986), *Voces femeninas en la literatura de la guerra civil española: una valoración crítica al medio siglo de historia 1936-1986*.

Among publications dedicated specifically to the discussion of women's issues and women's culture in Spanish-speaking countries, one should particularly point out the Mexico City-based *fem*. It has been successful in bringing together literary work, cultural criticism, and social analysis from writers living and working in many countries. It also is unusually strong in its historical view of feminism, drawing attention to the lengthy tradition of questioning standardly assigned male and female roles.

A related enterprise, of importance during the years when feminism was first entering literary studies, was the organization of bulletins, circulars, and bibliographies to disseminate information on women writers, feminist essayists, and their work. Kathleen O'Quinn originated the

San Francisco-based Clearinghouse on Latin American Women Authors, active in the early and mid-seventies. Diane E. Marting, during this same period, began coordinating, at first as a shoestring operation with bibliographical listings circulated in Xerox, the projects that would eventually result in the section "Spanish America," Margery Resnick and Isabelle de Courtviron, eds., *Women Writers in Translation: An Annotated Bibliography, 1945-1982* (New York: Garland, 1984), 227-46, and *Women Writers of Spanish America: An Annotated Bio-Bibliographical Guide* (Westport CT: Greenwood, 1987). Marting continues her reference and bibliographic work, currently organizing *Fifty Spanish American Women Writers*, under contract to Greenwood Press. As the listing of works later in this paper shows, providing bibliographic guidance to researchers working on women writers has since become the concern of a number of scholars and publishing firms.

Feministas Unidas is a group organized during the annual conventions of the Modern Language Association. Beginning as an informal network, it has attained the status of an allied organization of the MLA. It sponsors a newsletter, *Feministas Unidas*, and publicizes events of special interest to feminist critics attending MLA meetings. Indiana University's Chicano-Riqueña Studies program, which produces the journal *Third Woman*, has long been active as a coordinating center for matters concerning U.S. Latina writers. While the above organizations and publications are mentioned for their early work in bringing together the area of studies, many more have since arisen and fulfill varied functions.

* * *

Important in stimulating interest in women's writings were the new anthologies of such texts, often edited so as to showcase the work of women writers considered to have been unjustly neglected. In other cases, both male- and female-authored works have been included, the criterion being their ability to illustrate perceptions of women and of issues affecting women.

Anthologies of both Spanish and Latin American writing include:

Flores, Angel, and Kate Flores, eds. *Hispanic Feminist Poems from the Middle Ages to the Present.* New York: Feminist P at the City U of New York, 1986. [In series *The Defiant Muse*].

Spanish peninsular anthologies include:

Martín Gamero, Amalia, ed., *Antología del feminismo.* Madrid: Alianza, 1975.

Navajo, Imelda. *Doce relatos de mujeres.* Madrid: Alianza, 1983.

Zapata, Celia de, ed. *Detrás de la reja.* Buenos Aires: Ediciones de la Flor, 1980. Caracas: Monte Avila, 1980.

Latin American [including Chicano] anthologies include:

Agosin, Marjorie, and Cola Franzen, eds. *The Renewal of the Vision: Voices of Latin American Women Poets 1940-1980.* Peterborough, England: Spectacular Diseases, 1987.

Boza, María del Carmen, Beverly Silva, and Carmen Valle, eds. *Nosotras: Latina Literature Today.* Tempe AZ: Bilingual Press/Editorial Bilingüe, 1986.

Crow, Mary, ed. *Woman Who Has Sprouted Wings: Poems by Contemporary Latin American Women Poets.* Pittsburgh: Latin American Literary Review Press, 1984.

Denser, Márcia, ed. *O prazer é todo meu: contos eróticos femininos.* Rio: Editora Record, 1984.

Donoso Correa, Nina. *Poesía femenina chilena.* Santiago: Editorial Nacional Gabriela Mistral, 1974.

Gómez, Alma, Cherríe Moraga, and Mariana Romo-Carmona, eds. *Cuentos: Stories by Latinas.* San Francisco: Kitchen Table Press, 1982.

Handelsman, Michael H. *Diez escritoras ecuatorianas y sus cuentos.* Quito: Casa de la Cultura Ecuatoriana, 1982.

Manguel, Alberto, ed. *Other Fires: Short Fiction by Latin American Women*. Avenal NJ: Clarkson N. Potter, 1986.

Meyer, Doris, and Margarite Fernández Olmos, eds., *Contemporary Women Authors of Latin America: New Translations* (Brooklyn: Brooklyn College, 1983).

Prado, Adélia, et al. *Mulheres & mulheres*. Rio: Nova Fronteira, 1978. [Includes men and women authors].

Sefchovich, Sara, ed. *Mujeres en espejo*. México: Folios Ediciones, 1983. *Mujeres en espejo 2*. México: Folios Ediciones, 1985.

Silva-Velásquez, Caridad L., and Nora Erro-Orthman, eds. *Puerta abierta, la nueva escritora latinoamericana*. México: Joaquín Mortiz, 1986.

Steen, Edla van, ed. *O conto da mulher brasileira*. São Paulo: Vertente Editora, 1978.

Vigil, Evangelina, ed. *Woman of her Word: Hispanic Women Write*. Houston: Arte Público, 1984.

Villegas, Juan. *Antología de la nueva poesía femenina chilena*. Santiago: La Noria, 1985.

Weiser, Nora Jacquez, ed. *Open to the Sun: A Bilingual Anthology of Latin American Women Poets*. Van Nuys, California: Perivale Press, 1981.

Young, Ann Venture. *The Image of Black Women in 20th Century South American Poetry: A Bilingual Anthology*. Washington DC: Three Continents Press, 1987. [Includes men and women authors].

* * *

The next category of feminist works is book-length studies. These include monographic essays by a single author as well as collections of essays. The works listed range from detailed analyses of particular textual or historical problems to essentially informative, panoramic overviews of a given sector of women's writing or writing about women; bibliographic research guides are also included. In compiling this listing, an effort has been made to include those works that show significant traces of the new interest in feminism. Conversely, the goal has been to exclude studies that pursue some longstanding theme of discussion in Hispanic and Luso-Brazilian studies, such as the conventional literary idealization of female beauty or the representation of women's virtues and vices, unless there is some visible infusion of feminist thought as it has been developed in recent years. Literary commentary based on Jungian or archetypal notions of male and female has been included only if it takes into account the social and cultural implications of concepts of gender. An ahistorical view of archetypes in literature, however concerned it may be with women and femininity, cannot be an extension of recent feminist thought, which arises from a critical examination of phenomena existing historically in real-world societies.

Contemporary feminism has affected not only works whose most evident function is to help frame the discussion of gender questions in literature, but also author studies. An example is the criticism on María Luisa Bombal, which in recent years has been increasingly likely to draw on feminist thought. Examples include Hernán Vidal, *María Luisa Bombal: la femineidad enajenada* (Barcelona: Bosch/Aubí, 1976), Lucía Guerra-Cunningham, *La narrativa de María Luisa Bombal: una visión de la existencia femenina* (Madrid: Playor, 1981), and Marjorie Agosín, *Las desterradas del paraíso, protagonistas en la narrativa de María Luisa Bombal* (New York: Senda Nueva, 1982), only the first of these overtly a work of feminist cultural analysis. Because Bombal's work raises issues central to feminist discussion, commentary on her work almost inevitably has become tinged with such concerns, even when the critics writing are not coming from a background of feminist thought. This development is especially evident in the compilation *María Luisa Bombal: apreciaciones críticas*, eds. Agosin, Elena Gascón-Vera, and Joy Renjilian-Burgy (Tempe AZ: Bilingual Press/Editorial Bilingüe, 1987). The collection is also testimony to the above-noted extension of archetypal criticism beyond its traditionally timeless character to treat historical social concerns. Critics whose approach to Bombal's texts, as to literature in general, was initially ahistorically archetypal now have become more willing to take into account the social and cultural meanings of texts. Agosin, Guerra-Cunningham, and Inés Dölz-Blackburn are among the Bombal critics who show this effect of the spread of literary feminism.

There are many other cases in which the general scholarship centered on a particular author has begun to show the influence of feminism, a circumstance that is likely to become most visible in compilations of essays. Some cases involve authors who are themselves feminists; an example is *Homenaje a Rosario Castellanos*, eds. Maureen A-hern and Mary Seale Vásquez (Valencia: Hispanófila, 1980). In others, the author under discussion is not an overt feminist, but produced work that raises questions of concern to feminists. Perhaps the most striking example of the latter pattern is the recent tendency toward feminism in commentary on the works of Clarice Lispector, to be discussed in the concluding section of this paper. The current section, however, has as its focus book-length works of literary criticism with a directly feminist or women's-studies approach.

Certain types of essays have been omitted from this listing because they are not part of literary studies as such, but rather belong to the realm of the more informal essay. Particularly prominent in this category are the literary essays of creative writers, which may well provide ideas that become the starting points for the more closely governed commentaries produced by academic critics. An excellent instance, notable for its influence both on the general literary culture and for feminist scholars, is Rosario Castellanos, *Mujer que sabe latín...* (México: SepSetentas, 1973). Many other women authors have produced essays, position papers, and statements of their outlooks on women's expression: Rosario Ferré of Puerto Rico and Luisa Valenzuela of Argentina are two recently prominent cases. However interesting and stimulating these essays are, for the purposes of this survey they, like creative writing itself, material previous to literary scholarship.

For reasons of scope, this survey does not incude feminist studies of texts that are not strictly speaking literary, such as comic books, advertising copy, and the *novela rosa*.

It should be noted, though, that analysis of texts beyond literature has proven an especially suitable vehicle for the practice of feminist criticism.

Important enough to deserve mention, although not strictly in the present category, is Evelyn Picon Garfield's *Women's Voices from Latin America: Interviews with Six Contemporary Authors* (Detroit: Wayne State UP, 1986).

Of works in which Spanish and Spanish-American literature are jointly considered, especially noteworthy are:

Fox-Lockert, Lucía. *Women Novelists of Spain and Latin America.* Metuchen: Scarecrow, 1979.

Miller, Beth, ed. *Women in Hispanic Literature: Icons and Fallen Idols.* Berkeley: U of California P, 1983.

Myers, Eunice, and Ginette Adamson, eds. *Continental, Latin-American and Francophone Women Writers. Selected Papers from the Wichita State University Conference on Foreign Literatures, 1984-1985.* Lanham MD: UP of America, 1987.

Mora, Gabriela, and Karen S. Van Hooft, eds. *Theory and Practice of Feminist Literary Criticism.* Ypsilanti: Bilingual Press/ Editorial Bilingüe, 1982.

On Spanish peninsular literature:

Armas, Frederick A. de. *The Invisible Mistress: Aspects of Feminism and Fantasy in the Spanish Drama of the Golden Age.* Charlottesville VA: Biblioteca Siglo de Oro, 1976.

Cook, Teresa A. *El feminismo en la novela de la Condesa de Pardo Bazán.* La Coruña: Diputación Provincial, 1976.

El-Saffar, Ruth. *The Recovery of the Feminine in the Novels of Cervantes.* Berkeley: U of California P, 1984.

Foa, Sandra M. *Feminismo y forma literaria: estudio del tema y las técnicas de María de Zayas y Sotomayor.* Valencia: Hispanófila, 1979.

Friedman, Edward H. *The Antiheroine's Voice: Narrative Discourse and the Transformations of the Picaresque.* Columbia MO: U of Missouri P, 1987.

Manteiga, Robert, Carolyn Gallerstein, and Kathleen McNerney, eds. *Feminine Concerns in Contemporary Spanish Fiction by Women*. Potomac MD: Scripta Humanistica, 1988.

McKendrick, Malveena. *Woman and Society in the Spanish Drama of the Golden Age*. London: Cambridge, 1974.

O'Connor, Patricia. *Gregorio and María Martínez Sierra*. Boston: Twayne, 1975. [Notable for its attribution of co-author status to the wife of Gregorio Martínez Sierra; the latter habitually signed his works as sole author].

Sponsler, Lucy. *Women in the Medieval Spanish Epic and Lyric Traditions*. Lexington KY: UP of Kentucky, 1975.

Concerning Latin American literature:

Agosin, Marjorie. *Silencio e imaginación (Metáforas de la escritura femenina)*. México: Katún, 1986.

Arancibia, Juana Alcira, ed. *Evaluación de la literatura femenina de Latinoamérica, siglo XX. II Simposio Internacional de Literatura*. San José, Costa Rica: Instituto Literario y Cultural Hispánico, 1985.

Bradu, Fabienne. *Señas particulares: escritora*. México: Fondo de Cultura Económica, 1987. [On seven Mexican women writers].

Cicchitti, Vicente, ed. *La mujer, símbolo del mundo nuevo*. Buenos Aires: Fernando García Cambeiro, 1976.

Cortina, Lynn. *Spanish-American Women Writers: A Bibliographical Research Checklist*. New York: Garland, 1983.

González, Patricia, and Eliana Ortega, eds. *La sartén por el mango: actas del Congreso de Escritoras Latinoamericanas*. San Juan: Huracán, 1983.

Jackson, Mary H. *The Portrayal of Women in the Novels of José Joaquín Lizardi*. The Northwest Missouri State College Studies 32, 4. Maryville MO: Northwest Missouri State U, 1971.

Luchting, Wolfgang. *La mujer o la revolución*. Lima: Ecoma, 1974. [On the Peruvian novelist Enrique Congrains Martin].

Magnarelli, Sharon. *The Lost Rib: Female Characters in the Spanish-American Novel*. Lewisburg: University Presses of America/Toronto: Associated University Presses, 1985.

Meyer, Doris. *Victoria Ocampo: Against the Wind and Tide*. New York: Braziller, 1979. [Literary biography].

— and Margarite Fernández Olmos, eds. *Contemporary Women Authors of Latin America: Critical Essays*. Brooklyn: Brooklyn College, 1983).

Miller, Yvette, ed. *Latin American Women Writers: Yesterday and Today*. Pittsburgh: Latin American Literary Review Press, 1975.

Muriel, Josefina. *Cultura femenina novohispana*. México: UNAM, 1982.

National Association of Chicano Studies. *Chicana Voices: Intersections of Class, Race and Gender*. Austin: Center for Mexican American Studies, 1986. [Proceedings volume from 1984 NACS Conference; includes section on "Language, Literature and Theater"]

Phillips, Rachel. *Alfonsina Storni: From Poetess to Poet*. London: Tamesis, 1979.

Rosenbaum, Sidonia. *Modern Women Poets of Spanish America*. New York: Garland, 1985.

Saldívar, Samuel G. *La evolución del personaje femenino en la novela mexicana*. Lanham MD: U P of America, 1985.

Sánchez, María Ester. *Contemporary Chicana Poetry: A Critical Approach to an Emerging Literature*. Berkeley: U of California P, 1986.

Virgillo, Carmelo, and Naomi Lindstrom, eds. *Woman as Myth and Metaphor in Latin American Literature*. Columbia MO: U of Missouri P, 1985.

* * *

Alongside feminist publications, there has been a growing discussion of gender in nonspecialized journals. Editors on occasion have reserved all or part of an issue for this purpose. Of particular historical significance is a Latinamericanist example, *Revista/Review Latinoamericana* 4.2 (1974), edited by Ann Pescatello, notable for its early date, for the degree to which it focuses on literature, and for its abiity to represent the major issues then forming the agenda of feminist criticism. Subsequent special issues of journals have often featured a particular set of sub-questions in feminism or feminism as it affects a determined area of commentary. For example, *Literatura Chilena, Creación y Crítica* 6.3 (1982), Marjorie Agosín, guest editor, reflects new interest in women's expression as it appears in Chilean alternative and countercultural social and cultural thought. The issue of *Revista Iberoamericana* 51.132-33 (1985) dedicated to women's writing stands not only by virtue of the mainstream prestige of the journal and the many well-known critics (including many not customarily identified with women's studies), but also as a demonstration of contemporary topics of discussion: features of women's writing claimed or theorized to be distinctly feminine, and the possibility that "feminine" texts may be able to disrupt ingrained concepts of language, representation, and expression. "La mujer/la escritura," a thematic issue of *escandalar* 6.1-2 (1983), Octavio Armand, ed., is indicative of a more detached, vanguardist, and self-consciously esthetic approach to issues of women's writing and a more direct infusion of ideas from the French literary scene. Of special note is *The Américas Review* 15.3-4 (1987), eds. María Herrera-Sobek and Helena María Viramontes, *Chicana Creativity and Criticism: Charting New Frontiers in American Literature.*

* * *

Perhaps the most telling sign that feminist concepts had affected the study of Hispanic and Lusophone literatures was the publication, in significant numbers, of articles showing this orientation in the pages of "mainstream" journals. This development indicated that feminist thought was considered sufficiently part of the study of literature to be of possible interest to readers who were specialists in the literature written in Spanish and Portuguese, but not in women's writings or in the literary extensions of the current debate over sex role and identity. In addition, the possibility of publishing feminist criticism in journals considered important to the profession meant that feminist critics were less likely to stand apart from their colleagues and constitute a caucus or special interests group. The difficulty of obtaining professional advancement, or indeed professional survival, while pursuing such interests was not eliminated, but it was certainly lessened.

The following listing of journal articles includes no entries from such journals as *Letras Femeninas* or *fem.*, because these publications are essentially constituted of criticism with a feminist or at least a women's-studies basis of some type. For the same reason, the articles in the 1974 special issue of *Review/Revista Interamericana* and the 1985 special issue of *Revista Iberoamericana* have not been listed individually. Instead, this registry is a guide to the appearance of such criticism in journals read by a broad cross-section of Hispanists or Luso-Brazilian specialists. It should be noted that other feminist studies of Spanish- and Portuguese-language texts have appeared as chapters in multi-authored volumes on a variety of topics. Because of the focus chosen here to illustrate the main lines along which feminist thought spread to a particular area of studies, and because of the dispersion of book chapters among dissimilar volumes, essays appearing in this form are not included.

Articles have been selected following the same criterion used for book-length works. In some way, they must bear testimony to the impact feminism has lately had on the study of Spanish and Latin American literature. [NB: The *Revista de Estudios Hispánicos* cited is the journal of that name that originated at the U of Alabama and subsequently moved to Vassar, not the one based at the U of Puerto Rico.]

Concerning Hispanic literatures without distinction of geography:

Dölz-Blackburn, Inés. "Recent Critical Bibliography on Women in Hispanic Literature." *Discurso Literario* 3.2 (1986): 331-34.

Sullivan, Constance A. "Re-reading the Hispanic Literary Canon: The Question of Genre." *Ideologies and Literature* 16 (1983): 93-101.

Spanish peninsular and Portuguese articles:

Bluestine, Carolyn. "The Role of Women in the *Poema de Mio Cid.*" *Romance Notes* 18.3 (1978): 404-409.

Boring, Phyllis Zatlin. "Carmen Martín Gaite, Feminist Author." *Revista de Estudios Hispánicos* 11.3 (1977): 323-38.

— "Delibes' Two Views of the Spanish Mother." *Hispanófila* 63 (1978): 79-87.

Bretz, Mary Lee. "Naturalismo y feminismo en Emilia Pardo Bazán." *Papeles de San Armadans* 87 (1977): 195-219.

Cambria, Rosario. "Women's Rights in Spain: It All Began with Concepción Arenal." *The American Hispanist* 2.17 (1977): 7-10.

Chown, Linda E. "American Critics and Spanish Women Novelists, 1942-1980." *Signs: Journal of Women in Culture and Society* 9.1 (1983): 98-101.

Cook, Teresa A. "Emilia Pardo Bazán y la educación como elemento primordial en la liberación de la mujer." *Hispania* 60.2 (1977): 259-65.

Dille, Glen F. "Notes on Aggressive Women in the *Comedia* of Enrique Gómez." *Romance Notes* 21.1 (1980): 215-21.

El-Saffar, Ruth. "Tres imágenes claves de lo femenino en el *Persiles.*" *Revista Canadiense de Estudios Hispánicos* 3.3 (1979): 219-36.

Feal Deibe, Carlos. "La voz femenina en *Los pazos de Ulloa.*" *Hispania* 70.2 (1987): 214-21.

Feeny, Thomas. "More on the Antifeminism of Pérez de Ayala." *Hispanic Journal* 7.1 (1985): 115-21. [Reply to Sara Suárez Solís, "El antifeminismo de Pérez de Ayala." *Los Cuadernos del Norte* (Oviedo) 1.2 (1980): 48-52].

Fox, Linda C. "Power in the Family and Beyond: Doña Perfecta and Bernarda Alba as Manipulators of Their Destinies." *Hispanófila* 85 (1985) 57-65.

Galerstein, Carolyn L. "Carmen Laforet and the Spanish Spinster." *Revista de Estudios Hispánicos* 11.2 (1977): 303-315.

Giles, Mary E. "Feminism and the Feminine in Emilia Pardo Bazán's Novels." *Hispania* 63.2 (1980): 356-67.

Gold, Hazel. "Ni soltera, ni viuda, ni casada: negación y exclusión en las novelas femeninas de Jacinto Octavio Picón." *Ideologies and Literature* 17.4 (1983): 63-77.

Grieve, Patricia E. "Private Man, Public Woman: Trading Places in *Condesa traidora*." *Romance Quarterly* 34 (1987): 317-26.

Griswold, Susan C. "Topoi and Rhetorical Distances: The 'Feminism' of María de Zayas." *Revista de Estudios Hispánicos* 1.2 (1980): 97-116.

Halsey, Martha T. "Olmo's 'La pechuga de la sardina' and the Oppression of Women in Contemporary Spain." *Revista de Estudios Hispánicos* 8.1 (1979): 3-20.

Howe, Elizabeth Teresa. "A Woman Ensnared: Laureola as Victim in the *Cárcel de amor*." *Revista de Estudios Hispánicos* 21.1 (1987): 13-27.

Ibarra, Fernando. "Clarín y la liberación de la mujer." *Hispanófila* 51 (1974): 27-33.

Kirkpatrick, Susan. "On the Threshold of the Realistic Novel: Gender and Genre in *La gaviota*." *PMLA* 93 (1983): 323-40.

McKendrick, Malveena. "The 'Mujer Esquiva'—A Measure of the Feminist Sympathies of Seventeenth Century Spanish Dramatists." *Hispanic Review* 40 (1972): 162-97.

Miller, Stephen. "*La de Bringas* as *Bildungsroman*: A Feminist Reading." *Romance Quarterly* 34 (1987): 189-99.

O'Connor, D. J. "La mujer lectora y protagonista de la novela española de 1870." *Hispanófila* 84 (1985): 83-91.

O'Connor, Patricia. "A Spanish Precursor to Women's Lib: The Heroine in Gregorio Martínez Sierra's Theater." *Hispania* 55 (1972): 865-72.

— "José Ruibal: Feminist Unaware in *La secretaria?*" *Revista de Estudios Hispánicos* 8.3 (1974): 13-17.

— "Eros and Thanatos in Francisco García Pavón's *El último sábado*." *Journal of Spanish Studies: Twentieth Century* 4.1 (1976): 175-85.

— "Francisco García Pavón's Sexual Politics in the Plinio Novels." *Journal of Spanish Studies: Twentieth Century* 1.1 (1973): 65-81.

— "Gregorio Martínez Sierra's Maternal Nuns in Dramas of Renunciation and Revolution." *The American Hispanist* 2.12 (1976): 8-12.

— "Mercedes Ballesteros' Unsung Poetic Comedy: *Las mariposas cantan.*" *Crítica Hispánica* 7.1 (1985): 57-63.

— "Spain's First Successful Woman Dramatist: María Martínez Sierra." *Hispanófila* 60 (1979): 87-108.

Ordóñez, Elizabeth J. "The Decoding and Encoding of Sex Roles in Carmen Martín Gaite's *Retahílas.*" *Kentucky Romance Quarterly* 27.2 (1980): 237-44.

— "The Female Quest Pattern in Concha Alos' *Os habla Electra.*" *Revista de Estudios Hispánicos* 14.1 (1980): 51-6.

— "Paradise Regained, Paradise Lost: Desire and Prohibition in *La madre naturaleza.*" *Hispanic Journal* 8.1 (1986): 7-18.

— "A Quest for Matrilineal Roots and Mythopoesis: Esther Tusquets' 'El mismo mar de todos los veranos'." *Crítica Hispánica* 6.1 (1984): 37-46.

— "Reading Contemporary Spanish Narrative by Women." *Anales de la Literatura Española Contemporánea* 7.2 (1982): 237-51.

— "¿Y mi niña?: Another Voice in *Los pazos de Ulloa.*" *Discurso Literario* 3.1 (1985): 121-31.

— "Woman and Her Text in the Works of María de Zayas and Ana Caro." *Revista de Estudios Hispánicos* 19.1 (1985): 21-34.

Ortega, José. "La frustración femenina en *Los mercaderes* de Ana María Matute." *Hispanófila* 54 (1975): 31-38.

Pérez, Janet. "Inversion, Evasion and Negation of the 'Madonna' Stereotype in Postwar Spanish Fiction." *Discurso Literario* 4.1 (1986): 185-200.

Richards, Catherine G. "Social Criticism in Lorca's Tragedies." *Revista de Estudios Hispánicos* 17.2 (1983): 35-53.

Rodríguez, Alfred, and John Timm. "El significado de lo femenino en *La familia de Pascual Duarte.*" *Revista de Estudios Hispánicos* 11.2 (1977): 251-64.

Rodríguez, Luz. "Aspectos de la primera variante femenina de la picaresca española." *Explicación de Textos Literarios* 8.2 (1979-1980): 175-81.

Rogers, Elizabeth S. "Monserrat Roig's *Ramona, adiós*: A Novel of Suppression and Disclosure." *Revista de Estudios Hispánicos* 20.1 (1986): 103-121.

Rovira, Rosalina R. "La función de la mujer en la literatura contemporánea." *Explicación de Textos Literarios* 3.3 (197-75): 21-2.

Scari, Robert M. "Los Martínez Sierra y el feminismo de Emilia Pardo Bazán." *Romance Notes* 20.3 (1980): 310-16.

Schmidt, Ruth A. "Woman's Place in the Sun: Feminism in *Insolación*." *Revista de Estudios Hispánicos* 8.1 (1974): 68-81.

Seator, Lynne Hubbard. " *Ana Kleiber* and the Traditional Nature of Sastre's Unconventional Women." *Revista de Estudios Hispánicos* 12.2 (1978): 287-302.

— "Women and Men in the Novels of Unamuno." *Kentucky Romance Quarterly* 27.1 (1980): 469-77.

Semprún Donahues, Moraima de. "El 'chauvinismo' feminista en *La tía Tula*." *Explicación de Textos Literarios* 8.2 (1979-1980): 219-33.

Spencer, Janie. "Am American Co-ed Seen Through Spanish Eyes: Ramón Sender's *Nancy*." *Romance Notes* 26.3 (1986): 209-214.

Sims, Edna M. "Resumen de la imagen negativa de la mujer en la literatura española hasta mediados del siglo XVI." *Revista de Estudios Hispánicos* 11.3 (1977): 43-49.

Spieker, Joseph B. "El feminismo como clave estructural en las *novelle* de doña María de Zayas." *Explicación de Textos Literarios* 6.2 (1978): 158-60.

Swietlicki, Catherine. "Rojas' View of Women: A Reanalysis of *La Celestina*." *Hispanófila* 85 (1985): 1-13.

Tucker, Donald W. "The Emergence of Women in the Novels of Miguel Delibes." *Hispania* 71.1 (1988): 38-42.

Turner, Harriet. "Family Ties and Tyrannies: A Reassessment of Jacinta." *Hispanic Review* 51.1 (1983): 1-22.

Vance, Birgitta. "The Great Clash: Feminist Literary Criticism Meets Up with Spanish Reality." *Journal of Spanish Studies: Twentieth Century* 2.2 (1974): 109-114.

Vieira, David J. "Women in the Portuguese Theater: 1921-1981." *Luso-Brazilian Review* 23.2 (1986): 85-96.

Welles, Marcia L. "The *pícara*: Towards Female Virtue, or the Vanity of Virtue." *Romance Quarterly* 33.1 (1986): 63-70.

Wyers, Frances. "A Woman's Voices: Mercè Rodoreda's *La plaça del Diamant.*" *Kentucky Romance Quarterly* 30.3 (1983): 301-309.

Journal articles for Latin American literature:

Agosin, Marjorie. "Una bruja novelada: *La Quintrala* de Magdalena Petit." *Chasqui* 12.1 (1982): 3-13.

Andrade, Ana Luisa. "*O Visitante* Revisitado: um caso adulterado num romance de Osman Lins." *Hispania* 68.4 (1985): 695-99.

Araújo, Helena. "Escritura femenina?" *escandalar* 4.3 (1981): 32-36.

—"Narrativa femenina latinoamericana: La Scheherezade criolla." *Hispanoamérica: Revista de Literatura* 11.32 (1982): 23-24. [On María Luisa Bombal].

Arrom, José Juan. "Cambiantes imágenes de la mujer en el teatro de la América virreinal." *Latin American Theatre Review* 9.2 (1978): 5-15.

Barradas, Efraín. "El machismo existencialista de René Marqués." *Sin Nombre* 8.3 (1977): 69-81.

Barros, Alcides João de. "A situação da mulher no teatro de Consuelo de Castro e Leilah Assunção." *Latin American Theatre Review* 9.2 (1976): 13-20.

Beer, Gabriella de. "Feminismo en la obra poética de Rosario Castellanos." *Revista de Crítica Literaria Latinoamericana* 13 (1981): 105-112.

Bente, Thomas O. "María Luisa Bombal's Heroines: Poetic Neuroses and Artistic Symbolism." *Hispanófila* 82 (1984): 104-113.

Birkmoe, Diane S. "The Virile Voice of Marta Lynch." *Revista de Estudios Hispánicos* 16.2 (1982): 191-211.

Boschetto, Sandra María. "El canto de las sirenas: aproximación al mundo femenino en algunos relatos de Juan Carlos Onetti." *Explicación de Textos Literarios* 7.2 (983-84): 3-18.

— "La inversión de la figura femenina en 'El güero' de José Donoso." *Crítica Hispánica* 6.1 (1984): 1-10.

Calderón, Héctor. "Ideology and Sexuality: Male and Female in *El obsceno pájaro de la noche*." *Ideologies and Literature* 1.3 (1985): 31-47.

Carlisle, Charles Richard. "La mujer en la narrativa de Ana-Iris Chaves de Ferreiro." *Discurso Literario* 2.1 (198): 145-53. [On Paraguayan novelist].

Corominas, Juan M. "Incidencia femenina en la estructura de *Gabriela, Cravo e Canela*." *Hispania* 68.3 (1985): 484-89.

Courteau, Joanna. "The Problematic Heroines in the Novels of Rachel de Queiroz." *Luso-Brazilian Review* 22.2 (1985): 123-44.

Cypess, Sandra Messinger. "¿Alguien ha oído hablar de ellas? (Una revisión de las dramaturgas mexicanas)." *Texto Crítico* 10 (1970): 55-64.

—"La dramaturgia femenina y su contexto socio-cultural." *Latin American Theatre Review* 13.2 (1980): 63-68.

— "I, Too, Speak: 'Female' Discourse in Carballido's Plays." *Latin American Theatre Review* 18.1 (1984): 45-52.

Fiscal, María Rosa. "Identidad y lenguaje en los personajes femeninos de Rosario Castellanos." *Chasqui* 14.2-3 (1985): 25-35.

— "La mujer en la narrativa de Rosario Castellanos." *Texto Crítico* 5.15 (1979): 133-53.

Fitz, Earl E. "Freedom and Self-Realization: Feminist Characterization in the Fiction of Clarice Lispector." *Modern Language Studies* 10.3 (1980): 51-61.

Flori, Mónica. "La función de los personajes femeninos en 'Paseo' y 'Santelices' de José Donoso." *Explicación de Textos Literarios* 14.1 (1985-1986): 25-32.

Fontanella, Lee. "Mystical Diction and Imagery in Gómez de Avellaneda and Carolina Coronado." *Latin American Literary Review* 9.19 (1982): 47-55.

Francescato, Martha Paley. See Paley Francescato, Martha.

Franco, Jean. "Apuntes sobre la crítica feminista y la literatura hispanoamericana." *Hispamérica* 45 (1986): 31-43.

Ginsberg, Judith. "From Anger to Action: The Avenging Female in Two *Lucías.*" *Revista de Estudios Hispánicos* 14.1 (1980): 51-64. [On the film *Lucía* by the Cuban director and screenwriter Humberto Solís]

Guerra-Cunningham, Lucía. "Algunas reflexiones teóricas sobre la novela femenina." *Hispamérica* 28 (1981): 29-39.

— "El personaje literario femenino y otras mutilaciones." *Hispamérica* 15 (1986): 3-16.

— "Tensiones paradójicas de la femineidad en la narrativa de Rosario Ferré." *Chasqui* 13.1 (1983): 13-25.

— "La visión marginal en la narrativa de Juana Manuela Gorriti." *Ideologies and Literatures* 2.2 (1987): 59-76.

Gyurko, Lanin A. "Borges and the *Machismo* Cult." *Revista Hispánica Moderna* 36.3 (1970-1971): 128-45.

— "The Pseudo-Liberated Woman in Fuentes' *Zona sagrada*". *Journal of Spanish Studies: Twentieth Century* 3.1 (1975): 17-43.

— "The Vindication of La Malinche in Fuentes' *Todos los gatos son pardos.*" *Ibero-Amerikanisches Archiv* 3.3 (1977). 233-66.

— "Women in Mexican Society: Fuentes' Portrayal of Oppression." *Revista Hispánica Moderna* 38.4 (1974-75): 206-29.

Hancock, Joel. "Elena Poniatowska's *Hasta no verte Jesús mío*: The Remaking of the Image of Woman." *Hispania* 66.3 (1983): 353-59.

Handelsman, Michael H. "*Bruna, soroche y los tíos*: An Ecuatorian Woman Writer's Contribution to Contemporary Feminist Fiction." *Revista de Estudios Hispánicos* 15.1 (1981): 35-42.

Hughes, Psiche. "Love in the Abstract: The Role of Women in Borges' Literary World." *Chasqui* 8.3 (1979): 34-43.

Johnson, Julie Greer. "A Caricature of Spanish Women in the New World by the Inca Garcilaso de la Vega." *Latin American Literary Review* 9.18 (1981): 7-51.

Kaminsky, Amy. "The Real Circle of Iron: Mothers and Children, Children and Mothers in Four Argentine Novels." *Latin American Literary Review* 4.9 (1976): 77-86. [On Marta Lynch and Silvina Bullrich].

Kirsner, Robert. "De doña Bárbara a Luisiana: feminismo refinado." *Caribe* 1.2 (1976): 57-64.

Leal, Luis. "Mujer que sabe latín." *Letras de Buenos Aires* 2.7 (1982): 35-53.

Lemaître, Monique J. "Jesusa Palancares y la dialéctica de la emancipación femenina." *Hispamérica* 30 (1981): 131-35. [On the work of the novelist Elena Poniatowska].

Lewald, H. Ernest. "Aspects of the Modern Argentine Woman." *Chasqui* 5.3 (1976): 19-25.

— "Two Generations of River Plate Women Authors." *Latin American Research Review* 15.1 (1980): 231-36.

Lewis, Marvin A. "Rita Mendoza: Chicana Poetess." *Latin American Literary Review* 5.10 (1977): 79-85.

Lindstrom, Naomi. "Clarice Lispector: Articulating Women's Experience." *Chasqui* 8.1 (1978): 44-52.

— "A Discourse Analysis of 'Preciosidade' by Clarice Lispector." *Luso-Brazilian Review* 19.2 (1982): 187-94.

— "A Feminist Discourse Analysis of Clarice Lispector's 'Daydreams of a Drunken Woman'." *Latin American Literary Review* 9.19 (1982): 7-16.

— "Norah Lange: presencia desmonumentalizadora y femenina en la vanguardia argentina." *Crítica Hispánica* 5.2 (1983): 131-48.

— "Women's Expression and Narrative Technique in Rosario Castellanos' *In Darkness*." *Modern Language Studies* 13.3 (1983): 71-80.

López, Yvette. " 'La muñeca menor': ceremonias y transformaciones en un cuento de Rosario Ferré." *Explicación de Textos Literarios* 11.1 (1982-1983): 49-58.

Magnarelli, Sharon. "The Diseases of Love and Discourse: *La tía Julia y el escribidor.*" *Hispanic Review* 5.2 (1986): 195-205.

— "Gatos, lenguaje y mujeres en *El gato eficaz* de Luisa Valenzuela." *Revista Iberoamericana* 108-109 (1979): 603-611.

Maier, Carol. "A Woman in Translation, Reflecting." *Translation Review* 17 (1985): 4-8. [Principally on the work of the poet Octavio Armand].

Martin, Eleanor J. "Carlota O'Neill's *Cuarta dimensión* [Fourth Dimension]: The Role of the Female and the Imagination in Everyday Existence." *Latin American Literary Review* 8.15 (1979): 1-11.

Martínez, Z. Nelly. "*El gato eficaz* de Luisa Valenzuela: la productividad del texto." *Revista Canadiense de Estudios Hispánicos* 4.1 (1979): 73-80.

McCracken, Ellen. "Manuel Puig's *Heartbreak Tango:* Women and Class Culture." *Latin American Literary Review* 9.18 (1981): 27-35.

McNab, Gregory. "Sexual Differences: The Subjection of Women in Two Stories by Orlando Amarílis." *Luso-Brazilian Review* 24.1 (1987): 59-61 [NB: concerns a Lusophone Cape Verdean writer].

Meyer, Doris. "Divided Against Herself: The Early Poetry of Nellie Campobello." *Revista de Estudios Hispánicos* 20.2 (1986): 51-63.

— "Nellie Campobello's *Las manos de mamá*: A Rereading." *Hispania* 68.4 (1985): 747-52.

— "Woman's Space, Woman's Text: A New Departure in Inés Malinow's *Entrada libre.*" *Latin American Literary Review* 12.23 (1983): 1-50.

Miller, Beth. "Historia y ficción en *Oficio de tinieblas* de Rosario Castellanos." *Texto Crítico* 28 (1984): 131-42.

— "Rosario Castellanos's *Guests in August*: Critical Realism and the Provincial Middle Class." *Latin American Literary Review* 7.1 (1979): 5-19.

Milleret, Margo. "Entrapment and Flights of Fantasy in Three Plays by Leilah Assunção." *Luso-Brazilian Review* 21.1 (1984): 49-56.

Minc, Rose S. "Guadalupe Dueñas: texto y contexto de la nueva alquimia del poder." *Discurso Literario* 1.2 (98): 231-41.

Mora, Gabriela. "Las novelas de Isabel Allende y el papel de la mujer como ciudadana." *Ideologies and Literatures* 2.1 (1987): 53-61.

— "La otra cara de Ifigenia: una reevaluación del personaje de Teresa de la Parra." *Sin Nombre* 7.3 (1976): 130-44.

— "*Los perros* y *La mudanza* de Elena Garro: designio social y virtualidad feminista." *Latin American Theatre Review* 8.2 (1975): 5-14.

Nigro, Kirsten F. "Rosario Castellanos' Debunking of the *Eternal Feminine*." *Journal of Spanish Studies: Twentieth Century* 8.1-2 (1980): 89-102.

Novães Coelho, Nelly. "A presença, da 'Nova mulher' na ficção brasileira." *Revista Iberoamericana* 126 (1984): 141-54.

Nunes, Maria Luisa. "Clarice Lispector: ¿artista andrógina ou escritora?" *Revista Iberoamericana* 126 (1984): 281-89.

Paley, Martha Francescato. "The New Man (But Not the New Woman)." *Books Abroad* 50.3 (1976): 589-95. [On the fiction of Julio Cortázar].

Perelmutter Pérez, Rosa. "La estructura retórica de la 'Respuesta a Sor Filotea'." *Hispanic Review* 51.2 (1983): 17-58.

Pontiero, Giovanni. "Testament of Experience: Some Reflections on Clarice Lispector's Last Narrative *A hora da estrela*." *Ibero-Amerikanisches Archiv* 10.1 (1984): 13-22.

Reedy, Daniel R. "Magda Portal: Perú's Voice of Social Protest." *Revista de Estudios Hispánicos* 4.1 (1970): 85-97.

— "Aspects of the Feminist Movement in Peruvian Letters and Politics." *SECOLAS Annals* 6.5 (1975): 53-64.

Rodríguez-Peralta, Phyllis. "Images of Women in Rosario Castellanos' Prose." *Latin American Literary Review* 6.11 (1977): 68-80.

— "María Luisa Bombal's Poetic Novels of Female Estrangement." *Revista de Estudios Hispánicos* 15.1 (1980): 139-55.

— "Narrative Access to a Feminine Childhood World: A New Peruvian Novel." *Latin American Literary Review* 9.17 (1980): 1-8. [On the work of Laura Riesco].

Schanzer, George O. "Rubén Darío and Ms. Christa." *Journal of Spanish Studies: Twentieth Century* 3.2 (1975): 15-52.

Schlau, Stacy. "Conformity and Resistance to Enclosure: Female Voices in Rosario Castellanos' *Oficio de tinieblas* [The Dark Service]." *Latin American Literary Review* 12.24 (1984): 45-57.

— "Stranger in a Strange Land: The Discourse of Alienation in Gómez de Avellaneda's *Sab*." *Hispania* 69.3 (1986): 495-503.

Steele, Cynthia. "La creatividad y el deseo en *Querido Diego, te abraza Quiela*, de Elena Poniatowska." *Hispamérica* 41 (1985): 17-28.

— "Toward a Socialist Feminist Criticism of Latin American Literature." *Ideologies and Literature* 16 (1983): 323-29.

Ugalde, Sharon Keefe. "El discurso femenino en *Misiá Señora*: ¿un lenguaje nuevo o acceso al lenguaje?" *Discurso Literario* 4.1 (1986): 117-26 [On the Colombian novelist Albalucía Angel].

Umpierre, Luz María. "Inversiones, niveles y participación en *Absurdos en soledad* de Myrna Casas." *Latin American Theatre Review* 17.1 (1983): 3-13.

Urbistondo, Vicente. "El machismo en la narrativa hispanoamericana." *Texto Crítico* 4.9 (1978): 165-83.

Valdivieso, Mercedes. "Social Denunciation in the Language of "El árbol" [The Tree] by María Luisa Bombal." Trans. Ellen Wilkerson. *Latin American Literary Review* 4.9 (1976): 70-76.

Vásquez Arce, Carmen. "Sexo y mulatería: dos sones de una misma guaracha." *Sin Nombre* 12.4 (1982): 51-63. [On the Puerto Rican novelist Luis Rafael Sánchez].

Vientós Gastón, Nélida. "Concepción Arenal." *Sin Nombre* 7.3 (1976): 46-61.

Williams, Lorna V. "*The Shrouded Woman*: Marriage and its Constraints in the Fictions of María Luisa Bombal." *Latin American Literary Review* 10.20 (1982): 21-30.

Wilson, S.R. "Art by Gender: The Latin American Woman Writer." *Revista Canadiense de Estudios Hispánicos* 6.1 (1981): 135-37.

Zapata, Celia de. "One Hundred Years of Women Writers in Latin America." *Latin American Literary Review* 3.6 (1975): 7-16.

Zavala, Iris M. "Dos mujeres contra el mundo: Flora Tristán y Louise Michel." *Sin Nombre* 7.3 (976): 37-45.

Among new tendencies in the feminist criticism of Hispanic and Lusophone literatures, the one to claim the most attention has been the effort to perceive in certain texts, and especially in those written by women, the marks of a distinctively feminine writing. This current of thought clearly stems from the polemic over *écriture feminine* that occupied a considerable portion of the French literary scene during the 1970s. In the French debate, two essential positions were possible. To simplify, the concept of feminine writing promoted by Julia Kristeva and others did not require that the text so classified be female-authored, but rather that it deviate in a significant manner from literature in the dominant mode and have the potential to call into question generally-imposed assumptions. The principal competing notion, identified with Hélène Cixous, Luce Irigaray, and others, is that of writing by women that constitutes the inscription of the experience of woman's body into the literary text.

While in France these two notions remained apart during a polemic that produced many variants on the basic positions, in the criticism of Hispanic and Lusophone literatures critics frequently draw from both tendencies of thought at once. A common practice is to single out women writers and assert that their work shows features no male writer could have generated. At the same time that the sex of the author and her treatment of experiences or perceptions specific to women claim attention, so does the idea that these differences from men's writing are at work decentering and subverting the *modo standard*, as "feminine writing" in Kristeva's sense is believed to do. While critics from differing cultures are certainly free to adapt eclectically from the set of assertions advanced by French discussants, the conflation of these two positions can have some disturbing results. It is easy to slide into the assumption that any writing that can be claimed to reveal its female authorship automatically counts as dissident or healthily subversive work.

Of studies of Latin American writers cited in these notes, several stand out for their involvement with notions of feminine writing. An evident example is Sharon

Magnarelli's work on Luisa Valenzuela, an author who invites commentary in this vein by identifying her writing as incontrovertibly and radically feminine. Volume 6, issue 1 (1986) of the *Review of Contemporary Fiction*, with its focus on Valenzuela, demonstrates the author's position statements, her creative work, and discussion of the questions raised by both. The González and Ortega collection of essays and the special issue 132-33 (1985) of *Revista Iberoamericana* feature debate over the issues involved in calling writing feminine. *escandalar* 6.1-2 (1983) is especially explicit in its efforts to connect Latin American writing with the French polemics; this special issue juxtaposes texts by Cixous and Kristeva with statements and creative writing by Latin American women.

The search for textual markers of female authorship has led critics to reexamine writings by a number of Latin American authors. Of writers hypothesized to have written as women, Clarice Lispector has come in for the most spectacular and publicized reconsideration.

Lispector and her work became exemplary cases for the hypothesis of a distinctive women's writing when they were personally discovered by Hélène Cixous. (It should be noted that Lispector's work already enjoyed an international reputation). Cixous made known the extraodinary affinity she felt with Lispector's texts and began producing highly personal and tendentious commentaries upon them, combining her own response with assertions that the Brazilian writer's narrative is essentially feminine both in its unspecifiable essence and its observable traits. Representative of Cixous's work centered on these concerns is her book-length *Vivre l'Orange/To Live the Orange*, trans. Ann Liddle, Sarah Cornell, and Cixous, published in a bilingual edition by Editions les Femmes of Paris. In turn, feminist critics have studied Cixous's Lispector commentaries, producing such explications as Carol Armbruster, "Hélène-Clarice: Nouvelle Voix," *Contemporary Literature* 2.2 (1983): 15-57.

When seen through such manifestations as Cixous's much-discussed bond with Lispector, the effort to analyze feminine qualities in texts can appear to be a privatized and idiosyncratic quest, ungrounded in the issue of women's historical role and status and unmotivated by any drive to reorganize society. Indeed, this critical endeavor is constantly imperiled by the ease with which the identification of female writing, and the traits said to characterize it, are presupposed to be inherently worthy. Lacking, amid such assumptions, is a willingness to question whether writing that differs from presumably male-defined norms is therefore a challenge to or subversive of dominant modes. Without a hard look at these questions, critics are liable not only to make unfounded assertions about the identifying characteristics of feminine writing but also to celebrate mindlessly texts that exhibit the prized difference.

Though criticism focused on women writers' distinctions can provide extreme instances of idiosyncracy and hermeticism, the question of otherness can also be the starting point for discussion that takes social factors into account. This more grounded critical tendency involves the examination of women's writing as one manifestation of the type of discourse characteristic of groups occupying a disadvantaged place in society. According to this line of thought, women's texts may be analogous to the production of other minorities in their indirect means of expression and persuasion, which allow dissidence to be both manifested and hidden in the text. This concept avoids the difficult-to-verify assertion that a feminine quality can be at the core of a text. Instead, it gains support from the common-sense idea that many literary texts put forward, through their less direct logic and argumentation, propositions potentially too disturbing to be stated in non-literary discourse. As well as relying on an understanding of literary rhetoric that goes back to classical antiquity, this approach can draw upon recent developments in such areas as discourse analysis and pragmatics —or, as the case may be, it may draw upon many forms of analysis designed to examine rhetoric in which meanings are simultaneously concealed and made present.

A less-prevalent recent tendency is to draw upon the feminist psychology developed by Carol Gilligan and others, distinguished by its component of social observation and criticism as well as by its attention to the distinctive features of female childhood and adolescence. Applied to literature, this psychological but not "psychologizing" approach is sought as a means of reestablishing the link between literary commentary and the situation of real-world women. Marta Peixoto's "Family Ties: Female Development in Clarice Lispector," Eizabeth Abel, Marianne Hirsch, and Elizabeth Langland, eds. *The Voyage In: Fictions in Female Development* (Hanover NH: UP of New England, 1983) 3-19, is a Latin American instance of this undertaking. The sparse representation of this critical tendency in Latin American criticism makes evaluation difficult, though Peixoto's successful study is an exceptionally promising manifestation.

Writing about women can also have an exceptional interest because of the various conventions of decorum that have long inhibited the discussion of certain aspects of women's experience. For this reason, texts that make a point of presenting women as sexual beings, and particularly those that stress distinctive features of female sexuality, have been recognized as potential generators of a dissident, questioning statement about society's usual notions of woman and sexuality both. The discussion of female sexuality in Hispanic and Lusophone literatures could well be of considerable historical sweep, ranging back to the more raucous embellishments of medieval narratives. More typically, though, the critical attention has gone to recent texts in which there is a self-conscious effort to violate rules of decorum in such a way as to imply a form of cultural criticism. Good examples of work in this vein are David William Foster's discussion of female sexuality in *Alternative Voices in the Contemporary Latin American Narrative*. Columbia MO: U of Missouri P, 1985, 129-36, and his "Espejismos eróticos," on the work of María Luisa Mendoza, *Revista de la Universidad de México*, nueva época, 37 (mayo de 1984): 36-38.

In applauding forms of study that rely on newer concepts of discourse, theory from other fields, or other recent developments, one should not disparage the possibility of worthwhile feminist investigations whose theoretical model is not particularly recent, overt, or specifiable. There should always be some recognition for the contribution to

feminist studies of intelligent critics with an acute, historically informed sense of how male and female are defined
in society. An example of a critic who, while a freethinker
in matters of literary theory, writes scholarly and insight-
ful commentaries is Walnice Nogueira Galvão. Her long-
time pursuit of the topic of warrior maidens in both literature and in the general cultural imagination resulted in
the lengthy interpretive survey "Ciclos da Donzela-Guer-
reira," collected in her 1981 *Gatos de outro saco* (São Paulo:
Editora Brasiliense), 8-59.

* * *

As feminist thought continues to manifest itself in
more and more areas of literary criticism, including such
seemingly unlikely locales as archetypal criticism and
mainstream author-and-work studies, it becomes increasingly evident that no unitary body of feminist literary theory and practice is emerging. Feminist ideas have been
manifested equally well, and poorly, in criticism with an
explicitly-elaborated theoretical framework and in studies
in which literary theory as such has relatively little importance. These circumstances suggest that what makes criticism legitimately feminist is the set of issues at its core,
and that theory and criticism as they have been developed
for other purposes can be the immediate vehicle for the
exploration of these concerns. This is not to say that all approaches to literary criticism are equally well suited to
feminist work. As noted earlier, an approach such as Jungian or archetypal criticism, which customarily considers
literary phenomena *sub specie aeternitatis*, must be his-
toricized and made to refer to social realities by critics hoping to turn it to the purposes of feminist criticism.
Formalist approaches to textual analysis are by no means
inherently incompatible with or unadaptable to feminism;
the admixture of social and cultural analysis to studies of
literary form is common in our day. Yet it is difficult to include within feminist studies a commentary in which
considerations purely of form predominate over such issues as women's role and status and the expression

women adopt under these social constraints. All in all, it seems frivolous to call feminist any criticism that appears too detached from the original motivation behind feminism: a desire for justice in the real-world apportionment between men and women of power and the ability to provide for material needs.

Without devaluing the contribution of women to literature, one can recommend that feminist critics invest less time in the quest for a purely feminist body of theory and devote, instead, their efforts to mastering concepts and information that will enable them to maintain, refine, and clarify the connection between their literary commentaries and problems of society and culture. If feminist criticism is to have a basis of this type, then its practitioners will need to acquire a greater knowledge of the history of social thought than is possessed by the majority of critics trained in literary analysis. Not only is general knowledge of social theory and social criticism desirable, but also knowledge of specific societies as they existed at the moment particular literary works and movements came into being. The often-expressed concern that feminist thought as it arises in more developed countries will be applied too directly to Latin American realities seems really a concern that critics will not know enough about, or not be sufficiently aware of, the social factors that make the difference. What is needed is not the reinvention of feminism to suit each new society, or the attribution of some unspecifiable Latin essence to works written in Spanish and Portuguese. Rather, critics should be conceptually able to take social variation into account, knowledgeable enough to do so, and conscious of the need make this effort. Feminist criticism is a subcategory of all literary commentary that also generates a critical statement about society. Critics working in this area should examine what has been done to make literary studies serve this function, ranging from the sometimes crude, but often powerful, observations that social analysts make when they allude to literature to highly literary and theoretically refined new syntheses of Marxist thought, deconstructionism, psychoanalytic concepts, and other elements. While this urging to feminist critics to know things may seem self-evident, reading feminist criticism of Hispanic and Lusophone literatures shows that frequently the social thought behind the literary anaysis has not been worked out with any degree of consistency or understanding of what has already been asserted and demonstrated in social analysis and commentary. For these reasons, the development of original theory seems less urgent for feminist critics than the work of acquiring knowledge about societies and about society, and being able to bring this knowledge to bear on literary analyses.

Note: This paper represents an updating and expansion of "Feminist Criticism of Latin American Literature: Bibliographic Notes." *Latin American Research Review* 15.1 (1980): 151-59.

For the research for the present paper, I would like to acknowledge the support of the Dallas TACA Centennial Fellowship in Spanish and Portuguese, and for the earlier research, that of the University Research Institute of the University of Texas at Austin.

Un diálogo entre feministas hispanoamericanas

Gabriela Mora
Rutgers University, New Brunswick

Este diálogo quiere resumir algunas de las cuestiones teóricas y prácticas que discuten las feministas que ejercen la crítica literaria. Más que respuestas, recoge preguntas y opiniones sobre asuntos que siguen debatiéndose.

M. Gracias compañeras por elegirme como moderadora de esta sesión especial sobre el feminismo en y para Latinoamérica. ¿Qué les parece que como punto de partida tomemos uno de los tópicos que algunas de Uds. han venido anotando como posible tema de discusión? El primero que veo aquí pregunta: ¿Cómo se diferencia la representación de la mujer en la escritura latinoamericana de la de otras latitudes, y qué fenómenos históricos habrían influído en dicha representación?

A. A mí me parece que, con muy pocas excepciones, no hay grandes diferencias porque la mayoría de nuestras escritoras ha salido de la clase media alta, por lo que representa un campo reducido de vivencias casi siempre urbanas, de mujeres educadas, con acento en los problemas amorosos o maritales, parecidos a los que trata una europea o una norteamericana.

B. Que yo sepa esas no son las representaciones que hace una Ana Lydia Vega, una Rosario Ferré o una Rosario Castellanos, aunque las tres pertenezcan a la clase media. Yo me pregunto si es justo exigir que hablemos de la representación de la latinoamericana con la enorme diversidad étnica, de clase y de culturas que tenemos. Creo que cuando A dice que no existen diferencias, está considerando sólo lo que tiene que ver con mujeres no-indias, no-pobres, no-negras, no-mulatas. Es decir de una minoría no representativa de la condición femenina más general.

A. Pero, ¿existen representaciones literarias de esos grupos? Te agradecería me dijeras. Además de las autoras que nombraste, sólo puedo recordar a la Jesusa de la Poniatowska.

C. Te recomiendo *Un día en la vida* de Manlio Argueta, claro que aquí entra el problema de si deseas enseñar sobre la condición de la mujer en un texto escrito por un hombre.

M. Por favor, dejemos las listas de libros para el final, y tratemos de no desviarnos en muchas direcciones. ¿Sigues A?

A. Sí, quería decirle a B, que no puede negar que la escritora con medios suficientes para tener criada que le permita el tiempo para escribir, ha representado en su literatura los problemas que resultan de la condición general de inferioridad de la mujer. No puedes negar que el igualador del sistema genérico/sexual, borra las diferencias de etnias o de clases. Ese igualador nos ha relegado a todas, desde tiempos inmemoriales a las labores domésticas y a la crianza de niños. Por muchas criadas que la rica tenga, la responsabilidad de estas áreas cae sobre ella, no sobre el hombre. Por lo demás, escritoras como la Bombal, Bullrich o Guido, mostraron que las vidas femeninas de la clase alta no eran ajenas a la infelicidad y socavaron muchos valores apreciados por otras clases, sobre todo la media.

D. Si, pero al mismo tiempo reforzaron otros valores burgueses, y crearon heroínas cuyas vidas pudieron ser tomadas como modelos deseados por las lectoras. Y, aún si tuvieras razón en eso del igualador genérico, habría que preguntarse qué de común tiene una sirvienta india, analfabeta, con una escritora como Victoria Ocampo, pongamos por caso. ¿No crees que esa india se igualaría mejor con su hombre que con su semejante/mujer?

A. Perdóname M por pedir la palabra otra vez, pero creo que hay un punto importante que aclarar. D habló de "género", supongo para aludir a lo que en inglés las feministas llaman "gender system". A mí no me parece que la simple traducción funciona en el español, por las múltiples connotaciones de la palabra "género", por eso prefiero decir "sistema genérico/sexual", pero tampoco estoy satisfecha. Tal vez debiéramos buscar una manera más clara de aludir al fenómeno cultural que se implica. Hay otros vocablos extranjeros con este problema. Tengo una pequeña lista que podemos discutir.

M. Es un punto importante y te prometo que te llamaré al final para que lo retomes, pero ahora quisiera que continuáramos el asunto que se estaba discutiendo. ¿B?

B. Yo insisto en que no sabemos lo suficiente sobre muchos patrones culturales de grupos étnicos de América Latina. A pesar de que la radio y la televisión están arrasando con muchas costumbres, hay todavía algunas muy arraigadas que siguen vivas. Por ejemplo, me sorprendió leer que en las sierras del Perú, algunas comunidades indígenas obligan a las parejas jóvenes a cohabitar por un período extenso de tiempo, antes de que se casen. Como lo presenta Carol Andreas en *When Women Rebel*, es un regla que se impone con fuerza, que ella misma tuvo que obedecer. Estoy segura de que habrá estudios que muestran que algunas influencias africanas son origen de específicas conductas femeninas que ayudaron a la mujer a sobrevivir y a conquistar espacios de poder. Conocimientos de este tipo, cambiarían toda la perspectiva con que habría que leer en ciertos textos motivos como por ejemplo, la virginidad, o la jefatura doméstica.

D. Yo soy muy escéptica en esto de ver en las culturas antiguas soluciones o patrones laudables cuando se tiende tanto a mitologizarlos. Esa autora que mencionas, parece que no fuera peruana, y me pregunto qué y cómo entendió lo que vio.

A. Protesto por lo que has dicho D, que me parece un prejuicio bien peligroso. De acuerdo a lo que dijiste, si eres blanca no puedes escribir sobre el indio o el negro, si eres burguesa sobre el proletario, si eres mujer sobre el hombre.... Con lo que cuesta ganarse la vida en nuestros países, con la pobreza de las bibliotecas y recursos para la investigación, no sé cómo puedes objetar la contribución al conocimiento, venga de donde venga.

D. Por supuesto no quise decir eso, pero me acuerdo de los "científicos" europeos que estudiaban las llamadas sociedades "primitivas" según cartabones occidentales que consideraban superiores y universales, sin preocuparse de examinar las vivencias de los sujetos que estudiaban y la adecuación de su cultura al específico medio. Así se hizo también con la mujer, se la definió, se le otorgó un papel, y se la socializó para que se ajustara a esa definición. Es importante darse cuenta de quién habla por quién y por qué razones. Hasta ahora el hombre había hablado por la mujer cuidando sus propios intereses. Son las mujeres mismas las que a través de sus experiencias aprendieron a cuestionar esas definiciones y socialización.

A. ¡Las feministas querrás decir! La masa de nuestras mujeres está demasiado ocupada sobreviviendo para enterarse de lo que un pequeño grupo de nosotras clase media educada en su mayoría dice de todas ellas.

B. Quisiera creer que lo que dices es verdad sólo parcial. Si es cierto que el feminismo es todavía un movimiento pequeño, y peor, una gran cantidad de mujeres por ignorancia lo teme o se burla de él, creo que se han ido creando agrupaciones que directa o indirectamente se originan en el feminismo. El libro de Andreas me reveló, además de mi ignorancia sobre compañeras de otras culturas, una gran cantidad de trabajo político inspirado por feministas. Por eso, como dije antes no podemos hablar de la latinoamericana, sino de mujeres específicas de regiones específicas. Creo que todo trabajo antropológico, sociológico, económico, etc. que exponga la diversidad de soluciones culturales para las necesidades determinadas de grupos diferentes, ayuda enormemente a entender mejor las variadas formas que toman las relaciones entre el sexo y el poder.

C. Concuerdo con B. Necesitamos más estudios de la formación de nuestras culturas, y esto no va sólo en relación a las mujeres. Fíjense cómo todo lo que concierne al mestizaje todavía está rodeado de mitos y prejuicios.

Creo que hay mucho que investigar sobre este fenómeno que algunos llaman de la doble voz o visión mestiza. Henry L. Gates ha estudiado este asunto en relación al autor y literatura negra de Estados Unidos.

E. El problema es que precisamente por la condición subordinada de la mujer y de los grupos nativos en general, ha habido poco interés en estudiar esas prácticas diferentes de que habla B. Si no me equivoco, la mayoría de las investigaciones que tenemos son muy recientes, y todavía hay mucho por hacer. Mientras tanto ¿qué hacemos? ¿cruzarnos de brazos mientras los misioneros de cuanta rama protestante hay se agregan a los católicos y a las multinacionales para hacer su "faena civilizadora" y borrar o minimizar precisamente esos patrones culturales sobre los cuales queremos saber, y que a lo mejor pueden ser semillas de resistencia a las terribles condiciones presentes?

F. Eso de cruzarse de brazos es una exageración. Precisamente estamos aquí porque nos preocupan todas esas cuestiones que nombraste. Yo creo que si algo distingue a las feministas latinoamericanas, es la conciencia de que sus preocupaciones son parte de un proyecto mayor que incluye problemas específicos de cada nación, y globales que tienen que ver con prácticas colonialistas e imperialistas. Si se leen los informes del Congreso sobre la mujer de la región andina, que se hizo en Lima en 1982, se ve muy claro...

A. ¡Esto es lo que nos une a los compañeros! Ellos comparten nuestra preocupación sobre las horrendas condiciones de nuestros países. Sigo pensando que es injusto y poco solidario que no los hayamos admitido en esta reunión.

M. No vamos a repetir las discusiones de ayer. El voto para hacer reuniones libres, informales, solo nosotras, ganó y hay que respetarlo. Lo importante es recordar que también acordamos oponernos a cualquier programa oficial "separatista" entre los sexos, como impulsan algunas feministas norteamericanas. Yo creo que la inhibición de algunas compañeras ante los compañeros se está demostrando aquí porque muchas que han hablado ahora no habían abierto la boca antes. Esta es una solución provisional al problema que se mencionó ayer del acondicionamiento de la mujer, que la priva de la palabra pública. Con la práctica, poco a poco esperamos, ya no habrá necesidad de estas separaciones artificiales. ¿Decías E?

E. Estaba apoyando la idea de B sobre la necesidad de conocer mejor las culturas prehispánicas porque allí quizás se hallen, en la práctica, ciertos modelos que para algunas de nosotras son metas deseables, por ejemplo, tener la comunidad como la unidad básica social y no la familia. O una repartición de labores entre los sexos no tan tajante como la que establece la división entre lo público y lo privado de hoy, o una actitud más respetuosa y abierta ante el cuerpo y la sexualidad.

A. ¡La cosa es encontrar textos literarios que representen esas vivencias! Te ruego M que pongas el problema de los textos para las próximas reuniones.

G. Me pregunto si será posible, con la uniformación de modelos de conducta que la TV y el cine están produciendo, mantener un tipo de unidad familiar diferente a la que desea la propaganda capitalista. Los países desarrollados se opondrán a cualquier forma que vaya a herir sus intereses, como ya se han opuesto a discutir la propuesta de un 'nuevo orden' en el control de la información o de la economía, que vienen proponiendo los del tercer mundo. Pero, quisiera que B y F me dijeran si en esa literatura que han leído aparecen el alcoholismo y las golpizas de maridos a sus esposas entre las comunidades indias. De lo que sé, estos problemas son endémicos en casi todas las clases y culturas.

F. Hay mucha verdad en eso. En el informe del Congreso que mencioné, a pesar de que algunas investigadoras encontraron comunidades con criterios diferentes para escoger pareja, educar hijos o atender enfermos, la mayoría veía un patrón extendido de dominio, muchas veces abusivo, del hombre sobre la mujer.

B. Por mi lado, quiero dejar bien claro que estoy consciente del peligro de simplificar y mitologizar fenómenos muy complejos. Pero me parece que algunas de esas formas culturales podrían ayudar a explicar, por ejemplo, el valor y la resistencia de mujeres como Domitila Barrios o Rigoberta Menchú. Hay en ellas como una manera más 'natural' de afirmarse en y contar con la colectividad.

G. Si, pero acuérdate que tanto en *Si me permiten hablar* como en *Me llamo Rigoberta Menchú* se muestra el alcoholismo, el machismo, la superstición de sus hombres, además de la explotación económica de los de afuera.

E. Me alegra que se traigan a colación los libros de Domitila y Rigoberta porque justamente presentan vidas de mujeres del pueblo apoyadas justamente en la solidaridad comunitaria tanto o más que en la propia familia. Me parece crucial en estos testimonios el mostrar cómo los gobiernos, que se dicen defensores de la familia, las destruyen con su brutalidad y persecución. Es difícil olvidar la pateadura de las botas militares a la Domitila preñada, o el asesinato de familiares de Rigoberta. La prédica oficial sobre la sacrosanta maternidad y el valor de la familia queda totalmente desmentida con esos actos.

H. Por eso me parecen válidas las posiciones feministas empeñadas en revisar críticamente la familia como institución social e ideológica. No se trata, como proclaman las mujeres de la derecha, de destruir la familia u oponerse a la maternidad, sino en estar conscientes de cómo ambos fenómenos se vienen manipulando como instrumentos de propaganda y coerción, para impedir cambios sociales.

G. De acuerdo, pero acentuando lo de críticamente porque cuando se menciona a la familia se la piensa como una abstracción universal, con una sola forma. Aquí creo que la antropología ayuda a concebir patrones que se salen de la llamada familia nuclear tan extendida ahora, y la más reproducida en la literatura. Por lo demás el feminismo, en esta revisión crítica, ya ha hecho ver las contradicciones y conflictos de esta familia nuclear, sobre todo cuando se compara la propaganda oficial de sus bondades y virtudes, y la vida real de las mujeres. Por eso concuerdo con la compañera que dijo ayer que el feminismo no podía ignorarse en la lucha para transformar la sociedad.

H. Hay un ejemplo chileno muy expresivo sobre esto. La constitución de 1980 hace ilegal propagar doctrinas contra la familia. La Secretaría de la Mujer, un organismo creado bajo Pinochet, estipula que entre las funciones de este organismo está el "honrar la importancia de la mujer, y cooperar para prepararla mejor a realizar sus tareas como madre, esposa y dueña de casa". En un artículo de Rosa Bravo y Rosalba Todaro, se señala que esta disposición está en directa oposición a ciertos acuerdos internacionales que Chile firmó.

I. Yo no sé por qué H dice que no se trata de destruir a la familia, por lo menos la nuclear. Creo que aquí está el por qué se ve el feminismo con hostilidad y temor. Si se piensa que estamos cuestionando no sólo la familia, sino la sexualidad misma, y por lo tanto socavando cimientos de instituciones sociales, como esa que nombró H, además de los mismos estudios establecidos como la psicología, la sociología o el marxismo, no hay que sorprenderse. No sé cuántos se atreven a pensar como Rosalind Coward en *Patriarchal Precedents*, que hasta el instinto sexual es una construcción social.

J. ¡Pero cómo! ¿Entonces ella no reconoce la diferencia anatómica?

I. Sí, por supuesto, pero eso no quiere decir que la anatomía se corresponda con lo que se dice es cada sexo. Las conductas sexuales diferentes, las variedades de matrimonios, las distintas reglas sobre el incesto que van descubriendo la historia y la antropología, te destruyen las bases con que partieron muchas ciencias "universalistas". Pero, aún sin salir de la cultura europea predominante, se tiene que considerar que hay fenómenos humanos que los científicos no quisieron o pudieron ver porque estaban cegados por falsas premisas o temores inconscientes. Como dice Coward, el significado que se le da a la diferencia anatómica tiene que ver con las organizaciones del poder social. Por eso ella pide que se distinga entre fenómenos que ahora se toman como sinónimos, como el sexo (anatómico), la sexualidad, las relaciones sexuales y la división laboral por sexos. Así, entre otras cosas, se dejaría de considerar la heterosexualidad como patrón único de validez, y entraría la bisexualidad la homosexualidad, la masturbación, etc. a verse como prácticas no aberrantes.

J. Yo confieso que cuando oigo hablar de la sexualidad y de Freud y de complejos, me entra la desesperación. Creo que la obsesión del hambre que veo en mi país, me anula la importancia de lo sexual que las compañeras de los países más desarrollados discuten y discuten. Me fastidia que se defina al ser humano por su sexo, que es lo que compartimos con los animales. ¿Por qué no partir de la conciencia, o de los sentimientos, o de otra categoría humana más específica?

I. Lo que pasa J es que en el fondo, no se trata de sexo sino de la ideología de lo sexual que impone el poder. En inglés se habla del "sistema sexo-género", como A quiere que digamos, para designar los conceptos culturales agregados al sexo anatómico, que junto a otros aparatos ideológicos, son cruciales para la formación de la identidad. Como repiten muchas feministas, naces con vagina o pene, pero te hacen mujer u hombre, con todas las connotaciones de valores y jerarquías que esto significa. Esto sin entrar en el problema de que lo sexual y lo erótico abarca mucho más que lo genital, como se hace creer. Por eso, si cuestionas las nociones de lo 'femenino' o de lo 'masculino' que nos impone ese sistema sexo-género, vas sacando el hilo de un gran ovillo que te va a llevar a la familia, a la escuela, la iglesia, la economía y todo el aparataje estatal. La conciencia de que todas estas fuerzas te están continuamente presionando, o 'interpelando', como dicen algunos, ha contribuído a la noción aceptada hoy, de ver la formación de la identidad como proceso y no como fenómeno fijo...

G. Teresa de Lauretis dice en su *Feminist Studies/Critical Studies* que del discurso feminista va emergiendo un concepto de identidad múltiple, cambiante, muchas veces contradictoria, hecha con "representaciones heterogéneas y heterónomas" de género, raza y clase. Por no haberse visto así antes, se hablaba de la Mujer, como si se pudiera abarcar a todas las mujeres del mundo bajo una sola categoría, ocultándose sus diferencias.

A. Espérate un ratito G, por favor. A mí me confunde mucho esto de la identidad en proceso permanente, y el yo siempre diferido de que hablan las derrideanas. Por mucho aparato que me interpele, yo sé que soy mujer desde que nací y ...

G. Tienes que darte cuenta de que a la vez que somos sujeto en proceso, somos individuos que tenemos que identificarnos y elegir diariamente. ¿Puedes afirmar que tu sentirte mujer fue igual a los 14 años, cuando quizás para ti, el mantenerte virgen era un imperativo absoluto? ¿O que tus deseos y metas no variaron al estudiar y salir del ámbito del hogar? ¿O que al casarte y tener hijos no cambiaste?

C. Entiendo lo que dice A porque a veces una lee cosas que dan la impresión de que en esta infinidad de cambios no queda nada, todo se borra, y no hay de dónde agarrarse. Hay ya algunas feministas reaccionando contra la moda de la "inexistencia" del Yo, para decirlo en su forma más exagerada. Por ejemplo, Jane Flax sostiene que aunque ha sido muy importante deconstruir la noción del yo universal, elaborado con el patrón impuesto por la cultura blanca, occidental, masculina, ella como psiquíatra necesita la existencia de un "yo base" o "core self" para curar la fragmentación que sufren algunos enfermos mentales.

L. A mí no se me hace difícil aceptar esa glosa de Lauretis que hizo G. Puedo definirme en este momento como mujer, heterosexual, católica, maestra, antiimperialista; entre otras cosas, pero no puedo asegurar si en el futuro deje el catolicismo, me haga guerrillera, o comunista, o lesbiana, o lo que sea se me vaya imponiendo con mis experiencias y espero mayor conocimiento. Creo que estas nuevas nociones sirven para combatir las ideas conservadoras que se apoyan casi siempre en algo "esencial" como bases del ser humano y de las instituciones, para impedir cualquier cambio necesario.

D. Concuerdo contigo. Soy la primera en reconocer cómo la deconstrucción ha impulsado la práctica feminista por caminos más novedosos. Pero creo que debemos estar alerta al peligro de caer en la despolitización cuando se exageran o se malinterpretan ciertas nociones "postmodernistas". La popularidad del "yo descentrado" corre el riesgo de hacer olvidar que también somos agentes de cambios y de resistencias. Por esto recomiendo el libro de Ana Sojo *Mujer y política* que insiste en la heterogeneidad y pluralidad del sujeto político, justamente para no volar hacia abstracciones que se olvidan del ser concreto, de carne y hueso. Una cosa es rechazar las fijaciones esencialistas y metafísicas, pero otra es negar toda realidad.

J. Me pregunto por qué en el feminismo europeo y norteamericano tanto teórico como en la práctica escritural, figura el lesbianismo tan prominentemente, y aparece menos en Latinoamérica ¿Es porque como para mí el sexo resulta no relevante comparado con la sobrevivencia? ¿O nuestras escritoras son más pacatas? Puedo nombrar a Peri Rossi que escribe abiertamente sobre el lesbianismo y relaciona la opresión política y la sexual, pero no se me ocurre otro nombre.

L. A mí me parece que si hay temor al feminismo, hay terror a la homosexualidad. Ambos se ven atacando los fundamentos patriarcales. Fuera de los tabúes sembrados por la religión la prohibición de la homosexualidad tiene que ver con problemas económicos (no es relación productiva), además de los prejuicios generados por el machismo. Pienso que el afecto, que abre la comunicación entre los seres y exige la expresión erótica, es siempre positiva, y debería ser indiferente si se da entre miembros del mismo sexo. La verdad es que en nuestros países no se sabe o quiere saber cuán extensa es su práctica. Para nuestra perspectiva feminista, creo sería importante averiguar si es cierto, como se dice, que el lesbianismo es tolerado menos que la homosexualidad masculina, justamente por el desvalor de la mujer, y la hostilidad a que ella se salga del patrón asignado.

A. ¿Y qué me dicen de la homosexualidad en los países socialistas? No sé si lo de "antisocial" se lo ponen a los homosexuales porque si, obsesos con sus problemas personales, se niegan a colaborar en el proyecto colectivo, o por puro prejuicio.

D. Quizás al pensar que los homosexuales necesariamente tienen problemas personales, estás revelando tus propios prejuicios. Conozco homosexuales socialistas que viven muy contentos en Cuba porque están comprometidos profundamente con el proceso revolucionario. Por otro lado, se sabe que Cuba va muy lentamente erradicando el machismo.

H. Hablando del machismo tan arraigado en Latinoamérica, conviene recordar que aparece en formas tan poderosas como las legislaciones vigentes. El ejemplo más conocido es el tratamiento más severo a la adúltera que al adúltero, pero hay leyes que todavía determinan que la administración de la propiedad matrimonial es del marido, o que exigen que la esposa tiene el deber de cuidar a los niños y obedecer al esposo. Cecilia Medina tiene una lista de estos casos de leyes discriminatorias para la mujer.

D. Como siempre las leyes y las teorías andan atrasadas en relación a lo que ocurre en la realidad. Aquí en USA se habla con horror del gran porcentaje de familias mantenidas por mujeres solas. Tengo la sospecha de que este mismo fenómeno es viejo en Latinoamérica, y es más extendido de lo que se supone. Una gran mayoría de mujeres del pueblo alimenta a los hijos y al marido borracho, empuja la toma de tierras, los comedores populares, y otras maneras de mantener la vida.

G. Pero, ¿te das cuenta que las actividades que nombraste inciden justamente en las tareas de reproducción que es lo que cuestiona el feminismo como labor exclusiva de la mujer?

D. Si, me doy cuenta, y podemos discutir la cuestión de si la crianza de niños, porque forma la fuerza laboral futura, debe ser puesta también bajo la producción. Lo que yo quería era ejemplificar con la mujer del pueblo, una refutación categórica a las cualidades que se le dio tradicionalmente a lo femenino. Estas mujeres son, tienen que ser fuertes, decididas, activas, agresivas, si hay necesidad. Por lo demás, aunque su meta sea mantener a los hijos, lo que caería bajo la "reproducción", sus actividades, pongamos por caso, vender comida en la calle, producen dinero, tienen valor de cambio, son productivas. Otra cosa es que entren o no en las estadisticas de la economía "oficial". Aquí es donde los teóricos me dan dolores de cabeza con sus casilleros estancos de fenómenos fluídos, cambiables. Es absurdo mantener que la mujer pertenece al ámbito doméstico, cuando las necesidades económicas nos han tirado a la calle hace harto tiempo. Lo malo como todas sabemos, es tener que ganarse el pan, y ser responsable del trabajo casero también, sin que el hombre lo comparta.

F. Hay que tener cuidado en no idealizar o 'romantizar' rasgos de vidas que de verdad no se conocen. No sé si has leído las protestas de las feministas negras de este país contra el mito de la fortaleza de la mujer de color, que los sureños supieron explotar muy bien a su favor. Lo que no quiere decir que esa fortaleza sea inexistente. Las investigadoras peruanas del libro que cité, encontraron regiones en que la actividad productiva, como la agricultura o la ganadería estaba totalmente en manos de la mujer. Pero aún así, la obligación doméstica seguía sobre sus hombros.

H. Bueno, ¡de eso se trata, de borrar la separación entre lo doméstico y lo público como se ha asignado a los sexos! Las feministas quieren que se revalorice la reproducción, que se admita que ya no existe división: la política está en lo privado, lo que falta es transformar lo doméstico para que no sea sólo ámbito femenino. A mí me gustó lo que dijo ayer L en su trabajo, sobre el "pensar materno" que algunas norteamericanas propulsan se enseñe también a los hombres, no sólo a las mujeres, para que ellos cultiven desde que nacen esos rasgos maternales que se creían eran naturales.

L. Sí, pero recuerda que yo advertí que esas teorías de Rudduck y Chodorow tienen el peligro de hacer creer que los cambios fundamentales pueden ser individuales. ¡Se cambia la socialización de los sexos, ipso facto cambia la sociedad! Como dije, sin la transformación de las estructuras económicas y sociales, además de los cambios culturales, lo que proponen es ilusorio. No estoy segura de que una rica o un rico capitalista porque muda pañales y cocina va a cambiar fundamentalmente su deseo de hacer dinero y adquirir poder. No es sólo la ideología sobre lo privado lo que hay que cambiar, sino también la de lo público. Y con esto entramos en el problema de los valores, su jerarquización, y ya pisamos terreno más general, no sólo de las feministas. Creo que una de las razones por qué muchas norteamericanas han sido atacadas fue precisamente porque no pudieron ir más allá de programas liberales que iban a aliviar situaciones de injusticia, pero no a cambiar los sistemas que las generaban.

B. Yo creo que la corriente feminista que habla del "pensar materno" y todos esos rasgos positivos que Carol Gilligan halla en la mujer, está predicando una especie de 'superioridad' moral femenina parecida a la que sostenían los liberales del siglo XIX que sirvió para encadenarla al pedestal. Esto es peligroso porque se cae otra vez en esas dicotomías definidoras de lo masculino y lo femenino, que justamente originó el renacer del feminismo. Por otro lado, esta tesis simplifica el fenómeno de la maternidad que es mucho más complejo por estar sujeto a tantas fuerzas diversas. Si, por la parte positiva, es cierto que la socialización hacia la maternidad, en general, hace a la mujer más sensible al afecto, al énfasis en la relación en vez de la distancia, etc. se ocultan hechos como el placer erótico que obtiene la madre del contacto con su bebé, o las consecuencias de la limitada educación que recibe la mujer, que le impide hasta imaginar conductas diferentes. Tampoco se habla mucho del resentimiento que genera en muchas madres el trabajo constante a que las obliga la maternidad, ni de las madres que son tan posesivas, que pueden destruir a sus hijos.

A. ¿Conoces textos literarios en que se exponga esa complejidad de que hablas?

B. Bueno, no muchos. Quizás Peri Rossi y Albalucía Angel son las que van más lejos en desenmascarar a la madre burguesa posesiva y 'consumidora', y en explorar el placer erótico femenino. Pero creo que sigue imperando el modelo de la sacrificada entre nuestras escritoras. Pero esto no es extraño porque todavía la presión de los tabúes y la autocensura es muy fuerte. Por innombrables, esos fenómenos eran como inexistentes. Por lo demás, las mujeres mismas no han estado conscientes de ellos. Justamente es el feminismo el que está impulsando la exploración de estas zonas vedadas antes.

C. Yo no rechazo del todo ese pensar materno que Chodorow y Ruddick exaltan. La tesis psicoanalítica que explica cómo la formación de la identidad masculina es más difícil porque obliga al niño a separarse de la madre y adaptarse a un modelo más abstracto que el que la niña ve concretamente a su lado, parece plausible explicación del proceso de masculinización. El niño debe tapar su vertiente 'femenina' que reforzó al nacer con su contacto con la madre, para hacerse 'hombre'. Las implicaciones que puede tener este 'origen' de ciertos rasgos masculinos pueden ser enormes. Por ejemplo, en lo que concierne al belicismo. Sería estupendo que con una diferente socialización del hombre pudiera contribuirse a la disminución o extinción de las guerras.

D. A mí lo que no me gusta de esas autoras es que siguen enlazando la identidad, con el sexo y el desarrollo del niño en sus primeros cinco años, lo que niega la posibilidad de cambios de que hablábamos. Pero, aunque no soy muy optimista sobre los resultados de la socialización igual para los dos sexos, a veces pienso que una mayoría de las madres parece justificar con sus acciones ese "pensar materno" de que se habla. Un buen ejemplo lo dan las madres de los desaparecidos que bajo los regímenes totalitarios han hecho una labor política audaz y muy eficaz. Por esto me parece que no se puede adoptar actitudes tajantes de protesta contra la familia porque sólo resulta en divisiones. La literatura e historia del grupo negro en USA o de Latinoamérica, da ejemplos de núcleos familiares como asiento de ayuda, confianza, consuelo, lealtad...

B. Estoy de acuerdo, y pienso lo mismo sobre el papel de la iglesia en Latinoamérica. No se la puede atacar a rajatablas porque bajo las condiciones presentes muchas veces es una fuerza progresiva. Pero creo que éste es un caso explícito de praxis y creo que L estaba situada en lo teórico. Ya sé que me van a decir que no se pueden separar, pero de algún modo debemos llegar a explicar ciertas conductas. El caso de las "madres de los desaparecidos" no creo que esté impulsado por un 'pensar' o un 'sentir' diferente. Seguro que los padres, maridos o hijos, están igualmente afectados. La acción política de las madres puede ser resultado de una resolución táctica que vio como más efectiva la marcha de las madres, o de una contingencia de disponibilidad a ciertas horas, etc. Me da miedo que algunos principios teóricos de ciertas feministas, tapen o entierren la fuerza que ha tenido la penetración capitalista para contaminarlo todo con su ideología de la propiedad privada...

G. ¡Hasta la relación entre padres e hijos! Esto no es nada nuevo, si se acuerdan del uso que hicieron de la mujer y los niños los industriales en el siglo XIX. En otras palabras, creo que estamos diciendo que la ideología sobre la mujer y la familia es fundamental en la lucha política...

J. ¡Siempre y cuando esté informada por el feminismo y que los partidos participen de su visión, porque o si no tendremos que esperar hasta que triunfe la revolución! ¡Y aún así, no estamos seguras de que no nos sigan mandando a cocinar y a cuidar a los niños! En cuanto a lo que dice C, de la posible influencia antibélica del 'pensar materno', no sé cómo se explican entonces los casos de mujeres que llamaron a la guerra como en Chile en el 73, por ejemplo.

H. Este es el problema de algunas explicaciones psicoanalíticas que parecen estáticas e inoperables al situarlas en específicos momentos históricos movidos por fuerzas socio-económicas no contempladas en esos modelos. En

casos de contrarrevoluciones como la chilena, creo que
la primacía de una ideología política determinada borró
la diferencia entre los sexos. Claro que se me puede decir que esas mujeres que llamaban al golpe estaban mo-
vidas por el amor a sus hijos, y entonces no veo la ventaja de ese pensar materno.

G. Creo que las compañeras de los países más desarrollados
han puesto demasiado énfasis en separar lo privado y lo
público que quizás no sea división tan cerrada en muchas culturas. Para regresar a la literatura, ahí están los
libros de Domitila y Rigoberta para demostrarlo. A mí
me gustaría estudiarlos como una especie de épica contemporánea que en vez de héroe tiene una heroína que
habla desde la colectividad a la colectividad. El problema es que el curriculum de mi departamento no
tiene cabida para estos libros. Sólo se enseñan los géneros tradicionales -novela, cuento, teatro, poesía-. Mis
colegas dicen además, que no tienen valor literario, que
son sólo testimonios...

D. ¿Tampoco enseñan las cartas de Colón o Cortés o el Padre las Casas? o....

M. Desgraciadamente, aunque reconozco que aquí tenemos un problema práctico y urgente, tengo que cortar
esta dirección de la discusión. Esto de la validez del canon, afecta a los estudios feministas en general, que
como saben todavía son marginales. Reconozco también que en el caso de la latinoamericana la marginación es doble...

D. ¡Triple!: latinoamericana, mujer, feminista...

M. Bueno, como sea, la cuestión es que tenemos que tratar
de no dispersarnos en tantas direcciones.

C. Yo quisiera adherirme a lo que dijo D, y mencionar otro
libro de testimonios: *La mujer cubana en el quehacer de
la historia* que me gustó justamente porque se oyen voces de mujeres del pueblo. Muchas de las historias son
de compañeras que comenzaron analfabetas y terminaron como muy sofisticadas políticas. En otros casos, se
ve cómo las teorías con que empezaban tenían que mo-
dificarse o cambiar con los resultados de la práctica. El

puro sentido común y el espíritu de abnegación de esas mujeres...

L. ¡Cuidado con hacer fetiches del sentido común o de cualquier espíritu! La experiencia personal interpreta los hechos de acuerdo a las ideologías impuestas al sujeto. Mucho de lo que se ve a través del sentido común se cree que es 'natural', cuando ha sido impuesto por la cultura. Recuerda que, a propósito de la reproducción, una gran cantidad de mujeres es principal trasmisora y defensora del machismo, apoyándose en la experiencia y el sentido común. El feminismo está desenmascarando todas estas creencias y actitudes como ideologías, y no fenómenos inmutables de alguna 'esencia humana'. Este es el punto que B, creo, estaba tratando de presentar. Si los ejemplos que estamos viendo, muestran que muchas mujeres, sin educación, y con mínimos medios de subsistencia, pueden hacer lo que hacen, tienen un potencial tremendo para contribuir a los cambios que se desean. La cuestión no es sólo entender en algunos casos, qué es en su cultura lo que las ayuda a ser tan fuertes, sino cómo podemos nosotras, en nuestros respectivos trabajos, contribuir a encauzar ese potencial hacia una mayor autoconciencia para la acción personal y colectiva.

A. ¡No vamos a empezar otra vez con la cuestión del papel de la literatura en la vida real...y que si la pluma y el cañón por favor! Además que lo que dices L, me suena un poco al manipuleo de las mujeres por los partidos políticos del que algunas se han quejado amargamente.

M. No, no. Ya hemos decidido que partimos de considerar la literatura como un objeto ideológico con todas las consecuencias positivas y negativas que esto significa. Como aparato ideológico produce y reproduce modos de conducta, pero contribuye también a cuestionarlos. En cuanto a la relación con los partidos políticos, les ruego que no lo planteen ahora porque ya saben, se discutirá en sesión general mañana.

H. Sobre este asunto de las mujeres como trasmisoras de ideologías machistas, quiero mencionar otra vez la Secretaría de la mujer en Chile que une explícitamente la noción de Hogar con Patria. Recuerden que las mujeres de la derecha que azuzaban a los militares a insurreccionarse contra Allende, desafiaban su *hombría* para incitarlos. Esta invocación y el llamado 'peligro comunista' para la sobrevivencia de la familia y de los hijos, fueron el fundamento de su propaganda. La triste ironía es que hoy, más que nunca, se hace difícil esta sobrevivencia para las familias. Hay que reconocer que la derecha supo usar muy bien a sus mujeres.

D. Yo no sé si puedes decir *usar*. Esas mujeres estaban bien convencidas de donde estaban sus intereses. El hecho de que con sus conductas hayan roto los códigos más tradicionales sobre lo que una dama debía o no hacer, te demuestra la fuerza que pueden adquirir las mujeres cuando les tocan lo que consideran como más propio. La cosa es cómo cambiar esos intereses individuales, egoístas, reforzados ahora por cuanto medio de difusión se ha inventado.

N. Yo quisiera decir que junto con difundir los estudios antropológicos y sociológicos que se hagan sobre las mujeres de todas las clases sociales, habría que detenerse también a revisar los llamados "clasicos" del pensamiento latinoamericano. No hay duda que muchos de ellos, han contribuído a romper o a reafirmar los patrones de desigualdad; sobre todo si tuvieron algún poder, como Sarmiento, o Vasconcelos, por ejemplo. He leído afirmaciones de Antonio Caso, que te ponen carne de gallina. No sé si conocen unos artículos que escribió sobre el feminismo en que lo acusa de estar entre las teorías que producen la decadencia de la cultura. Entre otras cosas, este mexicano distinguido afirma que la menor duración de la función del ovario, demuestra la inferioridad de la mujer, en relación al varón. Como Spencer, Caso está convencido de que si no se realiza la función maternal, el organismo femenino se atrofia.

C. Bueno, si de clásicos se trata, yo estoy muy orgullosa de mi compatriota Eugenio María de Hostos que en sus trabajos sobre la educación científica de la mujer se muestra muy feminista. No sólo aboga allí por una mejor educación sino que va contra la opinión de hombres

como Spencer o Comte en cuanto a la supuesta inferioridad mental femenina. Me parece que en los atributos
que Hostos le da a la mujer va incluso más lejos que
John Stuart Mill.

G. Habrá que desenterrar también a las 'clásicas' Flora
Tristán, la Gorriti, Amanda Labarca, y otras tantas que
seguro nadie conoce. Pero es importante también revisar a los presentes, sobre todo cuando son reaccionarios
como Paz o Vargas Llosa, o misógenos como Arenas.
Creo que en este sentido Sharon Magnarelli hizo un
buen uso del feminismo en su libro *The Lost Rib*....

A. ¡Pero si no sólo hay que ir a los reaccionarios, fíjate en
los problemas que todavía tienen en Cuba con el machismo, a pesar del código familiar y todo!

C. Es verdad. En *La mujer cubana* se ve bien claro cómo
aun las mujeres que tenían padres o esposos o hermanos luchando al lado de Fidel, tenían problemas para
integrarse a los diferentes trabajos porque no querían
que ellas salieran de la casa. Ahora quizás sea menor la
resistencia, pero tampoco puedes esperar que se cam-
bien hábitos de centurias con sólo legislación. Lo bonito
del Código familiar es que fue discutido a todo nivel social, hubo participación masiva en su aprobación.

G. A mí me gustaría volver a la literatura y al problema de
la separación del juicio estético del contexto histórico, o
lo que algunas llaman las contradicciones entre la lectura "apreciativa" y la "política". Me parece que es demasiado fácil resolver esta cuestión diciendo "toda lectura es política". Quisiera más argumentos para con-
vencer a los que eligen textos sólo porque tienen ya reconocida "calidad" aunque representen una ideología
retrógrada y peligrosa. Reconozco que este problema es
bien complejo y no es exclusivo del campo
latinoamericano.

J. Bueno, esos textos no se pueden hacer desaparecer, sea
como sea, son parte de nuestra historia. La cuestión es
que hay que enseñarlos con un ojo muy crítico y usarlos
para destruir nociones injustas y prejuiciosas.

D. Pero también hay que saber quiénes son esos
"elegidores". En este momento, creo que nosotras mis-

mas entramos en ese saco, aunque claro, tenemos menos poder que la mayoría masculina que ha podido por más largo tiempo decidir qué se lee. Me parece que la necesidad de la teoría sale justamente de la insatisfacción que sentimos con modelos de práctica insensitivos a cuestiones que consideramos importantes. Aunque no hemos definido lo que vamos a llamar teoría literaria feminista latinoamericana, me parece que todo lo que se ha venido diciendo tiene que ver con el estado actual de nuestros países y nuestro quehacer profesional. El consenso a que lleguemos tendrá que partir de estos hechos básicos.

L. Yo creo que toda teoría está arraigada al momento histórico de su formulación, es inevitable. Pero recordemos la heterogeneidad de las mujeres latinoamericanas. Si la teoría pretende comprender, explicar el mundo de la mujer ¿puede ser tan comprensiva en nuestro caso? ¿Y qué pasa con las feministas que siguen líneas de partidos específicos? ¿Podremos mantenernos unidas o nos dividiremos, como el feminismo norteamericano separado según líneas políticas determinadas?

D. Yo no puedo ver entre las latinoamericanas un feminismo de derechas como ocurre aquí en USA. Me parece una contradicción de términos. Mi concepción del feminismo sólo encaja en presupuestos de cambios radicales de las estructuras socio-económicas. Las cuestiones de igualdad de sueldo, aborto, o pornografía, por ejemplo, que despiertan tanta pasión aquí, y divide a las feministas, me parecen secuelas de problemas estructurales más profundos que no se tocan en las discusiones. Importantes como son estas cosas, se esfuman un poco si se las compara con el hambre, con los altos porcentajes de cesantía de hombres y mujeres de nuestros países. Por esto no creo que podamos eludir el subdesarrollo económico cuando intentemos definir nuestros propósitos y elaborar una teoría.

B. Yo te diría amén D, siempre y cuando recordáramos que el desarrollo económico 'per se' no borra el sexismo. ¡Si fuera así no habría feministas en USA o en Europa!

M. Creo que ya se ha hecho hincapié en el peso de la cultura y otros factores decisivos en esa cuestión. Además, lamentablemente, ya se nos acaba el tiempo. Voy a darle la palabra a A, como lo prometí, y por último a F, que hace rato tiene la mano levantada.

A. Bueno, en realidad voy a ser portavoz de muchas que sentimos que hay que tener cuidado en la traducción y uso de términos extranjeros que no se dan con facilidad en el español. No tenemos soluciones ahora, y habrá muchos otros términos que se pudieran incluir. Mi propia lista tiene los siguientes del inglés: "womanhood", "femaleness", "gender system", "gendered subjectivity", "ageist society", "womanness", "nurturing being", "women's mothering".

M. Propongo que A y las que estén interesadas en este problema estudien las posibles mejores versiones para estos y otros vocablos y las presenten para discusión. F, te toca a ti.

F. Si soy la última, entonces voy a dejar la pregunta y a usar, cada loco con su tema, el libro sobre el Congreso de Lima para mencionar un problema que allí expresaron muchas compañeras. Se trata del temor que muchas tienen de que la labor académica sea demasiado elitista y apartada de las vidas concretas de la mayoría de las mujeres. Comparto grandemente este temor. En la mayoría de los trabajos allí presentados se leía una especie de ley no escrita de relacionar todo con tareas y metas específicas de política activa. Como dije antes, creo que aquí está la diferencia más obvia entre las feministas que están trabajando en nuestros países y nosotras. El problema es cómo podemos desde aquí, USA, y desde el medio académico, contribuir mejor a la lucha en que ellas están empeñadas.

M. Creo que F plantea la pregunta cuya respuesta vale un millón como se dice aquí. Desgraciadamente tenemos que terminar, así que agregaremos este asunto a los que ya tenemos.

J. Antes de retirarnos quisiera decir que no estoy muy satisfecha con esta reunión porque parece que hay dos canales que no se comunican: por un lado todas las cuestiones sociales y políticas que se han mencionado, y por el otro los textos literarios y los parámetros teóricos bajo los cuales deseamos leerlos. ¿Por qué no lees M la lista de tópicos que hemos venido acumulando para discutir, a ver si podemos añadir otros que ayuden a juntar estos canales?

M. Muy bien. Además, ya saben que tenemos que elegir a otra moderadora para la reunión libre de mañana. Quisiera sugerir que en vez de ser abierta en cuanto a temas, eligiéramos uno o dos como centro. Comparto lo que dice J y puede que así no nos dispersemos tanto como hoy. Los tópicos que tengo anotados son, sin orden de prioridad, y tal como lo mencionó cada una, los siguientes: 1) Poder cualitativo y cuantitativo de la televisión y otros medios masivos de información en la identidad de la mujer actual. 2) La lectura estética versus lectura política ¿falsa dicotomía? 3) Teorías de las francesas sobre la escritura femenina y su relevancia para el feminismo latinoamericano. 4) Relación entre mujer, feminismo y religión (sobre todo la teología de la liberación). 5) La literatura como invención de nuevas formas de convivencia. 6) Divergencias y convergencias entre el feminismo de España y el latinoamericano. 7) El problema del canon literario, criterios y justificaciones. 8) ¿Qué se entiende por teoría feminista latinoamericana? 9) Problemas de traducción de vocablos extranjeros para mayor comprensión de su significado y uso en la teoría y la práctica de las feministas hispanoamericanas.

POSTSCRIPTUM. El problema de la traducción de términos me fue sugerido por intercambios ocurridos en la reunión de abril, 1988. Agradezco a las/los participantes y a la Universidad de Minnesota por esta oportunidad para añadir este asunto y aclarar otros que presenté en la primera versión de este diálogo.

OBRAS CITADAS

Anderson de Velasco, Jeanine, editora. *Congreso de investigación acerca de la mujer en la región andina. Informe final,* Lima: Asociación Perú-Mujer, 1983.

Andreas, Carol. *When Women Rebel: the Rise of Popular Feminism in Peru,* Westport, Connecticut: L. Hill, 1985.

Barrios, Domitila y Moema Viezzer. *Si me permiten hablar... Testimonio de Domitila una mujer de las minas de Bolivia,* México: Siglo XXI, 1977.

Bravo, Rosa y Rosalba Todaro. "Chilean Women and the UN Decade for Women," *Women's Studies International Forum,* 8, Nº. 2 (1985), 111-116.

Burgos, Elizabeth. *Me llamo Rigoberta Menchú y así me nació la conciencia,* Barcelona: Argos Vergara, 1983.

Caso, Antonio. "Feminismo y sociología", *Obras completas,* Universidad Nacional de México, 1975, v. VIII, pp. 200-204.

Coward, Rosalind. *Patriarchal Precedents Sexuality and Social Relations,* London: Routledge and Kegan Paul, 1983, pp. 277-286.

De Lauretis, Teresa, editor, *Feminist Studies/Critical Studies,* Bloomington: Indiana University Press, 1986, p. 9.

Flax Jane. "Re-membering the Selves: Is the Repressed Gendered?," *Michigan Quarterly Review,* (Winter 1987), 92-110.

Gates, Henry Louis, Jr. *Black Literature and Literary Theory,* London: Methuen, 1984.

Gilligan, Carol. *In a Different Voice: Psychological Theory and Women's Development,* Cambridge: Harvard Univ. Press, 1982.

Hostos, Eugenio María de. "La educación científica de la mujer", *Obras completas,* Habana, Cuba: Cultural, 1939, v. XII, tomo 1, pp. 7-65. Preparamos una edición comentada de estos ensayos que publicará la Universidad de Puerto Rico.

Magnarelli, Sharon. *The Lost Rib: Female Charecters in the Spanish-American Novel,* Lewisburg: Bucknell University Press, 1985.

Medina, Cecilia. "Women's Rights as Human Rights: Latin American Countries and the Organization of the American States (OAS)," en *Women, Feminist Identity and Society in the 1980's, Selected Papers,* editoras Myriam Díaz-Diocaretz e Iris M. Zavala, Amsterdam: John Benjamins, 1985, pp. 61-79.

Ruddick, Sara. "Maternal Thinking," *Feminist Studies* 6, Nº. 2, (Summer 1980), 342-367.

Séjourné, Laurette con la colaboraciónde Tatiana Coll. *La mujer cubana en el quehacer de la historia,* México: Siglo XXI, 1980.

Sojo, Ana. *Mujer y política: Ensayo sobre el feminismo y el sujeto popular,* San José, Costa Rica: Departamento Ecuménico de investigaciones, (DEI), 1985.

THE PROBLEMATICAL PERMUTATIONS OF FEMINIST THEORY

Elizabeth J. Ordóñez
University of Texas, Arlington

In this poststructuralist, postmodernist generation we are by now quite accustomed to the archeological play of reading literature for intertextuality or the rewritings of textual precursors that resonate infinitely in their successors. However, though there is a growing body of critical theory which owes its own existence to intertextuality, we are less apt to think of our applications of the theories of others as a problematical and even ambivalent coming to terms with a critical intertext. And yet the critic, too, attempts to write her way out from an encircling "anxiety of influence" which only at her peril can she ignore.

The purpose of this paper will be to explore, from an admittedly personal and selective perspective, salient aspects of the feminist critical intertext as it echoes in the present generation of principally North American critics working with texts that may or may not be North American. In other words, my survey will acknowledge influences that have made themselves felt on my own readings, with the assumption that I am not unique in these experiences; rather I shall seek to speak as a metonymic representative of a particular generation which inhabits a specific time and place. Furthermore, this exploration of critical intertextuality will proceed with the knowledge that nothing is fixed, that what I may say today is but the latest utterance in a process undergoing constant flux and change. As do literary texts, the metatext or self-conscious critical reflection on texts is always a dynamic process, a series of negotiations and (ex)changes, a give and take that interacts, questions, seeks to break out of borders and restrictions while never forgetting that all critical discourse, indeed all writing, is "confined by the parameters of discourse at a particular moment" (Stanton 158). And perhaps disappointingly, that moment, too, is confined to what Domna Stanton has ruefully named the "imperfect present" (Stanton 158).

Imperfection, however, is certainly preferable to ossification or rigidity for the sake of purity of purpose or what we might call, echoing Stanton, a "present perfect." What feminist theory has done perhaps better than other modes of critical discourse is to welcome multiplicity or heterogeneity as postures essential for the destabilization of ideological or cultural hegemony. When Jerry Aline Flieger talks of the importance of "reconnaissance" or the acknowledgement of the work of the other critic as essential for one's own orientation within the existent critical interext, I realize that feminist criticism--perhaps because of its youth and desire to be taken seriously--has, especially most recently, an increasingly impressive track record of self-criticism and reflection. Here I think specifically of recent thoughts on feminist theory by such critics as Peggy Kamuf, Jean Bethke Elshtain, Jane Gallop and Gayatri Spivak. Conscious that all critics view reality "through an Imaginary grillwork of Ideology," as Flieger has warned (Flieger 55), feminist criticism is thus increasingly aware that it must become itself the "subject for critical inquiry" (Elshtain 129). For these reasons, this paper will reflect back on personal and generational milestones in feminist theory that have affected the way we read and write about literature by and about women, and it will attempt to place in perspective how these influences are shaping our present thoughts on the problematical issue of feminist critical theory.

In the beginning was the "raising of consciousness," that first sally into the stark awareness that gender arrangements were unbalanced and had been so for a very long time. This was bleak and disappointing terrain for these early explorers (of the present generation), for we were driven as much by a zeal to rearrange economies of power and authority which organize the sexes as we were by the disinterested quest for knowledge. (As you well know, initial American and European feminist scholarship was often motivated by anger and rage as research uncovered ubiquitous evidence of gender imbalance across cultures.) Anthropologists looking at gender relations found that in every human culture women are in some way subordinate to men. As Michelle Zimbalist Rosaldo discovered in the seventies: "Women may be important, powerful, and influential, but it seems that, relative to men of their age and social status, women everywhere lack generally recognized and culturally valued authority" (Rosaldo 17). More recently, historian, Gerda Lerner, broadens and further universalizes this disconcerting yet undeniable assymetry between the sexes: "There is not a single society known where women-as-a-group have decision-making power *over* men or where they define the rules of sexual conduct or control marriage exchanges" (Lerner, *Creation* 30).

Increasingly, we came to see how this assymmetry in the social sphere is inevitably undergirded and overdetermined by the reigning ideologies of each culture in question. In her classic *Second Sex*, Simone de Beauvoir established the essential imbalance structuring Western culture's concept of masculine and feminine. From ancient times to the present the figure for humanness has been man; woman has been the Other. But given Beauvoir's existential perspective, she refused to settle for this age old predicament. Instead she exorted woman to assert her right to humanness: "I believe that she has the power to choose between the assertion of her transcendence and her alienation as object; she is not the plaything of contradictory drives; she devises solutions of diverse ranking in the ethical scale" (Beauvoir 45). Interestingly, Beauvoir's existential ideology empowered us to "seek self-fulfillment in transcendence" (Beauvoir 46), but it left us largely unprepared to imagine humanness outside its masculine definition. Beauvoir's prescription for female liberation was still grounded largely upon the Aristotelian and hierarchical assumption that maleness signifies transcendence and is essentially less alienated than the corporeal immanence of the female. Implicitly, if not explicitly, to be truly human one had to be more like a man, repress the female body for the sake of transcendence to a higher rung of the "ethical scale."

A well-known American response to the asymmetry of gender roles in Western culture was, of course, Kate Millet's *Sexual Politics*, the "book that started it all!" (according to the publishers), certainly a primary catalyst for subsequent studies of misogyny in male-authored texts. Even my more tempered "Sexual Politics and the Theme of Sexuality in Chicana Poetry" clearly echoes Millet and owes its inspiration and orientation to Millet's perceptive anger. In fact, looking back on these earlier angry responses to gender differences, I see that the privileging in my own early work of thematic inventories of female oppression (issuing from the convincing assumption that the female experience in patriarchal culture must almost always be oppressive) is largely a result of my readings of these trailblazers in gender studies. Similarly, others in those earlier years concentrated on exposing stereotypes of women in literature (often negative or enfeebling), the misogyny of the literary tradition and/or canon, the exclusion of women from literary history and anthologies. In our field the work of Lidia Falcón and María Aurelia Capmany in Spain, and that of American Hispanists such as Beth Miller, Edna Sims, and Constance Sullivan broke new ground in the unveiling of the above-mentioned inequities. Both in this country and abroad, critics sought to establish connections between the socio-historical and literary mistreatment of women, and, as a result, the ways in which we would subsequently read or reread hallowed works underwent radical revision. As Lawrence Lipking has recently observed: "Something peculiar has been happening lately to the classics. Some of them now seem less heroic, and some of them less funny. Those 'irrelevant' scenes of cruelty to women, those obsessions with chastity and purity, those all-male debates about the nature and future of the human race, those sacrifices of feeling to duty have changed their character. Some old masters even look silly. Under the gaze of women, strong writers turn pale" (Lipking 79).

As feminist theorists continued to gaze into heretofor invisible places, they began to uncover other aspects of culture and other texts. In the early seventies two Oxford anthropologists, Shirley and Edwin Ardener, proposed that since past anthropological findings were based on male-oriented categories and models of history and culture, findings that did not fit these models were often classified as aberrant or deviant or were simply ignored. It turned out that not even anthropologists were always culturally neutral. As a corrective, the Ardeners advanced a theory of simultaneous cultural duality; that is, they suggested that women consitute a "muted group," the boundaries of whose culture and reality overlap, but are not wholly contained by, the "dominant (male) group." The articulation of this perspective conferred a certain authority on women, and more importantly, one which need not correspond to man's more publicly or dominantly articulated power. Indeed the critical eye shifted and began to see less visible, contrasting views; the ear learned to hear less audible voices of a different timbre. Historical scholars affirmed similar views, like this one by Gerda Lerner: "Women live their social existence within the general culture and whenever they are confined by patriarchal restraint or segregation into separateness (which always has subordination as its purpose), they transform this restraint into complementarity (asserting the importance of woman's function, even its "superiority") and redefine it. Thus, women live a duality —as members of the general culture and as partakers of women's culture" (Lerner, *Majority* 52). (It was Lerner's proposal that enabled me to formulate a theoretical framework for my article, "The Concept of Cultural Identity in Chicana Poetry," in which I focus upon some of the less visible areas of Chicano culture which find their expression in poetry by Chicanas.)

This recognition of women's culture corresponds to a second phase of feminist literary theory and criticism during which scholars began to discover that women writers had a "literature of their own." Patricia Meyer Spacks, one of the first of this tendency in the United States, found that women writing throughout the centuries shared similarities of experience and responses in writing. Probably deeply influenced by Beauvoir, Spacks studied, in *The Female Imagination*, aspects of female experience such as power and passivity, adolescent development, the female artist, and the independent woman. Though she has been criticized for her ahistorical and acultural use of the concept of "female" imagination, she heightened my awareness that female heroism may express itself in forms other than those defined by patriarchal standards, and thus provided a fresh perspective that eventually led to my recent study of female heroism in Dolores Medio's *Diario de una maestra*. Spacks' insistence on the idea of "taking care" as a form of female heroism enables us to recognize acts which may be muted by the cloistered hush of the drawing room, even as we may feel an ambivalent uneasiness about the troubling potential of this perspective to glorify the restrictions of women's lives. Here, as in other instances, the most promising option seems to be that of engaging in gingerly negotiations between the acceptance of those aspects of theory which open texts and experience to new light and possibilities and the rejection of those implications which might push us back into regions of discomfort and even oppression.

Two years after Spacks' study, Elaine Showalter's *A Literature of Their Own: British Women Novelists from Brontë to Lessing* went further to establish an historical and cultural framework for modern fiction by British women. Showalter replaced traditional literary periods with three stages in women's literary history, stages marked by an increasing growth of feminist consciousness: the first or *feminine* is characterized by an imitation of prevailing modes of the dominant tradition; the second or *feminist* protests against these standards and values and advocates minority rights and values; the *female* turns inward toward a search for identity and self-discovery.

Showalter's paradigm has been criticized for measuring its authors against an ideal of self-development belonging to the late twentieth century (a peccadillo that was rather prevalent at the time) and for assuming that history moves toward greater and greater degrees of self-consciousness and improvement. Still, her tentative categories helped us see that women may employ varied narrative strategies or write in different voices given differing cultural conditions, and in a more general sense they simply made us more receptive to and capable of discerning variety and change in literary expression by women.

The study from this period which was to have the greatest impact beyond the boundaries of Anglo-American criticism was Sandra M. Gilbert and Susan Gubar's *The Madwoman in the Attic: The Woman Writer and the Nineteenth-Century Literary Imagination.* I believe its influence has been proportionate to its size and weight (it boasts 719 pages), for one can hardly read or write about nineteenth century literature by women without considering its theoretical implications. Revising Harold Bloom's Oedipal model of literary history as a conflict between fathers and sons, Gilbert and Gubar replaced Bloom's concept of "anxiety of influence" with "anxiety of authorship," showing how women writers struggled with male precursors and patriarchal discourse to express themselves in a culture whose readers might feel antagonism and/or indifference toward the woman who claims the pen. Gilbert and Gubar succeeded in showing, elegantly and convincingly, that the endeavors of these writers often produce submerged, even subversive meanings which may at once conform to and deviate from dominant or patriarchal literary discourse. Interestingly, these theories correspond to the Ardener's concept of cultural duality, to Elaine Showalter's analogous concept of a "dominant" and "muted" story ("Feminist Criticism in the Wilderness"), and to Nancy K. Miller's theory of "another text" ("Emphasis Added"). One can certainly hear echoes of these theoretical influences in two of my recent articles on works by pre-contemporary Spanish women writers: "Woman and Her Text in the Works of María de Zayas and Ana Caro" and "¿Y mi niña? Another Voice in *Los pazos de Ulloa.*" Gilbert and Gubar's proposal thus effects a kind of quantum jump in considerations of how the female-inscribed text and its author negotiates with its literary and non-literary culture; it recognizes the possibility of an all-embracing both/and in women's texts, a perception toward which Showalter's earlier successive, but mutually exclusive, stages seemed to be gesturing.

Rounding out my selective view of this second phase of feminist criticism is a consideration of Annis Pratt's *Archetypal Patterns in Women's Fiction,* another study which has influenced my own work and has been useful in guiding the reading of my graduate students. Northrop Frye's *Anatomy of Criticism* is the central intertext of Pratt's contribution, but her uneasiness with the limitations of Frye's theories when applied to the experiences of the female hero led her to an investigation of a vast body of women's literature and to the discovery of certain archetypal patterns common to that corpus of texts. In her earlier "wave theory," she articulated the premise that was to structure her subsequent book: that "there is a considerable degree of continuity in the woman's novel, a uniformity of concern and an abundance of analogues that indicate the possibility that fiction by women is a body of material that can be described as a self-contained universe following its own organic principles" (Pratt, "Exploring" 181). Indeed, female hero or anti-hero plots in texts written by and about women often reveal differences from the contours of traditional patriarchal myth which present, in the main, a conception of man as hero and woman as other or helper. These differences in texts of women may even evince vexation with the traditional roles of women in the myths of Western culture.

Accordingly, I have read the disquieting stories of women diminished by the weight of male-defined myth; conversely, I have also discovered a tendency on the part of women writers to engage in alternate mythopoeic processes in which woman may fashion herself a hero according to her own terms. As Pratt's paradigmatic discoveries insinuated themselves into my own critical text, I found that in certain contemporary Hispanic narratives by women, female "heroes" embark upon quests for matrilinear identity and the elusive boon of androgyny. Feminist myth and archetypal criticism has thus especially helped illumine for me works by Concha Alós and Esther Tusquets. Still, as with the work of Spacks, one could level the charge against Pratt that her archetypal approach washes away the differences in female experience wrought by the workings of history and cultural specificity. Yet without doubt there are experiences that bind women across cultures, and the recognition of these links need not be mutually exclusive with a recognition of the ways in which such common patterns may express themselves within a specific cultural context. Even Fredric Jameson does not reject the theories of Northrop Frye, but instead seeks to historicize them by considering how, for example, the romance paradigm contains reality and seeks to transform it rather than escape from it or substitute for it (Jameson 110). The myths and archetypes of women's texts may be said to engage in a similar enterprise.

During the present decade, the widespread influence of deconstruction and French feminism, with its concepts of "l'écriture féminine," presents a felicitous convergence of theories which are as suggestive as they are problematical. In my recent article, "Inscribing Difference: 'L'Ecriture Féminine' and New Narrative by Women," I have summarized how French feminists have responded to Freud's reading of female sexuality as a lack and to Jacques Lacan's positing of the phallus as the ultimate signifier structuring desire, by attempting to circumvent this symbolic order of culture and language dominated by what Lacan has called the "law of the Father." Seeking to devise a mode of expressivity outside this paternal or dominant discourse, they attempt to structure a discourse closer to the female body and identified with the mother rather than the father. Thus one could say, at the risk of gross oversimplification, that all those engaged in the working out of these theories express a common desire to displace the reigning hierarchy with the primacy of what they have named the "feminine." The goals of theorists such as Julia Kristeva, Hélène Cixous and Luce Irigaray share a tendency toward subversion of and escape from the dominant paternal order and affirmation of some still-to-be defined feminine alternative, one which works to establish what Ann Rosalind Jones has named a "site of 'différence,' a point of view from which phallogocentric concepts and controls can be seen through and taken apart" (Showalter, *NFC* 362). Cixous, for example, proposes bringing "women to their senses and to their meaning in history" (*NFF* 245), a call I have found particularly helpful in perceiving a similar concern now surfacing in the works of Spain's youngest generation of women writers ("Rewriting Myth and History").

Since I have already addressed connections between current French feminist thought and recent critical and creative writing by Spanish women in "Inscribing Difference," I shall forego further echoes of those observations here. Suffice it to say that the influence of France on Spain in this area is not insignificant, the defiant posture of French feminist theory providing an energizing and liberating impetus to Spanish female expression which was until the present decade substantially supressed. For specific cultural and historical reasons the appeal of French feminist subversion became one which slipped quite naturally into the Spanish context and served the needs of the historical moment with almost tailor-made precision. And yet Spanish feminists have leveled critiques similar to those which we have cited for the theories of female culture or archetypes--chief among them is the one by Empar Pineda which I cite in "Inscribing": that by affirming a feminism of difference located principally in the maternal principle, we could end up right back where we started if the prior question of change in the structures of dominant ideology remains unposed (Pineda 261).

Here in the United States, Jane Gallop has voiced similar reservations to the deceptive difference of the maternal as outside and beyond the bounds and bonds of the paternal: "to move beyond the father, the mother looks like an alternative, but if we are trying to move beyond patriarchy, the mother is not outside... the institution of motherhood is a cornerstone of patriarchy" (Gallop 322). Domna Stanton, too, warns how the maternal of French feminism "is dangerously close to recreating in 'deconstructive' language the traditional assumptions on femininity and female creativity" (Stanton 174). As an antidote to this regressive lure, Stanton proposes replacing the maternal as metaphor with the maternal as metonymy, thus shifting the emphasis from "difference from" man to "differences within" and "among" women. This substitution of tropes would underscore "the desire for the other, for something/ somewhere else, a desire extended along an indefinite chain of signifiers...," and would be capable of exposing "specific cultural values, prejudices, and limitations" (Stanton 175). It certainly would foster continued openness to variety and heterogeneity in feminist theory, thus discouraging undesirable temptations to impose or fix forever any single, global or hegemonic theory on all. In short, Stanton's proposal would help insure the continued subversive indeterminacy and lack of finality in feminist discourse that Peggy Kamuf has named "plurivocality and plurilocality" (Kamuf 47).

Whatever we say or whatever we write, therefore, will always be part and parcel of an ongoing discourse into which we insert ourselves at particular and varying points. Our individual utterances can never be entirely encompassing, nor should they be; neither can they be separate or detached. Returning again to the comments of Jerry Aline Flieger, whatever position the feminist theorist or critic may take, she must begin by "relinquishing any claim to a position outside ideology" (Flieger 56). For the world, the text, and the critic are all caught up in an inevitable and indestructible paradox: the more they might wish to elude what Flieger has called the "grillwork of ideology," the more they become implicated among the plurality of its inmates. Our best, indeed our only, option is to learn to hear wisdom through the garble, and then hope to respond with sensitivity and boundless imagination.

Since the preceding remarks were written, read, and discussed, I feel obliged to add as a postscript some brief comments in response to the question: where do I presently locate myself/ourselves on the landscape I have just outlined? At the risk of sounding redundant (and perhaps exasperatingly noncommital), I feel the need to reiterate how each moment of the critical enterprise represents a unique confluence of ideologies, and how each self who acts as critic is engaged in an ongoing, dynamic process with a complex cultural totality made-up of elements from the present and the past. Each individual confronts these elements in ways that are at once shared and unique, the latter being those that render the occupation of criticism its vitality and transformative potential. However, since each one of us intersects with texts and their cultural contexts at subtly different points, it is our responsibility, as critics, to assess the meaning of those points of convergence. In so doing, we will inevitably find that the terrain —the cultural, political, ideological ground— on which we stand as we formulate our assessment will demand its own clarification.

The text will also make its own claims and demands. It, too, occupies a space and partakes in a moment. We thus owe it to the text to confront and assess its location with all the pertinent historical and cultural information we can muster. (Many papers of this collection illustrate just how this can be done, and they do so with solidity and brilliance.) Once we converge with a text, neither it nor we will ever be the same. We will have rewritten it; it will have rewritten us, for our next critical venture will be unlike any before it. Another nuance will have been added to the way we read, and our view of the world beyond the text will likewise be forever altered. The paradoxical task and joy of the feminist critic, then, is to revel in this adventure of process. More than likely, it will prove not at all inauspicious if we refuse to be definitively or absolutely pinned down. For in opting instead for the ongoing, all-embracing process of opening up texts, reading, and experience to as yet uncharted possibilites, we may break beyond the boundaries of the oppressive, the intransigent, and most importantly, the known.

WORKS CITED

Ardner, Edward. "Belief and the Problem of Women." *Perceiving Women.* Ed. Shirley Ardner. New York: John Wiley, 1975.

Beauvoir. Simone de. *The Second Sex.* Trans. and ed. H.M. Parshley. New York: Bantam Books, 1970.

Capmany, María Aurelia. *De profesión mujer.* Barcelona: Plaza y Janés, 1971.

—. *El feminismo ibérico.* Bracelona: Oikos-tau, 1970.

Elshtain, Jean Bethke. "Feminist Discourse and Its Discontents: Language, Power, and Meaning." In *Feminist Theory: A Critique of Ideology.* Ed. Nannerl O. Keohane, Michelle Z. Rosaldo, and Barbara C. Gelpi. Chicago: U of Chicago P, 1982. 127-45.

Falcón, Lidia. *Mujer y sociedad.* Barcelona: Edit. Fontanella, 1969.

Flieger, Jerry Aline. "The Prison-House of Ideology: Critic as Inmate." *Diacritics* 12 (Fall 1982): 47-56.

Frye, Northrop. *Anatomy of Criticism.* New York: Atheneum, 1968.

Gallop, Jane. "Reading the Mother Tongue: Psychoanalytic Feminist Criticism." *Critical Inquiry* 13 (Winter 1987): 314-29.

Gilbert, Sandra A. and Susan Gubar. *The Madwoman in the Attic: The Woman Writer and the Nineteenth-Century Literary Imagination.* New Haven: Yale UP, 1979.

Jameson, Fredric. *The Political Unconscious: Narrative as a Socially Symbolic Act.* New York: Cornell UP, 1981.

Jones, Ann Rosalind. "Writing the Body: Toward an Understanding of l'Ecriture féminine." In *The New Feminist Criticism: Essays on*

Women, Literature, and Theory. Ed. Elaine Showalter. New York: Pantheon Books, 1985. 361-77.

Kamuf, Peggy. "Replacing Feminist Criticism." *Diacritics* 12 (Summer 1982): 42-47.

Lerner, Gerda. *The Creation of Patriarchy.* New York: Oxford UP, 1986.

—. *The Majority Finds Its Past.* New York: Oxford UP, 1979.

Lipking, Lawrence. "Aristotle's Sister: A Poetics of Abandonment." *Critical Inquiry* 10 (Sept. 1983): 61-81.

Marks, Elaine and Isabelle de Courtivron, eds. *New French Feminisms: An Anthology.* Amherst: U of Mass. P, 1980.

Miller, Beth. *Mujeres en la literatura.* Mexico: Fleischer Editora, 1978.

Miller, Nancy K. "Emphasis Added: Plots and Plausibilities in Women's Fiction." *PMLA* 96 (Jan. 1981): 36-48. Rpt. *The New Feminist Criticism.* 339-60.

Millet, Kate. *Sexual Politics.* New York: Avon Books, 1970.

Ordóñez, Elizabeth. "A Quest for Matrilineal Roots and Mythopoesis: Esther Tusquets' *El mismo mar de todos los veranos.*" *Crítica Hispánica* 6 (1984): 37-46.

—. "Diario de una maestra: Female Heroism and the Context of War." *Letras Femeninas* 12 (primavera-otoño 1986): 52-59.

—. "Inscribing Difference: 'L'Ecriture Feminine' and New Narrative by Women." *Anales de la Literatura Española Contemporánea* 1 2 (1987): 45-58.

—. "Rewriting Myth and History: Three Recent Novels by Women." In *Feminine Concerns in Contemporary Spanish Fiction by Women.* Ed. Robert Manteiga, Carolyn Gallerstein, and Kathleen McNerney. Potomac, Maryland: Scripta Humanistica, 1988.

—. "Sexual Politics and the Theme of Sexuality in Chicana Poetry." In *Women in Hispanic Literature: Icons and Fallen Idols.* Ed. Beth Miller. Berkeley: U of Calif. P, 1983. 316-39.

—. "The Concept of Cultural Identity in Chicana Poetry." *Third Woman* 2 (1984): 75-82.

—. "The Female Quest Pattern in Concha Alós' *Os habla Electra*. *Revista de Estudios Hispánicos* 14 (Jan 1980): 51-64.

—. "Woman and Her Text in the Works of María de Zayas and Ana Caro." *Revista de Estudios Hispánicos* 19 (Jan. 1985): 3-15.

—. "¿Y mi niña? Another Voice in *Los pazos de Ulloa*." *Discurso literario: Revista de temas hispánicos* 3 (Fall 1985): 121-31.

Pineda, Empar. "El discurso de la diferencia. El discurso de la igualdad." In *Nuevas perspectivas sobre la mujer*. Ed. M. A. Durán. Madrid: Universidad Autonoma de Madrid, 1982. 257-71.

Pratt, Annis V. *Archetypal Patterns in Women's Fiction*. Bloomington: Indiana UP, 1981.

—. "The New Feminist Criticisms: Exploring the History of the New Space." In *Intellectual Sexism: A New Woman, A New Reality*. Ed. Joan Roberts. New York: David McKay, 1976. 175-95.

Rosaldo, Michelle Zimbalist, ed. *Women, Culture, and Society*. Stanford: Stanford UP, 1974.

Showalter, Elaine. *A Literature of Their Own*. Princeton: Princeton UP, 1977.

—. "Feminist Criticism in the Wilderness." *Critical Inquiry* 8 (Winter 1981): 173-205. Rpt. *The New Feminist Criticism: Essays on Women, Literature & Theory*. Ed. Elaine Showalter. New York: Pantheon Books, 1985. 243-70.

Sims, Edna. "Resumen de la imagen negativa de la mujer en la literatura española hasta mediados del siglo XVI." *REH*, 11 (Oct. 1977): 433-49.

Spacks, Patricia Meyer. *The Female Imagination*. New York: Avon Books, 1975.

Spivak, Gayatri Chakravorty. "French Feminism in an International Frame." In *In Other Worlds: Essays in Cultural Politics*. New York: Methuen, 1987. 134-53.

Stanton, Domna C. "Difference on Trial: A Critique of the Maternal Metaphor in Cixous, Irigaray, and Kristeva." In *The Poetics of Gender*. Ed. Nancy K. Miller. New York: Columbia UP, 1986. 157-82.

Sullivan, Constance A. "Re-Reading the Hispanic Literary Canon: The Question of Gender." *Ideologies and Literature* 4 (May-June 1983): 93-101.

THE NOVELNESS OF A POSSIBLE POETICS FOR WOMEN

Sara Castro-Klarén
Johns Hopkins University

A few years ago, at another large gathering of students of women's writing, I discussed the governing naivete with which the category woman was deployed in Anglo-American feminist literary criticism. In "Teoría de la crítica literaria feminista y la escritura femenina en América Latina" (1984), I also pointed out the growing differences between the Anglo-American school, a body of inquiry largely based on Freudian psychoanalysis, and the French school, a post-structuralist group investigating the constitution of the subject in language. I tried to designate the difficulties inherent in the wholesale adoption of both the categories informing the Anglo-American school and the essentialist configuration of woman that it constructed. It seemed to me that the mad-(creole) woman of Gilbert and Gubar, based as it was on Harold Bloom's Freudian and exemplarily paternalistic anxiety of influence, constituted questionable ground for an investigation of the activity of women writers in Latin America. Kristeva's argument or rather search for a space in which the feminine symbolic contract could be detected seemed more promising to me, provided that "feminine" be understood as nothing "other" than an historical event. As such, "the feminine" would have to be placed constantly in a dialectical relation to the masculine, itself an "historical event" rather than a category. In the paper read at Mt. Holyoke College, I argued further that the writing done by Latin American women was thus historically marked by the signs of marginality, race, and "the feminine" within such historic marginality.

In a way, what I would like to do here is to continue the essay written five years ago. In order to continue, rather than repeat what was then argued, I need to take into account the recent self-critical appraisals of Anglo-American criticism, which have since then delved into some of the questions I raised at Mt. Holyoke. Above all, consideration of further developments within the field of Latin American literary criticism, an enterprise which, in the praxis of some critics, has grown closer to a general cultural criticism, need to be included.

Less dogmatic than others and more open to the incorporation of criticism of her own initial basic assumptions, Elaine Showalter has written a cogent essay on the difference between *gynocritics* and *gynesis* or roughly a part of the Anglo-American school and a part of the French School. For Showalter, gynocritics, closer to her own criticism, focuses on the specificity of women's writing, whereas the French exploration of the textual consequences and representations of sexual difference that Alice Jardine proposes would constitute gynesis.

As Showalter understands history (facts in actuality and chronology):

> Gynocritics is, roughly speaking, historical in orientation; it looks at woman's writing as it has actually occurred and tries to define its specific characteristics of language, genre, and literary influence, within a cultural network that includes variables of race, class, and nationality.[1]

Implicit in gynocritics is therefore the opposition male/female, not as historically constituted figures, but rather as a ground, modified by such cultural "variables as race, class and nationality." In Showalter's definition, it would seem that the male/female opposition either precedes culture (history?), it is something which is located outside of culture, or it is placed at the center of culture. At any rate, the male/female opposition is the (biological) epistemological basis from which the "specificity" of the female is rescued or reconstructed by Gynocritics. With that assumption in mind, Showalter has rescued and reassessed a whole body of writings by North American Woman, and in doing so has forced a deep reconsideration of the canon in English language letters.

The French project, on the other hand, according to Showalter, rejects "the temporal dimension of woman's experience" (Kristeva's "le temps des femmes"), "and seeks instead to understand the space granted to the feminine in the symbolic contract" ("Woman's Time ..." p. 37).

Kristeva finds that in evoking "the name and destiny of woman" she prefers thinking of *space* rather than chronology because space makes possible inquiry into the notion of woman conceived as *the Other*. Thus "the gaps, the silences and absences of discourse and representation to which the feminine has traditionally been relegated can be seen" ("Woman's Time ..." p. 37).

It is bemusing, in the context of Latin American intellectual history, and in the contexts of the spaces opened by Borges and Lezama, Arguedas and Cortázar, to read Showalter quoting Alice Jardine, who in turn is of course quoting French thought, on the presence of the Other in Western consciousness. For both Anglo-American critics (Showalter, Jardine, etc.) the space "outside of the conscious subject has always connoted the feminine in Western Thought —and any movement into alterity is a movement into that female space" ("Woman's Time ..." p. 37). It is not necessary here to review the Bible, Greek tragedy, St. Thomas, Hegel, Freud, Nietzsche, Lacan et al to agree —hastily— that indeed, the space outside, the space denied from consciousness in the West's patriarchy, has been Woman, as it would be, by definition, in any other patriarchy. However, it would take almost a willful act of denial, not to say in the same breath, that in the historical constitution of the West's imperial hegemony, other groups —blacks, Indians, non-Christians— have also been repressed, kept outside of the tight circumference of consciousness and when represented, they have also been situated in the space accorded to the Other. This has been true not only in the West but in all societies saturated by the West's system of thought. And in order not to spare anybody at all and to cover the whole globe, I should say that the deployment of Woman as the Other, or others as the Other, is probably not a Western monopoly. It has been the most universal system of alienation and exploitation of human beings by human beings.

I believe that the late recognition on the part of *Gynesis* of Woman as Other, is almost ironic in relation to Latin American literature and literary studies, where, if not always hanging on Lacan's latest word, we have learned to posit an entire discourse, even the discourse of the national dominant classes, as the discourse of the Other. We could continue on this point ad infinitum; let me simply remind you of recent studies on El Inca Garcilaso (Susana Jaklavi Leiva), Sor Juana (Octavio Paz), Sarmiento (Noé Jitrik), Delmira Agustini (Sylvia Molloy), and Rosario Castellanos (Maureen Ahern), in which the question of the alterity and transformation of the Other is keenly examined. For the moment I should like to touch in greater detail on the main and most recent proposals being made in North American feminist studies, because they continue to be highly persuasive and well researched though uncritically adopted in the study of women writers writing in Spanish.

However, as Showalter writes, the original dilemma posited in the female/male opposition is not so much solved by *gynesis* and its positing of Woman as Otherness, for when that Otherness, in the end, does finally emerge, *gynocritics* would demand to know what of it is specifically female or feminine or womanly.

> "In the texts of gynesis very little attention is paid to woman writers; even the concept of *écriture femenine* developed by the most influential critic of the school, Hélène Cixous, describes the symbolically or metaphorically feminine attributes of avant-guard writing rather than writing by women. Finally, some of the most prominent French theorists of *gynesis*, including Kristeva, Cixous, and Sarah Kofman, reject the label of 'feminist,' or even regard themselves as anti-feminists, seeing feminism in its activist mode as a liberal anachronism, or as "the final hysterization of middle-class woman" ("Woman's Time ..." p. 37).

Faced with this devastating attack made upon Anglo-American feminism not only by the sophistication of French thought but also by the voice of a plain working woman such as the Bolivian miner, Domitila,[2] Gynocritics respond fiercely, by pointing out that *gynesis*, after all, depends heavily on the male masters and male theoreticians and their texts, the main villain being, of course, Lacan, who did not do himself any favors when, under heavy feminist questioning on the part of some of his female disciples (Luce Irigaray et al), emulating Freud, lashed out against his shadowy *inquisitors* and declared that: "It is just that they don't know what they are saying, which is all the difference between them and me."[3]

Showalter's article restates the dilemma which results from the essentialist search for Woman, posited in a-historical terms and above all without embedding the agent of the search (the scholar) in the web of his/her ideology and in the creation of his/her own strategies of containment. Shari Benstock, in her essay on the question of women's writing as re-formulated in the case of Gertrude Stein, a woman who said that she wanted to write like a man, recognizes that for the moment this issue of the chicken and the egg has reached an impasse. Her re-evaluation of Stein's "failed" linguistic modernism relies on the notion that Stein wrote against the grain of all linguistic (male) conventions, precisely because her enterprise emerged out of a clear consciousness of her lesbian (outsider) womanhood. Though Benstock is convincing in her examination of the *differences* between Stein's radical modernism and Joyce's less radical and more male (insider's) version of linguistic experimentation, the Anglo-American critic does admit that positing Stein's lesbianism as the field of reference for her non-sensical writing comes down to an a-priori assumption on the part of the reader. Benstock writes that

> the problem here is not how such a critical methodology would see Stein but how it sees *language*, a problem that Stein spent many years pondering. The gynocritical approach works best when it examines the links between women writers and their work in literary periods in which language itself was not under inspection, when language itself was not a crucial issue for writers, when language was accepted —as it was until the advent of modernism— as a transparent window through which the perception of reality found expression. [...] The writing situation is much more complex when the woman writer at the window does not see *through* the window to an

> external reality, but rather sees language as a palpable subject
> that is the 'subject' of the literary undertaking.[4]

Right here Benstock has touched on the point of dissention between gynocriticism and gynesis which is, of course, the questions of biography-gender, as well as gender in relation to autograph. If we want or if we assume autograph to reveal, all by itself, some indelible mark upon which the subject is constituted, we are sadly mistaken. The collection of essays in *The Female Autograph* inconclusively examines the relation of genre to autograph. In her keen essay "Autobiography: Is the Subject Different?" Donna C. Stanton addresses the "problematics of subjecthood" and the highly valorized notion of a female or male unified identity, but cannot see devalorizing the female signature for fear that texts autographed by females will once again sink into anonymity. Caught in the dilemma posed by autobiographical categories in the texts' encoding and decoding, Stanton concludes that

> even more problematic is the question of the referential status
> of the signature. To be consistent with my textual, non
> referential approach to the female subject, I should view the
> signature as a name that comprised various senses of gender,
> ethnicity, or class and that evoked various cultural and
> literary associations.[5]

Contrary to the purpose of the book, reflection upon *The Female Autograph* rather demonstrates the impossibility of the desired equation between autograph and the female subject/object. For Benstock the question, at least in Stein's case, is whether Stein's discovery was related to her own biologically determined womanhood and the problematic social definition of her as a woman who wanted to be a man. Anglo-American feminist critics of Stein would probably say "yes," that her discovery was directly linked to her womanhood *because* her womanhood was problematic to her. The French would also say "yes," but for different reasons. "Stein's writing is an example of *écriture femenine* by its formal characteristics of openness and irrationality" ("Beyond the Reaches ..." p. 25). More recently, *The Poetics of Gender* took up the whole question of feminine writing and its conceptualization within the frame of difference. In "Difference on Trial," Donna Stanton writes a paragraph that for me sums up the concerns and conundrums explored in the entire volume and the healthy re-vision that the field is undergoing. As "the moment of the maternal emerges as a new dominance, it must be put into question before it congeals as feminine essence, as unchanging in *difference*."[6] In agreement with Alice Jardine's call to discontinue reorganizing the relationship of difference to sameness through the dialectics of valorization , Stanton wonders if French theory of feminism is not closely dangerous to recreating, in deconstructive language, traditional assumptions of femininity and if neofeminism is not reinstituting an antisystem that would be just as repressive as a dictatorship.

While I am not sure that all the French women theorists would agree to the characterization made of their thought on women's writing presented in these paragraphs of Benstock, or for that matter in Showalter's portrait of the French "school," there is no question that the meditation on Stein's writing and her insertion among the modernists on the left Bank really takes us beyond the present reaches of feminist criticism. Incisive and well grounded as Benstock's analysis is of both Stein's *écriture* as well as feminist theory, it nevertheless still leaves us marooned at the doors of Nina Baym's essay, "Why I do not do theory." Baym argues that, thus far, feminist theory has mostly served to pit woman against woman. She takes four major instances in the analysis of woman's writing in North America. These instances have been proposed as indivisible from womanhood itself. They have been seen as all informing allegories of the person and personality of woman. Baym's summary and critique presents the search for Woman as: a) The Mad Woman [Gilbert and Gubar]; b) A Female language [D. Stanton, Cixous]; c) Freud the Father and company [mainly Lacan the Son]; d) The Pre-Oedipal or Phallic Mother. From this portrait Baym concludes that "theory" has basically been misogynist.

While it is true that Baym's reading of Chodorov's and Dinnerstein's studies overemphasizes the matricidal force evoked by the all powerful pre-oedipal mother, it never-

theless remains to be said that the terrifying mother, like
the terrifying father, of both oedipal theories, is actually a
portrait of a social formation which emerges in the capitalist nuclear family. As such it is not necessarily a
"universal" in the formation of the human psyche. The
extended and class-criss-crossed families of rural and even
urban Latin America, to cite but one example, afford the
child (male or female) a much larger number of presences
and models where to seek refuge and find resistance to
Freud's menacing father and Chodorov's terrifying
mother.

For cultural reasons which could bear discussion elsewhere, I have always been astonished at the obsessive
contemplation regarding the ownership, location and al-
location of the phallus which has informed the kind of
psychological literary criticism examined by Nina Baym.
Her conclusion that not only Freud himself, but practically all psychological, or rather, Freudian-derived studies
are in fact misogynous appears profoundly convincing.
Even when an attempt is made to set Freud's misogyny
on its head, and the Phallic Mother is erected in place of
the Father, Baym shows that she who erects the phallic
mother probably did not like her own mother very much.
Without apologies, Baym writes:

> the Freudian and the feminist agendas may coincide because
> feminists do not like their mothers, or because feminists prefer
> to endow women with a revolutionary power that we cannot
> have if we are part of the system all along. [...] These issues
> are sharply evident in recent feminist literary work on moth-
> ers and daughters. It provides testimony, often unwitting and
> in contradiction to its stated intentions, of the deep-seated
> hostility of daughters to mothers. [...] She (the feminist) re-
> veals that the mother she seeks is not *her* mother, but another
> mother, preferably an imaginary mother.[7]

Once again, what has been done in the name of theorizing
sets woman against woman, and this realization is very
humbling indeed.

Though humbling in its call for a new modesty, Baym's
essay clears the ground for the possibility of what I would
call a more integrating and therefore radical cultural study

of Women. Baym seems to conclude that if one is part of the system one cannot, at the same time, aspire to revolutionary change. She warns that "our powers are limited, and our agendas for change will have to take internal limitations into account" ("The Madwoman ..." p. 57). One of those internal limitations would seem to be the terrifying "matricidal impulse" that Baym sees in the difference, not between male and female, but between woman and woman. The author of *Responses to Fiction in Antebellum America* asks her reader for a pluralist indulgence in order to over-come the matricidal impulse, or the will to a univocal feminism. "Women's liberation didn't suggest we all had to be one thing. To find oneself again a conscript, within a decade, is sad," she writes ("Madwoman ..." p. 59). It is sad, indeed, but a free market pluralism will not take us beyond gynocritics/gynesis, or woman against woman. Pluralism, if it means a grab bag, will simply give us more of the same.

II

Feminism, like Marxism or deconstruction, is in fact a broad and complex cultural critique. (See Michael Ryan, *Marxism and Deconstruction*, 1982, and Fredric Jameson, *The Political Unconscious*, 1983.) It is not a methodology for literary criticism. In fact, that is what it lacks. Like Marxism and deconstruction, it is, therefore, an ideological inquest which reaches well beyond the bounds of any given discipline as currently constituted in the Anglo-American academy. The basic tenets of feminism, as it sprang in the United States, from the pen of journalists such as Betty Freidan or Gloria Steinem, have never come to grips with the following: a) if there is no such thing as human nature, how can Woman's essence, or womanhood, be posited? b) if after Marx, Sartre, and Anthropology, we posit only man's contingency, how can we justify a search for Woman, without indulging in anachrony?

Women, like men, are at best contingent categories, Sartrean situations. One is loaded down in silence, it is true, the other is contorted and malformed in the tangles of its own discourse, of its history and thus his quest for power. Thus Woman, whether she is to be re-constructed in philosophy, biology, theory of evolution, or textual reading, could be considered the locus of contending relationships. Woman would be a construct and not a given. The male/female opposition would always be present, but the terms and meanings of this opposition and its derivations would of course vary as the simple opposition gains density and multiplicity with historical grounding. Women would emerge rather than be a pre-condition, in the examination of power relations such as discourse, income, division of labor, biological reproduction, etc. Women as a multiple text need to be expanded in the way Jameson would expand a text in preparation for a totalizing reading capable of dealing not only with difference but also with contradiction.

Closer to home, in what we call literary criticism, the search for and emergence of Women would cause a total revamping of what we have thus done, because if Woman ceases to be encapsulated in the oxymoron of the known/but denied, or the known/but unknown, then as we research for Her we have to question what we think we know. If the Freudian family romance is basically misogynist, how then do we conceive of the development of personality and individual identity, a basic concept for the discussion of characters, and plot, and story, and thus the meaning of the novel we attempt to read? What does it mean then to read *Doña Barbara* in traditional Freudian terms, or *Facundo* in the context of Lacan's concept of the Other? What does it mean to read *Doña Barbara* in terms of a myth of national foundation? What does it mean to read *Hasta no verte Jesús mío*, or *Balún Canán* or, *Maldito amor* in terms of national myth?

While we cannot throw out the baby with the bath water, what the study of Women proposes is not exactly a degree zero in thought but the reconstitution of all the categories and tools of analysis to be found in the given or the Western arsenal of thought.

Nevertheless, we must start modestly. We can begin to question representation of authorship as the antechamber of person or vice versa. Foucault's essay on the question of the author proves very useful in this context. Recent theory in autobiography and its fictionality can also illuminate the problem of female/male authorship. We can begin to conceive of each one of our most basic categories as novelistic texts in Bahktin's sense. Authorship, the subject, the Other, story, language, would all cease to be unified, closed concepts. Instead, each would constitute a space for struggle between centripetal and centrifugal socio-ideological forces. Thus the heteroglossia of Bahktin's novelistic text would, in its dynamism, open up sufficient cracks as to enable us to re-draw the figure of women/men in history. History will of course have to be rewritten and *Doña Barbara* along with Rosas, may turn out to be not only Sarmiento's own other(s) but Mexico's distillation of machismo in the María Félix movie version of Gallego's novel. Such a comparative statement would in fact entail the dissolution of genre, and periodization as presently understood. Right now these categories hold the skeleton of our sense of history in Latin American literature. Any history or anthology seeking to encompass woman's writing would have to, practically, begin by re-vamping genre (see Ludmer's essay on Sor Juana and her period, or Adorno's book on Guamán Poma, or Cortázar on his own work). Such a re-construction would allow a more specific place and understanding, not only of the work of Sor Juana, but also of the canonization of Santa Rosa and the "canonization" of satirical poetry of their contemporaries. In turn, these texts would have to be re-plotted, as Jean Franco has suggested, in relation to discourse not previously regarded as "literary," such as the word given in the confessional, in letters and in diaries.

Feminism, women's writing, for historical reasons which affect the entire globe, comes into the picture of Latin American letters at a critical moment. For reasons that I have explored elsewhere, the study of Latin American literature is ripe for a re-writing of its history. The figure of Women and the subsequent problematics implied by its presence should cause a profound re-thinking of the possible history of Latin America and its symbolic systems.

NOTES

[1] Elaine Showalter, "Woman's Time, Woman's Space; Writing the History of Feminist Criticism," in *Feminist Issues in Literary Scholarship*, ed. Shari Benstock, Indiana University Press, Bloomington, 1987, p. 37.

[2] Moema Viezzed, editor, *"Si me permiten hablar,"* *Testimonio de Domitila, una mujer de las minas de Bolivia*, México, Siglo XXI, 2da ed., 1977.

[3] Quoted in Juliet Mitchell and Jacqueline Rose, eds., *Feminine Psychology: Jacques Lacan and the école freudienne*, New York, Norton, 1982, p. 144.

[4] Shari Benstock, "Beyond the Reaches of Feminist Criticism: A Letter from Paris," in Shari Benstock, ed., *Feminist Issues in Literary Scholarship*, op. cit., p. 22.

[5] "Autobiography: Is the Subject Different?" in *The Female Autograph*, ed. Donna C. Stanton, The University of Chicago Press, Chicago, 1984, p. 16.

[6] Donna Stanton, "Difference on Trial," in *The Poetics of Gender*, ed. Nancy K. Miller, Columbia University Press, New York, 1986, p. 174.

[7] Nina Baym, "The Madwoman and Her languages: Why I don't do Feminist Literary Theory," in Shari Benstock, ed., *Feminist Issues in Literary Scholarship*, op. cit., p. 57.

LIMITS UNLIMITED:
THE STRATEGIC USE OF FANTASY IN
CONTEMPORARY WOMEN'S FICTION OF SPAIN

Geraldine Cleary Nichols
University of Florida, Gainesville

"...repugna ante todo la confusión de fronteras. Es un síntoma de pulcritud mental querer que las fronteras entre las cosas estén bien marcadas." Ortega y Gasset, *La deshumanización del arte.*

"Yo empecé a escribir mis libros de niña. Entonces eran cuentos fantásticos, cuentos de gnomos, cuentos de conejitos. Para mí, escribir era crear un mundo donde yo pudiera habitar un espacio diferente, que no tuviera precisamente nada que ver con el mío, porque el mío no me gustaba." Ana María Matute, personal interview.

Over the past several years I have been concentrating my research on the literary works and the world of seven women writers —Mercè Rodoreda, Ana María Matute, Carmen Laforet, Esther Tusquets, Ana María Moix, Carme Riera, and Montserrat Roig. They are all closely associated with Barcelona, a city marked as no other in Spain by a bourgeois heritage which prizes the tangible and honors the pragmatic. This attitude is crystallized for me in two terms one frequently hears in Catalan: *seny* or common sense, considered the distinctive Catalan virtue; and *faves comptades* ("money in the bank"), a sure thing, something that can be counted and counted on.[1] Barcelona is a city where "discreet," as in the charm of the bourgeoisie, and "discrete," as in separate, visible, enumerable, come together to form the better part of *valor* and valor. As feminists we are all too aware of the place accorded women in a scoptic or oculocentric economy —their sex "n'en est pas un," is not one— and we are familiar with

the eye: the center

the analogous position reserved for ladies in a bourgeois culture; we are grounded theoretically, then, for understanding —*grosso modo*— how such a background may have impinged on these writers as they grew to maturity.

It is important to keep in mind the Barcelona connection while reading the fiction written by these daughters of the bourgeoisie, because it is an indelible part of the sociocultural matrix of all of their works, even those written in the fantastic mode. To be attentive to their background is to engage in what Nancy Miller calls "overreading": "To overread is to wonder... about the conditions for the production of literature... when we tear the web of women's texts we may discover... the marks of the grossly material, the sometimes brutal traces of a culture of gender; the inscription of its political structures" (274). Miller maintains that feminist critics must resist the deconstructionists' attempts to efface the writing subject insofar as this practice "kills off by delegitimating other discussions of the writing (and reading) subject" (271), namely those which take into account the subject's gender-, class- and race-inflected position in society. She advocates instead a critical positioning, an "arachnology," that would read "*against* the weave of indifferentiation to discover the embodiment in writing of a gendered subjectivity: to recover within representation the emblems of its construction"(272). More graphically, she writes that "the goal of overreading, of reading for the signature, is to put one's finger —figuratively— on the place of production that marks the spinner's attachment to her web" (288). Barcelona, built by industrial fortunes, is a vital coordinate in locating our writers' place of production.

Another coordinate as important as the geosocial in placing or grounding the fiction of these writers is of course the cultural, and particularly literary, tradition surrounding them. Given the fact that the predominant narrative mode in twentieth-century Castilian and Catalan literature is realism, it is not surprising to find that most of their fiction falls within the realist or neorealist tradition.[2] Indeed, the autobiographical or pseudo-autobiographical character of much of their writing —for which they have been roundly criticized— may similarly be attributed to their sociocultural background, rather than to a gender-linked lack of imagination, as many unreflexive critics would have it. This because there is no environment more propitious than the bourgeois to self-absorption; and because on another level, as José-Carlos Mainer has repeatedly pointed out, twentieth-century Spanish fiction is characterized by an unusual abundance of autobiographical elements.

In most of my published research on these seven authors to date I have traced the connections between their realist texts and their particular sociocultural and historical backgrounds; I have limned the outlines of a "tradition of their own."[3] The focus of this paper will be quite different, because I propose to leave aside the realist fiction deemed characteristic of these writers to turn instead to the fantasy fiction written by three of them: Rodoreda, Matute, and Riera. These three —and to a lesser extent Moix as well— stand out from the others insofar as they have recurred to a different mode of fiction altogether, one which is not particularly common in twentieth-century Spain, and one which we would not expect to emerge from a culture which, like an anti-Macondo, prizes *seny* and *faves comptades*. For some time I have wanted to explore how Rodoreda, Matute, and Riera use fantasy, to see in what way it is related to their realist fiction. It may appear far-fetched to search for references to the "grossly material" in a seemingly non-referential mode like the fantastic, but we will see that these writers' fantastic worlds are always related in a logical way to the "real" world around them; that their fantastic projections invert, distort, or otherwise unsettle a particular, specific, historically grounded status quo. While the scope of this paper will not allow me to detail the points of contact between the realist and fantastic modes in their work, I can begin to outline the common project I found to underlie their fantasy works: they propose nothing less than the reform of our perceptual grids, the wanton erasure of the frontiers and hierarchies so praised by thinkers like Ortega: the unlimiting of limits.

A note on my methodology for readers unfamiliar with the sort of criticism practiced in my field of specialization, Peninsular or Spanish literature. Close textual readings form a part of the Anglo-North American tradition of Peninsular Hispanism, and it is within this tradition that most of us must function if we aspire to be published, tenured, or granted research funds. Feminists who work in Peninsular literature have broadened the scope of their inquiry beyond the text to study the context —Miller's "place of production"— out of which or against which the texts have been written, but the approach even to contextual material is still that of close reading. When for example I became interested in the group of Catalan-based women writers —some of whom write in Castilian, others in Catalan— this tradition of close reading led me to undertake the study of Catalan, as well as of Catalonia's history, anthropology, sociology, literature, and culture. Without such grounding it would have seemed presumptuous at best to attempt to trace the specificity of the literature written by these women within the larger context of twentieth-century Spanish letters.

Yet it was not simply my training as a Peninsularist which convinced me to carry out this extensive research; my feminist convictions were equally important. Women's specificities have been effaced by the generic pronoun mentality for too long; feminist critics must reclaim them and give them voice. This fight against what Miller calls the "weave of indifferentiation" requires patience, research, documentation, and faith in the value of a project some will dismiss as excessively empiricist. To bring feminist politics to the study of literary texts is to require ourselves to pay attention to difference, to be attuned to the precise rhythms we are attempting to analyze. For this reason, I base my discussions on concrete works by authors, rather than generalizing about fantasy in women's texts. For the same reason, I cite them in their original language, for the Catalan specificity needs to be marked with respect to the "generic" Castilian (or "Spanish") reality. At the same time, I would like to be careful not to overstate the case for difference lest readers forget that Spanish women of all regions share a tradition of oppression which unites them and marks them as different from their French or English sisters, for example.[4] The fantasy fiction of Carmen Martín Gaite and Adelaida García Morales —to name two writers of other regions who come immediately to mind— may also have its genesis in (their desire to escape) the realistic, pragmatic, pan, pan y vino, vino Spanish mentality that Cervantes incarnated in Sancho Panza.

The specific stories referred to in this study are: for Matute, two of the stories included in Tres y un sueño, "La razón" and "La isla"; the fantastic sketches in Los niños tontos; and, from Algunos muchachos, "No tocar," "El rey de los zennos," and "Una estrella en la piel." Rodoreda's stories include "Una carta," "La salamandra," "El riu i la barca," "El senyor i la lluna," "La meva Cristina," "Semblava de seda," and "Un full de gerani blanc." Riera's fantastic stories are drawn from her critically neglected collection Epitelis tendríssims, with the following titles: "As you like, darling," "Mr. Flowers, un savi botànic," "Uns textos inèdits i eròtics de Victoria Rossetta," "Una mica de fred per a Wanda," "Estimat Thomas," "La senyoreta Angels Ruscadell investiga la terrible mort de Marianna Servera," and "Josep Lluís Jacotot agonitza."

Those who are familiar with these particular works will agree that, superficially at least, they have little in common. The term "fantasy literature" is broad, but it still must be stretched to accommodate the disparate types of stories these represent. Of the three, Rodoreda's come closest to classical fantasy, since they involve metamorphoses or the presence of supernatural forces. Matute's are more diffuse, verging at times on poetry (Los niños tontos); others on allegory ("No tocar," "El rey de los zennos," "La razón," "La isla"). Both genres are proscribed by Todorov in his classification of the fantastic, on the grounds that they tend to undermine the reader's belief in the events narrated by the story. Riera's stories are altogether different from the others; hers are what we might call "erotic" fantasies, although this is a somewhat misleading description of them, as we shall see and as Spanish critics protested to her when they were published. The sources I have found most helpful in attempting a preliminary analysis of these stories as fantastic literature are Tzvetan Todorov, *Introduction à la littérature fantastique*; Rosemary Jackson, *Fantasy: The Literature of Subversion*; Katherine Hume, *Fantasy and Mimesis: Responses to Reality in Western Literature*; and Christine Brooke-Rose, *A Rhetoric of the Unreal*. Finally, Robert Scholes' *Structural Fabulation* is useful for explaining the provenance of the broadly didactic aspects of this fantastic fiction, which he regards as a "special case of romance" (28). There are three closely related characteristics of the fantastic as defined by these critics which prove particularly relevant to the stories under consideration, characteristics which moreover suggest why a woman writer dissatisfied with the status quo might find fantasy congenial. First, the fantastic is intimately bound up with limits (Todorov, Jackson, Hume); second, it grows out of ancient taboos (Todorov, Jackson); third, it is an essentially subversive mode (Jackson). A brief consideration of each of these three points as they apply to our stories will show that Matute's, Rodoreda's, and Riera's seemingly disparate concretions of the fantastic are in fact quite similar; and that each author has used the fantastic in a way wholly consonant with the other realist works in her corpus.

All theoreticians of the mode or genre seem to agree with Todorov's statement that "the fantastic represents an experience of limits" (93). Bessière writes: "Because it is a narrative structured upon contraries, fantasy tells of limits, and it is particularly revealing in pointing to the edges of the 'real'" (cited in Jackson 23). Jackson goes beyond what she calls Todorov's "*poetics* of the fantastic" to talk about the "*politics* of its forms" (6), that is, the project or goal these works promote. In a sentence which could summarize the fantasy fiction of Matute, Rodoreda, or Riera, she writes: "Fantasy is preoccupied with limits, with limiting categories, *and with their projected dissolution*" (48. Emphasis mine). The limits broached or transgressed in what Todorov calls "pure fantastic" literature (written, he asserts, only in the XIX century) are those dividing life from death; the "real" from the unreal, i.e. supernatural; and permitted from forbidden practices in the sexual or behavioral realm. Jackson analyzes the commonalities of the fantastic's thematic concerns, and (consonant with her avowed political orientation) identifies these shared elements as *tactics:* "all of [these themes are] concerned with erasing rigid demarcations of gender and of genre. Gender differences of male and female are subverted and generic differences between animal, vegetable and mineral are blurred in fantasy's attempt to 'turn over' 'normal' perceptions and undermine 'realistic' ways of seeing" (49).

It is perhaps indefensibly categorical to say that all writers of fantasy are concerned with erasing rigid demarcations —with giving their readers a sort of lesson in tolerance— but it appears clear to me that Rodoreda, Matute, and Riera do have such an interest, amply demonstrated in their non-fantastic literature. No one who has met a Rodoredian heroine victimized solely or principally on the basis of her gender could doubt the writer felt strongly about the issue of gender stratification, in spite of her public repudiation of feminism.[5] Similarly, anyone who has read Ana María Matute's fiction could vouch for her profound commitment to the cause of human justice and equality. In her realist fiction, such as the novels *Primera memoria* and *Los hijos muertos,* she repeatedly traces and rejects the rigid divisions along class, economic, gender, race, generic, political, and regional lines which have characterized Spain; she uses fantasy in the same way. Riera longs to abolish conventionally imposed limits on our affective behavior: to free the signifier and the signifying person from foolish consistencies and exclusions. From her first story, "Te deix, amor, la mar com a penyora" to her latest novella, *Qüestió d'amor propi,* she has been looking for the way to fuse —and confuse— identities and roles: sexual, grammatical, generic. The fantasy written by these three conforms to Scholes' definition of fabulation, which is "fiction that offers us a world clearly and radically discontinuous from the one we know, yet returns to confront that known world in some cognitive way. Traditionally, it has been a favored vehicle for religious thinkers, precisely because religions have insisted that there is more to the world than meets the eye, that the common-sense view of reality —realism— is incomplete and therefore false" (29). Perhaps it is not so peculiar, after all, to find fantasy writers among these daughters of the Barcelona bourgeoisie, who have nothing to lose but their chains in insisting that there is more to the world than meets the eye.

Let us begin with the stories of Ana María Matute, whose works of fantasy predate Rodoreda's by about ten years. The protagonists of *Los niños tontos* fall on the losing side of an arbitrary line drawn by their peers: they are too fat, too ugly, too quiet, too poor, too fastidious, too imaginative; they have the wrong family, ears too big, dreams too real, fantasies too destructive. The broad range of these so-called infractions, mixing as it does the trivial with the accidental, the concrete with the incorporeal, exposes the capricious nature of the line drawn between normal and abnormal.[6]

On the formal level, Matute's sketches also blur a line, that between the mimetic or physical world and the fantastic or incorporeal. This effect is achieved in part by her prose style, well known for its ellipses and unexpected or nonexistent transitions from the concrete to the abstract or universal. This style has often been called "poetic," but in the context of her fantastic fiction, it strikes me that a more descriptive term for it would be "subtractive," as Hume defines it: "Subtractive worlds are either very narrow definitions of reality which leave out large portions of human experience, or they are worlds in which the author has deliberately erased expected material, especially the logical connections between actions" (83); "Erasure of such ordinary narrative features as logic and motive so lowers our assurance of what is real and what is fantasy that the distinction is almost meaningless... On us as readers, the effect of subtractive works is often very compelling... Subtraction overcomes our natural tendency to reject a comment based on fantastic material because fantasy may seem irrelevant to our reality" (94).

We may see the effect of this destabilization of the line between real and unreal by comparing two stories in *Los niños tontos*, "El niño de los hornos" and "El incendio." In the first, a macabre but realist story, a child acts on a desire to be rid of his new baby brother by incinerating him in a "play" oven. We accept as real or as plausible this actualization of desire; our bourgeois education allows us to see it as motivated, and to naturalize it within the context of sibling rivalry. In "El incendio," another child takes colored pencils and enacts his desire to temper the blinding whitewash covering his house; he paints flames over it, and the house then burns to the ground. In this case the leap from desire to its realization violates our sense of the real, which says that penciled flames can't burn anything. The miscegenation of fact and fantasy in "El incendio" calls into question our culture's epistemological and metaphysical system which "equates the real with the visible, and gives the eye dominance over other sense organs" (Jackson 45). In this oculocentric system words or other representations (such as painted flames), far from being real, are merely markers of absence, of lack. And yet as we compare these two stories, one canonized as "realist" and the other as "fantastic," we should pause to question our unthinking acceptance of this implicitly judgmental hierarchy.[7] After all, which of these two sorts of confusion between wish and fulfillment, fantasy and reality, is more common among children, more plausible? Without any doubt children are more apt to confuse books, pictures, movies and other signs with reality than to commit fratricide, but our rigid perceptual grid does not allow us to "see" that fact. Children who persist in never-never land are scorned as "fantasiosos" instead of being treasured as visionaries in touch with another reality, somewhere beyond the obtunding limits of the concrete.

Like much classical fantasy literature, Matute's fantasy fictions also explore, test, and repeatedly deconstruct the limit between life and death (interestingly enough, death is not a frequent concern in most of her realist fiction). A combination of subtractive and metaphoric writing renders inconclusive —phantasmic— the ends both of the protagonists and of the sketches in most of the works in *Los niños tontos,* as well as in "El rey de los zennos," "Estrella en la piel," "No tocar," and "La isla." When the sentences making up these sketches stop, we often suspect that the protagonist has died, but we cannot be sure of the fact. Eerily enough, they project no sense of an ending, and the reader, trained in hermeneutics, eschatology and other Western metaphysical doxa, finds this unsettling. Blind to the affirmative message behind this narrative strategy —that perhaps death is not so final, has no sting— such a reader misprizes the story, represented by its ending, as "poetic," "allegorical," unreal. Or, alternatively, as consonant with the "peculiar" nature of the protagonist, who has after all lived as though absent from (real) life, that is to say, as though dead. For such a character, death may not be an altogether different state (and may even be seen as a friend, as in "La niña fea" or "Mar"). What is important to underline in both interpretations is the well-trained reader's tendency to (dis)miss the liberating message that can be construed in these fictions.

In Rodoreda's stories —"La salamandra," "El riu i la barca," "Semblava de seda," and "Un full de gerani blanc"— death and the narrative are similarly deprived of finality because long before their end the protagonists seem to have passed to some other plane of existence where, for all we know, death isn't the same —or different, either. Whatever such a death is, it can no longer be envisioned as a discrete state but rather as somehow contiguous to life. As Jackson notes, the trope characteristic of fantasy is not metaphor, but metonymy: "it does not create images which are 'poetic', rather it produces a sliding of one form into another, in a metonymical displacement" (82). In the fantasy world of these authors, it is death which slides into or out of life; both states are ranged along a continuum with no clear ends.

This mention of the life-death continuum brings us to the second characteristic of fantasy literature, its (hypothetical) origins in ancient taboos. Common cultural prohibitions such as those forbidding intercourse between the living and the dead, and between certain family members, are regularly transgressed or tested under the cover of fantasy, giving rise to such classical fantasy themes as the un-dead, vampires, necrophilia, ghosts, and such forth. Another taboo, perhaps not widely recognized as such until deconstruction and Lacanian psychoanalysis foregrounded it, forbids the human's continuing in symbiotic unity with alterity (represented by the mother in the child's earliest years). The "no" or "name" of the father decrees that each being will have its own, unmergeable and deficient identity, as signaled by having a unique name. Two different items may not be called by the same name, or be the same or, as classical physics teaches, occupy the same place at the same time. It is but a step from this interdiction of symbiosis, which operates on an individual level, to the one Gayle Rubin calls the "taboo against the sameness of men and women, a taboo dividing the sexes into two mutually exclusive categories, a taboo which exacerbates the biological differences between the sexes and thereby *creates* gender" (178). I believe that the urge to transgress *this* engendering taboo, more than any other, lies at the heart of the fantasy enterprise in women's fiction; that the various limiting categories women fantasy writers seek to deconstruct all refer back in some way to gender categorization, the daily bread of their childhood, the *pan, pan* and *vino, vino* that taught them how the sex that is not one must speak and how reality must be.[8]

Rodoreda's tales of metamorphosis violate the taboo against symbiotic unity with alterity, against being simultaneously the One and the Other. Her woman-changed-into-salamander has an animal's body, but continues to think in a way that is clearly human; the same is true of the fish in "El riu i la barca." Both creatures live in something like "the borderline between clothing and habitation," as sculptress Shirley Federow calls it, a fecund area, a no-man's land. (Cited in Lauter 140) The transformations related in "La meva Cristina" and "El senyor i la

lluna" have been reversed by the time of narration, but
the sailor who had turned into a human pearl and the
man who had become a moonwalker are profoundly —
even physically— altered by their experiences. Within the
story's present they are at once the One —and the Other.
In such stories the fantastic transformation illustrates how
multiple and non-identical a single human being can be,
thus effectively destabilizing the notion of this being's
unity and integrity.

Once the categorical and founding division between self
and other is breached —a major project of fantasy
fiction— other similar divisions may also be violated, as
we see in "Una carta," where the line between thought
and its materialization, or subject and object, is
deconstructed, as is the line between male and female.
The story is narrated in the form of a letter written by a
nameless female protagonist who believes herself to be
suffering from a strange illness. The addressee is a doctor
to whom she has turned for a diagnosis. As she describes
it, her "mal" —and the use of this amphibologic word,
with its moral connotations, rather than the more
common, strictly denotative "malaltia" (a distinction lost
in the Castilian translation of the story by José Batlló), is
highly significant— has few but grave symptoms: her
thoughts materialize, her wishes turn into reality. Such
an illness eliminates the limits between (desiring) subject
and (desired) object, but under closer observation it can
also be seen to abolish another set of limits, those between
the male —he who is culturally empowered to impose his
will on reality— and the female —she who is defined as
powerless to resist being imposed upon. Any virus which
could wreak such generic havoc would indeed be a "mal,"
a dis-order of major proportions. The story suggests that
her symptoms can only be considered pathological because
they are suffered by a female; if a male were similarly
afflicted, they would be taken as signs of virility and
robust health. As the writer describes her life —or gives
her "medical history"— the reader cannot help but be
impressed by her enviable condition; still, the woman says

she is "sick," and so one reads on to discover the diagnosis of this peculiar "mala salud de hierro."

As she tells her life, one perceives that circumstances have conspired to allow this woman to overcome what Gilbert and Gubar call "the socially conditioned epidemic of female illness" (55) or the "social disease of ladyhood" (269). As a very young woman enamored of the man who would become her husband, her physical and mental state was impaired *comme il faut*: "Quan encara festejàvem... i va començar a agradar-me (jo era la rica i ell el pobre) així que el veia venir, en comptes d'esperar-lo tranquil.la per donar-li el bon día, em posava a tremolar. El tremolor em començava a les mans i se m'estenia fins a les cames i de les cames em pujava als llavis" (187). But no sooner had they married than she began to assert herself, to recover her health, as it were, by refusing him his "rightful" access to her body: "al cap d'un any de casada era ben verge, i els crits que em va costar" (187).

The antibody or element which allowed her to fight off the wasting disease of womanhood was present when she was a maid; it is even mentioned —coyly, in parentheses— in the previous quotation: "(jo era la rica i ell el pobre)." Wealth is a male marker in Rodoreda's fiction; it is one of the bludgeons men use on hapless women. A woman born wealthy, like the protagonist of "Una carta" and like Sofia en *Mirall trencat*, is not then fully a "female": she cannot be victimized with impunity. As the years passed, the woman of "Una carta" took on more cultural attributes of the male —becoming healthier and healthier— without undergoing any sexual change. She writes that she was forced to wear the pants in the family, because her husband was "un tou," a softie (with all of the sexual connotations implied in that word). And as writer of the letter that is this story, she —like the writer of "Una carta," Rodoreda— has also taken a male position vis à vis the signifier. Beyond this, she is widowed and middle-aged, with her children grown and gone, so that she is not a slave to anyone's whims except her own. In short, she has assumed all the prerogatives of a man by the time her "illness" declares itself, and yet she is still a woman: that is the "mal" represented in this story.

In what is surely her final concession to convention, she turns to a male authority figure for a diagnosis of her dis-order. But what name can be found for she who has defied both the no and the name of the father, for an ownerless woman well past the age of nubility who trangresses the line between subject and object and the taboo against sameness? Characteristically, she does not wait for the man to name her (condition); she names herself and her disorder, which by the end of her narrative she understands to be one and the same thing, a cultural category constructed to anathematize outlaw (or scofflaw) women: "Em penso que sóc bruixa." She sees herself as the fantasy creature, the witch, credited with the power to abolish normal limits, and on this realistic and autoreferential note, the story ends.

If we turn to Carme Riera's *Epitelis tendríssims* we can appreciate even more clearly the thrust —a word I use advisedly— of the strategic use these writers make of the fantastic. Riera's wry tales, like her well-known "Te deix, amor, la mar com a penyora," present a sort of literary riddle whose solution opens onto chaos —or at least revolution. The regressive ending of "Te deix" compels readers to reevaluate the whole experience: the story and their facile acceptance of the heterosexist assumptions that overdetermined their "mis"reading of it. The objects of desire and the desiring subjects of *Epitelis tendríssims* are equally beyond the pale of normalcy, and the love affairs are even more transgressive than in "Te deix." The brazen inscribed author writes in the prologue that her friends warned her not to try writing erotica, because women lack the capacity and the experience to succeed in such a genre. She is determined, nonetheless, and revealing her beancounting origins or literary training, she begins looking around her resort hotel for inspiration; alas, real life, even in resort hotels, is considerably less lubricious than such "fantasy" rags as *Playboy* would have one believe, and she finds no useful material. Until, that is, she stops looking at whole people—at unified subjects, whose erotic or boundary-fusing potential is nil, and fixes instead upon parts, fragments of these wholes—a foot, a graceful back—whose very incompleteness calls out for erotic fusion with its complement. Starting from the fragment, she then tries to imagine how the person attached would make love: sex by synecdoche. To start from the margins is a feminist or minority practice, and to deconstruct the integrity of the desiring subject is a typical practice of modern fantasy. Jackson comments on the importance of the latter practice: "It is important to understand the radical consequences of an attack upon unified 'character', for it is precisely this subversion of unities of self which constitutes the most radical transgressive function of the fantastic" (83).

Once the reader accepts the "absurd" premise that a nostril might provide the key to person's eroticism, it is difficult to draw a firmer line when it comes to the obscure objects of desire proposed by these stories; to say, for example, that certain objects cannot possibly function erotically. This difficulty is exacerbated by Riera's narrative style, one which was defined in "Te deix": her prose is affective or titillating, which makes it difficult for the reader to hold him- or herself back. Furthermore, Riera overdetermines the hermenuetic and proaeretic codes in her stories,[9] teasing the reader through the texts on an intellectual as well as erotic level. When she drops the last of the seven veils in this artful narrative dance, revealing the true nature of the lusted-after object, the reader's quickened breathing stops altogether for a moment. He or she has been caught again, *in flagrante*, misreading on the basis of conventional erotic expectations, and now must find a facesaving way to continue the play through to its conclusion. The drive toward closure, satisfaction —cunningly intensified by Riera's style— impels the reader to perform a crucial mental operation. S/he must try to naturalize, de-taboo, these bizarre *petits choux,* to render them desirable: to unlimit the limits imposed with monolithic force where sex and gender intersect, where desire itself is engendered.

To satisfy curiosities piqued by my own meta-striptease, and to show the level of Riera's daring in *Epitelis tendríssims*, I mention a few of the objects of desire. In "Mr. Flowers, un savi botànic," the protagonist turns to jelly over a pale, lovely, succulent... cabbage. Part of the literary charm of this story is that it takes the clichéd—and, let's face it, ridiculous—term of endearment, *petit chou*, to its logical —and, let's face it, illogical— limits. This particular treatment of metaphor is a common mark of fantasy fiction, as Jackson points out: "[fantasy] takes metaphorical constructions literally" (41).

A similar operation, where the metaphoric is interpreted literally, gives "As you like, darling" its double edge. Here it is a sexy, disembodied masculine voice over the telephone which arouses and satisfies the female protagonist. The intellectual cliché exploited here is the post-structuralist identification of logos and phallus. Another story which plays with the archetypal identification between the wind or *pneuma* and the male genesic urge is "Una mica de fred per a Wanda," in which the voluptuous Wanda finds her pleasure when standing in a strategic position before the air-conditioning registers as they blast cold air. "Uns textos inèdits i eròtics de Victoria Rossetta" similarly exploits two archetypal associations to create the illusion in the reader's cliché-ridden mind that the passionate Victoria has a marvelously endowed "playmate," when in fact she has fallen in love with the immense, phallically shaped but chaste lighthouse, with its pulsing, penetrating beams of light.

Most of the stories in *Epitelis tendríssims* are as iconoclastic and suggestive as these, and most could have the effect of widening one's vision of erotic possibilities, of erasing the limits one thought were natural. I use the word "could" advisedly, because this collection of stories was not well received in Spain. It had few reviews, and Riera was told repeatedly by male colleagues and critics that the book was a dud, a regular dose of saltpeter. It is her only book not to have been translated into Castilian. Testimonial readers —those who flock to her public appearances and write her long, confessional letters— have had a different reaction, however; little old ladies have told her they found it highly erotic. Her latest novella, *Qüestió d'amor propi*, currently on the best-seller list in Catalonia, has had a similarly skeptical reception by (male) critics, who find the male character one-dimensional and ridiculous. He is both of those things, which does not mean he lacks verisimilitude! I would like to suggest that the male critics and academics who have objected to these two books have done so because they cannot bear to be taken so lightly, or revealed as so dispensable. The admixture of humor in *Epitelis tendríssims* is undoubtedly the straw that broke these critics' backs. She is thumbing her nose at them, or, in the marvelously appropriate Catalan or Castilian idiom —appropriate since figs are associated with the female sex— *els fa la figa, les hace la higa.*

And yet Riera is quite serious in *Epitelis tendríssims*; in several important ways these unorthodox stories might be compared to the writings of the Marquis de Sade, who, in Jackson's words, "urges transgression of the limits separating self from other, man from woman, human from animal, organic from inorganic objects. He seeks a defiant and violent disorder, a fluidity, a lack of discretion" (73). In the comico-erotic stories I have discussed up to this point, there is no suggestion of the physical violence which marks Sade's texts, but it is present in the two remaining stories —"La senyoreta Angels..." and "Josep Lluís Jacotot agonitza." In them Riera depicts a form of boundary-breaking violence so regularly visited on defenseless women by men in positions of power over them that it has until recently seemed natural, un-remarkable. In one story she depicts stupration, in another incest; chillingly enough, they are undoubtedly the stories which work best as erotica in the collection.

* * *

After this brief survey of fantasy in the short stories of Rodoreda, Matute, and Riera, it is not difficult to perceive its subversive nature: it transgresses taboos, destabilizes dichotomies, and overturns the bean jar, gesturing toward a new disorder. The three writers use different sorts of fantasy thematics and techniques to effect a similar response in their readers: to knock their socks or their prejudices off, to give them a new and ultimately liberating vision of a world where the One is not enthroned at the expense of the Other, where the One and the Other are intertwined, warp and woof. Like Matute's fantastic creatures, the *zennos* —whose name echoes the Greek word for outsiders— these writers have installed themselves, in their fantasy fiction, "al fondo del mundo, en el envés del tapiz, en la trama del enorme bastidor: al otro lado de los hechos feroces" (118-19) —there to convey to the world the beauty of, as we say in English, the "wrong side" of the tapestry.

NOTES

[1] At some moment during the conference, when Cristina Dupláa and I were discussing our highly complementary papers, she used another common Catalan expression which fits into the same schema. It is "anem per feina," and means "let's get down to work"; it is often used in a laudatory sense as an adjectival complement meaning "businesslike."

[2] José-Carlos Mainer attributes this peculiarity to the Spanish writer's pragmatic and unremitting "búsqueda del lector." The fact that the Spanish reading public has always been extremely limited has also forced the writer, in Mainer's view, to adopt other ingratiating strategies such as: "el explícito diálogo con un hipotético lector... la referencia obstinada a puntos de unidad colectiva... la idea de lectura como experiencia vivencial, la pretensión obsesiva de 'sinceridad' como valor ético-estético" (*La historia de la literatura...* 36. See also Mainer's *La Edad de Plata* 66,70). It is interesting to note how closely these rhetorical strategies parallel others identified by gender-conscious critics as peculiar to women's writing. See for example Marta Traba on the differential features of women's writing (author's self-referentiality; extraordinary concern with establishing communication with the reader; unselfconscious admixture of real or autobiographical elements into fiction); Judith Kegan Gardiner on the woman writer's establishment of fluid boundaries between fiction and autobiography

and on her "manipulation of identifications between narrator, author, and reader" (179); Carme Riera on the woman writer's cultivation of complicity with the reader ("Literatura..." and "Vindicación...").

[3]See especially my "Caída/respuesta...," "Mitja poma...," "Codes of Exclusion...," "The Prison-House (and Beyond)...," "Sex and the Single Girl...."

[4] The thorny questions of Catalan specificity and Spanish commonalities will be broached in far more detail in the book I am presently writing on the Catalan authors mentioned at the beginning of this paper, provisionally titled *The Foundered Garden*.

[5] She called feminism "una bestiesa" in a television interview with Maria Antònia Oliver, as the latter recalls in a brief article (31). In another interview with Montserrat Roig she stated: "Tot això de les 'reivindicacions de la dona actual' és una mica literatura. Des del punt de vista social no m'interessa, i des del punt de vista íntim ja té la partida guanyada. Una dona sempre guanya; si no és amb la feina, serà amb la maternitat o amb l'amor" (174).

[6] Matute's hatred of divisions is frequently reflected in her literature. One of the sections of *Primera memoria* is titled "La escuela del sol," and the lessons learned in that school are those of inequality. Matia inveighs against the brightness of the Spanish sun because it creates such inescapable and clearly demarcated distinctions on the earth: sun/shadow, day/night; these distinctions then rationalize or reflect those of an inequalitarian society. See Nichols, "Codes...". In "El incendio" the child also reacts to the divisory properties of the sun: "El niño tenía los ojos irritados de tanto blanco, de tanto sol cortando su mirada con filos de cuchillo" (25). The protagonist of Riera's *Qüestió d'amor propi* also finds the Spanish sun too "categorical" and revealing: "per culpa d'aquesta poderosa llum el nostre entorn s'eriça de pues i, com si estigués en perpètua erecció, es torna desagradablement fal.lic" (14).

[7] In his study of speculative fiction, Robert Scholes comments on this hierarchization: "It is customary in our empirically based Anglo-Saxon criticism to distinguish between two great schools of fiction according to the relationship between the fictional worlds they present and the world of human experience: novels and romances, realism and fantasy.... because of our empirical bias, we have tended to value realism more highly than romance" (28). He later attributes this distinction—rather ethnocentrically, to my mind—to race, space, and time: "I have at times accepted the traditional Anglo-Saxon distinction between romance and

realism, and have at times rejected it. This needs some clarification. The distinction itself was made by an empirically oriented race in age of developing empiricism. Thus, it must have some value, if only a historical one. The distinction was originally and has been traditionally invidious, with realism being the privileged form. This suited a materialistic and positivistic age, and the science of that age seemed to lend support to a realistic notion of the cosmos" (101). Certainly the Hispanic critical and literary tradition takes an equally dim view of fantasy.

8 Class and "racial" or linguistic differences must also have been important factors in the formation of these writers as young girls in Barcelona. I develop these ideas more fully in *The Foundered Garden*.

9 See Brooke-Rose's description of this practice as it applies to fantasy fiction (105-27).

WORKS CITED

Brooke-Rose, Christine. *A Rhetoric of the Unreal: Studies in Narrative and Structure, Especially of the Fantastic.* Cambridge: Cambridge UP, 1981.

Gardiner, Judith Kegan. "On Female Identity and Writing by Women." *Writing and Sexual Difference.* Ed. Elizabeth Abel. Chicago: U of Chicago P, 1982. 177-91.

Gilbert, Sandra and Susan Gubar. *The Madwoman in the Attic: The Woman Writer and the Nineteenth-Century Literary Imagination.* New Haven: Yale UP, 1979.

Hume, Katherine. *Fantasy and Mimesis: Responses to Reality in Western Literature.* New York: Methuen, 1984.

Jackson, Rosemary. *Fantasy: The Literature of Subversion.* New York: Methuen, 1981.

Lauter, Estella. *Women as Mythmakers.* Bloomington: Indiana UP, 1984.

Mainer, José-Carlos. *La Edad de Plata (1902-1939): Ensayo de interpretación de un proceso cultural.* Madrid: Cátedra, 1983.

—. Introduction. *La historia de la literatura española* 6.1. Ed. Gerald G. Brown. Revised ed. Barcelona: Ariel, 1983.

Matute, Ana María. *Algunos muchachos.* 1968. Barcelona: Destino, 1982.

—. *Los hijos muertos.* 1958. Barcelona: Destino, 1981.

—. *Los niños tontos.* 1956. Barcelona: Destino, 1978.

—. *Primera memoria.* 1960. Barcelona: Destino, 1973.

—. *Tres y un sueño.* Barcelona: Destino, 1961.

Miller, Nancy K. "Arachnologies: The Woman, the Text, and the Critic." *The Poetics of Gender.* Ed. Nancy K. Miller. New York: Columbia UP, 1986. 270-95.

Nichols, Geraldine Cleary. "Caída/re(s)puesta: la narrativa femenina de la posguerra." *Literatura y vida cotidiana. Actas de las IV Jornadas de Investigación Interdisciplinaria.* Ed. María Angeles Durán y José Antonio Rey. Zaragoza: Seminario de Estudios de la Mujer, Univ. Autónoma de Madrid, 1987. 325-35.

—. "Codes of Exclusion, Modes of Equivocation: Matute's *Primera memoria. Ideologies and Literature* no. 1 (1985): 156-88.

—. "The Prison-House (and Beyond): *El mismo mar de todos los veranos." Romanic Review* 75 (1984): 366-85.

—. "Sex, the Single Girl, and Other Mésalliances in Rodoreda and Laforet." *Anales de la Literatura Española Contemporánea* 12 (1987): 123-40.

—. Oliver, Maria Antònia. "Dona i literatura." *Les dones i la literatura catalana.* Barcelona: Publ. de l'ICE, 1986. 29-32.

Riera, Carme. *Epitelis tendríssims.* Barcelona: Eds 62, 1981.

—. "Literatura feminina: ¿Un lenguaje prestado?" *Quimera* 18 (1982): 9-12.

—. *Qüestió d'amor propi.* Barcelona: Laia, 1987.

—. "Te deix, amor, la mar com a penyora." *Te deix, amor, la mar com a penyora.* Barcelona: Laia, 1975. "Te dejo, amor, la mar como una ofrenda." *Palabra de mujer*. Trad. Carme Riera. Barcelona: Laia, 1980.

—. "Vindicación de Teresa de Cepeda." *Quimera* 15 (1982): 4-7.

Rodoreda, Mercè. *Mi Cristina y otros cuentos*. Trad. José Batllo. Madrid: Alianza, 1982.

—. *Tots els contes*. Ed. Carme Arnau. Barcelona: Eds 62, 1979.

Roig, Montserrat. "L'alè poètic de Mercè Rodoreda." *Retrats paral.lels/2*. Montserrat: Publicacions de l'Abadia de Montserrat, 1976. 163-76.

Rubin, Gayle. "The Traffic in Women: Notes on the 'Political Economy' of Sex." *Toward an Anthropology of Women*. Ed. Rayna R. Reiter. New York: Monthly Review, 1975.

Todorov, Tzvetan. *The Fantastic: A Structural Approach to a Literary Genre*. Trans. Richard Howard. Cleveland: P of Case Western Reserve U, 1973. Trans. of *Introduction à la littérature fantastique*, 1970.

Traba, Marta. "Hipótesis sobre una escritura diferente." *Quimera* 13 (1981): 9-11.

LAS SOMBRAS DE LA ESCRITURA: HACIA UNA TEORIA DE LA PRODUCCION LITERARIA DE LA MUJER LATINOAMERICANA

Lucía Guerra Cunningham
University of California, Irvine

En la tradición cultural de Occidente, el repertorio simbólico dominante que reafirma y otorga supremacía jerárquica a lo visible ha asignado a la sombra significados que se insertan en la columna negativa de sus limitadas y rígidas oposiciones binarias. La sombra concebida como el doble incorpóreo de todo cuerpo tangible, como el reflejo engañoso de lo real y como imagen de la parte primitiva, maligna e inferior del ser humano es, sin lugar a dudas, un elemento temible. Dentro de este contexto, resulta significativo el hecho de que "lo femenino" como categoría incluida en este sistema haya sido siempre la sombra por excelencia y es precisamente esta imagen la que nos provee la primera inseminación en este acercamiento crítico a la producción literaria de la mujer. Pero yendo más allá de la estaticidad y rol pasivo de la sombra que convencionalmente es sólo el reflejo exacto de los contornos de un objeto cuya visibilidad y gravidez constituyen en sí los atributos de poder de "la presencia", nuestra imagen de la sombra se permite transgresiones momentáneas de espacio que desfiguran y subvierten lo tangible dominante. Se añade así una segunda dimensión al objeto legitimado que en su reflexión fantasmática adquiere fisuras desestabilizadoras; brechas, silencios y márgenes que la sombra instaura soterradamente negando la unicidad totalizante del objeto, haciendo de su presencia tangible sólo una alternativa que, por opciones claramente ideológicas, ha resultado favorecida por el sistema dominante.

La escritura de la mujer es, en muchos sentidos, una proliferación de sombras, la apropiación estratégica de

modelos masculinos (objetos legitimizados) que se des-
construyen de una manera aparentemente inofensiva
pues, en su posición de término subordinado, la experiencia femenina y sus posibles modelizaciones estéticas está
forzada a ocultar sus zonas disidentes. El análisis mismo
de este fenómeno implica incursionar en una sub-cultura
femenina que ha sido deliberadamente borrada para man-
tenerla en el nivel de lo no-existente y ahistórico, mecanismo hegemónico que responde a una ideología falologocéntrica y a factores infraestructurales propiciados por el
patriarcado. Por consiguiente, el presente estudio podría
calificarse como la exploración de espacios silenciados que,
según los parámetros dominantes, corresponderían a los
márgenes desechables de una sombra que malignamente
aumentó y desestabilizó las dimensiones del objeto legi-
timizado.

ENCUADRE Y FIJACION: LOS LAZOS PATRIARCALES DE LA SUBORDINACION FEMENINA

> Para qué hizo Dios a la mujer de
> miembros débiles y voluntad
> flaca sino para quedarse sentada
> en un rincón.
>
> *Fray Luis de León*

El fenómeno de la subordinación femenina se distingue
por una complejidad intrínseca ligada al cuerpo, las relaciones de parentesco, construcciones sociales específicas y
la producción material. Como acertadamente distingue
Engels en *Orígenes de la familia, la propiedad privada y el
Estado* (1884), esta última posee un carácter dual: la producción y reproducción de los medios de subsistencia y la
reproducción de los seres humanos. La institucionalización de la familia monogámica como unidad económica
por medio de la cual la propiedad se acumula y transmite
para el interés individual, marcaría, para el pensamiento
marxista decimonónico, la primera oposición de clases en
la evolución histórica y la opresión del sexo femenino correspondería a una situación de tipo eminentemente económico. Sin embargo, los recientes estudios antropológi-

cos han puesto de manifiesto el carácter generalizante de la estructura patriarcal bajo condiciones en las cuales el factor de la producción material varía considerablemente del modo económico capitalista. Razón por la cual se ha comenzado a otorgar una mayor importancia al factor biológico determinando que el rol materno de la mujer posee un efecto profundo tanto en los patrones sexuales e ideológicos como en la organización misma del trabajo.[1] Por lo tanto, es en el cuerpo femenino como *locus* de la reproducción de la especie donde se encuentran los orígenes mismos de una problemática de la subordinación que se hace evidente en la organización económica y las construcciones culturales de un grupo.

Si desde un punto de vista fisiológico es natural que ella "conciba" y "dé a luz", por extensión, es también natural que cuide de los hijos y se circunscriba al ámbito doméstico. Pero este sencillo proceso de naturalización no se restringe únicamente al regazo materno, por el contrario, se extiende a significaciones culturales que hacen del signo mujer una compleja construcción social estructurada a partir de un proceso de mutilación que reafirma su rol primario. Partiendo de una dimensión exclusivamente corporal —su capacidad biológica reproductora— la imaginación masculina le asignó el significado primario de Mujer-Matriz, un vientre que, como la vasija de las sociedades primitivas, se convirtió en el símbolo del principio de la vida al cual se le atribuyó una ecuación básica en los elementos cósmicos del agua y la tierra. No es de extrañar, por lo tanto, que su representación como forma redondeada en la cual se exagera la protuberancia del vientre y de los senos constituya en sí un símbolo visible de la unidimensionalidad atribuida por el patriarcado a la mujer. Simultáneamente, la muerte, en su calidad disyuntiva con respecto a la vida, vino a ser sinónimo de la distorsión monstruosa de la maternidad, de esa figura bestial que devora a sus propios hijos o consume las entrañas de los cadáveres y, en las figuraciones de la Madre-Terrible, es nuevamente el cuerpo femenino ahora despojado de redondeces armoniosas y benéficas el que revierte a la mujer como ente exclusivamente fijado en lo biológico.

Cercenación inicial que no obstante las prolíferas mitificaciones en lo sagrado o lo profano responden y se presentan a partir de este proceso de naturalización que en términos concretos resulta irrefutable. La mujer es madre del mismo modo como el hombre es padre, pero a diferencia de éste que se auto-adjudica la identidad jerárquica de Padre en el ámbito celestial, religioso, político y familiar, ella se estatiza y restringe en una identidad exclusivamente biológica.

Es más, la mujer que ontológica y socialmente es sólo madre se concibe como una prolongación del ámbito natural considerado en un orden inferior al de la Cultura o modificaciones del entorno. Su cuerpo —atado a la reproducción de la especie— es considerado un reflejo de lo cíclico y repetitivo que se opone a la invención y acción creativa del hombre en su impulso civilizador y, de igual manera como la Naturaleza se subordina a la Cultura, la mujer —sinónimo de ella— es subordinada al hombre como agente de todo proyecto cultural.[2]

En consecuencia, es válido afirmar que lo biológico se transforma no sólo en relaciones concretas establecidas por la división sexual del trabajo sino también en una devaluación de lo femenino que adquiere una función de objeto de intercambio.[3] Esta devaluación no se refiere, por supuesto, al valor mismo de los dones de la transacción que en algunos grupos culturales poseen cualidades mágicas sino, más bien, al hecho de que son los hombres y no las mujeres sus únicos agentes activos. Y en su capacidad de iniciadores y beneficiarios de dicha transacción, los hombres poseen el poder para establecer no sólo las regulaciones específicas de parentesco sino también de toda la organización social de su grupo. Por consiguiente, en el sistema del "tráfico de mujeres", ellas son las únicas que no reciben ningún beneficio de su propia circulación.[4]

La división genérica de los sexos no obstante se origina en un factor biológico concreto pasa por una serie de transformaciones que lejos de estructurar únicamente lo sexual se proyectan en todas las actividades humanas marcadas por un poder masculino que se atribuye, extendiendo la metáfora de Gayle Rubin, el rol de traficante del Hacer y la Palabra, de poseedor exclusivo de la Conciencia y la Actividad, de ente todo poderoso que mistifica o degrada el cuerpo femenino reproductor para crear un signo que antojadísamente fluctúa entre lo virginal y lo demónico. La mujer como individuo que en su rol primario de madre ha permanecido en el espacio marginal de la Cultura irónicamente es también la matriz de prolíferas construcciones culturales en su calidad de Otro. Un Otro creado por el Sujeto masculino como necesidad imperiosa para una economía que ideológicamente se sustenta a partir de lo Mismo. Poniendo de manera irreverente los mecanismos del falologocentrismo, se podría afirmar que la materialidad e inmanencia atribuidas a la mujer responden a las estrategias de un poder masculino que necesita ubicar en su tablero las fichas del No-Ser para imponer el Ser (el Sol y el concepto teleológico del Tiempo opuestos a la luna, a la menstruación, a la vivencia cósmica que fluye en los márgenes de todo lo "histórico", el Espíritu y la Razón iluminando todas las empresas culturales y reprimiendo la Carne que sólo figurativamente da a luz, el Logos consumiendo la Materia en aventuras metafísicas y trascendentales).

Pero si quisiéramos explicar el fenómeno de la subordinación femenina sólo en términos de la oposición Opresor-Oprimido estaríamos simplificando un tejido de múltiple y contradictoria faz. No se trata, como en el caso de las clases sociales oprimidas, de la visible explotación económica de un grupo cuyo *ethos* y valores culturales son aniquilados por un poder hegemónico, tampoco se puede explicar la subordinación femenina a partir de una exclusión absoluta o una imposición colonizadora. A diferencia de los grupos colonizados por una cultura dominante, la mujer, dispersa en todos los estratos sociales, tradicionalmente no ha poseído una conciencia de clase ni de cultura pues su Hacer doméstico y maternal ha sido relegado al espacio de la No-Cultura. Fenómeno que ha impedido, hasta ahora, la funcionalidad de una reinscripción de modos económicos y culturales alternativos. En contraste con otros grupos dominados, habría que afirmar que en el caso de la mujer ha sido el cuerpo femenino en su dimensión reproductiva el verdadero eje de la dominación. La relación sexual y eminentemente genérica que la mujer esta-

blece con el hombre mantiene esta subordinación en un
nivel cuya complejidad no admite explicaciones exhausti-
vas a partir de paradigmas ya desarrollados en términos de
clase social, cultura invasora o grupos excluidos. Su rol de
madre dentro de la institución del matrimonio hace de la
mujer un cuerpo que es también cómplice ideológico del
orden masculino de las cosas y junto con convertirse en
celosa resguardadora de dicho orden, ella también se asi-
mila a los valores de una clase social determinada, en última instancia, por la actividad económica del *Pater Familias*. Es precisamente este complejo mecanismo de asociación afectiva y sexual el que ha ocultado una estructura de
dominación dispersando, a la vez, al sexo femenino en
estratificaciones que previenen toda posibilidad de una
verdadera conciencia de grupo.[5]

Por consiguiente, la situación subordinada de la mujer
es un fenómeno que fluctúa simultáneamente entre la
participación/exclusión, práctica paradójica y no-disyun-
tiva que sitúa a la mujer en la zona fluida del Ser/No-
Ser/Deber-Ser. Si los explícitos códigos morales resultan
un firme asidero del Deber-Ser, la problemática del Ser
para el Sujeto femenino constituye un enigma que sólo se
resuelve parcial y mentirosamente en las vastas construcciones culturales de un sistema que, bajo la abstracción no
génerica denominada Hombre, estratégicamente postula
un Ser universal subsumiendo al Sujeto Ausente. Es más,
en un sistema donde Ser mujer equivale a No-Ser
(pasividad, carencia de racionalidad, intuición vencida por
la lógica), la dicotomía clásica del pensamiento falologocéntrico (Ser/No-Ser) se difumina para dar paso a un
flujo oximorónico bajo el cual yace de manera latente otra
instancia del Ser que correspondería a los impulsos transgresivos dominados por la represión de las organizaciones
sociales y las construcciones culturales de la estructura patriarcal.

Utilizamos la categoría del Ser no sólo en una acepción
exclusivamente metafísica puesto que, en nuestra opinión, el Ser se define en una relación concreta con la Historia. Y es en el devenir histórico donde se dan, de manera
más evidente, las contradicciones complejas y ambivalen-

tes del Ser femenino que en su particular posición de Sujeto simultáneamente participa y se mantiene ausente.
En las sociedades de occidente, según los parámetros
dominantes de la Historia oficial construida a partir de
eventos y personajes que configuran la "evolución" lineal
del desarrollo y "progreso" del proyecto capitalista, la mujer se relega a los espacios de la absoluta pasividad ahistórica y sólo figura en ella como compañera en la vida anec-
dótica de los "héroes" o como mujer excepcional que tras-
pasó los límites de su rol femenino para vestirse y actuar a
la manera de los hombres. Sin embargo, sería erróneo
aseverar que la mujer ha estado fuera de la Historia si ésta
se concibe no como una sucesión de hechos públicos en
una sociedad de carácter homogéneo sino como un con-
glomerado complejo de sub-culturas mantenidas a nivel
marginal por el poder hegemónico.

No obstante su exclusión en la economía, la política y
las actividades legitimizadas de la cultura, la mujer, aparte
de funcionar como eje diseminador de la ideología dominante en el ámbito familiar, ha participado tangencial-
mente en el devenir oficializado de la Historia utilizando
de manera estratégica su imagen convencional de ser débil
e inofensivo.[6] Es más, desde el espacio unitario y hegemónico de la ideología burguesa ha actuado contra dicha
ideología produciendo dislocaciones momentáneas que
sólo actualmente comienzan a ser estudiadas.[7] Por otra
parte, como ponen en evidencia las recientes investigaciones históricas, ella en su posición marginal ha sido el
agente activo de una "Sub-Historia" que posee como núcleo su intervención modificadora en el espacio doméstico, los valores éticos, el consumo y la diseminación de
los objetos culturales.[8]

Participación/Exclusión: praxis que incluye como uno
de sus elementos básicos la no-praxis, la tensión de un silenciamiento, la presencia latente de un "aquéllo" poster-
gado por la represión y la dominación. Espacio en blanco
que por no haber sido culturalmente codificado permanece como lo irrepresentado y lo irrepresentable. Y en los
recientes estudios que a partir de la categoría genérico-
sexual analizan una problemática hasta ahora sin voz, se

ha puesto de manifiesto esta dinámica de la fluidez dual de la subordinación.

En este sentido, las investigaciones socio-lingüísticas resultan altamente esclarecedoras para comprender el fenómeno de la escritura producida por la mujer. A partir de un concepto de lenguaje como código de conceptualización de las relaciones humanas e instrumento de poder, se ha comenzado a inquirir en la categoría del génerolecto que pone en evidencia la estructura de la organización patriarcal. Cheris Kramarae, por ejemplo, parte de una distinción básica entre las percepciones del mundo, experiencias y actividades de cada grupo sexual para postular la dicotomía entre lenguaje masculino dominante que funciona como norma y el lenguaje subordinado de la mujer que se mantiene de manera marginal.[9] En una situación de grupo silenciado, la mujer adecúa su ideolecto, claudica e incluso deja espacios en blanco para zonas de su realidad específica que carecen de un discurso manteniendo, simultáneamente, un conjunto de signos catalogados a nivel popular como "cháchara de mujeres" o, parafraseando a Lope de Vega, en palabras que llevan la firma del viento.

En consecuencia, la mujer utiliza y maneja simultáneamente dos códigos que se encuentran en una relación diglósica muy particular puesto que a la fuerza centrípeta homogeneizante y de carácter dominante se opone en un diálogo silenciado el código femenino que no alcanza a adquirir un poder dispersivo; y es precisamente en este proceso diglósico anclado en el silenciamiento y la represión donde se reitera la organización asimétrica impuesta por la estructura patriarcal en todas las actividades humanas.[10] La mujer entonces se encuentra en una situación discursiva ambivalente, entre dos aguas, la del discurso falologocéntrico de raíces "liberales" y "humanistas" que defienden como ideales la libertad, la auto-determinación y la racionalidad y el flujo turbio de un discurso femenino marcado por la subordinación, la difusión y la fragmentación. Apropiándonos de la teoría de M. M. Bajtín, podríamos aseverar que, como un eficiente ventrílocuo, la mujer asume las voces de un lenguaje ajeno permitiéndose en los intermedios el carnaval polifónico de su féminolecto marginalizado. Es más, si para el teórico ruso, usar la palabra de otro implica infundirle nuevos significados que le dan a ésta una doble voz, las interrelaciones siempre variables de este bivocalismo deberían también ser analizadas en términos de una categoría genérico-sexual que no sólo funciona en los espacios de una claudicación sino también en la zona silenciada de las subversiones.

LAS SOMBRAS DE LA ESCRITURA

> El rechazo y la exclusión de un repertorio imaginario femenino ciertamente pone a la mujer en la posición de experimentarse a sí misma sólo de manera fragmentaria en los márgenes poco estructurados de una ideología dominante como desperdicio, como exceso, como aquéllo que queda de un espejo investido por el "sujeto" (masculino) para reflejarse a sí mismo.
>
> *Luce Irigaray*

Era costumbre entre griegos y romanos que se le permitiera a los invitados traer al banquete a un familiar o a un amigo, individuo no incluido en la lista de comensales y que recibía el nombre de "sombra". Las escritoras, en este sentido del término, han sido siempre una sombra, personajes no oficialmente invitados a participar en el oficio de las letras. Obviando la discusión del uso de seudónimos masculinos, de la recepción negativa por parte de una crítica falologocéntrica y de las obvias exclusiones en un canon de carácter eminentemente masculino que funciona como la Ley del Padre, preferimos detenernos en las implicaciones estéticas de un fenómeno que se podría definir como la acción transgresiva de crear un texto literario en los espacios intertextuales de modelizaciones que no corresponden a una visión del mundo femenina.

Y significativamente han sido las escritoras y no la crítica quienes han estado conscientes de esta incursión en terreno ajeno. En uno de sus ensayos sobre la mujer publicados por Gertrudis Gómez de Avellaneda en 1860, la autora cubana afirma: "Si la mujer —a pesar de estos y

otros brillantes indicios de su capacidad científica— aún
sigue proscrita del templo de los conocimientos profundos, no se crea tampoco que data de muchos siglos su
aceptación en el campo literario y artístico: ¡Ah! ¡no!   también ese terreno le ha sido disputado palmo á palmo por el
exclusivismo varonil, y aún hoy día se la mira en él como
intrusa y usurpadora, tratándosela, en consecuencia, con
cierta ojeriza y desconfianza, que se echa de ver en el ale-
jamiento en que se la mantiene de las academias *barbu-
das*".[11]

Habiendo experimentado ella misma la masculinización de su talento pues, para sus coetáneos, el hecho de
que fuera una excelente escritora se debía a que ella era
"mucho hombre",[12] Gertrudis Gómez de Avellaneda define el éxito literario de la mujer como el producto de un
enmascaramiento audaz y estratégico; refiriéndose a
George Sand "lampiña disfrazada" (p. 304) por excelencia,
la autora afirma: "Otras que cubriendo sus lampiñas caras
con máscara varonil, se entraron, sin más ni más, tan
adentro del templo de la fama, que cuando vino á cono-
cerse *que carecían de barbas* y no podían, por consiguiente,
ser admitidas entre las capacidades académicas, ya no había medio hábil de negarles que poseían justos títulos para
figurar eternamente entre las capacidades europeas". (pp.
303-304)

La imagen de la máscara y el antifaz es indudablemente
un signo que si bien no metaforiza en toda su complejidad
la escritura de la mujer pone de manifiesto, sin embargo,
un elemento esencial: la impostura y el adulterio, dos actos transgresivos que modifican ilegalmente el objeto
"legítimo" en un proceso de usurpación. Concepto que
contrasta, de manera significativa, con "el dar a luz" o "el
parto de la creación" que los escritores, en un curioso proceso de apropiaciones del cuerpo femenino, han utilizado
tradicionalmente para referirse a la escritura.

Si el texto literario para estos últimos es, en principio,
un embrión que se alimenta y crece dentro del mismo Sujeto Creador, la mujer "concibe" su escritura dentro de
una gestualidad que implica ocultarse a sí misma, salirse
de los límites propios exiliándose en los espacios oficiales
y hegemónicos de modelos literarios masculinos. Y utili-

zamos la imagen del exilio porque, como en éste, se produce un dialogismo significativo entre lo propio y lo foráneo marcado, como en el caso de la diglosia del lenguaje, por la supremacía de lo masculino dominante. En este sentido, entonces, resulta apropiado el acercamiento teórico de Claudine Herrman quien analiza la producción literaria de la mujer en términos de la oposición entre colonizador y sujeto femenino colonizado.[13]

Son ya prolíferas las imágenes que intentan definir este complejo proceso estético que, en última instancia, revierte a la constitución del Sujeto en el lenguaje. Para Helena Araújo, escritora colombiana consciente de nuestra problemática tercermundista, la escritura femenina es la imagen especular de la invención como postergación de la muerte. Araújo afirma:

> Scherezada sería un buen sobrenombre kitch para la escritora del continente. ¿Por qué? Porque como Scherezada, ha tenido que narrar historias e inventar ficciones en carrera desesperada contra un tiempo que conlleva la amenaza de la muerte: muerte en la pérdida de la identidad y en la pérdida del deseo. Muerte-castigo. Seguramente también, la latinoamericana ha escrito desafiando una sociedad y un sistema que imponen el anonimato. Ha escrito sintiéndose ansiosa y culpable de robarle horas al padre o al marido. Sobre todo ha escrito siendo infiel a ese papel para el cual fuera predestinada, el único, de madre. Escribir, entonces, ha sido su manera de prolongar una libertad ilusoria y posponer una condena.[14]

Según la postulación de Helena Araújo, el acto de inscribir lenguaje en un papel significa para la mujer anular ese otro papel mitificado de madre que la ha relegado a la muerte de una verdadera identidad y de la anulación del deseo, transgresión que constituye en sí un acto de libertad condenado al castigo. Si el énfasis de la escritora colombiana se da en las imposiciones de lo social y convencional, Julia Kristeva, desde una perspectiva europea, define la escritura de la mujer como un proceso inscrito en el lenguaje mismo al decir: "En la escritura de la mujer, el lenguaje parece ser visto desde un terreno ajeno, ¿es tal vez contemplado desde el punto de vista de un cuerpo asimbólico y espasmódico? Virginia Woolf describe estados suspendidos, sensaciones sutiles y, sobre todo, colores como el azul y el verde, pero ella nunca disecta el lenguaje como lo hace Joyce. Apartadas y enajenadas del lenguaje, las mujeres son visionarias, bailarinas que sufren cuando hablan".[15] Escritura que interrumpe y posterga la condena de la muerte, gestos y movimientos de un cuerpo que aún no se ha incorporado a un sistema de construcciones simbólicas. El factor que se presenta como núcleo seminal de la escritura de la mujer en todas estas interpretaciones es la enajenación que pone en evidencia una marginalidad del Sujeto productor inserta en una infraestructura que se organiza a partir de la diferenciación génericosexual.

Lo importante, por supuesto, es analizar los movimientos de la bailarina, detenerse en las texturas narrativas que Scherezada teje como una anulación momentánea de la muerte. Y el primer problema que ella enfrenta es representarse a sí misma deslizándose por los márgenes de una identidad ya adscrita, sumergiéndose más allá del repertorio imaginario masculino que en prolíferas modelizaciones estéticas ha atribuido a "lo femenino", en su calidad de Otro, las categorías de la pureza virginal, el pecado, la inmanencia y la transgresión.[16] Identidad otorgada que para las escritoras contemporáneas es sinónimo de una mentira, como pone de manifiesto Mercedes Valdivieso al recordar la situación cultural chilena durante la década de los sesenta: "Aunque a las mujeres nos estaba permitido escribir, éste era un escribir acondicionado a un lenguaje que nos hacía mujeres y que nos mentía acerca de nuestras propias aspiraciones, nuestro cuerpo y nuestras emociones".[17]

Y es en este proceso de búsqueda de una identidad propia que se intenta fijar con el propósito de ficcionalizar — acto creativo que a su vez proporcionará un asidero tangible a dicha identidad— que la escritora vivencia las contradicciones de un Ser pluralizado en el Ser/No-Ser/Deber-Ser. Al respecto, Susan K. Cornillon ha dicho: "En la cultura masculina la idea de lo femenino se expresa, se define y se percibe por el hombre como una condición de ser mujer mientras que para la mujer esta idea de lo femenino es vista como una adición a la propia femineidad, como un *status* o meta que deben ser logrados".[18] Por consiguiente, representarse a sí misma significa transgredir las sólidas construcciones culturales del sistema falologocéntrico para incursionar en lo "no representado" y lo "no representable", bucear en las zonas silenciadas de ese otro Ser sitiado en el vacío y más allá de los límites asignados a un Sujeto masculino y un Otro femenino. En este proceso, indudablemente, el cuerpo resulta ser la primera trampa. En su análisis de la mujer como objeto de mercancía puesto que ella en su rol reproductivo ha sido subsumida en el ámbito natural dominado y el espacio doméstico de la propiedad privada, Luce Irigaray afirma: "—de igual manera como un objeto de mercancía no posee un espejo para reflejarse a sí mismo, la mujer sólo sirve como reflejo, como imagen de y para el hombre pero carece de cualidades propias. Su forma investida de valor equivale a lo que el hombre ha inscrito en y sobre su materia: es decir, su cuerpo".[19]

Y no obstante ella es poseedora de un cuerpo hecho objeto del Deseo, bajo las imposiciones patriarcales que protegen la propiedad legítima sobre los hijos, le está prohibido ser Sujeto de ese Deseo bajo la mirada plácida del modelo sagrado de la Virgen María —figura asexuada por excelencia. Luce Irigaray pone en evidencia los mecanismos de las operaciones simbólicas de una economía patriarcal que, con el objetivo de dominar y subyugar, escinde el cuerpo femenino en "sangre menstrual/perfil de apariencias, cuerpo/envoltura investida de valor, materia/medio de intercambio, naturaleza (re)productiva/femineidad fabricada".[20] Y, en esta escinsión, todo lo natural permanece en lo amorfo, en lo silenciado como tabú o en lo mistificado y degradado de las representaciones masculinas de un cuerpo femenino que funciona como signo mismo de la apropiación.

Como un modo metafórico de definir este fenómeno de la simultaneidad contradictoria del Ser, Adrienne Rich ha escrito: "We are translations into different dialects/ of a text still being written in the original".[21] En su discurso

142 LUCIA GUERRA CUNNINGHAM

feminista, Rich otorga a la traducción el significado de
transposición, de forzamiento distorsionador, de versión
alterada, al mismo tiempo que pone en evidencia el proceso inconcluso de una auto-codificación femenina. Por
otra parte y desde la perspectiva de la creación literaria
misma, Marguerite Duras afirma: "Creo que 'la literatura
femenina' es una escritura orgánica y traducida... traducida de la oscuridad. Por siglos las mujeres han estado en
la oscuridad. No se conocen a sí mismas. O sólo se conocen precariamente. Y cuando las mujeres escriben, ellas
traducen esta oscuridad... Los hombres no traducen. Ellos
parten de una plataforma teórica que ya ha sido elaborada
y está muy bien ubicada. La escritura de la mujer es realmente traducida de lo desconocido, más bien como una
nueva forma de comunicar y no como un lenguaje ya establecido".[22] Por lo tanto, en el doble proceso de transgredir los límites de la traducción falologocéntrica y de crear
un nuevo discurso que traduzca las zonas silenciadas de la
femineidad la escritora, bailarina a compás diglósico, enfrenta serios escollos que la condenan, como asevera Luce
Irigaray, a la fragmentación.

Y aparte de las fragmentaciones de la femineidad tanto
en su sentido social como ontológico se da, en el texto
literario, la modelización de circunstancias y espacios que
nuevamente circunscriben a la Subjetividad femenina
puesto que esta representación se realiza a partir de una
perspectiva ubicada en la alteridad de la subordinación.

ESTRATEGIAS DISCURSIVAS DE LA MUJER LATINOAMERICANA
COMO SUJETO/OBJETO DE LA ESCRITURA

Adscribiéndonos a las recientes teorías de la
intertextualidad, partimos de la hipótesis de que todo texto
es, en mayor o menor medida, una interrogación, una
respuesta o una absorción de otro u otros textos precedentes con los cuales constituye un sistema de relaciones. En el caso de la producción literaria de la mujer, habría que aseverar, tomando en cuenta todos los factores de
dominación anteriormente comentados, que el sistema
textual dominante ha producido, desde una perspectiva

masculina, discursos *sobre* la mujer y no *en* ella ni *por* ella. Tradicionalmente, esta producción ha carecido de un *corpus* literario propio al cual remitirse, puesto que tanto los mecanismos de difusión editorial como los juicios de valor establecidos por el canon sistematizado han contribuido al silenciamiento de los textos escritos por mujeres. En consecuencia, dicha producción se podría definir como una literatura derivada cuyo régimen natural es la hipertextualidad ya que su sistema de referencia corresponde a una literatura producida por el grupo hegemónico y originador de hipotextos.[23]

El proceso de inserción en el sistema textual dominante que pone en evidencia el complejo fenómeno de la subordinación ya brevemente esbozado se realiza, sin embargo, desde la posición descentralizada de un Sujeto cuya visión del mundo y perspectiva acerca de la problemática femenina no coincide con aquélla presente en el espacio intertextual. Es más, en su identidad socialmente adscrita de Otro y como Objeto de los discursos dominantes, el Sujeto femenino de la escritura se reconoce y parcialmente claudica a ese Otro en las representaciones literarias de ese espacio construido por hipotextos donde el signo mujer refiere a la pureza asexualizada, al pecado amenazante o a la marginalidad con poder subversivo. Fenómeno que en sí mismo desconstruye el concepto falologocéntrico del Sujeto de la escritura para hacer de él un Sujeto que es simultáneamente y, en mayor o menor grado, Objeto.

En consecuencia, el desfase básico a nivel de la concepción del mundo y la posición del Sujeto constituye su especificidad que responde a los movimientos antagónicos de la claudicación y la subversión. Y es a partir de este desfase básico que se pueden comprender los fenómenos estéticos del silencio y el vacío, el palimpsesto, la diglosia de lo femenino, la mímica con valor transgresivo y la feminización de otros grupos dominados, márgenes visibles o en blanco que modifican el espacio intertextual asimilado creando fisuras significativas en el sistema ideológico falologocéntrico.

En este punto es importante también subrayar que la escritora latinoamericana como Sujeto/Objeto de la escritura constituye una peculiar construcción social e ideológica puesto que asume una actividad cultural típica de los grupos dominantes en una hegemonía que marginaliza a los sectores populares, indígenas y negros. Simultáneamente, sin embargo, perdura y se mantiene latente su marginalidad genérico-sexual que, a la vez, y a nivel de la estratificación social propiciada por la estructura económica, le adscribe el rol de resguardadora de los valores y ritos de la burguesía. El texto producido en este complejo proceso que fluctúa entre lo hegemónico y lo marginal pone en evidencia una conciencia colectiva femenina que recién empieza a ser dilucidada.[24] Y como evidencia de la asimetría básica entre los sexos, la conciencia colectiva femenina ha seguido una evolución distintiva que, en el caso del siglo XIX, época en que la mujer latinoamericana no tuvo acceso a la educación ni a la política, dió origen a disidencias de carácter retardatorio.[25]

Desde las zonas de la alteridad propiciadas tanto por la subordinación social como por una subordinación de carácter estético, la escritora enfrenta el problema dual de asumirse como Sujeto productor en la escritura asimilando, a la vez y en un gesto mimético, las representaciones de lo femenino como Objeto de los discursos literarios dominantes. Y no obstante en el proceso imaginario ella logra esta posición de Sujeto, la máscara a la que aludía Gertrudis Gómez de Avellaneda posee trizaduras que delatan su alteridad o resulta insuficiente para encubrir áreas de la femineidad que, por razones obvias, no han sido literariamente representadas en el sistema textual de corte masculino.

Dentro de este contexto de la producción literaria de la mujer, no resulta fortuito que el primer aspecto que llama la atención en sus textos narrativos sea la omisión de experiencias típicamente femeninas como el embarazo, la maternidad, la subordinación social genérica y las relaciones cotidianas con objetos del espacio doméstico. Estos silencios y vacíos responden, por una parte, al concepto implícito de acontecimiento narrativo postulado por los hipotextos de una producción dominantemente masculina en la cual la "acción narrativa" se origina en una "zona de sucesos" donde se ignora, por razones obvias, la potencialidad literaria de las vivencias experimentadas por la mujer. Silencios y vacíos que no sólo ponen en evidencia la claudicación de la escritora a modelizaciones de carácter dominante sino también la ausencia, en los niveles simbólicos y culturales, de un discurso que reafirmando la diferencia genérico-sexual, produzca la constitución de la femineidad en el lenguaje.

Además, es importante señalar que los silencios y los espacios en blanco están también determinados, en la esfera de la organización social, por el discurso que ésta le atribuye a la mujer quien en el espacio público y convencionalmente aceptado de su Deber-Ser no ha tenido otra alternativa que sustituir la sexualidad por la sentimentalidad, el lenguaje explícito por el eufemismo y la ira o rebeldía por el silencio. Los textos narrativos de la mujer han estado tradicionalmente marcados por un pudor y una autocensura que corroboran la hipótesis de Judith Fetterley con respecto al control masculino de la textualidad, al dominio autoritario de la perspectiva androcéntrica que masculiniza al receptor y hace del fenómeno de la recepción un proceso determinado por una supremacía cultural que es también una supremacía genérica propiciada por la estructura patriarcal.[26]

Si bien estas omisiones constituyen en sí importantes elementos constitutivos del texto como "presencias de la ausencia", nos interesa en este ensayo destacar el silencio y los espacios en blanco como una estrategia textual que soterradamente transgrede el sistema impuesto por las construcciones ideológicas del falologocentrismo. En el discurso de la sexualidad impuesto por este sistema, el acto sexual, desde una perspectiva que propicia la heterosexualidad y el principio de la actividad masculina, éste se define como un acto entre hombre y mujer dirigido a un propósito de placer y reproducción en el cual el evento trascendente está constituido por la penetración fálica.

En novelas tales como *El abrazo de la tierra* (1933) y *Las cenizas* (1942) de María Flora Yáñez, *Extraño estío* (1944) y *El mundo dormido de Yenia* (1946) de María Carolina Geel y *La última niebla* (1934) y *La amortajada* (1938) de María Luisa Bombal, el Deseo se estructura a partir de una economía libidinal en la cual el cuerpo femenino experimenta el placer erótico en su contacto con la tierra y el agua, contacto definido como "enlace orgánico, integral y armonioso".[27] Si bien, desde una perspectiva freudiana y falologocéntrica, la actividad erótica en estas novelas podría considerarse como un fenómeno de sublimación y desplazamiento, la representación de la sexualidad femenina como instancia de la multiplicidad y fluidez pone de manifiesto la especificidad del placer sexual femenino que escapa a los procedimientos de computación de una economía escópica masculina. Es más, las omisiones de la penetración fálica no responden sencillamente a la autocensura o el pudor sino que transgreden las imposiciones de un sistema que le otorga a la actividad sexual el exclusivo propósito de reproducción en el caso de la mujer.

Un aspecto relevante es, por supuesto, el modo estratégico en que se realiza dicha transgresión puesto que en su contacto con la tierra, el agua o un amante imaginario y por ende lícito, la sexualidad femenina se presenta como "inofensiva" para las convenciones morales y, tomando en cuenta a un receptor masculino que le atribuye a la mujer un discurso sentimental y eufemístico, las imágenes poéticas resultan ser signos que refuerzan dicha preconcepción. En este sentido, los espacios en blanco otorgados a la penetración fálica y su sustitución por otro discurso de la sexualidad deben ser analizados como una práctica de oposición que recién empieza a ser analizada en la literatura de la mujer.[28] Y, en los textos antes mencionados, no sólo se produce la negación de la penetración fálica como único evento trascendente sino que también se desterritorializa la actividad sexual femenina borrando el falo, ampliando sus límites a una esfera cósmica íntimamente unida a lo femenino, según la posición ideológica de sus autoras.

Una táctica esencial en las prácticas de oposición realizadas por los grupos subordinados es, indudablemente, el enmascaramiento estratégico de los elementos subversivos, proceso que produce una bitextualización básica que en el caso de *Sab* (1841) de Gertrudis Gómez de Avellaneda asume la forma de un palimpsesto. Si en el nivel visible del relato se presenta la trayectoria típicamente romántica del esclavo Sab, bajo éste subyace otro relato "borrado" en el cual se presenta a Carlota quien en su condición femenina está condenada a la claudicación y el silencio. Sab resulta ser entonces un recurso estratégico cuya función como Sujeto Romántico es iluminar retrospectivamente la problemática social de la mujer, planteada en la novela, como peor que la esclavitud.

Y, en este sentido, habría que decir que la autora cubana realizó una verdadera apropiación femenina de la estética romántica del mismo modo como Soledad Acosta de Samper a través de un procedimiento de intensificación morbosa se apropió del leit-motif de la enfermedad como signo romántico de la sentimentalidad femenina. Sus relatos incluidos en *Novelas y Cuadros de la vida sur-americana* (1869) podrían considerarse como contra-textos de *María*, novela homónima de Jorge Isaacs, pues si en ésta la enfermedad realza el carácter pasivo y espiritual de la mujer que posee como modelo a la Virgen, en los textos de su coetánea, la figura de la leprosa acosada por cuartos cerrados viene a ser un correlato objetivo de la existencia femenina representada como la nada alienante cuando ésta no alcanza su realización a través del Sujeto masculino.

Los procedimientos de apropiación han producido en la novela de la mujer latinoamericana inversiones significativas, como es el caso de la estructura del *Bildungsroman* concebida, en esencia, como la trayectoria de un personaje en el proceso de incorporación a un orden de tipo social. Este modelo, dadas las inadecuaciones básicas de la mujer en su calidad de Otro siempre marginal a dicho orden, resulta una estructura de márgenes excesivos, razón por la cual la trayectoria femenina se interioriza excluyendo el Afuera que tradicionalmente posee un valor iniciatorio.[29] Teresa de la Parra partiendo de una ideología feminista que concibe la integración de la mujer en el orden burgués como un proceso que anula toda posibilidad de independencia y libertad, irónicamente invierte y contradice la estructura del *Bildungsroman* en su novela *Ifigenia. Diario de una señorita que escribió porque se fastidiaba* (1924). El proceso de formación en este texto deviene en una deformación y mutilación de los impulsos subversivos de la mujer planteando implícitamente una *anti-Bildungsroman* que constituiría la verdadera iniciación educativa de la mujer latinoamericana.

Si bien el importe ideológico y consciente, como en el caso de Teresa de la Parra, produce estas inversiones fácilmente discernibles, nos parece aún más interesante el fenómeno de aquellos textos en los cuales se hace evidente la contradicción entre una ideología asimilada al orden burgués y un conjunto disperso de disidencias no sistematizadas ni conceptualizadas con respecto a la problemática femenina. Tal sería el caso de Mercedes Cabello de Carbonera, escritora peruana que compartiendo una ideología positivista concibe a la mujer como un ser de superioridad afectiva e innata que complementa la superioridad del hombre en las actividades del entendimiento y la razón. Su novela *Blanca Sol* (1889) es, en uno de los niveles del relato, simplemente el proceso de degradación de la protagonista que simboliza también el deterioro moral de la burguesía limeña.

Pero el intento moralizante de Cabello de Carbonera le hace una mala jugada. La figura de la prostituta como anti-modelo de la mujer que en su rol de madre y resguardadora de la familia debe cultivar la virtud, establece una fisura en el discurso positivista de la femineidad. La prostitución añade márgenes contradictorios a la situación femenina dentro del orden burgués haciendo del matrimonio un tipo de prostitución aprobada por la sociedad, del mismo modo, el adulterio, en el relato de los desvíos no-disyuntivos de la virtud opuesto a aquél de la torcida senda, marca una significativa evolución espiritual de la protagonista. No obstante la posición ética dominante en la novela es aquélla que corresponde al relato de la moral disyuntiva que revierte al Deber-Ser, estas fisuras hacen de la problemática femenina una diglosia que conlleva transgresiones significativas.

Diglosia que en la narrativa de Rosario Ferré se convierte en estrategia beligerante puesto que en la escisión pecado/virtud la única opción válida está en la subversión motivada por las zonas reprimidas de la ira, la rebeldía y la sexualidad. En *Papeles de Pandora* (1976), las chágaras furibundas que salen de los ojos de la muñeca, signo convencional de la femineidad en su significado de pasividad, ornamentación y enajenación de la realidad histórica, son una amenaza que ha transgredido todos los silencios y la fusión de la mujer burguesa en el doble de la prostituta constituye la venganza a las imposiciones patriarcales sobre la sexualidad femenina.

Una de las estrategias más efectivas para los grupos dominados es indudablemente asumir el discurso que el poder hegemónico le adscribe. Proceso mímico que enmascara subversiones y que garantiza, en el caso de la producción literaria, un relativo éxito. Que una mujer imite el estilo de un patriarca como García Márquez es bien visto tanto por la industria editorial como por el público, tal es el caso de *La casa de los espíritus* (1984) de Isabel Allende. Que los conflictos en una novela escrita por una mujer pertenezcan a la zona etérea de los sentimientos que expresan la delicada alma femenina es también una indudable garantía.

El éxito inmediato obtenido por María Luisa Bombal se explica, a nivel de la recepción, por corroborar la imagen convencionalizada de la mujer. Amado Alonso en su ensayo publicado en 1936 a apenas unos meses de su edición comercial,[30] enfatiza en su análisis de *La última niebla* la presencia de un modo "típicamente femenino" en el cual predomina la emoción y la vida sentimental.[31] Desde los cuarteles de un sistema positivista que no parece evolucionar cuando se trata de distinciones genérico-sexuales, Alonso afirma: "Si la mujer vive para la vida afectiva del alma y el hombre para las creaciones y realizaciones del espíritu, éste es un temperamento íntegramente femenino. (¡Qué suerte que el oficio masculino de escribir no haya masculinizado a una escritora más!)". (p. 253)

Para la perspectiva de receptores que conciben a la mujer dentro de las construcciones sociales y culturales propiciadas por el falogocentrismo, la protagonista de *La última niebla* es el protipo femenino enclavado en las aventuras del corazón. Sin embargo, este uso deliberado de una retórica sentimental que supone un estilo femenino enmascara un discurso de la sexualidad que el receptor y no el texto hace invisible. Y en la presentación dialógica del "amar" y el "desear" es la sexualidad femenina la verdadera matriz de las instancias cardinales del relato, del mismo modo como la imaginación y la escritura están motivadas por el Deseo.

Al referirnos al fenómeno de la mímica con valor subversivo,[32] damos por descontada una prolífera producción de corte conformista en la cual la asimilación de un discurso femenino, según la ideología dominante, pone de manifiesto una subordinación de la cual las mujeres han sido sus mayores propiciadoras. Tal es el caso de *Aves sin nido* (1889) de Clorinda Matto de Turner, texto que corrobora la visión positivista de la femineidad en su dimensión sublime de la maternidad. Sin embargo, *Aves sin nido* es también una de las primeras novelas en las cuales se denuncia, como en el caso de *La cabaña del tío Tom*, la explotación de un grupo marginalizado por la organización latifundista.

Si bien, desde una perspectiva burguesa y masculina, se ha explicado este interés en los grupos marginales como una manifestación del espíritu humanitario de la mujer, nos parece que éste responde a una identificación con el Otro que en su posición de vencido y dominado funciona como imagen especular de la condición femenina. Y en textos más contemporáneos, esta identificación se hace evidente por una coincidencia en cuanto a la relación del indígena con la Naturaleza y su particular concepto del tiempo.

En *Recuerdos del porvenir* (1963) de Elena Garro, las categorías falologocéntricas del tiempo y la realidad se diluyen y difuminan en el pueblo de Ixtepec que mantiene las vivencias indígenas pese a la dominación de la Conquista Española y la Revolución Mexicana, subversión del vencido que se reitera significativamente en la oposición entre lo masculino y lo femenino representado por el General Francisco Rosas y Julia Andrade. El Poder, la violencia y la energía racionalizadora ubicada en el presente y lo tangible se enfrentan con los escollos de la memoria, la intuición y lo impenetrable configurando espacios cognoscitivos irremisiblemente condenados a la incomunicación.

De manera semejante, Rosario Castellanos modeliza el conflicto irresoluble entre los sexos postulando la posesión del lenguaje como elemento clave en todo sistema de dominación. *Balún Canán* (1957) y *Oficio de tinieblas* (1962) resultan, desde una perspectiva contemporánea, textos señeros con respecto a la relación entre discurso y estructuras de poder. Si el discurso ladino dominante impone la opresión y el silencio a los indígenas, en las relaciones hombre-mujer se reitera esta estructura. Significativamente, los personajes femeninos de *Oficio de tinieblas* son, en esencia, seres que no manejan las estrategias de un código lingüístico masculino poniendo en evidencia una subordinación que se manifiesta en el silencio, en el monólogo interior, en la comunicación con un interlocutor imaginado.[33]

Y desde una posición ideológica feminista que en el presente aún resulta de vanguardia, Rosario Castellanos opone a la civilización masculina de occidente las figuras de Teresa (narradora que transforma el lenguaje como instrumento de dominación en sistema sagrado que transmite lo mítico y perdurable) y Catalina (madre regestadora de los dioses ocultos que transgrediendo el signo de la Virgen María insta a su pueblo a la rebelión). Se reinscribe así el devenir cíclico y mítico de una Historia al margen de la linearidad occidental, del mismo modo como en el diálogo dispar entre lo masculino y lo femenino se mantiene latente un conjunto de valores que se oponen a las estructuras de poder impuestas por el patriarcado.

HACIA LA CREACION DE UN CONTRADISCURSO

En este ensayo, deliberadamente hemos utilizado el término "femenino" en dos sentidos contradictorios: por una parte, le hemos asignado los significados convencionales adscritos por el sistema falologocéntrico, por otra y de manera mucho menos explícita, hemos utilizado la palabra "femenino" para designar toda una zona enraizada en la subordinación, el silenciamiento y la represión. Por cierto, las construcciones culturales de "lo femenino" en la versión masculina de la realidad resultan ser fácilmente manejables en su tangibilidad del mismo modo como sería relativamente fácil describir un objeto concreto para el cual ya existen paradigmas conceptuales y sus respectivos discursos. Cómo definir, sin embargo, aquéllo que ha permanecido en la sombra sin caer en la contradicción de utilizar un acercamiento de tipo falologocéntrico. Cómo fijar esta sombra siempre movediza en un devenir histórico que propicia diferentes posiciones femeninas con respecto a "lo femenino", posiciones determinadas por una identificación e inclusión en clases sociales dominantes que han silenciado a otros grupos en un continente latinoamericano marcado por la discriminación racial y el poder imperialista. Qué hacer con esas otras sombras que corresponden a la representación literaria de "lo femenino", según una imaginación femenina siempre a medias y bajo el resguardo de una tradición masculina dominante.

Obviando las apropiaciones que ha hecho la modernidad con respecto a lo femenino como el aspecto negativo de las oposiciones binarias del pensamiento de occidente y, por ende, la brecha que permitirá desconstruirlo,[34]habría que destacar el campo polémico que se ha abierto en la nueva ideología feminista. Desde el esencialismo de Hélène Cixous quien a partir del *locus* concreto del cuerpo femenino y su *jouissance* le adjudica las metáforas también presentes en el falologocentrismo de la difusión, la liquificación y la vitalidad para posteriormente biologizarlo en la maternidad, en la voz de la madre que canta antes de la ley y en su seno, símbolo del centro y la esencia del Ser en una forma vacía y llena, grávida y aérea.[35] Hasta la posición radical de Julia Kristeva quien al considerar "lo femenino" como semiótico y anterior a lo simbólico amplía su significado definiéndolo como una praxis que corresponde a lo no representado, a aquéllo que permanece fuera de las nominaciones y las ideologías. Negatividad que le permite detectar lo femenino en escritores tales como Lautréamont, Artaud y Bataille.[36]

Lo importante, por supuesto, no es la respuesta que vendría a satisfacer los esquemas simplistas de las disciplinas aún insertas en la tradición positivista. Tampoco las elucubraciones de un nuevo intelectualismo europeo que hace del Sujeto una abstracción fuera de la Historia, la fase estratégica de lo irresoluto o incierto, según las postulaciones de Jacques Derrida.[37] Las escritoras latinoamericanas contemporáneas han descubierto al enemigo, han tomado una posición política con respecto a un sistema masculino que en el Tercer Mundo se expresa de manera homóloga tanto en las relaciones hombre-mujer como en las estructuras de opresor-oprimido.

Y es, desde esta nueva perspectiva ideológica, que se inquiere en la problemática femenina incursionando en la topografía hasta ahora tabú del propio cuerpo, dando voz a lo silenciado, insertando a la mujer en la Historia e incluso creando espacios utópicos.

Dentro de este contexto, la mirada del Otro en lo Otro ha resultado fuente prolífera para la inscripción de un contradiscurso. Los testimonios de Jesusa Palanqueres, Domitila Chúngara y Rigoberta Menchú ponen en evidencia la especificidad de una problemática femenina inserta en los espacios populares e indígenas marginalizados. Un Otro de lo Otro que se opone al poder masculino presente en su estrato social a partir de las tretas del débil y que, simultáneamente, solidariza con el Otro masculino para participar en la lucha de clases. Es más, la escritora de los estratos medios y altos que asume la posición de amanuense para editar dichos testimonios inicia, por fin, una relación con mujeres de otros grupos sociales expresando una conciencia social en vías de hacer de la población femenina una colectividad históricamente coherente.

Asimismo, se inicia un nuevo discurso de la sexualidad que se contrapone a las represiones y silenciamientos patriarcales. Escritoras como Albalucía Angel, Armonía Sommers y Griselda Gambaro no sólo describen la violación sexual con una explicitez que escandaliza a los receptores convencionales sino que también y, por primera vez, le otorgan un significado para la existencia femenina. Y Sylvia Molloy en su novela *En breve cárcel* (1982) astilla todos los espejos de la moralidad burguesa para presentar el problema de la identidad femenina en un triángulo amoroso lesbiano que difumina los límites impuestos por la heterosexualidad.

A pesar de las llamadas conquistas de los movimientos sufragistas en Latinoamérica alrededor de 1950, indudablemente la mujer aún se mantiene fuera de los espacios institucionalizados de la política y su acción se realiza, en muchos de nuestros países, desde la marginalidad de la resistencia. Isabel Allende, Luisa Valenzuela, Marta Traba, Elvira Orphée y Ana Vásquez son algunas de las escritoras que representan la tortura no sólo como un testimonio de la represión política sino también con una clara conciencia feminista que la ubica en el contexto mayor de la violencia masculina. Es más, en el caso de *Abel Rodríguez y sus hermanos* (1981), por ejemplo, Ana Vásquez opone una praxis política femenina a las organizaciones patriarcales de los partidos políticos.

Conciencia social de la problemática de la mujer que ha dado origen también a la utopía, género que pone en evidencia una insatisfacción esencial con el orden establecido y que modeliza una alternativa. *Las andariegas* (1984) de Albalucía Angel presenta un interesante contradiscurso inserto en la Historia silenciada de la colectividad femenina y en un futuro donde se han aniquilado las jerarquías masculinas del Poder. Transgrediendo los formatos tradicionales, la autora incursiona en un discurso que contradice la lógica, la objetividad y la linearidad de los discursos dominantes e incluso simbólicamente omite el uso de la mayúscula jerárquica. De manera simultánea, representa el espacio silenciado de una memoria colectiva femenina que posee como acervo la tradición europea e indígena.

La escritura se constituye así en acto fundador de una realidad inédita, develando asimismo la identidad femenina desde su propio centro —los círculos y semi-círculos del substrato mítico, literario e histórico que corresponde a las imágenes opacas o ausentes del espejo patriarcal. La travesía de las andariegas en una apropiación de lo épico masculino deviene entonces en una búsqueda de los orígenes que es también una reafirmación y rescate de la Historia y la Cultura femenina deslizándose en los márgenes del Hacer masculino y en una condición constante de exilio. Y desde este ámbito legendario y mítico se trasciende en viaje milenario a la utopía de la destrucción de la civilización masculina representada por la ciudad de Nueva York y al vuelo ascendente de las nuevas amazonas bajo la mirada sabia de la Tierra para iniciar un nuevo comienzo.

Pero, ¿será la utopía significativamente motivada por *Las guerrilleras* de Monique Wittig la respuesta para las mujeres del Tercer Mundo?

HACIA LA POLITIZACION DE LA ESCRITURA Y EL DISCURSO CRITICO

En la teoría feminista actual se enfatiza la diferencia genérica como una respuesta crítica a un sistema cuyas construcciones sociales y culturales han estado escindidas por la oposición binaria entre lo masculino y lo femenino. Se analiza, así, la escritura de la mujer como un proceso bilingüe, bifocal y bitextual que correspondería a la modelización ficcionalizada de la subordinación social y que, en alguna medida, inserta fisuras en los conceptos totalizantes de Texto y Sujeto. Y, desde esta perspectiva que personalmente y de manera transitoria comparto, se está realizando una reevaluación de la producción literaria de la mujer, actividad que en el caso de la literatura latinoamericana, pone en evidencia vacíos significativos especialmente cuando la práctica de la crítica literaria supone una praxis política.

Si bien mi discurso crítico marcado por una dependencia cultural podría resultar adecuado para un *corpus* literario producido por mujeres latinoamericanas que en el pasado siguieron las huellas de una literatura oficial y dependiente, las categorías básicas de este acercamiento indudablemente resultan insuficientes. La hipótesis de un Sujeto masculino y un Otro femenino se complejiza cuando ese supuesto Sujeto es también un Otro colonizado, ¿qué significa, por lo tanto, ser un Otro de Otro? ¿Qué mecanismos y qué relaciones se originan cuando el Otro a nivel de lo genérico-sexual asume simultáneamente una posición de Sujeto? En una sociedad de tajantes estratificaciones sociales, ¿no asumirá también ese Otro (femenino y burgués) mecanismos de poder cuando establece relaciones con mujeres de otros sectores sociales? La protesta de Domitila Chúngara en las reuniones del Año de la Mujer celebrado en México corroboran el hecho de que este Otro también se erige un lugar jerárquico entre las mujeres de otros grupos subordinados.

Por otra parte y en una etapa en la cual el discurso crítico feminista recién abre un par de brechas en la institución universitaria, el concepto mismo del falologocentrismo no deja de tener una posición estratégica que, en mi opinión, corre el peligro de una estaticidad histórica. Si, hasta ahora, ha resultado ser un recurso más o menos útil, éste y la estructura patriarcal que lo sustenta no deberían funcionar como abstracciones generalizantes, por el contrario, sería necesario investigar sus modalidades específicas en un devenir histórico marcado por la evolución del capitalismo. Modalidades que originarían una constante revisión de los elementos estructuradores del binomio Poder masculino-Subordinación femenina y un proceso de adecuación en nuestro acercamiento crítico.

Hasta este momento, gran parte del discurso crítico feminista se ha apropiado, en mayor o menor medida, de aquellos planteamientos teóricos masculinos que intentan desconstruir el falologocentrismo (Derrida) o que ponen en evidencia los mecanismos de una producción cultural marginal (Bajtín) insertando la categoría del Género como construcción social y cultural. Indudablemente, esta nueva categoría ha modificado, de manera significativa, las actuales investigaciones históricas, antropológicas, científicas y artísticas. No obstante las nuevas mediaciones originadas por la inserción de lo genérico-sexual, no deja de ser necesario, en el futuro, un acercamiento teórico que, yendo más allá de la perspectiva actual sobre la subordinación femenina, plantee parámetros femeninos y feministas para el análisis de la producción cultural del hombre y la mujer.

Pero estas son consideraciones que, en este punto del devenir crítico y por ende histórico, sólo ponen en evidencia una conciencia de las limitaciones actuales y una insatisfacción que es también un deseo ubicado en la zona utópica de la esperanza. Conciencia/Utopía que se duplica al asumir mi rol de escritora latinoamericana cuando se trata de definir lo femenino puesto que asumir una identidad genera el dilema de un proceso de inserción o un proceso de anulación de las categorías dominantes. A pesar de que algunas críticas latinoamericanas como Margo Glantz y Helena Araújo han adoptado el cuerpo femenino como estrategia discursiva siguiendo las postulaciones de Cixous e Irigaray, nos preguntamos hasta qué punto son válidos los significados atribuidos al cuerpo por un sector del feminismo francés en un continente teñido por la represión y la tortura. ¿No trasciende acaso este cuerpo su economía exclusivamente libidinal para ser un cuerpo político que es vejado por la tortura y que reacciona en una economía fecal como táctica desestabilizadora? ¿Hasta qué punto ese gran seno femenino que alimenta la escritura en la teoría de Cixous adquiere significados diferentes cuando aloja la fotografía de un desaparecido?

A Jacques Derrida le resulta poco problemático apropiarse del hímen para analizar el poema en prosa *Mimique* de Mallarmé como tejido que se dobla sobre sí mismo y que no posee centro ni dialéctica de la totalidad, apropiación que borra todas las marcas represivas impuestas a la sexualidad femenina.[38] Nos preguntamos si sería posible, desde una perspectiva feminista, astillar el hímen intacto de la Virgen María y reinscribir en ese espacio un concepto de valor político que modificaría a la vez las mitificaciones patriarcales acerca de la maternidad. Suplantando la trinidad sacralizada del Padre, el Hijo y el Espíritu Santo por la tríada de la reproducción como signo político: madre y padre en un proyecto conjunto que es cuerpo/ amor/ placer en una fluidez que connota la anulación del poder jerárquico. Proyecto conjunto y solidario liberado de las limitaciones de la heterosexualidad (hij: a/o), sin madres fálicas ni complejos de Edipo, ni envidias por ningún pene. Fuera del Orden Simbólico simbolizado por el Falo, en una nueva organización social que tendría a la difusión uterina como imagen especular.

Bien podría argumentarse que el uso estratégico del cuerpo femenino revierte, en última instancia, a la oposición binaria Mente/Cuerpo reafirmando un orden falologocéntrico que otorga a lo masculino la mente y a lo femenino el cuerpo. Sin embargo, se trata de hacer de este cuerpo un signo de valor político, la metáfora de una organización alternativa. Y, a diferencia de la teoría freudiana anclada en un falo monolítico y, a mi parecer, bastante unidimensional, por no decir aburrido, habría que afirmar que el cuerpo femenino en sí provee una metáfora muchísimo más compleja.

La condición biológica de la maternidad recién empieza a tener un discurso desde una perspectiva femenina que inquiere en la difusión de la Subjetividad erosionando las distancias y distinciones a nivel de Sujeto y Objeto. Del mismo modo, nos parece que la sangre menstrual (tabú por excelencia en todos los grupos patriarcales) posee la potencialidad de sustituir el signo sangre en sus connotaciones de muerte, territorialización y dominación para significar la vida en una sociedad libre de jerarquizaciones y estructuras de dominación (un asistema para nuestra perspectiva actual todavía restringida a la lógica de la negatividad)."Con vida los trajimos, con vida los queremos" gritaban las Madres de la Plaza de Mayo haciendo de la maternidad un derecho político, utilizando el cuerpo maternal como una táctica contra el poder fascista.

Aún hoy, el pensamiento feminista representa una amenaza, una especie de mujer diabólica que, como la Quintrala, mató a su padre, se deshizo violentamente de su amante y arrojó a Dios de su casa suplantando el poder masculino por un poder femenino que lo reproduce. La teoría feminista en su versión más positiva (y ya existen, por supuesto, varias versiones, algunas significativamente insertas en el liberalismo y el socialismo) aspira a no reproducir las estructuras de poder, a originar una eclosión del sistema binario hombre/mujer en un plano de igualdad política y social que recién empieza a configurarse a nivel teórico. Trascendiendo los esquemas del desconstructivismo, la anulación de la oposición binaria entre lo masculino y lo femenino no constituye simplemente un gesto filosófico sino la desestructuración de categorías sociales y económicas. Sin duda, en el camino actual se dan contradicciones que como los ladridos de los perros en el Quijote son una señal de que avanzamos, no obstante las limitaciones que toda contradicción implica.

Tal vez y dado el carácter hipotético de esta sección de mi ensayo, una manera de concluirlo sea refiriéndose a una novela escrita por una mujer latinoamericana contemporánea: *Por la patria* (1986) de Diamela Eltit. Coya, personaje femenino y andrógino a la vez produce a través de su identidad una desarticulación significativa al nivel de una sexualidad que se mantiene circundada por el poder dictatorial. Coya es también Coa, el lenguaje polifónico de un sector marginal acosado por la violencia militar. Coya/Coa podría ser el símbolo de esta apertura que actualmente está generando la teoría feminista para dar voz y cuerpo a una sombra que aún se ve forzada a asumir las máscaras del dominado.

Sin embargo y citando un subtítulo de esta novela, habría que decir que "son muchas las estacas en las esquinas alambradas"; el discurso mismo de este ensayo ha estado cercado por fronterizaciones típicas de un quehacer crítico tradicionalmente masculino, mi discurso ha sido feminista pero no femenino, claudicación estratégica que hoy día se hace necesaria para abrirse un espacio en los centros institucionalizados.

NOTAS

[1]Consultar, por ejemplo, el importante estudio de Nancy Chodorow titulado *The Reproduction of Mothering: Psychoanalysis and the Sociology of Gender*. (Los Angeles: University of California Press, 1978).

[2]Estas son las postulaciones básicas de Sherry Ortner en su ensayo que, pese a tener actualmente retractores, constituye, sin lugar a dudas, un análisis señero para los estudios feministas. (Ver "Is Female to Male as Nature Is to Culture?" publicado en *Woman, Culture and Society* volumen editado por Michelle Rosaldo y Louise Lamphere. Stanford: Stanford University Press, 1974).

[3]Como ha señalado Claude Lévi-Strauss en sus estudios antropológicos, el lazo recíproco básico para el matrimonio no se establece entre hombres y mujeres sino entre hombres y hombres por medio de mujeres que funcionan sólo como la ocasión principal. (*Elementary Structures of Kinship*. Boston: Beacon Press, 1969, p. 116).

[4]Gayle Rubin en su interesante exégesis de las postulaciones de Lévi-Strauss, Freud y Lacan señala lo siguiente: "If women are the gifts, then it is men who are the exchange partners. And it is the partners, not the

presents, upon whom reciprocal exchange confers its quasi-mystical power of social linkage. The relations of such a system are such that women are in no position to realize the benefits of their own circulation. As long as the relations specify that men exchange women, it is men who are the beneficiaries of the product of such exchanges—social organization" ("The Traffic in Women: Notes on the 'Political Economy' of Sex" publicado en *Toward an Anthropology of Women* editado por Rayna Reiter. New York: Monthly Review Press, 1975, pp. 157-210).

[5]El fenómeno de primacía de la clase social sobre la identificación y conciencia a nivel genérico ha sido analizado, por ejemplo, en las relaciones entre mujeres durante la época colonial en Hispanoamérica. (Ver el ensayo de Elinor C. Burkett titulado "In Dubious Sisterhood: Class and Sex in Spanish Colonial South America" publicado en *Women in Latin America: An Anthology from Latin American Perspectives*. Riverside, California: Latin American Perspectives, 1979, pp. 17-26).

[6]En la Historia latinoamericana son numerosos los ejemplos de mujeres, con un evidente compromiso político aún no analizado suficientemente, que han hecho un uso estratégico de la identidad femenina convencional para realizar sus acciones. En el caso de las guerras por la Independencia, aparte del espionaje y el apoyo que brindaban a los patriotas en el hogar, cabe mencionar que las "mamitas" del Alto Perú, mujeres que viajaban con el ejército para cocinarle a los soldados, muchas veces engañaron a los realistas al entrar a una ciudad llorando por la derrota de los patriotas. En el caso de La Regalada, esta mujer campesina   salió desnuda de su rancho para atajar al ejército realista fingiéndose loca mientras los patriotas se preparaban para el asalto. Las acciones de la resistencia contra las dictaduras de Argentina y Chile han sido en el presente otra manifestación de la utilización estratégica del cuerpo femenino en su significado convencional de madre.

[7]Así, por ejemplo, Carroll Smith-Rosenberg estudia los efectos subversivos de la New York Female Moral Reform Society, grupo fundado en 1834 que en defensa de los valores postulados por el Culto de la Verdadera Femineidad se opuso a la prostitución y en este proceso atentó contra el orden impuesto por la nueva burguesía comercial. En este sentido son también de gran valor los estudios de Mary Ryan (*Cradle of the Middle Class*. New York: Cambridge University Press, 1981) y de Bonnie Smith (*The Ladies of the Leisure Class*. Princeton: Princeton University Press, 1981).

[8]Para una síntesis de los planteamientos teóricos feministas y sus implicaciones metodológicas en las investigaciones históricas ver los siguientes ensayos: "The Social Relation of the Sexes: Methodological Implications of Women's History" de Joan Kelly-Gadol (*The Signs*

Reader: Women, Gender & Scholarship editado por Elizabeth Abel y Emily K. Abel. Chicago: The University of Chicago Press, 1983, pp. 11-25) y "The Feminist Reconstruction of History" de Carroll Smith-Rosenberg (*Academe* [septiembre-octubre 1983]), pp. 26-37. Entre las investigaciones que parten de esta nueva concepción de la Historia, se destacan *Latin American Women: Historical Perspectives* de Asunción Lavrín (Westport: Connecticut, 1978), *Prostitution and Victorian Society: Women, Class and the State* de Judith R. Walkowitz (Cambridge: Cambridge University Press, 1980) y *Sex, Politics and Society: The Regulation of Sexuality since 1800* de Jeffrey Weeks (Londres: Longman, 1981).

[9]Cheris Kramarae. *Women and Men Speaking: Frameworks for Analysis*. Rowley, Massachusetts: Newbury House Publishers, Inc., 1981.

[10]Para un análisis del fenómeno de la sexoglosia se puede consultar el interesante estudio de M.ª Jesús Buxó Rey titulado *Antropología de la mujer: Cognición, Lengua e Ideología Cultural* (Barcelona: Promoción Cultural, S.A., 1978).

[11]El ensayo en cuatro partes bajo el título de "La mujer" fue publicado originalmente en el *Album cubano de lo bueno y lo bello* en La Habana en 1860. En nuestra investigación hemos utilizado como fuente la reedición incluida en *Obras literarias de la Señora Doña Gertrudis Gómez de Avellaneda* publicada en Madrid por la Imprenta y Estereotipia de M. Rivadeneyra en 1871 (pp. 285-306). Esta cita corresponde a la página 303.

[12]Como detalle que ejemplifica la supremacía de valores masculinos en la actividad literaria, cabe citar las palabras de José Zorrilla quien comentó lo siguiente con respecto a Gertrudis Gómez de Avellaneda: "...su escritura briosamente tendida sobre el papel, y los pensamientos varoniles de los vigorosos versos con que reveló su ingenio, revelaban algo viril y fuerte en el espíritu encerrado dentro de aquella voluptuosa encarnación mujeril. Nada había de áspero, de anguloso, de masculino, en fin, en aquel cuerpo de mujer, y de mujer atractiva: ni coloración subida de la piel, ni espesura excesiva en las cejas ni bozo que sombreara su fresca boca, ni brusquedad en sus maneras: era una mujer; pero lo era sin duda por un error de la naturaleza, que había metido por distracción un alma de hombre en aquella voluptuosa envoltura de mujer". ("Gertrudis Gómez de Avellaneda", *Obras de la Avellaneda*, tomo VI, La Habana, Imprenta de Aurelio Miranda, 1914, p. 501).

[13]Claudine Herrman. *Les voleuses de langue*. París: éditions des femmes, 1976.

[14]Helena Araújo. "Narrativa femenina latinoamericana". *Hispamérica*, año XI, No 32, 1982, pp. 23-34.

[15]Entrevista con Xaviere Gauthier reproducida de *Tel Quel* en la antología *New French Feminisms* editada por Elaine Marks e Isabelle de Coutivron. New York: Schocken Books, 1981, p. 166. La traducción es mía.

[16]En mi ensayo "El personaje literario femenino y otras mutilaciones" analizo precisamente este aspecto en las construcciones simbólicas de una literatura masculina en la cual el personaje femenino caracterizado a partir de los modelos sociales asignados a la mujer funciona como signo del orden patriarcal o que, en una apropiación del Sujeto masculino, se transforma en símbolo de trascendencia o agente de la transgresión. (*Hispamérica*, año XV, No 43, 1986, pp. 3-19).

[17]"Encuentro con novelistas" realizado en el Congreso Internacional de Literatura Femenina Latinoamericana. (Santiago, Chile, 20 de agosto de 1987).

[18]Susan K. Cornillon. "The Fiction of Fiction" en *Images of Women in Fiction: Feminist Perspectives*. Bowling Green, Ohio: Bowling Green University Popular Press, 1972, p. 113. La traducción es mía.

[19]Luce Irigaray. *This Sex Which Is Not One*. Ithaca: Cornell University Press, 1985, p. 187. La traducción es mía.

[20]Ibid., p. 188.

[21]Adrienne Rich. *The Dream of a Common Language*. New York: Norton, 1978, p. 51.

[22]Entrevista con Susan Husserl-Kapit reproducida en la antología de Marks y Coutivron. Op. Cit., p. 174.

[23]G. Genette. *Palimpsestes*. París: Editions Seuil, 1982.

[24]En este sentido, estamos de acuerdo con la posición de Cora Kaplan quien postula la escritura de la mujer como una praxis inserta en la estratificación social y la organización genérica sexual. (Ver, por ejemplo, su ensayo titulado "Pandora's Box: Subjectivity, Class and Sexuality in Socialist Feminist Criticism" en *Making a Difference: Feminist Literary Criticism* editado por Gayle Greene y Coppélia Kahn. New York: Methuen, 1985).

[25]Como ejemplo de este fenómeno se podría citar la narrativa de Juana Manuela Gorriti, autora argentina que, a diferencia de sus coetáneos varones de la Generación de 1837, presenta la dictadura de Juan Manuel de Rosas desde una perspectiva conservadora y católica.

[26]Judith Fetterley. *The Resisting Reader: A Feminist Approach to American Fiction*. Bloomington: Indiana University Press, 1978. Dentro de esta perspectiva, se puede consultar también *Gender and Reading: Essays on Readers, Texts, and Contexts* editado por Elizabeth A. Flynn y Patrocinio P. Schweickart (Baltimore: The John Hopkins University Press, 1986).

[27]María Flora Yáñez. *Las cenizas*. Santiago, Chile: Casa Nacional del Niño, 1942, p. 73.

[28]Marie Maclean. "Oppositional Practices in Women's Traditional Narrative". *New Literary History*, vol. 19, No 1 (Otoño 1987), pp. 37-50.

[29]Consultar, por ejemplo, los análisis incluidos en *The Voyage In: Fictions of Female Development* editado por Elizabeth Abel, Marianne Hirsch y Elizabeth Langland. (Hanover: University Press of New England, 1983).

[30]*La última niebla* se publicó originalmente en 1934 en una edición limitada hecha por Oliverio Girondo y sólo se distribuyó comercialmente al ser re-editada por la editorial "Sur" en 1935.

[31]Amado Alonso. "Aparición de una novelista". *Nosotros* I, No 3 (junio 1936), pp. 241-256.

[32]Utilizamos este término siguiendo las postulaciones de Luce Irigaray quien define "mimétisme" como una estrategia discursiva en la cual la mujer asume deliberadamente lo designado por el falologocentrismo como estilo y postura femenina con el propósito de develar los mecanismos a través de los cuales se la mantiene en lugar subordinado. Op. Cit., p. 220. Si bien en su definición Irigaray da mayor énfasis a la conciencia política feminista, nos parece que ésta se presta adecuadamente para describir textos latinoamericanos producidos por la mujer.

[33]Para un excelente análisis de este aspecto, consultar el ensayo de Stacey Schlau titulado "Conformity and Resistance to Enclosure: Female Voices in Rosario Castellanos' *Oficio de tinieblas* (*The Dark Service*). (*Latin American Literary Review*, vol. 12, No 24 [primavera-verano 1984], pp. 45-57).

[34]Para un excelente estudio de "lo femenino" en pensadores modernos tales como Jacques Derrida, Jacques Lacan y Gilles Deleuze, consultar *Gynesis: Configurations of Woman and Modernity* de Alice A. Jardine (Ithaca: Cornell University Press, 1985).

[35]Entre sus textos feministas se destacan: *La Jeune Née* en colaboración con Catherine Clément. París: UGE, 1975, "Le Rire de la Méduse", *L'Arc*, 61, 1975, pp. 39-54, "Le Sexe ou la tete?", *Les Cahiers du GRIF*, 13, 1976, pp. 5-15 y "L'Approche de Clarice Lispector", *Poétique*, 40, 1979, pp. 408-419.

[36]Los textos claves para comprender esta asociación de lo semiótico y lo femenino en Julia Kristeva son: *La Révolution du langage poétique* (París: Editions du Seuil, 1974) y *Polylogue* (París: Editions du Seuil, 1977). Son de particular interés sus ensayos "Les temps des femmes", 33/34: *Cahiers de recherche de sciences des textes et documents*, No 5 (Invierno 1979) y "Hérétique de l'amour", *Tel Quel* (invierno 1974), pp. 30-49.

[37]Jacques Derrida ha hecho, por ejemplo, la siguiente afirmación: "Decir que la mujer está en el lado, para así decirlo, de lo incierto sólo tiene el significado de una fase estratégica. En una situación dada que es la nuestra, la estructura falogocéntrica europea, el lado de la mujer es el lado desde el cual se empieza a desmantelar dicha estructura. Por lo tanto se puede poner lo irresoluto y todos los otros conceptos que van con él en el lado de la femineidad, la escritura, etcétera. Pero tan pronto como se ha alcanzado la primera etapa de la desconstrucción, la oposición entre hombre y mujer ya deja de ser pertinente. Ya no se puede decir que la mujer es otro nombre, o un buen tropo para la escritura, lo irresoluto, etcétera. Necesitamos alguna manera de progresar estratégicamente. Necesitamos empezar con la desconstrucción del falogocentrismo usando, por así decir, la fuerza femenina en esta movida y luego--y ésta sería la segunda etapa o nivel--desechar la oposición entre hombre y mujer". ("Women in the Beehive: A Seminar with Jacques Derrida" en *Men in Feminism* editado por Alice Jardine y Paul Smith, New York: Methuen, 1987, pp. 189-203). Esta cita corresponde a la página 194 y la traducción es mía.

[38]Consultar el excelente ensayo de Leslie Rabine titulado "The Unhappy Hymen Between Feminism and Deconstruction" en el volumen *The Other Perspective on Gender* editado por Juliet Mac Cannell y que será publicado por la prensa universitaria de la Universidad de Columbia.

THE EVOLUTION OF PSYCHE UNDER EMPIRE: LITERARY REFLECTIONS OF SPAIN IN THE 16TH CENTURY

Ruth El Saffar

Northwestern University

The modern state that arose in Spain in the sixteenth century effected major changes in socio-economic and political groupings, and offered as part of the basis of its appeal a unification and order that promised accord among people across the Iberian peninsula, and perhaps, given the imperialistic aspirations of Spain's first united kingship, among people the world over. The aim of unity carries on its underside the visage of an Other—one who, as disrupter, heretic, or renegade, plays a treasonous role that keeps the royal image pristine. Coincident with the centralization of power in Spain at the end of the fifteenth century is the effort to expel or assimilate the sub-groups at odds with the norms imposed by the King and Queen. At stake are issues of power.

The centralized power in the process of being established in the Iberian Peninsula identified as threats to its aspirations of total control such smaller units as feudal lords, Jews, Moors, or others viewed as heretics. In order to break down the credibility and cohesion of the sociopolitical sub-groupings present at the time of the reconquest, the crown had to differentiate members of the smaller entities from the definition of nationhood being created. The new definition of belonging eluded earlier notions of regional or tribal loyalty, basing its claims on something more abstract—on values and belief systems that were in theory free of the taint of issues of origin..

The ruler of the modern state as it began to form in Spain in the late fifteenth century needed to create a network of alliances based not on the model of confederacy, but on an ideological linkage between the crown and the individual. Thus the edicts of expulsion in the 1480s in Spain were softened by the possibility that the Other, through conversion, could become one with the dominant culture. The process of extracting the individual from the group, of granting that individual a dignity and identification apart from the place and people with whom he (rarely *she*, as will be shown) originally belonged has far-reaching consequences for Western culture and Western cultural products, and effects much more than simply the groups singled out for the label of heresy. For what was evolving under the rulership of Ferdinand and Isabella in Spain was a new way of identifying the individual, one that depended less on social origins than on mentality, and that ultimately demanded that the individual break the bonds of home and family around which awareness of self had previously been based. That break, as will be explored in what follows, carried radical implications for the relationship among the sexes that is only now beginning to be taken into consideration in accounting for the literary and cultural phenomena of the period commonly called the "Golden Age."

The growth of urban centers, the establishment of schools and universities outside of the home, the professionalization of the military, and the discovery of the new world, while cooperating with the crown's need to break down competing power agglomerates to create conditions appropriate to the formation of a new individual, also provided the means by which men and boys were required to effect a severing from the feminizing forces in their lives. The process of collective differentiation from the feminine unfolds over the course of the sixteenth century and can be apprehended by looking into a series of literary texts written at approximtely fifty-year intervals between 1500 and 1605. Three extremely well known proto-novels, iconoclastic and at odds with the totalizing aspirations of the state in which they were incubated, will serve to track the advance of the process of differentiation. Chosen as much for their popularity at the time they were written as for their continued familiarity to present-day readers, the works—*La Celestina, Lazarillo de Tormes,* and *Don Quixote*—reflect phylogenetically the Western European movement away from an organic world view, and from a position of dependency on the cyclical system of filiations in which that view is grounded.[1]

I will concentrate on the ways that each text locates the male hero most interested in assimilating the values of the new state. That male figure anticipates the novelistic hero whom Edward Said has identified as celibate and Leslie Fiedler has called an escapee from home and family.[2] He emerges as the expression of the new man, the child of the modern state. His idealized, invulnerable predecessor, the wandering knight of the romances of chivalry, corresponds in conception to the period before the rise of the modern state when feudal structures precluded a realistic imagining of personal independence.

Although both the fifteenth century hero of the chivalric romance and the sixteenth century hero of the proto-novel engage in intense contests with male antagonists and live lives of wandering and solitude, they differ in the question of their relationship to their origins. The typical chivalric hero truly succeeds at the point where his valorous deeds earn him a recovery of his lost connection to his origins, which are invariably noble. The hero who begins to emerge in the prose fiction of the sixteenth century, on the other hand, gains power in relation to the degree that he succeeds in *dissociating* from those responsible for his birth and upbringing. As with Lazarillo, Guzman de Alfarache, Tomas Rodaja of *El licenciado Vidriera,* and of course Don Quixote, the new novelistic hero's origins are rural and/or marginalized in such a way as to represent for the hero's emerging self-definition a handicap. The new hero sheds his given name in favor of one cut to his own liking, one that will reflect not his condition as dependent and contingent, but his aspirations to autonomy and power.

The initially marginalized position, like that occupied by women and children in the nuclear families that the monarchical regimes strenthened,[3] is one of powerlessness and indefinition from which the new male seeks escape.

In the fifteenth century the hero is still motivated by the desire to please the female figure and to be recognized according to his place of origin, which is still exalted.[4] Increasingly, from the sixteenth century on, the figure of the mother and of the origin she represents will be repressed or debased.

In the chivalric works, the hero generally belonged to a setting in time and space entirely distinct from that of his readers, a setting in which dreams enjoyed immunity from the demands of the everyday. In the works to be examined in this paper, on the other hand, the males portrayed as seeking a place within the new social order are figures who seem cut from the cloth on which the readers themselves have also been woven. These new heroes' struggles to forge for themselves an identity appropriate to a lifeworld newly defined comment richly on the complexities of the task of separation. They show how the desire to enter the world of the father, with its promises of status, wealth and power, competes with the still unexpunged yearning to experience the pleasures and comforts of the world of the mother, who represents earth, food, sex, abundance, and companionship.[5]

The new male figure, as we shall see, is a lonely being, isolate, fearful, increasingly lettered and correspondingly alienated from the body and from women.[6] The works to be examined here reveal clearly the process by which, over a century, the figures associated with the female/ maternal/rural/oral world lose power. It is not coincidental, therefore, that, while in Spain the Inquisition set its sights primarily on Jews and false converts, in other European countries, and to some degree even in Spain, that same organ of pan-Christianity was identifying witches with heresy, thereby setting the stage for the protracted period, into the seventeenth century, during which witches were tortured and burned.[7] While the issue of religious heresy has some hope of being resolved through conversion, the deeper problem of the human connection to earth cannot be so easily settled. It would not be until the seventeenth century, with the rise of the mechanistic world view, that the identification of women with nature and its mysteries would lead not to a mania of persecution but to suppression and subordination of a more subtle variety.[8]

The drive toward individuality, meanwhile, engaged men in a need to disidentify not only with the natural world, and with nature, but with the image of the mother who represented the ties to tribal groupings and to the imponderables of life and death. As that which consistently eludes and undercuts the system, the mother and the feminine in general represent a threat, which, like the earth and nature and all other elements that challenge stability and order, must be subdued.

In her excellent study of Machiavelli Hanna Fenichel Pitkin traces the tradition of "Fortune" as a figure of feminine power from the time of the Romans to the Renaissance, focusing particularly on Machiavelli's complex use of her. Fortune in Machiavelli is imaged as a woman both dangerous and all-powerful. Pitkin says:

> For this reason, many consider her "omnipotent," but the poet [Machiavelli, in "Tercets on Fortune"] advises that there is "no reason. . . for fear" where a man is strong." (145)

Quoting further from the "tercets", Pitkin notes Machiavelli's observation that "Fortune's reign is always violent if prowess [*virtú*] still greater than hers does not vanquish her." While making clear the ambiguities in Machiavelli's treatment of Fortune, Pitkin sums up his reaction to her as follows:

> Machiavelli returns again and again to the struggle against Fortune's power by means of virtú. Perhaps it is that virtú consists neither of prudence nor of boldness, but of the extraordinary, almost superhuman power to modify one's character as the times change. (160)

I mention Machiavelli here because he presents a particularly engaging figure of the struggle between autonomy and dependence that characterized men in the urban, mercantile economies emerging in Europe in the Renaissance. The madmen, orphans and beggars that figure so predominantly in the literature of the period will be seen as those who most acutely experience the imbalances that result when those aspects of life representing mother and those representing father become torn asunder in the interest of creating a new figure, conceived as if independent and autonomous. The action of politics, economics, and education all come to bear on the social realities of the sixteenth century to force a sharp differentiation of the sexes, one that has major consequences for the development of the new novelistic hero.

In *La Celestina*, Fernando de Rojas presents himself from the margins of his work as caught within the embrace of a natural world which he experiences as frightening and disorderly.

The Nature that Rojas describes in the Prologue has all the qualities of Machiavelli's Fortune, and the all-powerful mother that the whore/witch Celestina will represent in Rojas' work. Escape from her becomes the task that most urges itself on the young men (Rojas in the prologue; Pármeno and Sempronio within the work) who chafe under her rule. Rojas captures that desire for escape, and for identification with the absent father, in his fable of the viper:

> La víbora, reptilia o serpiente enconada, al tiempo del concebir, por la boca de la hembra metida la cabeza del macho y ella con el gran dulzor apriétale tanto que le mata y, quedando preñada, el primer hijo rompe las ijares de la madre, por do todos salen y ella muerta queda y el casi como vengador de la paterna muerte. ¿Qué mayor lid, qué mayor conquista ni guerra que engendrar en su cuerpo quien coma sus entrañas? (41)

The fable of the viper accurately points to the place in consciousness that *La Celestina* marks, a place still embedded in the womb, but one in which the containment has lost its protective significance and has come to feel like constraint. The world of *La Celestina*, balanced at the border between the fifteenth and the sixteenth century is still a world of mother-rule. Another bestiary example from the Prologue, however, betrays a sense of the mother's whimsy, indifference and fundamental disinterest in those dependent on her. In this fable the Roc, a bird from the Indian Ocean, is the focus of Rojas' meditations, not now on procreation and parturition, but on care of those in a position of dependency. Of the fabulous and monstrous Roc Rojas writes:

> se dice ser de grandeza jamás oída y que lleva sobre su pico hasta las nubes no solo un hombre o diez, pero un navío cargado de todas sus jarcias y gente. Y como los míseros navegantes estén así suspensos en el aire, con el meneo de su vuelo caen y reciben crueles muertes. (42)

The citation is reminiscent of another contemporary of Rojas and Machiavelli. In his notes on the flight of birds, Leonardo da Vinci gives some potent early childhood associations to a bird whom he calls the nibio, or kite.[9] Further amplifying on the condition of helplessness he sees as common to mankind, Rojas goes on to attribute qualities of despotism and ungovernability to Nature herself, whose rule is one of earthquakes, storms, and other convulsions of terroristic behavior. The general condition of consciousness that Rojas describes has rendered him a person disquieted by conflict, seeking to please, and yearning for a way out of his connection to indefinition. He sees even the disposition of his book as a matter of contention among others, and the very writing of it a sign of a frivolity with which he is eager finally to dissociate himself. Speaking of the question of what to call his book he says:

> Y viendo estas discordias, entre estos extremos partí agora por medio la porfía, y llamela tragicomedia. Así que viendo estas conquistas, estos disonos y varios juicios, miré a donde la mayor parte acostaba, y hallé que querían que se alargase en el proceso de su deleite de estos amantes, sobre lo cual fui muy importunado; de manera que acordé, aunque contra mi voluntad, meter segunda vez la pluma en tan extraña labor y tan ajena de mi facultad, hurtando algunos ratos a mi principal estudio, con otras horas destinadas para recreación, puesto que no han de faltar nuevos detractores a la nueva adición.(43-44, emphasis added)

The desire for order, expressed in Rojas' hasty return to his "principal estudio", the study of law, may well reflect an underlying yearning, evident throughout the work, for a strong father image, something that would ally Rojas' vision with that of a whole generation for whom, in Spain, the centralized rule of Ferdinand and Isabel offered respite from chaos and disintegration.

Rojas presents us in the prologue with the image of a thoroughly reluctant author, a figure of authority little at ease with his role, ready to abandon it at any moment, worried about the conflict his words might stir, anxious to placate any and all, and desirous to get back to his study of the law. What is this "extraña labor" in which he finds himself engaged? The embarassing and unusual "vacation" Rojas takes in order to finish La Celestina has allowed him to expose to consciousness of the place of the mother, the place where her voice predominates, for what will be virtually the last time for many centuries in Western culture. For, as we will see later in more detail, *La Celestina* offers a view of the witch/mother not from the vantage point of the culture that is in the process of suppressing her, but from her own perspective. Rojas, who wrote *La Celestina* in his early twenties, while still in law school, never wrote another literary work.

The Other that Rojas both brings to life and condemns to death in the person of Celestina, is a figure of sensuality, who, like Circe, renders men foolish, dependent, and beast-like. the antidote to her, as Machiavelli appears to propose in his advocacy of the cunning use of power, is a strong father figure, and a unified state.

The socio-political changes taking place in Europe generally, and even more rapidly in Spain, made necessary, desirable, and inevitable the separation of men from a feminine environment, self from community, passion from reason, and disorder from will. Like the baby vipers of Rojas' prologue, the young men coming to consciousness in the sixteenth century were being prepared to burst the bonds of the body of the mother. Maravall, among others, has pointed to the relationship between the modern state and the growth of individualism, and has located the development of both at the turn of the 16th century, just when *La Celestina* was being written. Maravall says:

> Sin tener en cuenta la presencia de ese sustrato de individualismo, no se comprende el fenomeno del Estado moderno. Si, como tantas veces se ha dicho, el Estado absoluto tiende a constituirse en una relación inmediata con el individuo, de un lado basándose en él, de otro constrinendo sus tendencias disolventes, es porque ese Estado, desde su origen, corre paralelo al despertar del individualismo. (Estado moderno I, 408)

The appeal of the authoritarian state and the image of the autonomous individual lies in the promise they offer of relief from the feelings of chaos and uncertainty that Rojas describes so well in his prologue. There is in the notion of the absolute and the autonomous a reasuring sense of completion, of totality, of one-with-oneselfness that seems to preclude discord and war. Pedro Mártir de Anglería's 1488 explanation of why he chose to remain in Spain provodes one example among many of the advantages that the Catholic Monarchs' sucess in uniting the peninsula and wresting power from the nobles represented for contemporaries:

> En grado hasta entonces desconocido instauraron la fenecida paz y concordia en ambas Españas, de modo que ninguna región, de por sí segura, pudiera jactarse de haber tenido nunca mayor seguridad. Hicieron desaparecer de la escena los alborotos y sediciones serviles que hervían doquiera, no solo en los pueblos, sino tambien en las ciudades. Libraron los caminos de las emboscadas de los ladrones y de las violencias de los salteadores. Restablecieron la desterrada justicia y dieron firmeza a la región vacilante. (*Estado moderno*, p. j)

Jacques Lacan's analysis of the appeal to the child of the promise of a unified vision of self has a similar ring. Against the sense of helplessness and fragmentation that is his experience as an infant is held out the possibility, through socialization and language, of entering into an order that will give him power and a sense of self-control. As Ellie Ragland explains it, "His [Lacan's] mirror stage must, therefore, be understood as a metaphor for the vision of harmony of a subject essentially in discord." (27)

As Lacan himself makes clear, and as the writers of the period we are about to study in closer detail reveal, however, the sense of unity and freedom from discord is purchased at the cost of hypervigilance and repression. The discussion of *Lazarillo* to follow will show how anxiety regarding the formation and sustenance of the autonomous self surfaces in regimes designed to reject the mother and to incorporate in her stead the values represented in the father.

In addition to the effects on consciousness of the growth of the modern state, the impact of the printing press needs also to be mentioned as a factor in examining the changing relationship between the sexes and among social classes. The printing press brought with it an explosion of learning that had the effect of both expanding opprotunities for advancement across social classes and increasing the separation between men and women. Both phenomena—the increase in social mobility and the restriction of women's educational and economic development—are issues of major importance to the sixteenth century. Both can be seen working through the literary texts of the period.

Walter Ong has pointed out further that with the spread of colleges and universities in the 16th century came an increase in the learning of Latin, which became a male language of science and power clearly distinct from what he reminds us is the "mother tongue". Ong notes:

> An affinity seems to exist between early modern science, in its need to hold at arm's length the human lifeworld with its passionate, rhetorical, practical concerns, and Learned Latin as a tongue which had been isolated from infant development and thus from the psysiological and psychosomatic roots of consciousness and which had been given instead an artificial base in writing. (*Interfaces*, 35)

One more word needs to be said before returning to the literary texts through which the evolution of the concept of self in the sixteenth century in Spain is being represented. The sixteenth century provides an especially good stage on which to see the struggle of consciousness played out since the mix of political, sexual, racial, and educational discriminations allowed many people to experience both oppression and privilege. Several recent critics have turned attention to authors who live both within and outside the bounds of dominant Western ideology. Emilia Pardo Bazán is a good example of such a consciousness, as are Ana María Matute, Nadine Gordimer, and Rosario Castellanos. Such women novelists offer examples of privileged and highly educated women who have intense psychological identification with oppression due to their mixed condition as women and as members of an elite society of educated males. Henry Louis Gates has argued a similarly complex "double discourse" for the texts of African and African American critics and writers.[10]

In the cases of Fernando de Rojas and Cervantes, the conflicted vision of male power and the success of the social order of which they are a part derives, as Castro, Sicroff and Gilman have shown, from their place—as *conversos*—at the margins of the dominant society. Although the authorship question still haunts *Lazarillo* criticism, cogent reasons for believing that the author is Gonzalo Pérez have recently been advanced by Douglas Carey and Dalai Brenes.[11] Claudio Guillen's by now famous expression regarding the condition of the picaro as a "half-outsider" is apt in considering the psychological space from within which the proto-novel formed in Spain in the sixteenth century.

For purposes of this study, it is interesting further to note that psycho-sexual studies of Cervantes' work—I am thinking principally of Louis Combet's and Rosa Rossi's readings—find that the impeded sociological identification with the dominant order is doubled in the order of gender identification. Cervantes, and, I would augue, the author of *Lazarillo de Tormes*, construct works in which the imposed identification with masculinity is feigned on the part of the chief protagonists, whose impaired ability to make a sexual alliance with a woman suggests an imcomplete severing from the mother. The works selected for study here all share the quality of double-voicedness which allows them both the render and to undermine the image of male autonomy that the politics, education and economics of the age were calling into being. The works to be considered here capture both the striving for autonomy which is the dominant ideal and the desire for dependence that was everyman's dark secret.

In *La Celestina* Rojas projects onto the witch and the erotically-bonded couple the image of a way of being in the world which is both immensely appealing and ultimately eliminatable. There is, in other words, toward the figure of those things that order has pushed out to the margins of consciousness, a sentiment of affiliation and familiarity that will be presented and then suppressed. By the time of *Lazarillo de Tormes*, fifty years later, the mother/prostitute and the couple remain only a whisper across the lips of the gossiping masses, something to be known and desired but never named. By 1600, in *Don Quixote*, the male hero has become so isolated, so cut off from the instincts and the whole world that the mother represents that he reverts to the utter madness of imagining that by force of arms he can restore that long-lost age when the earth was bountiful and men were the children she suckled at her breast.[12] What was the suffocating rule of the mother for Rojas becomes for Cervantes a hundred years later once again the sacred place of containment.

Significant in these visions is the on-going expression of connection to that which the dominant society is in the process of denying. Cervantes's mad gentleman from La Mancha shows just how far the process has gone—how deeply writing and the dream of military conquest has penetrated consciousness, and how alienating the world of intellect and dominance has been. He also shows how insistently the repressed returns. His mad gentleman's world teems with women, sex, the body, the desire for companionship, and the pleasures of the spoken word. Cervantes shows how stubbornly the maternal and oral cultures resist the dominant society.[13]

The point is that empire creates, and then depends for an alliance with, individuality. What we have been slow to recognize is that that individuality is male, and that it is locked into an unconscious relationship with that which it is supressing. The issues only really become clear when we look at the novelistic texts—the texts which carry the figure of the "new man" as he evolves out of his unconscious embeddedness in the mother—to find another expression of his being in such concepts as individuality, autonomy, and loyalty to the king. The new literary forms that emerge in the sixteenth century neither support the dominant political rhetoric of harmony and order nor the fantasy and allegory of earlier narrative. Instead they establish a consciousness in the here and now that nonetheless resists the glorification of that lived reality.[14] They give us a view of the underside of unity and harmony, an insight into the world of the repressed in which both the structure of consciousness and the lifeworld against which consciousness has set itself can be seen.

Plays of the period, of course, serve another function. They tell what the dominant class wants to perpetrate, and what it has to offer to those who accept its values. In *Fuenteovejuna, El alcalde de Zalamea* and *Peribañez* we see that the king offers a sense of personal sovereignty that the nobles in a feudal state do not. Whereas the feudal lord claimed sexual rights over his vassals, as *Fuenteovejuna* shows, the king respects the marriage vows of his subjects. The king will in fact protect those vows if the subject will in his turn give him his loyalty. The rule by king over the modern state thus undercuts not only the territorial and sexual rule of the landed nobility, but also all communal ties. The new man is to consider himself a Spaniard, rather than Jew, or Catholic, or Catalunian. The arrangement intensifies, as Maravall has shown, both the autonomy of the individual and the absolute power of the king. It also encourages, as part of the agreement, the parallel power of every man over his wife.[15]

Pármeno, Lazarillo and Don Quixote are men who have in one way or another failed to achieve the promise that allegiance to a male authority promises. They want, all of them, to sever their ties to the social group from which they came, but none, having made that move, has managed to make the further step of assuming a kind of reign within the mini-kingdom of the family. All three appear, therefore, at a place between the figurative mother and the figurative father from which, belonging to neither, they are able to reveal the workings of the structures between which they are suspended.

Despite the obvious affiliations between *La Celestina*, *Lazarillo de Tormes*, and *Don Quixote*, differences are also apparant that suggest that a movement in consciousness needs also to be taken into account. Using a psycho-structural model, *La Celestina* might be considered a basically pre-Oedipal work. It is predominantly oral, offering fourteen voices in contrapuntal interaction; it introduces no explicitly "authorial" position; and it presents itself as a text extremely susceptible to the intervention of others, as Rojas noted in his prologue. The story proper as well as the Prologue suggest a continuing psychic embeddedness in the mother, as the work has to do with a female power and bonding that one escapes at one's peril. Like the viper who avenges the paternal death, the servants Pármeno and Sempronio funcion in *La Celestina* as characters both over-fed and fed up with the mother. They are ready to leave, but can do so only at the cost of falling into an authoritarian world which designates them as outlaws and strings them up.

It may be worth spending a little time looking into *La Celestina* with the idea of catching a glimpse of the world she represents, a world aging, as she is aged, and, though vital and capable of leaving progeny, one under threat of extinction. Celestina tells Pármeno of the dangers of uprooting:

> Por tanto, mi hijo, deja los ímpetus de la juventud y tórnate con la doctrina de tus mayores a la razón. Reposa en alguna parte. Y ¿dónde mejor, que en mi voluntad, en mi ánimo, en mi consejo, a quien tus padres te remitieron? Y yo, así como verdadera madre tuya, te digo, so las maldiciones, que tus padres te pusieron si me fueses inobediente, que por el presente sufras y sirvas a este tu amo que procuraste, hasta en ello haber otro consejo mío. (68)

She also warns him about the monied economy he longs to join:

> Deja los vanos prometimientos de los señores, los cuales desechan la substancia de sus sirvientes con huecos y vanos prometimientos... Estos señores de este tiempo más aman a sí, que a los suyos. (68-9)

She offers her own alternative: food, women, companionship, and, against Pármeno's budding sense of loyalty as an abstract notion to be applied to the idea of work and service, she insists on a more tribal, group-centered set of values. Pármeno says:

> "Riqueza deseo; pero quien torpemente sube a lo alto, más aina cae que subió. No querría bienes mal ganados," (69)

to which Celestina replies, "Yo sí. A tuerto o a derecho, nuestra casa hasta el techo"(69).

Celestina's is a world of passion and practicality, in which human relations vary according to the moment and the mood. Describing her mothering of Pármeno she says : "mil azotes y punadas te di en este mundo y otros tantos besos" (67). The treatment is mirrored in Pármeno's ambivalent attitude toward her. He has run from her already, and, having encountered her again, has denounced her as "flaca puta vieja" (67). Under the influence of her arguments, however, he begins to vacillate:

> "No sé que haga, perplejo estoy. Por una parte téngote por madre; por otra a Calisto por amo." (69)

Finally, against her promises of sexual love and the comradeship of friends, his efforts to propose to her a rule based on reason carry little power.[16]

In *La Celestina* we see a female system of relationships that reaches from the lowest to the highest figures in the social order. Everyone from Lucrecia to Melibea's mother Alisa are secretly devoted to Celestina's world, and so are most of the men, from the prelates to the ambassador from France. Pleberio, who is the only father of any substance in the work, and who represents the prosperous monied class which will be increasingly enfranchised under absolutist regimes, wakes up only to discover that he has lost everything—that the female world in which he also had invested his future has betrayed him.

Lazarillo de Tormes presents a view of the Oedipal process at a slightly more advanced stage. In *La Celestina* the move away from the mother, who had come to represent greed rather than bounty and ugliness rather than beauty, was precarious, indeed, impossible, because the paternal world was virtually a world of absence. Pármeno's father Alberto had long since left him and his inheritance in female hands. Pleberio lived in ignorance of the comings and goings of the women in his house, all of whom had intimate bonds to Celestina. By 1550, however, when *Lazarillo* was written, two elements of socio-technical history had become sufficiently established to render the figure of the all-powerful mother—already in decline as *Celestina* showed—a virtual anachronism. Lazarillo comes to adulthood, not in a mythic, never-named town as in *La Celestina*, but in Toledo. The journey of his life, a journey into masculine identity and into incorporation into the royal hierarchy, takes him to the heart of Spain—to the place where the emperor holds his court and celebrates his victories; the place where commerce has established itself as the avenue to wealth and success.

Lazarillo reaches the pinnacle of his success when he learns to accommodate to all the systems by which men achieve power in the time of Charles V. He shows himself capable of earning money buying and selling wine and water; he manages a place as town crier in the royal hierarchy; and he has found protection in the ecclesiastical establishment. In every *oficio* he reveals that the true function of the various male establishments is to secure access to the bodily pleasures whose major characteristic at the highwater of the empire is scarcity. The clergy, who enjoin against sex and food, become the means by which Lázaro finds both; the royal government, engaged in the denunciation of reprobates, collaborates with the church to take from the poor.

Lázaro learns that the new means of access to what all desire is through repression and dissimulation. Lázaro, whose real, first and best teacher was a blind beggar, figures out how to appear to make an alliance with the father in order to recover some portion of the maternal benefices from which he has been torn. His repression of the mother is far from complete, however. Lázaro is a conscious dissembler, pretending acquiescence to the values of the father in order to continue to enjoy the comforts of home. He never, therefore, truly leaves the position of the child in the family romance which in 16th century Spain has to do with increasing differentiation of self from mother, and with the concommitant embrace of the image and values of the father.

The monarchical/ecclesiastical alliance plays a major role in the creation of the Oedipal structure that was being forged in the nuclear families and the urban environment that began to emerge as central in the sixteenth century. The creation of paid armies, the colonization of the New World and the economic allurements of the city pulled young men from their maternal/rural environments and created the possibility of escaping cyclical time and the anonymity of repetition. Instead, the move from home emphasized the possibility of envisioning a new time measured by the span of one's own life and given value by one's own action.

The impact of the printing press, with the development of schooling that that invention allowed, cut even deeper into the developmental process, rolling back further the age at which boys would leave their maternal environments. Educators like Sir Thomas Eliot urged that boys as young as seven years of age be removed from women's company, including that of their mothers, and put into an all-male environment to assimilate the learning of Latin. Obviously all these forces come to bear differently on people depending on social class, but what becomes terribly clear when looking at the sixteenth century is the massive removal of males at varying ages from home, as if all the forces of history and culture were driving Pármeno from the womb and Lázaro from the protection of his mother.

Lázaro's portrait of his age, however, reveals how imperfect is the severing of the child from the desires associated with the mother. Throughout the first two chapters of his fictional autobiography Lázaro portrays himself as locked in intense struggle with a male mentor for possession of food, and, more generally, for the sustenance offered by women. Both of Lázaro's early masters possess the containers in which precious food is kept. The struggle reaches a climax in Chapter II when an old chest containing bread becomes the object of Lázaro and his master's battle. The phallic overtones are hard to ignore in this clearly post-Oedipal work situated around the boy's awakening into a male world. A neighbor tells the priest, who is baffled by the continuing signs that someone else is getting into the locked container for which the priest is supposed to have the only key:

> En vuestra casa yo me acuerdo que solía andar una culebra, y esta debe de ser, sin duda. Y lleva razón, que como es larga, tiene lugar de tomar el cebo y, aunque la coja la trampilla encima, como no entre toda dentro, tornase a salir. (144)

A "snake" enters and leaves the battered box that contains the precious loaves of bread that women in the parish have donated—a bread so revered by the starved Lázaro as to be likened to the face of God.

Lázaro's phallic competition with his master, however, leaves both him and the bread box beaten beyond recognition, and renders the master a slave to hyper-vigilance and anxiety. Having learned of the "snake" threatening his possession of the contents of the box, the priest is no longer able to sleep:

> Cuadró a todos lo que aquel dijo, y alteró mucho a mi amo. Y dende en adelante no dormía tan a sueño suelto. Que cualquier gusano de madera que de noche sonase pensaba ser la culebra que le roía el arca. Luego era puesto en pie, y con un garrote que a la cabecera, desde que aquello le dijeron, ponia, daba en la pecadora del arca grandes garrotazos, pensando espantar la culebra. (144)

When the priest finally is able to turn his rage directly on the interloper, he clubs Lázaro to the brink of death and ejects him from his house. From Chapter III on, it is clear that Lázaro has not succeeded in entering the male world represented by the priest and other figures of power. Hunger teaches Lázaro in Chapter III that women, even when the law goes to the contrary, can be counted on for food and shelter. In Chapter IV Lázaro leaves the Mercedarian friar who shows him how to enter women's houses for any pleasure he desires. In Chapter V he becomes a passive observer in a show that reveals how church and government collude to take material goods from the poor. Chapters VI and VII present Lázaro as a man who has learned to exploit a corrupt system in exchange for a symbolic return to the place of the child—a place of instability in which nonetheless he is given food and shelter while not having to assume sexual responsibility for a woman.[17]

Lázaro, in short, uses the new system to achieve his ends, which are a return to the mother. The return involves a change of dress, an assumption of urban living, a move to writing, a sense of ever-impending failure, an exchange of friendship for an environment in which the Other is judge. The new man that Lázaro has become must be constantly on guard, and must be engaged in denouncing those like him, those who have not achieved definition as men of honor and unity. He hopes all the while, by ruses of power and denunciation, not to be himself exposed.

If Pármeno and Sempronio act out of the psycho-sexual stage of early childhood in their abortive effort to separate from the mother, Lázaro presents the adolescent failure to usurp, or assume the place of the father. He remains locked into a place of indefinition and dissembling in which he feigns manhood and honor in order to hold onto a protection and nurturance that he is unready to relinquish.

Don Quixote presents the Oedipal process at another stage. If in *La Celestina* the mother was omni-present and all-powerful and in Lazarillo she was an explicit figure representing loss and desire, in *Don Quixote* her repression has been almost entirely successful. Don Quixote has so totally broken his connection to the body, the land, and the mother, that he lives as if a stranger to the environment which supports him. His life has become his books, for which he is willing to sell off parcels of land. The niece of marriagable age and a housekeeper in her forties tantalize but cannot awaken his dormant sexuality.[18] The books, which provide a means of escape from the erotic pressure of so much accessible yet untouchable female sexuality, are also instruments that exalt his suppressed desires. When Don Quixote is brought back from his first disastrous sally, beaten and delirious, his niece has finally to admit that her uncle has long been behaving in a strange manner:

> muchas veces le aconteció a mi señor tío estarse leyendo en estos desalmados libros de desventuras dos días con sus noches, al cabo de los cuales arrojaba el libro de las manos y ponía mano a la espada, y andaba a cuchilladas con las paredes, y cuando estaba muy cansado decía que había muerto a cuatro gigantes como cuatro torres, y el sudor que sudaba del cansancio decía que era sangre de las feridas que habia recibido en la batalla, y bebíase luego un gran jarro de agua fría, y quedaba sano y sosegado. (115)

Don Quixote represents the armored, hyper-lettered, alienated man whose rejection of woman and earth has almost entirely taken over his consciousness. Cervantes shows through him, however, how repression returns to consciousness as violence and idealism, how arms and letters, those quintessentially masculine pursuits, fail to account for or master the natural world. Women in *Don Quixote* show themselves more than capable of the self-defense Don Quixote would like to assume for them. They also reveal an ability to read, imagine, and manipulate events for the sake of their own interests. Don Quixote's madness is both the result of his extreme one-sidedness and the cause of his recovery of balance.

Cervantes takes his character on a journey that results in the breaking down of his armor, and his reincorporation into the lifeworld around him. Through Don

Quixote's madness, Cervantes is able to show us the underside of empire, its vast heterogeneity, its multi-linguistic and multi-caste population, its peasants and working class, its garrulous women, its soldiers, its orphans, its beggars—a whole world that belies the totalizing aspirations of the Hapsburgs, and the posturings of autonomy and individualism which that empire urges as its principal ally.

The growth of individualism in the 16th century, so clearly documented in the major literary texts of the period, moves consciousness out of the pre-Oedipal situation which Rojas' text presents. In *Moses and Monotheism* Freud identifies the entire construct of culture—its prohibitions and its cults of male ancestor worship—with the working out of that struggle between a dominant male—the father, the king—and his sons. The arrangement prevents further parricide, just as the modern state seeks to avoid regicide.[19] In exactly the same fashion the little boy is relieved of his feelings of rage and envy of his father by renouncing his attachment to his mother, on the understanding that he too will one day, learning from his father, take a position of power with respect to a woman.

The creation of the new man in Europe in the Renaissance is a reflection of the development of everyman in the culture of Western Europe as it has emerged since then.[20] The attitudes of dominance, separation, and repression of the feminine that evolved in sixteenth century Spain as the empire extended its power over larger and larger entities—political as well as religious and racial—are constructs of culture that are revealed in all of their pain and difficulty in the works of the imagination that captured the responses of psyche to that period.

NOTES

[1] For further development of the notion of organicism and its relation to the mechanistic world view that competed with it and ultimately overtook it, see Carolyn Merchant and also Brian Eslea. The term "filiation" is inspired by Edward Said's reflections on biologically determined bonds as opposed to those choosen consciously. See *The World, the Text, and the Critic.*

[2] See Said's *Beginnings,* and Fiedler's *Love and Death in the American Novel.*

[3] See Flandrin, p. 125.

[4] For more on the Renaissance courtier's changed attitude with respect to the competing demands of his lady-love and the lord to whom he owes obeisance, see Joan Gadol Kelly's excellent article.

[5] In "Feminism and Science" Evelyn Fox Keller writes:
> Our early maternal environment, coupled with the cultural definition of masculine (that which can never appear feminine) and of autonomy (that which can never by compromised by dependency) leads to the association of female with the pleasures and dangers of merging, and of male with the comfort and loneliness of separateness. The boy's internal anxiety about both self and gender is echoed by the more widespread cultural anxiety, thereby encouraging postures of autonomy and masculinity which can, indeed, may, be designed to defend against that anxiety and the longing that generates it. (239)

[6] Maravall says:
> Si se ha puesto en evidencia una situación de alienación, es en tanto que ha sido posible tomar conciencia de ella. La situación de alienación en todo régimen anterior al Estado es de tal naturaleza que ni siquiera queda una perspectiva que permita contemplarla. El régimen de Estado hizo posible esto último, al crear un distanciamiento entre el individuo y el poder. (418)

[7] For commentary on the relationship of the shifting attitudes toward Nature and women in the seventeenth century to the witch mania, see Merchant and Belsey.

[8]Brian Easlea discusses the effects on social and ethical consciousness of the embrace, in the seventeenth century, of a Cartesian view of the universe. While Easlea contends that the victory of the mechanistic over the animistic world view finally helped put an end to witch persecutions, he also points out that it worked further to sever the connection of self to world that other forces were also promoting in Western Europe.

[9]Leonardo's childhood recollection of the *nibio*, which Freud mistranslated as "vulture", appears in his notes on the flight of birds ("Questo scriver si distintamente del nibio par che sia mio destino, perche nella mia prima recordatione della mia infante e' mi parea che, essendo io in culla, che un nibio venissi a me e mi aprissi la bocca colla sua coda e molte volte mi percuotesse con tal coda dentro alle labbra") from the Codex Atlanticus, fol. 65, reprinted in Neuman, (p. 6, n. 8). Both Freud and Neumann discuss the memory, and see the bird, despite other differences in interpretation, as a figure for the all-powerful mother.

[10]Gates asks:
> If every black canonical text is, as I shall argue, 'two-toned" or 'double-voiced', how de we explicate the signifyin(g) black difference that makes black literature 'black'? (3)

Barbara Johnson, generalizing the issue to a question of the universal and the particular, says:
> There is no point of view from which the universal characteristics of the human, or of the woman, or of the black woman, or even of Zora Neale Hurston, can be selected and totalized. Unification and simplification are fantasies of dominion, not understanding. (218)

[11]Doug Carey, in private communications, and also in a lecture at the Midwest Modern Language Association, 1985. See also Brenes.

[12]Don Quixote justifies his entire mission as knight errant on the basis of his desire to restore the "Golden Age". I have elaborated on the importance of Don Quixote's Golden Age speech (*Don Quixote*, I, 11) in "Sex" and also in "In Praise".

[13]Bakhtin's study of Rablelais gives historical context to the continuing presence, throughout the Renaissance, of "carnival", or the "world turned upside down" within learned texts and sacred ceremonies. Popular culture is rooted in agrarian economies and world views which,

by the seventeenth century, have largely been displaced by the written and urban-centered cultures in Europe. Bakhtin counts Cervantes' Sancho Panza as among the last remnants of the figure of the wise fool and glutton in literary works in Europe.

[14]A good example of how the new novelistic form undermines the pretenses of empire even as it finds in the individual that empire creates the basis of its structure can be found at the end of *Lazarillo de Tormes*, where Lazaro compares the peak of his own good fortune with that of the Emperor Charles V.

[15]Virtually every commentator of domestic relations in the sixteenth century, whether in England, Spain, or France, notes the shift of power in the family toward the husband's authority. Lawrence Stone, writing about England, attributes the "apparent positive decline in the status and rights of wives in the sixteenth and early seventeenth centuries" (202) to, among other things, the "decline in kinship, which left wives exposed to exploitation by their husbands", and "the emphasis placed by the state and the law on the subordination of the wife to the head of the household as the main guarantee of law and order in the body politic." (202)

[16]The dialogue in which Celestina and Pármeno discuss love and reason goes as follows:

> *Pármeno:* No querría, madre, me convidases a consejo con amonestación de deleite, como hicieron los que, careciendo de razonable fundamento, opinando hicieron sectas envueltas en dulce veneno para captar y tomar las voluntades de los flacos y con polvos de sabroso afecto cegaron los ojos de la razón.
> *Celestina:* ¿Qué es razón, loco? ¿Qué es afecto, asnillo? La discreción, que no tienes, lo determina, y de la discreción mayor es la prudencia, y la prudencia no puede ser sin experimento y la experiencia no puede ser más que en los viejos. (71)

[17]For good analyses of the compromised sexual arrangements Lazaro makes in Chapters IV, VI and VII, see Sieber and Shipley.

[18]For more on the question of the housekeeper and the niece in *Don Quixote* see Carroll Johnson.

[19]Dian Fox has written extensively about the political theories extant in Spain at the time of the Habsburgs, and particularly notes, in her study of Calderón, the question of regicide.

[20]Evelyn Fox Keller relates the growth of science in the seventeenth century to peculiarities in the social division of the sexes, writing in *Reflections on Gender and Science:*

> Our inquiry confirms that neither the equations between mind, reason, and masculinity, nor the dichotomies between mind and nature, reason and feeling, masculine and feminine, are historically invariant. Even though the roots of both the equations and the dichotomies may be ancient, the seventeenth century witnessed a marked polarization of all the terms involved—with consequences as crucial for science as for our understanding of gender.(44)

Works Cited

Bakhtin, Mikhail. *Rabelais and His World.* Translated by Helene Iswolsky. Cambridge, Mass.: The M.I.T. Press, 1968.

Belsey, Catherine. *The Subject of Tragedy: Identity and Difference in Renaissance Drama.* London and New York: Methuen, 1985.

Brenes, Dalai. "*Lazarillo de Tormes*: Roman à clef." *Hispania* 69 (1986): 234-243.

Carey, Douglas. "Maternal Subtexts in the *Lazarillo de Tormes*: Gender and Authorship." Modern Language Association, December 1985.

Castro, Américo. *Cervantes y los casticismos españoles.* Barcelona: Alfaguara, 1966.

Combet, Louis. *Cervantès ou les incertitudes du desire.* Lyons: Presses Universitaires de Lyons, 1981.

Easlea, Brian. *Witch Hunting, Magic, and the New Philosophy.* Sussex: The Harvester Press, 1980.

El Saffar, Ruth. "In Praise of What is Left Unsaid: Thoughts on Women and Lack in *Don Quixote.*" *MLN* 103 (1988): 205-222.

—. "Sex and the Single Hidalgo." *Studies in Honor of Elias Rivers.* Edited by Bruno Damiani and Ruth El Saffar. Washington, D.C. Scripta Humanistica, 1989, forthcoming.

Fiedler, Leslie. *Love and Death in the American Novel*. New York: Criterion Books, 1960.

Freud, Sigmund. *Moses and Monotheism*. Translated by James Strachey. New York: Norton, 1961.

—. *Leonardo da Vinci*. Translated by A.A. Brill. New York: Random House, 1961.

Flandrin, Jean-Louis. *Families in Former Times: Kinship, Household and Sexuality in Early Modern France*. Translated by Richard Southern. Cambridge: Cambridge UP, 1979.

Fox, Dian. *Kings in Calderon: A Study in Characterization and Political Theory*. London: Tamesis, 1986.

Gates, Henry Louis. Introduction. *Black Literature and Literary Theory*. Edited by Henry Louis Gates, Jr. New York and London: Metheun, 1984.

Gilman, Stephen. *The Art of "La Celestina"*. Madison: U of Wisconsin P, 1956.

Guillén, Claudio. "Toward a Definition of the Picaresque." *Literature as System*. Princeton: Princeton UP, 1971, pp. 91-106.

Johnson, Barbara. "Metaphor, Metonymy and Voice in *Their Eyes Were Watching God*." *Black Literature and Literary Theory*. Edited by Henry Louis Gates, Jr. New York and London: Methuen, 1984, pp. 205-220.

Keller, Evelyn Fox. "Feminism and Science." *Sex and Scientific Inquiry*. Edited by Sandra Harding and Jean F. O'Barr. Chicago: U of Chicago P, 1987, pp. 233-246.

—. *Reflections on Gender and Science*. New Haven: Yale UP, 1985.

Kelly, Joan Gadol. "Did Women Have a Renaissance?" *Women, History, and Theory*. Chicago: U of Chicago P, 1984, pp. 19-50.

Lazarillo de Tormes. Edited by Joseph Ricapito. Madrid: Cátedra, 1982.

Maravall, José Antonio. *Estado moderno y mentalidad social*. Madrid: Alianza, 1972.

—. *La literatura picaresca desde la historia social*. Madrid: Taurus, 1986.

Merchant, Carolyn. *The Death of Nature.* London: Wildwood House, 1980.

Neumann, Erich. "Leonardo da Vinci and the Mother Archetype." *Art and the Creative Unconscious.* Translated by Ralph Manheim. Princeton: Bollingen Series, 1974.

Ong, Walter. *Interfaces of the Word.* Ithaca and London: Cornell UP, 1977.

Pitkin, Hanna Fenichel. *Fortune is a Woman: Gender and Politics in the Thought of Niccoló Machiavelli.* Berkeley: U of California P, 1984.

Ragland-Sullivan, Ellie. *Jacques Lacan and the Philosophy of Psychoanalysis.* Urbana: U of Illinois P, 1986.

Rojas, Fernando de. *Tragicomedia de Calisto y Melibea.* Edited by Dorothy Severin. Madrid: Alianza, 1972.

Rossi, Rosa. *Escuchar a Cervantes: Un ensayo biográfico.* Valladolid: Ambito, 1988.

Said, Edward. *Beginnings.* New York: Basic Books, 1975.

—. *The World, the Text and the Critic.* Cambridge: Harvard UP, 1983.

Shipley, George. "A Case of Functional Obscurity: The Master Tambourine-Painter of *Lazarillo,* Tratado VI," *MLN* 97 (1982): 225-253.

—. "Lazarillo and the Cathedral Chaplain: A Conspiratorial Reading of *Lazarillo de Tormes,* Tratado VI," *Symposium* 37 (1983): 216-241.

Sicroff, Albert. *Les controverses des status de 'pureté de sang' en Espagne du XVe au XVIIe siècle.* Paris: Didier, 1960.

Sieber, Harry. *Language and Society in "La vida de Lazarillo de Tormes".* Baltimore and London: Johns Hopkins University Press, 1978.

Stone, Lawrence. *The Family, Sex and Marriage In England 1500-1800.* New York: Harper & Row, 1977.

STUDYING GENDER IN THE SPANISH GOLDEN AGE

Anne J. Cruz
University of California, Irvine

No querría yo, hijas mías, que fueseis en nada mujeres, ni lo pare-
cieseis, sino varones fuertes, que si ellas hacen lo que es en sí, el
Señor las hará tan varoniles que espanten a los hombres.

Santa Teresa, *Camino de perfección*

The relations between the ideology of sex roles and the reality we
want to get at are complex and difficult to establish. Such views
may be prescriptive rather than descriptive; they may describe a
situation that no longer prevails; or they may use the relation of
the sexes symbolically and not refer primarily to women and sex
roles at all. Hence, to assess the historical significance of changes
in sex-role conception, we must bring such changes into connection
with all we know about general developments in the society at
large.

Joan Kelly, "Did Women Have a
Renaissance?"

At the onset, the study of gender in the Golden Age
presents critics with the problematics, not only of identifying a particular category of study within sexual and socio-
economic classes, but of defining gender and gender roles
in the sixteenth and seventeenth centuries. Moreover,
those of us whose main field of study is literature and its
production must also take into account, not only the
sociohistorical context of the work, but its intrinsically
literary aspects. The questions posed by gender studies of
the Golden Age, then, relate specifically to what is meant
by gender according to contemporary definitions, and
where gender relations are located textually in order to
focus on them as subject of study.

Both questions resist simple answers, and in turn expose other issues deeply embedded in the social construct
of literature, such as canon formation, periodization, and
collusion with dominant ideologies. Therefore, although

this essay discusses several approaches to these issues taken by Renaissance and Golden Age scholars, it by no means exhausts the topics or attempts all the possibilities of gender study. Rather, it offers an overview of early and recent trends in Renaissance and Golden Age literary criticism in order to emphasize the need, not only for more studies of this kind in the field, but for the application of new methodologies that contribute to the revision of received modes of thought on gender in literature.

GENDER IN THE RENAISSANCE

One of the major tasks of gender studies is to define what is meant by such a category at any particular time in history. An integral part of cultural symbolic code systems, gender has varied in meaning and significance throughout different historical periods.[1] In order to reach an understanding of the cultural function of gender in society, it is therefore necessary to historicize gender definitions—to understand them as forming part of an underlying sexual ideology that varies according to specific sociohistorical needs.

Yet the difference between male and female has been articulated as a constant at least since biblical times: an impenetrable boundary dividing men and women into sexual opposites.[2] While this mythical line between the sexes has frequently been transgressed, belief in its integrity continues to be fostered through the efforts and in the interest of one group alone. Thus, while stating that Christian morality developed from the problematization of attitudes on liberty and power held by classical societies, and not from an inconsequential refinement of sexual austerity, Michel Foucault nevertheless points out that the Western view of man as subject arose from an expressly male ethics:

> It was an ethics for men; an ethics thought, written, and taught by men, and addressed to men—to free men, obviously. A male ethics, consequently, in which women figured only as objects or, at most, as partners that one had best train, educate,

and watch over when one had them under one's power, but stay away from when they were under the power of someone else (father, husband, tutor).[3]

In the Middle Ages and the Renaissance, such an ethics was carefully maintained and nurtured by the debates on misogyny and feminism.[4] Whether viewed as naturally diabolical and wicked, or equally as naturally angelical and pure, woman remained, nonetheless, "other"—a creature placed either below or above man on the spiritual scale, but never his equal.

That her spirituality (or conversely, her materiality) was a natural given constituted the central issue in the numerous fifteenth- and sixteenth-century treatises on women. Erasmus is generally acknowledged to have dignified women's position in early modern Europe, in particular by encouraging their education.[5] Yet reform movements did not eliminate the opinion that woman was morally evil, a view heatedly debated earlier in religious misogynist writings and the secular literature which idealized her. In Spain, fifteenth-century defenses of women were represented by, among others, Diego de San Pedro's *Cárcel de amor*.[6] They continued well into the sixteenth century with Juan de Espinosa's *Diálogo en laude de las mujeres* (1580), dedicated to María de Austria, and Luis de León's influential *La perfecta casada* (1583). Carefully distinguishing between the specific and the general, Espinosa lauds most women for their superior virtue:

> [S]iempre ha sido mi intention, no de provar que, en general, los varones sean imperfectos o malos, y las hembras perfectas o buenas, por que en el uno y en el otro sexo, es cosa manifiesta, hauer en particular, buenos y malos, sino que, por la mayor parte, en las hembras resplandesce mucho mas la virtud, que en los varones.[7]

Evidenced in their moral qualities as well as in their physiognomy, women's "natural" difference thus structured gender definitions in the early modern period.

But if differentiation by sex originates from the distinctive natural functions of the sexual organs (especially

women's generative powers), it also implies the socially
assigned function of the gendered self. In their need to
maintain the status quo, patriarchal societies have considered as "masculine" certain characteristics such as authority, reason, judgment, command, and discipline, precisely
because these qualities are what keep males in power.
Similarly tautological, characteristics deemed weak or
vulnerable such as gentleness, compassion, nurturing,
emotionality, and love are assigned to women and thus
labeled female or maternal.[8] However, as Caroline Walker
Bynum notes in her study on the iconography of Jesus as
mother, these "feminine" traits have at times been assigned to men, and even to the male deity. Arguing that
sexual boundaries were quite fluid in the Middle Ages, she
points out that "authors found it far easier than we seem
to find it to apply chracteristics stereotyped as male or female to the opposite sex" (162). Medieval interest in the
theme of God's motherhood is explained in part by the
male religious' attributing feminine qualities to themselves, exactly at a time when such characteristics were socially and politically valuable in the development of religious communities.[9]

Arguably more constrained than their medieval counterparts, women in the Renaissance were relegated to private, familial roles which in turn were believed to reflect
their natural inclinations, obscuring the crucial factor that
distinctions between men and women, were socially—not
naturally—determined. Although appearing to laud
women's virtues, Spanish defenses of women in reality
sounded a moral alarm. Insistently prescriptive, treatises
as different as Luis Vives' Erasmian *De institutione femi-
nae christianae* (1524-28) and Luis de León's Counter-
reformational *La perfecta casada* both reveal an underlying
belief in women's intellectual, moral, and physical inferi-
ority predicated upon an equally strong conviction in the
superiority of men. To Luis de León, women were part of a
divine plan reaffirming male power:

Y pues no las dotó Dios ni del ingenio que piden los negocios mayores,
ni de fuerzas las que son menester para la guerra y el campo, mídanse con

lo que son y conténtense con lo que es de su suerte, y entiendan en su casa, y anden en ellas, pues las hizo Dios para ella sola.[10]

Artfully combining the "feminist" defense of woman's virtues with a denouncement of her "natural" proclivities, Luis de León thus establishes an ideal model for the Christian wife and mother which he grounds on a timeless and unassailable theological truth.

GENDER AS A SOCIAL CONSTRUCT

Historical studies of women's roles in society make clear, however, that their position depended, not upon natural differences, but on such factors as their social, economic, and educational status. In her seminal essay, "Did Women Have a Renaissance?" Joan Kelly-Gadol challenged the widely-held myth that women had reached a higher level of equality in the Renaissance. Studying the development of the modern state and the subsequent increased domination of women, she argued convincingly otherwise:

> [A] new division between personal and public life made itself felt as the state came to organize Renaissance society, and with that division the modern relation of the sexes made its appearance, even among the Renaissance nobility. . . . Renaissance ideas on love and manners, more classical than medieval, and almost exclusively a male product, expressed this new subordination of women to the interests of husbands and male-dominated kin groups and served to justify the removal of women from an "unladylike" position of power and erotic independence.[11]

Although Kelly bases her arguments on the development of the Italian state and the corresponding loss of power by Italian women, her conclusions apply as well to Spain and Spanish women. Indeed, Kelly points out that while cultures vary, there emerges a consistent pattern of female subordination when domestic and public activities are sharply differentiated (10). The division between female public and private roles was more noticeable in Spain than in other European countries: contemporary travellers, for instance, were shocked at the harsh treatment of women by their husbands, who kept them literally locked inside the home.[12]

The relatively recent concept of gender as a social construct thus offers a useful—in fact, essential—means of understanding Renaissance culture. The category of gender allows us to problematize Golden Age ideology which exalts the social order as natural and theologically determined. By questioning the ideological bases of gender, we may attain a broader comprehension of the ways women's position in society becomes increasingly institutionalized. We can also examine the tensions within gender order, which disclose that the Renaissance concept of gender was not so totalizing as it appears—that gender roles also proffered women the potential to subvert social categories, even while delimiting their actions.

The epigraph I have chosen for this essay, Santa Teresa's exhortation to her nuns that they behave in a specifically masculine way so as to "espantar hasta a los más varoniles," reveals an understanding of gender difference that goes beyond the merely physical or "natural." It is, in fact, a shrewd appraisal of the extent religious women could go to effect change within the community. As such, it is as subversive a statement of women's empowerment, as the female Picaresque novel's supposedly liberal attitude toward the *pícara* is instead a manifestation of the male author's power and control.[13] The nuns' desexualized role permitted them a more "masculine" and thus more active and powerful position, while the purported sexual freedom of the *pícara* —male- authored for a male audience—contrasted with the increasing regulation of prostitution throughout the sixteenth and seventeenth centuries. Gender studies of these two radically different texts thus reveal the ways in which prostitution and religious orders functioned as a means of gender control in the Renaissance, their potential for subversion, and the differing limitations imposed upon women by both systems.

GENDER LOCUS

The study of gender in the Golden Age requires locating the discourses wherein gender relations occur; determining, that is, the loci of the study, as well as defining its subject. Repeating what feminist criticism has long recognized in literary studies generally, Paul Julian Smith observes that there are at least two methods of analysis available to feminist critics of the Golden Age.[14] The first consists of studying the representation of women in literature, while the second analyzes the writings of women themselves. He questions, however, whether either approach offers a satisfactory means of gender research. According to Smith, since the Golden Age canon consists mainly of male-authored texts, the portrayal of women bespeaks a masculine bias that "tell[s] us little of women's lives in the period, and less about the enabling conditions of gender and sexual difference as a whole" (240). Similarly, to Smith, the paucity of women writers during the period severely limits the field of study. In view of such difficulties, Smith chooses to study what he calls the "stylistics or textuality" of two Golden Age women writers in an effort to find within their language those characteristics which set them apart from the male norm.

Smith's essay deserves much praise for applying recent feminist theory to a topic in Golden Age studies which has hardly, if ever, been addressed on its own terms—that of a feminine language and, by extension, of an explicitly feminine literature. Most critical studies continue to view women's language relative to men's, even when it transgresses social and linguistic norms. The studies thereby implicitly corroborate and maintain the binary opposition linking accepted male convention to a dependent female discourse. Indeed, with the exception of Smith himself, such critics as Emilio Orozco Díaz, Víctor García de la Concha, and Fernando Lázaro Carreter view Saint Teresa's language and style as based on a rhetoric of repression, appropriating male strategies, but ultimately reliant upon them.[15]

In contrast, Smith analyzes Saint Teresa's and María de Zayas y Sotomayor's writings according to Julia Kristeva's notion of the semiotic, the stage of pre-verbal consciousness expressed through discontinuity and fragmentation, and to Luce Irigaray's awareness of phallomorphic logic reconstructing anatomy in its own image.[16] Granting that discontinuity cannot be claimed as an essential characteristic of women's writing (240), he concludes that both Saint Teresa's and María de Zayas's writings conflate biological and historical differences in the mobile articulation of their discursive bodies. Smith offers an exciting alternative to the stalemate usually reached by critics who must choose between the biological and the historical, and effectively liberates women's writing from its perceived reliance upon male discourse. Yet, despite Smith's provocative analysis of female discourse, his essay perpetuates the belief that Golden Age literature does not extend beyond the orthodox canon traditionally revered by academics. I will return to Smith's essay, but for the moment, I would like to call attention to his unfortunate undervaluation of legitimate areas of study, since in neglecting them, he may, however unwittingly, discourage further—and much needed—research in the field.

THE REPRESENTATION OF WOMEN IN MALE-AUTHORED TEXTS

While breaking new ground in Golden Age criticism, Smith nevertheless adheres to certain conventional views on Hispanic literature. The first is his belief that male-authored texts do not offer sufficiently rich ground for feminist study. Smith is right, of course, in asserting that male writers are biased in their depiction of women, although not all are so "rarely sympathetic" or "overtly hostile" as he presumes. Francisco de Rojas Zorrilla, Lope de Vega, and Cervantes—to name but three—often portray women in a generally positive light, and while their perspective on women may in turn have occasioned such male- centered critiques as Rudolph Shervill's "Lope's Ways with Women," *Bulletin of the Comediantes* 1 (1963): 10-13; and

Anthony J. Close's "Don Quixote's Love for Dulcinea: A Study of Cervantine Irony," *BHS* 54 (1977): 107-114; it has also motivated Raymond MacCurdy's essay "Women and Sexual Love in the Plays of Rojas Zorrilla: Tradition and Innovation," *Hispania* 62 (1979): 255-65. Zorrilla's reputation as a feminist writer due to his female protagonists' vigorous protestations of arranged marriages and their insistence on equality has already been noted.[17] What MacCurdy discovers in reading the plays a bit more carefully, is the female protagonists' joyful expression of sexual love which, according to MacCurdy, is "probably the most significant measure of Rojas' feminism" (262).

Cervantes's growing interest in the independent female character has also inspired Ruth El Saffar's study, *Beyond Fiction: The Recovery of the Feminine in the Novels of Cervantes* (Berkeley: Univ. of California Press, 1984), which posits the qualities of the feminine as the redemptive factor in Cervantes's later works. Whether or not we agree with El Saffar that Cervantes documents his own liberation and final conversion through his fiction, it is clear that his female characters are increasingly liberated from the objectification of solely erotic conflicts. El Saffar's study is based on Jungian concepts, but these serve as well to point out that the absolute differentiation of male and female in the literary text is not a natural— but a social— construct. However much some aspects of El Saffar's study, as well as of Cesáreo Bandera's earlier work, *Mimesis conflictiva* (Madrid: Gredos, 1975), stress the desire for transcendence in—and from—fiction, they also contribute to our awareness of the feminine as an "other," as a difference created for the benefit of the entangled, less than transcendent male ego.[18]

Thus, while Smith dismisses such fictional figures as the "manly woman" in Golden Age drama as mere reinforcements of the status quo (220), we cannot forget that these same portrayals provided one of the first instances of feminist criticism in Golden Age studies. Indeed, Melveena McKendrick's *Women and Society in the Spanish Drama of the Golden Age: A Study of the 'Mujer Varonil'*, written in 1974, initiated a trend in gender studies that continues unabated: the study of the representation of women in male-authored texts. Following McKendrick's example, for example, are Ruth Lundelius's article "Tirso's View of Women in *El burlador de Sevilla* ," *Bulletin of the Comediantes* 27 (1975): 5-14; Ann Wiltrout's "Women in the Works of Antonio de Guevara," *Neophilologus* 60 (1976): 525-33; and her "Murder Victim, Redeemer, Ethereal Sprite: Women in Four Plays by Calderón," in *Perspectivas de la Comedia II*, Alva Ebersole, ed. (Valencia: Albatros-Hispanófila, 1979), pp. 103-20. Also examples of this trend are Edna Simms's "Notes on the Negative Image of Women in Spanish Literature," *CLA Journal* 19 (1976): 468-483; Sandra Foa's "Women in the Literature of Medieval and Golden Age Spain," in *Conversations in the Disciplines* (Syracuse, Onondaga Comm. Coll., 1979); Glen Dille's "Notes on Aggressive Women in the Comedia of Enríquez Gómez," *Romance Notes* 21 (1980): 215-21; Louise Salstad's bibliography, *The Presentation of Women in Spanish Golden Age Literature* (Boston: G. K. Hall, 1980); and *Women in Hispanic Literature: Icons and Fallen Idols*, Beth Miller, ed. (Berkeley: Univ. of California Press, 1983).

To this list, we should add several dissertations which have been written on women in literature and which we will most likely see soon in print: "The Women of the *Romancero*" (Frank Lynn Odd, 1975); "The Image of Women in Selected Spanish Golden Age Byzantine Romances" (Jane Frances Schneider, 1978); "The Image of Women in the Theater of Juan Ruiz de Alarcón" (Catalina Oliver- Prefasi, 1983); and "The Motif of the Woman Disguised as a Man in Shakespeare and Some Siglo de Oro Spanish Dramatists: The Portia Figure" (Margaret Ellen O'Connell, 1983). This year, the Kentucky Foreign Language Conference has sponsored a session on "Identities in Change," which includes the following papers: " *Jardín de nobles doncellas* y su influencia en la imagen femenina del siglo XVI"; "Portraits of Women in the Pastoral Novel"; and "Calderón's Figures of Women."

The titles of these studies indicate that a number of critics, as well as graduate students and their dissertation advisors, view the attempt to understand the role of women in literature, albeit through male-authored texts, as a valid approach in literary criticism. What we must ask is whether such studies contribute to an understanding of women in society—if the images of the text correspond to a homologous view of history. Anticipating Joan Kelly's 1977 essay on women in the Renaissance, McKendrick's important study argues that literature provides access to cultural attitudes toward women:

> While literary evidence must be approached with care if we are to establish the social *reality* of woman's life in any previous age, it is our most important source of information with regard to *attitudes towards* the concept of woman. And while these attitudes are often highly personal, they equally often reflect general trends which, however, stylized, always have some psychological truth. (4)

While Golden Age literature cannot be considered a mere reflection of historical reality, the depiction of women in Golden Age fiction through both its negative and positive images, and its ommissions as well as its distortions, reveals the pervasiveness of the patriarchal system in male-authored texts. Its study thus broadens our understanding of the social and physical limitations placed upon, and suffered by, real women.

CONTEXTUAL CRITICISM AND THE NEW HISTORICISM

But do male-authored texts in the Renaissance present a reliable view, however distorted, of real women? The studies we have examined lead us to conclude that literary constructions of women have little to do with reality, and everything to do with ideology. Although McKendrick asserts that Golden Age drama gave a more realistic appraisal of women, she is quick to add that this was not accompanied by any practical improvement in women's conditions (326). Moreover, McKendrick admits that her own example, the extremely popular *mujer varonil*, stood not for Hispanic tolerance of strong women, but for sexual fantasy, for Baroque conceit, and ultimately, for female subjugation (322-23). It is therefore not surprising that the play *La monja alférez* by Juan Pérez de Montalván, based on the case of a real *mujer varonil*, Catalina de Erauso, resolves her identity at the end as female, restoring gender order. Adducing historical data in her study of the play, historian Mary Elizabeth Perry points out that although it follows the life of Catalina de Erauso in that she is granted permission from the pope to live and dress as a man, the play's ending stresses her grudging revelation of her female nature and her acknowledgement of male superiority.[19] While McKendrick's method of analysis relies mainly on literary representations of women, Perry arrives at her conclusions by comparing historical sources with the literary text.

Perry's historical analysis expands the area of inquiry to discourses other than the literary. It thus exemplifies Kelly's methodology, which supplements McKendrick's by including contextual analysis of gender relations. To gauge the various relations between men and women in the Renaissance, Kelly applies the following criteria:

> 1) the regulation of *female sexuality* as compared to male sexuality; 2) women's *economic* and *political roles*, i.e., the kind of work they performed as compared with men, and their access to property, political power . . . 3) the *cultural roles* of women in shaping the outlook of their society, and access to the education and/or institutions necessary for this; 4) *ideology* about women, in particular the sex-role system displayed or advocated in the symbolic products of the society (20).

To Kelly, among a given society's symbolic products are its art, literature, and philosophy. While these ideological indexes offer direct knowledge of the attitudes of the dominant sector, she also argues that they yield indirect knowledge about what is not stated: in this case, the various social, sexual, political activities of women. Understanding that the relations between symbolic constructs and a particular reality are complex and tenuous, Kelly argues that the historian must relate historical changes to all that is known about society in general (21).

This methodology forms part of a wider critical development recently adapted to Renaissance studies under the title of "New Historicism" in the United States, and as a form of cultural materialism in England.[20] Taking as their field of study the nature and function of hegemonic culture, practitioners such as Stephen Greenblatt, Stephen Orgel, and Louis Montrose articulate what another New Historicist, Steven Mullaney, calls a "poetics of cultural production" which blurs disciplinary boundaries and situates literary texts within the broader social context.[21] Yet what differentiates Kelly's approach from the New Historicism is its emphasis on determining woman's place within cultural production. Recently, the New Historicists' neglect of this essential factor has been brilliantly addressed by Marguerite Waller in her essay, "Academic Tootsie: The Denial of Difference and the Difference it Makes," forthcoming in an anthology appropriately entitled *Seeking the Woman in Late Medieval and Renaissance Writings: Essays in Feminist Contextual Criticism.*[22] Exposing the desire for the epistemology of authority held by the (male) New Historicists, Waller points out that the history they invoke is one still privileged by a specific class and gender—those of white, male academics—and that their cultural critique is intended for this same audience.

The critical practice espoused by the New Historicism, however, need not be restricted to—or by—a privileged male perspective. The methods utilized by feminist historians to uncover the presence of women in the past—in Kelly's words, "to restore women to history and to restore our history to women"— are equally fruitful to the literary critic in recovering the woman in literature, and in restoring literature to women. As discursive practice, literature is a historical product as well as a symbolic construct, and encodes one locus of gender relations which, when compared with other social discourses, distinguishes and reveals both the dominant male as well as the muted female attitudes. Extending beyond McKendrick's and Kelly's arguments, in their Introduction to the volume *Seeking the Woman* editors Janet Halley and Sheila Fisher argue that the "[s]tudy of male-authored texts of [medieval and Re-

naissance] periods suggests, then, that the representation
of women does not merely distort or interpret but *altogether ignores* the historical existence of real women and
their experience of selfhood. In order to understand these
literary constructions of women, it is necessary to assess
them against the materiality of women's lives—the
conditions in which they grew up, worked, worshipped,
married, gave birth, and learned" ("Introduction" 6; emphasis mine). In order to reconstruct the presence of
women in society, it is also necessary to consult such extra-
literary texts as the economic, legal, political and religious
systems and codes which delimited women's access to
power.

What must be remembered, however, is that these prescriptive and proscriptive codes were also written by men
with their own interests in mind. When not dancing
through the minefield, Golden Age gender criticism walks
a tightrope between possibly erroneous conclusions as to
the historical status and welfare of women, and illumina-
tive insights into their actual conditions, all gleaned from
male-centered texts. As Halley and Fisher make clear, to
write women was to refer not to women, but to men
("Introduction," 4). In writing about woman, men wrote
about (male) desires: the demarcation of feminine absence
in the text, then, ultimately ensures male presence.

THE (MALE) TEXTUAL SELF

The difficulty in obtaining reliable information on
women in the early modern period has consistently hindered the feminist historiographical project. Such has not
been the case for male roles, since men have traditionally
been the subjects of most cultural—literary as well as extra-literary—texts. The male as represented in the literary
canon thus poses several challenges to feminist critics: to
demythologize the literary and social construct of masculinity, and to analyze and compare male representation
with historical reality. Both projects are thus central to the

New Historicism's goal of destabilizing cultural hegemony. But with a difference.

Itself arising from a decentered position, feminist criticism avoids the ideological blindness that Waller, in her
previously cited article, finds in Greenblatt's analysis of
the Wyatt sonnet "Whoso list to hunt; I know where is an
hind," where the poem's denial of the woman extends beyond its content to its selectively male readership. Greenblatt sees the poet's inner life shaped by the competitive
relationship that ensues between the poet and Caesar—the
hind's possessor, and the poet's lord— over the object of
desire (105). In contrast, Waller considers the poem predicated upon the woman's absence:

> The text (of Wyatt's poem) . . . not only masculinizes the place
> of the reader, but also actively usurps the place of woman as
> speaker or writer, as producer of language (4)

Waller concludes that when the woman disappears as
subject from the critic's text as well as from the text of the
Renaissance author, the critical text colludes with the
absolutism and misogyny it finds so reprehensible in its
sixteenth-century object of study. As demonstrated by
Waller's forceful argument, the role of feminist contextual
criticism, then, is both to uncover the ideological instability of the masculine figure represented in the literary text,
and to disclose the epistemological alliance of male-oriented criticism with male-centered textual authority.

With its complicitly male conventions, male-authored
Golden Age literature provides a wide arena in which to
practice feminist contextual criticism. The honor plays in
particular present a complex array of attitudes whose ambiguity is reflected in their critics' oftentimes conflicting
stances. According to Thomas O'Connor, for example,
Frank Casa's article, "Honor and the Wife-Killers of
Calderón," *Bulletin of the Comediantes* 29 (1977): 6-23, dis-
regards woman's dignity and inviolability in Casa's assertion that the murders affirm the dignity of man. This debate in turn spurred William McCrary to evaluate gender
behavior in Lope de Vega's *Los comendadores de Córdoba*

and *El castigo sin venganza*, and in Calderón's *A secreto agravio, secreta venganza*.[23] Following the logic of the plays, McCrary underscores the fact that masculine orientation is directed toward the world and theater of men, where women are mere stage props. In short, what these plays are about, according to McCrary, is the theatricalization of male transference anxiety.

I have argued elsewhere that while Calderón's own thoughts on the honor code are of little relevance to the wife-murder plays' structure, his *A secreto agravio, secreta venganza* dramatizes the consequences of male social behavior, which differentiate the masculine sphere of action from the feminine realm.[24] Ascribing Don Lope de Almeida's friendship with don Juan de Silva to the experiences both shared while in the military, I view their male associative behavior as an example of what Lionel Tiger has called "male bonding."[25] In interpreting this relationship as male bonding, rather than as an example of ennobling classical male friendship, I follow Waller's reading of Wyatt's sonnet in order to understand the play rhetorically, instead of mimetically.

Such a reading reveals that unlike other Calderonian wife-murder plays, the protagonists' relationship—not the wife-husband conflict—energizes the relations of power inherent to the honor code. The friends' covert competition propels the play's action and leads inexorably to the death, not only of the two lovers, but of don Lope himself. By comparing the relations between the protagonists with the extra-literary concept of male sex role identity, we arrive at an understanding of how the text at once infers culturally defined sex roles and is structured by them.

Golden Age plays are but one area where textual representation of male roles may be analyzed. In the same way that Waller interprets Wyatt's Petrarchan sonnet, the Golden Age lyric may be read as an attempt by male poets to forge their sexual identity at the expense of the woman. The first-person narrative voice of the lyric impels the reader to assume a male identity, creating an echo chamber where the male voice gathers strength by effectively "masculinizing" its readers through repetition. Even when addressed to women, lyric poetry diminishes the feminine position, dismembering the female image in order to create the male persona. The seventeenth-century parodies of Petrarchan love poetry can also be studied for their attitudes to women beyond their purely literary response to female idealization.[26]

Other genres provide equally valid fields for gender studies. Besides their idealization of the feminine, as textual representatives of the masculine code of honor, the novels of chivalry offer a particularly influential example of male rivalry and oedipal conflict. Moreover, the consumption of these novels had serious social and historical consequences not only for the New World, but for subsequent political symbolism and strategies.[27]Such disparate texts as the pastoral novel and the Picaresque may also be studied to reveal the socio-psychological gender constructs supporting the former's elite Neoplatonic love theory, and the deviant sexuality of the lower-class pícaro in the latter. Conventional approaches to the pastoral speak of its "affinity to noble love," with its corresponding valorization of female spiritual virtue and its rejection of eroticism, remarking on its similarity to mystical literature.[28] Yet, to my knowledge, only Elizabeth Rhodes has addressed the pastoral's understanding of female psychology and its attraction to women readers.[29]

The depiction of sexuality in the Picaresque has been studied by Harry Sieber, *Language and Society in 'La vida de Lazarillo de Tormes'* (Baltimore: Johns Hopkins Press, 1978), who reads the *Lazarillo's* fourth chapter as an unvoiced revelation of homosexuality; and the seventh as the willed suppression of cuckoldry.[30] Denying any direct homology between the text and society, Sieber's study nevertheless inquires into the social implications of honor, since to Sieber, the text *is* the linguistic sign of honor (vii-viii). It might also be said, then, that in their silence, the text's suppressed references to sexual activity are the linguistic signs of shame (*pudor*). Furthermore, the fact that certain kinds of sexual activity are (un)mentioned only in Picaresque literature raises important questions regarding the interrelations of class and gender in Golden

Age Spain. In texts depicting the lower classes, sexual deviance becomes interrelated with social difference. Thus, the *Guzmán de Alfarache's* linguistic excesses confirm his shame over his doubtful origins, as his braggadoccio cannot help but reveal the mother's whorishness, as well as the father's *converso* blood and homosexual tendencies.[31]

WOMEN IN THE GOLDEN AGE

Like his assertion that male-authored texts offer little or no information on the conditions of gender and sexual difference in Golden Age Spain, Paul Julian Smith's comment that "there are very few women writers in Spain in the period" (221), also needs correction. He might have stated instead that there are only a few *well-known* women writers from the period. Indeed, he chooses two of these women for his analysis: Santa Teresa and María de Zayas y Sotomayor. Traditional criticism has ensured our familiarity with Santa Teresa's writings, but we need to question why other women writers have met with far less success.

Citing Xavier Lampillas's list of sixteenth-century *mujeres ilustres* and Pérez y Pastor's list of seventeenth-century women writers, Melveena McKendrick mentions, among others, Luisa Siega, Oliva de Sabuco, Juana Morella, Isabel de Joya, Ana Caro, and Catalina Zamudio (21). According to McKendrick, four women alone have remained in the public's memory: Santa Teresa, María de Zayas y Sotomayor, Sor María de Agreda, and Mariana Carvajal y Saavedra (22-23). Yet the literary renown of even these four women is unequal at best. As McKendrick points out and Smith's essay illustrates, Santa Teresa has received the greatest attention of any Hispanic woman writer. Interest in her life remains strong; three biographies have recently been published (Efrén de la Madre de Dios (Montalva) and Otger Steggink, *Tiempo y vida de Santa Teresa* (Madrid: Editorial Católica, 1977); Rosa Rossi, *Teresa de Avila. Biografía de una escritora*, (Barcelona: Icaria, 1984); and Victoria Lincoln, *Teresa: A Woman. A*

Biography of Teresa of Avila (Albany: State University of New York Press, 1984). Her complete works have been twice translated into English (by E. Allison Peers, London: Sheed and Ward, 1958; and by Kieran Kavanaugh and Otilio Rodríguez, Washington, D.C.: ICS Publications, 1976-80). Indeed, her stature outside Spain is confirmed by her inclusion as Spain's sole representative in Katharina M. Wilson's study, *Women Writers of the Renaissance and Reformation* (Athens: The University of Georgia Press, 1987).

Although hardly comparable to the attention paid to Santa Teresa, interest in María de Zayas y Sotomayor is increasing. Besides Smith, Elizabeth Ordóñez, Sandra Foa, William Clamurro, and Mireya Pérez-Erdelyi have recently addressed Zayas y Sotomayor's writings—the latter critic focusing on the images of women in her novels.[32] In contrast, to my knowledge, María de Agreda and Mariana Carvajal have yet to become subjects of study. And if we include Manuel Serrano y Sanz's list to those mentioned, we find that there are many more women writers in the Golden Age whose names have been all but forgotten.[33]

Several of these women, such as Juana de Austria, Luisa de Carvajal y Mendoza,[34] and María de Agreda, Philip IV's correspondent, were not only writers, but played an important part in the history of the period, which they documented in their letters.[35]Others, such as Ana de Bartolomé and Jerónima Nicolini (Sor Inés de la Cruz) were mainly religious women whose autobiographies were written at the behest of their confessors. Still other women, both secular and religious, composed poetry and maintained voluminous correspondence, while anonymous women writers penned novels of chivalry such as the *Primaleón* and the *Palmerín de Oliva*.

What emerges from these lists, then, is compelling proof of an abundant literary production, one which remains in general unpublished and unstudied. The generic variety alone of this literature presents us with a wealth of material in critical need of such historiographical treatment as cataloguing, dating, and editing, as well as the sheer pleasures of the interpretive task. Poetry (cultured and popular, religious and secular), drama, autobiography, epistle, novel, and romance are all represented in the writings. That the literature was produced by women offers us a non-canonical view into the sixteenth and seventeenth centuries, one gleaned from the slant of a feminine—and at times, even feminist—perspective. No matter how conventional the genre, the fact that they have been appropriated by a woman offers us ample reason to study these works, and to approach them from a distinctly different critical angle than male-authored texts.

FEMINIST APPROACHES TO FEMALE-AUTHORED TEXTS

In the preceding pages, I have discussed the advantages of feminist contextual criticism in interpreting social discourses. Literature written by women also presents some of the difficulties evinced in male-authored texts, especially since Renaissance women writers cannot be supposed to incorporate an inherently feminist stance. This approach, then, is most useful for moving beyond women's roles in literature, whether as referents or participants.[36]

Before women wrote in the Renaissance, they read—and since both activities were conditioned by male-authored texts, women had little choice but to imitate men in their reading as well as in their writing. Yet, in the experience of women, the literary text represented the same male-centered perspective encountered in extra-literary texts. The study of women's literature, then, necessitates its comparison to male-authored texts in order to establish the differences, as well as the similarities, among genres.

Since women wrote in the genres with which they were most familiar, the pun "generic differences," based on the Spanish homonym "género" for both genre and gender, and thus resonating with both textual and sexual connotations, is an apt term for the tensions inherent to these literary relations. Feminist contextual criticism allows us to foreground genre/gender differences, by viewing male-authored texts as part of the social discourse within which women wrote. For instance, while generally ascribed to male poets, some anonymous cultured and popular poetry may indeed have been composed by women; critical studies comparing them to the traditional canon may be of help in elucidating their origins, as well as in revealing social attitudes toward gender.[37] Similarly, religious women writers must first be read within the context of canonical religious writers in order to distinguish them from the canon. As female autobiographical writings partake of the same conventions as saints' lives and confessions, so María de Zayas y Sotomayor follows the model of the exemplary novel when writing her own *novelas ejemplares.* And, to avoid possible conflicts with the Inquisition, some women write under male pseudonyms.[38] An extrinsic analysis of women's literature thus accords it a rightful place in literary history, ensuring that, by its very presence, writing by women be given the same attention as its male counterpart.

Yet, perhaps not so paradoxically, the inclusion of women in the canon has often resulted in their denigration. Traditional criticism has viewed women's writings as female versions of male texts, and tended to judge them according to conventional standards. "Lesser literature"— the value judgment most often passed on sixteenth- and seventeenth-century Hispanic women's writings—usually stems from its inability to transfer female experience completely into male terms, thus maintaining its difference. When not arriving at a negative opinion of female authorship, such masculinist criticism either acclaims it as "virile" (if the work is considered successful in its imitation of male models) or bespeaks a paternalistic attitude which effectively robs the work of its rigor and intelligence if in any way different from male authorship. Thus, Santa Teresa's "freshness and originality" (she writes unlike a man) are attributed to her lack of a good memory, which apparently hindered her ability to remember the male-authored texts she had previously read, and to the Inquisition, for keeping her from reading more.[39]

The most difficult task of the critic when confronted by a female-authored text, then, is to isolate those elements that may be read as "feminine," as opposed to "masculine." Either explicitly or implicitly, questions on the existence or manifestation of gender difference arise whenever a text is female-authored. Returning to Paul Julian Smith's essay on Santa Teresa and María de Zayas y Sotomayor, we read that to him, the question of how women writers manifest gender differences can be answered by an intrinsic analysis, studying what Smith calls "the texture of their very language" (221). The critic is no longer stymied by the oppositions in Santa Teresa's *Vida* between the personal (experiential) and the social (institutional), the spontaneous (of an essentialist nature) or artificial (culturally acquired). To Smith, these questions may be "circumvented if we accept the hypothesis that there is a pre-verbal stage of human consciousness, associated with the female body, to which the reader may regain access through certain kinds of writing" (232). Relying on Irigaray, Smith analyzes María de Zayas y Sotomayor's novel *Mal presagio casarse lejos* as social exchange outside the world of men, as an example of "women's writing":

> Irigaray . . . asks us to read the "blanks" of patriarchal discourse and suggests the possibility of a space beyond its dominion. . . . Irigaray calls for a text that will overturn syntax . . . and suspend teleology through the breaking of linguistic threads . . . To read Zayas (and Teresa) as a "woman's writing" would thus be to refuse the temptation to construct a "personal identity" as source of the text, and to attempt (provisionally at least) to experience *all* writing as an alternating play of continuity and rupture, stasis and impulse. (239)

Based as it is on Kristeva's and Irigaray's work, Smith's approach forms part of recent French critical studies which Alice Jardine has named gynesis:

> [T]he putting into discourse of "woman" as that *process* diagnosed in France as intrinsic to the condition of modernity: indeed, the valorization of the feminine, woman, and her obligatory, that is historical connotations, as somehow intrinsic to new and necessary modes of thinking, writing, speaking.[40]

To Jardine, the object produced is neither a woman nor a thing, but a horizon toward which the writing process tends; that is, it is a reading effect of the "feminine" or the appearance of women (defined either metaphorically or historically) in the text, and as such, need not be written by a woman.[41]

Recently, this criticism, whether in its different versions by Kristeva, Irigaray, or Hélene Cixous, has come under attack by Anglo-American feminists for depending too heavily on male theoreticians and male writers, as well as for relegating women solely to a spatial dimension, and denying them a temporal one. Claiming that the texts of gynesis pay little attention to women writers, Elaine Showalter posits instead gynocritics:

> [looking] at women's writing as it has actually occurred and [trying] to define its specific characteristics of language, genre, and literary influence, within a cultural network that includes variables of race, class, and nationality.[42]

Despite their oftentimes antagonistic stances, it is important to observe that one school does not necessarily refute the other; indeed, while grappling with the very real differences between the two cultural systems, Jardine's study provides much of the context for a rapprochement between them.[43] Neither propounds a totalizing system: If gynocritics privileges women writers by focusing exclusively on their writing—a focus long overdue—it risks ignoring male-authored texts' influences on women, both representationally (textually) and culturally (extratextually), and remaining within patriarchal ideologies. And while gynesis reasserts the value of the feminine, as Showalter herself has stated,[44] its most radical practitioners have been accused of reverting to essentialism, of positing some form of utopia, or of remaining within the binary oppositions construed by the same master narratives they mean to criticize.

Yet perhaps most importantly for our study, these two systems, while essential to our understanding of the postmodern condition, are equally of value to Golden Age texts. In effect, by bringing together Kristeva and Irigaray, Smith's essay illustrates the importance of gynesis in revalorizing the feminine, in giving a new language to the spaces which open up in the literary text, whether male- or female-authored. Moreover, his choice of two women writers redirects our reading to those texts not included in the canon: gynocritics thus compels a revision of the literary tradition previously ignored by male-centered criticism. Rather than contradict one another, the critical systems discussed in this essay overlap in their explorations of gender difference. In the textual rereadings of gynesis, as well as through the historically grounded approaches of new historicism, feminist contextual criticism, and gynocritics, we may formulate a critique of gender in the Golden Age that allows us to understand not only the dominant and muted voices of our past, but those of our own changing spaces and times.

NOTES

[1]For modern views on gender and gender difference, see *"Femininity," "Masculinity,"* and *"Androgyny": A Modern Philosophical Discussion* Mary Vetterling-Braggin, ed. (Totowa, N.J.: Rowman & Allenheld, 1982).

[2]Anne Dickason points out that the concept of "the feminine" has been "defined as early as the third century B.C. in Western and Eastern thought; the Pythagorean Table of Opposites and the dualisms of Yin-Yang express similar divisions of nature clustered around 'masculine' and 'feminine' characteristics." See her essay, "The Feminine as a Universal," in Mary Vetterlin- Braggin, p. 10.

[3] Michel Foucault, *The Use of Pleasure: The History of Sexuality* Vol. 2. Robert Hurley, trans. (New York: Vintage Books, 1986), p. 22.

[4]For the debate, see Barbara Matulka, *The Novels of Juan de Flores and Their European Diffusion* (New York, 1931); and Jacob Ornstein, "La misoginia y el profeminismo en la literatura castellana," *RFH* 3 (1941): 219-32.

[5]See Américo Castro, "Algunas observaciones acerca del concepto del honor en los siglos XVI y XVII," *RFE* 3 (1916): 382-84; and Ricardo del Arco y Garay, *La sociedad española en las obras dramáticas de Lope de Vega* (Madrid, 1941), 405b, cited in Melveena McKendrick, *Woman and Society in the Spanish Drama of the Golden Age: A Study of the 'Mujer Varonil'* (London: Cambridge University Press, 1974), p. 6. McKendrick cautions: "This does not mean that women were now regarded as men's equals. The Erasmian reformers did not themselves create or propagate a new image of woman, and in many respects their basic premises are still those of the medieval moralists" (6).

[6]See Joseph F. Chorpenning, "Rhetoric and Feminism in the *Cárcel de amor* ," *BHS* 65 (1977): 1-8.

[7]Juan de Espinosa, *Diálogo en laude de las mujeres,* ed. Angela González Simón (Madrid: Biblioteca de Antiguos Libros Hispánicos, 1946), pp. 155-56.

[8]Caroline Walker Bynum, *Jesus as Mother: Studies in the Spirituality of the High Middle Ages* (Berkeley: University of California Press, 1982), p. 148.

[9]See Chapter Four, "Jesus as Mother and Abbot as Mother: Some Themes in Twelfth-Century Cistercian Writing," Bynum, pp. 110- 169.

[10]Luis de León, *La perfecta casada y poesías selectas,* ed. Florencia Grau (Barcelona: Editorial Iberia, n.d.), p. 116.

[11]Joan Kelly Gadol, "Did Women Have a Renaissance?," in *Becoming Visible: Women in European History,* Renate Bridenthal and Claudia Koons, eds. (Boston: Houghton Mifflin, 1977), pp. 137-64; reprinted in *Women, History, and Theory: The Essays of Joan Kelly* (Chicago: The University of Chicago Press, 1984), pp. 19- 50. Although Kelly has been criticized for basing herself too narrowly on courtly love literature and the Italian nobility, her essay inspired a re-examination and re-thinking of the period. See *Women in the Middle Ages and the Renaissance: Literary and Historical Perspectives* Mary Beth Rose, ed. (Syracuse: Syracuse University Press, 1986). For a study of middle- and lower-class women, see Natalie Zemon Davies, "City Women and Religious Change," *Society and Culture in Early Modern France* (Stanford: Stanford University Press, 1965).

[12]"Los maridos que quieren que sus mujeres vivan bien, se hacen tan absolutos que las tratan casi como esclavas, temerosos de que una honesta libertad las emancipe de las leyes del pudor, poco conocidas y mal observadas en el bello sexo." Cited in José Deleito y Piñuela *La mujer, la casa y la moda (en la España del rey poeta)* (Madrid: Espasa-Calpe, 1966), p. 18.

[13]See Edward H. Friedman, "The Voiceless Narrator: *The Spanish Feminine Picaresque and Unliberated Discourse," The Anmtiheroine's Voice" Narrative Discourse and Transformations of the Picaresque* (Columbia: University of Missouri Press, 1987), pp. 69-118; and my essay, "Sexual Enclosure, Textual Escape: The Pícara as Prostitute in the Spanish Female Picaresque Novels," in *Seeking the Woman in Late Medieval and Renaissance Texts*, Sheila Fisher and Janet Halley, eds. (Knoxville: University of Tennessee Press, forthcoming).

[14]Paul Julian Smith, "Writing Women in Golden Age Spain: Saint Teresa and María de Zayas," *MLN* 2 (1987): 220-240. As an introductory approach to feminist criticism, Mary Ellmann's *Thinking About Women* (New York: Harcourt, Brace, & World, 1968) remains useful.

[15]See Emilio Orozco Díaz, *Expresión, comunicación y estilo en la obra de Santa Teresa* (Granada: Diputación Provincial de Granada, 1987); as well as Víctor García de la Concha, *El arte literario de Santa Teresa* (Barcelona: Ariel, 1978); and Fernando Lázaro Carreter, "Fray Luis y el estilo de Santa Teresa," in *Homenaje a Gonzalo Torrente Ballester* (Salamanca, 1981).

[16]Smith cites Jane Gallop's *Quand nos levres s'ecrivent:* Irigaray's body politic," in *Romanic Review* 74 (1983): 77-83; he takes Kristeva's concept from her "Sémiotique et symbolique," in *La Révolution du langage poètique: L'Avant-garde a la fin du XIXe siècle: Lautréamont et Mallarmé* (Paris: Seuil, 1974), pp. 17-100.

[17]See Francisco de Rojas Zorrilla, *Cada qual lo que le toca y La vida de Nabot*, Américo Castro, ed. Vol. 2, Teatro Antiguo Español (Madrid: Hernando, 1917), pp. 246-47; and Angel Valbuena Prat, *Literatura dramática española* (Barcelona: Editorial Labor, 1930), p. 249-53.

[18]That this difference also encompasses a loss is eloquently made evident in Ruth El Saffar's recent essay, "In Praise of What is Left Unsaid: Thoughts on Women and Lack in *Don Quijote ," MLN* 2 (1988): 205-22.

[19]Mary Elizabeth Perry, "*La monja alférez*: Myth, Gender, and the Manly Woman in a Spanish Renaissance Drama," *La Chispa '87: Selected Proceedings*, Gilbert Paolini, ed. (New Orleans: Tulane University), pp. 239-49.

[20]For a discussion of the development of these critical trends, and a defense of their application, see Steven Mullaney's preface to his study, *The Place of the Stage: License, Play, and Power in Renaissance Literature* (Chicago: University of Chicago Press, 1988), vii-xii. See also *Political Shakespeare: New Essays in Cultural Materialism*, Jonathan Dollimore and Alan Simfield, eds. (Ithaca: Cornell University Press, 1985); and Raymond Williams, *Marxism and Literature* (Oxford: Oxford University Press, 1978).

[21]See, for instance, Stephen Greenblatt, *Renaissance Self-Fashioning: From More to Shakespeare* (Chicago: University of Chicago Press, 1980); Louis Montrose, "Renaissance Literary Studies and the Subject of History," *English Literary Renaissance* 16 (1986): 5-12; and Jean Howard, "The New Historicism in Renais sance Studies," *ELR* 16 (1986): 13-43.

[22]Edited by Sheila Fisher and Janet E. Halley, and forthcoming from University of Tennessee Press.

[23]William C. McCrary, "The Theatricality of Male Orientation in the *Comedia*," *Studies in Honor of William C. McCrary*, ed. Robert Fiore et al. (Lincoln, Neb.: Society of Spanish and Spanish- American Studies, 1986): 27-34.

[24]"*Homo ex Machina?* Male Bonding in Calderón's *A secreto agravio, secreta venganza*," paper read at the Louisiana Conference on Hispanic Literatures, Tulane University, New Orleans, La., February 16-18, 1987.

[25]Lionel Tiger, *Men in Groups* (London: Thomas Nelson and Sons, 1969), xv-xvi.

[26]For an analysis of the literary transformations of women depicted in poetry, see John D. Smith, "Metaphysical Descriptions of Women in the First Sonnets of Góngora," *Hispania* 56 (1973): 244-48.

[27]While not dealing specifically with gender issues, Margarita Zamora's essay "Historicity and Literariness: Problems in the Literary

Criticism of Spanish American Colonial Texts," *MLN* 102 (1987): 334-46 discusses the related phenomena of historiographical concepts of truth, and the mediative role of institutions and ideologies in the formation of Spanish-American colonial literature. It is not coincidental that gender studies find themselves in alliance with third-world critiques of imperialism.

[28]See Jorge de Montemayor, *Los siete libros de la Diana,* Francisco López Estrada, ed. (Madrid: Espasa-Calpe, 1946), lvxxii; and Bruno Damiani, "Nature, Love, and Fortune as Instruments of Didacticism in Montemayor's Diana ," *Hispanic Journal* 3 (1982): 7- 19.

[29] Elizabeth Rhodes, "Skirting the Men: Gender Roles in Sixteenth-Century Pastoral Books," paper presented at the MLA, San Francisco, Ca., December 28, 1987.

[30]See also B. Bussell Thompson and J.K. Walsh, "the Mercedarian's Shoes (Perambulations on the fourth *tratado* of *Lazarillo de Tormes)*," *MLN* 2 (1988): 440-48.

[31]See Friedman, p. 37.

[32]Elizabeth Ordóñez, Women and Her Text in the Works of María de Zayas and Ana Caro," *Revista de Estudios Hispánicos,* 19 (1985): 3-15; Sandra M. Foa, *Feminismo y forma narrativa: estudio del tema y técnicas de María de Zayas y Sotomayor* (Valencia: Al batros, 1979); Mireya Pérez-Erdelyi, *La pícara y la dama: la imagen de las mujeres en las novelas picaresco-cortesasas de María de Zayas y Sotomayor* (Miami: Universal, 1979); William Clamurro, "Eros, Honor, and the Decadence of Empire in María de Zayas' *Desengaños amorosos,*" paper presented at Louisiana Conference on Hispanic Languages and Literatures, Tulane University, February 26-28, 1987.

[33]Manuel Serrano y Sanz, *Apuntes para una biblioteca de escritoras españolas* (Madrid: Atlas, 1975).

[34] See my "Chains of Desire: Luisa de Carvajal y Mendoza's Poetics of Penance," paper presented at the MLA San Francisco, December 27-30, 1987.

[35]I have not seen Joaquín Pérez Villanueva's article "Sor María de Agreda y Felipe IV. Un epistolario en su tiempo," in *Historia de la Iglesia en España,* vol. 4 (Madrid, 1979).

[36]For examples of contextual feminist criticism applied to women's writings and experiences, see *Becoming Visible: Women in European History;* and *Women in the Middle Ages and the Renaissance: Literary and Historical Perspectives,* ed. Mary Beth Rose (Syracuse: Syracuse University Press, 1986).

[37]For a discussion of generic transformations and the representation of women, see my "Genre Transformations and the Question of Gender: *La bella malmaridada* as Ballad and Play," *Scandinavian Yearbook of Folklore,* forthcoming.

[38]Such is the case of Luisa Enríquez Manrique de Lara, Countess of Paredes de Nava who, no doubt ironically, wrote her meditative treatise *Año santo: Meditaciones para todos los días* (1658) under the name and title "Licenciado D. Aquiles Napolitano, Clérigo Presbítero, Comisario del Santo Oficio de la Inquisición, Protonotario Apostólico." Joaquín Pérez Villanueva, *Felipe IV Y Luisa Enríquez Manrique de Lara, Condesa de Paredes de Nava: Un epistolario inédito* (Salamanca: Caja de Ahorros y M. de P. de Salamance, 1986), p. 44.

[39]Ciriaco Morón-Arroyo, "The Human Value of the Divine: Saint Teresa de Jesús," in *Women Writers of the Renaissance and Reformation,* p. 405.

[40]Alice A. Jardine, *Gynesis: Configurations of Woman and Modernity* (Ithaca: Cornell University Press, 1985), 25.

[41]Hence the application of Cixous's *écriture femenine* to the avant-garde. What we should note, however, is that such an approach would be of great help in understanding mystics such as San Juan de la Cruz, who consistently appropriates the feminine voice.

[42]Elaine Showalter, "Woman's Time, Woman's Space: Writing the History of Feminist Criticism," in *Feminist Issues in Literary Scholarship,* Shari Benstock, ed. (Bloomington: Indiana UP, 1987), 37.

[43]For a discussion of the contradictions between the two systems, see the essays in *Writing and Sexual Difference* , Elizabeth Abel, ed. (Chicago: Univ. of Chicago Press, 1982); especially, Jane Gallop, " Writing and Sexual Difference : The Writing Within," 283-90.

[44]Elaine Showalter, "Feminist Criticism in the Wilderness," in *The New Feminist Criticism,* Elaine Showalter, ed. (New York: Pantheon Books, 1985), 249.

LESBIAN CARTOGRAPHIES:
BODY, TEXT, AND GEOGRAPHY

Amy Kaminsky
University of Minnesota, Minneapolis

This paper argues the need for an acknowledged lesbian feminist textual criticism for Latin American literature. Since the terms "lesbian" and "feminist" are slippery and highly charged, I will begin by offering some working definitions. "Feminism" recognizes and seeks to redress the subordination of women, which it sees as culturally determined. Feminist theory and criticism take as a primary task the empowerment of women as producers and readers of texts. "Lesbian feminism" assumes that the devotion of sexual energy to women is a part of the general commitment to women that feminism implies. Though a lesbian can be devoid of political consciousness, lesbianism carries within it the potential for a powerfully pro-woman theory and practice.

While feminist theory, always self-critical, has in recent years incorporated into its analysis the specificities of class, race, and nationality that inform and shape the oppression of women, in most feminist accounts sexuality remains the constant of women's subordination. Whether it is the will to fix paternity and thus rights of inheritance in the aristocracy, the sexual use of female slaves throughout history, the obsessive drive to contain what is perceived as female excess, or the categorizing of women's work as reproductive rather than productive, what is specific to women's oppression is the impulse in phallocentric culture to regulate female sexuality. According to legal theorist Catherine MacKinnon, "Sexuality is to feminism what work is to Marxism: that which is most one's own, yet most taken away" (MacKinnon, 515). That is to say, women's sexuality has been defined and legislated in culture so that women get cast as primarily sexual beings, with our sexuality understood in reference to androcentric needs or fears. Reproducer or temptress, madonna or whore, are, broadly speaking, our two choices. MacKinnon continues, "As the organized expropriation of the work of some for the benefit of others defines a class —workers— the organized expropriation of the sexuality of some for the use of others defines the sex, woman" (MacKinnon, 516).[1] Anthropologist Gayle Rubin has argued that the constraints on female sexuality, which depend on the enforcement of heterosexuality, are at the root of the rigid, hierarchical gender polarities that characterize androcentric culture. The resulting polarized and rigid, gender-identified sexuality runs so deep that it has been used as a metaphor in ascribing meaning to such diverse cultural phenomena as imperialism and electrical wiring. The radical recovery of women's sexuality that lesbian feminism implies, then, is a profoundly political act.

Needless to say lesbianism is not embraced as a liberatory act by Latin American culture. The virtually intractable heterosexism of that culture accomodates homophobia on the right, where lesbianism (like male homosexuality) is seen as a sin born of permissiveness, and on the left, where it is characterized as bourgeois decadence. Alternatively, lesbian sex is dismissed out of hand as "not sex" since no penis is involved (ie. there is no category for women as sexual actor as opposed to passive recipient). Or, perhaps most insidious of all, since it seems so benign, is the equation of lesbianism with mental illness, an unfortunate but conceivably curable disorder.[2]

Given phallocratic culture's will to control women's sexuality it is not surprising that sexual expression on the part of women that does not include men is the most forbidden of all. It is still possible to silence potentially feminist women with the epithet *lesbian*. Heterosexuality is so deeply ingrained, that it is passed off not only as "natural" but as the *sole* natural expression of sexuality. To be called "lesbian" is to be called "monster". Yet heterosexuality as we know it is hardly the natural, unmediated sexual expression we are led to believe it is, and there is simply no way to know what women's sexuality would look like in what philosophers once called the State of Nature. The taboos and rituals surrounding sexual behavior, as well as those invoked at such events as menarche, menstruation and menopause, pregnancy, childbirth and nursing, are deeply entrenched in culture and internalized by the individual. The definitions and circumstances of sexual behavior —whether it must always include a penis, if genital penetration is the sine qua non of sexual interaction, if by defintion the penetrator is "male" and the penetrated one "female"— are also elaborated in culture. The lines between prescription and description blur, so that normative behavior gets defined as natural behavior, and the punishment for non-normative behavior is justified as correcting or eliminating an aberration of nature.

As Adrienne Rich has argued, heterosexuality in Western society is compulsory, and transgression is severely punished. While it is demonstrably risky to invoke lesbianism as a critical stance,[3] to posit a feminist criticism that denies the possibilty of a non, or even anti-heterosexual position is to foreclose on a rich source of counter-hegemonic thought. Furthermore, for feminists to comply with the taboo of lesbianism is to hand anti-feminists a convenient device with which to frighten us into submission.

One of the reasons that academic feminism (which might be defined as the intellectual legitimation of feminist thought) is so slow to grow in Latin America and practically non-existent in its literary criticism and theory, is women scholars' fear of having their sexuality impugned.[4] The Latin American continent's halls of academe ring with the claim, "No soy feminista, pero...." Feminist activity is much more vital and diverse among political activists than among academics. There are women's centers and rape crisis centers in cities, and a feminism that incorporates, and is incorporated by, the oppositional politics of revolutionary movements. But until women are no longer terrorized by the threat of the mark of deviance whenever they shift their glance from the male cultural project, as long as women fear being called lesbians for giving their energy and attention to other women, there will be no free women.[5] Consequently, the feminist critical project is incomplete without the infusion of lesbian theory and criticism.

Moreover, a literary criticism that takes as one of its goals the transformation of repressive cultural practice, as both feminist literary criticism and Latin American materialist literary criticism do, needs to take into account that which is most marginalized, most repressed, and most forbidden. This project not only opens the culture to as full a view as possible but also stands to liberate those subjects positioned on that often invisible margin.

Lesbianism is a profound rejection of androcentrism (the ontological and epistemological privileging of the male subject). According to philosopher Marilyn Frye, lesbians, *as* women, pay attention *to* women, where "attention" is understood as a "kind of passion" (Frye, 172). Similarly, the first, and still most crucial, move of feminist scholarship is the shift of focus from men to women, which in turn brings about a remapping of meanings and the sudden appearance of formerly unnoticed phenomena. Unreflexively hererosexual feminist criticism began simply with looking at individual women characters and authors. When it began to consider relationships between women, questions arose whose consideration has been greatly enhanced by a lesbian feminist perspective.

Though the notion of woman-centeredness goes beyond sexuality, sexuality remains central to it. This is so because women are constructed in culture primarily as sexual beings, so to redefine women's sexuality is to call into question the basic definitions of "woman" (not least the definition that limits her existence to a sexual one). It is crucial, then, both to demystify the cultural construction of normative sexuality and to insist on valuing lesbianism. This may look like the deconstructionist move of decentering and reversal, and there are indeed connections to be made. But while deconstruction has been fascinated by woman as alterity, lesbian feminism holds that "woman" is an essentializing fiction that masks the existence of *women*, who in their diversity are very much a historical phenomenon. Furthermore, unlike heterosexual psychoanalytic readings from Freud to Lacan, lesbian sexuality posits woman as *presence* rather than absence or lack.[6]

Woman ceases to be merely temptation, or a figure of the desired. A woman can be writer, not just muse.

The analysis developed in the United States and France by lesbian feminist theorists can serve as a useful catalyst for work in this area to be done in Latin America. While I have previously questioned the extent to which foreign critical concepts can be used in analyzing Latin American texts, I have also claimed that going outside a repressive culture has made it possible for lesbian writers to write openly about lesbianism.[7] It is no doubt true that foreign definitions and theoretical constructs can go only so far in theorizing lesbian texts and naming lesbian experience in Latin America, but the debate can be opened up with the tools these lesbian-feminist theorists have begun to fashion and hone.[8]

There remains the question of the definition of lesbian literature and lesbian criticism. In fact, the category "lesbian" itself is contested. Marilyn Frye, for example, argues that the word "lesbian" is as yet undefinable, because "lesbians' existence is not countenanced by the dominant conceptual scheme" (Frye, 153). Ann Ferguson, Jacquelyn Zita, and Kathryn Pyne Addelson do attempt to construct —and then question— definitions of "lesbian" as they grapple with Adrienne Rich's notion of lesbianism as resistance to patriarchal dominance. Bonnie Zimmerman exhaustively rehearses the difficulties of definition in dealing with lesbian literary criticism: "The critic will need to consider whether a lesbian text is one written by a lesbian (and, if so, how do we determine who is a lesbian?), one written about lesbians (which might be by a heterosexual woman or by a man) or one that expresses a lesbian "vision" (which has yet to be satisfactorily described)" (Zimmerman, 188). Without attempting to resolve the problem of definitions, Bertha Harris sees the emergence of new lesbian literary forms, set free from male tradition and evolving from the "monster literature" she claims it necesssarily is in patriarchy (Harris, 8). The very notion of "lesbian literary forms" raises theoretical issues such as authorial intention and the relationship of biography to the literary text. The fact that it is too early, and probably strategically unwise, to settle on definitions just yet, does not mean that we are exempt from dealing with these and other issues.

GENDER AND SEXUALITY

According to social scientists Suzanne Kessler and Wendy McKenna, gender is determined in culture by means of a complex interaction of gender assignment, gender attribution and gender identity.[9] On this interpretation sexuality does not necessarily play a major role in the construction of gender. The relation between sexuality identity —heterosexual, homosexual, bisexual, asexual— and gender identity is itself complex and historically and culturally determined. In cultures that are ideologically heterosexual, and in which women are, if not reduced to their sexual-procreative function at least primarily seen with reference to that function, to call a woman a lesbian is to come close to calling into question her gender and therefore her deepest sense of self. In such cultures homosexual behavior might result in a confusion about gender —anyone attracted to a member of one sex must, by definition, belong to the other. On the other hand, gender might exist in a less oppressive system, in which the sexual definitions of women are differently construed. In fact, we are now seeing among feminists in the United States and elsewhere a desire to retain gender difference, obviously a precondition of retaining the category "women," while undoing gender hierarchy.

The nature of the relationship between gender identity and sexuality identity in women is closely tied to the extent to which lesbianism is understood as a political choice as well as an intimate behavior.[10] For women whose lesbianism is an affirmation of womanhood expressed in their total commitment to women, being a lesbian means embracing and valuing the self as a woman as well as valuing other women. Sexual expression may be the most important element of this commitment or it may play a negligible part. On the other hand, and in the extreme, lesbianism may be seen as a rejection of womanhood, in that women get defined only as the sexual complement of men so that the individual attracted to a woman can not, by definition, be a woman herself. Underlying both conceptualizations is a radical refusal of gender norms. In the latter, androcentric/phallocratic, case the word "woman" stays fixed within its rigid definition and the individual breaks free to be a man or a monster, but no longer a woman, while in the former, feminist, case the individual woman breaks free of the rigid role definition, taking the concept "woman" with her.

Vera, Sergio Toledo's 1987 movie produced in Brazil, shows conflicting ways in which sexuality and gender intersect. Within a culture forcefully divided along gender lines, and with that division clearly marking woman as vulnerable and violated, particularly within the institutionalized world of the orphanage where Vera Bauer goes through puberty, Vera and the other strong girls in the orphanage redefine themselves as men and create a simulated patriarchal family structure. The girls assign themselves and each other social genders that do not obviate biological categories. Pronouns clash with nouns in such dialogue as, "She's going to be your father," or "Paizão is my grandfather. My father (another girl) is her son." Vera becomes a male syntactically: that is, she takes the place of "man" in the structure of the orphanage, but she retains the morphology of a woman.

The strong girls, redefined as men, demand obedience but also offer protection and even affection. When Paizão, the dominant girl, leaves the orphanage she bequeathes her power to the chosen "son," Vera, in order to make sure the other, weaker, girls survive. Vera thus defines herself socially/ syntactically as a man before she is fully aware of her sexual feelings. When she does feel tenderness toward one of the other girls the viewer recognizes the beginnings of sexual attraction. But lesbian sexuality in the orphanage remains suppressed and barely acknowledged. The family relationships the girls set up are generational: there are grandfathers, fathers and daughters, but no wives, and the personal services we see the daughters render are not of a sexual nature.[11] Vera's love for her seductive and vulnerable friend is expressed in terms of tenderness, protectiveness, and comfort. What is acknowledged as sex is the brutal and coercive behavior perpetrated by the older male guards on the girls.

It is when Vera leaves the orphanage, trying to come to terms with her identity, that she decides to be a man morphologically as well as syntactically. She changes her sexually ambiguous clothing (jeans and workshirt) for the prestigious masculine signature costume of suit and tie, and openly publicizes her attraction to Clara, a self-proclaimed heterosexual woman who nevertheless refuses to enter into what she characterizes as oppressive long term relationships with men. After first telling her that women don't interest her sexually, Clara becomes willing to enter into a sexual relationship with Vera, since the promise of a new kind of relationship between equals appeals to her. But Vera channels her feelings into traditional gender terms, insisting on her maleness.

According to one viewer, Vera comes close to creating the category "lesbian" but fails.[12] She identifies herself as a male first, and then begins to want women *as a man*. Instead of envisioning different forms of sexuality available to her as a woman, Vera tries on a different gender identity. When she first cross-dresses she succeeds in convincing Clara's parents, whom she has not previously met, that she really is a man. At the same time, she acts in a gentle, nurturing, traditionally feminine way toward Clara's son. In her relationship with Clara, however, Vera mimics —in fact winds up in a painful parody of— overbearing, sexually possessive machista behavior. For her protector, the kind, intellectually and socially powerful man who tries to fit Vera into Brazilian culture after she has been brutalized in the orphanage, Vera's gender transgression is childish and irresponsible. Though his intentions are good, he operates fully within the phallocratic system and cannot, therefore, help her. His attempt to integrate Vera into Brazilian society depends on his belief that the brutalization she experienced at the orphanage resulted in temporarily aberrant behavior. He "understands" that Vera's coworkers, his social and intellectual inferiors, reject her crossdressing because they believe it is "unnatural" for the young woman to exhibit such behavior. While they undoubtedly perceive Vera's crossdressing as an announcement of sexual preference, it is the claim of maleness they most fear.[13]

For Vera, sexuality is an effect of gender; and sexuality identity is not separable from gender identity. In Vera's inner world there is no such thing as a lesbian: Her attraction to Clara must be a result of her being a man and functions as retroactive proof that she is a man. Vera cannot be a lesbian; since a lesbian is first a woman —and Vera denies her womanhood. That is, her gender identity, however tenuous, is masculine.[14] Clara recognizes that a relationship based on sameness is potentially liberating, but Vera is incapable of disassembling gender hierarchy, particularly once she has decided to join the dominant gender. At the end when she is confronted with evidence of her womanhood —her menstrual blood— she suffers a psychic break.

Vera Bauer resists being oppressed as a woman, but she is unsuccessful in her resistance because she does not question the structure in which women's oppression operates. Her rebellion is individualistic and, given the terms of the culture, wrongheaded and impossible. It is only by questioning the terms of the construct itself that she could possibly begin to break free.

Because she believes that she must reject her womanhood both to keep from being victimized and to act sexually with another woman, Vera is severely troubled by her body. She reacts violently when she thinks she is being observed undressing at the orphanage, she binds her breasts and she refuses to get undressed, or even to become aroused, while making love to Clara. It is her extreme disjuncture with her body, her refusal to acknowledge it, that ultimately wrecks her, since her woman's body simply won't go away.

While *Vera* documents the destruction of its protagonist due to the cultural proscription of lesbianism, Sylvia Molloy's novel, *En breve cárcel*, presents an already lesbian protagonist in retreat from culture. Like Vera Bauer, who announces her love for Clara by publishing a poem dedicated to her, Molloy's character is a writer whose writing is bound up in her lesbianism.[15] Also like Vera, the unnamed protagonist of Molloy's novel is alienated from her body. She is, however, by no means uncomfortable or unhappy with her lesbianism.[16] If at the end of *Vera* the disjuncture between the character's body and her gender identity results in fragmentation —the character's physical being is disbursed in multiple t.v. monitor images—, Molloy's novel charts the restoration of the lesbian body. In *En breve cárcel*, the text is a recuperation of the body, necessitated by and in a patriarchal structure that disallows the female body for itself (por sí and para sí). In the novel, as in the film, it is the character's sexuality, not just her gender, that most forcefully elucidates the dispossession of the body. For a reader to repress the question of sexual affinity and marginalize the lesbian aspect with the implication that it is not meaningful, as critics of *En breve cárcel* have, is to do violence to the novel and to reinscribe the silence around lesbianism that Molloy, in her text, has broken. Since the almost obsessive interiority of this novel can be understood as a consequence of the invisiblity of lesbianism of the culture, to remarginalize lesbianism in the criticism of the novel is profoundly ironic.[17]

Published in 1981, *En breve carcel*, Molloy's first novel has already had a certain amount of scholarly attention paid to it. Insofar as I have been able to ascertain, however, that attention has been paid only by women critics.[18] While the published critics of Molloy's novel, Francine Masiello and Magdalena García Pinto, have not tried to disguise the fact that the novel concerns lesbian characters, neither have they seen fit to foreground the lesbianism in the text. I want to make it clear that I find these readings extremely useful pieces of criticism. At the very least, they made my foray into Molloy's text a lot less lonely, and their readings in many ways lit my way through the novel. But they both marginalize lesbianism.

García Pinto begins by saying "La primera novela de Sylvia Molloy [. . .] sorprende por su prosa tersa, su tono contenido y por un modo narrativo novedoso " (687), despite the fact that none of these characteristics is particularly surprising in a writer who has spent a good part of her career studying the work of Jorge Luis Borges. Lesbianism, which *is* a surprise —particularly in a writer who has spent a good part of her career studying the work of Jorge

Luis Borges—is not mentioned as a surprising, or any other kind, of element. When García Pinto first suggests there might be lesbianism in the text she does so with consummate ambiguity: "En *En breve cárcel* la representación de recuerdos y sueños genera fragmentos textuales que forman el tejido del *récit*, al cual se bordan una serie de textos que contienen una suerte de meditación sobre *el amor y las relaciones personales entre mujeres* y un discurso sobre la escritura de ficción, todos articulados por una narradora que se plantea desde el inicio como sujeto de la narración" (688, emphasis added).[19] While in one reading of the sentence "entre mujeres" can refer to both "amor" and "relaciones interpersonales", in an equally grammatically correct reading "entre mujeres" can modify nothing more than "relaciones personales" suggesting that "amor" carries its unmarked meaning —heterosexual love. It is not until several pages into the essay that we finally find the unambiguous "las dos amantes" (690).

Francine Masiello does a brilliant job in showing the relationship between space and the production of the subject in an article that places Molloy in the context of "la narrativa rioplatense moderna" (103). While it is incontestable that Molloy belongs in this company, there are other contexts— lesbian narrative, to be precise— into which she might be as readily placed. Critics have noted "that lesbian literature is characterized by the use of the continuous present, unconventional grammar and neologism; and that it breaks boundaries between art and the world, between events and our perceptions of them, and between past, present and the dream world" and that before the advent of lesbian feminist writing "the lesbian character creates for herself a mythology of darkness, a world in which she moves through dreams and shadows" (Zimmerman, 195; Stanley, 18).[20] These descriptions of lesbian narrative sound like readings of Molloy, and in fact are remarkably like descriptions of the contemporary Latin American novel. Insofar as the broad categories — lesbian writing and Latin American writing— derive from late twentieth century cultures in a conscious process of creating themselves within complex and often painful political circumstances, it is not surprising that they have found similar formal solutions. My point is that Masiello chooses to locate *En breve cárcel* in one of these categories to the exclusion of the other, while the text fits in both.

Nevertheless, Masiello's formalist analysis seems less deliberate in its marginalization of lesbianism than García Pinto's. Finessing the lesbian question by eschewing discussion of content altogether, Masiello takes a swipe at "heterosexual legality" in the second half of the piece that indicates an awareness of the political and hermeneutical issues at stake.[21] Still, at the beginning Masiello uses "feminist" as a code word for "lesbian" in describing the textual project as "una resistencia narrativa específica cuya articulación toma forma por medio de una reconstrucción feminista de la realidad" (104). Though I agree that Molloy's work articulates a "specific narrative resistance", I believe that the "reconstruction of reality" that is going on within the text is not feminist but lesbian in its least political variation. Feminism suggests some sort of interaction with societal structures —a political consciousness— which is thoroughly lacking in the protagonist of *En breve cárcel*. What we have in the novel is the protagonist/writer who constructs her text in articulation with two other women, who have been both her and each other's lovers, and with her own past (where the emphasis on dreams suggests a Freudian, and, by extension, sexual, meaning to the past) —a very closed world. Molloy's character is not a feminist, or not discernably so, even if the text lends itself to a feminist reading. Her relationships with other women have no apparent etiology in the text —she is completely obsessed by her body, her writing and her dreams; the relationships with her lovers are deliberately wrenched from their cultural context. Her flight at the end of the novel is to no specific place —it is simply away from the places she has been before. This is not to say that Molloy's final object may not be to come up with a new way to write novels that valorizes women's interactions with each other and a particular sort of interiority which can later be connected to a larger feminist project — indeed my claiming her novel for a lesbian-feminist reading suggests that this may be the case.[22] But the "reconstruction of reality" that occurs within the text does not go beyond the self. When the world finally enters — paradoxically by means of the dreams that demand to be transcribed faithfully and therefore reveal the real-world place names that connect the women back to the places they inhabit, the writer's text comes to an end.

While at first sight the glance-averting approaches Masiello and García Pinto take may appear to be done as a favor to Molloy, a claim that her book has universal appeal and should not be considered merely a lesbian text, such a move is analogous to criticism that claims Latin American writing for world literature, conveniently bypassing the cultural ground that gives it its essence. The painful investigation of self that is the center of Molloy's novel is an investigation of the lesbian body. It is about the creation of a text that gives form and meaning to a body that is culturally meaningless. And a woman's body is only free of meaning in Western culture if she has already refused the heterosexual meanings ascribed to it. This is the ground on which the novel is written, implicit in the text and crucial to it.

BODY AND TEXT

The human body is not just a physical phenomenon in the natural world. It is one of the most heavily burdened bearers of meaning in culture, and one of its richest sources of meaning derives from the gendered character of the body. The meaning of the body-gendered-female is tied to an ideological structure of heterosexuality —women's bodies "mean" in relation to men's needs —nurturance, sex, physical care, a respository for human physicality when what men value is intellectual or spiritual. *En breve cárcel*, as a text, takes as a focus the relation between body and writing wherein the body in question is not part of the heterosexual economy, but rather is in the process of forging new meanings. The text does not rehearse everything the writer's body is not —mother, wife, mistress, whore, celibate for God—, but rather repeatedly lights on the body as uncharted and unbounded. The text is so tightly focused, the room so claustrophobic, that unless we remember that we are readers reading and as such make the text meaningful in terms of the knowledge we bring to it, we can forget that outside the room the writer must walk in a heterosexual world. Her few forays into the street are brief and laden with anxiety. The decision to contain the body, to closet it as it were, functions as a textual strategy that permits the refusal (or perhaps shedding) of old meanings and offers the physical space in which the writer can risk formlessness in her search for form. The writer's body is not what the world expects it to be, but it is not yet anything else.

Since there are no meanings "out there" already made that could be employed usefully to shape this body, it is in danger of collapsing. It is crucial to *make* meanings so that the lesbian body is neither dismembered, nor absorbed by heterosexual meanings/needs/interpretations. In fact, the lesbian body has been taken up by male heterosexual representation, usually in a pornographic or quasi pornographic context, where lesbian sexuality is enacted for men. So despite the fact that in *Vera* and *En breve cárcel* the body is no longer doing what, according to the dominant culture, it is supposed to be doing, it is possible that, in the movie particularly, given the visual medium, the women's aborted lovemaking might get reabsorbed into the male sexual economy; two women's bodies, overtly sexualized, offered up to the male gaze.[23] While this may well be an issue for the novelist, the writer/protagonist of *En breve cárcel* encloses herself in her room away from any uninvited intrusion. Lesbianism in *En breve cárcel* is normative to the extent that the heterosexual world is excluded.

Her body, formless and always threatening to disintegrate is, not surprisingly, foreign to the writer. "El cuerpo —su cuerpo— es de otro. Desconocimiento del cuerpo, contacto con el cuerpo, placer ó violencia, no importa; el cuerpo es de otro" (31). Her childhood memories include no bodily memories, except as they refer to someone else. No recollection of pleasure, none of pain, and she only remembers her illnesses because they have been rendered textual —her parents told her the stories of her being born

with a broken collarbone and of a serious childhood illness. What she recalls independently is not the sensation
of pain or illness but the presence of her parents, that
which is external to her. Similarly, her efforts at control
and containment begin with the more manageable task of
mastering the environment when she herself threatens to
go out of control. As a child she learned to keep sane by
regulating her environment, making sure her room was
in perfect order. Later, when she is ill, she gets her room in
order, under control, before she gives in to the sickness.

As an adult illness, violence, and pain become ways to
know the body. In a step toward wholeness, the writer has
to acknowledge her own sick body —her mother is not
there to do it for her. Science and society can confirm the
illness (the thermometer shows she has fever; the
concierge comments on the way she looks), but only after
she recognizes the illness herself.[24] Once the writer has
done this she deliberately exacerbates the distance between
mind and body —alienating herself from her pain, trying
to force her body to accept food, until, pushed to its limits,
the split is healed and she can sleep "entera" (107). Push-
ing the body to its limits is to encounter her own boundaries, or even to find out if they exist. In an invocation of
her body's presence, the writer does violence to herself,
seeks pain (33-34). "También ella se ha dejado pegar, consciente" (33). The writer also, with no little pleasure, in-
flicts pain: she invokes a childhood memory of hitting her
sister with a belt. Pain inflicted on the sister is tantamount
to pain inflicted on the self, however; since the writer
comes closest to experienceing her own body as a child by
observing the naked body of her sister. Looking at her own
body is another form of violence —watching it age. "A su
cuerpo lo violenta, a solas, con la mirada" (34). Yet her
alienation from her body is so complete that often she
doesn't even feel its pain: "Los tajos, las mutilaciones, son
sin duda dolorosos pero está tan acostumbrada a las grietas, desde chica, que las imagina y aunque se las inflija deja
de sentirlas" (35).

The writer's self-assigned task is to construct a text that
will hold her. She feels her body is forever threatening to
come apart. Early in the novel she remembers her lover

Vera (not of the movie) telling her, in French, that when they first met she looked uncomfortable in her skin,[25] and skin remains an important motif: "Mal en su piel, mal de su piel, irritada con esa apariencia llena de fallas, de grietas. De chica le impresionaban mucho más que los esqueletos —que siempre le parecían cómicos— esos cuerpos que ilustran el sistema muscular en los diccionarios" (15-16). She has repeated nightmares of skinlessness, of lack of boundaries and vulnerability. "Más de una vez ha soñado con despellejamientos, con su propio depellejamiento. Por ejemplo, se ha desdoblado, queda como una corteza pero no se ve, ve en cambio a un muchacho enfermo que tiene de la cintura para abajo el cuerpo despellejado, y a ella le ha tocado conservar la piel inútil de él" (16) She is "mal protegida por su piel ineficaz" (16).[26]

Martha Noel Evans, writing on contemporary French literature, recently used an almost identical metaphor in a way that helps explain the fascination and repulsion we see in this text toward the flayed body. "One might say that the mask of male discourse adheres to the female body; when the mask is dismantled, the body parts come with it" (185). To the extent that the culture's dominant discourse is internalized as our own, it gives shape —meaning— to our bodies both as external and self-generated constraint. Like Molloy, Monique Wittig removes the skin from the lesbian body:

> I discover that your skin can be lifted layer by layer, I pull it, it lifts off, it coils above your knees, I pull starting at the labia, it slides the length of the belly, fine to extreme transparency, I pull starting at the loins, the skin uncovers the round muscles and trapezii of the back, it peels off up to the nape of the neck, I arrive under your hair, m/y fingers traverse its thickness, I touch your skull, I grasp it with all my fingers, I press it, I gather the skin over the the whole of the cranial vault, I tear off the skin brutally beneath the hair, I reveal the beauty of the shining bone traversed by blood vessels . . . (Wittig, *The Lesbian Body*, 17).

The removal of the skin becomes an act of love that on one level opens the woman to her lover and on another permits a new definition of self and body that includes the lover.

This peeling away of the skin causes the body to spill over, to flow outward. It is associated, in other words, with excess. Indeed, the writer's desire to gain control over her body, expressed throughout the text, is modulated by her desire to throw off restraint and exceed limits. Both these desires are informed by her sense that her body is alien to her. Giving the body over to pain is connected to her desire to defy limits: "En espejos enfrentados vio en una ocasion una de sus nalgas, surcadas de líneas rojas que interrumpían cada tanto los moretones dejados por una hebilla. Resultado de un encuentro más —y el último— con alguien que estaba decidido a sacarla de sí misma" (33). This sort of sexual excess is what the writer values in Renata, the lover whose absence is the generating factor in the text: "Con Renata ha vivido —como no con Vera— la falta de límites, ha compartido un lugar (que ahora se le antoja este lugar, donde escribe) donde todo le parecía posible, donde cabía el exceso: gritos, gestos, exageraciones, violencia, todo lo que sintió como vedado" (27). The notion of space here is no longer the physically measurable space of the room, but the mental/spiritual/sexual space of "no moral/cultural boundaries" in particular acts. "Donde escribe" —"where she writes"— is the literary space she is forging for this text.

Simultaneous with her desire for the order imposed by narration, the writer wants to break out of that which confines her (71). Significantly, the only explicit sex scene in the novel represents both the defiance of limits and their imposition. Renata's insistence she remain standing during the encounter is a restriction of the writer's movements, but the pleasure, humiliation and muted violence of the lovemaking are forms of excess.

Ultimately, the old skin (which in this text has already been rejected, if not entirely shed) must be replaced by new. Not surprisingly, the act of writing is repeatedly figured in *En breve cárcel* as the creation of an organic, self-generated cover. The pages of the text become like layers of skin, or scales —text as a bodily secretion that contains, protects, and gives form to the body. The narrator struggles

to find this metaphor and offers it up with no little sense
of accomplishment:

> Una clave, un orden para este relato. Sólo atina a ver capas,
> estratos, como en los segmentos de la corteza terrestre que pro-
> ponen los manuales ilustrados. No: como las diversas capas de
> piel que cubren músculos y huesos, imbricadas, en desapacible
> contacto. Estrecimiento, erizamiento de la superficie: ¿quién no
> ha observado, de chico, la superficie interior de una costra ar-
> rancada y la correspondiente llaga rosada, sin temblar? En ese
> desgarramiento inquisidor se encuentran clave y orden de esta
> historia (23).

It is only after the story is fully written, however, that
the strands the writer is pulling together —the story of
Vera, the story of Renata, the story of her childhood—
might in fact come together to reveal "como las capas de
piel en el libro de anatomía, el sistema de su imbricación"
(24). On the other hand, it might not. Language holds no
easy promise for the writer, since it figures so prominently
in the cultural system that has produced the bodily configuration she refuses.[27]

Molloy rings numerous variations on the theme of
verbal representation as the generation of skin.[28] The story
that Vera, the writer's lover, tells is " [un] relato que se
deleitaba en sí mismo, piel que había logrado componer"
(22). Later, during a reverie both produced and captured in
a session of free writing, the writer's words take on a float-
ing corporeality and attach themselves to her body:

> Ve que las palabras se levantan una vez más, como se levanta
> ella, agradece la letra ondulante que la enlaza, reconoce las
> cicatrices en un cuerpo que acaricia. Vuelven a romperse cuerpo
> y frase, pero no en la misma cicatriz: se abren de manera dis-
> tinta, le ofrecen una nueva fisura que esta tarde acepta, en la
> que no ve una violencia mala, en la que sospecha un orden
> (p.67).

Still another version of the text as secretion is writing as
exorcism, expelling the words so not only do they no
longer poison from within, but "lo que escribe es una
manera de ir tachando para seguir adelante" (139).

At one point the writer connects the completion of her task with death: "Se pregunta si es miedo o impotencia, si teme morirse escribiendo —*incrustar una anécdota y luego desaparecer*" (20 emphasis added). But what dies at the end of the novel is the possibility of any future relationship with Renata or Vera. Once the skin or scab or shell is encrusted, the text made material, the writer goes away, both leaving the text behind and taking it with her. The snoopy narrator, who doggedly records the writer's writing, retains her text —the one we read—, while the writer flies off wrapped in the protective pages of her manuscript: "Ha decidido armarse para el ejercicio: no hay alcohol, ni droga, ni tabaco que la ayuden. [. . .] Desamparada, se aferra a las páginas que ha escrito para no perderlas" (158).

Through words/texts/pages/voice the writer longs to order and delineate, create the boundaries between the pleasures of writing, sex, and dreams (71). Similarly, she will create order out of the chaos of events that touch her day: "Escribe hoy lo que hizo, lo que no hizo, para verificar fragmentos de un todo que se le escapa. Cree recuperarlos, con ellos intenta —o inventa— *una constelación suya.* " (13, emphasis added). She chooses in her writing to make a form that will contain and order chaos.

In a recuperative move, skin becomes a product of voice, and voice is associated with health. "En cambio no se ve sin voz (como no se ve sin piel) y acaso el riesgo de esa imaginación sea su major amenaza: reconoce la salud, se aferra a ella, en términos de una entonación. Algo, la voz ronca de su tía, la voz cascada de Renata, su propia voz cuando escribe, algo, una piel de voces, para entonar los fragmentos" (35). Here the writer combines the fear of being without skin —vulnerable and raw— with the surety of always having a voice. The "no se ve sin" in one case is the fear of losing —skin; in the other it's the knowledge of having —voice. They come together at the end of the paragraph when her own writerly voice meshes with the voices of her aunt and her lover, transformed into a skin that "tunes the fragments." "Entonar" with its aural connotations of music, also carries the meaning of harmonize or modulate, bring together the disparate pieces of the fragmented self into a coherent whole. And it also recalls its reflexive meaning: "to strengthen the muscular fibres by means of tonic medicine." Skin (or, more precisely, its equivalent) and voice are further equated in a pleasurable way: Vera's voice is like the sleeve of her black velvet jacket.

Neither Molloy nor her writer is "writing the body," but rather spinning it a protective covering—weaving a skin, making an order, giving shape. Feminists have called this naming, coming out, finding a voice, empowerment. When she has completed the text, the writer emerges from her room/cocoon —which had been a temporary and only partially protective covering—no longer vulnerable and formless, but rather defiant, clad in the text she spun out of her need. Lest this seem like an overly optimistic result, we are reminded that her fear remains, though she now can be in the world despite it.

Although the production of the text is, finally, a healthy act, it is not without its difficulties and perils. The first chapter of the novel can be read as the avoidance of storytelling, since the story to be told is so painful:

> Hoy no quiere hablar más de Vera, no quiere extrañar más a Renata. [. . .] Desvía una narración, se dice que la dilata para contarla mejor; por fin la posterga porque no la puede contar. Quisiera que estos trozos de relato fueran como los cuentos de Vera, mejores que los cuentos de Vera: imperturbables. Pero teme anotarlos porque sabe muy bien que le duele mucho contar esta historia" (24-25).

The loss of the lover, Renata, is doubly the occasion for the text. It is both an important element in the narration, and when Renata does not appear, the writer occupies herself with writing. So Renata's absence from the writer's room effects her presence in the text. In perhaps the only truly amusing moment in the novel, Renata learns that her ex-lover is writing a book and so she pays her a visit, behaves perfectly charmingly, and rewrites a little of their personal history so that she will come off well as a character.

Renata knows, as does the writer, that stories can do harm. Renata tells gratuitous lies that fail to hide her infidelities, and the writer elaborates tales of infidelity with which to wound her lover. Vera is also a storyteller who uses her sad tales of betrayal to seduce and control potential and actual lovers. And the writer hates the idea that Renata has probably turned her into an anecdote with which to entertain her current lover.

The distinction between spoken and written stories is also a factor here. Because it feels like a breach of confidence, the writer does not repeat Vera's childhood story to her hosts —but she goes home and writes it down into this narrative (85). Spoken texts too easily do harm; written ones are healing. In the end, though, writing and speech converge in the desire for communication. The writer wants to write a spoken language as Renata sleeps, to declare her love for Renata: "Renata duerme y ella quiere escribir, una vez más, en este cuarto. Decir que la quiere a Renata, decirle —me haces falta. Decirle: Renata, yo estoy en tu cuerpo y por tu cuerpo, como por el mío hablo. [. . .] Pero Renata duerme" (157). What she longs for here is an integration of writing and speech, a way to express the integration of herself and this lover, to write a spoken declaration of love. The narrator then backs up and shows us that she *has* been writing (this?): "Deja de escribir." Paradoxically, she can write, but cannot speak, and both because Renata is asleep.

GEOGRAPHY

The dialectical relation between containment and excess played out in terms of the writer's body is echoed in the treatment of geographical space in the novel. The text establishes a relationship between place and self that it also works to suppress: "Para viajar es necesario saber de dónde se parte" (148). The relationship is elsewhere figured in atypical grammar, where the adverb of place wrests new meaning from the verbs: "Soy donde fui —o donde no fui—, soy donde seré" (148).

The writer is a traveller who moves between three continents. Yet the issue of language is buried—it is implied that she speaks English with Renata and in French with

Vera—, and with few exceptions such action as there is in this text takes place in tightly enclosed spaces. *En breve cárcel* is, in a way, an exercise in lesbian separatism. In order to construct and solidify meaning, to the extent they are able, the writer removes her self, and Molloy removes her story, from the heterosexual world.

The figuring of geography in this text is problematic. The relationship between places and names, which attach them to a reality external to the novel but at the same time are fictionalized as part of a literary text, is not easily resolved. The writer has experimented with various ways of dealing with the problem, and the narrator recognizes these ploys as a form of flirtation. The sexually nuanced term is intriguing in this context, since part of the reason for suppressing the names of the cities is to forge a new and separate lesbian space:

> "Querría describirla, evocar el primer encuentro hace cuatro años en casa de Vera, en pleno centro de aquella ciudad sofocada por la nieve. Ciudad que no nombra por ahora, que acaso no nombre: en cada nueva copia de este texto propone geografías vagas, una latitud frígida aceptable, un invento nevado que no la convence, que tacha. Querría no nombrar, por coquetería, con desenfado. Sabe que nombrar es un rito, ni más ni menos importante que la inscripción de una frase trivial. Pero también sabe que los nombres, las iniciales que había escrito en una primera versión, han sido sustituidos; la máscara del nombre que recuerda, del nombre con que dijo, con que creyó que decía, ha sido reemplazada por otra, más satisfactoria porque más lejana. Se pregunta por qué disimula nombres literalmente insignificantes cuando pretende transcribir, con saña, una realidad vivida" (19).

Barely eleven pages before the end of the novel the narrator, following the writer's decision, finally reveals the external geography of the novel.

> "En estos sueños que sin cesar la hacen visitar ciudades—Amberes, París, Roma, Buenos Aires— donde con su madre, donde con su hermana, recorre espacios sin saber adónde va. En todas hay un punto secreto y ella no lo encuentra.
> Ha tenido que mencionar nombres de ciudades. Esto la molesta, pero son parte de sus sueños. La ciudad nevada donde conoció a Renata y volvió a ver a Vera es la ciudad de Buffalo, en el es-

tado de Nueva York. La ciudad donde volvió a encontrar a Renata y Vera es París. Y la ciudad donde creció y —si le dieran
la elección— volvería a crecer, es la ciudad de Buenos Aires.
Ha dado claves, se siente tranquila. Pero sabe que ha caído en
estas revelaciones tardías para no seguir enfrentándose con
presencias femeninas, para protegerse de ellas (147).

Once the cities have made their way into her dreams,
the writer concludes that they are indeed part of her internal landscape and therefore must be revealed. It is also
only fair that she reveal the cities' names to the astute
reader who has read the clues along the way and deserves
the reward of finding out for sure if s/he was right.[29] But
telling also serves a psychological cause: to protect the
writer from the presence of the women she knew in those
places.

Giving the places a real geography engulfs the women
in the meanings extant in those places and summons the
preexisting definitions of relationships, body, texts that
she's been working, painfully, to undo and remake. But it
doen't work, since after naming the places and invoking
the ready-made reality they come with, the women reap-
pear: "la acosan, tremendas" (147), whereupon she claims,
with bravado "Yo las convoqué."[30] She then tempers her
statement in recognition of her need of these figures: "Yo
quería —madre, hermana, amante— que estuvieran conmigo, yo no vivo sino por ustedes" (147). This final
admission effectively brings the narration to a resloution.

These cities that press their meanings onto the characters are rendered usable when they become dream spaces
for the writer, her mother, and her sister that at least contain the promise of new meaning, even if the writer cannot as yet get hold of it ("En todas hay un punto secreto y
ella no lo encuentra" (147). Real geography, in the company of the mother and the sister, can, potentially, be
transformed. The mythical geography with which her father exhorts her, on the other hand, is static; and it is ultimately rejected.

The internalized voice of the dead father tells the writer
to go to the shrine of Artemis the fertility goddess, the
other aspect of Diana the virgin huntress, to whom the
writer is drawn. The geography of this dream is unlike the

other geography of the novel since in a material sense it is not anywhere. It only exists as a cultural imperative, the father's exhortation to the daughter to worship at the shrine of heterosexuality and conventional motherhood. "Sabe que al decirle Efeso está rompiendo la geografía apenas nombrada de este relato para llamarle la atención sobre un lugar único al que nunca podrá llegar" (153). The temple of Artemis on Ephesus was burned down the night Alexander the Great was born. There is literally no way to go there. What her father wants is for her to return to a heterosexual mythology that in fact no longer exists.

MAPMAKING

The most obvious geographical question this novel presents is, Why Buffalo? Everybody writes between Paris and Buenos Aires: that's practically a canonical trope in Argentine literature. But Buffalo? Molloy lived there, but since she doesn't exploit the local color (except as shades of white and gray, the colors of snow), the only explanation that makes sense is that *En breve cárcel* is to some extent autobiographical. The author's porteño childhood and her trips to Paris support such a reading. In no other way can we assert the autobiographical nature of the text, without going outside the book itself. But the book tells us (on the back jacket, in author's notes written, presumably, by her) that the geography of the novel is congruent with Molloy's personal geography.

Molloy plays with the autobiographical mode —her narrator reports on a writer who is piecing together the contours of a textual self—, but she knows enough about autobiography as a genre to know that what her writer is writing is not an autobiography.[31] It is, rather, "una serie de violencias salteadas" that have touched her and others (68). The writer's text lacks both a sustained narrative and a focus on an individuated self, and in particular it avoids the single most important characteristic of Spanish American autobiography identified by Molloy, to wit, the subject's desire to be representative: "The Spanish American 'I' (if one dare generalize in this fashion) seems to rely more than other 'I's' —to rely in a nearly ontological manner— on a sort of national recognition. Representativeness and identity are closely linked in Spanish American self-writing." (Molloy, "At face value," 3). Molloy's writer not only eschews any sense of representativeness; she hides her geographical origins until the very end, so that she ostensibly cannot even have representativeness thrust upon her. Of course the disenfranchised lesbian is not likely to constitute herself as representative of her culture or even of her sex as, say, Victoria Ocampo did.[32]

Since she reads the writer's text in order to fashion her own, the narrator of *En breve cárcel* is connected to the reader as well as to the writer. The narrator has access to the writer's written words, the texts that she produces — including the writing she does in the room waiting for Renata and the already transcribed dreams she keeps in a folder left over from when she was a student. So the narrator becomes, above all, a reader of texts and an explorer of the writing process.

I have been deliberate in calling Molloy's protagonist "the writer", both because that is what she is, and also because the term constantly threatens to refer to Molloy herself. While it is critically fashionable to proclaim the death of the author, this text not only represents women writing, but it places the narrator in uncomfortably close proximity to the protagonist. Events get reported with very little lag time —barely enough to see that there are events that are being edited out of what the writer is writing, not just by the writer but by the voice narrating her as well. The claustrophobic sense of space is so present that there seems to be no place for the narrator to be but in the room with the writer. The relationship between the narrator and the writer is like the relationship between the writer and the other women characters. They are not conflated, but neither are they totally separable. They are bound to each other, similarly situated in the world (women writing/ women loving women/ beings with women's bodies), and their position in the universe depends on their relationship to each other.

In this text there is no individuated self. The writer does not break free of the others — Vera, Renata, mother and sister —she incorporates them into her text which is the shape she gives her self. The defining of a self through relationships with others is a frightening notion to a male writer-friend of hers, whose self is created through rigid boundaries separating him from "the other". But for her the idea of being a self in process and in relation is liberating.

> "El tiene miedo, rechaza la idea de que la novela que ha escrito integre la realidad no como objeto sino como relación vivida. Cuando lo oyó hablar se sintió tocada, se dio cuenta de que ella también corteja un espacio intermedio: reconoce que al transcribir ordena y se permite cambiar nombres pero pretende dilucidar, en un plano que sabe de antemano inseguro, un episodio cuyas posibilidades ignora, cuyos antecedentes fluctúan, y que querría definitivo" (20).

Though the promise of fixity is tempting (querría definitivo), she knows she seeks that intermediate space between chaos and control (Ella también corteja un espacio intermedio).[33]

At the end of the novel when, closed in on by the women she loves —mother, sister, Renata, Vera—, the writer declares that she bade them come: "Yo las convoqué" (147). But she corrects herself: she does not decide imperiously when and if they should appear, but rather she needs them: "Yo quería —madre, hermana, amante— que estuvieran conmigo, yo no vivo sino por ustedes" (147). These women have never been completely separable from her or each other, but now they form a whole, and together they achieve the recuperation of a past that gets beyond the father. The writer's bond with Vera and Renata enables her to dream the not so buried female past of mother and sister and supercede the dream of the father.[34]

FINAL WORDS

En breve cárcel ends at the brink of the writer's emergence into the world. Though unlike Toldeo's Vera Bauer she is strengthened, not destroyed, at the end of her story, like Vera, Molloy's writer does not challenge the world with a lesbian vision. Yet the very existence of these texts, film and novel, invite the feminist critic to a public reading that makes that challenge. *En breve cárcel* and *Vera* are two very different works. As a novel, one is singly authored, while the other, a film, is collaborative. One is written by a woman, the other written and directed by a man. Obviously, my concern in this paper has not been to identify lesbian-produced texts, but to engage texts to which lesbianism as an issue is central and, in my analysis, to respect that centrality in order to open a proscribed area to serious textual inquiry. *En breve cárcel* and *Vera* are two of the texts that break the long-held silence around lesbianism, opening up a space, as García Pinto says, that allows the conversation to begin.

NOTES

[1]Like all aphoristic statement's MacKinnon's oversimplifies to make a point.

[2]Any critique of homophobia and heterosexism to take hold in Latin America will undoubtedly attach itself to the left, just as traditional sexist attitudes and behavior that cross the political spectrum have become less respectable on the left with the rise of international feminism.   Perhaps the best known novelistic treatment of the relationship between politics and sexuality is Manuel Puig's *El beso de la mujer araña*, in which the revolutionary "hero" must question his sexism, his homophobia, and his class assumptions when he is confronted with his ostensibly apolitical homosexual cellmate.

[3]Bonnie Zimmerman recounts the decimation of a women's studies program that occured when the lesbian faculty were fired from their California university. Other, less obvious problems are the trivialization of the work and the difficulty in getting it published. In "Straight Minds," during an analysis of the ways discourse causes material oppression, Monique Wittig points out that what is outside dominant discourse gets labeled trivial, so it can't legitimately be brought in.

[4] Exceptions can be found primarily among critics who have lived for a considerable amount of time outside Latin America.

[5] The IV Encuentro Feminista Latinoamericano y del Caribe, reported on in the Peruvian feminist magazine *Viva* 13 (March 1988),19-27, esp. p. 22, included a lesbian workshop which generated the following goals: to gain space within the feminist movement, to build a lesbian identity, to reject discrimination. The publications from earlier Encuentros have also included reports from lesbian workshops, which, unlike other reports, were submitted without naming the workshop leaders.

[6] See Luce Irigaray, *This Sex Which Is Not One* for a discussion of the Freudian misreading of female sexuality.

[7] "Reading the Body Politic: Alicia Partnoy's *The Little School* and "The Monumental Time of *Los recuerdos del porvenir*" are examples of the first stance, while "Gender and Exile in Cristina Peri Rossi" takes the second position.

[8] For example, it is possible that gender definitions are tied to sexual behaviors differently in parts of Latin America than they are in the US, or that similar demonstrations of affection between women have different cultural meanings.

[9] Simply put, "gender identity" is the gender (male or female) the individual perceives him or herself to be, "gender attribution" is what others perceive the individual to be, and "gender assignment", made at birth, is a one-time —albeit crucial— form of gender attribution.

[10] I apologize for the clumsly term, "sexuality identity," but I could find no phrase that was both elegant and unambiguous to denote an individual's sense of her or himself as herterosexual, bisexual, lesbian, gay, etc.

[11] Ie: age, like gender, is an indicator of power, and like gender it is derived not from the natural world but from the power relations it legitimates.

[12] Naomi Scheman, personal conversation.

[13] In earlier heterosexist representations of lesbians on film (*The Killing of Sister George, The Fox*) one of the women is considered more

or less innocent, insofar as she is potentially redeemable for heterosexuality, a vicitim seduced by the evil masculine woman. The latter is to be punished for transgressing gender norms more than sexual ones. Similarly, in parts of Latin America, among men the active partner in homosexual relations retains his prestige as "male", while the penetrated partner is devalued as female.

14 On the other hand, Vera's coworkers and benefactor inisist she is a woman, and her cross-dressing and behavior toward Clara signifies to them that Vera is a lesbian. Gender attribution and gender identity are in colflict. The filmmaker enters into this conversation as well. While the character herself refuses to answer to that name, preferring the sexually ambiguous last name, Bauer, he titles his movie *Vera*, disposing the viewer to attribute to the protagonist a femaleness she rejects. Of course the character's choices are the filmmaker's as well. Toledo's choice of gendered title underscores the conflict in/of the film.

15The fact that they are writers also gives them access to their culture. Vera's benefactor is interested in rescuing her from the certain marginalization that is the typical Brazilian orphan girl's plight because she writes poetry. The relationship between Molloy's protagonist's writing and her culture will be discussed below.

16Furthermore, she is not locked into rigid gender categories: in her dreams the writer becomes a boy or identifies with male figures in non-sexual situations.

17I am indebted to Sara Evans for this insight.

18 Sara Castro-Klarén names Molloy as one of a group of Latin American women writers who might belong to a Latin American women's literary tradition, and Francine Masiello and Magdalena García Pinto each devote an article to *En breve cárcel*. In addition, Maribel Tamargo presented a paper on *En breve cárcel* at MLA in 1986.

19García Pinto's opening sentence mentions "una brecha" that Molloy opens in Latin American women's writing, but this seems not to be an allusion to lesbianism, attached as it is to narrative mode.

20Zimmerman here is referring to the work of Susan Wolfe and Julia Penelope Stanley.

21In her study of *El beso de la mujer araña* Laura Rice-Sayre also criticizes Masiello for a formalist reading that leads away from, rather than towards, a fully political reading of a text.   Given Masiello's commitment to scholarly work that maintains its relevance as a form of political practice, this is ironic.

[22]Since lesbianism is disobedience it is a handy metaphor for disruption and social change (cf. Albalucía Angel's *Las andariegas* and Reina Roffé's *Monte de Venus*).   However, lesbianism as defiance of patriarchy is a subtext at best in *En breve cárcel*, where the protagonist unpeels layers of her psyche in a self-exploration (though she denies that's her aim) stripped as thoroughly as possible of social/cultural/ historical context.   Though it would be nice to be able to claim this novel for feminism, in these postmodern times the critic is not likely to be in the business of reporting on authorial intention.   Furthermore, Molloy's other published texts hardly indicate a feminist politics. Molloy is best known as a prolific and incisive critic of Spanish American literature.   If the lesbian content of her novel places it at the margin of contemporary writing in Latin America, her criticism is well within the mainstream, dealing with such canonical writers as Borges, Sarmiento, Darío, and Rulfo, and such upright themes as the diffusion of Spanish American literature in France and the status of autobiography in Spanish America.   Her few forays off the path of the annointed —an article on Felisberto Hernández, another on Delmira Agustini— hardly constitute a break with mainstream criticism.

[23] Given the way the shots are framed, I do not believe this to be Toledo's intention.   Viewers accustomed to seeing women as objects of titillation might well reframe the scenes according to their own expectations, however.

[24]Cheri Register, in *Living with Chronic Illlness: Days of Patience and Passion*, describes this phenomenon.   Register's book documents the control chronically ill people come to experience over their illness when they can, in Register's words, name the unhealthy self.

[25]It is perhaps more than coincidence that this name, meaning "truth," is attached to lesbian characters in both the film and the novel.

[26]This fear of disintegration is figured throughout the novel, in both dream and memory.   One instance is the writer's recollection of the accident that killed her father and her aunt, with its emphasis on their broken bodies.

[27]Here I take issue with García Pinto where she quotes and amends Benvéniste: "Es en y por el lenguaje cómo el hombre [o la mujer por

supuesto] se constituye como sujeto" (688). García Pinto's bracketed feminist correction is a friendly insertion which unintentionally (I think) points to the very problem it means to solve by fiat. Men may have constituted themselves as subjects by means of words, but words have trapped women in meanings that threaten to constitute them as object (in a subject/object dichotomy) or absence (in the subject/other split). The idea that women might be able to constitute themselves as subjects through language is contested and problematized in the novel, where it's not at all clear that the protagonist will be able to constitute herself via language.

28The affirmative value of skin is underscored in the scene where the writer finally sleeps with Renata and the primary body reference is to the lover's skin: "Nunca tocó una piel, la piel de otro, como esa noche" (55).

29Either too clever or not clever enough, I was thrown off by the mention of White Plains, a suburb not of Buffalo but New York City.

30Molloy, in "Sentido de ausencias," an essay on the absence of women writers in her life, writes that she will make sure that in the future to be aware of the women writers who preceded her and accompany her. The verb she uses to bid them to her is the same one that the writer uses when she acknowledges her need for her mother and sister: "Es hora — o por lo menos lo es para mí— de reconocerme en una tradición que, sin que yo lo supiera del todo, me ha estado respaldando. No sólo eso; es hora de contribuir a *convocarla* en cada letra que escribo" (Molloy, "Sentido de ausencias," 488, emphasis added).

31As a prominent critic, Molloy is something of a public personage whose other published works also cast light on this novel. Her writer sits in a room forging this text, but what she meant to be doing was a safely ditstanced scholarly study of autobiography. As far as we know, the writer never wrote that piece, but Molloy did. She presented it to the Department of Romance Laguages at the University of Michigan in 1984, which subsequently published it in its journal, *Dispositio*.

32According to Molloy, "Victoria Ocampo, in her *Autobiografía* (1979-1983), [. . .] aspires to construct a figure, a *persona* representative of woman's role in Argentina at a given time" ("At Face Value," 3).

33I am not claiming some biologically determined way of understanding the self, divided forever along gender lines. In fact, I believe that issues of identity presented in this novel are also influenced by male writers: Molloy's 1982 article on Felisberto Hernández' autobiographical text, *Diario del sinvergüenza* brings up some of the issues of the problems of the unified self.   She quotes Hernández, "He andado buscando mi propio yo desesperadamente como alguien que quisiera agarrarse el alma con una mano que no es de él" (*Tierras de la memoria*, 69). And it is likely that her close reading of Borges has also made some mark on her thinking: "esa certeza de que no hay 'yo de conjunto'"(ibid.). She does not resolve the problem the way they do, however.

[34]Here I am in disagreement with Masiello, who considers the writer's relationships with Vera and Renata "nefastas relaciones de pareja," and later claims that "la relación entre Renata, Vera y la heroina delimita modos negativos de relacionarse" (110). I don't think Molloy is either modelling or judging the relationships —or that the novel has to do with getting free of these women.

WORKS CITED

Angel, Albalucía. *Las andariegas*. Barcelona: Biblioteca del Fénice, Editorial Argos Vergara, 1984.

Castro-Klarén, Sara. "La crítica literaria feminista y la escritora en América Latina." *La sartén por el mango: Encuentro de escritoras latinoamericanas*. Ed. Patricia Elena González and Eliana Ortega. Río Piedras, P.R.: Ediciones Huracán, 1984.

Clarke, Cheryl. "Lesbianism, an act of resistance." *This Bridge Called My Back: Writings by Radical Women of Color*. Ed. Cherríe Moraga and Gloria Anzaldúa. New York: Kitchen Table Women of Color Press, 1981.

Evans, Martha Noel. *Masks and Tradition: Women and Politics in 20th Century France*. Ithaca: Cornell University Press, 1987.

Ferguson, Ann, Jacqueline N. Zita, and Kathryn Pyne Anderson. "On 'Compulsory Heterosexuality and Lesbian Existence': Defining the Issues." *Signs. Journal of Women in Culture and Society*, 7:1 (Autumn 1981): 158-199.

Frye, Marilyn. "To See and Be Seen: The Politics of Reality." *The Politics of Reality: Esssays in Feminist Theory*, Trumansburg, NY: Crossing Press, 1983.

García Pinto, Magdalena. "La escritura de la pasión y la pasión de la escritura: *En breve cárcel*, de Silvia Molloy." *Revista Iberoamericana* 51: 132-133 (July-Dec. 1985): 687-696.

Harris, Bertha. "*What we mean to say:* Notes toward Defining the Nature of Lesbian Literature." *Heresies* Fall 1977: 5-8.

Irigaray, Luce. *This Sex Which Is Not One.* Translated by Catherine Porter with Caroline Burke. Ithaca: Cornell University Press, 1985.

Kaminsky, Amy. "Gender and Exile in Cristina Peri Rossi." *Continental, Latin American, and Francophone Women Writers: Selected Papers from the Wichita State University Conference on Foreign Literature, 1984-1985.* Ed. Eunice Myers and Ginette Adamson. Lanham, MD: University Press of America, 1987.

—. "The Monumental Time of *Los recuerdos del porvenir*," *Latin American Review* in press.

—. "Reading the Body Politic: Alicia Partnoy's *The Little School.* Unpublished paper, MLA, Dec. 1987.

Kessler, Suzanne J. and Wendy McKenna. *Gender, an Ethnomethodological Approach.* New York: Wiley, 1978.

MacKinnon, Catherine A. "Feminism, Marxism, Method and the State. An Agenda for Theory." *Signs. Journal of Women in Culture and Society* 7: 3 (Spring, 1982): 515-544.

Masiello, Francine R. "*En breve cárcel*, la producción del sujeto."*Hispamérica* 14: 41 (Aug. 1985): 103-112.

Molloy, Sylvia. "At Face Value: Autobiographical Writing in Spanish America." *Dispositio* 9: 24-26: 1-18.

—. *En breve cárcel.* Barcelona: Seix Barral,1981.

—. "Inscripciones del yo en *Recuerdos de provincia.*" *Sur* 350-351 (Jan.-Dec. 1982): 131-140.

—. "Sentido de ausencias." *Revista Iberoamericana* 51: 132-133 (July-Dec. 1985): 483-488.

—. "*Tierras de la memoria*: La entreapertura del texto." *Escritura*, 7:13-14 (Caracas, Jan-Dec. 1982): 69-93.

Peri Rossi, Cristina. *Lingüística general.* Editorial Prometeo, 1979.

Register, Cheri. *Living with Chronic Illness: Days of Patience and Passion* New York: MacMillan Free Press, 1987

Rice-Sayre, Laura. "Domination and Desire: A Feminist-Materialist Reading of Manuel Puig's *Kiss of the Spider Woman.*" *Textual Analysis, Some Readers Reading.* Ed. Mary Ann Caws. New York: Modern Language Association of America, 1986: 245-256.

Rich, Adrienne. "Compulsory Heterosexuality and Lesbian Existence." *Signs. Journal of Women in Culture and Society* 5: 4 (Summer, 1980): 631-660.

Reina Roffé. *Monte de Venus* . Buenos Aires: Corregidor, 1976.

Rubin, Gayle. "The Traffic in Women: Notes on the Political Economy of Sex." *Toward an Anthropology of Women.* Ed. Reina Rapp. NY: Monthly Review Press, 1975: 157-210.

Stanley, Julia Penelope. "Uninhabited Angels: Metaphors for Love," *Margins* 23 (1975), quoted in Zimmerman, p 194.

Tamargo, Maribel. "*En breve cárcel*: texto, género, transgresión" unpublished paper MLA, Dec. 1986.

Velázquez Spanish and English Dictionary. Chigago: Follett, 1974.

Wittig, Monique. "Straight Minds." *Feminist Issues* (Summer 1980).

—. *The Lesbian Body* trans. Peter Owen. Wm Morrow, 1975, repr. Boston, Beacon Press, 1986: 17.

Wolfe, Susan. "Stylistic Experimentation in Millett, Johnston and Wittig" unpublished paper, MLA 1978.

Zimmerman, Bonnie. "What has never been: an overview of lesbian feminist criticism." *Making a Difference.* Ed. Coppélia Kahn and Gayle Greene. NY: Methuen, 1985: 177-210.

LA CRITICA LITERARIA FEMINISTA HISPANOAMERICANA COMO PROBLEMATICA DE DEFENSA DE LOS DERECHOS HUMANOS

Argumentos en apoyo de una arquetipificación universalista

Hernán Vidal
University of Minnesota, Minneapolis
Para Alicia, Begoña, Bernardita y Susana.

ACOTACIONES Y PRECAUCIONES

Mi contribución a este momento de la crítica literaria feminista hispanoamericana es explorar la posibilidad de trasladar a ella las categorías propias del discurso en defensa de los derechos humanos. Un examen de la bibliografía muestra que esa crítica ha sido institucionalizada sólo con criterios privativos de la profesión de lector académico, desdibujándose en un trasfondo muy distante el hecho de que la desmerecida situación social de la mujer es fundamentalmente cuestión de derechos humanos. Puesto que hasta la fecha no se conocen estudios que planteen este asunto en lo literario, corresponde meditar sobre el modo en que tales categorías podrían tener una función teórica e instrumental en el análisis.

Esta exploración se da en un momento de redefinición de la crítica literaria feminista, según muestran dos ensayos de importancia publicados recientemente. Jean Franco ha comentado[1] que la "teoría contemporánea parte de un examen consciente de la institucionalización de los géneros literarios, tarea de deconstrucción en la cual tiene particular interés el feminismo. Aquí quiero hacer hincapié en una distinción entre la teoría feminista y la crítica que rescata textos olvidados o reivindica el valor de textos del pasado. Esta crítica muchas veces define la literatura feminista en una forma muy general como 'textos por mujeres' [...] La teoría feminista, en cambio, tiene una meta más ambiciosa. Falla como teoría si no logra cambiar el estudio de la literatura de modo sustancial. Debe, por lo tanto, abarcar una lectura de la cultura que altere sustancialmente los marcos del sistema literario y nos dé, al mismo tiempo, nuevos instrumentos de análisis" (p. 32).

Por su parte, en un ensayo de argumentos irrebatibles, Sara Castro Klarén ha puesto en tela de juicio[2] los presupuestos fundamentales de aquellos análisis que intentan la caracterización de una identidad y de una imaginación esencialmente femeninas: "Desde un punto de vista histórico, la 'identidad femenina' ofrece problemas análogos a aquellos ya examinados con relación a la 'imaginación femenina'. Esto sucede en parte porque ambos términos responden al sentido idealista y tradicional de identidad como algo visible, fijo, constante y siempre igual a sí mismo" (p. 35). Ambas evaluaciones plantean cuestiones radicales, si tomamos en cuenta que, en un estudio reciente de la institucionalización académica de la investigación feminista, precisamente se dice que esas son las áreas constituyentes de la disciplina: "los métodos de las investigadoras literarias feministas incluyen la reinterpretación de la obra de autores femeninos reconocidos o el redescubrimiento de autores femeninos que han sido desterrados del canon literario, y la exploración de una tradición literaria específicamente femenina"[3].

Sin desconocer en absoluto sus aportes de material empírico, por mi parte creo que, además, debería cuestionarse si la práctica positivista en el análisis interpretativo de la representación literaria de la mujer realmente puede llamarse feminista. Por práctica positivista entiendo aquellos ejercicios analíticos hechos sobre un texto literario para aplicar algún otro texto de teoría feminista nada más porque coinciden en el uso de categorías fundamentales, sin que el trabajo dé *evidencia textual* de estar motivado por una crítica cultural conscientemente asumida por el practicante como parte de un programa de reforma social de cierta trascendencia en lo que afecta a la mujer[4]. Sin embargo, más que descontar la validez de la crítica positivista, la cuestión de interés sería recuperar el material que ha acumulado para reconstelarlo desde la pespectiva de una crítica cultural que realmente sirva los objetivos del movimiento feminista.

Si el momento actual de la crítica literaria feminista está caracterizado por la necesidad de tan drásticas redefiniciones, y continuando emblemáticamente el espíritu de las cuestiones planteadas por algunas investigadoras en el estudio de la producción discursiva proveniente de la cultura femenina de los conventos[5], quiero atribuir a mi exploración la utilidad de "navaja de Occam", concepto creado ya en la filosofía medieval por el franciscano de Surrey William Occam, con el cual abogó en el siglo XIV por la sedimentación de un conocimiento real que evitara la producción de categorías pseudo explicativas innecesarias. Esto me obliga a intentar un esbozo y una evaluación de la forma en que se ha institucionalizado la crítica literaria feminista hispanoamericana en el medio académico. Dado que no se ha inaugurado una sociología del hispanismo, ese esbozo no puede sino ser limitado. Esto crea problemas de diverso orden, que he tratado de solucionar de un modo más bien informal.

Por ejemplo, he basado ese esbozo en observaciones y discusiones personales que he tenido con colegas también preocupados del tema. En especial me dirijo a la forma en que la crítica literaria feminista hispanoamericana concibe el espacio político y el modo en que se inserta en él el problema de la mujer. Esto lo hago instalándome en la tradición gramsciana del materialismo histórico y a través de la producción de lo que podría llamarse un perfil de tipicidad colectiva, compuesto con la integración de ideologemas de diversa procedencia y ubicados en una narración única y continua. Sin duda habría que decir mucho más sobre la parte burocrática de esa institucionalización académica, proyecto que debería emprenderse con un formalismo sociológico que no corresponde a los propósitos de este trabajo específico.

Por otra parte, al hablar de crítica literaria feminista hispanoamericana me refiero más bien a su institucionalización académica norteamericana. La razón está en que el gran volumen de esta producción intelectual sin duda está en Estados Unidos, debido a la alta formalización burocrático-académica que han tenido aquí los estudios de la mujer. Este dato debe complementarse con otros dos: parte importante de este personal académico proviene de los países latinoamericanos; además es frecuente la contratación de las críticas literarias feministas latinoamericanas más conocidas para dictar cursos esporádicos en universidades norteamericanas. Con ello se produce un cierto nivel de homogeneidad discursiva, puesto que este personal debe referirse a un cuerpo de teoría ya generalizado, lo cual es reforzado por la alta circulación mundial de escritos feministas anglo-norteamericanos y franceses. Por lo demás, cualquier observador del feminismo en Latinoamérica podrá haber comprobado que la activación o mayor visibilidad de las formas actuales del movimiento con frecuencia han sido gestadas con ese referente internacional, muchas veces con desconocimiento de su historia local.

En rigor, a través de este trabajo debí haber utilizado el término "crítica literaria feminista hispanoamericanista", más bien que "hispanoamericana". No lo hago simplemente para evitar la cacofonía.

Quizás la parte más cuestionable de mi trabajo sea el análisis de la crítica literaria feminista hispanoamericana a través de esa composición de un perfil típico único, a pesar de la diversidad de origen de los ideologemas usados. Deseo llamar la atención sobre este problema por razones éticas y técnicas: como analista, asumo la responsabilidad sobre la forma en que he elaborado esa tipificación, pero a la vez señalo que cualquiera distorsión de identidad que involuntariamente pueda haber causado se debe a la configuración sociológica del movimiento feminista, del cual la crítica literaria es una extensión. Como solución parcial he seguido la estrategia de acotar al máximo mi foco de discusión, utilizando únicamente material producido por hispanoamericanistas. Aún más, de ese material sólo he usado aquél que demuestra una conciencia de crítica cultural, lo cual lo reduce apreciablemente. Por tanto, en sentido estricto, mis argumentos de ningún modo pueden entenderse como una evaluación de la teoría feminista anglo-norteamericana y francesa, por mucho que la crítica examinada integre esa teoría a su discurso. Más adelante veremos que la construcción de un perfil típico único para caracterizar a un discurso institucionalizado expone aspectos insospechados hasta para quienes lo han producido, lo cual gravita sobre el uso de argumentos evaluatorios.

Pero, por sobre todo, la cuestión fundamental de mi contribución yace en un entendimiento de la configuración sociológica del movimiento feminista. Por tanto, quiero explayarme al respecto, con la esperanza de que así mi proposición sea puesta en mejor perspectiva.

CONFIGURACION SOCIOLOGICA DEL MOVIMIENTO FEMINISTA

En la literatura sociológica[6] un movimiento es descrito como una alianza temporal de individuos y organizaciones que dependen mutuamente para actuar sobre un objetivo limitado. Surgen en circunstancias de profundas crisis sociales que impiden que las luchas políticas sean canalizadas por las instituciones general o normalmente preocupadas de su conducción, como los partidos políticos. En estas circunstancias los partidos establecidos bien pierden su legitimidad y credibilidad ante la población y amplios sectores disidentes llevan adelante su actividad reivindicativa fuera de ellos; o bien el aparato represivo del Estado impide que esos partidos puedan manifestar su actividad organizativa y, por tanto, deben crear una nueva modalidad de negociación a través de los movimientos. Huelga decir que esta forma de inestabilidad institucional abre dinámicas sociales que significan un profundo desafío teórico para los partidos políticos establecidos y para su capacidad de influencia social.

Por estas circunstancias los movimientos pueden entenderse como coaliciones transitorias e inestables, basadas en una red de relaciones institucionales y personales preexistente, que redirige sus recursos para enfrentar las tareas que surgen de la crisis social colectiva. Recordemos que generalmente los programas universitarios de estudios de la mujer en Estados Unidos han sido formados con la redistribución de personal ya adscrito a otras unidades y que en el trasfondo de su gestación están los procesos sociales de la movilización por los derechos civiles y de la protesta contra la guerra de Vietnam durante las décadas de 1960 y 1970, y la crisis económica que ha causado nuevamente un debate público sobre la situación de la mujer como masa laboral. La transitoriedad e inestabilidad de los movimientos se origina en el hecho de que las circunstancias que motivan la coalición inevitablemente cambian y de que los compromisos adquiridos se modifican de acuerdo con ello. A esto se agregan las tensiones que surgen en su seno: puede que los miembros de la coalición tengan un acuerdo básico sobre la naturaleza de las tareas comunes, la forma de realizarlas, y ciertas normas de conducta, derechos y deberes. Sin embargo, a la vez los miembros cuidan celosamente el perfil de su identidad individual y de grupo menor asociado, rehusando fundirse en la mayor homogeneidad corporativa que logran organizaciones más estables, como los partidos políticos.

Por esto es que se habla de la naturaleza segmentaria y policéfala de los movimientos. Segmentaria porque las rupturas originadas por la crisis social que motivara la organización del movimiento siguen presentes en su seno, lo cual lleva a constantes discusiones y debates para mantener el foco consensual que los vertebra. Policéfala porque todo observador, aunque puede percibir una coherencia en el movimiento, tiene dificultades en determinar quiénes son sus representantes y portavoces autorizados o más representativos, puesto que, como indicaba, cada individuo y grupo menor asociado cuida celosamente su identidad distintiva, a la vez que lucha esforzadamente por proyectar una imagen de unión general fuera del movimiento. Esto obliga a los miembros de la coalición a un extremo cuidado en la modulación de la imagen pública, lo que se refleja en una gran quisquillosidad frente a quienes son considerados como extraños a la coalición; ante ellos se enmascara el lenguaje. Generalmente ello resulta en un delicado y difícil acto interno de balance en la cuerda floja que desenfatiza cualquiera discordancia ideológica fundamental y privilegia a veces excesivamente el potencial de cohesión que pueda generarse en la retórica y el ceremonial protocolar acumulados en el tiempo. Ante estas circunstancias el movimiento puede sufrir profundas crisis en la tarea de alcanzar sus objetivos o serias distorsiones en su producción de conocimiento histórico.

Todo movimiento tiene la necesidad crucial de producir una retórica y un ceremonial protocolar que perfilen tanto su identidad y sus relaciones internas como las públicas.

Prueba de ello está en que la retórica y los protocolos pueden llegar a ser la sustancia metafórica y simbólica de la que se nutre un arte quizás generado por un movimiento. Por ejemplo, es un hecho concreto que diversas formas de teoría feminista ya han sido utilizadas en la literatura hispanoamericana. No obstante, dada la diferente formación intelectual de sus miembros, puede que algunos confundan la producción de conocimiento real —es decir, válido para avanzar la teleología del movimiento— con la manipulación de las metáforas y símbolos emblemáticos producidos retóricamente por la coalición. Por ejemplo, en el movimiento feminista se podría señalar el énfasis en una solidaridad de la mujer *(sisterhood)* a través de toda diferencia histórica, racial, étnica y de clase. A mi juicio, los escritos recientes a que me he referido demuestran una intranquilidad al respecto, de allí el deseo de redefinir la identidad de la crítica feminista. Espero que este trasfondo explique más concretamente la importancia que pudiera tener la introducción de la "navaja de Occam" que propongo.

GENERACION DE HEGEMONIA, FEMINISMO Y CRITICA LITERARIA FEMINISTA

A pesar de la diversidad ideológica del movimiento feminista, es posible afirmar que la comunidad esencial que lo vertebra es su intento de crear o articular una crítica de la cultura que, a través de su teoría y metodología, le permita interpelar y transformar las relaciones de poder institucionalizadas en términos genéricos que limitan la plena manifestación social de la mujer. Este cuestionamiento propone una utopía: "La teoría feminista analiza las relaciones entre lo femenino y las instancias del poder y propone la misma pregunta que Derrida al decir: '¿Qué sucederá si tratamos un área de las relaciones con el Otro en el cual el código de señales sexuales no fuera ya determinante'" (Franco, p. 33). Dentro de este proyecto, en sus formas más lúcidas, la crítica literaria feminista se concibe como intento de revelar y exponer las estrategias lingüísticas con que el discurso literario, entendido como institución, constituye la subjetividad de los agentes sociales, permitiendo la subordinación de la mujer a un orden patriarcalista. Esta contribución sería un acto fundacional en el proceso de regenerar sensibilidades sociales que luego permitan alguna forma de movilización social en demanda de la reivindicación de la mujer. A juicio de muchos, esto es lo que otorga un perfil genuinamente revolucionario al movimiento feminista. Este pone en tela de juicio las definiciones genéricas en que se ha basado el poder patriarcal a través de la extensión de la historia humana, en todo lugar, más allá de toda categorización racial, étnica y clasista, mientras que, a la vez, el conocimiento producido por el movimiento es condicionado por esas categorías.

Ahora bien, todo desafío del poder generado por la institucionalidad social —bien sea entendida ésta como padrones de conducta tipificados y repetidos constantemente en el tiempo o como organizaciones burocráticas que administran algún sector de la sociedad— es, en última instancia, un acto político. Como tal, un movimiento de transformación social de tan vastas aspiraciones como el movimiento feminista debe estar preparado para confrontar y enfrentarse a la necesidad sistémica que caracteriza a una sociedad, a la vez que debe plantear alternativas de reorganización de efectividad práctica. Por necesidad sistémica se entiende la facticidad material de instituciones burocráticas con poder coercitivo que administran la sociedad de acuerdo con programas aplicados causalmente, que impelen efectos sobre la colectividad, aplicaciones hechas sobre la base de una planificación de medidas administrativas fundadas en premisas a las que se da rango de certidumbres a largo plazo, las cuales confieren estabilidad a las definiciones de lo real impuestas por el poder social y económico imperante. Quienes confrontan y se enfrentan a esa facticidad material deben cumplir con la tarea de superar el reino del azar, es decir, organizar a individuos dispersos, de intereses potencialmente afines, pero cuya conducta es incierta, inestable y sólo potencialmente reivindicadora, a menos que se les pueda entregar un conocimiento global del funcionamiento de la sociedad y una organización que los movilice con cierto grado de homogeneidad y disciplina hacia objetivos de liberación racional y consensualmente definidos.

Para las vastas aspiraciones de transformación social propuestas por el movimiento feminista, esos objetivos implican la generación de una contrahegemonía. Si nos atenemos a términos gramscianos, la hegemonía política se basa en la capacidad de alianza y coordinación estable y a largo plazo de los intereses y acción de ciertos sectores sociales como para imponer un programa de desarrollo social y económico que trascienda los límites de sus intereses corporativos específicos y consensualmente integre bajo su orientación las diversas relaciones de clases y géneros que se dan en las diferentes actividades económicas, políticas e ideológicas dentro de un territorio nacional. En la historia de los modernos Estados-nación, las maquinarias más eficientes para la expresión, conformación y modelamiento de opciones hegemónicas son los partidos políticos. Como instituciones burocráticas, ellos son capaces de congregar los más variados recursos de personal, instalaciones, medios comunicativos y doctrinarios para el análisis de las coyunturas, conflictos y contradicciones sociales, como paso configurador de la acción de los intereses colectivos que reune, representa y expresa. A nivel de negociación o conflicto colectivo, estos intereses son primordialmente de clase.

El requisito de generar una contrahegemonía política revela la contradidicción fundamental que caracteriza tanto al movimiento feminista como a los otros dos movimientos de relevancia actual en Latinoamérica, el de defensa de los derechos humanos y el de la teología de la liberación: aunque para ser una posibilidad histórica efectiva el feminismo debe ser capaz de generar una hegemonía que cree las condiciones reales para la máxima materialización del ser social de la mujer en la totalidad del espacio social, *el objetivo único* de la reivindicación de ella *por sí solo* es inadecuado para la tarea. De allí que a lo sumo pueda constituir un movimiento transitorio e inestable. No se conocen partidos feministas de estabilidad y duración prolongada; todos ellos sucumben finalmente a las inevitables e inescapables tensiones de clase que se desarrollan en su interior.

La conciencia de la incapacidad de generación de hegemonía lleva a las feministas políticamente efectivas a una estrategia doble y quizás combinada: la de militar en los partidos políticos establecidos para luchar desde su interior contra el patriarcalismo, a riesgo de ser neutralizadas; o la estrategia de formar grupos independientes de presión que establezcan alguna forma de relación de apoyo crítico con los diferentes partidos políticos existentes. Ambas estrategias quedan marcadas bien por un sello reformista o revolucionario, en la medida en que las feministas demanden nada más que un mejor espacio dentro del orden socioeconómico imperante o militen en partidos políticos o grupos de presión que buscan transformaciones sociales más radicales. Las feministas que abandonan estas dos opciones se entregan a una acción política de marcado perfil anarquista, en cuanto rehusan una participación altamente estructurada en la negociación o conflicto social colectivo y deciden dirigir sus esfuerzos a una transformación del poder a nivel comunitario molecular. No se conocen sociedades que hayan sido radicalmente transformadas por movimientos de postura anarquista.

Así es como queda configurado el amplio espectro de opciones de la acción política feminista en una lucha que debe darse en todo interesticio de la sociedad civil y de la sociedad política puesto que, de acuerdo con la experiencia empírica más inmediata y el conocimiento antropológico acumulado, la dominación patriarcalista de la mujer parece ser, en efecto, un fenómeno transhistórico, transnacional y transcultural.

A mi juicio, la contradicción entre las aspiraciones revolucionarias del feminismo y su incapacidad de generar hegemonía es el principal factor condicionante de la forma en que se ha institucionalizado académicamente la producción discursiva de la crítica literaria feminista hispanoamericana. Es preciso considerar que, para la intelectualidad que participa en un movimiento, toda producción discursiva implica la creación de tipificaciones de conducta y acción social que mejor perfilen la identidad histórica del agente de transformación social en nombre de quien se habla y de las tareas de transformación que se le atribuyen. Como se podrá comprender, el gran desafío para los intelectuales involucrados en esta tarea es la de crear las condiciones de confianza y representatividad que avalen la legitimidad de ser portavoces y vanguardia de un movimiento masivo. Si aceptamos la premisa de la necesidad fundamental de construir hegemonía, esa legitimidad sólo puede provenir de un referente directo o indirecto en alguna agencia política real, organizada colectivamente para la generación de esa hegemonía. El enfrentamiento con esta necesidad fáctica implica, inescapablemente, la asunción de una posición de clase.

Aquí es donde surge la problemática fundamental que debe enfrentar quien emprenda el estudio de la crítica literaria feminista: en su gran mayoría ella es asumida como ejercicio intracadémico que responde primordialmente a incitaciones profesionales. La consecuencia es que, *en sus escritos*, esta crítica no busca o no puede demostrar esos referentes políticos reales de mayor amplitud y efectividad social. Aunque el estudioso pueda percibir en ellos la existencia de matrices de pensamiento liberal, marxista, marxista-leninista, socialdemócrata o anarquista, esas identidades rara vez son explicitadas en aras de la cohesión del movimiento y deben ser, más bien, atribuidas por sus obvias conexiones con el pensamiento político predominante en la actualidad. Puesto lo político en sordina, sobre este trasfondo se ha construido un agente social "mujer" abstracto, de naturaleza homogénea, uniforme, constante, equilibrada y no contradictoria en cuanto a que se la presenta siempre como objeto universal de la opresión, de la discriminación y de la explotación masculina y nunca a ella como agente de opresión, discriminación y explotación de otras mujeres. Por el contrario, la orientación de las ciencias sociales ha sido mostrar que la mujer, como ente social, está sujeta a discontinuidades, contradicciones y conflictos, en la medida en que, aun desde una posición subordinada ante el hombre, todo ser humano puede encarnar estructuras sociales opresoras, discriminatorias y explotadoras de grandes masas de seres humanos; y también en la medida en que en diversas épocas han existido zonas de la actividad social en que la mujer es también dueña o controla medios productivos, logra una gran medida de independencia personal y prestigio social que le otorgan la autoridad necesaria para influir sobre las relaciones sociales y la política comunitaria de producción y apropiación de plusvalía.

Se podría decir que la crítica literaria feminista hispanoamericana, en la forma en que actualmente se la practica, está caracterizada por una fuerte censura de la opresión, la discriminación y la explotación de mujeres por mujeres. Esto hace del proyecto feminista en la crítica literaria una construcción simbólica *arquetipificadora y universalista* que involucra aun a aquellos análisis literarios que conscientemente buscan una historificación de su discurso al situar la producción de autores femeninos en su contexto histórico. Sin duda, esta arquetipificación debe atribuirse a la dificultad de los intentos por perfilar a la mujer como agente social que no se diluya totalmente en lo político y adquiera así una identidad distintiva, de manera que los problemas de su condición social queden estructuralmente resaltados. Esta estrategia es lo que permite a esta crítica literaria la adopción de una retórica marcadamente denunciatoria y, por tanto, negativista de los órdenes sociales conocidos. No obstante, en la medida en que la dimensión política deba ser puesta en sordina, esta crítica tiene dificultades para entrar en una estrategia afirmativa de un orden social concreto más satisfactorio por lo que, en su reemplazo, debe hacer énfasis en un protocolo de solidaridad femenina por sobre diferencias raciales, étnicas y de clase.

Es necesario detenerse en este punto, aun a riesgo de desviar la atención, pues pareciera plantear dos problemas delicados. Desde una perspectiva materialista histórica como la que adopto es frecuente una suspicacia sobre toda arquetipificación universalista, ya que tales arbitrios generalmente tienen una orientación ontologista ahistórica de tendencia reaccionaria. Si así fuera, tendríamos que colegir que mi trabajo, en realidad, dirige una crítica del todo negativista a la crítica literaria que nos preocupa, lo cual, ciertamente, no es mi intención.

Al respecto, entonces, es necesario recordar que en el materialismo histórico hay una base fundamental de ontologismo, pero no metafísico, sino histórico. El esfuerzo más reciente por relevar este tema ha sido Norman

Geras, quien ha demostrado[7] que Marx, en todas las etapas de su desarrollo intelectual, utilizó una concepción universalista de la naturaleza humana de modo descriptivo y normativo en su crítica al capitalismo, mediada ella por las categorías históricas de clase y etnia: "... el materialismo histórico mismo, esta aproximación distintiva y global a la sociedad que se origina en Marx, descansa rectamente sobre la idea de una naturaleza humana. Ella hace resaltar ese nexo específico de necesidades y capacidades universales que explican el proceso de producción humana y la transformación del entorno material organizada por el ser humano; proceso y transformación que trata a su vez como base tanto del orden social como del cambio histórico. Por tanto, no es cierto, [...] aunque frecuentemente se lo suponga, que por ser general y constante, la naturaleza humana misma no puede intervenir en la explicación del cambio. Por el contrario, si los seres humanos tienen una historia que da surgimiento a la más fabulosa variedad de contornos y formas sociales, se debe a la clase de seres que son, todos ellos..." (pp. 107-108). Este es precisamente el meollo del asunto al que se dirige el discurso en defensa de los derechos humanos. Al utilizar el concepto de persona como eje central de su argumentación, el movimiento en defensa de los derechos humanos adopta una neutralidad sexual que puede resultar en un decidido apoyo a las arquetipificaciones feministas, a la vez que establece un criterio diferenciador frente a sus esencialismos privativos, los cuales son, ciertamente, ahistóricos.

Volviendo a mi línea de argumentación central, es preciso agregar que, por otra parte, cuando a la escritura femenina se le imputa la identidad de acto políticamente subversivo, la arquetipificación universalista de la mujer con frecuencia mayoritaria asume *una matriz analítica funcionalista*. Este contorno surge con la premisa espacial de que tanto el Estado nacional como las formas de institucionalización de la cultura nacional son centros de poder desde los cuales se manifiesta la mentalidad patriarcal y falócrata. Desde allí, con su control del logos, con su capacidad para manipular un lenguaje y una historia oficializadas como tradición universal y Signo Supremo, el poder masculino se erige en Hacedor y Transformador ra-

cional de lo real, hace ciencia de las jerarquías discriminatorias y excluye a la mujer de la historia, de la opción de
verbalizar su propia historia, propalando periódicamente
nuevas definiciones del cuerpo femenino. Estas jerarquías
lo reducen a mero aparato reproductor y objeto del deseo
masculino, atándola a la cotidianidad doméstica. Esas definiciones dictan la identidad de los géneros y de su función en la familia y en el hogar con un propósito triple:
reitera la apropiación nacionalista de la imagen femenina
representada como sacralidad descorporizada que mutila
su humanidad, circulándola como valor simbólico
máximo que legitima su sistema social y un supuesto bien
común; a la vez circula y agresivamente promueve un
discurso totalizador único que, con una lógica lineal y binaria, intenta uniformar toda identidad para mejor controlarlas; también enmascara lingüísticamente los mecanismos de su dominación.

En la periferia, sin embargo, se darían espacios de resistencia en que se gestan nuevas solidaridades comunitarias
entre los marginados, particularmente las mujeres, para
oponerse a la autoridad tradicional que domina la cotidianidad. Allí el feminismo arma un nuevo discurso para
poner fin al silenciamiento de la mujer y ofrecer una visión descentralizada de la historia. A través de él los marcos de la limitación genérica son subvertidos con un lenguaje vanguardista que proyecta simbólicamente los procesos naturales del cuerpo de la mujer a la aprehensión y
conformación de lo real; lenguaje que enfatiza las organicidades de relación de lo real frente a los criterios
fragmentadores de la mente masculina; lenguaje que resemantiza positivamente el significado de la maternidad,
de los espacios y las ocupaciones estereotípicas de la mujer
y afirma la heterogeneidad de identidades y proyectos sociales. Ese lenguaje, inestable en sus significaciones, ambiguo y contradictorio, funda un sujeto femenino autónomo
que rearticula su identidad fragmentada por la instrumentalización racionalizante de los hombres. Acentúa lo
amorfo, la identidad plurívoca, los cursos de acción indefinidos, los orígenes inciertos, tensando los confines de la
heterosexualidad, explora la expresividad de los silencios,
de la locura, de la vitalidad excesiva y gozosa del placer

sexual ubicado en la vagina, en el clítoris, en la vulva, en los labios, en los senos, excesos de vitalidad que auguran la potencial liberación de las disciplinas del principio de realidad masculino. Desde los espacios de esa marginalidad ese feminismo intentará incursiones al espacio falogocéntrico para regenerarlo. Lucía Guerra-Cunningham postula[8] que "Tal vez —imitando una estrategia hasta ahora masculina—valga la pena conocer mejor al enemigo para subyugarlo tanto en el sentido bélico de vencerlo como en su connotación erótica (más femenina y más humana, según visión feminista) de integrar al Otro a uno misma fusionándose para integrar, logrando así un equilibrio entre hombre y mujer que se perdió en época anterior a la pérdida del Paraíso y restaurar la armonía de aquel día en que Lilith y Adán fueron igualmente hechos en la tierra" (p. 34).

El contorno funcionalista de esta argumentación se hace evidente al considerarse la demarcación de la cultura masculina como espacio ante el cual la mujer debe distanciarse escépticamente, puesto que, desde la marginalidad universal de la subcultura en que se la ha mantenido, no puede hacerse responsable ni comprometerse con ella. Desde esta perspectiva queda implícita la noción de que la cultura de los hombres opera con la inercia de una máquina milenaria que busca su reproducción automática y su estabilidad, aun a pesar de la disidencia y de la resistencia femenina, fortaleciendo a la familia como institución confinadora para la mujer y decantanddo roles sexuales normativos que la mutilan.

Esta representación de la sociedad tiene claros paralelos con la sociología funcionalista de Talcott Parsons[9], quien precisamente concebía la sociedad como un orden sistémico que desarrolla un servomecanismo cibernético de autocontrol y reproducción automáticos al hacer circular entre sus unidades y aparatos un *input* y un *output* de energía canalizada a través de conductos. El principal de estos conductos es la familia, dentro de la cual se disciplina la energía sexual de los individuos mediante la interiorización de los valores que constituyen el capital simbólico (el aparato L=*latent pattern- maintenance)* de la sociedad y se lleva a cabo la socialización en roles genéricos heterosexuales que imponen normas óptimas para la reproducción social. En el pensamiento de Parsons, la disciplina sexual, ganada a través de la represión de toda desviación, hace de la familia la institución estabilizadora de la sociedad por excelencia, en su triple función de unidad consumidora de los productos y servicios del aparato A (adaptativo= económico), de unidad productora de fuerza laboral y de unidad de implementación articuladora a nivel microsocial de los proyectos de desarrollo socio-económico definidos por el sistema político (aparatos G= *goal attainment* e I= integración). En la adscripción de funciones, el marido tiene claramente un predominio de roles asociados con lo instrumental-adaptativo, en que se privilegian las tareas externas al hogar, mientras que en la esposa predominan los roles expresivo-integrativos, es decir, donadores de amor y cariño, llevados a cabo en la interioridad hogareña.

Sobre la base de esta estabilidad, y a la vez afianzándola, circula el capital simbólico (L) que define necesidades sociales, motivaciones y normas mediante un sistema de representaciones que promueven la confianza en el orden establecido, el interés común y la solidaridad. Parsons define el poder social como la capacidad para mantener el sistema sobre estas bases fiduciarias. De allí que para él la administración social óptima constele los aparatos sociales sobre el pivote de la circulación del capital simbólico. Si la población interioriza esos valores y se adapta a los roles genéricos heterosexuales, no es necesario el uso de la violencia en la administración social. Este ideal fue expresado por Parsons en su conocida fórmula L-I-G-A.

En la forma en que Parsons concibe el poder hay, en última instancia, una equiparación entre dinero, influencia, sexo y lenguaje. El dinero es el símbolo más visible de la forma en que un sistema social puede crear la confianza en su administración, puesto que el poder político ha sido capaz de dar garantías a la población de un valor real a través de pedazos de papel que en sí ciertamente no lo tienen. Es el mismo efecto creado por los mensajes, códigos y representaciones que el poder hace circular en la sociedad a través del lenguaje. La circulación de dinero, lenguaje e imágenes sexuales reelaboradas por la normatividad genérica realmente da surgimiento y dinamiza las sanciones negativas y positivas, las coerciones y persuasiones, la motivación de dependencias y compromisos que provocan el funcionamiento efectivo, congruente y homogéneo de todos los aparatos y subsistemas sociales, otorgándoles un carácter de sacralidad.

Sin duda que en el entendimiento de la circulación de dinero, sexo, lenguaje y símbolos en la administración de la influencia y del poder encontramos las bases de la actividad llamada "relaciones públicas". Se podría decir que la mayoría de los estudios feministas en la literatura hispanoamericana, como crítica de los mecanismos del poder patriarcalista, han sido hechos dentro de estos parámetros —principalmente en lo que respecta al predominio analítico de la categoría género. Por tanto, de manera consciente o inconsciente se han ubicado dentro de una orientación funcionalista.

NEGACION DE LA NEGACION: EL CONCEPTO DE GENERO FRENTE A LA CATEGORIA PERSONA

Discutir el posible aporte de las categorías relacionadas con la defensa de los derechos humanos requiere, previamente, una evaluación crítica de la institucionalización a que me he referido. Este es el momento en que tal vez graviten los aspectos sorprendentes de ese perfil de tipicidad única en los argumentos evaluatorios, según señalaba en la introducción de este trabajo.

Si mis suposiciones anteriores son mínimamente correctas, en primer lugar habría que señalar la marcada tendencia liberal romántica en la elaboración arquetipificadora y universalista del agente social "mujer". Con esto me refiero a la metaforización espacial que divide la sociedad civil de la sociedad política (el Estado y la institucionalización de la cultura nacional) para imaginar en la primera la existencia de espacios "marginales" del todo libres de la influencia estatal, en que los individuos logran el resguardo necesario para constituir su autonomía como agentes revolucionarios. Como se sabe, este mito fue creado por el iluminismo burgués en el siglo XVIII en sus luchas revolucionarias contra las arbitrariedades del Estado feudal absolutista. Se trata de un mito en la medida en que se argumenta la negación de las condiciones sociales imperantes, instalando la perspectiva de la imaginación crítica en un sitio ubicado totalmente fuera de ellas. Obviamente es una variación del ideologema del "contrato social", que concebía una naturaleza humana del todo libre, anterior a la sociedad, que accedía a someterse a las limitaciones legales para preservar el bien común.

Por el contrario, la experiencia histórica demuestra la continuidad dialéctica entre la sociedad civil y la política. Nada puede constituirse fuera de la sociedad y de los recursos ideológicos y materiales acumulados dentro de ella. Tanto nuestra personalidad como el sentido de la cotidianidad que ella habita están conformadas por las definiciones, diagramaciones y reticulaciones que le impone la legalidad administrada por el Estado y por los recursos materiales e ideológicos que éste pone en circulación. En esa cotidianidad, con nuestro trabajo material, fisiológico-reproductivo y/o ideológico, inevitablemente todos —pertenezcamos a las cúpulas de la hegemonía social o a las clases subordinadas— contribuimos a la reproducción de la sociedad, de su orden simbólico y del poder político que la administra. A la vez, todos consumimos en alguna medida los bienes producidos colectivamente. Quizás podamos criticar la forma instrumental en que las clases hegemónicas administran las relaciones sociales y sus normatividades en el proceso de explotación de personal y de medios productivos, así como podemos criticar las desigualdades con que se retornan esos bienes a los diversos sectores de la colectividad. Quizás lleguemos a condenar la pauperización de que son objeto ciertas clases sociales en el proceso de superexplotación capitalista. Quizás podamos poner en evidencia que, en la medida en que ciertos bienes sean distribuidos en menor cantidad y calidad, limitamos la posibilidad de que los seres humanos afectados puedan concretar el máximo de sus potenciales. Sin embargo, es incorrecto decir que pueda existir algún sector social totalmente privado de algún bien, como se afirma de la mujer en cuanto a su exclusión de la escritura. La debilidad de este argumento se hace patente al señalar la situación paradojal de que las mujeres que protestan la exclusión del poder estatal y de su orden simbólico sean precisamente intelectuales feministas en quienes los Estados-nación han invertido grandes recursos de las culturas nacionales para constituirlas en tales intelectuales e instalarlas en centros académicos. La paradoja es aún más intensa en el caso de las intelectuales latinoamericanas, si tenemos en cuenta las estadísticas de la selectividad piramidalmente creciente con que el sistema capitalista distribuye en nuestros países el ingreso a la educación primaria, secundaria, universitaria y de postgrado.

En segundo lugar, no está de más indicar que la defensa de los derechos de la mujer se exilia al reino de la ciencia-ficción si desahucia radicalmente la cultura establecida por ser manifestación del patriarcalismo y de la falocracia. Aunque nuestra imaginación tenga la capacidad de crear una utopía que augure un orden social más justo, ella debe anclarse de algún modo en la forma fáctica como se administra el reino de la necesidad tal como existe en nuestros días, bajo riesgo de que, al no ser así, esa utopía sea considerada retórica vacía de contenido histórico. No podemos vivir fuera de esa cultura, pero dentro del confinamiento de la actividad académica sí podemos contribuir en medida modesta a la creación de condiciones ideológicas que en el futuro permitan una lucha más decisiva por reconstelar sus componentes y reorientar su sentido para la reivindicación y la liberación de todos los seres humanos. Una utopía que emprende un vuelo para instalarse directamente en el futuro, sin pasar por las tareas terrenales de enfrentarse a la facticidad social no puede sino minar la credibilidad política de un proyecto cultural de tal trascendencia como el feminismo, y de su capacidad movilizadora. No se trata de abandonar la tarea obligatoria de crear utopías. Más bien se trata de que nos hagamos responsables de los sacrificios que han tenido que hacer las generaciones anteriores para acumular la cultura que nos han legado y desarrollar el juicio crítico que nos permita discernir, seleccionar y tomar de ella aquéllo que nos sea de mayor utilidad para esa tarea.

Esta responsabilidad histórica es de especial importancia en la lucha antimperialista de los países dependientes:

aunque ciertamente tenemos el derecho y la obligación de
protestar por la forma en que la figura femenina ha sido
manipulada por el nacionalismo para legitimar estructuras sociales opresivas, las poblaciones que sufren el flagelo
imperial no pueden permitirse el subjetivismo de declarar
la irrelevancia de los Estados y las culturas nacionales,
acto, por lo demás, que en el mundo real de las luchas políticas concretas está totalmente desprovisto de sentido.
Más bien deben luchar por la creación de un nuevo Estado
y de una nueva cultura que garanticen la autonomía en la
definición de las necesidades nacionales y los sistemas
económicos, las estrategias, los medios y los recursos para
satisfacerlas. En el materialismo dialéctico esto plantea el
problema de la negación de la negación, lo cual nos lleva a
examinar el aspecto funcionalista de la crítica literaria feminista.

Mediante el uso de la categoría género, esta crítica ha
enjuiciado la forma en que la mujer se ve constreñida al
micronivel social (la familia, las instituciones de la cotidianidad) en el trabajo de crear un sentido simbólico para
sí y para su entorno bajo la influencia directa o indirecta
del macropoder (el Estado y sus instituciones). Esto indica
una antinomia, puesto que se intenta criticar al poder a
partir de una categoría discursiva creada precisamente por
el poder —recordemos que la teoría sociológica funcionalista ha sido uno de los principales instrumentos de administración del capitalismo. Toda definición genérica es la
proyección de un poder capaz de validar, difundir e interiorizar entre la población determinados estereotipos. Al
adscribir a los individuos ciertas normas de conducta, la
socialización en esos estereotipos los involucra en un proceso de sumisión y capacitación dentro de jerarquías que
fundamentan una división sexual del trabajo. Ella contribuye a la dominación social en medida paralela con la creación en el sujeto de una autoconciencia que le permita
construir su universo simbólico dentro de esas definiciones estereotípicas. Sospecho que esta antinomia es el origen de las tautologías que repetidamente se han señalado
en las argumentaciones de algunas formas de feminismo.
Entre las muchas que se podría mencionar, consideremos
la concepción de la ciudadanía propuesta por el movi-

miento maternalista. Mientras los más amplios sectores
del feminismo condenan los estereotipos que se han adscrito a la mujer por reducírsela a mero agente de administración familiar y de reproducción biológica, el materna-
lismo propone la regeneración de la sociedad patriarcal
precisamente en términos de los estereotipos de un fun-
cionalismo conservador:

> El feminismo maternal está expresamente dispuesto a poner
> freno a lo que considera como cualidades áridas y poco imagi-
> nativas de la posición liberal prevaleciente y, más enfática-
> mente, presentar un sentido de alternativa en cuanto a la vir-
> tud cívica y la ciudadanía. Como primer paso, desea establecer
> la primacía moral de la familia. Aunque para algunos esto
> pueda parecer un inicio extraño para una política feminista,
> las maternalistas nos interpelan para que revisemos la rígida
> distinción liberal entre los ámbitos público y privado y consi-
> deremos en vez lo "privado" como el foco de una moral pública
> posible y como un modelo para la actividad ciudadana misma.
> O, para decirlo de otro modo, el feminismo maternal critica la
> política "estatista" y a los individualistas, y ofrece en reem-
> plazo la única alternativa que ve —una política informada por
> las virtudes del ámbito privado, y una noción de persona com-
> prometida con la promoción de capacidades de relación, amor y
> afecto por el prójimo [...] Lo que hace de esto una perspectiva
> netamente feminista (más bien que, por ejemplo, un
> conservadurismo tradicional) es su afirmación de que la expe-
> riencia de las mujeres como madres en el ámbito privado las
> dota de una capacidad especial y de un "imperativo moral"
> para poner freno tanto a la visión masculina del individua-
> lismo liberal como a su noción masculinista de la ciudadanía[10].

Tales tautologías podrían ser resueltas en la medida en
que hubiera entre los proponentes la conciencia de que
aquellos rasgos maternalistas de la sensibilidad social son
promovidos como formas de conducta positiva, generadas
dentro de la sociedad que se rechaza, pero elevadas a la
utopía de un estadio de acción social superior y preserva-
das allí por su carácter progresista. Esta negación de la negación requiere, sin embargo, la introducción consciente
de conceptos que se enfrenten antagónicamente a las categorías conservadoras que han creado la conducta deseable
y que posibiliten la transferencia de ella a ese estadio superior, manteniéndose la continuidad de los elementos

positivos nacidos en el vientre de la sociedad vieja en el augurio de la nueva.

En lo que concierne a las categorías operativas de la crítica literaria feminista, ese antagonismo implicaría la estrategia de poner en tensión los importantes logros obtenidos mediante el análisis genérico funcionalista en un enfrentamiento con las categorías más universales del discurso en defensa de los derechos humanos. Aún más específicamente, esta fricción debería darse entre la categoría género y la categoría persona. La primera propone examinar el efecto de las adscripciones normativas en la personalidad de la mujer y su potencial de acción social, de acuerdo con las imposiciones del conservadurismo social, pero ahora serían puestas en estrecho contacto con la utopía implícita en el concepto persona, según la entiende el derecho internacional: el derecho de acceso irrestringido de todo ser humano, por el mero hecho de ser humano, a la acumulación cultural existente en una sociedad; el derecho, por tanto, a que todo ser humano materialice el máximo de sus potencialidades a través del gozo de esa acumulación cultural; que ese acceso y esa materialización se den en términos de proyectos individuales y colectivos autónoma y soberanamente definidos. Como se observa, de ningún modo propongo el abandono de la categoría género, sino, más bien, la magnificación de un contexto heurístico con la contraposición de las dos categorías discutidas. Si es que existe el peligro de subsumir el discurso feminista en el de defensa de los derechos humanos, éste se daría por el descuido en el balance de ambos términos.

El concepto de persona[11] ha llegado a ser noción central del derecho internacional y de las luchas sociales en los Estados nacionales. Implica que tanto los individuos como las organizaciones sociales, los gobiernos y los Estados deben reconocer que todo ser humano, por el mero hecho de ser humano, tiene la conciencia, la autonomía, los valores, los programas emocionales y la capacidad de elección y planeamiento necesarios para tener libre acceso a los espacios públicos, usarlos, habitarlos, desplazarse por ellos, trabajarlos, establecer relaciones con otros seres, desarrollando allí actividades que intrínsecamente redundan en el enriquecimiento y complejidad del bien individual y común. En esto se origina la concesión, demanda y el gozo en común de la dignidad de persona. Al concederse esta dignidad se reconoce que la persona, como agencia social, tiene la capacidad de interiorizar los códigos del universo simbólico que da sentido a las relaciones sociales, de socializarse en sus tipificaciones, usos, hábitos, protocolos, rituales y ceremonias con una actitud evaluativa y crítica, de manera que la interpretación de ellos que haga para su propia acción contribuya material y espiritualmente a la reproducción y transformación óptimas de la sociedad. De esta forma, los derechos humanos pueden llegar a ser un proceso de permanente creación, expansión y refinamiento. Todo esto implica una concepción racional de la personalidad como ente que, de acuerdo a un cálculo prudencial, posee un autocontrol por el que finalmente actuará sintetizando el bien individual y el colectivo. Esto permite el juicio moral y legal de los individuos, los grupos, las organizaciones, los gobiernos, los Estados nacionales y los sistemas de reproducción social, en la medida en que permitan el gozo y expansión de los derechos de la persona o los restrinjan y violen.

Los derechos de la persona han quedado decantados en la Declaración Universal de los Derechos Humanos de las Naciones Unidas y los convenios complementarios posteriores, instrumentos que tienen rango de derecho internacional. Son de dos tipos: los derechos civiles y políticos garantizan la protección del individuo frente al Estado en cuanto a protección de la privacidad y de la integridad personal, a tratamiento según procedimientos legales, a protección igualitaria ante la ley, a protección ante la discriminación y garantías de participación política. Los derechos económicos y sociales garantizan el derecho al trabajo, al seguro social, a la educación y a un nivel de vida adecuado a la dignidad de persona. Son normas mandatorias, de alta prioridad para la conducción de las relaciones comunitarias, colectivas, estatales e internacionales[12]. Los derechos que afirman son de naturaleza universal, inalienables e indeclinables. Estos tres términos implican lo siguiente: primero, son normas morales aplicables en todo el mundo, supranacionales, supraculturales, indiscriminatorias en cuanto a raza, etnia, sexo, religión, creencia, clase social y nacionalidad; segundo, no existe autoridad legal que pueda repudiarlos o suspenderlos sin mediar consideraciones de orden superior —las llamadas *causas prima facie* — que en nombre de emergencias de naturaleza potencialmente catastrófica legitimen su suspensión en la medida permitida por los convenios internacionales y el escrutinio de los organismos internacionales pertinentes; tercero, como individuos o grupos no tenemos el derecho a abandonar su gozo, hasta el extremo que, si lo hacemos, otros tienen la obligación de abogar por ellos aun ante nuestra oposición. Con este aval, la Declaración Universal de los Derechos Humanos constituye un cartabón básico de principios éticos para la crítica de la política social de los gobiernos nacionales, independientemente del hecho de que esos derechos hayan sido incorporados o no en el sistema legal de cada país. Como norma internacional, este cartabón impone la obligación universal de velar por la implementación de esos derechos a todo individuo, organización social, gobierno y Estado. Por lo tanto, la violación de los derechos humanos constituye un objeto de legítima preocupación, organización y movilización nacional e internacional, con el propósito de demandar y obtener de la autoridad su reconocimiento, respeto, aplicación, cumplimiento, junto con las compensaciones para los afectados y el castigo para los infractores.

Se podrá observar que el lugar central de la noción de persona en la argumentación en defensa de los derechos humanos supone un largo proceso de arquetipificación universalista. La Declaración Universal de los Derechos Humanos de las Naciones Unidas (1948) y sus convenios complementarios demuestran un proceso acumulativo a través de la historia. Aunque por razones de contexto histórico esto fue expresado a veces con un lenguaje sexista, en la noción de persona se decanta una tradición revolucionaria que se inicia con la proclamación de la Magna Carta inglesa en 1215, la Declaración de Independencia de los Estados Unidos (1776), la Constitución norteamericana, la Declaración de los Derechos del Hombre y del Ciudadano de la Revolución Francesa (1789), la Constitución francesa de 1791, la Declaración de la Convención Revolucionaria Francesa (1793), la Constitución soviética de 1918, la Constitución mexicana de 1919, la Constitución de Weimar. Por ser un proceso acumulativo de logros de la humanidad, los documentos fundamentales de las Naciones Unidas listan los derechos humanos sin prioridades, sin calificaciones y sin exponer las bases teóricas y filosóficas que los originaron. Podríamos hablar de un estilo monumental y oracular en cuanto a que esos documentos simplemente exhiben y enuncian ante la humanidad los avances de su maduración ética sin comentarios, llamando a los seres humanos a que den realidad a esos derechos con la movilización dentro de su sociedad y en la comunidad internacional de naciones y den sustancia argumentativa a esas enunciaciones desde las plurales perspectivas de su origen cultural y de su posición de clase.

Por lo dicho se podrá apreciar que en la arquetipificación universalista del concepto de persona hay una clara diferenciación legal entre lo sincrónico y lo diacrónico. El aspecto diacrónico corresponde a la forma en que se dan los conflictos sociales en cada Estado-nación, espacio en que los intereses en juego afirman una voluntad de poder y deben atravesar el laberinto catastrófico del devenir fáctico de la historia, que contrapone necesidad y azar, libertad y alienación, deseo y realidad. Frente a esto, la labor de las Naciones Unidas para la creación de cartabones universales de derechos humanos implica un eje sincrónico de acumulación histórica abstracta: de cada una de las magnas cartas generadas en los grandes episodios de las luchas históricas, la Declaración Universal de los Derechos Humanos ha decantado una voluntad de justicia y un imperativo categórico que, transformados jurídicamente en derechos humanos filosóficamente justificados, constituyen una teleología histórica en versión moral y ética. Dicho en otras palabras, la relación sincrónico-diacrónica demuestra una concepción sistémica de la historia humana basada fundamentalmente en la noción de praxis. La historia humana surge como la constante creación de necesidades y nuevos modos de satisfacerlas a través del tiempo, lo cual introduce un aspecto dinámico a la confrontación de las categorías del discurso en defensa de los derechos humanos frente al concepto funcionalista de género, el cual, con su perspectiva desde la cúpula de poder, tiende a hacer de la historia una concepción más estática.

La existencia de estos ejes sincrónico y diacrónico en la arquetipificación universal de los derechos humanos revela, además, la capacidad humana de crear mitos y luego hacerlos realidad material a través de su praxis. Se ha señalado que la Organización de las Naciones Unidas, como institución, es la concreción material e histórica del mito de la ley natural propuesto por el liberalismo iluminista en su separación de la naturaleza humana como esencia anterior a la historia que luego accede a la regimentación social en aras del bien común[13]. Este planteamiento llevó a la diferenciación jurídica de dos áreas: los derechos humanos como una de las áreas constitutivas del derecho internacional y el derecho constitucional que, en realidad, configura el modo en que los ciudadanos pueden gozar esos derechos humanos dentro de la estructura de poder de su Estado-nación. Conocida es la relación supervisora que mantienen las Naciones Unidas con respecto a las naciones miembros y signatarias de los diferentes instrumentos respectivos en cuanto a velar por la implementación de los derechos humanos. En particular deben mencionarse la Comisión de Derechos Humanos, la Sub-Comisión para la Prevención de la Discriminación y la Protección de Minorías y la Comisión sobre el Status de la Mujer, la Organización Internacional del Trabajo, además de otras instituciones gubernamentales e interguber-namentales como la Corte Internacional de Justicia, la Corte Europea de Derechos Humanos y la Corte Interamericana de Derechos Humanos. En este mismo sentido, demás está llamar la atención sobre la relevancia que han tenido en los últimos años las actividades de organizaciones no gubernamentales como Amnistía Internacional, la Comisión Internacional de Juristas, la Liga Internacional de Derechos Humanos, la Comisión de las Iglesias sobre Asuntos Internacionales del Consejo Mundial de Iglesias, la Comisión Pontificia de Paz y Justicia y el Comité Internacional de la Cruz Roja, entre otras.

El punto concreto que deseo marcar con todo esto es que no toda arquetipificación universalista es necesariamente ahistórica, según lo demuestran tanto las Naciones Unidas como el gran vigor que ha demostrado el movimiento mundial en defensa de los derechos humanos en las últimas décadas. Espero, además, que haya quedado claramente relevada la gran cercanía que existe entre ese movimiento y la crítica literaria feminista hispanoamericana en su mutua necesidad de establecer arquetipificaciones transhistóricas, transnacionales y transculturales: la defensa de los derechos humanos debe darse en todo lugar y sistema social. Esta crítica literaria puede evitar ataques de subjetivismo ahistoricista si se asume como una problemática directamente conectada con el discurso en defensa de los derechos humanos y la institucionalidad histórica y efectiva de las Naciones Unidas, por mucho que el problema de generar una contrahegemonía quede sin solución. Además de que esta conexión le daría un aval de legitimidad institucional extracadémica incuestionable, la introducción del concepto de persona en el análisis literario podría tener las siguientes repercusiones prácticas:

CUESTION DE UTOPIA: En el movimiento feminista intracadémico norteamericano conviven posiciones ideológicas que en la arena estrictamente política tenderían al antagonismo —tales como el liberalismo, el marxismo, el marxismo-leninismo, el anarquismo, la socialdemocracia, además de posturas privativas del movimiento, tales como el esencialismo sexual. De allí que este movimiento feminista pueda ser caracterizado como segmentario y policéfalo. Sin embargo, profesionalmente sus participantes han podido proyectar una imagen de razonable homogeneidad de objetivos, deflectando las percepciones de discrepancias internas con la construcción de ese agente social mujer arquetípico y universal de que he venido hablando. Esta estrategia de neutralización de conflictos resulta en una reducción de las divergentes teorías sociales en juego a la calidad de instrumentos analíticos que el feminismo puede o no sintetizar con algún grado de eclecticismo[14]. Este eclecticismo es el que abre la posibilidad para la proliferación de un positivismo que entiende la interpretación feminista como la simple aplicación de cualquiera teoría que dé mejor resultado en el análisis de un texto sin que el/a crítico(a) haya madurado algún programa de crítica cultural globalizante.

Y ya instalado en esta matriz positivista, la preocupación del crítico puede caer en la misma desorientación técnica observable en otras áreas de la crítica literaria hispanoamericana: por sobre todo querer estar al día en la aplicación de las últimas novedades del discurso crítico, sin sopesar sus diferencias de sentido y significación social. Así un gran subjetivismo adquiere aspecto de gran objetivismo, en la medida en que cada análisis demuestre la presencia de la más amplia parafernalia técnica. En última instancia, el criterio de verdad que anima a todo movimiento de reivindicación social entra en crisis, puesto que, al desdibujarse la directa relación teleológica de un escrito análitico con la utopía histórica propiciada, se crea un pluralismo ideológico en que cualquier afirmación da lo mismo. Como lo ha señalado Jean Franco, este peligro aqueja particularmente a un feminismo que, haciendo fe de hablar desde una posición de marginalidad, se reclama como propulsor de pluralismos ideológicos en contrarreacción a un centralismo de signo falocrático supuestamente homogenizador de identidades sociales: "Estamos entrando en un período de crisis que ha visto el derrumbre de las 'narrativas maestras' —las teorías globales y totalizantes basadas siempre en la exclusión de lo heterogéneo. Desde este punto de vista contemporáneo es relativamente fácil deconstruir los sistemas binarios del pensamiento colonial o nacionalista. Sin embargo el pluralismo también tiene sus riesgos: si todo es válido, nada importa. Las mujeres, tanto escritoras como críticas, tienen mucho interés en cuestionar la validez de un pluralismo que no trasciende el nivel del consumo" (p. 42).

Para explicar la viabilidad que ha tenido este eclecticismo se podrían avanzar tres hipótesis, a partir de las cortapisas que opone al desarrollo de un pensamiento progresista la realidad palpable del conservadurismo de la mayoría de los programas de enseñanza de las literaturas hispánicas en Estados Unidos, particularmente la peninsular: primera hipótesis, dada la baja gravitación de los partidos de izquierda en la cultura nacional norteamericana y la intensidad menor con que parecen percibirse los conflictos sociales a través de la forma en que los elaboran los medios de comunicación masiva, el potencial conflictivo intracadémico de las diversas posturas políticas feministas pierde la urgencia que podría tener, por ejemplo, en las agudas crisis sociales de los países dependientes. Segunda, que la configuración de este horizonte social permite, entonces, el predominio de ideologías de corte tecnocrático que precisamente separan la teoría social de la teleología de los agentes políticos que la esgrimen. Tercera, a partir del dato de que la institucionalización de la crítica literaria feminista es ya un hecho irreversible, es inevitable que las discusiones teóricas y metodológicas adquieran su dinámica profesional propia y llegue a predominar la discusión técnica y el propósito principal de producir crítica para asegurar un futuro profesional, desdibujándose, hasta el extremo de hacerse confuso, el perfil de la utopía reivindicadora o liberadora que da sustancia a esos esfuerzos. Si se atuviera a diversos escritos, y sin ánimo de ser exhaustivo, el/a lector(a) podría colegir que la crítica literaria hispanoamericana feminista bien busca el abandono radical de la "cultura masculina" y la construcción de un espacio exclusivamente femenino; o bien busca su regeneración reinsuflándole un vitalismo esencialmente femenino, perdido en algún momento de la historia; o bien busca la regimentación de los estadios de desarrollo psíquico del individuo para evitar el trauma edípico; o bien busca garantías para el uso total de los espacios públicos del capitalismo sin alterar sus estructuras fundamentales; o bien concibe la liberación de la mujer conjuntamente con la revolución socialista; o bien busca la síntesis de algunas de estas opciones. Sobre esta indefinición redundan los intentos de preservación del mínimo común denominador del movimiento, lo que impide que las feministas discutan sus objetivos sociales hasta sus últimas consecuencias.

La confusión del/a lector(a) podría llegar a convertirse en alarma si atiende a una retórica que a veces descuida el delicado paso de las mediaciones entre estructuras sociales impersonales, como el patriarcalismo y el falocentrismo, y los individuos que puedan encarnarlo o no, para crear la impresión de que se condena a los hombres en general. A pesar de la justicia de la condena de esas estructuras, a veces su vehemencia parece reemplazar la discriminación contra la mujer por una contra el hombre. Así surge la pregunta, ¿es posible luchar contra una discriminación creando otra? No está demás considerar que buena parte de estos lectores son estudiantes cuyo criterio en cuestiones sociales está sólo en formación.

Ante esta diversidad, la introducción del concepto de persona a la crítica literaria feminista proporcionaría un perfil utópico claro en cuanto a los objetivos del feminismo, de gran economía discursiva, precisamente en el sentido que se lo otorga las Naciones Unidas y el movimiento en defensa de los derechos humanos: el de ser una base mínima de entendimiento en la conducción de los conflictos ideológicos, políticos y armados.

CUESTION DE LECTURA: Como proponía en una sección anterior, el modo en que se construye discursivamente el agente social por el que hablamos condiciona, en cuanto a la crítica literaria, la forma en que realizamos y proponemos nuestras lecturas, nuestros análisis e interpretación de textos y los instrumentos teóricos y metodológicos que constelamos para estos efectos. Aquí es donde la inserción de la problemática de los derechos humanos serviría de "navaja de Occam": el monje inglés abogó por un principio de parsimonia en la creación de universales filosóficos para no caer en entidades pseudo explicativas. Arguyó que "la pluralidad no debe ser asumida sin necesidad" y que "lo que se puede realizar con el mínimo de suposiciones con muchas se hace en vano".

El beneficio de esta actitud ya fue indirectamente demostrado por Sara Castro Klarén en el ensayo ya citado. Aunque Castro Klarén no introduce la problemática teórica del discurso en defensa de los derechos humanos a la crítica literaria, su discusión coincide en parte con él al afirmar que "la reforma feminista busca la igualdad y la eliminación de los prejuicios sexistas en el mundo, en cuanto se constituyen en poder masculino, como una forma de solucionar la injusticia de la situación" (p. 28). Esto le permite una impresionante economía de recursos en el acto de poner en tela de juicio la operatoria de aproximaciones esencialistas. A la vez, con equidad, Castro

Klarén rescata sus aportes empíricos: "Si presumimos que los textos de mujeres, textos escritos y firmados con nombres de mujer, de hecho contienen o se convierten en una categoría para el análisis y la constitución del sujeto femenino, se podría decir que construimos una tautología en vez de un implemento analítico. Presumiríamos aquí que una identidad fija, casi fuera del contexto cultural, establece lo que las mujeres son y lo que las mujeres hacen, de acuerdo con los dictados de la interpretación de una 'imaginación femenina'" (p. 31); "No se puede tan llanamente ir de ida y vuelta entre identidad sexual y roles sociales, y salir luego con la conclusión de que entre escritoras como Jane Austen, las Brontë, George Eliot y otras menos conocidas se formara una sororidad de autoría femenina" (p. 32); "Cuando se lee a feministas provenientes de otra vertiente de la tradición de occidente, parece que el problema de la identidad como una herramienta crítica de análisis residiera en la manera global en que se lo ha concebido. Desde un punto de vista histórico, la 'identidad femenina' ofrece problemas análogos a aquellos ya examinados con relación a la 'imaginación femenina'. Esto sucede en parte porque ambos términos responden al sentido idealista y tradicional de identidad como algo visible, fijo, constante y siempre igual a sí mismo" (p. 35).

CUESTION DE RETORICA: Consideraciones como las reproducidas rememoran ecos de la consigna occamista de que "no se debe multiplicar los entes sin necesidad". En este sentido, otro pasaje clave del ensayo de Castro Klarén introduce el problema de la importancia real de la retórica feminista en la crítica literaria: "Aunque Showalter admite que hay repeticiones y preocupaciones temáticas en común, su estudio reconoce la necesidad de deshacerse de muchas de las presunciones actuales sobre la mujer y sobre la escritora para comenzar a cuestionar algunas de las frases claves en que estas presunciones se fundamentan. Frases tales como 'imaginación femenina', 'estética femenina', 'cuartos propios', 'literatura propia' (prescripción de J. Stuart Mill), 'la mente femenina'" (p. 33). Por nuestra parte agregaríamos la preocupación por las locas, las brujas, las histéricas y las sororidades.

Como emblemas de la situación social de la mujer, apelar a estas figuras retóricas señala dos órdenes de problemas de contenido histórico: primero, ellas pueden tener la crucial importancia de toda consigna emitida en forma razonada en el contexto de las funciones y tareas de propaganda y activismo de todo movimiento de aspiraciones políticas —la de fijar en la imaginación de las masas un símbolo que de modo certero y económico concentre en sí toda una programática de tipo intelectual y emocional ("las locas de la Plaza de Mayo", por ejemplo). Segundo, la reiterada aparición de esos emblemas en el lenguaje de las masas puede indicar algún tipo de preocupación social no explicitado, el cual la intelectualidad de vanguardia debe analizar, revelando y verbalizando su significado como aspiraciones no del todo conscientes. Sin embargo, como en cierto modo lo sugiere Castro Klarén, sería un serio revés intelectual que un movimiento cediera al hechizo de proyectar su bagaje metafórico a otros niveles discursivos y fetichizara su propia retórica para elevarla a la categoría de instrumento de producción y organización de conocimiento. Como ha señalado Jean Franco, esto es de particular importancia cuando se hacen analogías apresuradas de la situación de la mujer con lo popular, el exilio, las etnias y razas sojuzgadas, los pueblos dependientes: "... fundir la teoría feminista en una teoría general del colonialismo tampoco sirve. No es suficiente decir con Julia Kristeva que la 'mujer' como categoría discursiva está incluida entre los marginados de la sociedad y 'es la misma lucha... nunca pueda darse la una sin la otra'. Definitivamente NO es la misma lucha" (p. 35).

CUESTION DE COMPLEJIDAD HISTORICA: Aunque, como propongo, debemos reforzar la arquetipificación universalizante con que se ha institucionalizado la agencia social de la mujer en la crítica literaria feminista que nos concierne, también debemos tomar conciencia de las distorsiones históricas que esa conceptualización pueda poner en movimiento. Perfilar a la mujer como objeto transhistórico, transcultural y transnacional de opresión corresponde a la información y evidencia antropológica de que disponemos. No obstante, censurar el hecho histórico de que ella es también agente de opresión de otras mujeres es empobrecer la riqueza de los seres humanos. Permítaseme que aquí yo mismo introduzca una analogía, que no creo apresurada: esa censura puede caer en la misma trampa en que se vieron los cultores deficientes del realismo socialista cuando intentaron hacer hagiografía con la imagen de un proletariado incapaz de hacer mal e instintivamente propenso a las luchas de liberación. Sospecho que esa censura es otro de los orígenes de la creación de universales innecesarios sobre la condición social del ser humano: si partimos de una hagiografía similar sobre la mujer, en algún momento deberemos echar mano de algún arbitrio pseudo explicativo para enfrentar la irrebatible evidencia histórica de la lucha de clases con que está mediado el conocimiento de la mujer. En mi experiencia, la más clara demostración de esta trampa potencial ocurrió cuando, en un análisis textual, una estudiante feminista de gran inteligencia y talento explicó el maltrato que sufría una empleada doméstica de origen indio en un hogar acomodado con la afirmación de que los valores masculinos de la cultura nacional impedían que la dueña de casa expresara su natural feminidad solidaria con otra mujer.

El uso de las categorías del discurso en defensa de los derechos humanos evitaría tales recovecos y nos permitiría ir directo al grano: la cuestión es mostrar el gran espectáculo de seres humanos que deben crear y exhibir su dignidad de tales dando sentido simbólico a sus cuerpos y a su entorno en medio de las más grandes contradicciones impuestas por su condición social; la cuestión es, además, demostrar que, aun en su calidad de opresora de otras mujeres, una mujer burguesa, en el marco de la opresión que ella misma sufre dentro de su clase, también debería tener las opciones para concretar el máximo de los potenciales de su personalidad. Desbrozar esta situación permitiría a la crítica literaria feminista calibrar finamente el uso de la retórica y el protocolo de solidaridad sin que ello distorsione el conocimiento histórico.

Aceptar la premisa del derecho irrestringido a la acumulación cultural, desembarazarnos a partir de esto de toda construcción retórica que nos entrampe en la metafísica permitiría no sólo que la crítica literaria feminista avanzara estratégicamente desde posturas de denuncia negativista a una clara afirmación transcultural positiva de los derechos de la mujer, sino también a la posibilidad de vislumbrar más concretamente la promesa del potencial revolucionario que se le imputa. En las condiciones expuestas, la crítica literaria podría realizarse como una reflexión sobre la forma en que las obras analizadas han elaborado una visión de la sociedad y de su orden simbólico. Para estos efectos, la lectura del texto literario analizado debería ser considerada como un eje diacrónico de manifestación de una circunstancia histórica concreta al cual debería introducírsele el eje sincrónico abstracto del estado actual de los derechos humanos existentes. Esta yuxtaposición podría desnudar la forma como se oscurecen los mecanismos del sistema de opresión social prevaleciente, exponiendo la forma en que impiden o habilitan la concreción del ser social de la mujer. Esta reflexión se vería forzada a asumir una postura eminentemente ética, señalando los límites restrictivos de la conciencia histórica de los autores en el momento de transar en el juicio social para proteger algún interés consciente o inconscientemente asumido, desmontando los artilugios de la mala conciencia que los llevan a tales transacciones, a la vez que se rescatan sus logros progresistas. Inevitablemente, en la asunción de una postura ética frente a su trabajo, el crítico literario mismo no tendría más opción que la de historificarse a sí mismo al cuestionar su propia ideología en cuanto a las restricciones de su conciencia y a posibles claudicaciones en su análisis e interpretación, al contrario de una crítica positivista que presume una objetividad espúrea en la aplicación de un instrumental teórico aparentemente neutral, o de una crítica feminista que se desvía a los circuitos cerrados del juego retórico.

CUESTION DE TRANSFERENCIA CULTURAL: Por otra parte, en el contexto de que la defensa de los derechos humanos es una obligación universal que compromete a todo individuo, organización social, gobierno y Estado, el problema de la transferencia de implementos intelectuales en condiciones de dependencia toma otro cariz. En razón de esta obligación universal, en defensa de los derechos humanos la transferencia discursiva es deber incuestionable, en la medida en que grupos e instituciones extranjeras apoyan a grupos y organismos locales —como las comisiones nacionales de derechos humanos— en el desarrollo y protección de sus objetivos. En las últimas décadas la intelectualidad progresista latinoamericana alcanzó gran lucidez en cuanto a una conciencia de los efectos culturales de tal importación como factores favorables o negativos en las tareas históricas de definir las necesidades continentales reales y los medios para satisfacerlas con algún grado de autonomía política. También en este período ha quedado expuesta la visión retrógrada con que los fascismos latinoamericanos conciben las relaciones genéricas, reiterando ellos los estereotipos de la mujer que el movimiento feminista contemporáneo ha venido condenando ya largamente. Por otra parte, en los países afectados por el fascismo, la violenta represión de los estamentos políticos, predominantemente masculinos, ha creado condiciones en que la actuación pública de la mujer en defensa de los derechos humanos ha alcanzado enorme relieve. En el caso chileno, durante un largo período esta movilización femenina a nivel político abrió los únicos espacios concebibles de actividad para la oposición antimilitar. Estas acciones de mujeres, no necesariamente feministas, tuvieron un impacto que puede ser analizado en dos vertientes: bien como una reactivación del movimiento feminista chileno entre una intelectualidad pequeñoburguesa progresista que se ha constituido en diversos grupos de estudio; o como mayor visibilidad política y legitimidad social para un movimiento que había continuado desarrollándose fuera de la conciencia pública. Estos grupos de estudio a la vez irradian sus reflexiones hacia alguna forma de actividad social, particularmente con vistas a un nexo con la mujer de las clases subordinadas, y a la reconstrucción de la historia anterior del movimiento feminista en Chile. En cierta medida el estímulo intelectual para estos esfuerzos de recuperación de raíces perdidas provino de los escritos del feminismo anglo-norteamericano y francés. En este contexto, entonces, cualquier forma de feminismo que cuestione los límites conservadores y autoritarios de las definiciones genéricas, aun en sus formas más esencialistas, es un aporte hacia la redemocratización. Dado que entre estas intelectuales feministas han predominado las cientistas sociales, en su apropiación teórica de esas importaciones han demostrado un gran discernimiento en el uso de las diferentes variedades de argumentación feminista, bien para fines retóricos y protocolares de enorme importancia para la expresión artística o para la producción de conocimiento histórico, sin que ambos aspectos se obstaculicen mutuamente[15].

CUESTION DE LUCHA DE CLASES Y DEFENSA DE LAS CULTURAS NACIONALES LATINOAMERICANAS: Aunque espero que el curso de mis argumentos haya sido explícito al respecto, para terminar, quiero dejar en claro que estoy lejos de un idealismo y de un voluntarismo que con frecuencia vician la comprensión del movimiento en defensa de los derechos humanos y que indirectamente afecta al movimiento feminista por la gran cercanía que los une. Se trata de la expectativa de que la madurez ética de la humanidad expresada por el movimiento quizás pueda superar los antagonismos contemporáneos de la lucha de clases a nivel nacional e internacional. La urgencia mundial creada por una contaminación ambiental que afecta aun a países y regiones no directamente conectadas; la posibilidad de un holocausto nuclear y la violación masiva de los derechos humanos acarreadas por un militarismo guiado por la Doctrina de la Seguridad Nacional; los masivos desplazamientos mundiales de poblaciones marginadas; la preocupación por hambrunas catastróficas en diferentes lugares del globo; la rápida difusión mundial de enfermedades antes desconocidas, como el SIDA, todo esto ha encontrado expresión en movimientos como Amnistía Internacional, el Partido Verde europeo, el movimiento Greenpeace y el mismo movimiento feminista, que parecen haber creado un estilo, una agenda y una movilización políticas instaladas directamente en un plano universal al abogar por el bienestar de la especie humana, al parecer soslayándose el espacio de los Estados nacionales, en que se dirimen intereses más específicos.

No puede negarse la existencia real de cantidades masivas de individuos inspirados por un sentimiento sacro de la humanidad, sea de tipo secular o religioso. No obstante, las luchas que puedan dar estas organizaciones por presio-

nar en defensa de los derechos humanos —ya sea en atención a violaciones locales o en solidaridad con lo ocurrido
en otros países— tendrán el marco inescapable de las
instituciones estatales y el universo simbólico de cada cultura nacional y, por ende, la articulación de un poder
hegemónico de clase. Por lo tanto, es inevitable caracterizar al movimiento en defensa de los derechos humanos
como una modalidad especial de la lucha de clases. Esto se
hace evidente si consideramos que, como ocurre en los
países latinoamericanos afectados por el fascismo, además
de individuos independientes, buena parte de las personas
involucradas en estas organizaciones son familiares de
militantes políticos dañados por la represión o son personas designadas por los partidos. Lo que otorga a esta forma
de lucha de clase su modalidad especial es que los activis-
tas en defensa de los derechos humanos, bien sea de manera consciente o inconsciente, en efecto proponen a la colectividad un estilo de conflicto político en que se redefine
el uso de la acumulación simbólica de la cultura nacional
en su relación con las actividades que giran en torno al Estado. Ese estilo privilegia los elementos retórica y protoco-
larmente integrativos y cohesionadores de la experiencia
histórica elaborados por la memoria y la conciencia colectivas. Con ese estilo se afirma que, en tributo a ella y en referencia a la madurez moral y ética de la humanidad expresada en el derecho internacional, los conflictos sociales
deben ser dirimidos sin echar mano de los recursos extremos e innecesarios que permiten los instrumentos de violencia y los aparatos estatales de disciplinamiento social,
opresión y represión existentes, bien sean ideológicos, po-
liciales o militares. Esto podría servir como una hipótesis
para explicar el hecho de que los movimientos de derechos
humanos, en las grandes coyunturas de crisis mundial, se
activen tanto en países de gran estabilidad como de inestabilidad en sus instituciones políticas. Esta hipótesis expone, además, que el espacio en que se dan estas luchas es,
inevitablemente, el de los Estados y las culturas nacionales, cuya autonomía y soberanía debemos preservar para
que la defensa de los derechos humanos llegue a ser una
utopía concretada.

NOTAS

[1]Jean Franco, "Apuntes sobre la Crítica Feminista y la Literatura Hispanoamericana". *Hispamérica*, año XV, N° 45, 1986.

[2]Sara Castro-Klarén, "La Crítica Literaria Feminista y la Escritora en América Latina". *La sartén por el mango*, Patricia Elena González y Eliana Ortega, eds. (Río Piedras, Puerto Rico: Ediciones Huracán, 1984).

[3]Ellen Carol DuBois, Gail Paradise Kelly, Elizabeth Lapovsky Kennedy, Carolyn W. Korsmeyer, Lillian S. Robinson, *Feminist Scholarship. Kindling in the Groves of Academe* (Chicago: University of Illinois Press, 1987) p. 58. La traducción es mía.

[4]Se recordará que uno de los aspectos operatorios centrales de la investigación positivista es la de limitar el conocimiento válido a lo empírico y a los resultados entregados por los instrumentos de captación de lo empírico que se apliquen.

[5]Me refiero al panel 713 "Social Bodies, Spiritual Selves: Religious Women Writers of the Golden Age" organizado por Jean Franco (Columbia University) en la Convención de la Modern Language Association, 1987. En él participaron, además, Georgina Sabat-Rivers (State University of New York, Stony Brook), Electa Arenal (College of Staten Island, City University of New York), Anne J. Cruz (University of California, Irvine).

[6]Ver: Jo Freeman, ed. *Social Movements of the Sixties and Seventies* (New York: Longman, Inc., 1983); Luther P. Gerlach and Virginia Hine, *People, Power, Change, Movements of Social Transformation* (Indianapolis: The Bobbs-Merrill Co., Inc., 1970).

[7]Norman Geras, *Marx and Human Nature. Refutation of a Legend* (London: Verso Editions, 1983). La traducción es mía. Además, es preciso tener en cuenta el ontologismo histórico de un Georg Lukács: Theo Pinkus, ed. *Conversations with Lukács* (Cambridge, Massachusetts: The MIT Press, 1975).

[8]Lucía Guerra-Cunningham, "Los Recursos del Cuerpo: Evaluación Crítica de la Teoría Feminista". Manuscrito de próxima aparición en *Eutopías* (Minneapolis, Minnesota).

[9]Ver: *The Structure of Social Action* (1937); *Family, Socialization and Interaction Process* (1955); *Economy and Society* (1956); *Sociological Theory and Modern Society* (1967).

[10]Mary G. Dietz, "Context is All: Feminism and Theories of Citizenship". *Daedalus*, Vol 116, Nº 4, Fall, 1987. La autora se dirige a las dificultades que ha tenido el movimiento feminista para generar una teoría política. Al mismo problema se refiere Mary E. Hawkesworth en "Re/Vision: Feminist Theory Confronts the Polis". *Social Theory and Practice*, Vol. 13, Nº 2 (Summer, 1987).

[11]Charles Taylor, "The Person". Michael Carrithers, Steven Collins, Steven Lukes, eds. *The Category of the Person* (Cambridge: Cambridge University Press, 1985); Hernán Montealegre, *La seguridad del Estado y los derechos humanos* (Santiago de Chile: Edición Academia de Humanismo Cristiano, 1979).

[12]Para un entendimiento global de la problemática de los derechos humanos ver: James W. Nickel, *Making Sense of Human Rights* (Berkeley: University of California Press, 1987); Karel Vasak, Rédacteur général, *Les dimensions internationales des droits de l'homme* (Paris: UNESCO, 1978); Theodor Meron, ed., *Human Rights in International Law. Legal and Policy Issues* (Oxford: Clarendon Press, 1985).

[13]Imre Szabo, "Fondaments historiques et développement des droits de l'homme". Vasak, op. cit.

[14]Como muestra de un eclecticismo en sus esfuerzos por evitar consideraciones políticas fundamentales, tómense en cuenta los intentos de definir neutralmente la investigación feminista como mera manipulación y cambio de paradigmas heurísticos en la obra ya citada, *Feminist Scholarship*. En las conclusiones se afirma lo siguiente: "Una fuente de problemas es que los debates considerados como centrales en el pensamiento feminista evolucionan y cambian. A medida que un conjunto de cuestiones se hace menos productivo y estimulante intelectualmente, otras avanzan al primer plano. En los años iniciales los problemas teóricos no resueltos se centraron en torno a "reforma" versus "revolución" y en torno a la primacía de las estructuras económicas y sociales, a diferencia de las sexuales y psicológicas, en el objetivo de explicar la subordinación de la mujer. Más recientemente el debate feminista ha desplazado su foco para hacer resaltar el género en el futuro que se ambiciona para la mujer: Algunas feministas piensan que las diferencias genéricas son un producto social pernicioso y debería ser eliminado; otras afirman que las características femeninas proveerán de valor y fortaleza a las mujeres y a la sociedad en el futuro. A medida que se acumula información sobre la mujer, las investigadoras aplican diversos marcos analíticos a ese conocimiento para tratar de comprender la condición de la mujer y sugerir como cambiarla. Una vez que la investigación sobre la mujer llegue al nivel interpretativo, el problema no será determinar qué esquema es feminista, sino qué marco feminista es

mejor, qué ideas tienen la mayor capacidad para explicar la opresión, para analizar la injusticia social, y proyectar un futuro de liberación. La existencia de marcos analíticos feministas en competición es extremadamente importante —el intercambio entre ellos es el modo en que nuestro pensamiento crece en complejidad y poder— pero hace imposible que se marquen líneas divisorias exactas entre ideas feministas y no feministas en referencia a contenido teórico" (196-197).

[15]En particular tengo en mente *Ser política en Chile* (Santiago de Chile: Facultad Latinoamericana de Ciencias Sociales (FLACSO), 1986), de Julieta Kirkwood. Para los propósitos de configurar un perfil colectivo de un pensamiento feminista, esta obra tiene el mérito de ser una compilación y organización póstuma de notas de la autora por parte de un colectivo feminista.

THE OTHER WITHIN: CLASS AND ETHNICITY AS DIFFERENCE IN MEXICAN WOMEN'S LITERATURE

Cynthia Steele
University of Washington

Cuando desaparezca la última criada, el colchoncito en que ahora reposa nuestra conformidad, aparecerá la primera rebelde furibunda. Rosario Castellanos, 1970

I. INTRODUCTION: WOMEN'S EXPLOITATION OF WOMEN

This quotation, which ends Rosario Castellanos' essay "La liberación de la mujer, aquí" (*El uso* 56-60), points to a theme that is pivotal not only in this author's works, but also in the narrative of her closest literary heir, Elena Poniatowska. It also constitutes a secondary theme in fiction by other Mexican women writers of the past thirty years, among them Amparo Dávila and Elena Garro. This is not altogether surprising, in view of the centrality of the mistress-servant relationship in the lives of most upper- and middle-class Mexican women of their generations. In highly stratified Latin American nations like Mexico, dependent development has perpetuated, in modified form, the precapitalist institution of domestic service. In fact, during the past three decades, massive, predominantly female, immigration from the countryside to Mexico City, along with the incorporation of middle-class women into the work force, has ensured the survival of this seemingly anachronistic institution, which is characterized by the exploitation of the peasantry by the urban upper and middle classes, of Indians by *mestizos* and whites, and of women by other women.

Mexican women authors of this period, in writing about the frustrations of bourgeois and petit-bourgeois women characters, return time and again to metaphors of enclosure and isolation. Frequently, the female protagonist's seclusion in the private sphere excludes insensitive or tyrannical males and females of her own social class, but includes the character's nanny, cook or maid in a relationship characterized by mutual emotional dependency, unilateral support, and conspiracy against patriarchal power. Both Rosario Castellanos and Elena Poniatowska have made clear, in autobiographical fiction and essays, the psychological significance that such relationships have had throughout their own lives (Castellanos, *Balún-Canán* and *El uso*; Poniatowska, "Presentación" and *La "Flor de lis"*). Moreover, Poniatowska and other Latin American women intellectuals who have undertaken oral histories of working-class, *lumpen*, and peasant women seem— consciously or not—to draw on the dynamics of the mistress-servant relationship as a basis for establishing rapport with their informants (Poniatowska, "Hasta" and "Presentación"; Burgos). Thus, both in fiction and history, female solidarity across lines of class and ethnicity at times paradoxically has grown out of a common experience— from opposite ends of the power dialectic—of female exploitation.

The labor relationship between female employer and servant occurs in the highly problematic context of dependent capitalist development. It is inextricably linked to the problem of massive internal migration resulting from urban industrialization, coupled with rural impoverishment and unemployment. At present the problems of underdevelopment are greatly exacerbated by a major economic crisis, which in turn has been aggravated by the effects of the devastating earthquakes of 1985. In this context, the cities cannot absorb rural immigrants' labor on more than a substandard level; thus, a large, nonunionized surplus labor pool is created which perpetuates substandard employment. In 1980 (before the crisis and earthquakes undoubtedly deteriorated the situation), a Mexican domestic servant typically earned the equivalent of between twenty and eighty dollars a month for a six-day working week with unlimited hours and duties and, usually, no social security benefits (Goldsmith 1). However, it would be a mistake to view the victimization of servants as solely economic. They frequently are subjected to rape and systematic sexual abuse by male employers and their sons. Nor can one underestimate the psychological effects over time of a relationship that posits the servant as childlike and inferior, greatly limits her independence and undervalues her work. As Judith Rollins has observed, "What might appear to be the basis for a more humane, less alienating work arrangement allows for a level of psychological exploitation unknown in other occupations. The typical employer extracts more than labor" (156). Moreover, the phenomenon is increasingly international in scope. In recent years, because of the economic and political crises in Mexico, Central America and the Caribbean, and the marked increase in two-income professional households in the U.S., the number of Latin American and Caribbean maids and nannies has grown significantly in this country, particularly in New York and cities in the Southwest. Poor women are beginning to move from the urban labor market in the neocolonial microcosm to similarly exploitative but better-paying positions in the metropolis. Questions of cultural alienation and exploitation along class and racial lines, which are raised by internal migration, become even more pressing in this context.

There are a number of reasons that the Latin American middle classes—and, increasingly, their U.S. counterparts—continue to tolerate this institution. On a pragmatic level it entails obvious advantages for the female employer; since the sexual division of labor assigns housework and child care to her, she is able to free herself of most of these responsibilities—and thereby create time for other economic, cultural, or social activities—by relegating this 'woman's work' to another woman, one from a lower social class (and, frequently, another racial and ethnic group). Thus, for a working woman without recourse to the support system traditionally provided by female members of the extended family, having a maid partially solves the problem of the double day. For a married woman, it may, in addition, defer the need to confront her husband regarding the sexual divison of household labor and childcare. Even for women that aren't employed outside the home, the organization of Latin American societies makes such activities as shopping and dealing with bureaucracies time-consuming, thus encouraging dependence on servants to do household labor while the employers carry out errands (Rollins 40).

On a less conscious level, the mistress—especially if she is not employed—achieves a certain amount of social power by virtue of supervising another person's labor, which may to some extent compensate for her feeling of powerlessness within the patriarchal order. That is, her isolation and lack of integration into the marketplace—which consigns the production of exchange values to men and the production of private use values to women—deprive her of economic, political and social power, limiting her sphere of authority to her children and servants (Sacks 234). Ironically, the presence of a domestic worker further reduces the housewife's participation in the economy, reducing her traditional role as producer of use value and consumer of merchandise to the single role of consumer (Goldsmith 7). Beyond this, a servant can act as a buffer to absorb tensions between herself and her husband and other family members. Finally, Rollins has noted that the domestic worker offers her employers "the self-enhancing satisfactions that emanate from having the presence of an inferior and validating the employers' lifestyle, ideology, and social world, from their familial interrelations to the economically and racially stratified system in which they live" (156).

Middle-class liberals and progressives may justify their participation in this institution by arguing that the urban alternatives to such employment for young, uneducated and unskilled female immigrants from rural areas are even more odious: nonunionized factory work (i.e., sweat shops and *maquiladoras*), or employment in the 'informal sector' (such as street vending and prostitution). Furthermore, they may argue that domestic employment is transitional, that it will provide the servants with a livelihood while they train themselves for less exploitative work, such as white-collar jobs or work in the (public) service sector. However, the data regarding whether such employment tends to serve as a stepping-stone in Mexico City is, at best, ambiguous. It seems more likely that servants' daughters, rather than they, may benefit professionally from greater access to education in an urban context (Goldsmith 6). Lourdes Arizpe's research indicates that the most common movement for the servants themselves is from live-in to live-out work (from "trabajo de planta" to "trabajo de entrada por salida"), generally beginning at the time of their marriage. However, when this situation changes, the fundamental nature of the job (salary and working conditions) doesn't improve significantly (*Campesinado* 101-109). In psychological terms, Mary Goldsmith has found that women who work "de entrada por salida" tend to be the most resigned to and defeated by their situation (7). Moreover, Arizpe's interviews with female Mazahua street vendors in Mexico City (so-called 'Marías') revealed that they overwhelmingly preferred the independence, flexibility, and family and peer companionship, not to mention the relatively higher pay, of this precarious form of self-employment, to the alternative of working as maids (*Indígenas* 138).

Only within the past decade have feminist social scientists and activists begun to turn their attention to domestic service, which accounts for the employment of approximately one-half of female urban workers in Latin America (in Mexico City, more than half a million women) (Grau 17; Goldsmith 1). There are a number of possible reasons for this. For one thing, its very omnipresence may lead people to take it for granted, to view it either as natural or, at best, as an inevitable part of dependent capitalist development. (Carlos Monsiváis notes, with regard to the Mexican garment workers whose plight was brought to light by the earthquakes, that up until then a similar mentality had prevailed vis-a-vis their situation: "¿Qué se le va a hacer? Las costureras eran 'esclavas tradicionales,' y su humillación resultaba 'algo imposible de modificar, un mal del siglo'." His description of these women's working conditions reveals a close resemblance to the situation of domestic servants [92-93].) Furthermore, the power dynamics of the mistress-servant relationship tend to reinforce in the employer feelings of what Judith Rollins has termed "maternalism"; she rationalizes that she is doing her servant a favor by 'giving' her work, that in so doing she is protecting and sponsoring the less fortunate. Paradoxically, in its very omnipresence, this institution is also, in a sense, invisible, by virtue of its relegation to the private sphere. During the past decade, however, a number of Mexican social scientists have begun to conduct research on domestic workers, and several organizations have been formed to educate servants regarding their rights and to support their efforts to achieve higher salaries and better working conditions (Urrutia).[1]

Feminist literary critics have been even slower to deal with this problem, in spite of its prominence in the works of twentieth-century women writers and its obvious implications for issues of feminism and social justice. When so much remains to be written about women's subjectivity, it might at first glance seem counterproductive for feminist critics to focus on fictional portrayals of women's objectification of other women. Yet what is compelling about the treatment of this theme in Mexican women's narrative is precisely the complex, problematic portrayal of the mistress-servant relationship as a form of female complicity against patriarchy, across barriers of class and race. By way of illustration, I will briefly discuss how the mistress-servant relationship relates to the imaginative distribution of space and the construction of female subjectivity in two short stories from the late 1950s and early 1960s by Amparo Dávila and Elena Garro, as well as in autobiographical fiction and essays, written during this period and more recently, by Rosario Castellanos and Elena Poniatowska.

II. AMPARO DAVILA AND ELENA GARRO: FANTASY AND COMPLICITY

In Amparo Dávila's story "El huésped," which was originally published in 1959, an unhappy middle-class housewife, isolated in a rural town, is confronted with the danger posed to herself, her maid Guadalupe, and the two women's children by a wild creature that her husband has brought home. The animal, like the protagonist/narrator and her husband and children, is never named; "...nunca lo nombrábamos, nos parecía que al hacerlo cobraba realidad aquel ser tenebroso" (19). However, a number of clues identify it as a mountain lion. The narrator's husband, who regards her with marked indifference and whom she suspects of infidelity, refuses to acknowledge the danger that the ferocious animal poses to his family and servants. In her loneliness and fear, the protagonist finds some comfort in traditional domestic labor: garden work and sewing, with her children playing at her side. Since she is confined to the house and cannot venture outward into public space, she retreats radically inward, into the interior garden of the large house (her unconscious?), a space which she associates with creativity, fertility and a domestic harmony that excludes men. However, in the kitchen and bedroom, the spaces associated with her wifely duties, she is stalked by the vicious cat and forced to retreat. Moreover, the narrator is especially vulnerable in her bedroom, since she cannot close the door when she is alone at night, for fear of provoking her husband's jealousy when he returns home.

While the story is tantalizingly ambiguous, it seems clear that the cat is a projection of oppressive—even sadistic—patriarchal authority (and aggressive sexuality?), the flip side of her husband's apparent indifference. The two women eventually band together to protect their children and themselves, but their maternal solidarity is not without its contradictions. Early in the story the narrator tells us that the creature hates and pursues her, but has no interest in Guadalupe and her baby Martín. (Apparently, servants are the only characters who are 'real' enough to have names). Yet when the cat eventually strikes, it chooses Martín as its (his) victim. Earlier Guadalupe had saved her mistress from nearly burning down the house in her attempts to ward off the beast; however, when the situation is reversed and the servant leaves her baby with her mistress, the latter doesn't manage to effectively reciprocate the maternal protection. Moreover, in attempting to persuade her husband to remove the creature from the household, the protagonist argues for the safety of her own children, not that of Martín, although he already has been singled out by the predator. Her indifference to his welfare is also apparent in her hope that Guadalupe won't leave her employ after this brutal incident. The narrator tells us that, in spite of Martín's brush with death and her husband's refusal to take the animal away, Guadalupe decided to remain, out of the fierce loyalty that masters traditionally have expected of their servants, coupled with a (female) desire for revenge, a desire that, as we learn, the narrator herself shares: "...era una mujer noble y valiente que sentía gran afecto por los niños y por mí. Pero ese día nació en ella un odio que clamaba venganza" (21).

The two women's anger, deriving from their maternal instinct and a burning hatred, leads them to conspire to turn the master's own weapons against his vicious pet: they kill it through enclosure (as the narrator has been isolated and encloistered by her husband) and starvation (as the narrator has been emotionally starved). (While these two parenthetical observations presumably apply to Guadalupe as well, the narrative systematically ignores her loneliness and oppression.) When the husband returns, the secret assassins conspire once again, to practice the sort of deception that conventionally is associated with femininity: "...lo recibimos con la noticia de su muerte repentina y desconcertante" (23). The first-person singular with which the narrator began her tale has become first-person plural, suggesting a continuing bond of female solidarity against patriarchy,[2] although without breaking out of the patriarchal edifice. What the narrator fails to acknowledge—but the story unwittingly lays bare—is that Guadalupe, beyond sharing her mistress' vulnerability to the abuses of patriarchy, is also the victim of her mistress' relative indifference, which is, to a certain extent, comparable to the husband's callousness. And, as the story eloquently demonstrates with regard to the master, in unequal power relations, indifference can mask sadism.

Elena Garro's short story "La culpa es de los tlaxcaltecas" was published in 1964, at a time of widespread intellectual disillusionment with the bourgeoisie that had emerged victorious from the revolution and, for the previous two decades, had been leading Mexico down a road to modernization that was proving to be a dead-end littered with corruption. (For instance, Fuentes' *La muerte de Artemio Cruz* had been published two years earlier.) In Garro's story, Laura, another unhappy wife, this one bourgeois and childless, confides in her servant Nacha about her alleged rendezvous with her Aztec cousin/husband from an earlier life. The setting for the women's private conversations—essentially monologues by Laura—is Nacha's domain, the kitchen, which Castellanos once referred to as "el espacio sagrado," and which is described here as "separado del mundo por un muro invisible de tristeza, por un compás de espera." (Are the sadness and anticipation attributes only of Laura? of Nacha? of all women? [76]) The story draws on two conventional associations with the notion of betrayal, with the *tlaxcaltecas* who formed an alliance with Cortés' forces to defeat the Aztecs, and with women. Through her marriage to Pablo, a jealous *mestizo* associated with the upper echelons of the national government, Laura has been disloyal to her Aztec husband; in fact, she is committing a "permanent betrayal." By extension, the story suggests, in their support of the postrevolutionary bourgeoisie that governs the country, contemporary Mexicans are betraying the nation's prehispanic roots, posited as a native aristocracy which can be a source of spiritual authenticity. Laura establishes a bond of female complicity with Nacha by eliciting the cook's admission that she, like Laura (and all women), is "treacherous" ("traicionera").

This female, nurturing (yet sad and waiting) space of the kitchen is implicitly contrasted with other, dangerous or corrupt spaces. The house in general is associated with the reflection or multiplication of luxury and alienation: "Desde que entré, los muebles, los jarrones de cristal y los espejos se me vinieron encima y me dejaron más triste de lo que venía" (p. 81). The dining room is the theater in which Laura's bourgeois husband, Pablo Aldama, exhibits his self-importance. His obsessive chatter about Presidential visits bores Laura (as well as Nacha, who calls him "fregón"), while his "cuerpo deshabitado" and "ojos muertos" (like those of the only other *mestizo* man in the story, a mechanic) suggest that the official power with which he flirts masks an impotence or lack of authenticity (i.e., truth, loyalty, courage, sensuality—all the values associated with the Aztec husband). By contrast, the Indian's "ojos brillantes...chispas negras" suggest spiritual insight, a notion that is reinforced by his repeated appearance at windows. He is also associated with the highway (movement, journey, quest), and with two traditionally aristocratic spaces that, by the early 1960s, had been appropriated by popular culture: the streets of downtown Mexico City (the heart of the ancient Aztec empire) and Chapultepec Park (the site of Maximilian's castle, heart of the French empire in Mexico). Even before her rendezvous with the Aztec begin, the jealous Pablo fears his wife's ventures into the public sphere and tries, in vain, to confine her to the patriarchal house. Thus, Laura's bedroom, like the narrator's bedroom in "El huésped," far from being a refuge or intimate space, is associated with the exertion of oppressive male control: Pablo's angry accusations and violence, and the psychiatrist's paternalistic interrogations. Only the kitchen, the servants' domain, is neutral territory in the gender war. In the last scene of the story, when Laura, who had disappeared weeks earlier, has returned to say good-bye to Nacha, it is the latter who opens the kitchen window for the Aztec, facillitating Laura's final escape with him. (The kitchen's "sad wait" has ended.)

Nacha is drawn into the role of co-conspirator through a combination of a matter-of-fact faith in romantic love (which allows her to recognize that Laura was "meant for" the Aztec and not for Pablo) and stubborn loyalty to her mistress. In other words, it is by virtue of attributes that are traditionally associated with women and with servants, respectively. At times she seems to be humoring Laura, while silently sharing the family's fears for her mistress' sanity. Yet, when faced with choosing between her loyalty to Laura and obedience to the patriarchal authority of Pablo and his dowager mother, Margarita, Nacha unhesitatingly chooses Laura.

At the end of the story, Laura definitively escapes the claustrophobic confines of postrevolutionary bourgeois Mexico into the alternative reality of romanticized prehispanic culture, which constitutes a sort of aristocracy of passionate sensibility. In casting her lot with the Aztecs, she renounces the passive, 'female' role of complicity with oppression that identified her with the *tlaxcaltecas*.

If Pablo cannot fathom Laura's sensibility and therefore fears it, Nacha, by virtue of her femininity and, one might speculate, her Indian heritage, can intuit and enjoy it vicariously. At the same time, the story seems to imply that centuries of subordination have robbed the Aztecs' ancestors of the capacity for feeling deeply themselves; in this sense, the bourgeoisie's emotional sterility is mirrored in its servants. Nacha's extreme identification with her mistress, her habit of living through her, is apparent in the cook's final departure, which follows on her realization that, with Laura's 'liberation' (into a time warp and death alongside the Aztecs? into madness?), her own life has lost its purpose: "Ya no me hallo en casa de los Aldama. Voy a buscarme otro destino" (93). Nacha's failure to collect her salary before leaving underlines the personal—as against the economic—nature of her involvement in the mistress-servant relationship. While the female protagonist (unlike her counterpart in "El huésped") makes a definitive break with patriarchy, her servant unquestioningly moves on to another mistress, to her own, decidedly less romantic, "destiny."

III. ROSARIO CASTELLANOS: CIRCLES OF OPPRESSION

As we have seen, both Dávila and Garro create an idealized, semifeudal fictional world in which the maid's complicity with her mistress is primarily a function of her loyalty as a servant. However, in both stories the maid—like the mistress—is also reacting against some form of male oppression. This female conspiracy also appears, but in a more complex and problematized form, in the fiction of Rosario Castellanos and Elena Poniatowska, Mexico's most important women writers since Sor Juana. The differences in the perspectives of these two writers—with regard to the other two authors and to each other—correspond to significant differences in the sociohistorical contexts that they have drawn on in their works. Castellanos' best fiction deals with postrevolutionary Chiapas, which, during the 1950s, continued to be rigidly stratified along racial lines. Indian servants maintained strong ties with Tzotzil and Tzeltal communities and ideologies, which allowed them to maintain a separate cultural identity from their employers, as well as a potential base of support. At the same time, the caste system of Chiapas posited them as objects, as inheritable property of their masters. For Poniatowska, the frame of reference is Mexico City during the period from 1945 to the present. In this context, the servants' isolation and alienation combines with the growing predominance of capitalist labor relations to radically change their cultural identity, while increasingly inhibiting identification with their employers' ideology. The change, then, is from an Indian or *mestizo* peasant culture (in the context of the capitalization and impoverishment of the countryside) to various forms of popular urban culture. Poniatowska has observed this as a movement from community tradition and folk art, as sources of identity and values, to a loss of cultural roots ("el desarraigo"), accompanied by "la negación de todo aquello que es admirable" ["Presentación" 12, 15-16, 80-81]. Lourdes Arizpe, however, cautions against the temptation to see this process as a simple one of acculturation entailing loss; rather, she posits the hypothesis, based on her extensive research on urban immigrants, that it may be only the most visible aspects of an Indian culture which disappear in the city, while the basic world view and system of values remain fundamentally intact, permeating urban Mexican culture (*Campesinado* 127).

In an essay of self-criticism written in 1971, Rosario Castellanos identified the central thematic thread woven throughout her fictional works as:

> ...la de la situación de la mujer en México y la de las situaciones en las que tienen que realizar los actos que se le proponen como válidos y alcanzar, a través de ellos, su plenitud de persona. O todo lo contrario...la unidad de esos libros la constituye la persistencia recurrente de ciertas figuras: la niña desvalida, la adolescente encerrada, la solterona vencida, la casada defraudada. ¿No hay otra opción? Dentro de esos marcos establecidos, sí. La fuga, la locura, la muerte. La diferencia entre un cauce y otro de vida es únicamente de

grado. Porque si lo consideramos bien, tanto las primeras como las otras alternativas no son propiamente cauces de vida, sino formas de muerte (*El uso* 228-29).

If the central concern of Castellanos' fiction is the limited possibilities for fulfillment and self-realization available to upper- and middle-class Mexican women, an important secondary theme is the exploitation of lower-class, particularly Indian, women. The many portrayals of oppression, rebellion and revenge that we find in her novels and short stories were heavily influenced by Simone Weil's theories of the dialectic of oppression, which Castellanos described as "...la corriente del mal que va de los fuertes a los débiles, y que regresa otra vez a los fuertes" (Carballo 3).

Her autobiographical first novel *Balún-Canán* (1957) portrays the close relationship that develops between two outsiders to the power structure: the lonely seven-year-old daughter of the oligarchic Argüello family who is marginalized by virtue of her age and, especially, her gender, and her Tzotzil nanny. In contrast to the two stories discussed earlier, here oppressive patriarchy is embodied by the girl's mother, the mistress of the household. In many respects, the nanny represents the nurturing, maternal figure that the girl's mother is not. In addition, she initiates the girl into Tzotzil history and mythology, a magical, pantheistic view of reality, and a vivid sense of indignation before social injustice. Specifically, the girl's primary emotional bond with the servant is combined with feelings of guilt regarding the woman's victimization by the girl's family and class: "Ella, siempre desde que nací, me arrima a su regazo. Es caliente y amoroso. Pero tendrá una llaga. Una llaga que nosotros le habremos enconado" (17). As this passage suggests, the emotional complexity of the adult mistress-servant relationship may be influenced by the surrogate maternal role that female servants play in the early lives of many upper- and middle-class Mexicans. Thus, the nanny represents for the child a female role model, but one that is stigmatized and powerless (the wound is in her knee, suggesting immobility and stasis), not only because of her class and gender, but also, in many

cases, by virtue of her ethnic identity and beliefs, which
frequently conflict with the dominant ideology: "...mi
nana...[n]o sabe nada. Es india, está descalza y no usa
ninguna ropa debajo de la tela azul del tzec. No le da
vergüenza. Dice que la tierra no tiene ojos" (10). By the
end of the novel the girl acknowledges that she could
never recuperate the intimacy that she shared with her
nanny; her statement implies, moreover, that she herself
has been incorporated into oligarchic power relations and
ideology: "Nunca, aunque yo la encuentre, podré reconocer a mi nana. Hace tanto tiempo que nos separaron.
Además, todos los indios tienen la misma cara" (291).
Thus, the psychological loss also entails a loss of moral integrity.

Castellanos' second novel, *Oficio de tinieblas* (1961),
contains another version of the same sort of relationship,
one deformed by its immoral foundations. Teresa, an Indian woman who has just given birth, is forced to wean
her own baby too early—leading to its death—in order to
nurse her *ladina* mistress' child, Idolina. The resulting relationship is neurotically symbiotic, perpetuating Idolina's
hysterical paralysis and converting Teresa into a machine
of female self-sacrifice and ruling-class dogma.[3]

In a series of newspaper articles published during the
1960s and 1970s, Castellanos explains, with characteristic
self-irony, the autobiographical bases for her fictional portrayals of servants. She describes "dos largas servidum-
bres" in which she has participated: that of María Escandón, her Tzotzil *cargadora* (childhood ser-
vant/companion), who lived with Castellanos until the
latter's marriage; and that of Herlinda Bolaños, the Náhuatl woman who worked for Castellanos for thirty years, after having been her husband's nanny. Castellanos describes her awakening to the exploitative nature of the relationship with her first servant:

> El día en que, de una manera fulminante, se me reveló que esa
> cosa de la que yo hacía uso era una persona, tomé una decisión
> instantánea: pedir perdón a quien había yo ofendido. Y otra
> para el resto de mi vida: no aprovechar mi posición de privi-
> legio para humillar a otro. ¿Qué ocurrió entonces? ¿Entre una
> María rebosante de gratitud y una Rosario cargada de es-

crúpulo moral se estableció una amistad respetuosa? No, entre
una María desconcertada y una Rosario inerme ya no hubo contacto posible (El uso 262-63).

After Castellanos' marriage, when María Escandón
went to live with Gertrudis Duby, the anthropologist re-
proached the writer for not having educated her servant:

> Yo andaba de Quetzalcóatl por montes y collados mientras
> junto a mí alguien se consumía de ignorancia. Me avorgoncé. Me
> prometí que la próxima vez (si es que había una próxima vez)
> no sería lo mismo. Mi política en relación con Herlinda Bo-
> laños fue totalmente diferente. Pero no me atrevería a decir
> que más adecuada (263-64).

While living in Israel, where Castellanos served as the
Mexican ambassador, Herlinda came into contact with
servants from other Latin American countries and acquired a certain degree of class consciousness. In retrospect,
the author admits to having attempted to undermine this
process, albeit unconsciously: "Yo estaba de acuerdo...en
principio. Pero en la práctica procuraba convertirla no en
mi adversario de lucha de clases sino en mi cómplice. Le
di autoridad para que mandara a otros y ambas comen-
tábamos—como lo hacen siempre las señoras— la inepti-
tud total de sus subordinados" (264).

IV. ELENA PONIATOWSKA: *RESSENTIMENT* AND SOLIDARITY

In an essay on domestic servants in Mexico, Poniatowska has written, "Ninguna escritora mexicana le ha
rendido mayor homenaje a las 'nanas'...que Rosario
Castellanos. Ninguna además se ha sentido [tan] culpable
(como si la culpabilidad sirviera de algo)" ("Presentación"
67). With the recent publication of her own
autobiographical novel *La "Flor de Lis"* (1988), Poniatowska's description of her predecessor's accomplishment
could apply equally to her own works. Moreover, she
shares Castellanos' profound sense of class responsibility
and guilt, as well as her tendency toward candid self-reve-
lation and self-criticism. As she has written elsewhere of

Castellanos, "Pocos escritores mexicanos han propor-
cionado tanta información acerca de su persona, pocos lo
han hecho tan emotivamente" ("Rosario" 57).

In La "Flor de Lis" and several of the short stories collected in De noche vienes (1979), Poniatowska also examines the other side of female complicity: the exploitative
and, at times, neurotic psychodynamics of the mistress-
servant relationship. In her portrayals, she eloquently captures the "maternalism," dehumanization, and ressentiment that Judith Rollins subsequently has identified as
fundamental characteristics of such relationships. In
"Esperanza, Número Equivocado," the maid derives
vicarious enjoyment from imagining her mistress' possible romances. With the passing years, the gifts she receives
from her employer increase her identification with the
upper class, and at the same time reify the class difference
between them, since the gifts are second-hand and not reciprocal (Rollins 192). Esperanza's identification increases
to the point that, when given responsibility over the other
maids, she becomes a tyrant. Her small act of rebellion at
the end of the story suggests a belated awareness of her
loneliness and the impossiblity of changing her situation,
i.e., the beginnings of the ressentiment that we find full-
blown in "Love Story."

"Love Story" relates the opposite of its ironic title: a tale
of disdain and neurotic emotional dependency, on the part
of the mistress, Teleca, and of resentment and rebellion,
on the part of the maid, Lupe. The verbal duels of the two
women eloquently capture the push-and-pull of a continual power struggle, in which Teleca is continually de-
manding a deference (both linguistic and behavioral) that
Lupe steadfastly denies her. Teleca's attitude toward Lupe
is profoundly ambivalent; her disdain and need to control
alternate with an obsessive fascination, motivated by
loneliness and insecurity:

> ...nada le interesaba sino Lupe, saber qué pensaba Lupe,
> seguirla, pararse junto a ella frente al fregadero, mirar sus
> brazos redondos y macizos, sus brazos, dos manzanos con termi-
> naciones de hojas—qué bonito se arrugaban sus yemas con el
> remojo—oir su joven voz, jugosa como sus manos (121).

Teleca regards Lupe as what Rollins has termed a "window to exotica"; her apparent interest in the maid masks voyeurism and an impulse to confirm the differences between the two, in order to implicitly reassure herself of her own superiority (166).

Lupe's final revenge, before abruptly leaving Teleca's employ, is equally impassioned, at once a product of the body that her mistress fetishizes and a total reversal and rejection of her role as servant: "...ahí sobre el lino blanquísimo [de su cama]...bajo el escudo de familia, [Teleca] vio el excremento, una enorme cagada que se extendía en círculos concéntricos, en un aterrador arcoiris, verde, café, verdoso, amarillento, cenizo, caliente" (131). This incident acknowledges the irony of a situation in which the servant is—explicitly or implicitly—admonished to stay in her place, but, paradoxically, that 'place' is precisely the inner sanctum of the aristocratic or bourgeois home. The maid's ultimate insult (in both senses) reaches the center of the privileged female space which she co-habits with her mistress but which is forbidden to her through a rigid hierarchy of spatial deference.

In "El limbo," Mónica, an adolescent aristocratic girl, is faced with the implications of a servant's attempt to strangle her newborn child. She is drawn into a complicity that is initially unwelcome (since it subverts Rosa's desperate act), by a veteran maid who identifies with the mistress of the house and seeks to distance herself from and disclaim responsibility for her fellow servant. Rosa's act is itself the ultimate refusal to accept responsibility, apparently motivated by a combination of post-partum depression and *ressentiment* (and, perhaps, by a fear of losing her job). After she has told Mónica that she has left the baby for dead in the closet, the narrator imagines the maid's vengeful enjoyment of the girl's shocked reaction: "¿Cómo te quedó la cara, rota, catrina, hija de gente decente? A ver, trágate esa, pollita de leche, a ver, reacciona bestiecilla de salón" (49).

Mónica's efforts to save the infant's life push her out of the sheltered world of the immigrant European aristocracy into a public space marked by female poverty and powerlessness: a lower-class women's hospital. Her experiences there awaken her to social injustice and responsibility, but the hospital's clients scornfully reject her ingenuous attempts to organize them, as Rosa had rejected her help earlier. Rather, they, like the household servants in *La "Flor de Lis,"* admonish the privileged girl to stay in her place. Both girls, Mónica and Mariana, whose sensitivity and social concern set them apart from their aristocratic families, feel uncertain about where that place might be; but for the poor women this is unambiguous. In *La "Flor de Lis,"* The servants accept their class position vis-a-vis Mariana as a given, a source of stability and security that should not be questioned. For the poor mothers in the hospital, Mónica is a bleeding-heart liberal whose ultimate loyalty will be to her own class; and subsequent events seem to bear out their suspicion. Like the ending of *Balún-Canán,* the conclusion of "El limbo" suggests that the girl will conform to her class' expectations, which her grandmother communicates to her at the dinner table, that metaphor for class and intrafamilial hierarchy. Monica will allow her social indignation to subside before family pressures and the selfish concerns of everyday life. She will continue "...rayando a taconazos el corazoncito del niño de Rosa, bailaría encima de las mujeres a quienes los hijos se le caen de entre las piernas como frutas podridas...después de todo, la vida de uno es más fuerte que la de los demás" (65).[4]

For the most part, then, Poniatowska's fictional treatment of servants and other lower-class women is decidedly less romanticized than her predecessors' characterizations. If Castellanos had shifted the focus from servants' nurturing and loyalty to the social and psychological consequences of their oppression, Poniatowska delves even more deeply into the psychodynamics of the mistress-servant relationship. Nevertheless, some of her portrayals contain elements of primitivism. In these stories, her essays, and *La "Flor de Lis"*, a radical sense of Otherness is conveyed through association of servants with two sets of images. On the one hand, they are linked to sensuality and proximity to nature (lustrous black hair, perfect teeth like corn).[5] Comparisons to trees, branches and fruit are especially frequent ("sonrisa de manzana jugosa"). For instance, in *La "Flor de Lis,"* the child protagonist learns from her European aristocratic family to look down on the middle class but to accept the lower class as part of Mexico's picturesque scenery: "Si acaso algún pescador cuchillo en mano prepara su carnada del día siguiente, o unos acapulqueños retozan en el agua como delfines. Ellos no afean el paisaje. El pueblo-pueblo es otra cosa. Lo terrible es esta clase media baja que avanza pujando por el mundo..." (80). This aspect of their characterization is reminiscent of Garro's Aztec noble savage, except that here contemporary servants are portrayed as having retained much of the nobility of their prehispanic ancestors.

On the other hand, servants in Poniatowska's works are also associated with taboo bodily fluids, blood and excrement, suggesting a dark underside to the primitivism. In "El limbo," when Mónica ventures into the servant's quarters for the first time, she is repelled by its stench and uncleanliness. (Teleca, in "Love Story," has a similar reaction of repulsion when she enters Lupe's room for the first time, after the maid has left.) Mónica tries not to look at the blood stains that attest at once to birth and violence, new life and attempted murder, even as they bear witness to subhuman living conditions: "...la sangre, la mancha en el piso...los cuajarones sanguinolentos envueltos en el papel periódico como las entrañas de un pollo, de una totola, de una guajolota, amarillas y verde espinaca, el cordón umbilical y la bolsa de la placenta..." (52). The narrator compares Rosa's newborn infant to chunks of meat that the other servant buys for the family's dogs; his mother has treated him as a pile of inert flesh, just as she herself has been dehumanized completely: "...el cuerpo de Rosa que había contenido un niño sin que nadie se diera cuenta porque a nadie le importaba..." (52). One is reminded of Castellanos' portrayals of vicious circles of oppression and violence; except that here the circle closes on the lower class, leading it to cannibalize itself.

If, in "Love Story," excrement is the ultimate weapon that the servant uses against the mistress, a form of retribution for her own humilliation, in *La "Flor de Lis"* it is a symbol of the growing complicity between the aristocratic sisters, Mariana and Sofía, and their French peasant nanny, Nounou. When their mother learns that the girls have been defecating on the floor of their nursery, defiling an aristocratic space, she blames Nounou's peasant background and fires her. She replaces the beloved nanny with a strict disciplinarian who maintains her distance from the girls, addressing them as "usted" and refraining from touching them.[6] This incident addresses the upper classes' fear of relegating their children's socialization—traditionally the mother's role—to someone who is an outsider to the family and class. Yet the banishment of Nounou is portrayed as the girls' fall from paradise, from the plenitude of maternal love into an upbringing that stresses form over content, propriety over self-expression. As if in defiance of the maternal prohibition and painful separation from Nounou, the sisters retain a scatalogical fixation (20, 77).

Furthermore, Mariana, who narrates the novel, remains obsessed with the image of her mother, Luz, forever holding out the promise of maternal love, forever asking for tenderness, yet always aloof: "No es que la extrañe es que la vivo...Mamá es la gran culpable de mi esperanza" (95). This sense of maternal loss—of Nounou; of Luz; and, to a lesser extent, of Magda—is the novel's symbolic center. While Mariana and Sofía's father is even more distant than their mother, his going to war and then his own insecurity have always precluded his emotional presence in their lives: "Está en la orilla. Así será siempre; se quedará en la orilla...A papá lo quiero cuando me rehuye, cuando sus ojos son ese verdor de inseguridad y de expectación que después sabré que jamás se cumple, porque mi padre no sabe por dónde entrarle a la vida" (87). Of all the male characters in the novel, only Father Teufel will temporarily exercise a fascination over Mariana comparable to that of her mother; and this desire is triangular, since the girl's attraction to the priest increases when he begins to demonstrate interest in Luz.[7]

In Mexico, several years after the painful separation from Nounou, Mariana and Sofía find another loving accomplice in a second peasant nanny, Magda: "Ese amor ha de durar toda la vida...En realidad Magda es nuestra cómplice....Es sabia, hace reir, se fija, nunca ha habido en nuestra casa presencia más benéfica" (*La "Flor"* 54-58).[8] In addition to indulging them in forbidden activities (prohibited games, comic books and street food) in prohibited or 'exotic' spaces (la Villita, el Zócalo, Magda's village, their mother's closet),[9] Magda opens up to Mariana and Sofía an alternative world view based on natural cycles and on folk culture, religion, and medicine. Like the nanny in *Balún-Canán*, she introduces them to the oral tradition as a source of wisdom and prophesy. As a result, Mariana comes to associate popular culture with Mexicanness.[10] When she later suffers from her schoolmates' accusations that she isn't Mexican, she fantasizes about being poor as a proof of citizenship: "Quisiera vender billetes de lotería en alguna esquina para pertenecer. O quesadillas de papa. Lo que sea" (75).

As in *Balún-Canán*, love for the nanny leads the girl to become aware of her insertion in the class structure,[11] with its unequal responsibilities and privileges, distributed spatially in the aristocratic home:

> ...al regresar en el camión siento un desconcierto cada vez mayor, una mano me aprieta las tripas, la tráquea, no sé si el corazón. Porque nosotras pasaremos a la mesa, con nuestra mamá y la visita en turno, y Magda se irá a comer a la cocina.
> ...Por qué no soy yo la que lavo los platos?...Por qué no es Magda la que toma las clases de piano si se ve que a ella se le ilumina el rostro al oír la música que teclearo con desgano?
> ...A ver, doña Blanca, a ver Naranja dulce, limón partido, a ver jicotillo, a ver mexicana que fruta vendía, a ver qué oficio le daremos matarilirilirón, a ver cómo respondo yo, por sus buenas manos ajadas y enrojecidas sobre su delantal, sus manos como dos manzanitas pachiches que se repegan la una a la otra para protegerse? (58-59).

However, Mariana's nascent class consciousness is limited to the case of Magda and soon recedes. By the time that Father Teufel interrogates her about the inferior status of servants in her home, and specifically about the hierarchy of eating arrangements, she replies, startled, that she has never thought about it: "Como un relámpago, Magda atraviesa frente a mis ojos, pero Magda es Magda." She then proceeds to parrot her grandfather's explanations about the inferior intellectual capacity of servants (145).

(When the priest moves in with Mariana's family, he too forgets his earlier indignation regarding the servants and treats them as if they were invisible. According to Mariana, "El padre no les presta atención, simplemente no las ve. Yo soy la sirvienta del Señor" [166].) Moreover, the insults that Sofía directs at Magda when she is angry suggest that even the girls' affectionate relationship with their nanny contains the seeds of exploitation; through their dealings with servants, upper- and middle-class children train to become adult masters (55, 58).

Teufel, a precursor of Liberation Theology, temporarily exerts a powerful, essentially patriarchal influence over Mariana, her family and her girlfriends in the Colonia Francesa. This influence, which draws on the Catholic tradition of mysticism, is eventually proven to mask a virulent *machismo*, manifested in the priest's abuse of his patriarchal authority to seduce his female followers, and in his tirade against female sexuality: "Empiezo a creer que es cierto aquello de que el cuerpo de cualquier mujer es fácil. Todas se abren paso con él, lo llevan a la proa de su vida..." (187). In Teufel's farewell to Mariana, his earlier exhortations that she work with the poor and collaborate in founding a new, socialist order, are replaced by a more existentialist and individualistic understanding of the concept of commitment: "El único compromiso del hombre sobre la tierra, Mariana, es vivir" (251). Teufel represents Liberation Theology as a new variant of female oppression, the patriarch masquerading as social messiah.

The female servants are the only ones who initially sense that something is amiss: "Mucho antes de que el común de los mortales salga de su modorra, el padre, terminadas sus abluciones, invoca a su Señor, y yo fui escogida para seguirlo, aunque a Felisa y a Victorina el padre les parezca medio raro" (166). Although, in the second half of the novel, the appearance of Teufel, the Father, engulfs Mariana's mother and overshadows the servants, the more enduring influence of these women on Mariana is apparent in the final scene. As Mariana, now a young adult, sits in the Alameda, Mexico City's public space par excellence (along with Chapultepec Park), she at last feels that she belongs to the Mexican *pueblo* in which she is immersed:

> ...escojo una banca junto a la estatua *Malgré tout* y miro como los hombres al pasar, le acarician las nalgas. Las mujeres, no. Me gusta sentarme al sol en medio de la gente, esa gente, en mi ciudad, en el centro de mi país, en el ombligo del mundo...mi país es la emoción violenta, mi país es el grito que ahogo al decir Luz, mi país es Luz, el amor de Luz. '¡Ciudado!', es la tentación que reprimo de Luz, mi país es el tamal que ahora mismo voy a ir a traer a la calle de Huichapan número 17, a la FLOR DE LIS. 'De chile verde' diré: 'Uno de chile verde con pollo' (261).

Mexico is Mariana's home by virtue of two female relationships: with her biological mother, Luz, her beacon of desire (and archetype of the voluptuous female body symbolized by the statue); and popular Mexican culture (the tamales), which, implicitly, is linked to Nounou, Magda, and the other female servants that have nurtured (fed) Mariana over the years.

Poniatowska has analyzed the mistress-servant relationship at length in "Presentación al lector mexicano," the prologue to Ana Gutiérrez's *Se necesita muchacha,* a collection of oral histories of twenty-four Peruvian domestic workers. Gutiérrez's book is one of the most complex examples of the ways in which Latin American women intellectuals have begun crossing class and ethnic barriers in their efforts to forge bonds of female solidarity through their intellectual work. It juxtaposes the Peruvian case with the Mexican one, even as it takes the oral history situation one step further than usual. In most oral histories (including Poniatowska's own *Hasta no verte Jesús mío),* the writer limits her/his role in the text to that of transcriber/editor, at most providing an introduction which describes the process of interviewing and editing. Here, however, Poniatowska reflects at length on the history of her own relationships with domestic servants, from her childhood nanny to her collaboration and eventual twenty-year friendship with another poor woman and occasional servant in wealthy households, Josefina Bórquez (alias Jesusa Palancares). In effect this personal essay constitutes a sort of oral history from the other side of the class/color line, a counterpoint of Otherness to the oral histories of domestic workers for which it serves as prologue. To my knowledge it is unique in providing this kind of juxtaposition of complementary testimonies about the servant relationship by women from two different Latin American contexts and opposite poles of the power dialectic.

It was her early emotional ties with female servants and her consequent interest in poor women that prepared Poniatowska to undertake the oral history of Josefina Bórquez which she fashioned into *Hasta no verte Jesús mío* (Bearse 136), now a classic work of documentary fiction. In creating Jesusa's language for the novel, the author incorporated elements of the dialects of a lifetime of female servants: "En su voz oía yo la voz de la nana que me enseñó español, la de todas las criadas que pasaron por mi casa como chiflonazos; sus expresiones, su modo de ver la vida, si es que la veían porque sólo vivían al día y no tenían razón alguna para hacerse ilusiones" (Poniatowska, "Hasta" 10).

Subsequently, Poniatowska has undertaken three novels based on the lives of privileged women artists: Angelina Beloff, Tina Modotti, and now herself. At the same time, she has continued to chronicle the lives and struggles of poor women and victims of political repression, including Rosario Ibarra de Piedra, the leader of the mothers of disappeared political prisoners (and now, for the second time, a leftist candidate for the Presidency); and the "Sindicato 19 de Septiembre," the garment workers' union that was formed after many women perished in sweatshops during the earthquakes of 1985.

V. WOMEN'S TESTIMONIAL LITERATURE

In a number of Latin American societies in which class stratification is rigid and the gulf between classes wide, intellectual women like Poniatowska, Elizabeth Burgos, Moema Viezzer and Medea Benjamin thus have begun acting as conduits to the publishing industry and mediators to the middle-class reading public for women whose socioeconomic, political and/or educational situations make it difficult or impossible for them to write and find publishers themselves. At the same time, there are certain problems inherent in the process of transcribing, editing and arranging another's words and in the attempt to represent faithfully the viewpoint of someone whose life experiences and ideological perspective are so radically different from one's own; that is, in the process of speaking for another.[12]

It is clear from Poniatowska's short stories and from what she has written about *Hasta no verte Jesús mío* that her motivations in choosing to act as an interpreter of poor women's histories include a passionately felt commitment to the cause of social and political justice in Mexico, a sense of guilt and responsibility for her own situation of privilege; and an idealization of the presumably greater strength and vitality of the popular classes (Poniatowska, "Hasta"). She, like Elizabeth Burgos, found her personal history of relationships with servants to be springboards for achieving trust, communication, even a sense of intimacy, with Josefina Bórquez. On the other hand, it seems apparent, from both the novel and Poniatowska's essays, that Bórquez's attitude toward her vacillated between: i) growing affection, ii) resistance bordering on rebellion, iii) deference, and iv) disdain for the writer's ineptitude in tasks associated with physical labor, with 'real' rather than intellectual work.

Without minimizing the potentially problematic nature of these attempts at mediating without "betraying," to use Burgos' term, the bonds that Latin American intellectual women are beginning to forge with women undertaking struggles against socioeconomic and political oppression (or with women like Josefina Bórquez who refuse to participate in such struggles, which is instructive in itself) are enormously significant. John Beverley has referred to testimonial literature as a transitional form, because "se ubica en el intersticio entre las culturas del opresor y del oprimido; es una forma de dialéctica de opresor y oprimido" (15).

Mexican women writers of subsequent generations have not foregrounded the theme of the mistress-servant relationship, as many of their predecessors did. To a large extent this may be due to changing labor relations in Mexico. With the development of capitalism, the phenomenon of live-in servants, particularly lifelong domestic workers who identify with and feel loyalty toward their employers, is much less common than it was during the childhoods of Dávila, Garro, Castellanos and Poniatowska. Consequently, in recent years women intellectuals concerned with the issues of poverty and exploitation have followed Poniatowska's lead in taking their project from the kitchen or nursery to the streets. The work of Cristina Pacheco is an outstanding example of this recent trend. In her books, newspaper articles, and television program "Aquí nos tocó vivir," Pacheco collects and recreates personal tesimonies by residents of Mexico City's shantytowns and slums, particularly poor women.[13] Like Poniatowska, she draws heavily on popular dialects in her chronicles, thus foregrounding the dialogic dimension of her work. At the other end of the social spectrum, Guadalupe Loaeza has begun chronicling, with scathing irony, the everyday life and ideology of bourgeois women. Testimonial literature, then, that most public of literary genres, paradoxically continues to be a largely female domain in Mexico. Its development mirrors the greater economic polarization of Mexican society, in the throes of the crisis and in the wake of the disastrous earthquakes. At the same time, it documents that society's increasing organization into popular social movements,[14] exemplified in the public imagination by the militant, female garment workers' union.

NOTES

[1] In the case of Peru, where there is a relatively high level of organization and class consciousness on the part of domestic workers, Cecilia Blondet, of the Instituto de Estudios Peruanos, reports that domestic workers are reluctant to form political bonds with middle-class feminists, because they distrust women who themselves have

servants (Latin American Studies Association convention, New Orleans, 1988).

[2] This shift was pointed out to me by members of my graduate seminar at the University of Washington.

[3] For a more detailed discussion of female power relations in Castellanos' fictional works, see Steele, *Narrativa indigenista* 81-90.

[4] Compare Poniatowska's description of her own guilt toward her nanny, Magdalena Castillo: "Sus años más importantes...nos los dio. Nos dijo: Tómenlos, para que...le bailáramos el jarabe tapatío, le zapateáramos encima bien y bonito. Y de hecho lo hicimos. Le hundimos nuestros taconcitos de catrinas cebadas a lo largo de todo el cuerpo" (Poniatowska, "Presentación" 63).

[5] See Flori's discussion of female body imagery in this and other short stories by Poniatowska.

[6] For an account of the autobiographical basis of this character and a number of other characters and episodes in the novel, see the interviews with Poniatowska conducted by García Flores, Leis Márquez, and Zalce. The author discusses her childhood relationships with her parents, her sister, and her American and Mexican grandmothers, as well as nannies and other servants. She also tells several of the autobiographical anecdotes that are portrayed in the novel as occurring to Mariana (including some of her early experiences with reading and writing and her first awareness of social injustice). In a paper read at the public presentation of *La "Flor de Lis,"* Antonio Lazcano Araujo identified some of the correspondences between the novel and the author's life (7).

[7] In one of the first reviews of *La "Flor de Lis,"* Enrique Mercado has commented on the overwhelmingly female world of the novel ("Un mundo infinito de mujeres en el que los hombres no cuentan sino de ornato"), as well as on its fascination with the female body (6).

[8] It seems likely that Magda is a representation of the author's nanny, Magdalena Castillo. See Poniatowska, "Presentación" 63.

[9] The mother's closet, even if forbidden to her daughters, would logically not be forbidden to her maid.

[10] Compare Poniatowska's comments regarding her growing sense of belonging to Mexico as a result of her relationship with another poor woman, 'Jesusa Palancares':

Lo que crecía o a lo mejor estaba allí desde hace años era el ser mexicana; el hacerme mexicana; sentir que México estaba adentro de mí y que era el mismo que el de la Jesusa y que con sólo abrir la rendija saldría. Yo ya no era la niña de ocho años que vino en un barco de refugiados 'El Marqués de Comillas,' hija de eternos ausentes, de viajeros de trasatlántico, hija de barcos, hija de trenes, sino que México estaba dentro, era un animalote adentro...un animal fuerte, lozano, que se engrandecía hasta ocupar todo el lugar. Descubrirlo fue como tener de pronto, una verdad entre las manos, una lámpara...y esta lámpara sólida, inmóvil me daba la seguridad de una casa. Mis abuelos, mis tatarabuelos tenían una frase clave: 'I don't belong.' Una noche, antes de que viniera el sueño, después de identificarme largamente con la Jesusa y repasar una a una todas sus imágenes, pude decirme en voz baja: 'Yo sí pertenezco'" (Poniatowska, "Hasta" 8).

[11] It is another female servant, Crisófora, who first introduces the girls to the concept of poverty: "En el campo, la carne de caballo la comen los cristianos" (37).

[12] For a more detailed discussion of this problem, see Steele, "La mediación en las obras documentales de Elena Poniatowska."

[13] In 1978 Elena Poniatowska was the first woman to be awarded the Premio Nacional de Periodismo; in 1985 Cristina Pacheco won it as well.

[14] See Carlos Monsiváis' *Entrada libre* (1987), a collection of chronicles acutely analyzing popular social movements of the 1980s.

WORKS CITED

Arizpe, Lourdes. *Campesinado y migración*. México: Secretaría de Educación Pública, 1985.

—. *Indígenas en la ciudad de México: El caso de las 'Marías.'* México: Secretaría de Educación Pública (SepSetentasDiana), 1979.

—. *Migración, etnicismo y cambio económico (un estudio sobre migrantes en la ciudad de México)*. México: El Colegio de México, 1977.

Bearse, Grace M. "Interview with Elena Poniatowska." *Hispania* 64 (March 1981): 135-36.

Benjamin, Medea. *Don't be Afraid, Gringo: A Honduran Woman Speaks from the Heart (The Story of Elvia Alvarado)*. San Franciso: The Institute for Food and Development Policy, 1987.

Beverley, John. "Anatomía del testimonio." *Revista de Crítica Literaria Latinoamericana* 13.25 (1er semestre de 1987): 7-16.

Bradú, Fabienne. *Señas particulares: escritora (Ensayos sobre escritoras mexicanas del Siglo XX)*. México: Fondo de Cultura Económica, 1987.

Burgos, Elizabeth. *Me llamo Rigoberta Menchú y así me nació la conciencia*. México: Siglo XXI, 1985.

Carballo, Emmanuel. "Rosario Castellanos: la historia de sus libros contada por ella misma." *La Cultura en México* (suplemento de *Siempre!*) 44 (19 de septiembre de 1962): 2-5.

Castellanos, Rosario. *Balún-Canán*. México: Fondo de Cultura Económica, 1973 (1957).

—. *Ciudad Real*. México: Organización Editorial Novaro, 1974 (1960).

—. *Oficio de tinieblas*. México: Joaquín Mortiz, 1975 (1961).

—. *El uso de la palabra*. Ed. José Emilio Pacheco. México: Excélsior, 1974.

Chevigny, Bell Gale. "The Transformation of Privilege in the Work of Elena Poniatowska." *Latin American Literary Review* 26 (July-December 1985): 49-62.

Dávila, Amparo. "El huésped." *Muerte en el bosque*. México: Secretaría de Educación Pública, 1985 (1959).

Díaz-Polanco, Héctor, et.al. *Indigenismo, modernización y marginalidad: una revisión crítica*. México: Juan Pablos Editor, 1979.

Fiscal, María Rosa. *La imagen de la mujer en la narrativa de Rosario Castellanos*. México: Universidad Nacional Autónoma de México, 1980.

Flori, Mónica. "Visions of Women's Symbolic Physical Portrayal as Social Commentary in the Short Fiction of Elena Poniatowska." *Third Woman* 2.2. (1984): 77-83.

Franco, Jean. "Beyond Ethnocentrism: Gender, Power, and the Third-World Intelligentsia." In *Marxism and the Interpretation of Culture.* Ed. Cary Nelson and Lawrence Grossberg. Urbana: University of Illinois Press, 1988, pp. 503-15.

Franco, María Estela. *Rosario Castellanos: Semblanza psicoanalítica (Otro modo de ser humano y libre).* México: Plaza y Janes, 1985.

García Flores, Margarita. "Entrevista con Elena Poniatowska." In *Elena Poniatowska* (Material de Lectura No. 10). México: Universidad Nacional Autónoma de México, 1983.

Garro, Elena. "La culpa es de los tlaxcaltecas." In *Narrativa mexicana de hoy.* Ed. Emmanuel Carballo. Madrid: Alianza Editorial, 1969, pp. 75-93. (Originally published in *Revista Mexicana de Literatura,* Segunda Época, 3-4 [marzo-abril de 1964].)

Goldsmith, Mary. "Trabajo doméstico asalariado y desarrollo capitalista." *Trabajadoras domésticas aslariadas en México: Lecturas seleccionadas de fem* 4.16 [septiembre 1980-enero 1981]): 1-9.

Grau, Ilda Elena. "Domestic Servants in Latin America." In *Latin American Women* (Report No. 57). Ed. Olivia Harris. London: Minority Rights Group, 1983, pp. 17-18.

Jelin, Elizabeth. "Migration and Labor Force Participation in Latin America: The Domestic Servants in the Cities." *Signs* 3 (1977): 129-41.

Lazcano Araujo, Antonio. "La flor más bella, sus pétalos de hoja de tamal." *La Jornada* 172 (30 de abril 1988): 1 and 7.

Leis Márquez, Amilcar. "La muchacha de la leña: Elena Poniatowska." *La Plaza* (Guadalajara), Segunda Epoca, 2.25 (septiembre de 1987): 8-11.

Loaeza, Guadalupe. *Las niñas bien.* México: Editorial Océano, 1987.

Meillassoux, Claude. *Mujeres, graneros y capitales.* México: Siglo XXI, 1977.

Mercado, Enrique. "Ya lo dijo el vate Velarde: empitona la camisa el mujerío." *La Jornada* 172 (30 de abril 1988): 3 and 6.

Monsiváis, Carlos. *Entrada libre: Crónicas de la sociedad que se organiza.* México: Ediciones Era, 1987.

—. "Mira, para que no comas olvido...": Las precisiones de Elena Poniatowska." *La Cultura en México: Suplemento de Siempre!* 1007 (15 de
julio 1981): 2-5.

Pacheco, Cristina. *La última noche del "tigre."* México: Ediciones
Océano, 1987.

—. *Zona de desastre.* México: Ediciones Océano, 1986.

Poniatowska, Elena. *De noche vienes.* México: Editorial Grijalbo, 1979.

—. *La "Flor de Lis."* México: Editorial Era, 1988.

—. *Hasta no verte Jesús mío.* México: Editorial Era, 1969.

—. "Hasta no verte Jesús mío." *Vuelta* 24 (noviembre de 1978): 5-11.

—. "Presentación al lector mexicano." *Se necesita muchacha.* Ed. Ana
Gutiérrez. México: Fondo de Cultura Económica, 1983, pp. 7-86.

—. "Rosario Castellanos: ¡Vida, nada te debo!" *¡Ay vida, no me mere-
ces!* México: Joaquín Mortiz, 1985.

—. "Testimonios de una escritora: Elena Poniatowska en micrófono." In
La sartén por el mango: Encuentro de escritoras latinoamericanas. Ed
Patricia Elena González and Eliana Ortega. Río Piedras, Puerto
Rico: Ediciones Huracán, 1984, pp. 155-62.

Rollins, Judith. *Between Women: Domestics and their Employers.*
Philadelphia: Temple University Press, 1985.

Sacks, Karen. "Engels Revisited: Women, the Organization of Production and Private Property." In *Toward an Anthropology of Women.*
Ed. Rayna R. Reiter. New York: Monthly Review Press, 1975, pp.
211-34.

Steele, Cynthia. "La mediación en las obras documentales de Elena
Poniatowska." In *Mujer y literatura mexicana y chicana: Culturas en
contacto.* Ed. Elena Urrutia and Aralia López. México: El Colegio de
México, 1988.

—. *Narrativa indigenista en los Estados Unidos y México.* México:
Instituto Nacional Indigenista, 1985.

Urrutia, Elena. "Experiencias de organización." *Trabajadoras domésticas asalariadas en México: Lecturas seleccionadas de fem.* New York:
Women's International Resource Exchange (from *fem* 4.16 [septiembre
1980-enero 1981]): 10-12.

Viezzer, Moema. *'Si me permiten hablar'...Testimonio de Domitila, una mujer de las minas de Bolivia*. México: Siglo XXI, 1977.

Weil, Simone. *Oppression et liberté*. Paris: Gallimard, 1955.

Zalce, Beatriz. "¿Mil miradas? Mil oídos y una sonrisa: Elena Poniatowska." *La Plaza* (Guadalajara), Segunda Epoca, 2.25 (septiembre de 1987): 5-7.

FEMININE DISCOURSE IN CHICANO LITERATURE

Rosaura Sánchez
University of California, San Diego

In the last decade the topic of feminine as well as feminist discourse has often been approached from a deconstructive or Lacanian framework. Proponents of these models have given rise to numerous studies on sexuality as the essential difference, and on woman as the male subject's Other. The assumption of these theories is that discourse is gender-specific and that it interpellates or addresses individuals as gendered subjects. Although the term "feminine" is used by feminist critics to refer not to sex, which is biologically determined, but to gender, which is culturally determined, a biological and psychological essentialism clearly underlies this theory of subjectivity, which is ahistorical and undialectical in nature. This entire focus on discourse as the point of departure points to an even more important presupposition: the poststructuralist assumption that all we know, all we can know, in fact, that all culture, is textual, that we experience the world phenomenologically as a vast text. Once we assume that the history of Western thought, Western culture itself, is the Logos, that vast text which encompasses the sum total of human symbolic systems, then the struggle for women should come at the level of the text, through a deconstruction of phallo-logocentrism, as indicated by Irigaray (Stanton, 74-75).

The notion of feminine subjectivity and feminine discourse thus offers several problems. The main problem is the reduction of history to text. Even the positing of discourse as part of material reality does not solve the problem if in the process one excludes other aspects of reality, neglecting thereby the nondiscursive which is infinitely vaster and definitely not a product of the mind or of language. However much these textual games may fascinate academics, the exploitation, subordination and oppression of women cannot be simply opposed at the discursive level, for the socially condoned brutal beating, disfigurement and killing of women in India, the Middle-East, Brazil, and other areas of the world as well as the various form of oppression to which women are subject throughout the world are more than oppressive discursive practices.

The second major problem of these theories of difference is the positing of gender as essentialist, as if there were a universal feminine subjectivity. This notion is particularly problematic to Third World women who do not see themselves as forming part of a single sociological or cultural group determined by a "sex/gender system." In fact, women of the Third World and ethnic minorities in the United States see dominant feminist theory as ethnocentric. Black women in particular have strongly criticized the work of white feminists, arguing that in these feminist texts, black groups are either typecast, stereotyped and ghettoized, reproducing the dominant ideology, or simply invisible, absent and silent (Barrett and McIntosh, 24). For this reason, feminists, especially socialist feminists, are beginning to consider the relation between ethnicity, gender and class; here the preference is for the consideration of "ethnicity" rather than "race" as they find that race itself is too comprehensive a category that does not account for class differences within races nor account for the particular needs of different groups of women within and across races. This consideration of the interplay of various factors that cut across gender and across ethnicity while noting cultural particularities has led some feminists to a recognition that there is no universal female point of view, no universal woman.

If there is no universal female subject, then can there be a universal feminine discourse, as posited by feminists? What would characterize this discourse? Would it include all female discourse or refer only to a particular type of discourse, one that could ostensibly be produced by both men and women? In general this discourse has been defined in terms of both its opposition to patriarchal culture and its liberating capacity, that is, its capacity to free women from repression. In describing feminine discourse in opposition to phallocentric discourse, feminists also posit the patriarchy as a universal and historical form of oppression (Rowbotham, 365). Recently feminists working with the *History Workshop Journal* have begun to question some of these postulates of feminist theory. Sheila Rowbotham, for example, argues that the term "patriarchy" implies a fixed structure and a fatalistic submission while allowing "no space for the complexities of women's defiance" (Rowbotham, 365). More specifically she argues for a historical analysis of sex-gender relations given differences of class, culture, mode of production and social movements within different periods of time. For other feminists, however, for whom sexual difference is the essential problem, "patriarchy" best describes oppression that is of both social and psychological origin and form (Alexander and Taylor, 370). Here the social inequalities of gender are seen to be cultural signifying practices inscribed on the unconscious psyche during a child's transition from the Imaginary to the Symbolic Order or Oedipal stage (Moi, 100). The patriarchy thus becomes a strategy to be eliminated; with it will come the end of women's oppression.

In the process of theorizing about the polarity of feminine and patriarchal discourses and practices, feminists have thus, for the most part, simply offered a new essentialism. What is feminine is thereby reduced to the opposite of masculine and defined in negative terms, as what is absent or repressed. More specifically, feminine discourse is said to be revealed in the gaps and silences in phallocentric discourse, those gaps and silences which reveal the unconscious. Affirming feminine discourse is as a result seen to imply affirming the libidinal, desire, and bodily pleasure (a-la-Irigaray), all of which are perceived as means of countering sexual repression and challenging phallo-logocentric authority (Cixous, 66). For Helene Cixous, it is female writing ("l'ecriture feminine") which has the potential for liberation; woman must write herself; female writing will unblock both female and male sexuality and "dephallocentrize" the body. Cixous' poetic vision of feminine writing as ecstatic self-expression has in this way reinforced the assumption that feminine discourse is erotic and biological (Jones, 105).

In all of these cases, it is the private and the personal spheres which are the matrices within which gendered discourses are seen to interact (Fraser, 63). With a cry that the personal is political, feminists have in fact made gender and sexual difference the essence of feminine discourse, relegating other considerations to a secondary plane. Although the objective is clearly the interpellation of a feminine subject, different in her own right, not merely the opposite of man, nor identical with the male subject, the entire proposition in terms of "Otherness" unfortunately affirms what it wishes to negate: male domination.

Whatever its appeal among a number of academic critics, this Franco-feminist criticism can be said to fail to consider real differences among women, particularly class differences, while closing off the possibility of an ideological analysis that examines not only contradictions within dominant patriarchal ideologies but also the unlimited number of subjectivities that a single human being may act out. One can only conclude that feminists of difference, like post-structuralists, although calling attention to the importance of discursive practices in culture, prefer to distance themselves from material causes of oppression in order to focus endlessly on the deconstruction of male texts; in so doing they merely produce a new mystification of the "feminine" or female unconscious (MacKinnon, 1983). Juliet Mitchell's response to this linguistic perspective is to question the notion of a "woman's voice." She states: "I do not believe there is such a thing as female writing, a 'woman's voice'. There is the hysteric's voice which is *the woman's masculine language* (One has to speak 'masculinely' in a phallocentric world) talking about feminine experience." Mitchell, who assumes the existence of only dominant discourse, sees the Kristeva school as apolitical and as projecting the feminine (the semiotic) into what is obviously the ludic space of masculine symbols, yet another level of word and mind games to be toyed with within the male dominant logos (Mitchell, 101).

Whether following the French school or not, feminists for the most part reject the very notion of being contained within phallocentric discourses. Moreover, they increasingly see feminine discourses as an alternative or counter-discourse which resists the male symbolic sphere while building upon the very discourse that it disassembles (Moi, 140). But can one counter without assuming the countered as a given? Foucault, in rejecting binary models, warns that counter-discourse can be an affirmation of the dominant discourse just as otherness affirms the self (Horowitz, 62). A feminine discourse which merely opposed patriarchal discourse would in effect further cement male subjectivity. Additionally Foucault cautions that no discourse is immune from the possibility of cooptation; thus even feminine discourses can be used as instruments of domination (Fraser, 66). Yet, even while stressing the political nature of discourse and its potential for serving as an instrument of domination, Foucault's micro-level approach fails to consider extra-discursive dimensions, that is, social nondiscursive practices, the historical matrices within which discursive practices compete and interact.

These historical matrices are of particular importance to Chicano women, whose victimization and oppression is tied to particular historical conditions of exploitation which have included a history of working class experience (primarily), immigration, deportations, racism, low wages, occupational and residential segregation, low educational attainment, lack of political power, labor stratification, labor struggle, as well as urbanization, industrialization, occupational mobility, consumerism and ideological assimilation. It is only within this broad material context that one can begin to examine patterns of socialization, sexual freedom, and repression, reproduction, female roles and functions and the extent of personal liberties for women in the Chicano community. Since history is marked as much by ruptures and discontinuities as by continuities, the network of discourses available to women in general and Chicano women in particular are also constantly in flux; the subjectivities they address are thus also varied and multiple.

Feminine discourse, like all discourses within the literary text, must be studied then as ideological practices which are part of a network of interacting signifying practices; feminine discourse is a nonclass ideology but it is linked to class ideologies and interacts as well with a multiplicity of discourses of ethnicity, religion, family, nationality, age, etc., all of which appear within specific historical and material matrices and produce different feminine subjectivities, according to the combinations at play (Therborn, 53-74). This analysis denies then the possibility of postulating a single feminine subjectivity or a single feminine discourse. We cannot therefore postulate one Chicana voice nor will we be able to find it in the literature, since a multiplicity of Chicana voices will be necessary to respond to the articulation of particular discursive practices which emerge within changing social formations.

To test our hypothesis we will look at the short stories of Helena Maria Viramontes, in her collection *The Moths and Other Stories*. The multiple discourses within these stories establish various subjectivities, among them, that of the autonomous, rational subject and its other, the criminal subject (Horowitz, 62). These two are especially evident in "Birthday" and "Broken Web." The moral, rational subject is marked by rational self-awareness, self-examination and self-analysis, all strategies of domination used by modern power, that is, by the dominant capitalist structure as the individual tries to discipline herself for getting an abortion or for witnessing the murder of her father. The discourse of sexuality is a constant thread weaving through all of the stories. As Foucault warns, this discourse sets up sex as the truth of our being; this essentialism in turn creates its own counter discourse, that is, its own apparatus of domination: sexual liberation (Horowitz, 63).

True resistance cannot then take the form of mere transgression but must posit alternative practices. For this reason, the pleasure centered women in the stories, while opposing sexual norms, find themselves alone and tormented by their transgressions. Throughout these stories the discourse of feminine sexuality is thus always in competition with that of the patriarchy, which assumes a particular form: men's control over women's sexuality and fertility. "Sexuality is, " as Foucault states, "the site of power relations," because it has been "made to play the role of the bearer of our nature" (Horowitz, 70).

The stories' focus on individual and private struggles rather than on collective struggles does not however totally obliterate the macro-social, especially in stories like "The Long Reconciliation," "The Cariboo Cafe," and "The Broken Web," where class discourses define the Mexican *terrateniente* and the landless peasant, the petty bourgeois cafe owner and the undocumented garment workers, the working class waitress, farmworkers and lumpen *coyote*. Class ideologies thus also compete and overlap with gender discourses.

One of the typical gender discourses in the stories is the discourse of maternity, which posits a nurturing role for women. Like the other discourses it is a strategy which constrains women within particular roles and affirms the dominant patriarchal structure by buttressing the family unit and the social-economic structure of society. Maternal discourse is also presented as an instrument of domination for in its nurturing and submissive capacity it condones and normalizes the subjugation of others, especially of other women, since it is often the mother who transmits the discourses of self-denial and subordination. This process is especially evident in "The Moths," in which the rebellious daughter, often punished for going against family norms, eventually becomes aware of her own mother's despair and silent plight. In the end she too assumes the mothering role as she bathes her grandmother's cadaver for burial, closing and thereby reaffirming the family cycle for women.

The discourse of maternity is often strongest when conveyed as a normative principle, an ethical necessity, the rejection of which brings on a number of social sanctions. The primary strategy of rejection seen in the stories is abortion, as evident in "Birthday" and "The Long Reconciliation." The need to see these practices as historically and materially determined forms becomes especially clear in a comparison of these two stories, for the combination of class, family and religious discourses during late capitalism, as seen in "Birthday," is quite different from that present in rural pre-Revolutionary Mexican times. If in today's world liberated women are expected to take full control of their bodies, leaving men free of any responsibility for conception, as in "Birthday," in oligarchic times in Mexico when the local *cacique* and landowner controlled an area, and farmworking families depended on family farmhands, children were an important commodity, as evident in "The Long Reconciliation." Children represented additional family income and a form of security against old age and infirmity. In an area of developing capitalism they also were a promise for the maintenance of property within the family. For this reason the dream of owning his own land was tied to Chato's dream of having a child. The patriarchy is thus reinforced by the practices of capitalism as reproduction and private property are linked. When his wife Amanda aborted and the ruling *terrateniente* deceived him by selling him worthless desert land, Chato's future was sealed. While unable to change his childless status, Chato would rebel against the state patriarchal system by killing don Joaquin. His revolt however gains social acceptance as it is viewed as part of a new network of discourses: those of revolution. His wife's rebellion against the dictate of the patriarchal ideological discourse through her unfaithfulness and abortion, on the other hand, is scorned by society, although her choice of erotic pleasure over reproduction in fact represents a stronger threat to the capitalist economic and political structure. In the story, child repudiation and betrayal lead to severe sanctions as she is abandoned by her husband.

Obviously abortion is a practice that is not limited to one historical period or class, but it is historically bound and subject to varying conditions. Within modern industrial societies, for example, the practice is generally no longer in the hands of *curanderos*, as in "The Long Reconciliation," although its accessibility to poor working-class women is constantly facing government threats to cut funding. Middle and upper-middle class women do not whoever have to resort to free or low-fee clinics, as described in "Birthday," for they can have the procedure performed in a hospital with a gynecologist. These ideo-

logical discourses are thus in articulation with class ideologies and affected by different modes of class existence.

The discourse of domesticity is also closely linked to
that of maternity and the patriarchy; maternity and domesticity could in fact be seen as subsets of the patriarchy.
The control and discipline which domesticity imposes
could only be compared to that established in prisons and
in the army. The primary strategy here is the normalizing
mechanism. Thus domestic life within marriage is established as the norm and all that lies outside of it is deemed
to be deviant and insignificant, without meaning.
Women's work within the home is of course non-wage-
labor, but this fact is accepted as normal, as the way it
should be, and women like Olga in "Snapshots," are only
too happy to perform double duty. The day her husband
divorces her, Olga's life ends and she becomes a prisoner
of the past, a past that she never really enjoyed. In the end
those snapshots, those "imaginary representations" of the
past consume all her waking hours, for without those
externally imposed constraints Olga is functionless. Resig-
nation is Olga's primary response but even this strategy
becomes an instrument for domination as she uses her
depression and lethargy in power plays to punish her
daughter and ex-husband for her abandonment and loneliness.

Religion is another important practice in these stories,
as it too establishes its own strategies of containment. In
modern society, one of the primary strategies of Catholicism is the practice of confession. It too, as Foucault stated,
functions as a mechanism of control, even today. If in
previous times in Latin America the priest was often the
one who turned in the thief after confession, today it
functions as a means of ensuring external control through
the process of self-examination. The strategy here is
metaphysical in nature, in the sense that the individual
assumes that he/she will find some hidden repressed
truth through the self examination of consciousness with
the assistance and intervention of the confessor, the spe-
cialist, who possesses the right hermeneutic for
interpretation (Dreyfus and Rabinov, 174). Although this
role is often in the hands of psychoanalysts in today's

modern age, for working classes, the practice of confession is accessible and free in the church confessional. "Western man," says Foucault, "has become a confessing animal" (Foucault, HS,59). It is "a central component in the expanding technologies for the discipline and control of bodies, populations, and society itself" (Dreyfus and Rabinov, 174).

Confession is an important strategy in these stories, for not only does it function as a strategy of power that reinforces the patriarchy but it also affirms the role of the Church. It is of course women who are expected to confess, since men, who know full well the disciplinary and controlling aspect of the confessional mechanism, place themselves in positions of power and beyond this subordination. This strategy is countered in several of the stories. In "The Moths" the adolescent daughter rebels against what is an important strategy in "Birthday," "The Long Reconciliation," and "The Broken Web," as well. In these three stories the counter-strategy, which in fact reinforces the confessional strategy, is pleasure; yet although "pleasure" is the practice and discourse which leads these women to their particular revolt, it also, by tapping feelings of guilt, eventually leads them back to confession.

The discourse of adolescence in these stories is primarily the discourse of confusion, signalling as it does that period of transition in which the individual becomes aware of a number of cultural practices which will now control her life. What becomes evident is the molding and socialization that occurs through discursive practices so that despite initial resistance, the child eventually participates in the reproduction of existing ideologies. Yet beyond these general patterns of behavior, each narrative case is different and responds to the particular family, class and interclass interaction within a particular historical period. Thus although at an individual or family level particular discourses are established, these are seen to compete and overlap with other class and non-class ideological practices. The younger generations are also constantly seen to be interpellated by the varied discourses of other generations and other groups, giving rise to new subjectivities and new problems as different practices clash. It is these inter-societal relations that lead to the production of new discourses and new social practices.

Although most of the stories in *The Moths and other stories* deal with the subordination of women to family, fathers, men, religion, and culture, the female characters are all different. Each story offers particular combinations of interacting class and non-class ideologies and particular strategies of domination which ensure that a power structure is maintained even when cases of resistance and rebelliousness are evident. Because these discourses and ideologies exist in historical form, they articulate with various class ideologies and modes of class existence. The effects of domination, obedience and rebelliousness that these ideologies produce in the characters must be examined then within the historical context of late capitalism and its ideological hegemony. As urbanization and redevelopment have fragmented the *barrio*, as violence has increased in the form of police brutality, exploitation, gang violence and drug addiction, social fragmentation has also increased. Women interpellated by all of these ideologies respond in fear, as in the case of Aura in "Neighbors," who sat petrified in her house with a gun in her hands, ready to shoot the first intruder or innocent caller who knocked at her door. Women also respond with violence themselves, as in the case of Olivia in "The Broken Web," who ended the abuse by killing her husband, or with inertia, like the woman in "Snapshots," who, after 30 years of marriage was left with nothing but a snapshot of moments she had mechanically and unconsciously lived through. These women function as the Others of male subjects and although they too seek to assert themselves as individual autonomous subjects, even while struggling with alienation and with reification, their counter-discourses inevitably serve primarily to assert the power of the dominant patriarchal discourses. Within their particular spheres of action, however, they are involved in a struggle to be heard, in a struggle for power with whatever strategies are within their reach.

The discourses interpellating these working-class women are varied and include discourses of gender, class, ethnicity, age, religion and occupation; their voices and subjectivities are thus a response to a network of interacting signifying practices, different historical moments, and different strategies of acquiescence or rebellion. There is no idealization of the feminine here. The differences are multiple, but undoubtedly countering patriarchal discourses, even while affirming them, is the salient task of all these characters in Viramontes' stories.

WORKS CITED

Alexander, Sally and Barbara Taylor, 1981. "In defence of 'patriarchy'," in *People's History and Socialist Theory*, edited by Raphael Samuel. London: Routledge & Kegan Paul, pp. 370-374.

Barrett, Michele and Mary McIntosh, 1985. "Ethnocentrism and Socialist-Feminist Theory," *Feminist Review*, No. 20, pp. 23 -28.

Brenner, Johanna and Nancy Holstrom, 1983. "Women's Self-Organization: Theory and Strategy," in *Monthly Review*, vol. 34, no. ll, pp. 34 - 46.

Cixous, Helene and Catherine Clement, 1986. *The Newly Born Woman.* Minneapolis: University of Minnesota Press.

Dreyfus, Hubert L. and Paul Rabinow, 1983. *Michel Foucault. Beyond Structuralism and Hermeneutics.* Chicago: The University of Chicago Press.

Elshtain, Jean Bethke, 1986. "The New Feminist Scholarship," in *Salgamundi*, no. 70-71, pp. 3 - 26.

Fraser, Nancy, 1983. "Foucault's Body-Language: A Post-Humanist Political Rhetoric?" in *Salgamundi*, no. 61, pp. 55 - 70.

Horowitz, Gad, 1987. "The Foucaultian Impasse: No Sex, No Self, No Revolution," in *Political Theory*, vol. 15, no. l, pp. 61 - 80.

Jones, Ann Rosalind, 1985. "Inscribing femininity: French theories of the feminine," in *Making a Difference: Feminist Literary Criticism*, edited by Gayle Greene and Coppelia Kahn. London: Methuen, pp. 80 - 112.

MacKinnon, Catherine A. "Feminism, Marxism, Method and the State: Toward Feminist Jurisprudence," in *Signs*, Vol. 8, No. 4, Summer 1983, pp. 635-658.

Mitchell, Juliet, 1986. "Feminity, Narrative and Psychoanalysis," in *Feminist Literary Theory. A Reader*, edit. by Mary Eagleton. Oxford, UK: Basil Blackwell, pp. 100 - 103.

Moi, Toril, 1985. *Sexual/Textual Politics: Feminist Literary Theory*. London: Methuen.

Rowbotham, Sheila, 1981. "The trouble with 'patriarchy'," in *People's History and Socialist Theory*, edited by Raphael Samuel. London: Routledge & Kegan Paul Ltd, pp. 364 - 369.

Stanton, Donna C., 1985. "Language and Revolution: The Franco-American Dis-Connection," in *The Future of Difference*, edited by Hester Eisenstein and Alice Jardine. New Brunswick, New Jersey: Rutgers University Press, pp. 73 - 87.

Therborn, Goran, 1980. *The Ideology of Power and the Power of Ideology*. London: Verso Editions and NLB.

Viramontes, Helena Maria, 1985. *The Moths and Other Stories*. Houston: Arte Publico Press.

SEGUNDA PARTE

EL SIGLO XIX PENINSULAR Y
LATINOAMERICANO

THE FEMALE TRADITION IN NINETEENTH-CENTURY SPANISH LITERATURE

Susan Kirkpatrick
University of California, San Diego

Insofar as feminist literary scholarship takes as its point of departure a critique of the gender bias that historically has informed the social and cultural institutions associated with literature, it challenges dominant versions of literary and cultural history in which female experience and activity have remained largely invisible. Sometimes by exposing the biases resulting from unexamined assumptions about gender difference, sometimes by bringing to light the suppressed struggles, defeats and accomplishments of women as cultural producers, feminist criticism has forced us to revise our interpretations of past and present culture. I am particularly aware of how feminist scholarship in my own field, nineteenth-century Spanish literature, has, in the process of recovering information about women's place in literary production and consumption, called into question certain standard narratives about Spanish literature and even social history. The feminist scholarship to which I am referring includes my own and that of such scholars as Alicia Andreu, Bridget Aldaraca, Geraldine Scanlon, Maryellen Bieder, Alda Blanco, Maricarmen Simón Palmer, Iris Zavala. This is scholarship still very much in progress, but its momentum is accelerating. Drawing mostly from my own current research,[1] I would like to sketch the pattern of female participation in literary production that is emerging from this research and discuss how these new insights require us to rethink common assumptions about nineteenth-century Spanish literature and society. I will proceed by first outlining what is now known about the origins and development of a continuous tradition of women's writing in Spain, a tradition that started with the Romantic movement. For purposes of discussion, the second part of my paper will draw from the emerging history of women's writing the following theses, which, if accepted, would modify our current understanding of the cultural history of nineteenth-century Spain: a) *only if we take into account the women poets' feminization of the Romantic subject can we form a complete picture of the Romantic discourse of subjectivity* and b) *literary evidence showing the rapid acceptance of the domestic angel as the model of true femininity suggests that certain fundamental ideological structures of bourgeois society were in place in Spain by 1850 even though bourgeois hegemony, measured in economic or political terms, had not yet occurred.* I will take up each of these theses after examining the broad patterns of women's literary production during the period in question.

1. NINETEENTH-CENTURY WOMEN'S WRITING

Although the late eighteenth century produced a few women writers (Josefa Amar y Borbón and María de la Hore, for example), this potential beginning of female participation in the Spanish press was cut short by the Napoleonic War and the severe restriction of the press by Ferdinand VII. I can find no evidence of women publishing in the 1810s or 20s, and only rare instances of woman-authored publications in the 1830s, even though the press rapidly expanded in that decade under the auspices of liberal reform. It was only in 1841 that women definitively entered the world of print culture in Spain as producers. In that year, a Catalan, Josefa Massanés, initiated the trend with her *Poesías,* and the Cuban-born Gertrudis Gómez de Avellaneda followed with a book of poetry and her first novel, *Sab.* Carolina Coronado, who had been publishing poetry regularly in the Madrid press since 1839, brought out her first volume of verse in 1843, when Gómez de Avellaneda's second novel had already appeared. By mid-decade Spanish periodicals were regularly soliciting pieces by women from around the peninsula: among them were

Angela Grassi in Barcelona, Amalia Fenollosa in Valencia, Dolores Armiño in Asturias, Dolores Cabrera Heredia in Aragon, Manuela Combronero in Galicia, Vicenta García Miranda in Extremadura, Rogelia León in Andalusia, and Victoria Peña in the Balearic Islands. These pioneering women were not exclusively poets: a mid-decade list of contemporary dramatists (*Revista Literaria del Español* 8 June 1845) included Angela Grassi and Josefa Robirosa de Torrens as well as Coronado, Gómez de Avellaneda and Cambronero. Both Coronado and Gómez de Avellaneda published novels; at the end of the decade, Cecilia Boehl von Faber, *Fernán Caballero*, had her first great novelistic successes.

This sudden breaking of women's silence coincided with the peak of the Romantic movement (Espronceda's *El diablo mundo* began publication in 1841) and of liberal reforms (the Espartero dictatorship began in 1841). This chronology suggests an explanation for the timing of Spanish women's entry into print culture. As the press was expanding, modernizing, seeking new readerships, two related movements—liberalism and Romanticism—made ideological inroads into traditional upper class culture, introducing ideas and attitudes that women could use to justify their self-expression in writing. New conceptions of the individual and of the importance of inner life and the emotions helped to create a climate in which women might feel authorized to assert themselves as subjects of writing rather than objects of representation by men. Women could—and did—appeal to the liberal ideal of the right to self-expression as legitimizing their literary activity. The Romantic emphasis on spontaneity and feeling over learning and intellect as the basis of poetic inspiration also made the appalling education most Spanish women received less of an impediment to writing.

The women who began to publish in the 1840s comprised the first generation of Spanish women who conceived of writing for the public as an accessible outlet for their creative and intellectual activity. They came from the same tiny stratum of Spanish society as their readership—that roughly 15% of the population, members of the professional and property-owning classes, whose literacy habits included regular reading of books and the periodical press. As far as I have been able to ascertain, the family background of these writers placed them among the landowning *hidalguía* (Carolina Coronado), the professional classes (Massanés's father was an architect, García Miranda's a pharmacist, Gómez de Avellaneda's a naval officer), or the merchant classes (Boehl von Faber). Their families were preponderantly liberal (the fathers of both Massanés and Coronado, for instance, were persecuted by the government of Ferdinand VII), which is no surprise, since these women often drew on liberal discourse to legitimize their writing during the early 1840s. What is surprising to me is that this first generation of women writers is largely made up of women from the provinces. The two well-known women writers who resided in Madrid, Coronado and Gómez de Avellaneda, moved to that city after beginning their careers in the provinces. Otherwise, as we have seen, the women who published regularly were sprinkled around the peninsula in provincial capitals and small towns.

Many of the women who had begun to publish by 1845 saw themselves as forming a kind of "hermandad lírica." They wrote to one another, dedicated poems to one another and steered one another toward sympathetic editors and periodicals. Their common theme was the suffering produced by the lot of women, particulary the anguish caused by finding the means of self-expression blocked to them. Carolina Coronado, the leader and model of this group of poets, wrote in 1846 about "lo triste que es la suerte de las mujeres a quienes las preocupaciones no permitían hace poco el desahogo de expresar sus pensamientos" ("Al señor director" 97). The language of this remark suggests the ideological underpinnings of these women's break with their former silence: Coronado uses a discourse that combines liberalism's concept of the individual right to freedom of thought and expression with Romantic psychology's view of the self's need to grow and expand through expression. Vicenta García Miranda's 1851 poem, "A las españolas," provides a good example of how the women writers of this generation sometimes asserted their sense of grievance through an even more militant language, one associated with the Fourierist currents that entered Spain in the 1840s: "¡Oh, mujeres¡ luchar a vida o muerte,/Sin que el ánimo fuerte /Desmaye en la pelea a que briosas/Algunas se han lanzado/Del sexo esclavizado/Por romper las cadenas ominosas." Gómez de Avellaneda had already equated the position of women with slavery in her 1841 novel *Sab* by representing two women and a mulatto slave as the socially marginalized subjects of Romantic angst. Avellaneda and Coronado, the leading writers of this generation, struggled to affirm their rights to self-expression and their position as subjects of writing in texts that, like *Sab* and *Dos mujeres*, subtly attacked the male bias inherent in Romantic representations of the self or, as in Coronado's poem, "Libertad," criticized liberalism's exclusion of women from its benefits: "¡*Libertad!* ¿qué nos importa?/¿qué ganamos, qué tendremos?/¿un encierro por *tribuna*/y una aguja por *derecho?*" (1852: 72). Thus, the difficulty these early writers faced in assuming the discourse through which they justified their break with the tradition of female silence led them toward a critique of those very discourses.

By the end of the decade of the 1840s, the numbers of women writers appearing in print had grown remarkably and the careers of many professional women writers were well established: besides Avellaneda and Coronado, there were Concepción Arenal, Angela Grassi, Robustiana Armiño, Cecilia Boehl, Pilar de Sinués, all of whom had long and active careers. But as the numbers of women writers grew, so did the cultural pressure to justify themselves by putting their writing to the service of a newly reformulated ideal of womanhood. Studies by Alicia Andreu and Bridget Aldaraca identify the stereotype that from the 1840s on dominated nineteenth-century representations of women as "el ángel del hogar" (Aldaraca) or "la mujer virtuosa" (Andreu). Aldaraca has shown how this image of woman derives from an earlier definition of female difference epitomized in Fray Luis de Leon's *perfecta casada* (66-67, 73-74). In the nineteenth-century version, new social realities modified the meaning of the earlier distinction male and female spheres of activity: in the context of a capitalist mode of production, the distinction was now seen as that between public and private, state and family, market and home, self-interest and love. In this new definition of the domestic as the sphere in which women preserved the values that had been driven out of the hard, materialist, but all-powerful world of the marketplace, the irrationality that had previously been considered a central feature of female nature was sublimated into the tender sensibility, the self-forgetful lovingness, that was supposed to make women naturally suited to their domestic role as wives and mothers. As the customs of "civilized" bourgeois Europe began to spread to Spain in the early nineteenth century, bringing greater social mixing of the sexes, the physical separation of men and women that had characterized the habits of much of precapitalist Spain was replaced by a moral separation that strictly regulated the psychological life of women. Passion and sexuality were banished from the female psyche and defined as contrary to feminine nature; women who exhibited these attributes (as, indeed, did many lower-class women whose circumstances hardly permitted them to retire to a domestic haven) were classified as degraded or monstrous. The true woman, the domestic angel, gained a moral authority previously denied to women. She was honored as a redeeming force in a society sinking into amoral materialism, but her redemptive powers were bought at a heavy price: they only functioned through her self-abnegation and patient obedience (Aldaraca 64, Andreu 53-54, 87-91).

The pressure of this feminine ideal is evident in the texts produced by women throughout the 1840s, even when these texts exhibit the bolder, more self-assertive impulses of Romantic liberalism. The cultural norm of femininity, for example, is surely a factor in the women poets' choice of an idiom closer to the refined sentimentality of Meléndez Valdés than to Espronceda's efforts to invigorate and energize the poetic vocabulary with street language. The mounting force of the domestic ideal reveals itself in the distinct shift in attitude among women writers after 1849. Many of those who at the beginning of the decade had claimed liberal, Romantic paradigms of the self for the female subject began to shape their representations of women in conformity with the ideology of female domesticity. In 1857, the same year in which Severo Catalina's influential treatise on women and their domestic nature appeared (Andreu 188, Aldaraca 74), Carolina Coronado recanted her earlier feminist positions: "Fuerza es confesarlo, en la sociedad actual hace ya más falta la mujer que la literata. El vacío que comienza a sentirse no es del genio, sino el de la modestia; la luz que empieza a faltarnos no es la luz de las academias sino la luz del hogar" ("Galería" 3). This insistence on the overriding importance of woman's domestic mission placed Coronado squarely in line with the reiterated message of the arch-conservative Cecilia Boehl's novels, which, starting in 1849, had met with immediate critical and popular success. Indeed, most of the first generation of women writers whose careers continued and flourished through the 1850s and 60s became identified with the "literatura de consumo" that exalted the image of the pure, submissive, domestic woman: Angela Grassi (see Andreu 1982, Pilar Sinués, Micaela de Silva, and Robustiana Armiño, all of whom began to write in the 1840s, are examples. Members of the next generation, like Faustina Sáez de Melgar and Patrocinio de Biedma, followed this model of writing women's literature. In her study of nineteenth-century Spanish women writers, Maricarmen Simón Palmer sees their conservatism with regard to feminine roles as a distinctive feature: "La inmensa mayoría de las escritoras optaron por hacerse portavoces de los valores tradicionales de la familia cristiana y defendieron la figura de la mujer madre y esposa, para poder de esa forma hacerse perdonar la 'falta' de escribir" (489). Thus the trend that took over women's writing in the 1850s remained dominant for the rest of the century.

Spanish women writers, then, collaborated in the proliferation of a discourse that aimed, through popular (that is, intended for the broadest reading public) fiction and the conduct manuals and psychological studies of women that began to appear in Spain in the 1850s, to define and confine femininity, as Geraldine Scanlon notes (21). Even so, it would be a great mistake to assume that women's writing from 1850 on was a monologic confirmation of the bourgeois ideal of domestic womanhood. In my own analyses of works by that most inveterate of sermonizers about women's domestic mission, Cecilia Boehl, I have found disruptive traces of a rebellious, ambitious, even sexual female subjectivity (see "On the Threshold" and *Las Romanticas*, Chap. 8). Careful scrutiny of texts by such writers as Grassi and Sinués would, I am confident, yield similar examples of a female perspective that subverts or revises the reductive norm of the domestic angel. Certainly, through their production of thousands of magazine stories, *folletines*, and *novelas por entregas*, these women writers of the 1850s and 60s contributed to the storehouse of textualized types, emotions, predicaments, and fantasies that supplied the materials of the critical realism of the following decades. They also sustained and nurtured a female readership whose indirect impact on late nineteenth-century literature has not been fully studied or acknowledged.

Within and against the framework imposed upon feminine subjectivity by the presiding bourgeois ideal of womanhood, women poets continued to rework the Romantic paradigms of self and desire in the 1850s and 60s. Rosalía de Castro, one of the handful of women writers to be included in the institutionalized canon of nineteenth-century Spanish literature, was presented to the public (largely through the efforts of her husband, Manuel Murguía, literary critic and Galician cultural nationalist) as the inspired poet of the Galician revival associated with the Romantic revaluation of local cultural tradition. To this perspective, still very much alive in our century (see Ribeiro Carballo Calero for recent examples), twentieth-century critics have added an appreciation of how her reworking of Romanticism anticipated modernist poetic innovation (see López-Casanova). But only very recently and very unevenly have scholars begun to uncover the fundamental connections between Castro's construction of feminine identity in her poetry and the other aspects of her work (see Albert Robatto). From the start of her career she inscribed herself in a female tradition: the title of her first book of poetry, *La flor*, aligns itself with an important motif in the work of the female Romantic poets, and in the prologue of her first novel, *La hija del mar*, she places herself in the same line of women writers to whom Avellaneda and Coronado had appealed—Sappho, Saint Teresa, Mme de Staël and George Sand. Both in the great poetry in Galician written in the 1860s and 70s, which voices the anguish and hope of the doubly marginalized Galician woman and in her eccentric—that is, non-realist—novels, which dealt with such issues as the objectification of women by male sexual obsession, the debilitating effects of women's economic and emotional dependence on men, and the unsatisfactory alternatives available to independent-minded women, Castro's writing raised to new levels of literary discourse the awareness of women's oppressive social destiny, the empathy with the marginalized and the aspiration for free self-expression and self-determination that had characterized Spanish women's writing in the early 1840s. The central, masculine tradition of literary scholarship has not recognized the female consciousness expressed in the texts by Rosalía de Castro, even while accepting those texts as part of the established canon.[2]

Another fine woman poet, Concepción de Estavarena, was given no place at all in the canon. Recovered from total obscurity only in 1979 by Josefina Romo Arregui's reedition of a poetry collection that had appeared in 1877, Estevarena's work constitutes an important moment in the female Romantic tradition. She rewrites themes and images associated with the female lyrical subject in Avellaneda and Coronado in the pared-down, evocative idiom of Bécquer, with whom she establishes an inter-textual dialogue. The chilling story of her short life—having spent her youth caring for her impoverished, elderly father, she was sent on his death away from her native Seville to keep house for a distant cousin in a damp, northern cli-

mate where her tuberculosis advanced rapidly and killed
her at the age of 23—dramatizes the precarious economic
position of the middle-class domestic angel, just as her
poetry exposes the psychic consequences of the angel's
confined existence:

> ¡Que es la vida mudable! ¡Que varía!
> Mi vida es siempre igual;
> horas que lentamente ya pasaron,
> y horas que lentamente pasarán.
> ¿De qué sirve el pasado, si no existe
> y qué es el porvenir sin esperar? (Romo 80)

This voice, lost in the turbulence of the demise of the first
Republic, speaks for that other reality obscured and denied
by the oppressive image of the *angel del hogar*.

Our picture of the emergence of a female Spanish literary tradition would be incomplete, however, with no
mention of the women writers who explicitly contested
the reigning definition of feminine nature. In the 1850s
and 60s some of the bases of the bourgeois construction of
women were attacked in the writing of María José Zapata
and Margarita de Celis of Cádiz, who developed a libertar-
ian feminism from the utopian socialism of Fourier
(Perinat 22-24). Far more influential, though less radical,
were the writings of the dauntless Concepción Arenal. A
member of the same generation as Avellaneda and Coronado, Arenal acted out her non-conformity in everyday
life, attending the university when it was forbidden to
women and earning money to support her family through
writing and through her work as prison inspector. Her critique of the inequities of nineteenth-century Spanish society led her to attack the juridical and economic inequality
of women and to call into question the ideal of the
domestic angel. In *La mujer de su casa* (1881) she argued
forcefully that "La mujer de su casa es un ideal erróneo..;
señala el bien donde no está; corresponde a un concepto
equivocado de la perfección, que es para todos progreso, y
que se pretende sea para ella inmovilidad" (202). Progressive liberal arguments about the need for an active and
informed as well as a free citizenry shaped Arenal's advo-

cacy of improved education and access to the means of economic independence for women. Yet she did not reject one of the fundamental ideological constructs on which the feminine ideal was based—the idea of the essential distinction between the home and the world of political struggle and the moral superiority of the former—and therefore, like many nineteenth-century women writers, opposed women's suffrage as entanglement in a morally degrading and corrupt system (275).

Although Arenal's first feminist book, *La mujer del porvenir*, appeared in 1868, the majority of her works on women date from the 1880s and 90s, years when the feminist attitudes that for many years she had been nearly alone in modeling were gathering momentum. Sofía Tartilán and Concepción Gimeno de Flaquer had published books in the 1870s urging better education for women and greater respect for their intellectual and moral capacities, although they offered their arguments as a refinement rather than a critique of the ideology of the domestic angel. But in the late 1880s a powerful new voice, that of Emilia Pardo Bazán, joined Arenal's in criticizing the forms of subjection masked by the ideology of female domesticity— and sometimes prodded the formidable older woman into taking firmer feminist positions.[3] Pardo Bazán polemicized vigorously in journalistic essays and public addresses on behalf of giving women access to better education, to the university, to the professions, and to the Royal Academies, refuting the anti-feminist authorities with wit and authority. Recent feminist scholarship has brought Pardo's feminist work to our attention again (see Schiavo, for example), for established literary tradition had de-emphasized this aspect of her production in favor of the fictional works that appeared to adopt the standard masculine perspective. But even Pardo Bazán's fiction challenged the image of the domestic angel by focusing on the relation of lower class women to work and politics in *La tribuna*, for example, or by explicitly attacking the norm for bourgeois women in *Memorias de un solterón*. Feminist critics now engaged in rereading the novels categorized as classics of Spanish naturalism (as opposed to "women's fiction") are deciphering the discourse of a female voice embedded in these novels as well.[4]

The work of these late nineteenth-century feminists seems only to have had an effect on everyday practices in the field of education: increasing concern with female education was reflected in the shift in attitude perceptible in the Congreso Pedagógico of 1892, in which the majority of speakers urged equal education for women (Scanlon 49). Yet in the arena of literary discourse, the women writers of the nineteenth century had developed a number of possible languages for expressing the difference of their experience and perspective, varying from the rewriting of the Romantic and late-Romantic lyrical paradigms to the projection of female subjectivity in the realist novel, from the apparently conformist appropriation of the authority of the domestic angel to the uncompromising critique of the norm itself. Structured into the space women made for themselves in print culture, this network of tensions and intersections formed a living tradition inherited by women of the twentieth century, a tradition that exerted its influence on readers and writers of both sexes, on literary discourse in general. Now, after a century in which gender relations have been perceptibly altered, if not by any means transformed, we can look back from our standpoint as women in the U.S. and in Spain, united by our consciousness of the historical determination of the structures we inhabit, and see what remained obscure to a perspective that ignored gender difference; we can see the dynamic place of women's discourse in Spanish cultural history.

Let me now elaborate briefly on two theses that I think can be drawn from this "other" literary history, theses that revise or modify the conventional version of nineteenth-century Spanish culture.

2.1 THE FEMINIZED ROMANTIC SUBJECT

My first proposition is that the women poets' feminization of the Romantic subject must be taken into account if we are to form a complete picture of the possibilities and limits of the Romantic discourse of subjectivity. The Romantic self, as Espronceda articulated it for Spanish literary culture, was coded as masculine insofar as the lyrical subject is premised on an active, appropriative desire. Indeed, one of the principal tropes in Espronceda's poetry figures the relationship between self and world as the erotic connection between a masculine subject and a feminine object. In this recurrent figure (in "A Jarifa" "A una estrella," "Canto a Teresa," for example) the beloved or desired woman stands for the object world that fails to correspond to the values imagined and desired by the lyrical—and masculine—self. Despite the tormented dissatisfaction produced by the Promethean desire of Espronceda's Romantic subject, the status of that subject as a coherent and authentic center of values is never in question: El diablo mundo makes it clear that this desiring and suffering subject, in a ceaseless quest for knowledge, produces the utopian vision that moves mankind forward toward the making of his own destiny. Given the powerful codes of gender identity that structured their culture and language, the women writers who used Romantic paradigms could not, as female lyrical subjects, adopt precisely the same position in relation to desire and world as the Esproncedian model. Their revisions stripped away some of the "naturalness" of the Romantic image of the self, revealing its social determinants on the one hand and its denied internal divisions and incompleteness on the other.

One example of such a revision is Gómez de Avellaneda's first novel, Sab. By positioning two women characters and a mulatto slave as the subjects of Romantic desire and its inevitable disappointment, she rewrites Espronceda's relation of subject and world: what the male poet saw as a metaphysical inevitablity, she represents as the product of social and historical inequity. The novel's three main characters fail to fulfill their desires for love and self-realization not because fulfillment is inherently impossible, but because their social destiny as women or as a slave prevents them. Sab, the mulatto, lays the blame firmly on the social power structure:

> Pero, si no es Dios, Teresa, son los hombres los que me han formado este destino, si ellos han cortado las alas que Dios concedió a mi alma, si ellos han levantado un muro de errores y preocupaciones entre sí y el destino que la providencia me había señalado...(226)

The novel (the first published abolitionist work in Spanish) explicitly criticizes the racism that prevents the larger society from recognizing the mulatto as a feeling, thinking, acting subject—as indeed, a *Romantic* subject, an "alma superior." Implicitly, the text also and more consistently attacks patriarchal society's negation of women's subjectivity, making this negation the source of the female characters' Romantic consciousness that the world is inadequate to their utopian desire. Avellaneda provides a suggestive alternative version of Espronceda's paradigm by making the subject of desire and disillusionment female and presenting in the case of Carlota, one of the two women protagonists, the optimal destiny of a bourgeois woman—love and marriage—as the very source of her final alienation.

To illustrate the necessity of including the female re-elaboration of Romantic discourse in our accounts of it as a significant phenomenon, let me give another example, one from the poetry of Carolina Coronado. In her first book of poetry (1843), Coronado evaded the claims of the domestic feminine ideal by placing the female lyrical self, the speaking subject of her poems, in a natural setting, a *locus amoenus* inherited from neo-classicists like Meléndez Valdés. Conventionalized through poetic language, the fields and woods of her native town provided the female lyricist with an environment that was outside the domestic circle, but not part of that conflictive outer world forbidden to women. But in an 1846 poem titled "Ultimo canto" Coronado presented this environment in quite a different light, associating it with a sense of claustrophobia and suffocation that was extinguishing her poetic vocation.

Addressed to her little brother, Emilio, the poem draws an analogy between the insect that the boy has captured in a bell jar and the woman speaker's own situation as a poet.

> Cuando aspira todo el viento
> Que circula en su fanal,
> El insecto que aprisionas
> En su cóncavo perece
> Si aire nuevo no aparece
> Bajo el cerrado cristal. (30)

The rhyme *fanal-cristal* and the idea of enclosure in glass create an intertextual echo with a key passage in Espronceda's *El diablo mundo*, published four years before, in 1842. Espronceda's protagonist, Adán, compares his situation—desiring what is beyond his reach—with that of a goldfish in a bowl. "¿Vistes aquel pez dorado / Que en tu casa en un fanal, / Breve lago de cristal, / Da vueltas aprisionado...?" he asks La Salada, his lover, adding that just as the goldfish seems to want to break past the glass to enjoy the world it sees on the other side, so he longs to do things that he does not know how to make possible. Later La Salada, at this point in the epic placed in the position of a constraining female reality principle, tells Adán that if he escaped from his own element, he, like the fish, would die. This figure of Romantic Promethean desire has been significantly modified by Coronado in constructing the subjectivity of the female poet. In "Ultimo canto" the feminine voice does not warn that death will result from overstepping boundaries, but instead announces that the boundaries, the enclosure, imposed on women suffocates them. For Espronceda the bell jar represents the metaphyscial limits of man's condition; for Coronado it represents the socially dictated constraints that smother women's spiritual life.

"Ultimo canto" also rewrites Coronado's earlier poetry by equating the glass enclosure with the *locus amoenus* that had served as an alternative to the domestic circle. Now the outdoor haunts of 1843 are made explicitly analogous to the bell jar:

> Celebré de mis campiñas
> Las flores que allí brotaron
> Y las aves que pasaron
> Y los arroyos que hallé,
> Mas de arroyos, flores y aves
> Fatigado el pensamiento
> En mi prisión sin aliento
> Como el insecto quedé. (30-31)

Unable to explore the larger world—"Mar, ciudades, campos bellos"—the poet finds the limited circle of her previous "feminine" poetic inspiration to be claustrophobic. The insect in the glass jar calls to mind the bee that in an earlier poem had figured the limits of the female poetic project. "Más quiero, humilde abeja, aquí en el suelo / Vagar de flor en flor siempre ignorada, / Que al águila siguiendo arrebatada / Con alas cortas, remontar mi vuelo,"(14) she had written earlier. But in "Ultimo canto" the lyricist declares, "Agoté como la abeja / De estos campos los primores" (31). Now she is unwilling to concede high-flying poetic power to men exclusively and presents herself as an eagle:

> Tal ansiedad me consume,
> Tal condición me quebranta,
> Roca inmóvil es mi planta,
> Aguila rauda mi ser.
> ¡Muera el águila a la roca
> Por ambas alas sujeta;
> Mi espíritu de poeta
> A mis plantas de mujer!
> Pues tras de nuevos perfumes
> No puede volar mi mente.... (31)

The opposition between the winged and the earthbound that had represented a gender distinction in the earlier poetry is here transformed into the internal tension that constitutes female lyrical subjectivity in Coronado's poetry from 1844 on. The contradictory pull between wings and roots recurs again and again in Coronado's poetry as the image of a female self split between its creative powers and aspirations and its limiting social condition as woman.

Negotiation of this conflict in the poetic writing of Avellaneda as well as that of Coronado produces an image of the self that tends to reveal the fractures and self-divisions that the male versions of the Romantic subject could more easily cover over. It is, then, to the female Spanish Romantics that we must look to find the "shadow" of the Romantic construction of the self—to find the social determinants and the fractured identity hidden by the grand Romantic image of the self as autonomous, coherent, value-giving and male.[5]

2.2. "ANGEL DEL HOGAR" AND THE INSTALLATION OF BOURGEOIS SOCIETY

My second thesis belongs to a slightly different order than the first, for it uses evidence from the emerging history of Spanish women's role in producing print culture to propose that we modify current views on nineteenth-century Spanish social history. One of the most clear-cut phenomena brought to light in recent feminist studies of women in nineteenth-century Spanish literature is the rapidity and decisiveness with which the "angel del hogar" was consolidated as a feminine ideal in the modern press that came into being with the demise of absolutism. This feminine norm is a version of the domestic model of womanhood that was closely associated with bourgeois values and social practices in England and France; its rapid acceptance in the written discourse of mid-century Spain signals one of the earliest triumphs of a bourgeois social ideology in a nation whose bourgeois revolution was attenuated and uneven. I will advance the hypothesis that as the physical gender segregation of traditional Spain dissolved, the emerging ideology of domesticity helped to provide the psychological, moral separation and subordination of women that was more appropriate to bourgeois culture.

Recent research has suggested that in European culture in general there was a shift in the social definition of gender difference that coincided, in very broad, even crude terms, with the transition from an aristocratic, feudal society to a bourgeois, capitalist society. Historians of the history of the family (Ariès, Stone) tell us that a new ideal, that of the sentimental, nuclear family, began to replace the older extended family in the eighteenth century. Along with this model of the family appeared the idea of the natural domesticity of its emotional center, the woman. According to Thomas Laqueur, eighteenth-century science supported this notion by substituting for the Aristotelian model of the differences between the male and female body and sexual organs, which represented the female body as essentially like but inferior to the male, a new model that emphasized the difference between male and female. In the differences stressed by the new model— the reproduction-related features of the female body, the female's supposed lack of sexual passion—we can see the premises of the domestic angel norm. Jean-Jacques Rousseau, a fundamental source of liberal theory, articulated the new scientific view of sexual difference as a moral and social imperative in his influential *Emile*: because nature made women inherently different from men, suiting them physically, morally and intellectually to their primary task of reproduction, he asserted, their education, their activity, their place in society should reflect this difference, channeling natural feminine instincts into civilized domesticity.

The reinterpretation of the female body by Enlightenment medical science and by Rousseau and his followers legitimized the development of a characteristically bourgeois ideology of womanhood, with its corresponding social practices. These included such things as nursing infants at home instead of fostering them out, replacing the arranged marriage with the marriage of controlled choice, socializing *en famille* in small gatherings in the home or short outings, giving the mother responsibility for the early education of the child. A forth-coming book by Kathryn Shevelow finds basic features of the ideology supporting these social practices already in place in the periodical literature of early eighteenth-century England, but in Spain the elements of this model of womanhood first come into literary discourse only late in the eighteenth century. In José Cadalso's *Cartas marruecas*, for example, we see in Carta LXIX the appearance of a domestic ideal of family life in which the husband-wife relationship, though clearly hierarchized, approaches the companionate marriage: in her husband, the wife "halló un compañero, un amante, un maestro" (128). In elaborating about this ideal wife, however, Cadalso still dwells principally on the questions of fidelity and chastity, the main concerns of the aristocratic honor code. *El sí de las niñas*, Moratín's well-known comedy, so popular during the first decades of the nineteenth century when a shift in the mores of family life was taking place among Spain's middle and upper classes, makes an effective case for basing marriage on the mutual attraction of the spouses and for giving value to the feelings and judgment of the bride. Jovellanos adds a crucial element, derived from Rousseau and associated with the bourgeois struggle against the ancien regime, in defining the wife not as simply the trustworthy reproducer of legitimate heirs, but as the mother of future citizens. In the *Elogio de Carlos III* he calls on the nation's women to play the role that "nature and religion" has entrusted to them: "a vosotras toca formar el corazón de los ciudadanos" (193). Here he concisely spells out the idea of sexual difference that characterized the new view of women's nature and mission: while men are in charge of thinking and acting, women are responsible for feeling.

This view of the domestic mission of women was linked with liberal ideology in the early 1820s in one of Spain's first periodicals directed to women, *El Periódico de las Damas* (1822). The periodical's explicitly stated objective was to educate women about the liberal revolution that was underway and to win them to the liberals' point of view so that with their "dulce influencia doméstica, contribuyáis a consolidar el benéfico sistema constitucional" (No. 6, p. 48). But it also devoted considerable effort to providing an anti- or non-aristocratic model of the domestic space within which women were to exercise their gentle, emotional influence. Reiterating that women's natural state was as wives and mothers and that their main study should be domestic management, the journal ran a series called "Letters of a Mother to her Daughter About to be Married." The first maxim was "Jamás excedan los gastos de tu casa a las facultades de tu marido" (No. 6, p. 4). Besides thrift, these letters urge the young bride to create a domestic interior in which the values of comfort and practicality prevail over those of ostentation. The Spanish style—that is, the Spanish aristocratic style—of constructing houses with grand entryways, showy staircases and rooms designed to admit numbers of outsiders is criticized; rooms and furnishings designed exclusively for domestic use are advised. Above all, the letters argue, the husband and wife's bedroom should be a private, carefully appointed space where the couple can withdraw from visitors, servants, even children. (No. 7, pp. 2-5) The model of domestic space that this periodical proposes corresponds closely with the kinds of changes that Ariès documents in English and French upperclass households in the eighteenth century. I have no other evidence to support the *Periódico*'s claim that in 1822 the predominant Spanish style still corresponded to an older norm associated with feudal aristocratic culture, but this article does suggest that progressive forces in Spain saw the introduction of a new domesticity as a yet-to-be-accomplished part of the revolution they were undertaking.[6]

Indeed, while the basic social history of this period remains to be done, there is evidence that some kind of shift in the social mores of the educated classes was in process in Spain in the first decades of the nineteenth century, that the diffusion of bourgeois social forms in Spain's cities was modifying the traditional Iberian separation of the sexes and cloistering of women. From the Middle Ages onward, Spanish custom had segregated women from men more strictly than was usual in other parts of Europe (Pescatello 20): in public places such as the church and the theatre, women were restricted to sections where men were not allowed, and even at home female space was differentiated from male space by furniture as well as partitions, for women sat on cushions, Moorish style, while men had chairs (Domínguez Ortiz 234-5). By the 1830s, however, urban customs had relaxed considerably with respect to the social mixing of the sexes. Domínguez Ortiz affirms that "by about 1800 the ladies had abandoned the Moorish cushions and mixed with men in the same room, as we see later in Romantic representations of social gatherings" (235). Indeed, the literature of this period suggests that urban women accompanied by servants, friends or relatives freely associated with men in public spaces such as the promenade, the theatre (only in 1836 was the law restricting women to the *cazuela* of the theatre repealed), masked balls or cultural events, as well as at private gatherings at home.

As the upper classes moved away from strict physical separation of the sexes, the emerging ideology of domestic womanhood offered a symbolic system, more appropriate to bourgeois culture, for maintaining the separation of women from men on the psychological plane, and justifying their economic and political subordination. One symptom of the shift toward the new symbolic forms in Spain was the middle and upper classes' adoption of the French genitive of possession in married women's last names (López-Cordón 85). Although Spanish law had never required women to change their names upon marrying, the custom of identifying a woman with the possessive plus her husband's last name (e.g. Pilar Sinués *de Marco*, instead of Pilar Sinués) became widespread in the nineteenth century, as though the more socially mobile women of bourgeois society required this appellative mark of their domestic subordination in lieu of physical enclosure. In much the same way, there developed in Spain as in other nineteenth-century societies, an ideology of gender difference that distinguished the domestic sphere from the arenas of economic and political activity not only as the physical space of the home, but also as a distinct emotional ambiance supposed to be identical with feminine subjectivity. Thus, it is precisely in the 1840s, following a shift in urban customs and coinciding with women's literary advance into the previously all-male terrain of the press, that the normative image of woman not only as the heart of domesticity but further, as the domestic angel, began its meteoric rise.

In 1842—the year following the first salvo of woman-authored books in the press—Pedro Sabater declared that the female of the species was "una especie de ángel descendido del cielo." What made her angelic was that her subjectivity consisted entirely of love in its domestic aspect—love of parents, family surroundings, husband and children. "[E]l torpe vicio de la voluptuosidad y el sensualismo" is explicitly ruled out for the true woman. It was through this kind of regulation of female subjectivity that the new ideology gave women a degree of moral authority while keeping them firmly circumscribed by domestic and reproductive functions. The early Spanish exponents of this version of the female psyche stressed the intellectual incapacity produced by the hypertrophy of sentiment, but a refinement of the model, more appropriate to an increasingly "civilized" and cosmopolitan bourgeoisie, was introduced by a visitor from the France of Louis-Phillipe. In 1844 Gustave Deville, a writer residing in Spain for a time, directly confronted the issue of Spain's emerging women poets and demonstrated a rhetoric that would confine them within the the ideological constraints of the domestic angel. "Influencia de las poetisas españolas en la literatura" argues for the cultivation of women's talents in order to make them more stimulating companions for men and credits women with natural qualities that endow them with a particular aesthetic sensibility: they are more sensitive to the harmony of forms, the beauty of detail, as befits creatures designed to console men and lead them toward virtue. But, says Deville, women must observe the limits of their gender-determined nature: "La mujer debe ser mujer, y no traspasar la esfera de los duros e ímprobos destinos reservados al hombre sobre la tierra" (193). Thus women should not attempt to write genres that require knowledge of a conflict-ridden and harsh public reality, but attend instead "tan sólo a las pacíficas investigaciones de la vida íntima, a las nobles y santas emanaciones del corazón y a la expresión coloreada y simpática de los sentimientos tiernos y religiosos" (194).

The triumph of the line that Deville elaborates here can be gauged in the fact that with very few exceptions Spanish women writers toed it for the rest of the century. As I suggested in my earlier sketch of the development of the female literary tradition, by about 1850 Spanish women writers had internalized—not without conflict—the norm of the "angel del hogar" and in their writing regulated— again not without conflict—their own subjectivity and that of their women readers according to the prescribed version of the female psyche. (See Alda Blanco's essay in this collection for a discussion of the complexities of this kind of writing.)

What is surprising in all this is that the basic outlines of the ideological norm and the moment of its decisive consolidation in Spain should so closely correspond to those of England, for example, where beginning of bourgeois hegemony supposedly occurred earlier than in Spain. Sarah Stickney Ellis's *The Daughters of England*, one of the canonical works of English domestic ideology, was published in 1842, for instance. I can discern few clear differences between the stereotypes of the English "angel in the house" and the Spanish "angel del hogar:" both center female subjectivity in familial relations, proscribe any form of sexual passion, urge self-abnegation and service, and grant women a redemptive moral mission. This parallel suggests that although certain economic and political patterns of nineteenth-century bourgeois society—industrialization and the liberalization of the state, for example—did not take definitive hold in Spain until late in the century, the patterns of gender relations characteristic of bourgeois society were in place by mid-century, among the literate classes at least.

One explanation of this manifestation of uneven development in Spain can be found in the particular situation of the Spanish Church in the early nineteenth century. As the most politically vulnerable of the institutional powers of the ancien regime in Spain, the Church was in the process of being despoiled of its economic base by a bourgeoisie eager to acquire land, a nobility anxious to expand its holdings and a state desperate for resources. The

Church's cultural prestige and power was also on the wane; its support of reactionary movements and leaders had stimulated the anti-clericalism of many liberals. At this moment of weakness, the Church sought to regain influence through a strategy focused on women, who for various reasons (less access to education and through it to enlightenment values, a cultural tradition that associated female piety with sexual chastity) had remained largely within the fold. Therefore, López-Cordón tells us, from the 1830s on "se desarrolló una pastoral específica, y se acentuó el carácter femenino de ciertas prácticas religiosas. El objetivo era 'reconquistar' a los hombres através de las mujeres" (91). In this conjuncture, the redemptive aspects of the "angel del hogar," so compatible with one of catholicism's own traditional images of womanhood—the Virgin Mary—coincided perfectly with the Church's aims and it began to promulgate this vision of femininity (rather than the misogynist tradition focused on Eve) in pulpits and confessionals.[7] Alicia Andreu's study of popular literature addressed to women in the second half of the nineteenth century reveals how widely the Church's image of the redemptive power of the self-sacrificing domestic woman was disseminated in fiction; time after time the loving submission and angelic purity of the fictional heroine brought straying husbands or suitors back to the saving embrace of the Church (87-91). The Church's cultivation of this image of womanhood can have played no small part in the rapid consolidation of the angel as the dominant norm.

The conservative thrust of the domestic ideal, especially as elaborated by the Church, also helps to account for the ease with which this version of gender ideology triumphed in Spain. During decades of disturbance and revolution (1840-1880) when Spain's propertied classes were fragmented by political, economic and regional differences, the image of the naturally domestic, virtuous and submissive woman became particularly important as a shared cultural norm that preserved traditional gender—and class—hierarchy. Elsewhere I have shown how Mariano José de Larra focused his anxieties about letting class revolution get out of hand upon the issue of the domestic and reproductive function of women ("La retórica de la familia"). The response to those anxieties can be found in the image of the domestic woman propagated later in the century, whose close association with conservative bourgeois ideology Andreu has pointed out.

In concluding, let me point out the dialectic at work in the rise of the domestic angel as the female norm in Spain. Although it reincarnated the traditional patriarchal hierarchy that subordinated women to men and received impetus from conservative forces within Spanish society, this image also had a certain empowering effect for women. The new version of gender ideology, by stressing women's difference from men, granted them a degree of authority and even superiority in their designated sphere, the sphere of the heart and home. And it was on this strictly limited but generally accepted terrain that Spain's women writers established the bridgehead from which they could eventually expand their role as active participants in the production of Spain's print culture.

NOTES

[1] A full account of my research on women writers of the Romantic movement will be available in my forthcoming book, *Las Románticas: Women Writers and Subjectivity in Spain, 1835-1850.*

[2] In this, the tradition follows the example of the male critic who established Castro as part of the canon—that of her husband, Murguía. Research in progress by Eugene Del Vecchio suggests that Murguía edited out of his wife's work elements of female subjectivity that did not conform to the passionless ideal.

[3] For example, Arenal retracted her statement that women should not be judges after it had been mocked by Pardo Bazán. See Scanlon 75.

[4] An example of such rereading was the session at the 1986 MMLA in Chicago, in which Ruth El Saffar, Diane Urey and Maryellen Bieder offered new readings of *La madre naturaleza*.

[5] While the image of the self in Espronceda and other male Romantic poets reveals itself on close analysis to be less stable and unified than the exaltation of the "yo" would lead us to expect, in general this male-authored poetry does not thematize self-division and instability of identity as the female-authored texts do.

[6] In the 1830s, articles of Larra and Mesonero Romanos on the new buildings going up in Madrid complain about the lack of spaciousness in these "casas nuevas," suggesting a shift toward smaller living spaces in those years.

[7] Carmen Martín Gaite's representation of a young woman's confession in *Entre visillos* suggests that the Church's version of the "angel del hogar" has lasted well into the twentieth century.

WORKS CITED

Albert Robatto, Matilde. *Rosalía de Castro y la condición feminina*. Madrid: Partenón, 1981.

Aldaraca, Bridget. "'El ángel del hogar:' The Cult of Domesticity in Nineteenth-Century Spain." *Theory and Practice of Feminist Literary Criticism*. Ed. Gabriela Mora and Karen S. Van Hooft. Ypsilanti, MI: Bilingual Press, 1982. 62-87.

Andreu, Alicia G. "Arte y consumo: Angela Grassi y *El Correo de la Moda*." *Nuevo Hispanismo* 1 (1982): 123-135.

—. *Galdós y la literatura popular*. Madrid: Sociedad General Española de Librería, 1982.

Arenal, Concepción. *La emancipación de la mujer en España*. Ed. Mauro Armiño. Madrid: Jucar, 1974.

Ariès, Philippe. *Centuries of Childhood: A Social History of Family Life*. Trans. R. Baldick. New York: Vintage, 1962.

Cadalso, José. *Cartas marruecas*. Buenos Aires: Espasa-Calpe, 1952.

Carballo Calero, Ricardo. "A Poética de *Follas novas*." *Nuevo Hispanismo* 1 (1982): 27-38.

Coronado, Carolina. "Al señor director." *El Defensor del Bello Sexo* 8 Feb. 1846: 96-97.

—. "Galería de poetisas españolas contemporáneas. Introducción." *La Discusión* 2 (1 May 1857): 3.

—. *Poesías de la señorita Carolina Coronado*. [Madrid]: n. p., 1852.

Deville, Gustave. "Influencia de las poetisas españolas en la literatura." *Revista de Madrid* 2nd ser. 2 (1844): 190-199.

Domínguez Ortiz, Antonio. *Hechos y figuras del siglo XVIII español*. Madrid: Siglo XXI, 1973.

García Miranda, Vicenta. "A las españolas." *Gaceta del Bello Sexo* 2 (15 Dec. 1851): 100-11.

Gómez de Avellaneda, Gertrudis. *Sab*. Ed. Carmen Bravo-Villasante. Salamanca: Anaya, 1970.

Jovellanos, Gaspar Melchor de. *Obras en prosa*. Ed. José Caso González. Madrid: Castalia, 1969.

Kirkpatrick, Susan. "La retórica de la familia en el discurso liberal: Larra ante *Anthony*." Forthcoming in *Hispanismo en los Estados Unidos*. Ed. Bridget Aldaraca, Edward Baker and John Beverley. Amsterdam: Rodopi.

—. *Las Romanticas: Women Writers and Subjectivity in Spain, 1835-1850*. Berkeley: Univ. of Calif. Press, 1989.

—. "On the Threshold of the Realist Novel: Gender and Genre in *La gaviota*." *PMLA* 98 (1983): 323-340.

Laqueur, Thomas. "Orgasm, Generation, and the Politics of Reproductive Biology." *The Making of the Modern Body: Sexuality and Society in the Nineteenth Century*. Ed. Catherine Gallagher and Thomas Laqueur. Berkeley: U. of Cal. Pr., 1987. 1-42.

López-Casanova, Arcadio. "La palabra poética rosaliana: Claves de modernidad." *Insula* 40, no. 463 (1985):1,10.

López-Cordón Cortezo, María Victoria. "La situación de la mujer a finales del antiguo régimen (1760-1860)." Ed. Rosa Capel Martínez.

Mujer y sociedad en España: 1700-1975. Madrid: Dirección General de Juventud y Promoción Socio-Cultural, 1982. 47-107.

Perinat, Adolfo and María Isabel Marrades. *Mujer, prensa y sociedad en España: 1800-1939.* Madrid: Centro de Investigaciones Sociológicas, 1980.

Pescatello, Ann M. *Power and Pawn: The Female in Iberian Families, Societies and Cultures.* Westport, CT: Greenwood Press, 1976.

Ribeiro, Orlando. "Rosalía de Castro: Símbolo da Cultura Galega." *Minas Gerais, Suplemento Literario* Sept. 14 1985 20(989): 9.

Romo Arregui, Josefina, ed. *Poetas románticos desconocidos: Concepción de Estevarena (1854-1876).* Madrid: Librería Romo, 1979.

Sabater, Pedro. "La mujer." *Semanario Pintoresco Español.* 2nd ser. 4 (1842): 115-16.

Scanlon, Geraldine M. *La polémica feminista en la España contemporánea: 1868-1974.* 2nd. ed. Madrid: Ediciones Akal, 1986.

Schiavo, Leda, ed. *La mujer española.* By Emilia Pardo Bazán. Madrid: Editora Nacional, 1976.

Shevelow, Kathryn. *Women and Print Culture: The Construction of Femininity in the Early Periodical.* London and New York: Routledge, 1989.

Simón Palmer, María del Carmen. "Escritoras españolas del siglo XIX o el miedo a la marginación." *Anales de Literatura Española de la Universidad de Alicante* 2 (1985): 477-490.

Stone, Lawrence. *The Family, Sex and Marriage in England: 1500-1800.* New York: Harper & Row, 1977.

DOMESTICITY, EDUCATION AND THE WOMAN WRITER: SPAIN 1850-1880

Alda Blanco
University of Wisconsin, Madison

Quiero a la mujer enteramente femenina, con su llanto, su graciosa risa, sus coqueterías; en una palabra, quiero que sepa zurcir y tejer bien un par de medias, y bordar con gracia una flor....Quiero que escriba para las buenas madres, las buenas esposas, las buenas hijas... María del Pilar Sinués

La observamos [a la literata] minuciosamente, y vimos que era una mujer que hablaba con discreción, que limpiaba su casa, se hacía los trajes, zurcía calcetines, llevaba la lista de la lavandera, y dirigía a sus amigas en algunas labores...Creen algunos hombres que la mujer, al tomar la pluma, abandona la aguja y todos sus deberes domésticos. ¡Fatal error! Concepción Gimeno de Flaquer

Sobre todo los que escriben y se tienen por graciosos, no dejan pasar nunca la ocasión de decirte que las mujeres deben dejar la pluma y repasar los calcetines de sus maridos, si lo tienen, y si no, aunque sean los del criado. Cosa fácil era para algunas abrir el armario y plantarles delante de las narices los zurcidos pacientemente trabajados, para probarles que el escribir algunas páginas no les hace a todas olvidarse de sus quehaceres domésticos... Rosalía de Castro

Las escritoras que por entonces (1887) figuraban, no muchas, desdeñaban como cosa vulgar cuanto podía hacerse con la aguja, incompatible con la pluma, por más que alardeaban de ser además de inspiradas poetisas o románticas novelistas, mujeres de su casa... Julio Nombela

Recuerdo que María del Pilar Sinués...no podía sufrir las chanzonetas de que las literatas eran blanco lo mismo en España que en los demás países, y cuando iban a visitarla señoras se presentaba a ellas con una labor en la mano, para dar a entender que la habían sorprendido dedicada a tareas femeniles. Es seguro que aquel trabajo, solo comenzado, la duró toda su vida y también es seguro que quedó sin terminar cuando la sorprendió la muerte en medio de la mas completa y triste soledad. Julio Nombela

In those days—the last of Queen Victoria—every house had its Angel. And when I came to write I encountered her with the very

first words. The shadow of her wings fell on my page; I heard the rustling of her skirts in the room.... Though I flatter myself that I killed her in the end, the struggle was severe... Killing the Angel in the House was part of the occupation of a woman writer.
Virginia Woolf [1]

Writing under the sign of the domesticity, a group of women writers flooded the Spanish print culture between 1850 and 1880 with novels and conduct books which embraced the figure of the domestic woman and exalted her ethos as socially necessary. Born between 1826 and 1837 they can be characterized as the younger sisters of the Romantic writers and the mothers of the women writers which would appear on the literary horizon in the latter part of the 1870's and the 1880's. Their seemingly wholehearted acceptance of domestic ideology can be read as a repudiation of the "protofeminist" Romantic women writers who, according to Susan Kirkpatrick in her admirable book *Las Románticas*, had extended the Romantic quest to women thereby elaborating a discourse of female subjectivity which empowered women to write. Kirkpatrick and Simón Palmer have sought to understand the reasons why at mid-century women writers veered from the enabling Romantic tradition and allowed the constraining angel of the domestic woman to enter into their homes. They have convincingly argued, in Simón Palmer's words, that: "the immense majority [of women writers] opted to make themselves spokeswomen for the traditional values of the Christian family and defended the image of women as mothers and wives, hoping thus to be pardoned for the 'offense' of writing (489). Kirkpatrick sees the rejection of this tradition as "a strategy [that] responded to the domesticating, repressive measures that....were applied to women writers by families, mentors, critics, editors and general social opinion" (9:5).

That women writers after 1850 acquiesced to this new configuration of domesticated womanhood did not, in fact, translate into a surrender of their authority to write. Nor did their feminine "domesticity" inhibit them from becoming professional writers, moving them into the public sphere of literary production where, from the pages of their journals and novels, they took up, among many other subjects, the empassioned defense of the woman writer. In doing so, they not only used a language uncharacteristic of the discourse of domesticity but we find that the "feminine" attribute of patient and obedience recedes in these texts giving way to a most "unfeminine" one; a bold critique of contemporary attitudes towards the "literata". In what could be called defense narratives, the women writers of this generation often create the figure of the domestic reading and writing woman and grant their fictional women of letters the respect and dignity which they themselves did not receive from the culture. But perhaps more importantly, by forging women characters that move from illiteracy to reading and then to writing-even if this activity is often only for private or familial consumption-these writers, in fact, "naturalized" the act of writing. Yet, simultaneously, they sought to contain women's writing by promoting the domestic novel as the appropriate genre for their designated audience: the middle class female. I would like to suggest that the writers of this generation envision and articulate a multifaceted and contradictory middle class domestic woman which is from the outset in potential conflict with the patriarchal social order.

Three writers came to dominate during this period: Angela Grassi (1826-83), Pilar de Sinués (1835-93) and Faustina Sáez de Melgar (1834-95). They produced single volume novels and conduct books which appeared in journals—for a male and female audience—and on occasion wrote serial novels.[2] These professional writers moved within the public sphere of print culture: Sinués, Sáez de Melgar and Grassi edited journals,[3] and Sáez de Melgar was the president of the prestigious Ateneo Artístico y Literario de Señoras. Some, like Grassi, had started their careers in Romantic journals and had, as Susan Kirkpatrick has documented, shared the Romantic ideology.[4] Not in isolation from each other, they continued the tradition, forged by Romantic women writers, of "literary sisterhood" by writing prefaces for each other's books and lauding each other's literary production. Angela Grassi, winner of a literary prize given by the Real Academia, for example, prefaced Sinués' novel/conduct book *El Angel del hogar*. They were not only aware of each other's existence but, more importantly, they perceived their literary objectives as similar: to educate the young women of Spain to become angels of the house.

These same years saw the proliferation of texts which contributed to the ever growing debate taking place in Spanish society over gender roles and the place of women in society.[5] Some of the women writers who participated in this polemic, although not belonging to the mid-century generation as outlined above, had, however, convergent ideas about the societal function of women and/or about the imperative for defending female writing and writers. Writing under the sign of the angel of the house and sharing the domestic spirit of the time,[6] Gertrudis Gómez de Avellaneda (1816-1873) and Concepción Gimeno de Flaquer (¿1860?-1919), nevertheless, addressed the question of gender and authorship producing texts which sought to expand the "literata's" writing authority. Rosalía de Castro, for whom it has become a literary commonplace to point out how unclassifiable she was, belongs to the mid-century generation by birthdate (1837) but not in terms of a shared domestic ideology or as a producer of domestic fiction. Yet, she shares the felt oppression as a female author and writes an enraged landmark piece on the subject: the very important "Carta a Eduarda" which directly engages the problematic of the woman writer.

The emergent modern bourgeois culture redefined sexual difference and created a new representation for women: the domestic woman which, according to Kirkpatrick, recast "the feminine as complementary—rather than simply inferior—to the masculine" creating a "new representational system [which] permitted women a legitimate arena of self-expression and artistic authority in place of the silence that the sexual hierarchy of an earlier social formation had enjoined on them" (9:12).[7] Yet, it seems as if the new paradigm of womanhood, in one of its many articulations, sought to construct writing and domesticity as incompatible for this new female figure. In the male and female-authored texts of the period, characteristic of which are the introductory epigraphs, we encounter the usage of "sewing" and "domesticity" as tropes which signal the social sanction against writing by women. Sewing, domesticity and femininity constitute a metonymic chain which stands in opposition to writing, education and the imagination, that is to say, the transgression of femininity. In spite of being generally in collusion with the ideology of domesticity which, according to Andreu, Aldaraca and Kirkpatrick had become dominant in mid-century Spain, the female authors during this period sought to conflate these activities by inscribing the act of writing onto the notion of femininity in their texts. Their various textual negotiations reveal their unwillingness to relinquish either one of these discourses of the self in a patriarchal culture which endeavored to keep them divided. Some fifty years later male authors continue to oppose writing and domesticity. So, for example, we encounter Valera in 1902 still insisting on the same issue: "No va encaminada esta educación general a que la mujer sea artista, literata o aprenda y ejerza este o aquel oficio mecánico...Por tanto, lo primero que hay que procurar en la mujer es que sea o que pueda ser perfecta casada, buena madre de familia" (III, 1415).

The reason for this unwillingness is that this generation of writers saw writing as primarily: the access of women to basic education, writing *was* literacy; a skill which would permit women to educate their daughters, training which the state did not provide; the ability to communicate with others outside of the immediate sphere of the home, the desire to socialize women's education. In their texts, the virtuous woman in any one of her three functions as a feminine female—daughter, wife and/or mother—is always educated or is receiving an education. Pilar de Sinués, the self proclaimed spokesperson for the domestic woman and author of over one hundred novels and courtesy books, images this educated middle class woman as a new social type, differentiated from other women in society by the fact of the education she receives. In *El ángel del hogar* (first published in 1859), she lays out for her female audience the different types of

education available to the young women of Spain and
points out the reasons why they are unsatisfactory.

> [L]a educación en España está reducida a tres clases. La edu-
> cación de la grandeza, encomendada al aya. La educación a la
> francesa. Y la educación a la antigua. Las jovenes formadas por
> la primera viven demasiado agitadas para que piensen en es-
> cribir, aunque algunas mujeres de talento han salido de la aris-
> tocracia. A la segunda pertenecen las que devoran libros a su
> placer. Las de la tercera no son generalmente de organización
> poética....No se le dan libros libros de ningún género; pero en
> cambio, se la exige que sea buena esposa y buena madre, sin
> pensar en que no puede dar ni enseñar lo que no le dieron ni
> aprendió....Un término medio entre esos dos extremos es lo que
> hace falta en la educación de la mujer....Enseñadles a leer y
> escribir con perfección. Si es posible, enseñadles la música y el
> dibujo....(231-33)

In this fragment, writing takes on its various meanings
but nevertheless Sinués' stresses the linkage between
writing and education underlining their joint importance
to the formation of the new type of woman. In it we can
read an implicit and veiled critique of a society which did
not see fit to educate its female population. In Spain primary schools for girls were not established until 1857 and it
was not until after 1868 that girls were permitted to enter
secondary schools. If the future women of Spain were to be
literate, so goes the argument of Sinués and her contemporaries, it would be the mothers, not the state, who
would primarily impart this education. Women, they argued, should be willing to accept this essential responsibility, and, moreover, they should be prepared for it intellectually. Thus, education in these texts is always a domestic
activity. The promoters of the angel in the house propose
that women be trained not only in the skills of domesticity
making them and, by extension the home, the balsam for
the violent world of man, but also as their daughter's
teachers.

Among one of the many themes in her novel *El hogar
sin fuego*, Sáez de Melgar addresses the lack of education
received by middle class girls. She clearly rejects the Sinués
model for educating girls—that mothers be the ones to
educate their daughters in and for the home—by creating a

female character, Julia, who must go outside of the domestic arena in order to provide for her family. Educated to be a domestic angel, Julia had soon realized that this type of training could not put the "cocido" on the table and, in the retelling of her story, indicts the limited and limiting assumption of such restrictions on the education and educative role for women.

> En dos años que duró la cesantía, sufrimos toda clase de disgustos; enfermos mis padres; pequeños mis hermanos, y yo que tenía veinte años, sin poseer una carrera o una profesión sólida que me hubiese permitido subvenir con mi trabajo a los gastos de mi casa. ¡Cuánto lamenté en esos terribles días la educación que se da en España a la mujer! Yo era una perfecta ama de gobierno que sabía cumplir todas las atenciones domésticas; pero en una casa sin dinero no sirve de nada el saber distribuirlo más o menos economicamente. 40

But this is not the only female character who has been restrained economically, emotionally and psychically by the prevailing notion of women's educational needs. Situated at midcentury, this novel is melodramatically structured through the themes of love and duty, love and passion, male and female education and the relation of an educated woman to society. Whereas Luis, the son of illiterate peasant parents, is given an education and becomes one of the most eminent doctors in Madrid, Elena, the daughter of the richest and most important family in a La Mancha town, is deprived by her parents of an education because they fear that she will turn into a "literata". Instead, she is brought up to be a "mujer de gobierno". But Luis, her childhood sweetheart, in an egalitarian gesture foreshadowing the sensitivity which will set him apart from all other male characters in the text, shares his education with Elena until his departure for Madrid. In this work, Saéz de Melgar, constructs a character whose angelic attributes of empathy, idealism, good taste, sacrifice, nurturing and domestic knowledge are not taught by the mother, but are rather cultivated by Elena, on her own, through reading and study. Elena, the self educated angel, is forced by her parents into a marriage of convenience with her uncle, twenty years her senior, in order to consolidate the family land holdings in the area. Portrayed totally unsympathetically as a mean bully, the husband constantly accuses Elena of being a "necia romanticona" when she takes no interest in their children or their education. He sees her indifference as a consequence of her bookish education and her "selfish" desire for a private space within the home where she can read. Elena, on the other hand, feels no mother-love because, as she herself points out, these children are not extensions of herself; they are, rather, reproductions of her husband, who is morally uneducated. There is no admonition of Elena's indifference towards husband and children in this text. Moreover, the narrator constantly points out her "naturaleza superior" underscoring that it has been "desarrollada en la soledad de la lectura y el estudio" (35). Because what she has learned from her books is to really love. And who she truly loves is Luis.

Love is therefore exhalted as the foundation of happiness and well being. But this love, in another variant of the domestic plot, inevitably enters into conflict with the Christian notion of moral duty. At a key moment in the text, Luis and Elena find themselves on the abyss of passion and it is precisely their shared education that had taught them how to love that holds them back. Not willing to become adulterers, they both keep their passion in check. Many different elements are functioning in this scene but, in order to limit my discussion, it is important to point out that Elena's education contributes significantly to this morally edifying moment. Although she has, for the first time in her life, felt passion, she has also been able to control it. Significantly, both Elena and Luis react and behave in the same manner when faced with the possibility of transgressing the moral and social codes. There can be, suggests Sáez de Melgar, moral equality between men and women. The reader, who has shared with Elena and Luis a moment of high melodrama, which has passed from desire to repression, is now addressed by the narrator who steps in to deliver the lesson of the scene which surprizingly shifts not only in language, but in discourse. Sáez de Melgar's narrative recourse is to incorporate the discourse of Enlightenment ideology to explain and justify the need for equal education for men and women.

> Por eso mientras la luz avance en nuestros horizontes, es un deber de todos los hombres dotados por Dios con genios superiores, trabajar con todas sus fuerzas a fin de ensanchar los limites. Cuando la instrucción progrese, la humanidad, que tiende inevitablemente a su perfeccionamiento y el género humano entrarán en el periodo de moralidad y armonía que es necesario para que la sociedades no choquen en continuo empuje. 71

Whereas, in this fragment the narrative strategy is to adopt the Enlightened discourse which claims to speak for all humanity and thus momentarily trascends gender, the end of the novel is clearly gendered. Sáez de Melgar sacrifices both Elena and Luis. Yet, in a curious plot twist it is Luis who dies while Elena survives. Death, in this narrative is a priviledge because it takes Luis out of his misery. Elena, who becomes crazy, has to live out her misery and in a sense live out the rhetoric of domesticity which articulates life as "un valle de lagrimas" and "la vida como amargura". This strategy underlines the unrelenting toll that the society doles out to women. It is not her education that has driven her to madness, but rather society and its laws.

Before the Revolution of 1868, women writers were seriously involved in reworking this theme of education for middle class girls whereas only a handful of male writers were so involved. The two most noted men during this period who addressed this question were: Severo Catalina (1832-1871) and Father Claret (1807-1870) who authored best selling books on the subject of women and their education. Their stances with regard to this polemic can be read as representative of the two extremes positions. Catalina, conservative politician, professor of Hebrew and Director of Public Instruction after the 1868 Revolution, in one of the most quoted books of the period, *La mujer, apuntes para un libro* (1857) argues that women require an education in order to fulfil their "noble misión de hija obediente, esposa fiel y de madre tierna y próvida" (268). In an operation very similar to Sinués', he conflates education and writing and goes on to defend women writers against "los partidarios de la rueca y de la aguja" when he proposes that, in fact, "la mujer nunca escribe bien ni con verdad para los que entienden que la mujer no debe escribir nunca" (267). Yet, he includes a caveat in his "grand" defense of women writers: he asks them to honestly assess their talent and, if they do not have what he calls "verdadero talento", to please give up writing (268). Father Claret, confessor to Queen Isabel II, "Apostle of Spain" and, in Raymond Carr's words, "fountainhead of political catholicism" (262) published a Catechism that sold over four million copies and a conduct book in 1862 for young girls entitled *Instrucción que debe tener la mujer para desempeñar bien la misión que el todopoderoso le ha confiado.* In it, education for young girls is restricted to the teaching of "las virtudes más propias de su vocación, que serán también siete, a saber: Humildad, Castidad, Devoción, Prudencia, Paciencia, Caridad y Ocupacion" (16). If these are not taught, he warns, "la vida de la mujer no es más que un doloroso enigma" (21).

These texts, like the pre-1868 texts on the subject, foreshadow the debates which will take place after the Glorious Revolution when the education of women, promoted by men like Fernando de Castro and the Institución Libre de Enseñanza, finally becomes a significant item on the social agenda. I would like to suggest, here, that education and one of its corollaries, writing, are marked differently by males and females at this moment society even if they share the ideology of domesticity. For women writers, it is a constantly repeated, and therefore important, theme; for male writers it is not. If woman is to be the pivot of society, argue even the most angelic of women, she must be educated or in Pilar de Sinués' utopian sounding words: "No me cansaré de repetirlo: educando bien a la mujer, se obraría un cambio saludable en todo el universo" (242). I want to stress this point—the everpresent argument in favor of educating the angel in the house—because I believe it begins to position female writers in a conflictual relationship to their society; education and writing are articulated as sites for contestation within the midcentury Spanish society. Seemingly constructing an image of womanhood which neatly and unproblematically fits the needs of a bourgeois society—the passive sacrificial woman—, they also inscribe within it a subversive element, which in its first moment, is the need for literacy.[8] In the latter part of the century, the legacy of this fight will continue, but the demand will be for the institutionalization of education for women. Again, it will be women writers, like the illustrious Pardo Bazán and Concepción Arenal, who will be in the forefront of this struggle

As we have seen in Sinués and will again encounter in the essays of Gimeno de Flaquer, the domestic women writers of this period always construct themselves in opposition to the aristocratic woman whose illiteracy and contempt for domesticity they see as backward, frivolous and selfish. The identification with the middle class—particularly the middle class woman—is so complete that, for example, Sinués metaphorically depicts this sector of society as if it were a virtous woman. In *El angel del Hogar* she compares the English to the Spanish social structure and claims that in England "no existe esa fracción [la clase media], tan estimable y la más desgraciada de la sociedad, cuyos instintos delicados están siempre martirizados por el escaso de sus medios de vida" (I, 324). From the pages of their novels and conduct books, women writers are forging and imaging an alternative model for women, particularly middle class women, and establishing themselves as the voice of this new and domestic woman. Writing on the threshold of the Revolution, Concepción Arenal publishes her essay entitled *La mujer del porvenir*, written in 1861 but published in 1868, which underlines the changing role for women. She states that:

> Esta mujer de ahora, de que tanto se queja el hombre no es a veces muy propia para contentarle; es, permítasenos la frase, *una mujer de transición*, con todos los defectos y las desdichas de quien vive en medio de la lucha del pasado y del porvenir, marchando por el caos a la luz de los relámpagos y queriendo comprender en vano las armonías de la tempestad. 148

Anticipating the accusations of advocating "la emancipación de la mujer", she argues that the meaning of these words is not yet well defined and that "nosotros deseamos consignar con claridad nuestro pensamiento" (185). She

ends her essay with a long list of demands—written in the
plural form, queremos—through which she delineates "la
mujer del porvenir". Both she and Sinués look to a future
woman, one which they are trying to construct from the
present. Neither one rejects the domestic woman , rather
they both make this educated new woman pivotal for a
society in dire need of regeneration. In words that resound
of Sinués, Arenal casts her "mujer del porvenir" in the
following light:

> Dulce, casta, grave, instruida, modesta, paciente y amorosa;
> trabajando en lo que es útil, pensando en lo que es elevado, sin-
> tiendo lo que es santo, dando parte en las cosas del corazón a la
> inteligencia del hombre, y en las cuestiones del entendimiento
> a la sensibilidad femenina; alimentando el fuego sagrado de la
> religión y del amor; presentando en esa Babel de aspiraciones,
> dudas y desalientos el intérprete que todos comprenden, la
> caridad; oponiendo al misterio la fe, la resignación al dolor, y
> a la desventura la esperanza....tal es la mujer como la com-
> prendemos; tal es la mujer del porvenir. 187

Elements of contestation, therefore, can be seen from
the outset in the essays written between 1850-1880. Generally framed within a more general discussion of the need
for women's education and a revisionist rewriting of
woman and her talents in history, two central themes are
elaborated in the essays of this period: the unequivocal defense of writing as a private and public activity and the defense, sometimes even the exhaltation of the female
writer. Woven into this figure, with the rhetorical needle
of domesticity, are the discourses of writing, education and
middle class virtuosity. In spite of the heavyhanded
rhetoric of domesticity and the acceptance of the Angel in
the House as emblematic, the discourse of the domestic
woman is, in the writings of female authors, contradictory;
sometimes it is in collusion with, and others times defiant
of the dominant ideologies. The unstable relationship of
this discourse to gender ideology revealed the contradictions and created the fissures through which male writers
were to mount their attack. Whereas later generations of
male writers and critics focused on the literary production
of the domestic authors, their contemporaries put into

question their authority to write. We shall see how the women authors at mid-century not only had to defend the figure of the woman writer in general, but also their own writing. They contested the social sanction against writing not only as a private activity—"artistic authority"—but also as writing for the literary marketplace—the public and social dimension of writing. Yet, their stance is not merely defensive; they also take the offensive and reproach men for their masculinist attitudes.

Common to all of the following essays is the narrative strategy of splitting and engendering the audience through the inscription of the distinct male voice and his arguments against writing women and writing by women. This strategy permits the essayists to isolate and specify the sector of the audience which she knows to be the aggressor and present him as such to the female audience. Sinués, again, in *El Angel del Hogar* argues that:

> Muy pocos seres se encuentran que sean defensores del talento de la mujer. Los hombres, en general, declaman contra él, porque, preciso es confesarlo, su instinto orgulloso y egoísta les hace desear que la condición de la mujer sea siempre esclava de la suya, como si el talento de esta débil mitad del género humano pudiese ser nunca gemelo del talento del hombre. (219)

Her characteristic strategy of apparent modesty serves to offset her very immodest—given its unladylike defiance—analysis of woman as slave. In the following fragment, she undertakes her self-defense by literally inscribing into her text the voice of male writers so that her audience can hear its language of belittlement:

> Yo sé que los grandes escritores dicen: "¡Pobrecilla! dejadla: va por su senda sin incomodar a nadie".¡Ah¡ ¡cuánto bien me hacen esas palabras! Sí, yo seguiré mi senda, sin afan, sin ambición....Dios bendicirá el pan que mi pluma me gane para la vejez, y solo os pido por recompensa, madres jóvenes y hermosas doncellas, que enseñéis mi nombre a vuestros hijos....(211)

Gómez de Avellaneda, in a series of articles written in 1860 and republished in 1877 as *Leyendas, novelas y artículos literarios*, takes Sinués' argument—which focuses soley on herself, as individual writer—one step further by exploring the relationship of gender to the literary world and institutions of the period. Avellaneda knows there is a difference between praise for individual female writers by male critics and the acceptance of these writers by male institutions. In 1853, a seat for her in the Real Academia had failed to materialize when her candidacy was rejected because she was a woman. She writes:

> Si la mujer....aún sigue proscrita del templo de los conocimientos profundos, no se crea tampoco que data de muchos siglos su aceptación en el campo literario y artístico: ¡ah! ¡no! también ese terreno le ha sido disputado palmo a palmo por el exclusivismo varonil, y aún hoy día se la mira en él como intrusa y usurpadora, tratándosela, en consecuencia, con cierta ojeriza y desconfianza, que se echa de ver en el alejamiento en que se la mantiene de las academias barbudas.—Pasadnos este adjetivo, queridas lectoras, porque se nos ha venido naturalmente a la pluma al mencionar esas ilustres corporaciones de gentes de letras, cuyo primer y más importante título es el de tener barbas. (303)

Whereas Sinués presents the world of a female writer as a static one of slavery in which she is willing to accept a position of marginality—as long as she has a place which she sees as granted initially by men and ultimately secured by women—Gómez de Avellaneda's poetic representation of this world is that of a war: literally as the site of the battle of the sexes where terrain must be contested inch by inch. Talent, in this war, is gender specific and wears a beard.

According to Gómez de Avellaneda, women are represented, in what we can read as a very anxious male discourse, as intruders into and usurpers of the male terrain. Rosalía de Castro (1866) and Concepción Gimeno de Flaquer(1877), in two surprisingly similar fragments, also point out the male resistance to women of letters. In the *Carta a Eduarda*, Castro through her narrator, Nicanora, writes: "Pero es el caso, Eduarda, que los hombres miran a las literatas peor que mirarían al diablo...."(955). Gimeno de Flaquer introduces her essay on women of letters in her book *La mujer española* with the following statement, echoing the discourse we have already encountered in Avellaneda's text.

> Muchas mujeres brillarían si no se alzase el hombre a cada
> paso, diciéndoles que al tomar la pluma usurpan un derecho que
> sólo a ellos está concedido.
> Hay mujeres que careciendo de valor para sostener la perpetua
> lucha con el hombre, abandonan la pluma y matan su
> inspiración, guardando mutismo eterno.
> El hombre español le permite a la mujer ser frívola, vana,
> aturdida, ligera, superficial, beata y coqueta, pero no le per-
> mite ser escritora. (211)

For them, women writers—and women in general—
live within the structure and language of patriarchy. They,
clearly, blame men for the prohibition against the female
writer and for her representation as Evil. In the following
texts, they create the character of the female writer and sit-
uate her within a social milieu where she has to endure
and live out the hostility of patriarchy. They spin a narrative strategy which incorporates the voices of this society
into their texts. This voice, no longer attributed solely to
the male, is articulated as homogeneous, dominant and
unrelenting and narrativized as a neverending drone. It is
the voice of Spanish society, now constituted by males and
females, unwilling to accept the woman of letters. For
both, the inclusion of the collusive female into this voice
expresses their felt marginality to society as a whole. Rosalía de Castro writes:

> [A]miga mía, tú no sabes lo que es ser escritora ....Si vas a la
> tertulia y hablas de algo de lo que sabes, si te expresas siquiera
> en un lenguage algo correcto, te llaman bachillera,...Si guardas
> una prudente reserva, ¡qué fatua!, ¡qué orgullosa!;...Si te haces
> modesta y por no entrar en vanas disputas dejas pasar
> inadvertidas las cuestiones con que te provocan, en dónde está
> tu talento?...Si vives apartada del trato de gentes es que te
> haces la interesante, estás loca, tu carácter es atrabiliario e
> insoportable.(955)

Concepción Gimeno de Flaquer adds that:

> Si la literata es reservada, la apellidan orgullosa; si es
> expansiva, charlatana; si es seria, altanera; si es alegre, loca;
> si es triste; romántica.

> Si habla poco, dicen que se desdeña de tratar a las gentes
> porque no las ve a su altura; si habla mucho, que quiere impo-
> nerse y lucir sus conocimientos.
> Si su conversación es sencilla, la encuentran vulgar y poco en
> armonía con sus escritos; si sus frases son elegantes, dicen que
> escogita los términos que usa para deslumbrar, haciéndose in-
> comprensible. (215)

In the case of Gimeno de Flaquer, the defense of writing women is also linked to a class discourse which articulates the importance of writing and education for the middle class woman. This text, written almost twenty years after Sinués' *Angel del hogar*, continues to intertwine the question of writing, education, and the domestic middle class woman. Again, we encounter the critique of the aristocratic woman because of "el ocio [en] que viven algunas de nuestras aristocráticas damas, sin saber escribir siquiera una carta" (222). In both of these fragments the juxtaposition of the enumeration of the hypothetical activities of the woman writer to the voice of society signals the lack of space, bordering on claustrophobia, felt by the woman writer. This lead Castro to implore Eduarda, her fictional friend, to "no, mil veces, no, Eduarda; aleja de ti tan fatal tentación, no publiques nada y guarda para ti sola tus versos y tu prosa, tus novelas y tus dramas: que ese sea un secreto entre el Cielo, tú y yo" (952). Yet, neither Castro, nor her contemporaries took heed of her plea.

In this paper, thus far, I have discussed writing as a function of education and literacy and have proposed that the women writers who promoted education for women, albeit domestic, positioned themselves in an oppositional space within patriarchy. Spanish society was quick to understand that even the most benign suggestions for the education of women would have far reaching effects—as Sinués had rightfully predicted—among which was the proliferation of a large corpus of writing by and for women. Because of this the female writer, as advocate of the educated middle class woman, becomes the ideal target for patriarchal attack. The following section illustrates another facet of writing and domesticity: the constraints placed on writing by women writers. I will focus primarily on Sinués not only is she the most ideologically self-conscious of the domestic fiction writers; she also proposes a reinterpretation and a fine tuning of the ideology of domesticity. What we notice in Sinués is that writing, as part of her program for women's literacy, is transformed into the writing of narratives. I will read Sinués in conjunction with Father Claret, also a promoter of domesticity, in order to point out their important differences.

Sinués takes on the figure of the Romantic woman and her literary production as the point of departure for her long and elaborate argument in favor of domesticity in *El Angel del hogar*. Father Claret, the moral authority of the period undertakes the same project. In *Instrucción que debe tener la mujer* he argues against young women as readers of novels with an altogether familiar argument from this period: "porque ellas son susceptibles como la pólvora; y por esto se las apartará de ver y oir cualquier cosa que las pueda provocar a esta fatal pasión. No se las permitirá leer libros de amores, singularmente novelas y romances..."(18). In place of novels and romances he instructs young girls to read the lives of saints, particularly female saints like St. Monica. Pilar de Sinués, on the other hand, does not recommend in her conduct book that young women be steered away from reading fiction. Instead, she proposes that a very specific and special type of literature be written for a very concrete audience: young girls training for their social "mission" as wives, daughters, and mothers. Her suggestion is that that they be offered "historias dulces, llenas de sentimiento y de verdad" (239). Sinués rejects the romantic tradition of novel writing, in a parallel argument to Claret's, because "las tiernas lectoras....siguen en cuanto pueden los pasos de las heroínas de sus novelas, y....entonces procuran desfogar su imaginación, ardiente de sí y acalorada por la indigestión de ideas, escribiendo a su vez novelas y versos que necesariamente han de tener el impuro colorido de la literatura que conocen" (227). Both Claret and Sinués have, in Cora Kaplan's words, "gendered and sexualized the interaction between women and the narrative imaginative text, one in which women become the ultimately receptive readers easily moved into amoral activity by the fictional representation of sexual intrigue" (160). But, in a curious and symptomatic twist, Sinués takes her argument one step further, than does Claret, by presuming that reading naturally leads to writing. Because she sees these two activities as inextricably intertwined, the propriety of a woman writing is not put into question. It becomes, rather, a question of what she reads and, therefore, what she reproduces in her writing. In *El angel del hogar*, among the many embedded narratives, there is a touching autobiographical fragment which narrates the production of her first novel, *Rosa*. In it she sets up a characteristic contradiction which reveals her ambivalence and unease about writing fiction. On the one hand, the narrating "I" seems to be driven to write by some inexplicable, yet, natural force. On the other hand, she clearly believes that her noctural martyrdom was her just atonement for the sin of creativity.

> Recuerdo que cuando a la edad de ocho años escribí y dí a luz mi novela *Rosa*, mi primer ensayo en este género de literatura, nadie quiso creer que fuese obra mía....[L]uego pasaba a otra habitación, encendía la luz y me ponía a escribir en pedazos de papel de todas clases, tamaños y colores, porque entonces yo carecía hasta de papel....Aquella noche llovía agua helada, y yo no tenía más abrigo que mi bata....Al amanecer, cuando la criada encargada de la limpieza abrió el balcón para barrer el aposento, me halló inmovil, fría y entregada a un sueño que, según todas apariencias, debía ser eterno. Aquella noche de martirio me conquistó el perdón de haber escrito una novela...(114-117)

Sinués always depicts herself as typical which, therefore, enables her to present her experience as paradigmatic for all. If the eight year old Sinués writes a novel without anyone's encouragment, her conclusion is that the creative impulse is a natural one. The question then becomes, how to channel woman's imagination and, therefore, her desire. Her solution is to propose that specialized narratives be written for women, that will, in turn, beget those same type of narratives. Yet, this neat solution hinges on the producer of these texts because "la escritora deber ser, o a lo menos debe procurar serlo, un modelo de las virtudes que enaltezca con su pluma; y al mismo tiempo deber haber armonía entre la belleza de sus pen-

samientos y la belleza de su ser" (236). As her negative example of writers, she uses the Romantic woman of letters.
Her criticism is not that she writes, but rather that she is
not "el modelo de todas las virtudes; en vez de ser gen-
erosa, sumisa y tierna, es, por lo regular, egoista, altanera o
insensible" (222-3). The new virtuous woman writer and
her texts will be specular images of each other and, like
facing mirrors, will reproduce virtuosity into infinity.

Both Claret and Sinués, I believe, are acutely aware that
femininity is a social construction and that the act of reading—and in the case of Sinués, the act of writing—is an
important element in this process. Fueled by the same fear
of uncontrollable female desire and the belief that literature has a didactic function, Claret and Sinués, both advocates of the virtuous woman, nevertheless, propose different literary solutions for the feminization of the female.
The female reader has become the site for the struggle of
competing ideologies: on the one hand, Claret's reactionary evangelical Catholicism, on the upswing after the
Concordat of 1851 and, on the other, Sinués' moderate
Catholicism which was seeking to accomodate religion,
education and progress.[9] In the end, it would be the domestic and sentimental novel, not the hagiography, which
would populate the literary terrain between 1850 and 1880.

For Sinués, writing, then, was to be circumscribed
within the new paradigm of womanhood and contained
in two ways: First, literally within the private sphere of the
home and, secondly, thematically. So, in one of the many
novelettes intercalated within her hybrid conduct book, *El
angel del hogar*, the narrator has the character of the
mother, structured as a paragon of virtue, give her two
daughters the diaries she had kept since childhood so that
they can learn from her experiences. She encourages them
to keep similar diaries so that they, in turn, could pass
them on to their daughters. If we read this novelette as an
allegory about women's writing, we find that Sinués articulates writing by women as the vehicle through which
women teach women—mothers to daughters—the hard
and important lessons to be learned in life. For Sinués
these include the acceptance of one's place in the world as

a woman, the boundaries confining women, and the necessay suffering endured by women.

> ¡Hijas de mi alma!—prosiguió la señora de Rivera, estrechando de nuevo contra su pecho a las dos niñas;—si llegara un día en que alguna reprensión mía os parece injusta, abrid este diario y me perdonaréis mi injusticia en gracia de lo que he sufrido; si en alguna ocasión dudáis de la senda que debéis seguir, quizá en él encontraréis consejos saludables que os servirán de guía en el revuelto y dificultoso camino de la vida...Angela y Rosa devoraron ansiosamente todo el libro, aquel libro que, según la misma autora decía en él, había sido escrito con inauditos trabajos y ocultando con el mas prolijo afán.... (127-8)

The mother, therefore, encourages them as future women to write but only as long as their writing does not extend beyond the four walls of the home. Because writing, in this articulation, is for the private sphere and for private consumption, Sinués-as-mother, proposes that women adopt the diary as their genre; the content of which should be didactic. The diary, as envisioned by Sinués, is, one could argue, a rather prosaic, unheroic and middle class version of the hagiography where daughters learn how to be virtuous mothers and wives rather than how to be saints. What is important for Sinués is that the content of these narratives of life, always metaphorically depicted as "a vale of tears", address the question of education towards virtue, that is to say, moral education. Yet, although Sinués' characters take their author's advice seriously and write only for their daughters and the private sphere, Pilar de Sinués herself was one of the most prolific novel writers of the nineteenth-century, producing almost one hundred domestic and virtuous novels between the 1850's and the 1890's.

The writers of the mid-century generation continue to broaden the cultural space for women writers and create a literary paradigm, the domestic novel, within which both characters and author can negotiate domestic ideology. In these the feminine role and identity are of pivotal importance in the construction and the reproduction of social life. We have seen Sinués and others argue against the aristocratic woman and the romantic woman of letters, proposing instead the angel of the house both as the figure for the writer and character of domestic fiction. Yet they have all fallen through the crack of literary history and the history of Spanish feminist theory and practice. Certainly, the succeding generations could not, and would not, look to this group of writers in their search for literary models or inspiration given that the ideology of domesticity was to become anathema for feminism, then and now. I have portrayed them as essentially contradictory but, nevertheless, contestatory because I think it helps explains the ways in which the legacy of Susan Kirkpatrick's "protofeminist" romantic writers is handed down to the feminist authors of the latter part of the century. They could be said to constitute the literary and historical missing link between two formidable generations. In and of themselves, though, they represent a type of female subjectivity where "femininity" and "feminism" dialogue, revealing the contradictory forces at work in the midcentury construction of womanhood.

NOTES

[1] The epigraphs are from the following sources: María del Pilar Sinués, *El Angel del hogar* (Madrid, 1874), 210; Concepción Gimeno de Flaquer, *La mujer española* (Madrid, 1877), 222; Rosalía de Castro, *Obras Completas* (Madrid, 1980), 953; Julio Nombela, *Impresiones y recuerdos* (Madrid, 1911), 429; Julio Nombela, *Impresiones y recuerdos* (Madrid, 1911), 430; Virginia Woolf, *Women and Writing* (New York, 1979).

[2] There is no systematic study of the production of women's literature during this period equivalent to what Ferreras has done for the male authored "novelas por entrega". Ferreras, who devotes a footnote to the novels written by women, does give some interesting information. He has found that very few women who specialized in the female audience published "novelas por entregas" preferring, rather, single volume novels or to publish in specialized magazines. Ignacio Ferreras, *La novela por entregas (1840-1900)* (Madrid: Taurus, 1972) 26.

[3] Sinués founded the journal, *El Angel del Hogar. Páginas de la familia* (Madrid, 1864-9) and she also directed *Flores y Perlas, Periódico literario, recreativo y moral dedicado al bello sexo* (1883-4). Sáez de

Melgar edited *La Violeta* (1862-5), *La Mujer* (1871), *La Canastilla de la Infancia* (1882-95) and *Paris Charmant* (1884-95). Angela Grassi was the director of the magazine *Correo de la Moda* from 1867 to 1883.

[4] Susan Kirkpatrick documents this phenomenon in chapter 9 of *Las Romanticas*.

[5] Some two thousand works on the subject of 'la mujer' were written in the nineteenth-century according to the bibliographical list compiled by primarily by Simón Palmer. María del Carmen Simón Palmer, "La mujer en el siglo XIX: notas bibliográficas", in *Cuadernos Bibliográficos* (Madrid: CSIC), 31 (1974), 114-198; 32 (1975), 109-50; 37 (1978), 163-206 and 38 (1979), 181-211; also "Libros de religión y moral para la mujer española del siglo XIX" in *Primeras jornadas de bibliografía de la Fundación Universitaria Española* (Madrid, 1977), 355-85.

[6] Catherine Jagoe, "Ambivalent Angels. Galdos' Representations of Women and Ideology of Domesticity." Diss. Cambridge University, 1988, 1-48.

[7] Nancy Armstrong, *Desire and Domestic Fiction, A Political History of the Novel,* (New York: Oxford UP, 1987) 1-27. Susan Kirkpatrick, *Las Románticas: Women Writers and Subjectivity in Spain: 1835-50.* (Berkeley: University of California Press, 1989).

[8] Literacy, argues Nancy Armstong is a double-edged sword. She presents this point in reference to the English working class at the beginning of the nineteenth-century. I believe the same point can be made for women's literacy at mid-century in Spain. "Education did not necessarily make newly impoverished laborers safe for an industrializing world; it could in fact have made them extremely dangerous. If education helped to produce a more tractable working class, working class radicalism was predicated on literacy too". Nancy Armstrong, *Desire and Domestic Fiction, A Political History of the Novel,* (New York: Oxford UP, 1987) 17.

[9] Sinués contributes to two liberal papers: *La Epoca* (1849-1936) and *El Imparcial* (1867-1930). Andreu describes *El Imparcial* in the following way: "Este periódico se identificó totalmente con los valores de la Revolución de 1868 y se declara partidario especialmente de las reformas educativas inspiradas por los krausistas. De tendencia anticlerical y libre pensadora". Alicia G. Andreu, *Galdós y la literatura popular,* (Madrid: SGEL, 1982) 166.

Works Cited

Aldaraca, Bridget. "El Angel del Hogar: The Cult of Domesticity in Nineteenth- Century Spain." *Theory and Practice of Feminist Literary Criticism.* Ed. G. Mora and K.S. Van Hooft. Ypsilanti, Mich.: Bilingual Press, 1982. 62-87.

Andreu, Alicia. *Galdós y la literatura popular.* Madrid: SGEL, 1982.

Armstrong, Nancy. *Desire and Domestic Fiction, A Political History of the Novel,* New York: Oxford UP, 1987.

Carr, Raymond. *Spain 1800-1975.* 2nd ed. Oxford: Clarendon Press, 1982.

Castro, Rosalía de. *Obras Completas.* Vol. 2. Madrid: Aguilar, 1980. 2 vols.

Catalina, Severo. *La mujer, apuntes para un libro.* 2nd ed. Madrid, 1861.

Claret, Antonio. *Instrucción que debe tener la mujer para desempeñar bien la misión que el todopoderoso le ha confiado.* Barcelona, 1862.

Ferreras, Ignacio Ferreras. *La novela por entregas (1840-1900).* Madrid: Taurus, 1972.

Gimeno de Flaquer, Concepción. *La mujer española.* Madrid, 1877.

Gomez de Avellaneda, Gertrudis. *Leyendas, novelas y artículos literarios.* Madrid, 1877.

Jagoe, Catherine. "Ambivalent Angels. Galdos' Representation of Women and the Ideology of Domesticity." Diss. Cambridge University, 1988.

Kaplan, Cora. *Sea Changes: Essays on Culture and Feminism.* London: Verso, 1986.

Kirkpatrick, Susan. *Las Románticas: Women Writers and Subjectivity in Spain: 1835-1850.* Berkeley: Univ. of Calif. Press, 1989.

Nombela, Julio. *Impresiones y recuerdos.* vol. 4. Madrid: Casa editorial de "La última moda", 1911. 4 vols.

Simón Palmer, Carmen. "Escritoras españolas del siglo XIX o el miedo a la marginación." *Anales de literatura española* 2 (1983): 477-490.

Sinués de Marco, María del Pilar. *El angel del hogar.* 7th ed. Madrid, 1874. 2 vol.

Valera, Juan. *Obras completas.* vol. 2. Madrid: Aguilar, 1949. 3 vols.

Woolf, Virginia. "Professions for Women." *Women and Writing.* ed. Michele Barrett. New York: Harcourt Brace Javanovich, 1979.

THE MEDICAL CONSTRUCTION OF THE FEMININE SUBJECT IN NINETEENTH-CENTURY SPAIN

Bridget Aldaraca
University of Florida, Gainesville

I have titled my paper "The Medical Construction of the Feminine Subject in Nineteenth-Century Spain" but I believe that the material in my paper can best be introduced by a brief discussion of the concept of construction and deconstruction of the unified or integral subject. In any discussion of contemporary theories of the subject, the concept of the deconstruction of the subject is inevitably based on the premise of its original construction. Within the philosophical tradition of early-modern and modern rationalism, the stable and homogeneous subject— the I of Descarte's *cogito* — is defined as an identity: A always equals A and can never equal non-A. This identity principle is called into question by feminist criticism from the vantage point of two disciplines: linguistics and psychoanalysis. These two disciplines also merge in the work of Jacques Lacan, with his development of the theory of the construction of subjectivity as taking place in the realm of symbolic meaning, that is to say, language.

Derridian theories of the deconstruction of the subject state that the signifier takes its meaning from its place in the signifying chain and can only be ascribed meaning in relation to other signifiers. Meaning is derived from the process of differentiation. Thus the concept of a subject which can be abstracted and moved unchanging from discourse to discourse, narrative to narrative, always recognizable and comprehensible because it maintains its identical properties, is blown apart. The process of deconstruction permits the questioning of the construction of the subject, or in other words, the construction of the subject engenders its deconstruction. However, most feminist critics agree that the categories of masculine/feminine difference can be neither ignored nor easily transcended because our own subjectivity is derived from within the same signifying chain that constructs the categories which are our point of reference. We cannot place our subjectivity outside the signifying chain which signs the social relations of capitalist patriarchy. As Toril Moi reminds us, a total rejection of the symbolic order—in itself a utopian proposition— and, I would add, the consequent necessary creation of our own personal symbolic order, is the Lacanian (and not only Lacanian) definition of psychosis.[1]

Much feminist criticism then, takes the form of a critique of the content of the socially constructed categories of masculine/feminine, underscoring the process by which these idealizing and reductive categories function to rationalize and justify relations of power and the oppression of women in patriarchal society. Because the categories of feminine/masculine are generally engaged rather than avoided in feminist criticsm and theory, the work of some feminist writers is criticized as essentialist; that is to say, dependent on abstract and homogenizing categories of man/woman or feminine/masculine in a framework which ignores other categories of difference or which does not take into account the historical genesis of concepts of difference and the role of ideology in their creation. What is clear is the divergence of political projects among the diverse groups of feminist writers, a divergence which usually is described in political terms as the difference between radical feminism, bourgeois humanist feminism and Marxist or socialist feminism. What is not absolutely clear by any means is that the tendency to slip into an essentialist perspective is more germane to one group than to another, although Marxist-feminists obviously must take into account the element of class in their theorization. However, it is not class itself but rather historical materialism—and most signally, Marxism's awareness of its own historicity—which allows it to avoid the pitfalls of essentialism.

Much of feminist literary criticism and theory has been oriented towards an attempt to discover or identify and thus to name (and to reappropriate) a unique female/feminine experience by circumscribing characteristics found in female-authored texts which may be considered uniquely female/feminine because they are not present in male-authored texts. In this search to establish a women's tradition which would both question and parallel the Great Tradition of the established canon, it is, in theory, the critic's 'feminist' consciousness which permits her to recognize the truth or authenticity of the female experience and to interpret or fill in the gap of the textual silences pregnant with repressed meaning. Critical to this project is the definition of 'feminist consciousness' which is generally understood to be the product not only of personal (lived) experience but also of all those various paths to knowledge which permit the individual to transcend personal experience and to identify with a politicized constituency. A feminist consciousness must be, by definition, related to a concept of a collective consciousness and a collective project, since feminism is a political position which insists on the common interests of all women within both socialism and capitalism.

Nevertheless, feminist literary criticism is replete with arguments which are premised on the authority of experience defined in the most limited way as personal, lived or individual. Experience engenders consciousness (the writer/critic's): consciousness (subjectivity) engenders the creative act (authorship/interpretation). Thus we read Cora Kaplan's statement in her excellent essay on the relationship between female subjectivity and class identity that: "the subjectivity of women of other classes and races and with different sexual orientations can never be 'objectively' or 'authentically' represented in literary texts by the white, hetereosexual, middle-class woman writer, however sympathetically she invents or describes such women in her narrative."[2]

Kaplan places the terms objectively and authentically in single quotes to reminds us of the various arguments against the concept of mimesis in realist fiction. "The Marxist critic (..) assumes the author and text speak from a position from within ideology—that claims about fictional truth and authenticity are, in themselves, to be understood in relation to a particular historical point of view of culture and art which evolved in the Romantic period. Semiotic and psychoanalytic theories of representation go even further in rejecting the possibilitiy of authentic mimetic art. They see the literary text as a system of signs that constructs the subjectivity of speaker and reader. Fiction of bourgeois women writers is spoken from the position of class-specific femininity." (..) It is hard for feminism to accept the implications of this virtual refusal of textual realism..."[3]

Kaplan's careful insistence on the non-funcionality of the concept of mimesis or textual realism defined as a reflection of "real life" is, however, contradicted by her assertion that the "white, hetereosexual, middle-class woman writer" *cannot* create 'authentic' black, lesbian, female working-class (male?) characters because this argument carries within it the implicit conclusion that black writers *can* (because they are black) create 'authentic' black characters, that lesbian authors (and only lesbian authors) *can* 'authentically' represent the lesbian experience in a literary text, and so on.

The assertion that the subject which sits within the pigeonhole of 'white, heterosexual, middle-class woman writer' cannot transcend her "class-specific femininity" is an example of the epistemological argument that experience—defined in the most limited way as lived or conscious—is knowledge. It is an argument which remits unavoidably to a mechanistic conception of mimesis and the diad of fiction/reality unmediated by narrative technique. Experience becomes a utopia of immediacy in which *becoming* is reabsorbed by *being*, dialectics reverting to ontology. To be sure, it is hard for all of us as feminists, or as non-feminists, to avoid discussing literary texts without the concept of resemblance or some similar mechanism which speaks to our desire to identify with the characters and the fictionally represented world they inhabit.

It is important to note that Kaplan is referring to the writing of fiction, and the supposed limitations of the author of fiction. It is all too obvious in this heyday of the religious right, that white women and white men usurp the political power of marginalized groups. But of greater importance is the fact that white middle-class hetereosexual women do not necessarily speak in the interests of all women within that limited category. The ultimate extrapolation of the statement cited is that only the Black female critic (or whatever category is established) can 'correctly' interpret the Black female writer, and so on. At this point it becomes clear that what we are really talking about is power: who will have the authority to say what is 'authentic' or what is 'objective', to define or negate the 'true' female experience; ultimately, the power to define what is feminism itself and who has the right to call herself/himself, a feminist. In the case of the feminist literary critic, control over the exercise of this political power is being fought over mainly in the arena of the Academy.[4] In the political arena outside the Academy, where French feminist literary criticsm is not the topic of the hour, the anatagonism of interests between political projects as articulated, for example, by a Phyllis Schlafley and a Bella Abzug, helps to create the ideological conditions which permit a white, hetereosexual, middle-class feminist to transcend the limitations of her class consciousness. Indeed, one could go further and state that it is the political proposition of feminisim, that *all* women share a position of mutual interest, which inevitably forces us to transcend politically our own specific and limited 'lived' experience. The extent to which one's 'raised feminist consciousness' translates into the successful writing of fiction, is, of course, another story.

There are several corrollaries to the argument which privileges experience as the only source of 'objective' or 'true' knowledge .

1. The argument places the critic in control of the author who in theory *can/not* speak/write with authority only or except within the limits of the category within which she is placed by the critic. As I have just stated, this mechanism can also be used to silence the critic's reflection on a category-different author. The creation of categories places the control in the hands of the creator of the categories which is why, as feminists, we insist on redefining categories and inventing new ones. In fact, the process of thinking in categories, that is, the process of differentiation, is inherent to symbolic representation and is the *sine qua non* of consciousness itself. Self-perception is a process of awareness of what we are *not*. Self-definition through the process of differentiation is inherent in language. We are continually establishing and recreating new categories of difference. In the paper I read this morning the following statement:

"For weeks I was in a daze. My thoughts were strange, esoteric. Suddenly I related to the world in terms of just two groups, the living and the dead." The speaker is a thirty-eight year old male, sexual preference and race unclassified, probably middle-upper or middle class who is dying of AIDS. [5]

2. The recreation of categories which assert the power to define social existence is a necesssary political act but one that tends towards the reification of the subject-as-finished product of the circumscribed category rather than holding in tension a concept of the subject- in - process. The Marxist concept of classes as the subject of history and/or the Derridian textualized subject-in-process which changes according to its place in the signifying chain, cannot operate within the same conceptual framework that includes a reified—abstracted, non-functional— subject which can be moved from category to category, as we change and redefine the categories. It is the I of Individual, the identical and idealized I of I am, which is germane to the statement that the white, hetereosexual middle-class woman writer *can/not*. The abstract I of bourgeois individualism, so deeply ingrained in our modern psyche, looks over the fences of our own constructed categories. In spite of our

advocation of a subject-in-process, feminist attempts to revindicate or to critique the class-bound specificity of a female consciousness are still often made to be dependent on the concept of a stable identity, a "yo" which is shifted from one set of circumstances to another.

3. At its most reductive level, the equation of experience = consciousness precludes both the Marxist concept of false consciousness (the uncritical internalization of the dominant ideology) and Freud's concept of an unconscious which is dependent on the subconscious repression of experience. The recent vindication of 'the feminine' through an attempt to create a new 'authentic' feminine writing— the project of a *feminine écriture* of Irigaray and Cixous— is an example of the utopian tendency which posits a political strategy based soley in the realm of ideology. An insistence on the specificity of the conditions under which women experience social relations in capitalist and socialist societies is indispensable to the formation of any feminist political strategy which has as its goal the betterment of those conditions. We can not banish the categories of male/female difference from our feminist discourse as long as these differences are grounded in material conditions which exist to the detriment of men and women of all classes.

In the last decade, the construction of female subjectivity has been the object of analysis of feminist psychoanalysts (Chodorow, Dinnerstein), who emphasize the preoedipal period and the mother-daughter bond, as well as feminist literary critics working with psychoanalytical concepts (Mitchell, Rose, Gallop, Gardiner, et al.)The result has been a flowering of provacative essays on Freud and the post-Freudians and a renewed interest in the genesis of psychoanalysis, an interest which has narrowed in on Freud's case of Dora and the disease of hysteria. The period in Spain which I will discuss is the period which immediately pre-dates the rise of Freud and which is dominated for two decades by the figure of the French clinician Jean- Marie Charcot.

Charcot's famous Tuesday lectures take place during the
late 1870s and the 1880s . In his lectures to a Parisian audience of physicians, writers, artists and intellectuals, Charcot describes the various diseases which he is observing
and in some cases, naming for the first time, in his clinc at
the Salpetrière. One of the diseases, certainly not a new
one, is hysteria. Using female hysterics as models in his
lectures and relying on hynotism to produce on the stage
the various dramatic symptoms that he was observing in
the hospital setting, Charcot detailed with precision the
numerous symptoms produced by hysterical attacks: dis-
tortion of the senses such as tunnel vision and partial or
total deafness, anesthesia or its contrary, hypersensitivity,
disruption or weakening of the motor forces, especially a
sensation of falling known as *astasia-abasia* (tottering and
swooning), *afonia* or loss of voice, *afasia* or loss of speech,
extreme loss of appetite or refusal to eat, *anorexia nervosa*,
inappropriate mood changes marked by crying or laughing
and finally, the awesome and terrifying spectacle of *la
grande hystérie*, the thrashing about, convulsions and
contractions of the full-blown hysterical fit. Charcot's description of hysteria became the text-book definition which
permitted the nineteenth-century physicians and alienists
to distinguish hysteria from epilepsy, dementia, and the
ravanges of alcoholism, tuberculosis and syphillis.

The debate concerning hysteria in the nineteenth century revolves around three issues which are also in one
way or another, interrelated: 1)the question of inherited
pathology, 2)the definition of gender, and 3)the problem of
sexuality. Some of the questions asked were, does male
hysteria exist? Should female hysterics marry? Is marriage
a cure for hysteria? Can hysteria be inherited, and if so,
how is it transmitted? But the most telling question which
permeates the medical discourse of the last decades of the
nineteenth century was the question which asked, is
hysteria a disease? *What* is hysteria?

Charcot's work in observing and describing his hysterical patients forms the dividing line bewteen a premodern
and a modern concept of hysteria. His use of hypnotism to

provoke and thus to demonstrate to his admiring public the bizarre symptoms of his attractive female patients made evident the fact that hysterical symptoms could be manipulated, by the hypnotist, and therefore possibly by the hysteric herself. Charcot's hypotheses concerning the cause of hysteria relied on current theories of an inherited predisposition to nervous diseases following the thinking of Morel and Moreau de Tours, as well as the organic orientation of the French school of medicine, which held that all diseases were caused by an anatomical lesion of a specific organ. Nevertheless, his dramatic use of hypnotism highlighted the role played in hysteria by the human mind or personality.

But although Charcot, in the words of the medical historian George Drinka, was "flirting with psychological explanation",[6] he remained firmly within the French tradition that attributed all disease to an anatomical lesion of a specific organ and he continued to search for the physical evidence of organic damage which would clarify the etiology of this mysterious and evasive disease. His modernity rests in part on the fact that the organ thought to be responsible was not the reproductive organs but the brain. Drinka says: "Charcot saw hysterics as victims of moral degeneration or faulty heredity, and therefore as possessing faulty cerebellums. Their neurolgical system lived on the edge of dissolution. To Charcot, in the fight for survival of the fittest, hysterics were creatures burdened with central nervous systems that could not stand any variety of stress, psychic or physical. Furthermore, the majority of hysterics were women, creatures more emotional than men, with smaller brains and muscles." [7]

Charcot's presence in the Spanish medical press and his contribution to the evolution of ideas and attitudes towards hysteria is readily evident. It is Charcot who is credited with establishing the medical fact of the existence of male hysteria. One physician exclaims: "...al Dr. Charcot ...debemos los mayores adelantos, y en particular cuanto se refiere a la histeria, de la cual hizo una descripción tan magistral, que bien puede decirse será imprecedora en los fastos de la Historia." And he goes on to say:"...hoy es cosa bien probada que la padecen de igual modo uno y otro sexo..."[8] But although male hysteria may have been accepted as medical fact on a theoretical level, in practice the association of hysteria with the female sex permeates medical discourse before, during and after the rise and fall of Charcot.

Middle and late nineteenth-century physicians insisted on a physiological basis for the supposedly natural or innate hypersensitivity of the female nervous system. The prescriptive recipe for the idealized *ángel del hogar*, a romantic image of women which develops in part as a reaction to women's demands for greater participation in bourgeois society,[9] details the supposed exclusivity of feminine/masculine qualities: woman is love not logic, controlled by passion rather than reason, she is not sense but sensibility, dominated by her heart rather than her head.[10] The female capacity to feel, to love, is a result of her hypersensitive nervous system: "La sensibilidad altamente exquisita de la mujer, es el origen de sus más tiernos afectos, es la base de su carácter moral: la estremada delicadeza de su sistema nervioso, la finura escepcional de sus fibras elementales, es la condición física de su organismo, la razón anatómica de su exquisita sensibilidad."[11] Nevertheless, the belief that a woman's moral character is grounded in her female biology, in the hypersensitivity of her "elemental fibers" creates an inevitable contradiction because it grounds both the Angel and her counterparts, the various images of the bad woman— the spendthrift, the fallen woman, the slut and the whore—in the same female anatomy. This contradiction meets in the terrain of female sexuality.

Dr. Campá's exalted description of the female nervous system tends to obfuscate what he means by the woman's "finura excepcional de sus fibras elementales" and it needs to be underlined that the title of his lecture is "Las dos edades críticas de la vida de la mujer, " that is puberty and the onset of menopause, considered in the nineteenth century to be the beginning and the death of the female as a sexual being. His description of the effect on the female organism of menopause fills in many of the blanks.

> "el organo generador no es asiento del orgasmo que antes le dominaba, y siguen indiferentes los demás factores del aparato, y duermen las sinergias y las simpatías orgánicas, y cesan de levantarse turbulentas reacciones, y tranquila la economia toda, parece volver a aquellos tiempos anteriores a la pubertad...
>
> Pasa una epoca en este silencio, y luego otra, y cada vez es mayor la indiferencia, y los fulgores que de cuando en cuando atestiguaban la existencia, bien que desfallecida, de los antiguos procesos, van haciendo más raros, acabando por no poder apreciar en el aparato sexual, ni cambios celurares definidos, ni congestiones sanguineas, ni eretismo fibrilar, ni *irritación nerviosa*,...[12](my underlining)

This passage, written in 1876, is not atypical of explicit clinical descriptions of female sexual arousal, but what is important for our understanding of nineteenth-century definitions of hysteria is the specfic link made between "nervous irritability" understood as the physiological basis of female sexuality and "nervous irritability" designated as the material grounding of women's moral character, the cite of her capacity for romantic love and passionate female abnegation. The fear and awe surrounding the discussion of the female nervous system which permeates medical discourse, becomes much more intelligible if we understand the term "irritación nerviosa" to function as a code for female sexuality. It is a code which both conceals the existence of female sexual desire and displaces it from the female sex organs *per se* into the nervous system where it can be diffused and renamed as an obiquitous non-sexual passion, or even idealized as the source of motherly love, "el origen de sus más tiernos afectos."

Previous to the nineteenth century, the uterine theory of hysteria, which originates in Greek thought, predominates as an explanation for female hysterical symptoms. This theory places female sexual desire at the source of the disturbance in the female organism and anthropomorphizes the womb as a sexually hungry animal, which when unsatisfied by normal coitus, rises in the female body in search of the sperm that will satisy its sexual longing, coming ultimately to rest in the throat where it is caught and held prisoner, forming a suffocating impediment to the respiratory process, the *globus histericus*. It is a theory which depends on the recognition of the existence of female sexual desire, and which links hysterical symptoms directly to an unsatisfied biologically-based (albeit anatomically incorrect) sexual need.[13]

Male fear of female sexuality is expressed in the nineteenth century by the insistent unlinking of hysteria from the demands that female sexuality might make upon the male. The idealized *ángel del hogar* is asexual, or rather, she satisfies her sexual needs, not through intercourse with the male, but through childbirth. In the opinion of many physicians, women's susceptible nervous system is the weak link which predisposes them to insanity and is the means of the transmission of hysteria from mother to child. The renowned hygienist, Pedro Felipe Monlau, reinforces the idea of an innate predisposition to hysteria in the female while denying a sexual etiology of the disease when he asserts that hysterics should not marry, because they stand the risk of transmitting their disease to their daughters.

> La propiedad hereditaria, al parecer, respeto a esta enfermedad, no procede sino de la madre, hecho que se comprende facilmente, si se reflexiona que casi solamente la mujer goza de aquella impresionabilidad del sistema nervioso, de aquella disposición afectiva, de la cual el histerismo no es más que un modo particular, una especie de exageración especial.[14]

The unlinking of hysteria from a sexual etiology and the linking of it to an inherited predisposition to "nervous irritability" also unlinks the female from the male and forces the responsibility for the disease onto the female. The condition of nervous irritability is 'natural' to the female organism and the hysterical woman is responsible for reproducing the disease through the reproduction of her diseased daughters. Monlau's stricture against marriage is an attempt to police the reproduction of an illness which is perceived more and more, as the century progresses, as a problem for the male and his family. Thus, social control over hysteria through the control over female sexual activity within the private institution of the bourgeois family—hysterics should not marry—parallels the attempt to control venereal diseases in the public sphere through the regimentation of the prostitute.

While the denial of a sexual etiology for hysteria removes the responsibility for the disease from the male, the definition of hysteria is continually colored by attitudes of condemnation and suspicion towards the female sex which embodies it and reproduces it. The idea of an inherited *predisposition* to nervous disease is, in the nineteenth century, as Drinka points out so succintly,"the Christian notion of original sin embodied in the nervous system".[15] This moralistic concept of disease as a kind of original sin also coexisted with a more liberal medical point of view which emphasized environment and the hope of holding at bay morbid tendencies through proper nutrition and a combination of physical and moral hygiene. The key to health was education. Women, who because of their weak nervous systems were considered a time-bomb waiting to explode, were also judged to have the capacity to gain control over their innate hysterical tendencies. Or rather, women could be controlled through proper education. Indeed, education was the mechanism of social control of both sexes. Dr. Sanchez y Candela insists that: "Debe empezar la educación de ambos sexos en la primera infancia, inculcándoles desde el principio la obediencia y el amor al prójimo, a fin de combatir el egoismo y encauzar la voluntad; tratando de despertar al mismo tiempo el amor a Dios, a la familia y al trabajo, sin los cuales no hay sociedad posible.[16]

The question of *what* is hysteria comes to rest on the question of the hysteric's possible moral responsibility for her disease, a question which is inextricably linked to the nineteenth-century concept of will, autonomy, or *voluntad*. Charcot's work reinforces a view of hysteria as a

moral—in modern terminology, functional—disease because he demonstrates through his use of hypnotism that
although hysteria might look like epilepsy or manifest
symptoms of paralysis or blindess, one of histeria's distinguishing characteristics was its capacity to *imitate* other
diseases. (The term functional distinguishes between neurotic conditions which are produced by the patient's reac-
tions to trauma or to the conditions of his/her environment and those conditions which are primarily organically
based and which therefore respond to medication with or
without the assistance of psychotherapy.) One of the most
important medical writers of the period, Dr. J. Grasset,
states in his *Enfermedades del sistema nervioso*, compiled
from classes given in the Academy of Medicine in Mont-
pellier in the 1870s and first published in Spanish in
Barcelona in the 1880s:"la afección histérica imita a casi todas las enfermedades que son patrimonio de nuestra especie". Although Grasset goes on to to insist on the
distinction of hysteria as either "una neurosis pura' or accompanied by "alguna lesión,[17] the idea that hysteria has
the capacity to disguise itself as "todos los malos conocidos",[18] reinforces the growing belief that hysteria is a disease of fakery, a fake disease, and the hysterical woman, an
imposter.

As hysteria is perceived more and more as a non-or-
ganic and non-fatal disease, sympathy for the hysteric
shifts from the woman to her family. Grasset, quoting
Frank, asks: "Se puede imaginar alquien más desgraciado
que el marido de una histérica?"[19] The disease of hysteria
begins to be associated in the medical texts of the period
with something called the "hysterical character"—the
nineteenth-century equivalent of today's "hysterical personality"—a judgement which has a great deal more to do
with proper female behavior and decorum than it does
with medical symptoms such as fever and blood pressure
or only as they are elevated in the hysteric's loving atten-
dants. The idea of a hysterical character reverts back to the
belief that women have an essential nature which is undifferentiated from individual to individual woman:

"Respecto al carácter y aun al espíritu, encuéntranse menos diferencias de mujer a mujer que de hombre a hombre: apártanse menos de su natulareza las mujeres que nosotros de la nuestra."[20] The idea that women are born hysterics would seem to contradict the idea that hysteria is a disease of the will, or rather that hysterical symptoms are willed voluntarily. The following description of hysteria taken from the first comprehensive diagnostic manual of mental illness written in Spain reinforces once more the idea that hysteria is an exaggeration of the basic female nature which is typified by its moral and physical weakness.

> En edad temprana ya demuestran las histéricas lo que han de ser, presentando la emotividad tan propia de ellas, por lo que tan pronto rien como lloran, por cualquier pretexto que impresione: precoces, coquetas, procurando llamar hacia sí la atención, dadas a la mentira, sujetas a pesadillas, a palpitaciones y a la anemia. La movilidad más exagerada es el principal distintivo intelectual; susceptibles de una instrucción extensa y brillante, les es imposible dedicarse a nada serio y constante. Son el espiritu de contradicción, dadas a la controversia, fantásticas, y con las mayores rarezas de carácter, su sensibilidad es exagerada y las variaciones de sus sentimientos no guardan proporcion con la causa que las motiva; cambian a cada instante de pensamientos y afectos; tienen una aficion inata al engaño, a la calumnia y a los chismes, inventando, para justificar cualquier cosa, una bien urdida novela...se les nota ademas una debilidad marcada de voluntad y de inteligencia.[21]

This quote demonstrates aptly the lack of sympathy felt for the hysteric now that hysteria is no longer considered an organically-based disease. Indeed, it is not clear from this quote that hysteria is considered a disease at all, since the only medical symptom mentioned, if we except the reference to weak intelligence which would make possible a diagnosis of mental retardation, is the symptom of anemia, which even in the nineteenth century is recognized as linked to improper nutrition and is treated with tonics. What we have instead is the traditional diatribe against the rebellious female; she is a liar, seductive, flighty and scatter-brained, not to be trusted, deceptive, and soft in the head. And she is a threat, often guilty of inventing stories, of calumny, about who? About what?

The opinion that hysteria is not so much a disease as an exaggeration of the natural weakness of the feminine character is reinforced not by denying the existence of male hysteria but by attributing affeminacy to the male hysteric. In 1893, in a speech to the Royal Academy of Medicine and Surgery of Granada, Dr. Velázquez will reaffirm the now established opinion that hysteria is a female disease and a disease of the will. "La cuarta parte de las mujeres, si no la mitad son histéricas, por cada cinco de éstas solo se cuentan cinco histéricos, cuanto más afeminado es el hombre tanto más propenso está, la virago es la que menos aptitudes tiene. ... La debilidad volitiva o la absoluta carencia de la voluntad, constituye en efecto, el principal factor del carácter histérico."[22]

I would like to conclude my discussion of hysteria in nineteenth-century Spain by returning once more to the question of socially-constructed categories and the social construction of the feminine subject. The medical categories of diseased and healthy can be understood as empirical categories, or rather, categories which can be empirically substantiated when the disease in question has a definite organic basis as in the case of venereal disease, cancer or tuberculosis. Although the etiology of these diseases was not fully understood then (or in the case of cancer now either, for that matter) still the causal relation between, for example, syphillis and sexual activity was known and the necesasary means to control it could be ascertained. Hysteria, with its apparently unfathomable causality and its dramatic symptoms, lent and lends itself to mystification. Freud's question, what do women want, is not the abstract question of the philosopher, it is a question born out of frustration and annoyance: at Dora's abandonment of her analysis, perhaps, or at all the women hysterics whom he treated day after day .

Socially constructed categories operate in the realm of ideology to exercise control over the categorized group by those who define the category. In the nineteenth century, scientific concepts of health and disease in medical discourse replace—or operate alongside—the moral theological categories of good and evil established by the Church fathers to control female behavior and especially, the expression and repression of female (and male) sexuality. The Perfect Wife, the Virtuous Woman, the Angel are posited against the social outcast, the Witch and the Whore. As I have commented elsewhere, the ideological constraints on women embodied in the image of the *ángel del hogar* are directed towards the wives and daughters of the middle-class in order to rationalize their exclusion from the public sphere and to prevent their access to education and the professions. The category of the sick hysteric operates in part to solve the problem of the rebellious female (both middleclass *and* working class) *in the house* that is to say, within the institution of the patriarchal family. It will be in the power of the doctors to say who is ill and who is well and to prescribe the cure. The new medical construction of the feminine subject borrows from traditional prejudices and invents, with the image of the hysterical female, a new and potent one, an image which is used to chastise and compell women to silence under pain of the accusation of insanity. From the nineteenth century down to the present moment, religion and science will both compete and reinforce each other in the struggle for control over women in bourgeois society.

NOTES

1 Moi, Toril. *Sexual/Texual Politics*. London: Methuen,1985, p.170.

2 Kaplan, Cora. "Pandora's Box: Subjectivity, Class and Sexuality in Socialist-Feminist Criticsm". In *Making a Difference*, eds. G. Greene and C. Kahn. London: Methuen, 1985, p.162.

3 Kaplan, p.161.

[4] For a lively example of the current power struggle to define feminism and to defend the limited and precariously possessed turf carved out by academic feminists, see *Men in Feminism*, eds. A. Jardine and P. Smith, London and New York: Methuen, 1987.

[5] *The Miami Herald*, 2/27/88: D-1.

[6] Drinka, George Frederick, M.D. *The Birth of Neurosis: Myth, Malady and the Victorians*. New York: Simon & Schuster, Inc., p.106.

[7] Drinka, pp.100-101.

[8] Dr. Candela y Sanchez, Pascual. "El concepto médico-social de la histeria", Discurso leído en la Real Academia de la Medicina, Madrid,1899, pp.7-8.

[9] See Geraldine M. Scanlon's *La polémica feminista en la España contemporanea:1868-1974*, Madrid:Siglo XXI, 1976, also reedited Madrid: Akal, 1986, for a detailed documentation of the conservative reaction to liberal feminist thinking in Spain during this period.

[10] For an analysis of the social construction of femininity in nineteenth-century Spain see Bridget A. Aldaraca, "El ángel del hogar: The Cult of Domesticity in Nineteenth-Century Spain" in *Theory and Practice of Feminist Literary Criticsm*, eds. G. Mora and K. S. Van Hooft, Michigan: Bilingual Press, 1982, pp.62-87.

[11] Dr. Campá, F. de P. "Las dos edades críticas de la vida de la mujer", Discurso leído en la Real Academia de la Medicina, Valencia, 1876, p.8.

[12] Campá, p.20.

[13] See Ilza Veith's classic study of hysteria entitled *Hysteria: The History of a Disease*. Chicago and London: The University of Chicago Press,1965.

[14] Dr. Monlau, Pedro Felipe. *Higiene del matrimonio o el libro de los casados*, first published in Madrid in 1853. Palua cites 11 subsequent editions, including a French translation in 1879, and two editions in Spanish published in Paris by Garnier. I quote from the Paris edition of 1892, p.502, which is designated the *séptima edición considerablemente aumentada*, although if Palua is correct, it would have to be an eighth edition. It is important to note that this textbook spans the entire second

half of the nineteenth century and was necessarily extremely influential.

[15] Drinka, p.53.

[16] Candela y Sanchez, p.11.

[17] Dr. Grasset, J. *Enfermedades del sistema nervioso*, Barcelona, 1880, tomo II, p.465.

[18] Candela y Sanchez, p.8.

[19] Grasset, tomo II, p.466.

[20] A.P., "La influencia de la mujer en la sociedad," *El Museo de las familias,*1863, cited in Aldaraca, pp.66-67.

[21] Dr. Martinez y Valverde, Joaquín, *El guía del diagnóstico de las enfermedades mentales*, Barcelona: 1900, pp.242-3.

[22] Dr. Velázquez de Castro, A. "La responsabilidad en las histéricas" Discurso leído en la Real Academia de Medicina y Cirugia, Granada: 1893, p.39.

MATERNIDAD, ECONOMIA Y PODER EN EL MATRIMONIO BURGUES DEL SIGLO XIX: EL EJEMPLO DE *FORTUNATA Y JACINTA*

Teresa M. Vilarós
University of Wisconsin, Madison

A través de toda la historia, y naturalmente, a través de toda la historia literaria, la mujer ha permanecido escondida, relegada a un plano silencioso y secundario. O, cuando su presencia se ha creído necesaria, ha servido como pantalla o espacio blanco en que el hombre ha proyectado sus miedos, deseos, fatigas o fantasías. La historia de la mujer es la historia de una imagen: la mujer como imagen fantasmal, como pantalla en la que el hombre se inscribe.

Precisamente por ello, la crítica literaria feminista encuentra más estimulante (y necesario) el estudio de los textos escritos por mujeres. El trabajo en este sentido está en estos momentos produciendo sus frutos, ya desde la relectura de textos escritos por mujeres "canonizadas" por la crítica masculina, ya desde la investigación y nueva lectura de las mujeres escritoras olvidadas (rechazadas) por las historias de la literatura.

Sin embargo, la búsqueda de una escritura femenina no debe implicar un abandono del cuestionamiento de la imagen femenina proyectada por el hombre. Al contrario, leer los textos femeninos puede servirnos para hacer hablar a estas mujeres marcadas (al fin y al cabo, como todas nosotras) con el nombre del padre. Dar la palabra a estas mujeres nacidas de varón y emanciparlas así de la tutela patriarcal. Y, una vez dotadas de nueva voz, escucharlas. Ellas también, y quizás ellas más que nadie, tienen mucho que contarnos desde su intrincada prisión textual. Prisioneras seminales de las construcciones teóricas de los hombres, del lenguaje, de la metafísica, del psicoanálisis, son, a pesar de todo, "lo otro."

Este trabajo quiere mostrar esa lectura diferente. Una lectura de textos masculinos desde mi diferencia sexual, desde "ce sexe qui n'en est pas un" como reza el título de un libro de Luce Irigaray. Lectura femenina en busca de la feminidad de un texto nacido de hombre.

No trato en este estudio de revelar el texto de Galdós como freudiano sino de revelar lo freudiano del texto. Y al mismo tiempo entablar un diálogo con los escritos de Freud de mano de algunas de las cuestionadoras de sus teorías.[1] La marca de género es aquí esencial porque implica por mi parte una toma de posición, un intento de interpretación distinto del tradicional masculino, una búsqueda de lo oculto, de lo velado, de lo olvidado de estas mujeres galdosianas.

Solamente así Fortunata, Jacinta y las demás mujeres dejan de ser clichés, blancos en los que se proyectan los deseos masculinos, para susurrar, balbucear más que decir, su diferencia.

Y en ese susurro de Fortunata y Jacinta, mucho se nos dice de la historia silenciosa de la mujer burguesa española del siglo XIX.

* * *

El subtítulo de *Fortunata y Jacinta* es "dos historias de casadas."Carlos Blanco Aguinaga señala acertadamente cómo el subtítulo y especialmente la conjunción copulativa del título indican al mismo tiempo las diferencias y las similaridades entre las dos mujeres: "Cada una de las mujeres se identifica con la otra en más de una ocasión, pero una y otra vez están separadas por su diferencia de clases. Tal vez sea suficiente recordar . . . que mientras Jacinta no produce pero compra, Fortunata produce y vende" ("Having No Option" 19).

La novela es, desde luego, una historia de relaciones y transacciones económicas y comerciales. Recordemos que los miembros de la familia Santa Cruz (a la que pertenece Jacinta por matrimonio) provienen de un medio pequeño-burgués específico, el de la clase de tenderos y comerciantes. Recordemos también que uno de los miembros más sobresalientes de la familia Rubín (la familia del marido de Fortunata), doña Lupe, es prestamista. Y Fortunata y Jacinta, a su vez, y según Blanco, compran, producen y venden. Sin embargo, no hay en toda la novela un episodio en el que Fortunata participe activamente en una venta (excepto cuando actúa como prostituta). Tampoco Jacinta, al contrario de su suegra, Barbarita, que sí tiene "la chifladura de las compras . . . y adqui[ere] por el simple placer de adquirir" (506), se caracteriza especialmente por el comprar o el derrochar. Antes al contrario, Jacinta conserva "los hábitos de economía adquiridos en su niñez" y "gastaba siempre mucho menos de lo que su suegra le daba para menudencias" (503).

¿Cuál es entonces la mercancía que está en juego? ¿Dónde está la conexión señalada por Blanco? La función económica en *Fortunata y Jacinta* está relacionada esencialmente con la maternidad. Pero la maternidad, como vamos a ver, controla institucionalmente no sólo la expresión de la sexualidad femenina, sino la misma definición de lo femenino como sexo otro, casi como carencia, y claramente desde luego ausencia, de sexo. Veremos incluso cómo una de las labores de producción doméstica más comunes, y una de las pocas que puede tener relevancia económica, la costura, está radicalmente asociada en el universo de la novela a esa ausencia de sexo a la que la maternidad como función única, condena a la mujer. La costura será presentada precisamente como el encubrimiento inconsciente, la sutura, del espacio vacío dejado por la castración original.

La maternidad en *Fortunata y Jacinta* juega un papel principal dentro de una estructura de poder específica como es la institución matrimonial y en particular el matrimonio burgués de fines del siglo XIX. Quiero recordar parcialmente qué significaba entonces el matrimonio según la interpretación de Luce Irigaray en *Speculum* (150-154). Engels, en *El origen de la familia, de la propiedad privada y del estado*, nos dice que el primer antagonismo de clase que aparece en la historia coincide con el antagonismo entre el hombre y la mujer en la relación monogámica y la primera opresión de clase con la opresión del sexo femenino por el masculino (76). Y Marx y Engels, en *La ideología alemana*, afirman que la separación de la sociedad en familias aisladas implica una división del trabajo que, a su vez, implica una distribución desigual de este trabajo tanto en cantidad como en calidad, así como también determina ideológicamente la noción de propiedad. Propiedad que en su primera forma, en germen, reside en la familia, donde la mujer y los niños son, estructuralmente, siervos del hombre (52). Tal vez estas afirmaciones puedan parecer exageradas, pero no podemos negar que el tipo de familia monogámica que conocemos permite la concentración de bienes y de riquezas en las manos del hombre, del jefe de familia, para poder pasar después esa herencia a los hijos de esa familia, es decir, a los hijos de este hombre y no a cualesquiera otros hijos de cualquier otra familia (Engels, *El origen de la familia* 86).

La estructura económica familiar exige que la mujer cumpla una función reproductora. La mujer es ante todo y por todo, *madre*. Desde esta posición, la compra, producción y venta de Fortunata y Jacinta en la novela de Galdós puede leerse como la compra, producción y venta del hijo, el hijo *necesario* (y enfatizo el término) para la aceptación y reconocimiento de la mujer por parte del hombre simultáneamente en tanto mujer y como parte de una estructura familiar de tipo patriarcal. Jacinta no produce hijos, pero compra uno, el llamado falso Pitusín. Fortunata, por su parte, produce al verdadero Pitusín y, aunque no lo vende, se lo regala a Jacinta. Esta conexión económica en lo maternal es lo que une a las dos mujeres, es lo que las atrae a la vez que las opone, lo que las hermana y lo que las separa más allá de la constatación obvia de su diversidad de clases. Fortunata y Jacinta van a buscarse y a perderse una a otra a través del texto, para al fin hermanarse y reconocerse en este hijo en común, este hijo que les es necesario a las dos para poder encontrar su puesto, y por tanto su ser, en la estructura socio-matrimonial de su época. Esta búsqueda especular es también el viaje al origen, búsqueda de la propia feminidad. Viaje circular. Y en el centro, en su centro y en el centro del matrimonio, el hijo. Porqué es necesario dar a luz a un hijo, a un varón, y cómo la ausencia o presencia de este hijo es el que determina la feminidad de la mujer en el sentido freudiano (y, por tanto, masculino) es lo que presento en este estudio. Por razones de espacio, voy a ocuparme más extensamente de Jacinta y los Santa Cruz y no de Fortunata y la familia Rubín.[2]

En la novela, las referencias a la institución del matrimonio son múltiples. El principio de *Fortunata y Jacinta* está dedicado en gran medida a la narración de las circunstancias que llevaron al matrimonio a Baldomero y a Bárbara, padres de Juanito. Juanito, andando el tiempo, se hace amante de Fortunata y después, marido de Jacinta. Fortunata, abandonada, contraerá un matrimonio poco afortunado con Maxi Rubín. El matrimonio de Jacinta con Juanito debería a su vez producir un heredero que continuara la dinastía santacruciana, heredero que llega al final de la novela no en forma "natural," es decir, no a través de un parto de Jacinta, sino como regalo de Fortunata a Jacinta del hijo que la primera ha tenido de Juanito Santa Cruz. Gracias a este regalo de Fortunata, Jacinta puede al fin honrar el contrato matrimonial en todos los aspectos, incluida la presentación de un hijo a la casa. Puede "realizarse." Es decir, como diría Luce Irigaray, Jacinta asume una sujeción histórica donde la mujer--con la posible excepción de la madre propia--es, sobre todo, objeto económico: valor de uso y/o valor de cambio entre los hombres. Mercancía marcada fálicamente y así apropiada por sus padres, por su maridos y sus proxenetas, siendo esta marca lo que decide su valor en el comercio sexual (*Ce sexe* 30-31).

En el caso del matrimonio de Fortunata, la posibilidad de un heredero para la dinastía Rubín está totalmente fuera de cuestión y no únicamente debido a la impotencia sexual de Maxi. A diferencia de Jacinta, Fortunata no quiere asegurarse ninguna posición dentro de su matrimonio con Maximiliano Rubín. Tiene sus propias ideas sobre los vínculos legales que unen a una pareja y, además, quiere ponerlos en práctica. La existencia textual de Fortu-

nata está siempre marcada por la consecución de su "idea,"
la famosa "idea blanca" que Guillermina Pacheco resume y
condena llamándola: "Aquel disparate de que el matrimonio, cuando no hay hijos, no vale ... y de que usted, por te-
nerlos, era la verdadera esposa de ...[Juanito]" (973). Idea
disparatada, desde luego, o quizás idea reprimida por los
cánones reglamentados, pero no tan "fuera de lugar," no
tan fuera del sistema económico de la institución decimonónica si pensamos que la idea de Fortunata revela directamente la importancia del hijo varón en la estructura
familiar monogámica que exige que la mujer sea, ante
todo, madre. La idea de Fortunata se traduciría más o menos así: "Yo soy la que puedo proporcionar un heredero a
los Santa Cruz. Por tanto, esto es lo que me convierte en
esposa. Pero si no aceptan lo que yo digo, y ya que el hijo
les es tan importante, voy a negociar con él a mi favor.
Voy a cambiarle a Jacinta el nene grande (Juanito) por el
nene chico (el hijo)."

"Cambiar un nene chico por el nene grande" (714) es
cita literal. Fortunata, con su "idea blanca," resume y
asume una equivalencia fundamental que Freud expone
sobre todo en "La sexualidad femenina" y en "La
feminidad:" los términos de mujer, esposa y madre son
inseparables e indiferenciables. En la novela de Galdós, los
términos freudianos no se˙ igualan. El equilibrio
estructural familiar que implica la ecuación freudiana se
rompe debido a la discordancia que produce un excedente.
Y éste es el gran descentramiento galdosiano: Tenemos
una esposa, pero es estéril. Tenemos maternidad, pero por
causa de la amante. Y como en el juego infantil del corro y
las sillas, una persona (una mujer) está de más, algo está
descolocado: Una esposa estéril, una amante fértil. ¿Cómo
igualar la ecuación mujer=madre=esposa? Porque es
evidente que hay que solucionar el problema ya que, en
este tipo de estructura, la mujer es la responsable de la
felicidad conyugal. Para Freud: "Las relaciones entre madre
e hijo son las únicas capaces de dar a la mujer una
satisfacción plena, porque de todas las relaciones humanas,
éstas son las más completas y las más desprovistas de
ambivalencia" ("La feminidad" 133); a partir de aquí, es

fácil llegar a la conclusión de que "la felicidad conyugal queda mal establecida si la mujer no consigue hacer de su esposo su hijo" ("La feminidad" 133-134). Así, si la mujer se iguala a la esposa y a la madre, por su parte el hombre se refleja a sí mismo en cuanto hijo. La dinámica familiar, de forma más o menos abierta, sigue líneas curiosamente cercanas al incesto. Por eso Fortunata no tiene inconveniente en cambiar "los niños." Por eso Jacinta, ya que no puede proporcionar el hijo real, se esfuerza en cumplir con la otra maternidad, la dirigida al esposo. Como ejemplo, la breve conversación entre Juanito y Jacinta: "—Mamá . . . — ¿Qué? — Teta" (565).

Doble responsabilidad, doble maternidad. Carga tremenda que nos lleva de la mano a una noción aterradora: la mujer que no es madre, no es. Y la que es madre lo es a la vez del esposo y del hijo, del hijo varón. A riesgo, en caso de fracaso, de ser puesta en duda su feminidad, su esencia, su "eterno femenino." Preparadas para la maternidad, para servir de canal de transmisión de los bienes paternos, de la propiedad, no es extraño que, como dice Freud, las mujeres no hayan contribuido "más que muy débilmente a los descubrimientos e invenciones de la historia de la civilización" ("La feminidad" 132) y que tengan "menos intereses sociales que los hombres" ("La feminidad" 134). Recordemos por ejemplo las múltiples alusiones a la falta de preparación intelectual de todas las mujeres en Fortunata y Jacinta, y de su falta de interés en lo social-masculino, la política por ejemplo. A las mujeres de nuestra novela no les interesa la historia sino su historia de maternidad.

¿Qué pasa entonces si la maternidad se frustra? ¿Cuál es el papel de una mujer casada, de la esposa que no cumple su función? La respuesta me parece evidente: ningún papel se reserva para la mujer estéril. La mujer estéril no es mujer en la ecuación mujer/madre. Nada hay previsto para ella y nada se espera de ella. No es nadie y no existe, pero su no-ser pone de manifiesto aún de forma más aterradora esa Ausencia específica a la que la cultura occidental parece condenar lo femenino. Lo femenino es siempre "lo otro," lo que no es masculino. La teoría freudiana sobre el desarrollo de la sexualidad infantil apunta claramente hacia esa otredad (otredad por otro lado siempre necesariamente parcial), cuando marca la necesidad de retroceso de cualquier impulso activo, masculino, para dar paso a la pasividad específica femenina. La mujer "normal" debe inhibir su masculinidad (actividad) infantil centrada en la zona erógena clitorial y cambiar a lo pasivo, a la zona erógena vaginal (remito, por ejemplo, a los estudios "La sexualidad femenina," "La organización genital infantil," "La diferencia anatómica entre los sexos" y "La feminidad," entre otros). Y a pesar de que el mismo Freud nos ponga en guardia sobre los peligros de una asociación simplista entre lo activo-masculino y lo pasivo-femenino, él mismo considera lo psicológico femenino como lo que da preferencia a objetivos pasivos ("La feminidad" 115).

La feminidad, asociada con la maternidad, queda así marcada por la pasividad y por la castración de la masculinidad: Carencia de acción y ausencia de pene. Por eso la búsqueda maternal de Fortunata y Jacinta es una búsqueda en la que todo el esfuerzo se vierte, paradójicamente en tapar la culpa, la ausencia, la falta. En tapar, precisamente lo que puede ser femenino. Una búsqueda que sigue las líneas del pensamiento freudiano: "Dar preferencia a objetivos pasivos. . . no es, naturalmente, lo mismo que pasividad; conseguir un objetivo pasivo puede necesitar grandes dosis de actividad" (La feminidad" 115). Esfuerzo inútil, en que todo está ya pre-fijado. Actividad hacia la pasividad. Pensemos en Jacinta, por ejemplo, Jacinta la casada estéril. Flor sin fruto, Jacinta es la malcasada, la malquerida. A pesar de todas las favorables predicciones, a pesar de sus prendas adecuadísimas, el matrimonio de Jacinta y Juanito es un fracaso. ¿Qué errores se han cometido? ¿Quién es el culpable? Aparentemente, no es el marido el que está en falta. Juanito es el puntal, el principio. El es el que necesita una mujer para procrear(se), no Jacinta. Juanito es el sujeto: está en el texto desde el primer momento. Recordemos que la novela, después del título y subtítulo, empieza con los enunciados "Parte primera," "Capítulo primero," "Juanito Santa Cruz" (aunque no olvidemos que, en realidad, el principio y origen de la novela se indica por el nombre de las dos mujeres del título). Jacinta es (o parece) el atributo, lo circunstancial. Solamente al final del tercer capítulo aparece Jacinta en escena, indirectamente, casi anónimamente, dentro del rebaño de las chicas Arnáiz: "La tercera de las chicas, llamada Jacinta, pescó marido al año siguiente. ¡Y qué marido!" (468).

Todo parece favorecer a Jacinta. "Pesca" un marido estupendo y va a tener hijos estupendos. El uso del verbo "pescar" refuerza la idea de la conveniencia de un marido como Juanito así como también insinúa que la mujer/esposa/madre de Juanito puede ser cualquiera, mientras que un "pez," una adquisición como él, un "delfín," es única. Muchos pescadores (muchas mujeres) para un solo varón. O muchas gallinas para un solo gallo. Pero Jacinta, ya lo sabemos, no pondrá los huevos. El pollo y el huevo (recordemos la escena del primer encuentro entre Juanito y Fortunata en la huevería)[3] son, serán, de Fortunata. Fortunata y no Jacinta es la calza para el pollo que pretende Barbarita:

> Barbarita iba muy contenta. . . y se decía por el camino: "Ahora le voy a poner a mi pollo una calza para que no se me escape más". . . Instaláronse en su residencia de verano, que era como un palacio, y no hay palabras con que ponderar lo contentos y saludables que todos estaban. El Delfín, que fue desmejoradillo, no tardó en reponerse, recobrando su buen color, su palabra jovial y la plenitud de sus carnes. La mamá se la tenía guardada. Esperaba ocasión propicia, y en cuanto ésta llegó supo acometer la empresa aquella de la calza, como persona lista y conocedora del ave que era preciso aprisionar. Dios la ayudaba, sin duda, porque el pollo no parecía muy dispuesto a la resistencia. (478).

La empresa que intenta Barbarita es la de casar al pollo y la esposa escogida, Jacinta. Futura esposa perfecta, "Jacinta era una chica de prendas excelentes, delicada, cariñosa y además muy bonita."(479) Escogida por Barbarita para nuera desde la infancia. Es decir, educada para sustituir a la suegra, o sustituir a la madre, Jacinta debe ser madre del hijo que ha de venir y madre de su esposo. Dice Bárbara a su hijo:

Es preciso que te cases. Ya te tengo la mujer buscada. Eres un chiquillo y a ti hay que dártelo todo hecho ¡Qué será de ti el día que yo te falte! Por eso quiero dejarte en buenas manos. . . No te rías, no; es la verdad, yo tengo que cuidar de todo, lo mismo de pegarte el botón que se te ha caído que de elegirte la que ha de ser compañera de tu vida, la que te ha de mimar cuando yo me muera ... Pon tu porvenir en mis manos. No sé qué instinto tenemos las madres, algunas quiero decir. En ciertos casos no nos equivocamos; somos infalibles, como el Papa. (478-479)

Pero sí se equivoca. Jacinta no poseerá valor de cambio en el negocio del matrimonio. Jacinta es una mercancía inútil que, aunque satisface a Juanito en cuanto objeto sexual materno en su relación peligrosamente incestuosa, no es capaz de cumplir con el contrato y dar a luz al hijo de la casa. La esterilidad de Jacinta la anula como mujer. Por eso Jacinta *tiene que* solucionar esa ausencia angustiosa, debe procurar un pequeño Santa Cruz a toda costa. Es por eso que se lanza a la calle para comprar un heredero. Los capítulos dedicados a la compra por Jacinta del primer Pituso, un niño que ella supone hijo de Fortunata y de Juanito, son los únicos que muestran a Jacinta en un papel activo. Y es precisamente la impropiedad de la asociación maternidad-actividad en la economía estructural de la familia burguesa decimonónica la que rechaza al niño comprado: El primer Pitusín suena a falso, es moneda falsa: "Habría dicho del Pituso lo que de las monedas que no sonaban bien: 'Es falso, o por lo menos, tiene hoja'." (569) El hijo que Jacinta busca y compra de manera desesperada, ilógica y casi histérica, de manera femenina, no se acepta en la estructura familiar patriarcal: El hijo materno no tiene valor económico.

No es pues casual, que el final del episodio de la compra del hijo de Jacinta cierre la primera parte de la novela, detenga la focalización en este personaje y nos haga entrar en el mundo de Fortunata. El pollo es para Fortunata, no para Jacinta. Fortunata es la otra mitad, el complemento de Jacinta, que tiene lo que a Jacinta le falta, el heredero de los Santa Cruz, pero a la que le falta lo que Jacinta tiene, la legalidad de esposa respecto a Juanito. A Fortunata, la madre, pero también la amante, la prostituta, le falta algo fundamental, su garantía de fidelidad. Y la fidelidad es esencial en este estado de cosas. A la mujer le está prohibido el adulterio porque la fidelidad de la mujer es el garante del hombre, la única certidumbre de que sus bienes, sus riquezas y su ser, van a pasar a sus hijos y a sus nietos. La fidelidad de la esposa es la garantía de la inmortalidad del marido.

A Fortunata le corresponde entonces el gallo del gallinero. El "pijo" Juanito Santa Cruz, retratado espléndidamente por Galdós, lejos de las gracias y virtudes que le encuentra su madre, más se acerca a la descripción que Jane Gallop, siguiendo a Lacan, hace de este tipo de hombre:

> El pijo es el que simultáneamente ofende y atrae a las mujeres. En uso vulgar y no filosófico, el "pijo" se refiere tanto al órgano sexual [masculino] como a una persona odiosa y desagradable, un hombre creído y autosuficiente que abusa claramente de los otros, y que caprichosamente exhibe poco o ningún respeto por la justicia. (36-37)

Fortunata, como Jacinta, cae seducida por Juanito. Pero Fortunata, a diferencia de Jacinta, va a recoger y transformar el derroche seminal gratuito del pijo Juanito. Fortunata va a ser madre, quedando establecida la impropiedad. Y una vez producido el descentramiento ninguna de las dos puede acceder a la "feminidad" según la sistematización de la fórmula freudiana (mujer=esposa=madre). Las dos pierden. En este excedente no puede haber ganadoras. Una y otra van a quedarse fuera. Jacinta, por su esterilidad inapropiada. Fortunata por su fertilidad inapropiada. Y aunque ninguna de las dos cumple completamente con los términos de mujer, esposa y madre, es a Jacinta, no a Fortunata, a quien se le exige responsabilidad por su condición de esposa legal.

Recordemos que Jacinta "pescó un marido estupendo." Es decir, a Jacinta se la rescata de la nada, de la masa femenina de su propia familia, y se le da un nombre y un estatus, un ser social. Jacinta, por su matrimonio, pasa a ser miembro de la casa Santa Cruz. Es su puesto como esposa y madre el que le va a conferir identidad, el que le da su razón de ser. Jacinta debe, a toda costa, mantenerse allí con un hijo, bajo riesgo de perder su identidad. Un hijo. Y de sexo, varón.

Porque hijas, aunque sean muchas, no redimen a la madre de la deuda. Eso lo sabe Jacinta por propia experiencia. Hija de Isabel Cordero y de Gumersindo Arnáiz, de sus progenitores se nos enfatiza la condición prolífica de la madre, y el atontamiento esencial del padre ("Isabel Cordero, esposa de Gumersindo ... tenía más pesquis que éste" [464]):

> Aquella gran mujer, Isabel Cordero de Arnáiz, dotada de todas las agudezas de traficante y de todas las triquiñuelas económicas del ama de gobierno, fue agraciada además por el Cielo con una fecundidad prodigiosa. En 1845, cuando nació Juanito, ya había tenido ella cinco, y siguió pariendo con la puntualidad de los vegetales que dan fruto cada año. Sobre aquellos cinco hay que apuntar más en la cuenta; total, diecisiete partos ... Si los chiquillos hubieran vivido, habría sido preciso ponerlos en los balcones como los tiestos, o colgados en jaulas de machos de perdiz ... En 1870 no quedaban más que nueve. (465)

Jacinta, la que no va a tener hijos, es hija de familia numerosa. Lo que a ella le falta le sobra a su madre. Este exceso productivo, sin embargo no hace a Isabel Cordero más valiosa en la economía de mercado patriarcal. El exceso, como la escasez, es un defecto en la cadena de productividad. Y más aún en el caso de Isabel, en que la "calidad" del producto destaca por su ausencia: de los nueve hijos vivos, siete son hijas. La barbaridad de tal fiasco se nos repite de forma insistente:

> De estas nueve cifras, siete correspondían al sexo femenino.¡Vaya una plaga que le había caído al bueno de Gumersindo! ¿Qué hacer con siete chiquillas? Para guardarlas cuando fueran mujeres se necesitaba un cuerpo de ejército. ¿Y cómo casarlas bien a todas? ¿De dónde iban a salir siete maridos buenos? ... La fecunda esposa ... siempre que pensaba en el porvenir de sus hijas se ponía triste, y sentía como remordimientos de haber dado a su marido una familia que era un problema económico. (466)

Isabel Cordero fracasa, como fracasará también su hija por defecto, en el cumplimiento de su deber. Deber que exige a la esposa/madre la sobrevivencia de un hijo, el varón que debe recoger la herencia de su padre, el encargado de la transmisión del discurso masculino. Más allá de este varón, todo es anecdótico. Y cuando, como en el caso de Isabel, ese más allá se define como un rebaño de féminas, lo anecdótico se convierte en penoso. Penoso para la madre y gravamen económico para el padre. Siete hijas son demasiadas hijas que guardar, que vigilar. Se necesita un ejército para ello. ¿Pero para qué? ¿Para qué tanto gasto, físico y moral? Para "guardarlas cuando fueran mujeres." Para guardarlas como esposas, porque inmediatamente después de su floración, hay que buscar siete maridos, siete maridos que van a ser su porvenir. Rebaño anónimo, las hijas de Isabel Cordero tejen su propio texto:

> [Isabel Cordero] cuidaba principalmente de que sus niñas no estuviesen ociosas. Las más pequeñas y los varoncitos iban a la escuela; las mayores trabajaban en el gabinete de la casa, ayudando a su madre en el repaso de la ropa ... En lo que mayormente sobresalían todas era en el arte de arreglar sus propios perendengues. (466)

Coser, tejer son primordialmente tareas femeninas. Y aunque como dijo Freud, las mujeres no hayan contribuido más que marginalmente a los descubrimientos e invenciones de la historia, sí tienen una técnica que les es propia: "[Las mujeres] han encontrado, sin embargo, una técnica, la del tejer y la del trenzar" (La feminidad" 132). Técnica que, de nuevo según Freud, ha tomado como modelo a la naturaleza que:

> habría dado el modelo para una copia semejante, haciendo crecer sobre los órganos genitales [femeninos] el vello que los enmascara. El paso que queda por dar es el de enlazar las fibras plantadas en la piel y que forman como una especie de fieltro ... Está uno tentado de adivinar el motivo inconsciente de esta invención. ("La feminidad", 132)

Es decir, que el tejido y el trenzado, únicas posibles aportaciones femeninas, no son sino técnicas ya en sí mismas defectuosas, incompletas, marcadas, como la mujer, por la castración original, por la falta fálica, intento inconsciente de cubrir la desnudez radical de la carencia. La mujer no puede salir de este círculo opresivo. Las hembras Arnáiz deben guardarse (guardarse ellas mismas y ser guardadas) por pudor, para esconder el sexo, para esconder el tejido primitivo, el texto que, como dice Sarah Kofman, "sea el que sea, es siempre un tejido que, por miedo a la castración, disimula una horrible y tentadora desnudez" (114). Las niñas Arnáiz, y Jacinta entre ellas, tejen y cosen para esconder su avergonzante feminidad, tapan el vacío, los agujeros, la brecha del canal vaginal, el abismo. Tejido (texto) femenino.

Curiosa esta asociación entre el tejido y la feminidad. Curiosa porque Jacinta, la que cose con Guillermina para cubrir, vestir su falta, nace de la renovada tienda de pañoletas y mantones de Manila que vio nacer a Barbarita, su suegra y tía paterna. Las telas chinas que tanto tienen que ver con Barbarita, se transforman en telas de ropa blanca. Flores, colores llamativos e intrincados dibujos para Bárbara, la mujer activa, el tipo freudiano de mujer fálica. "[B]atistas finísimas de Inglaterra, holandas y escocias, irlandas y madapolanes, mansouk y cretonas de Alsacia" (465) para la virginal Jacinta. Y es otra mujer, Isabel, la que es capaz de hacer el cambio de negocio, de los mantones de Senquán a las puntillas y las crinolinas. La que salva los tejidos (¿los textos?), la que sigue en el negocio de las telas. Gumersindo no sabe hacerlo. Gumersindo "no era hombre de gusto, y trajo unos adefesios que no tuvieron aceptación" (464). ¿Cómo hubiera sido posible? Telas, tejidos, costura son tareas femeninas. Gumersindo debe limitarse a su papel de guardián, a guardar las hijas como guarda los chales:

> Era quizás Gumersindo la persona que en Madrid tenía más arte para guardar [los mantones de Manila] ... Muchas damas, que en algún baile de máscaras se ponían el chal, lo mandaban al día siguiente, con la caja, a la tienda de Gumersindo Arnáiz, para que éste lo doblase según arte tradicional, es decir, dejando oculta la rejilla de a tercia y el fleco de a cuarta, y visible en el cuartel superior el dibujo central. (465)

Guardar las hijas ocultando cualquier orificio, dejar oculta "la rejilla" y "el fleco," esconder el sexo, y dejar en cambio visible lo lleno, el dibujo, la marca. Gumersindo, hombre casi sin presencia en la novela de Galdós, incapaz de manejarse en un negocio de telas y mantones. Apocado y medio tonto, y sin embargo, el amo de la tienda. Las mujeres van a doblar su chal a la tienda *de* Gumersindo Arnáiz (no de Isabel Cordero) y él es el guardador, el usufructuario en cierto modo, de hijas y mantones, por mucho que Isabel maneje el negocio y vista y muestre a las niñas.

Coser, tejer, trenzar. Las mujeres de *Fortunata y Jacinta* se dedican a las labores de aguja. Cose Jacinta con Guillermina:

> Concluida la comida, se diseminaban los comensales, unos a tomar café al despacho y a jugar al tresillo, otros a formar grupos más o menos animados y chismosos, y Guillermina a su sillita baja y al tejemaneje de las agujas. Jacinta se le ponía al lado y tomaba muy a menudo parte en aquellas tareas tan simpáticas a su corazón. Guillermina hacía camisolas, calzones y chambritas para sus ciento y pico de hijos de uno y otro sexo. (510)

Cose doña Lupe la de los pavos:

> Tomando la sillita baja que usaba cuando cosía, [doña Lupe] la colocó junto al balcón ... Lugar y ocasión admirables eran aquellos para reflexionar, con los trapos sobre la falda, la aguja en la mano, los espejuelos calados, la cesta de la ropa al lado. (632-633)

Cose Aurora, la segunda amante de Juanito, la que traicionará a Fortunata, cose la mayor parte del tiempo, fuera de su taller incluso, que "por cumplir y hacer las entregas a tiempo se [traía] alguna labor para trabajar en casa" (898). Y también Fortunata cose, aunque no sea de su agrado, cose con Aurora para poder "hablar largo y tendido sobre diferentes cosas" (898).

Labor de aguja constante la de estas mujeres. Labor femenina. Labor maternal, por tanto, si seguimos igualando los términos en el sentido freudiano. No es casualidad pues, que las prendas en las que trabajan Guillermina y Jacinta sean para los "ciento y pico de hijos" de la primera. Que las de Aurora sean ropa blanca, ropa para bautizos, para recién nacidos. Que la ropa que cose doña Lupe sea la de su hijo adoptivo, su sobrino Maxi. Y que Fortunata, la única madre real, la que no necesita coser, no cosa más que para ayudar a otras mujeres.

Guillermina, Jacinta, doña Lupe, Aurora. Cosen y tejen para los niños que no tienen, para unos hijos ausentes. Fortunata no cose por su cuenta. Ayuda a coser. Las demás, madres sin serlo, enhebran la aguja, tapan remiendos, zurcen y cosen ávidamente. Tapan los agujeros del tejido (texto) femenino, para tapar con hilo la brecha vergonzante de su sexo, para hacer *como si* el canal vaginal estuviera taponado por ese hijo imposible que va a nacer. Todas, en imitación inconsciente, en asociación, se clavan y desclavan agujas en y del pecho, pecho seco de Aurora, o cortado de doña Lupe ("a doña Lupe le faltaba un pecho, por amputación a consecuencia del tumor escirroso de que padeció en vida de su marido," (637) el posible pecho autoflagelado de Guillermina, porque a Guillermina "no se le hacía cuesta arriba la disciplina espiritual" (510). La falta de leche real para el hijo real se sustituye, a la vez que se castiga, con las agujas: "A cada momento se arrancaba Aurora del pecho una aguja enhebrada o se la clavaba en él, pues el pecho era su acerico, y allí tenía también una batería de alfileres" (898).

Cosen mientras charlan, reflexionan y piensan. ¿Sobre qué? ¿Qué les interesa a estas mujeres que, en realidad, como dice Freud, tienen "menos intereses sociales que los hombres?" Los hijos, naturalmente. La maternidad. A Jacinta

> se le había despertado vivo entusiasmo por las empresas de la Pacheco, y a más de reservarle todo el dinero que podía, se picaba los dedos cosiendo para ella durante largas horas. Es que sentía un cierto consuelo en confeccionar ropas de niño y en suponer que aquellas mangas iban a abrigar bracitos desnudos. (513)

Jacinta cose para consolarse de sus penas: "No hay existencia sin gusanillo . . . y ella [Jacinta] tenía dos: los apartamientos de su marido y el desconsuelo de no ser madre" (518). Dos penas que en realidad son una. Porque por no cumplir el contrato, por no tener ese hijo tan ansiado, Jacinta "solía decir en tono quejumbroso que 'no tenía gusto para nada'" (504). Jacinta no tiene hijos y el marido le es infiel. ¿Cómo va a "tener gusto" para algo? Jacinta se sabe culpable mientras cose, mientras tapa su falta. Y es realmente culpable por mostrar esa ausencia, ese agujero, esa falta. Doble ausencia, como mujer (falta de pene) y como madre (falta de hijos). El destino de la estéril Jacinta debe ser el mismo de su madre, pagar con su ser la deuda contraída, de la misma manera que Isabel dedica su vida y sus esfuerzos a pagar por el exceso y el sexo de su producción. Ella, y no su marido, será la encargada de sacar el dinero de debajo de las piedras, de arreglar los asuntos comerciales de su marido, de encargarse de la economía familiar para "colocar bien las siete chicas" (466). Sus esfuerzos la convierten en "una mujer desmejorada, pálida, deforme de talle, como esas personas que parece que se están desbaratando y que no tienen las partes del cuerpo en su verdadero sitio" (466). Retrato terrible, se castiga su falta con la descuartización corporal. Mujer-vegetal, mujer-ganado, mujer-gallina. Sin cuerpo. Sin imagen, porque, paradójicamente, sus descendientes hembras lo son a su imagen y semejanza, no a la del padre. El exceso o el defecto, la impropiedad, lleva a la muerte, como ocurre necesariamente en el caso de Isabel Cordero. Como debe ocurrir en el caso de Jacinta.

Pero Jacinta no muere. Jacinta se salva en un último desplazamiento, en una última impropiedad que, aunque deja las cosas finalmente en su sitio (una mujer, Jacinta, esposa y madre) las destruye también definitivamente. Jacinta se salva por el regalo de Fortunata. Con la posesión del Pítusín verdadero, ocupa por fin el lugar que le corresponde en la casa Santa Cruz. Pero también, gracias a este regalo, Jacinta se libera del yugo de su esposo: "—Haz lo que quieras," le dice Jacinta a Juanito al final de la novela, "—eres libre como el aire. Tus trapisondas no me afectan

nada./ Esto no era palabrería, y en las pruebas de la vida
real vio el Delfín que aquella vez iba de veras" (977).

Fortunata y Jacinta son pues inseparables la una de la
otra, hermanas que se buscaron a través del texto para en-
contrarse en el centro, espejo una de la otra, envés y re-
verso de una idea de mujer, de una idea de madre:

> [Jacinta] recordaba, sí, que la muerta [Fortunata] había sido su
> mayor enemigo; pero las últimas etapas de la enemistad y el
> caso increíble de la herencia del Pituso envolvían, sin que la
> inteligencia pudiera desentrañar este enigma, una reconcilia-
> ción. Con la muerte de por medio, la una [Jacinta] en la vida vi-
> sible y la otra [Fortunata] en la invisible, bien podría ser que
> las dos mujeres se miraran de orilla a orilla, con intención y de-
> seos de darse un abrazo. (976)

Hermanas que comparten un mismo corazón: la necesidad del hijo. Hermanas siamesas, entonces, que no pueden vivir separadas pero tampoco juntas. Fortunata lo
sabe. Y también sabe de legalidad. Sabe que la Ley que
marca a su hijo como el Pituso Verdadero, la ley que le da
el nombre del padre, es la misma que la anula como esposa. Los espacios, los agujeros están ya llenos: Hay una
esposa, hay una madre, hay un hijo. Lo único que queda
por hacer es igualar los términos y eso es precisamente lo
que hace Fortunata con su muerte. Fortunata y Jacinta,
pero también Fortunata o Jacinta. Las últimas palabras de
Fortunata son "Soy ángel ... yo también ... mona del cielo"
(974). Y a Jacinta, a su vez, ya con el niño en su poder,
"tanto le podía la imaginación, que la madre putativa lle-
gaba a embelesarse con el artificioso recuerdo de haber lle-
vado en sus entrañas aquel precioso hijo y a estremecerse
con la suposición de los dolores sufridos al echarle al
mundo" (977).

Fortunata o Jacinta, lo importante era la maternidad
dentro de la Ley, la maternidad dentro de una economía
seminal. Maternidad para tapar, esconder, la carencia femenina. Con el regalo de su hijo a Jacinta el poder masculino queda re-establecido. Fortunata muere y desaparece en
un charco de sangre. Edipo, de nuevo, asesina a su madre.

¿O no? Porque Fortunata renace de nuevo en cada lectura.

NOTAS

[1] Este trabajo pretende la lectura de algunos aspectos de *Fortunata y Jacinta* de la mano de Luce Irigaray. El diálogo con los textos de Sigmund Freud relacionados con la sexualidad femenina que la pensadora francesa propone en "La tache aveugle d'un vieux rêve de symétrie," (Speculum 9-162) es la base para este análisis de la novela de Galdós.

[2] La situación de Jacinta, desde otra perspectiva, ha sido estudiada por Harriet Turner. Remito a su trabajo "Lazos y tiranías familiares" a las personas interesadas en este personaje galdosiano.

[3] El primer encuentro entre Fortunata y Jacinto ha sido analizado ampliamente por Stephen Gilman en su libro *Galdós and the Art of the European Novel*. Gilman, con estupenda intuición, ha calificado a este episodio como "emblemático" (308). Este episodio anticipa y define las relaciones sexuales y de poder que van a existir entre los dos jóvenes.

OBRAS CITADAS

Blanco Aguinaga, Carlos. "Having No Option: The Restoration of Order and the Education of Fortunata." *Conflicting Realities: Four Readings of a Chapter by Pérez Galdós (Fortunata y Jacinta, Part III, Chapter IV)*. Peter B.Goldman, ed. London: Tamesis, 1985.

Engels, Friederich. *Der Ursprung der Familie, des Privateigentums und des Staats*. Frankfurt: Verlag Marxistische Blätter, 1971.

Freud, Sigmund. "The Infantile Genital Organization (An Interpolation into the Theory of Sexuality)." *The Standard Edition of the Complete Psychological Works of Sigmund Freud*. Translated and Edited by James Strachey in collaboration with Anna Freud, assisted by Alix Strachey and Alan Tyson. 24 vols. London: The Hogarth Press and the Institute of Psycho-Analysis, 1953-1974. 19: 141-145.

—. "Female Sexuality." *SE* 21: 225-243.

—. "Feminity." *New Introductory Lectures on Psychoanalysis*. Newly translated and edited by James Strachey. New York: W. W. Norton, 1965. 112-135.

—. "Some Psychical Consequences of the Anatomical Distinction Between the Sexes." *SE* 19: 248-258.

Gallop, Jane. *The Daughter's Seduction. Feminism and Psychoanalysis*. Ithaca, NY: Cornell, 1982.

Gilman, Stephen. *Galdós and the Art of the European Novel: 1867-1887*. Princeton: University Press, 1981.

Irigaray, Luce. *Ce sexe qui n'en est pas un*. Paris: Editions de Minuit, 1977.

—. *Speculum de l'autre femme*. Paris: Editions de Minuit, 1974.

Kofman, Sarah. *L'enigme de la femme. La femme dans les textes de Freud*. Paris: Galilée, 1980.

Marx, Karl, and Friederick Engels. *The German Ideology*. Part One. C.J. Arthur, ed. New York: International Publishers, 1970.

Pérez Galdós, Benito. *Fortunata y Jacinta. Dos historias de casadas*. En *Obras completas*. Vol. 2. Federico Sainz de Robles, ed. Madrid: Aguilar, 1970.

Turner, Harriet. "Lazos y tiranías familiares: una reevaluación de Jacinta." En *Fortunata y Jacinta. El escritor y la crítica*. Germán Gullón, ed. Madrid: Taurus, 1986. 277-298. Traducción de "Family Ties and Tyrannies: A Reassessment of Jacinta." *Hispanic Review* 51 (1983): 1-22.

Mentalidad, vida cotidiana y literatura. Las actitudes femeninas socializadas en la novela española de la Restauracion

Guadalupe Gómez-Ferrer
Universidad Complutense de Madrid

I. Introduccion

La historia de las mentalidades ha tenido una trayectoria bastante agitada; sus pioneros actuaron al margen de la historia oficial.[1] En los años treinta, los fundadores de la escuela de *Annales* atraídos por este sector de lo histórico le dedican algunos estudios; pero ni éstos ni otros publicados por aquellos años[2] tienen apenas resonancia, ensombrecidos, tal vez por el auge que adquiere en esos momentos la historia económica. Será en la década de los sesenta cuando se despierte de nuevo el interés por la historia de las mentalidades, si bien todavía veinte años después continúa ofreciendo este campo cierta novedad, constituyendo actualmente uno de los sectores punta de la investigación histórica. En nuestras aulas se habla mucho de historia de las mentalidades, aunque, de hecho, se ofrezcan escasos estudios convincentes.

En realidad no hay una definición clara de lo que son las mentalidades. Vovelle ha señalado que la más ajustada tal vez sea la dada por Mandrou: "una historia de las 'visiones del mundo'"[3], aunque no deja de reconocer su imprecisión. Maravall afina un poco más al precisar que la mentalidad hace referencia a una actitud espontánea pero no inconsciente "solo que, —escribe—, 'conscientes' no puede hacerse aquí equivalentes a fenómenos que se tomen como contenidos críticamente o reflexivamente elaborados, de la conciencia, sino que caben también contenidos recibidos, asimilados y que llegan a ser el fondo sobre el que emergen las opciones, las voliciones, las ideas, los modos de comportamiento que los individuos asumen no ya conscientemente, sino con plena responsabilidad del sentido que les dan. A esta última sedimentación consciente que queda por detrás de la reflexión crítica y personalmente asumida, en la que ésta se apoya, es a lo que llamo mentalidad"[4].

Por lo demás es evidente que el objeto de las mentalidades es lo colectivo. Su campo de análisis es el mundo de lo cotidiano, de lo espontáneo; sus resultados no son referibles a determinados sujetos individuales de la historia sino que por el contrario son reveladores del contenido impersonal de su pensamiento[5]. Obviamente, para un adecuado conocimiento de la historia de las mentalidades será necesario contar con una historia de la cosmovisión, ideal de vida, actitudes, comportamientos, papeles, etc., asumidos y desempeñados por las mujeres; porque ellas constituyen aproximadamente una mitad de ese conjunto humano cuyas reacciones espontáneas se trata de determinar.

Por otra parte, hasta fechas muy recientes la historia se ha centrado fundamentalmente en el análisis y en la descripción de los procesos en que se insertan los individuos —preferentemente hombres— en la esfera de lo público y lo institucional, excluyendo de su discurso la faceta privada y cotidiana de la sociedad. Actualmente el historiador ha tomado conciencia de la parcialidad de este enfoque —muy lejano en su esencia de la historia integral propugnada hace ya muchos años por Lucien Febvre[6]—, que deja fuera del objeto de investigación histórica ese tercio de la vida humana que el individuo dedica a rezar, a comer, a beber, a divertirse, a viajar o a establecer relaciones amistosas o amorosas[7]. Dentro de los escasos aunque valiosos estudios existentes sobre la vida cotidiana[8], se advierte el protagonismo de la mujer: sobre ella gravita en buena medida la cotidianeidad. Este nuevo enfoque de la historia social ha creado la urgencia de establecer un línea de investigación que permita tanto el conocimiento de la historia centrada en la vida pública o privada, como la determinación de las múltiples relaciones entre ambas. Dentro de esta perspectiva se va evidenciando la necesidad de contar con una historia de las relaciones humanas centradas no ya en las relaciones de poder o de clase sino en las relaciones de género[9].

En suma: por una parte el ensanchamiento de lo histórico demanda un conocimiento de la historia de las mujeres, sin el cual no se puede llegar a resultados válidos y científicos; y por otra, el trabajo de las mujeres profesionales en el campo de las ciencias sociales ha venido a constatar la parcialidad de conceptos, fuentes y métodos empleados en la construcción de aquéllas. El tema no es baladí, y constituye un reto intelectual, ya que obliga a una relectura de las llamadas ciencias sociales y humanidades. En el campo de la historia, que es el mío, el desafío es evidente. Ello exige la introducción de nuevos conceptos, el empleo de nuevas metodologías y un distinto enfrentamiento con las fuentes: nuevas preguntas a las fuentes clásicas e incorporación de otras no consideradas hasta fechas muy recientes.

En este contexto se inserta mi comunicación. Creo que la literatura constituye una fuente imprescindible para el análisis de las mentalidades y de la vida cotidiana, y me parece de capital importancia la lectura histórica del texto literario desde una perspectiva que tenga en cuenta, en sus dimensiones reales, el papel que ha correspondido y corresponde a la mujer en el proceso histórico. Es obvio que mis observaciones no estan hechas desde el campo del filólogo o del crítico literario, que me son ajenos, sino desde el mío propio, desde el de una historiadora de oficio.

II. LAS FUENTES

Mi interés se centra pues en el análisis del texto literario en cuanto fuente histórica. Ha señalado Hernán Vidal que la crítica socio-histórica del texto literario ofrece múltiples áreas de observación, y que es necesario al investigador "perfilar con cuidado el foco de estudio" y "establecer prioridades sobre los problemas que *se pone ante* sí"[10]. Mi objetivo en esta ocasión es el de señalar los papeles a través de los cuales ha sido socializado un modelo de mujer, partiendo del análisis de unas obras literarias surgidas en el último cuarto del siglo XIX, dentro de un horizonte cultural concreto y en el seno de una sociedad en proceso de modernización[11].

Las coordenadas temporales elegidas obedecen a mi interés por un periodo de la historia española sobre el que vengo trabajando desde hace muchos años con miras a un estudio de las estructuras sociales, de las mentalidades y con vistas también a un conocimiento de su vida cotidiana. Desde este punto de vista, la literatura de estos años ofrece un interés excepcional[12]. Por otra parte, al analizar el texto literario conviene partir de una afirmación de principio: ninguna creación cultural puede ser entendida fuera de su contexto social[13], y ello se acentúa mucho más en el caso de la novela[14]. Es justamente a partir del testimonio histórico, exterior a las obras, como el crítico social está en condiciones de advertir lo que hay en ella de coincidencias y de divergencias respecto a la realidad; de advertir los distintos "discursos" insertos en ella[15]. Ahora bien, el crítico social puede percibir o no el conjunto de discursos que se le ofrecen, en función, no sólo del sistema de prioridades que establezca en su análisis, sino del sistema de preguntas que le haga al texto.

Actualmente la crítica ha subrayado la viva conexión literatura-sociedad que manifiesta la novela española de la época de la Restauración, y, me refiero a la Restauración por ser ésta la época preferentemente estudiada por mí. Ahora bien, a pesar de la larga enumeración de problemas sociales que hacen los distintos críticos literarios que se ocupan de este periodo, en casi todos se advierte una laguna: la ausencia de referencias feministas[16], es decir, el desconocimiento de las relaciones entre los sexos, y la conexión que puede haber entre el proceso de modernización de la sociedad española y la posición de la mujer dentro de la misma. ¿Se beneficia aquélla de las transformaciones socioeconómicas que se producen en la realidad del país? ¿Aprovecha las ventajas que le ofrece el nuevo marco legal? ¿Se incorpora a las nuevas posibilidades que le brinda una educación cada vez más accesible y socialmente mejor vista? ¿Se capacita para realizar un trabajo que legalmente puede desempeñar? ¿Tiene conciencia de la discriminación existente entre los sexos en lo que se refiere a los derechos civiles consagrados por el reciente Código Civil? La ausencia de estas perspectivas feministas en la actual crítica social de la literatura de la Restauración, urge una relectura de la misma, con el fin de lograr una mejor aproximación al conocimiento de las relaciones humanas de la época. Dos aspectos de la misma han atraído mi atención: los manuales escolares y la novela de este periodo. Por ello, el proyecto de trabajo a que van dedicadas estas páginas consiste esencialmente en un análisis de los manuales escolares y de determinadas novelas, en las cuales he intentado rastrear el papel adjudicado a la mujer en el marco de la sociedad de la época. Debo advertir que, por distintos motivos, mi indagación se ha proyectado sobre la mujer perteneciente a las clases medias.

III. LA SOCIALIZACION DE LOS PAPELES FEMENINOS

Desde mi perspectiva de historiadora, la simple enumeración de papeles, funciones o actitudes con que la mujer aparece en los manuales escolares o en las novelas del periodo que me propongo analizar, quedaría reducida a una labor descriptiva, positivista y un tanto ahistórica. Para evitar estos peligros creo necesario partir, 1) de una breve referencia a la realidad española del último cuarto del siglo XIX, es decir, a las coordenadas históricas a que corresponden los textos; 2) de un conocimiento del ideal femenino socializado por los libros escolares dedicados a las niñas, y 3) del análisis de las actitudes y papeles femeninos que aparecen en las novelas de la época de la Restauración.

1. EL CONTEXTO HISTORICO.

En el último cuarto del siglo XIX se produce en España una serie de transformaciones que cambia la fisonomía del país[17]. En el proceso de modernización puesto en marcha durante esos años, hay un tema que me interesa destacar:

la medida en que aquél afecta a la vida de la mujer. No es momento de entrar en ello, pero sí de recordar el debate que se inicia en la década de los años ochenta acerca del papel y la posición que ocupa aquélla en la sociedad, acerca de su misma relación con los hombres[18].

Para valorar adecuadamente la situación de las mujeres en la época finisecular, es necesario partir del contexto real de una sociedad condicionada por una serie de factores que ha contribuído decisivamente a configurar su concreta vida material y su determinado horizonte mental. Recordemos los límites en que se mueve el sector terciario y el escaso índice de alfabetización existente; recordemos las altas tasas de natalidad y la práctica de la lactancia continuada; recordemos también la fuerte mortalidad infantil; pensemos, en fin, lo que era la vida del hogar en el marco de una economía ajustada, con un sistema que tenía mucho de autárquico tanto en el ramo de la alimentación como en el del vestido, y en un espacio domésticocon deficientes sistemas de aprovisionamiento y de evacuación de aguas, con calles polvorientas, con unas cocinas que requerían continuamente la vigilancia del fogón...; recordemos en fin, la presencia cotidiana de la enfermedad y de la muerte, y el complicado sistema de higiene, alimentación y relaciones sociales que esto llevaba consigo. Todo ello ocupaba gran parte de la vida de la mujer.

Junto a estas realidades hay que constatar la aparición de un conjunto da cambios técnicos, científicos y culturales, y en menor medida mentales, que, por una parte posibilitan cierta liberación del quehacer femenino en el espacio doméstico, y por otra permiten tomar conciencia — aunque de forma lenta y precaria—, de que la mujer apenas se ha beneficiado de la modernización que se ha puesto en marcha a partir de la doble revolución. En suma, en un contexto social claramente androcéntrico, se observa un desajuste entre las posiblidades que ofrece el nuevo horizonte histórico y la actitud inmovilista existente en lo que se refiere al quehacer femenino. Todo un conjunto de tradiciones invita más a la persistencia que al cambio, y hace difícil el ajuste de la posición de la mujer a la nueva realidad del país[19]. Desde este punto de vista el ideal de mujer propuesto por los manuales escolares y los arquetipos femeninos puestos en pie por la novela de la Restauració, suponen unos documentos muy reveladores del "tejido creencial" de la época; y unos datos muy útiles para entender el conjunto de vigencias sociales que preside la vida cotidiana y que determina los principios que informan la educación femenina, en función de unos patrones de conducta y de una formas de convivencia, que toda una serie de prejuicios y temores hará difícil remover.

2. EL MODELO DE MUJER SOCIALIZADO POR LOS MANUALES ESCOLARES

En la segunda mitad del siglo XIX, ante los avances del pensamiento liberal y de las ciencias naturales, se desecha la vieja idea de inferioridad fisiológica de la mujer y se difunde el principio de la igualdad moral e intelectual entre los sexos. En la práctica, estos principios de igualdad tendrán muy diversas oportunidades de aplicación. De hecho, se consagra una clara división de esferas de influencia que da por obvio la subordinación de la mujer al varón, tanto en el terreno jurídico como en el plano psicológico.

El ámbito de influencia de la mujer es el mundo doméstico. Su creciente responsabilidad y protagonismo en él, son recordadas repetidamente con objeto de justificar y ensalzar unas tareas que empiezan a llamarse "misión de la mujer" o "carrera maternal". Obviamente, en el seno de una sociedad burguesa, ávida de títulos que la legitimen, estas denominaciones o etiquetas que establecen cierto paralelismo con la vida profesional del hombre satisfacen las aspiraciones de la mujer. De una mujer que, satisfecha por el reconocimiento social de su función, trata de cumplirla con puntualidad y se esfuerza por salvaguardarla. Ella, ávida de respetabilidad, es la primera interesada en cumplir las pautas socialmente difundidas, volviendo la espalda a posturas innovadoras que pueden poner en entredicho aquélla. Los manuales escolares, las revistas, la propia literatura ponen de relieve la importancia de las obligaciones o deberes femeninos, y subrayan su alcance y trascendencia, superior, señalan algunos, a los que desempeña el varón, ya que afecta a los mismos fundamentos de la sociedad.

Dentro de este contexto, quisiera hacer algunas reflexiones acerca del modelo femenino socializado por unos textos escolares, orientados a la educación de las niñas. He trabajado con esta finalidad sobre algunos manuales aparecidos en el último cuarto del siglo XIX, y he podido advertir que los modelos propuestos guardan una gran semejanza. Por razones de claridad centro mis observaciones en dos obras de Pilar Pascual de Sanjuán: *Flora* (1881) y *Escenas de familia* (1891), y en otra de Mariano Carderera, *La ciencia de la mujer al alcance de las niñas* (1875). Las tres fueron objeto de numerosas reediciones en los años finales del siglo y primeras décadas del siglo XX. No he podido averiguar la amplitud de las tiradas, ni siquiera me es posible afirmar que conozco todas las ediciones, pero sí estoy en condiciones de señalar que fueron obras muy difundidas, utilizadas en la escuela laica y en la religiosa[20].

El objetivo de estos manuales es claramente didáctico. Tratan de establecer las normas que deben guiar el comportamiento femenino para ajustarse a un modelo ideal de mujer. Carderera, partiendo del principio de que "la obligación de la mujer consiste en gobernar la casa y su gloria en mandar en ella"[21], intenta mentalizar a las niñas acerca de la importancia de su misión en la sociedad, —ya que "del buen gobierno de la casa no sólo depende el bienestar interior, sino también la tranquilidad y la satisfacción en las relaciones exteriores y la dicha entre los pueblos"[22]—, y trata de proporcionarles una serie de conocimientos específicos que las capaciten para realizar sus funciones que les corresponde.

Pilar Pascual expresa claramente su objetivo en el prólogo y en el epílogo de su primer libro:

> Flora es ya una señora casada y copia exactamente las virtudes domésticas de su buena madre (...) os he ofrecido un modelo; el imitarle no es difícil. Dichosas vosotras si podeis superarle [23].

¿En qué consiste el ideal femenino promovido desde la escuela? Llama poderosamente la atención en estos tres libros el interés de sus autores por orientar a la mujer a los quehaceres domésticos. Leemos en Flora y en la obra de Carderera respectivamente:

> La mujer, sobre todo, parece destinada por la Providencia para vivir retirada en el modesto hogar, perfumándole con la escencia de su ignorada virtud, embelleciéndolo con su gracia sencilla; de modo que las mismas que han recibido del Cielo un valor varonil, un talento privilegiado y otros
> dones, han sido más desgraciadas que la generalidad de su sexo.
> No desdeñéis la instrucción y las dotes que distinguen en la sociedad a la joven y a la mujer bien educadas, pero no olvidéis tampoco que vuestros dominios están circunscritos principalmente por el estrecho círculo del hogar doméstico. Aspirad a la vida tranquila, modesta y retirada, a ser mujeres caseras y hacendosas [24].

El tema de la educación intelectual aparece como algo secundario. Carderera apenas le presta atención; sus consejos van dirigidos al comportamiento en el hogar. Pilar Pascual se refiere al riesgo que puede traer consigo el talento en una mujer. Apego a la tradición establecida, constante referencia al mundo del hogar y prevención ante el cultivo de las capacidades intelectuales es la escencia del mensaje de esta obra[25].

Escenas de familia, aparecida diez años después que *Flora*, se hace eco del cambio de horizonte histórico que ha tenido lugar. En esta obra se aborda directamente el problema de la enseñanza media y superior de la mujer, discutiendo sus ventajas y desventajas. El resultado es alicorto, estrecho y desalentador visto con perspectiva histórica; ya que, en un momento en que legalmente la muchacha tiene acceso a la universidad y a determinados empleos públicos, los esquemas mentales que se socializan desde la escuela permanecen anclados en los viejos modelos. De todas maneras, la autora, en los capítulos XVII y XVIII, deja clara la posibilidad de que la mujer acceda a la carrera universitaria, si bien se apresura a indicar que no debe ser esta su aspiración, ya que no es en el mundo abierto a la competencia con el hombre, sino en otro, es decir, en el hogar, que le es específico y propio, y en el que resulta insustituíble, donde se realizará plenamente. A precisar cuál debe ser este papel femenino está dedicado el capítulo XVIII, titulado significativamente "La misión de la mujer".

Ahora bien, el hecho de que la mujer deba permanecer al margen de la vida profesional y aun de la vida universitaria no significa que aquélla no tenga obligación de instruirse y cultivarse. Es conveniente que vaya a la escuela porque allí aprenderá "lo que necesita una mujer para ser buena *esposa* y buena *madre* y excelente *ama de casa*". Se indica que en ese momento, no basta para "ser mujer de su casa", con saber "guisar, barrer, coser y remendar la ropa, y a lo sumo leer y mal escribir"[26]. Pilar Pascual aborda también un tema muy difundido en la sociedad española de aquellos años: el peligro que entraña la instrucción femenina en orden al cumplimiento de los deberes domésticos. La autora examina la cuestión y se pronuncia por la conveniencia de la instrucción, si bien señala que ésta no debe servir de obstáculo para que se mantenga un orden de prioridades y, éste, para la mujer, siempre pasará por anteponer las tareas de orden doméstico a las de carácter intelectual,

> pero bien entendido, que los estudios a que se dedique nunca deben impedirle el que se dedique se ejercite en *trabajos de aguja*, es decir, en las *labores* propias de nuestro sexo, y sobre todo que adquiera práctica en el *arte culinario*, que sepa limpiar una habitación, hacer una cama y llevar el gobierno de la casa (...).
>
> La misión de la mujer es ser respetuosa hija, amable esposa, madre previsora y prudente ama de casa, y tanto mejor cumplirá estos deberes cuanto mejor se haya educado su inteligencia y su corazón. Por lo demás, por instruida que sea una señora, como quiera que sus deberes la retienen en el hogar, y los libros no la privaran de atender a cosas tan gratas como necesarias, experimentará un placer al coser la ropa blanca de su marido, al bordar y guarnecer con encajes las camisas del niño de pecho, al coser el traje de la niña ...[27]

El trabajo doméstico de la mujer de la clase media, que es a la que me estoy refiriendo, es objeto de la atención de los pedagogos que difunden a través de unos manuales no sólo los principios que deben guiarlo, sino hasta la forma misma de realizarlo. La obra de Carderera resulta paradigmática a este respecto. Parte el autor de la división de esferas de actividad en función del propio sexo: al varón le corresponde el ámbito de la vida pública, y a la mujer, en cambio, le cabe el ámbito de lo privado; es decir, los negocios que se "ventilan en el hogar", cuya fiel realización por otra parte, la hará merecedora del título de "buena ama de casa". Subraya Carderera que el cumplimiento de las tareas domésticas transciende su propio marco y tiene un carácter social: "la mujer como encargada del gobierno y la administración interior de la casa, es el eje de la familia" y "cuando el eje se enmohece o se sale de quicio, la familia peligra y por fin se arruina".[28] Señala también la estrecha relación existente entre el comportamiento doméstico de la mujer y la valoración social y moral de la familia, indicando que la tarea del ama de casa ha de ser vivida como "un trabajo amoroso realizado por devoción a la familia";

> la vida de la mujer será una cadena no interrumpida de tareas y ocupaciones incesantes. No tendrá una mirada para sí misma, ni podrá consagrar una sola hora al reposo y a su vida particular.[29]

Y lo subraya desde una determinada óptica, desde la idea de que "la resignación para trabajar y sufrir" es inherente a la condición de la mujer. Por ello, sacrificio y abnegación deben ser tomados como componentes de la vida diaria, no en virtud de la condición humana, sino en virtud de la específica condición femenina. Por lo demás, el libro de Carderera señala con minuciosidad los quehaceres y deberes de la mujer en el marco del hogar, y hasta reglamenta prolijamente la distribución de su jornada a lo largo del día y a lo largo de la semana.

En suma, la finalidad de estos textos escolares es evidente: intentan socializar desde la propia escuela, de manera sistemática y clara, un ideal femenino cuyo nivel educativo y laboral tratan de delimitar y reglamentar. El trabajo se centra única y exclusivamente —salvo en el caso de urgencias económicas— en el espacio del mundo doméstico: consiste en el cuidado material y moral del marido, aludido repetidamente como suprema autoridad de la casa; de la familia, que aparece escasamente subrayada; y de la casa, objeto de gran atención. La educación intelectual aparece claramente limitada tanto en su grado como en su proyección social; tan sólo es valorada en cuanto ayuda a la mujer a cumplir mejor su misión de ama de casa.

Esta "misión" o papel femenino puede parecer limitado o reduccionista desde nuestra perspectiva actual; conviene sin embargo situarlo en su propio contexto y considerar la escasa conciencia que existía en aquel momento de las desigualdades que podía comportar. En general, la mujer se sentía satisfecha de su protagonismo en el hogar, un protagonismo que se veía motivado y alentado por unos medios de comunicación: manuales, textos, revistas femeninas, novelas... que son los encargados, por otra parte, de neutralizar los atisbos emancipadores de la mujer, al subrayar que, es precisamente por la vía del trabajo en el hogar, por la que ésta logrará su igualdad con el varón. El autor es contundente al respecto:

> Nuestra igualdad con los hombres consiste en cumplir las obligaciones que nos son propias tan bien como ellos cumplen las suyas, pues para eso nos ha dotado Dios de cualidades especiales.[30]

Esta sublimación que se hace de la misión doméstica — que enmascara o esconde las limitaciones impuestas al libre desarrollo de la personalidad de la mujer—, potencian a mi entender, la resistencia espontánea a las tímidas iniciativas de emancipación que hubieron de surgir en aquel momento en el seno de la misma clase media.

3. LA NOVELA NATURALISTA ESPAÑOLA: ACTITUDES Y PAPELES FEMENINOS

Parece evidente que un estudio de los tipos femeninos presentados por la novela, exigiría al menos la atención a tres modelos: la mujer de la alta clase, la de las clases medias y la de las clases populares; y aún dentro de estos grupos, a las diversas categorías que en cada uno de ellos aparecen. Por razones de tiempo y espacio no es éste mi propósito. Motivos de claridad me aconsejan referirme a un solo grupo social. He elegido el mundo de las clases medias por tres razones fundamentalmente: 1) porque las clases medias constituyen en amplia medida, el sujeto y el objeto de la literatura; 2) porque, también en un buena parte, son las clases medias las que establecen los juicios morales de la sociedad española[31] y 3) porque los modelos socializados en los manuales, van dirigidos a ellas: la alta tenía sus institutrices, y la baja apenas estaba alfabetizada[32]. Además, los ejemplos presentados en los textos se refieren generalmente al mundo de las clases medias.

Ya he advertido que centro mi atención en la novela de los últimos lustros del siglo XIX; dentro de ella he elegido tres autores que me parecen muy significativos: Armando Palacio Valdés, Benito Pérez Galdós y Emilia Pardo Bazán[33]. Ahora bien, creo necesario hacer una división del periodo analizado; consideraré primero los años ochenta, en los que predomina el arquetipo de mujer tradicional, y luego la década de los noventa en los que este modelo aparece cuestionado y surge una nueva propuesta.

a) Años ochenta: la apología de la mujer tradicional.

En el contexto de los años ochenta, el término "mujer tradicional" tal vez no fuera de uso corriente, la historiografía posterior tiene, sin embargo, ideas claras sobre ello[34]. Yo utilizo el término para referirme a una mujer exclusivamente doméstica, que no cuestionaría una apreciación social generalizada que la situara por debajo del varón. En 1882, tuvo lugar en Madrid el primer Congreso Pedagógico en el que se plantea el papel de la mujer en la sociedad. Palacio Valdés escribe al año siguiente, en 1883, su segunda novela, *Marta y María* que es a mi entender una respuesta al mismo. Su objetivo es hacer "la apoteosis de la mujer vulgar"[35] y realmente lo consigue; y no sólo con esta obra, sino con otras posteriores en las que continúa ahondando en el tema: *Riverita* (1886), *Maximina* (1887), *El cuarto poder* (1888), *La hermana San*

Sulpicio (1889). Paralelamente, don Armando hace la crítica de dos tipos femeninos: el de la mujer romántica que alimenta su imaginación con lecturas religiosas llegando a la intransigencia[36]; y el de la que aspira a un ascenso social y abandona las pautas de comportamiento propias de su grupo social de procedencia. Ello comporta, desde su punto de vista, una traición a la familia y un grave desorden social[37].

Pérez Galdós se hace de los problemas que en torno a la mujer se debaten en la sociedad, pero su opción se decanta a favor de una mujer tradicional. He elegido tres personajes galdosianos: Irene, Amparo y Camila, correspondientes a *El amigo Manso* (1882), *Tormento* (1884) y *Lo prohibido* (1885). Todas ellas son referibles a este modelo.

Finalmente, Emilia Pardo Bazán, si bien presenta unos tipos femeninos que están sometidos a unas pautas sociales que denuncia, no ofrece en esta década ningún modelo alternativo. Ahora bien, la continua repulsa que manifiesta su obra hacia unos personajes alicortos, carentes de iniciativa y con escasas posibilidades de desarrollo, preparan al lector para cuestionar el problema de la posición de las mujeres en la sociedad y discutir o emitir ciertos cambios que ella misma propugnará en sus novelas de los años noventa. *Un viaje de novios* (1881), *Insolación* (1889), *Morriña* (1889), *Una cristiana-La prueba* (1890-1891), son buena muestra de ello.

Veamos con algo más de detenimiento la propuesta hecha por los escritores. Palacio Valdés, se orienta claramente por el modelo tradicional. He elegido cinco novelas que me parecen muy significativas: *Marta y María, Riverita, Maximina, El cuarto poder* y *La hermana San Sulpicio*.. Intentaré referirme a ellas conjuntamente, tratando de perfilar el arquetipo femenino que presenta el autor; porque ni aquél evoluciona, ni cambia la perspectiva desde la que éste último aborda la creación de sus personajes.

El tipo de mujer de la clase media valdesiana es un ser sencillo, ignorante, humilde, algo infantil y ajeno a toda preocupación política o cultural. La presentación novelesca de Marta subraya su sencillez y su elementalidad; la de Maximina su humildad y su bondad; la de Cecilia su "condición reservada y silenciosa"[38]. En general, estos personajes saben leer y escribir; no son pues analfabetos, pero carecen de preparación cultural. Recordemos la semblanza de Maximina: "no pasa por bonita, ni es gallarda, ni tiene talento, ni educación esmerada."[39]

Ahora bien, junto a esta somera educación cultural, es común a todos los personajes femeninos valdesianos una buena educación de tipo práctico, encaminada a que la muchacha sepa desempeñar cumplidamente sus tareas domésticas. Tareas que realiza con alegría, sosiego y precisión; Marta, Maximina o Cecilia poseen en alto grado esas cualidades que harán de ellas unas perfectas amas de casa: el gusto por la limpieza, por el orden, por el aseo, por el cuidado del menaje y de las ropas es común a todas ellas. La importancia de esta preparación está cumplidamente justificada si tenemos en cuenta que el objetivo de la mujer en la sociedad no es el trabajo profesional o el cultivo del espíritu, sino llenar las obligaciones de su *estatus* de casada. Casarse y crear un hogar constituye el sueño de toda mujer española en el último cuarto del siglo XIX; de ahí que el desarrollo de unas aptitudes encaminadas al cuidado de los aspectos materiales de la casa y a la atención al marido y a los hijos adquiera tanta importancia en la obra.

Paralela a esta educación de tipo práctico, resulta indispensable a la mujer de las clases medias, y sobre todo de la clase media alta, el conocimiento y buen uso de unas normas sociales. Es cierto que la posición del marido determina la situación económico-social de la familia; pero no es menos cierto que el comportamiento femenino sanciona en cada momento esta posición dentro de la clase. Una posición tanto más valorada socialmente, cuanto más cercana se manifieste en sus aspectos formales al comportamiento de la élite. Por ello, el buen manejo de las formas sociales se convierte en requisito esencial de la joven que aspira a obtener "un buen partido", es decir, un matrimonio ventajoso. Recordemos a este respecto la semblanza que se hace de la madre de Riverita:

era una verdadera dama, noble, distinguida, de modales muy finos y que se hacía respetar de todos. En este concepto, nuestra familia nada tuvo que oponer al matrimonio de Fernando, por más que tu madre no fuese rica, que no lo era en verdad. La distinción, los modales, las relaciones compensan muy bien la falta de fortuna. Mercedes estaba relacionada con la mejor sociedad de Madrid y sabía hacer los honores de un salón como la primera. [40]

Por el contrario, el desconocimiento de estas convenciones puede acarrear dificultades aun dentro del matrimonio. Pero, ¿en qué consisten estas convenciones? El narrador de *Riverita* ofrece una espléndida respuesta al trazar el talante de doña Martina, explanchadora —esposa de don Bernardo Rivera— y dar cuenta del gran salto que había tenido que dar para salvar la distancia existente entre su origen humilde y el nivel social en que la había situado su matrimonio:

¿La salvó en efecto esta señora? En concepto de don Bernardo no (...). Sin embargo, hay que convenir en que ella había hecho todo lo que estaba de su parte (...). Porque doña Martina supo muy bien, al cabo de pocos años, recibir a los amigos de su esposo con dignidad, ya que no con distinción, y supo también preparar una mesa con elegancia y pasear en carretela por la Castellana sin ir rígida e incómoda en el asiento. Aprendió igualmente a no dormirse en el Teatro Real y a saludar a sus amigas desde lejos abriendo y cerrando repetidas veces la mano; ofrecía la casa bastante bien, aunque siempre con las mismas frases; se enteraba de las últimas modas y se las aplicaba, se echaba polvos de arroz y se pintaba las cejas cuando iba a algún sarao. Por último, aunque con marcado acento español, había llegado a hablar medianamente el francés.
A pesar de todo esto, el señor Rivera no estaba satisfecho (...). Hallaba don Bernardo que su cara esposa reñía demasiado con los criados y a gritos; que sus frases de cortesía eran siempre las mismas y pronunciadas en retahíla como una lección; que daba confianza a cualquier amiga y la iniciaba sin reparos en los asuntos domésticos; que no observaba, en fin, con las personas que frecuentaban la casa, aquella dignidad y reserva, aquel sosiego imponente propios de una perfecta señora. [41]

La religiosidad femenina apenas es tratada por Palacio Valdés. Pero en general sus mujeres son más inclinadas a la práctica que el varón. El tema aparece explícitamente aludido en *Maximina*[42]. Por otra parte, la religiosidad femenina en los mundos valdesianos, como ocurre en la obra de Galdós, es valorada positivamente. La connotación negativa aparece, sin embargo, cuando la mujer utiliza la religión para adquirir prestigios sociales o cuando el espíritu religioso cae en fantasía o intransigencia: es el caso de María Elorza o de doña Perfecta[43]. Los rasgos morales más destacados en esta mujer de la clase media valdesiana son la generosidad, el sentido de solidaridad, su recidumbre y el valor ante la adversidad. La actitud de Maximina ante la ruina familiar o la de Cecilia cuidando al marido y a los hijos de su hermana resultan paradigmáticas. Por lo demás, es conveniente recordar, que la mujer se convierte en el marco familiar, en la depositaria de unos "mores", de una serie de valores de orden estético y moral, que están en la misma entraña de las clases medias.

El ideal femenino propuesto por don Armando queda bien explícito en la *La hermana San Sulpicio*:

> es viva y ardiente, pero no vanidosa, lo cual suprime uno de los grandes incentivos, acaso el más capital, que la mujer tiene para caer. El fuego de su alma, al casarse, se convierte en ternura y abnegación. Exige que se la ame, no que se la adorne. (...) Luego, por la tradición árabe quizá, la mujer casada vive casi siempre retirada. (...) El orgullo de la esposa es ser amada por el marido. Si éste es una mijita calavera, se me figura que le quiere más. Dicen que hay en ella algo de odalisca todavía; pero con una mujer que no exige más que se la acaricie tiernamente al llegar a casa, la vida es muy fácil y muy dulce[44].

Presenta, pues, don Armando un tipo de mujer hogareña carente de iniciativa que contrasta con la mujer de alta clase. La calle aparece como un peligro, y el recogimiento en la casa es valorado como una virtud. Pienso que ello puede obedecer fundamentalmente a una triple motivación. En primer lugar, ya lo he indicado, el cuidado de la casa, misión prioritaria de la mujer, debe acaparar su atención; en segundo lugar, el callejeo puede facilitar el contacto con otros hombres y esto supone un peligro para la honradez y decoro de la familia; finalmente, la experiencia positiva que la mujer pudiera aportar al hogar, o recibir ella misma tras el contacto con otras realidades, es considerada como superflua. En el hogar, el varón debe ser el único punto de unión con el mundo exterior; a la mujer le incumbe mantener vivas unas tradiciones y unas costumbres en el seno de aquél. En fin, en la óptica del novelista asturiano, la mujer es un ser elemental, muy próximo a la naturaleza, especie de enlace entre la tierra y el infinito, entre la materia y el espíritu. El final del capítulo XXIX de *Maximina*, resulta altamente siginificativo.

Carente de ambiciones, la primera aspiración de la mujer valdesiana, consiste en realizar un matrimonio por amor. No puede decirse que pierda libertad al casarse ya que nunca ha disfrutado de ella, y el hecho de depender de un hombre al que ama colma su felicidad. En *Maximina* encontramos una referencia explícita al respecto, por más que la valoración indicada quede patente a lo largo de la narrativa de don Armando,

> Maximina ni exigía ni le suplicaba siquiera. Con ser esposa del hombre que adoraba se consideraba enteramente feliz. Y los actos cotidianos y vulgares de la existencia eran para ella unos momentos de goce inefable[45].

Resulta interesante observar el juego de dependencias en el seno del matrimonio que presenta Palacio Valdés: la mujer aparece subordinada al varón en el orden material y físico; pero el marido queda subordinado en el orden moral, ya que tanto el equilibrio y la felicidad familiar como la propia realización del varón dependen del comportamiento femenino. En el marco del hogar, el hombre aparece como suprema instancia y suprema autoridad, mientras a la mujer le corresponde el papel de ser abnegada, dedicada por entero a los quehaceres domésticos, destinado a ser el pararrayos de toda preocupación familiar. Candor, ternura, laboriosidad, sencillez, limpieza interior, reciedumbre moral, serán las cualidades subrayadas en esta mujer de las clases medias valdesianas que ha de ser portadora de la felicidad para la familia.

Por último, quisiera llamar la atención acerca de un hecho que aparece muy claro en los mundos de ficción valdesianos; me refiero al papel que cabe a la mujer como factor homogenizador de las clases medias. Es muy significativo comprobar la medida en que los distintos tipos femeninos pertenecientes a las clases medias que aparecen en la novelística del escritor asturiano, guardan entre sí una enorme semejanza. Semejanza en la escala de valores, en el ideal de vida, en las preocupaciones cotidianas. Socialmente pueden pertenecer a sectores distintos de la misma clase, pero en todos ellos se advierte una identidad de reflejos morales. Podría decirse que la mujer contribuye en forma decisiva a mantener el "nosotros" por encima de las mismas diferencias ideológicas o económicas existentes en el seno de las clases medias.

Benito Pérez Galdós, como he señalado anteriormente, se inclina también por un modelo de mujer tradicional. Obviamente, no voy a señalar los distintos rasgos con que el escritor canario caracteriza a sus tipos femeninos de las clases medias, porque en líneas generales coinciden en lo fundamental con los presentados por Palacio Valdés. Voy a referirme únicamente a alguno de los problemas recogidos en su novelística en torno al debate planteado por aquellos años, acerca del papel que la mujer debe ocupar en la sociedad, señalando cual es su enfoque y su solución a los mismos.

El amigo Manso, escrita en 1882, es una obra muy interesante desde este punto de vista; la tesis de Galdós resulta sugestiva y adecuada para una reflexión. Tras el Sexenio, algunos krausistas se interesan por la situación de la mujer, poniendo de manifiesto la necesidad que ésta tiene de acceder a la educación y al mundo del trabajo; si bien en este último caso por motivaciones de orden principalmente económico. El ideal propuesto por el krausismo lo encarna Pérez Galdós en la protagonista de *El amigo Manso*, Irene, a la que sitúa en unas condiciones propicias: es huérfana, vive con una tía, es inteligente, "aficionada a los libros", va a la escuela con

aprovechamiento, cursa estudios en la Escuela Normal y
entra como institutriz en una familia emparentada con la
suya propia. Irene queda situada, pues, por el autor en
unas condiciones adecuadas para hacer de ella un nuevo
arquetipo femenino.

¿Qué rasgos aparecen ponderados en este personaje
como positivos? Por supuesto un tipo de belleza que hace
referencia no a cánones determinados, sino a un
panorama espiritual sano y equilibrado; la mujer es
valorada por "el fondo" y por "el estilo". El primero se
manifiesta en el carácter y el comportamiento; el segundo
en el lenguaje y en el atuendo; un atuendo, se apresura a
explicar el autor, que no es lujoso sino "correcto, limpio,
sencillo". El principio que informa el talante de este ideal
femenino es el del equilibrio; un equilibrio presidido por
la razón. El modelo, señala don Benito, tiene una clara
filiación extranjera, proviene del Norte, y está influído por
el positivismo; la "mujer positiva" se la denomina en el
capítulo XIII. Y, junto al sentido común, se valora la
religiosidad auténtica, las virtudes domésticas y el nivel
cultural: afición a la lectura, sensibilidad artística,
conocimientos... Frente a esta mujer encarnada por Irene,
que representa de alguna manera el ideal de "mujer
nueva", el escritor alude a otro tipo femenino, corriente
en la sociedad española, definido por la falsa religiosidad,
la instrucción deficiente mal encubierta por un aparente
barniz cultural, el carácter frívolo, vanidoso, ambicioso; el
deseo desmedido de ascenso social a través de un
matrimonio ventajoso.

Ahora bien, en la contraposición de estos dos tipos, en la
aparente opción de Galdós por Irene, cabe preguntarse
hasta dónde llega el novelista en su planteamiento de esta
"mujer nueva". Galdós está a favor de una mujer religiosa
—no intransigente— e instruída; pero no se cuestiona
siquiera la primacía del varón en las relaciones entre los
sexos[46], no alude a la emancipación —tema que empezaba
a discutirse por aquel entonces[47]—, plantea el trabajo
femenino como algo transitorio en la vida de la mujer y
sale al paso de aquella señalando los peligros que de la
misma pueden derivarse para la familia y la sociedad[48].
Por lo demás, la instrucción y la cultura femenina

constituyen en la óptica galdosiana un enriquecimiento moral que permite a la mujer cumplir más adecuadamente sus funciones de madre y de esposa[49]. Las limitaciones del arquetipo femenino presentado por don Benito son evidentes; en la primera mitad de la novela, cuando bosqueja a su personaje, hace concebir esperanzas: "He aquí la mujer perfecta, la mujer positiva, la mujer razón contrapuesta a la mujer frivolidad, a la mujer capricho"[50], pero al final da por fracasada la experiencia: Irene ha caído en la misma medianía que el escritor criticaba,

> Sentencia final: era como todas. Los tiempos, la raza, el ambiente, no se desmentían en ella. Como si lo viera... desde que se casó no había vuelto a coger un libro. Pero hagámosle justicia (...) Tenía, sin género de duda, grandes dotes de manejo social y arte maravilloso de tratar a las personas. Manuel empezó a recibir en su salón, por las noches a varias personas de viso ....[51]

A primera vista, el autor parece que lamenta lo ocurrido; pero, ¿estaba de acuerdo con los cambios sociales que podían derivarse en el caso de que hubiera prevalecido este nuevo modelo? Creo que no. La respuesta, aunque no pasa todavía de ser una mera hipótesis, se basa en argumentos que ofrece la misma obra.

Es posible que Galdós, que en el terreno de la política critica la influencia del positivismo[52], tenga distintas perspectivas respecto al influjo de éste en el mundo femenino: pondera las ventajas del predominio de la razón, pero evidentemente expresa sus temores frente a los afanes individualistas que el nuevo horizonte cultural pudiera propiciar; por lo demás, y en esto es muy claro, manifiesta su repulsa frente al pragmatismo y al utilitarismo que se ha impuesto en la vida cotidiana: el autor advierte el peligro que puede derivarse en las relaciones entre los sexos, el peligro de que los intereses económicos prevalezcan sobre los amorosos. Y hace a la mujer principal responsable de ello: la actitud de doña Javiera o de Irene contrastan con la de Mario o la de Manuel Peña.

En fin, si en *El amigo Manso* Galdós presenta la inviabilidad de una "mujer nueva", en *Tormento* (1884), a pesar de la fuerza con que se evidencia la injusticia de que es objeto una muchacha, víctima por una sola vez de los abusos sexuales de un hombre, Galdós no se atreve a romper los prejuicios sociales existentes y a ofrecer una alternativa. Amparo no se puede casar con Agustín Caballero, que la lleva como "querida" a Francia, para dejar a salvo su honor varonil: es decir, su virginidad involuntariamente mancillada la degrada socialmente, la priva de respetabilidad y la relega a un mundo marginado[53].

En *Lo Prohibido* (1885), nuestro novelista ofrece otro arquetipo femenino. De las tres hermanas —Elisa, María Juana y Camila— que protagonizan la obra, las dos primeras "son el resultado de lo que llega a ser una mujer en una sociedad determinada, la madrileña de 1880, muy condicionadas ambas por su ambiente y circunstancias". En cuanto a la tercera, Camila, la "mujer salvaje", está presentada muy de otro modo: "ser exento de todos los soportes que los otros deben a su tiempo, menos precisa y por lo tanto más significativa —significativa además de nuevas inquietudes de su creador..."[54]. Según Montesinos, —a quien sigo en este punto—, Camila no responde tanto a un modelo real como a un ideal del novelista. El objetivo de este último consiste en presentar un arquetipo que sirva de contrapunto a la realidad social. ¿Qué rasgos escoge y destaca don Benito? Señalaremos la espontaneidad, la franqueza, la generosidad, la ausencia de formalismos, la lealtad, la solidaridad: carácteres que, en la obra galdosiana aparecen encarnados generalmente en las clases populares. Desde este punto de vista, Camila significa la bondad de lo natural y supone una apelación a las virtudes populares. Pero puesto que el escritor la sitúa en un contexto social de clases medias y el personaje supone una denuncia de determinados carácteres mentales propios de estas últimas, conviene indagar de dónde proceden las rectificaciones de Galdós. El resultado que nos ofrece una primera aproximación es interesante: en Camila se ponderan, además de los rasgos señalados, la fidelidad conyugal, el amor maternal, la abnegación, el desprecio del lujo, la sencillez, el ideal de vida doméstica.... El novelista subraya la importancia del papel desempeñado por Camila en su pequeño mundo familiar; casada con un hombre bueno y honrado, elemental y primitivo, Camila no precisa cultura para relacionarse con él —Galdós la presenta casi analfabeta—, pero sí necesita tacto, lealtad y buen sentido para gobernar la casa y lograr que prevalezca en ella la alegría y la felicidad en medio de una serie de contrariedades. En fin, Galdós presenta en Camila un tipo de mujer rebelde ante las convenciones sociales; pero su rebeldía no se orienta a buscar la libertad, o la igualdad con el hombre en el plano laboral, educativo o sexual, haciéndose eco de las peticiones de núcleos feministas que empezaban a cuestionarse la posición de la mujer en la sociedad. Galdós, por el contrario, acentúa los aspectos domésticos de su personaje y pondera los excelentes resultados que, en orden a la economía, la convivencia, la armonía social puede suponer tal comportamiento femenino. En suma, rebeldía sí, pero orientada fundamentalmente, a subrayar, en buena medida, el comportamiento tradicional de la mujer.

En suma, en la obra de Galdós de los años ochenta, encontramos, como en la de Palacio Valdés, una opción por un modelo de mujer tradicional, —equilibrada y volcada al área doméstica—, y una crítica de la mujer intransigente, y de la que, seducida por los prestigios sociales de la élite, se orienta hacia este grupo social.

Los personajes femeninos creados por Emilia Pardo Bazán en la década de los ochenta, se ajustan, salvo muy contadas excepciones, al modelo de mujer tradicional. En esto coincide con Palacio Valdés o Pérez Galdós, si bien doña Emilia observa de distinta manera la dependencia de la mujer respecto al varón en el seno de la familia, y denuncia lo limitado de una educación orientada exclusivamente al matrimonio. Al analizar los personajes de Pardo Bazán, lo primero que se advierte es la profundización que la autora hace sobre este tema a lo largo de su carrera literaria. Teniendo en cuenta que los carácteres de los tipos femeninos creados por la escritora gallega coinciden en lo fundamental con los ofrecidos por Palacio Valdés o Pérez Galdós, prefiero guardar para el próximo apartado las observaciones críticas hechas al respecto por doña Emilia, ya que ello me permite presentar una visión global, aunque sea sintética, de sus propuestas. Conviene, sin embargo, señalar ahora el distinto enfoque que, a la altura de los años ochenta, hacen los tres autores de un mismo tema. Don Armando, a pesar de conocer el debate que estaba teniendo lugar y la propia posición de Pardo Bazán, no llega a cuestionarla novelescamente y opta por un modelo tradicional; don Benito lo cuestiona pero se orienta también hacia el modelo establecido; doña Emilia en cambio, asume en todo momento una actitud crítica ante las limitaciones que la sociedad impone a la mujer y siente el imperativo de remover los obstáculos que marcan estos límites.

b) *Años noventa: la propuesta de una mujer emancipada*

En las últimas décadas del siglo XIX el debate en torno al problema de la mujer encuentra un marco adecuado en diversos Congresos Pedagógicos, y cristaliza en una modificación del marco legal que tiende a disminuir las desigualdades entre los sexos[55]. La novela se hace eco de ello; algunos novelistas no pueden soslayar el nuevo horizonte cultural y limitarse a la mera apología de la mujer tradicional. Es el caso de Palacio Valdés, finísimo observador de su tiempo, que plantea el tema en un capítulo de *La alegría del capitán Ribot* (1899). El novelista, a través del diálogo entre sus personajes —tras uno de los cuales se esconde él mismo— se orienta de nuevo hacia el tipo de mujer tradicional[56]. Por otra parte, desde fines de los años ochenta, en muchas de sus obras se advierte la presencia de dos tipos femeninos en función, frecuentemente, antagónica. Al tipo "Maximina" cuyos rasgos he señalado más arriba, contrapone el tipo "Amalia"[57] —al que son referibles Ventura, Clementina, Alicia...—, mujeres estas últimas de acentuado atractivo sexual, egoístas y propicias a anteponer sus gustos e intereses a los del conjunto familiar con consecuencias nefastas para éste. Esta contraposición un tanto elemental y maniquea, polariza sin embargo, unos componentes socioculturales que el autor enfrenta en sus mundos de ficción.

Pérez Galdós muestra una mayor sensibilidad hacia el debate feminista y convierte este problema en el eje de *Tristana* (1892). Aunque plantea el tema con mayor hondura que Palacio Valdés, no difiere mucho su opción de la del escritor asturiano. Se manifiesta interesado por la educación femenina, pero tiene grandes dudas acerca del papel que corresponde a la mujer en la sociedad moderna. Por ello, si bien defiende su promoción cultural, sostiene la clara delimitación entre las respectivas esferas de influencia de ambo sexos. El mundo moral y religioso es el que corresponde a la mujer, y a él debe circunscribirse. La igualdad y aún la superioridad sobre el varón la logrará en el terreno moral, pero nunca en el plano de las capacidades intelectuales. En fin, Galdós, al igual que Palacio Valdés, deja entrever que la mujer es la encargada de mediar entre el mundo de la materia y el mundo del espíritu[58].

Pardo Bazán, que vive activamente el debate feminista, da cuenta a lo largo de su obra de las desigualdades existentes entre los sexos. Desigualdades que, en su óptica no se fundamentan en la biología o en la religión, sino en las conveniencias sociales. Doña Emilia, sin renegar de la mujer doméstica, pone en evidencia las barreras que la recluyen en el marco del hogar, y hace de Feíta un personaje que esgrime argumentos claramente feministas. La protagonista de *Memorias de un solterón* (1896), exige el derecho a la educación y al trabajo, y denuncia ante su padre y ante Mauro Pareja, —el protagonista masculino— las discriminaciones que pesan sobre la mujer, y las desventajas sociales que de ello pueden derivarse.

En este punto, y por razones obvias, voy a centrar mis reflexiones, sobre Emilia Pardo Bazán. En su discurso feminista desearía destacar cinco aspectos: las limitaciones y discriminaciones que la desigualdad de sexos comporta en las relaciones sociales; la existencia de una doble moral; la denuncia del matrimonio como única vía respetable para la mujer; las dificultades de un cambio; y finalmente, la mujer "emancipada" como propuesta de la novelista.

Pardo Bazán subraya la posición secundaria de la mujer respecto al varón, y señala la minoría de edad permanente a que la sociedad la condena. Tutelada primero por el padre y luego por el marido, la hija y la esposa apenas pueden reservarse ninguna esfera de su intimidad: todos sus actos e iniciativas deben pasar por la censura marital o paternal. Los personajes expresan en varias ocasiones el desasosiego que esta situación les produce y se orienta hacia el matrimonio como vía de emancipación[59]. Son numerosos los testimonios de la satisfacción que, en orden a la liberación de la autoridad paterna, experimenta la joven al casarse. Doña Emilia recoge en *Un viaje de novios* (1881), ejemplos ingenuos. Recordemos el simbolismo de emancipación de la autoridad paterna que adquiere un hecho tan trivial como pedir una taza de café: "sucedíale a veces decir a Rosalía o a Carmela. Deja, que en casándome, yo tomaré café. ¡Pues no!". Llegada la ocasión la protagonista degusta el café en el primer "fondín" que encuentra en su viaje de novios, y al tomarlo, no puede menos que pensar: "Si viniese papá ahora, qué diría"[60]. Numerosos los sentimientos de satisfacción, decía, pero numerosas también las manifestaciones de los límites en que se mueve la iniciativa femenina después del matrimonio; iniciativa que estaba muy condicionada por la propia legislación[61].

Otro tema que cuestiona la autora gallega es el de la doble moral: lo plantea abiertamente en *Insolación* (1889). Recordemos las observaciones que hace Pardo a la protagonista:

> Es hipocresía detestable eso de acusarlas e infamarlas a ustedes con tal rigor por lo que en nosotros nada significa (...) Pues si tratamos de creyentes, la cuestión de conciencia es independiente de la del sexo (...) Puedo decirle a usted de corrido los diez mandamientos..., y se me figura que rezan igual con nosotros que con ustedes. Y también sé que el confesor las absuelve y perdona a ustedes igualito que a nosotros. Lo que pide a la penitente el ministro de Dios es arrepentimiento, propósito de la enmienda. El mundo, más severo que Dios, pide la perfección absoluta (...) En el fondo ningún confesor le dirá a usted que hay un pecado más para las hembras. Es decir, que la cosa queda reducida a las consecuencias positivas, exteriores..., al criterio social. (...). Convendrá en que eso siempre realza a

una mujer; pero, en gran parte, depende del criterio social. La mujer se cree infamada, después de una de esas caídas ante su propia conciencia, porque le han hecho concebir desde niña que lo más malo, lo más infamante, lo irreparable es eso; (...). A nosotros nos enseñan lo contrario, que es vergonzoso para el hombre no tener aventuras, y que hasta queda humillado si las rehuye... De modo que lo mismo que a nosotros nos pone muy huecos, a ustedes las envilece[61].

El texto es claro y contundente. La autora denuncia la raíz social de la doble moral; señala la hipocresía que ello comporta, y apunta más adelante, las consecuencias sociales que de ello pueden derivarse.

La obra de Pardo Bazán evidencia en diversas ocasiones que el matrimonio es el único camino digno para la mujer[62], y ello por varios motivos: le confiere respetabilidad; es una buena vía de promoción social, y le permite lograr el título más codiciado: el de "buena ama de casa". Pero, además, en ocasiones viene a ser el medio de salvar la economía familiar. Recordemos la conversación entre Feíta y doña Milagros:

> Es lo que yo le digo a papá (...) No hay mayor desgracia que reunirse tantas marías como aquí nos hemos reunido. Si en vez de mujeres fuésemos hombres, saldríamos adelante, ¡vaya si saldríamos! Pero esto es un gallinero. No entiendo qué será de nosotras, porque realmente no servimos más que de estorbo.
> —Hija..., de estorbo precisamente, no (...) si os quedáis para vestir santos, no digo...; pero..., encontrando maríos buenos, como el mío o como tu padre...[63].

Por otra parte, razones de decoro, impulsan también a la mujer hacia el matrimonio, ya que la consideración social y la respetabilidad del hombre y de la mujer solteros son radicalmente diferentes: el hombre es tenido por un pillo simpático que teme adquirir responsabilidades y disfruta viviendo su sagrada libertad; en cambio la mujer es mirada con cierto grado de compasión ya que su soltería es el resultado de causas ajenas a su voluntad[64]. Este conjunto de circunstancias que rodea la vida cotidiana de la mujer hace que el matrimonio sea el primer objetivo de toda mujer al salir de la pubertad. Una vez logrado, la mujer tiene en muchas ocasiones el sentimiento de ser deudora respecto al hombre que la ha redimido de una soltería un tanto vergonzosa.

Sobre la base de estos supuestos, doña Emilia indica reiteradamente que es difícil que el matrimonio proporcione una relación amistosa y satisfactoria a los cónyuges. Los ejemplos de Carmiña Aldao, Lucía, doña Milagros o el matrimonio Neira, a pesar de sus trece alumbramientos, son significativos. El matrimonio se convierte así en una institución falta de contenido, de ahí que las resistencias que hacia el mismo manifiesta Mauro Pareja o la misma Feíta, personajes con los que de alguna manera se identifica la autora.

Llegados a este punto, conviene preguntarse si la escritora gallega veía alguna posibilidad de cambio para la mujer, a la altura de 1890. Su obra no se presta al optimismo, al sugerir que la sociedad exige la persistencia de la mujer tradicional. La novelista hace responsable al varón que se muestra muy reacio a que evolucione la mujer: "Para el español por más avanzado que sea, no vacilo en decirlo, el ideal feminista no está en el porvenir sino en el pasado"[65]. Estos presupuestos mentales obligan a la joven —destinada socialmente a la caza de un marido— a mantener su respetabilidad y su decoro, y para ello es imprescindible permanecer dentro de los patrones establecidos, ajustarse a las normas tradicionales. El hombre, que es el que tiene la iniciativa en la relación entre los sexos, no busca en la mujer afinidades que permitan una relación amistosa. El hecho aparece denunciado en *Una cristiana:*

> A nuestra edad todos soñamos con la mujer; y es bien natural que soñemos; pero debiéramos soñar con la mujer cortada para nosotros y no precisamente con la que nos haría infelices si nos uniésemos a ella. ¡Qué tu tía es muy buena, muy pura, muy santa! Bondad pasiva; sumisión al destino, rutina moral, hijo..., y se acabó. Tú, casado con tití Carmen, procederías como don Felipe: no le dirigirías la palabra a las horas de comer, y la dejarías sola todo el tiempo posible, porque ni os entenderíais, ni os desistiríais el uno del otro. Divorcio del alma más completo no se concibe. Créelo, no te forjes ilusiones bobas. ¿Serías tú íntimo amigo de un neocatólico? ¿No? Pues tampoco de tu esposa...

Pardo Bazán se refiere también a la confusión existente en la sociedad: se magnifica todo sacrificio de la mujeres, sin tener en cuenta que la razón debe presidir su conducta también en este aspecto; de lo contrario, actos incluso nobles pueden acarrear graves consecuencias sociales, hasta para la institución matrimonial:

> Luis —exclamé— ¿te atreves a negar el heroísmo de una mujer que por no presenciar los extravíos de su padre sacrifica su juventud y se casa con un hombre a quien no puede amar (....) — ¡Pués por eso, pués por eso!— vociferó Portal ya fuera de sí. Yo te replico desde mi punto de vista ¿Te atreves a calificar de virtud la acción de la mujer que acepta un esposo repugnante y no prefiere salir a cantar en un teatro como Cintia, o fregar pisos, como la alcarreña que nos sirve en casa de doña Jesusa[66].

Esta serie de prejuicios, convenciones y tabúes que condicionan la vida de las mujeres comporta un empobrecimiento social y un reduccionismo para el desarrollo de la personalidad femenina. Ejemplo de este empobrecimiento social lo constituyen las señoritas de Barrientos[67]. Ejemplo también del reduccionismo aludido es la respuesta de Neira al doctor Moragas. Señala éste el peligro de trastornos físicos que accecha a la mujer, incapacitada socialmente para dar cauce a sus propias energías: "¡Pobrecillas! ¿Qué quiere usted que hagan, don Benicio?" La respuesta de éste, padre de doce muchachas, es rápida y contundente: "¿Qué? ¡Lo que hicieron siempre..., lo que hizo mi santa madre! ¡Mucho coser..., mucho rezar..., en casita, y a querer a su marido y a sus hijos!"[68].

Piensa doña Emilia que son muchas y muy fuertes las inercias que dificultan la mejora de los papeles femeninos. Y cree que las transformaciones no serán propiciadas por la sociedad ni por los mismos intelectuales; es a la mujer a quien corresponde tomar la iniciativa[69]. Y ella toma la iniciativa en 1896: pone en pie a Feíta, arquetipo de la "mujer nueva", de la "mujer emancipada". ¿Qué se entiende por emancipada? Feíta lo expresa en diversas ocasiones: "salir", "andar sola", "no depender de nadie". Ello, obviamente, comporta tener acceso a la instrucción, tener derecho al trabajo, no verse obligada a recurrir al matrimonio por necesidad, considerarse libre en el seno de una sociedad llena de prejucios. Ahora bien, esto no significa la negación de la mujer doméstica, ni la vulneración de la moral sexual existente. La escritora, a través de Feíta, intenta demostrar que ni las responsabilidades hogareñas ni el cumplimiento estricto de las normas morales entran en colisión con el nuevo tipo femenino[70].

El comportamineto divergente de Feíta, —que se orienta hacia la libertad que se basa en el estudio y en el trabajo, que rechaza la tutela del varón y reclama el derecho a ser considerada como ser adulto y responsable produce un sentimiento hostil en el mundo de Marineda[71]. El desacuerdo radica fundamentalmente en la estrechez de miras y en el corto horizonte de una sociedad que se muestra incapaz de volver la espalda a unos prejuicios y rutinas ancestrales. Que la protagonista vulnere la tradicional esfera de influencias establecida para la mujer resulta incomprensible e imperdonable. Ante este argumento, Feíta denuncia la hipocresía de una sociedad que de hecho lo infringe en el marco del hogar, pero que se muestra intransigente a la hora de admitirlo socialmente:

> —Vamos, vamos, juicio.... Mete esa cabeza en agua fresca, y que se te quite la fiebre. Como yo vuelva a oirte barbarizar... Hija mía, Dios hizo a la mujer para la familia, para la maternidad, para la sumisión, para las labores propias de su sexo...¡de su sexo! No lo olvides nunca, y que nadie tenga que recordártelo, o serás la criatura más antipática, más ridícula y más despreciable del mundo: un *marimacho*; ¡puf! La mujer a zurcir medias...; no se ha visto ni se verá nunca que truequen los papeles a no ser en San Balandrán.
> —Pues sí, señor, que se ha visto— respondió con brío (...); porque mamá le mandaba a usted..., y usted obedecía a mamá lo mismo que un borrego. ¿Y sabe en qué consistía? En que mamá tuvo más disposición para el mando que usted. Cada quisque debe hacer aquello para que tiene disposición. ¿Dios me da a mí talento para estudiar? Estudio. ¿Dios le dió a Froilán disposición para jugar a la billarda y tirar piedras? Que juegue y que las tire. Y, ¡vamos!, es una picardía muy gorda eso de que las mujeres cuando sirven para esto o para aquello..., hagan precisamente lo otro y lo de más allá. Yo sé barrer y coser de una casa, y sé criar un chiquillo como crié a las gatas monas...;

pero me gusta estudiar, y estudiaré. ¡Sólo faltaba! Aquí todo el
mundo se pronuncia por hacer disparates... Pués me pronuncio
yo para hacer una cosa justa y buena. Quiero estudiar,
aprender, saber y valerme el día de mañana sin necesitar a
nadie. Yo no he de estar dependiendo de un hombre. Me lo
ganaré y me burlaré de todos ellos[72].

En fin, la escritora gallega, al presentar en sus obras la
posición de la mujer en el seno de la sociedad, denuncia
insistentemente los prejucios y dificultades que
condicionan y limitan el desarrollo de su personalidad;
pone de manifiesto los aspectos negativos de la
desigualdad existente entre los sexos, y trata de hacer ver a
los lectores la urgencia de una revisión de los papeles que
la mujer tiene asignados. La escritora apuesta por una
mujer nueva, en la que encarna sus propios ideales
femeninos; somete a su personaje a una serie de peripecias
novelescas destinadas a probar la validez de su postura, y
llega a conseguirlo. La protagonista logra en buena medida
su objetivo y muestra la viabilidad y la conveniencia del
cambio.

IV. CONCLUSIONES

Tras este somero análisis de los arquetipos y modelos de
la mujer de clase media socializados a través de la escuela
y de la literatura durante el último cuarto del siglo XIX, ha
llegado el momento de formular unas conclusiones:
1. Salvo en el caso de Pardo Bazán, los modelos
propuestos parten de una perspectiva androcéntrica y
coinciden en una orientación reduccionista de la
personalidad y actividad femenina.
2. Emilia Pardo Bazán, feminista activa[73], intelectual de
fina sensibilidad para percibir los problemas del momento,
realiza primero una crítica de la sociedad patriarcal
existente, para hacer a continuación una propuesta
alternativa basada en la igualdad de los sexos. Doña
Emilia, aristócrata que apenas presta atención a las
desigualdades de clase, denuncia en su obra las
desigualdades entre los sexos, poniendo en boca de sus
personajes muchas de las razones que setenta años más

tarde serían utilizadas para la construcción de una teoría feminista.

3. Desde un punto de vista histórico, el intento de abrir a la mujer las parcelas de actividad reservadas para el hombre, es un paso en el proceso de modernización. La revolución francesa supuso el inicio de la revolución burguesa y el intento de poner fin al Antiguo Régimen, terminando con las funciones reservadas, y abriendo las carreras al talento. ¿No se trata ahora de que esta vieja propuesta liberal alcance al mundo de las mujeres? Sin duda, pero el proyecto encontrará en España tantas dificultades, al menos, como había encontrado el desmantelamiento del Antiguo Régimen.

4. Los cambios producidos en el ámbito económico, social, político y cultural, apenas se han proyectado en el mundo femenino de las clases medias. ¿Por qué? Es difícil encontrar una respuesta. Quizá se pueda aventurar una hipótesis: en una situación de *inseguridad* para la burguesía y las clases medias —como la que viven en la etapa finisecular[74]—, es lógico que todo lo que pudiera conmover el fundamento de la sociedad —la familia y el hogar, en la forma establecida—, suscite especial temor y levante las resistencias más cerradas. Por otra parte, la exaltación que se hace de la misión doméstica y de la "carrera maternal" coloca a la mujer ante una vía de "promoción" y de legitimización en la nueva sociedad burguesa; la coloca ante una especie de carrera abierta al talento: si logra cubrir las etapas marcadas, recibirá una positiva consideración social.

NOTAS

[1] Hervé Coutau-Begarie,*Le phenomene "nouvelle histoire" stratégie et idéologie des nouveaux historiens.* Paris: Economica, 1983.

[2] M. Bloch publica en 1924 *Les rois thaumaturges;* L. Febvre, en 1944 *Le problème de l'incroyance au XVI siècle. Le religion de Rabelais;* Ph. Aries, en 1948 *Histoire des populations françaises et de leurs attitudes devant la vie .*

3 Vid. M.Vovelle, *Ideologías y mentalidades*. Barcelona: Ariel, 1985. p. 12.

4 Vid. J. A. Maravall, "La historia de las mentalidades como historia social", en *Actas de las II Jornadas de Metodología y Didáctica de la Historia*. Cáceres: Universidad de Extremadura, 1983. p. 404.

5 J. Le Goff, *Hacer la Historia*. Barcelona: Laia, 1980. vol III. pp. 83 ss.

6 L. Febvre, *Combats pour l'histoire*. Paris: A. Colin, 1953.

7 B. Bennassar, *Los españoles, actitudes y mentalidad*. Barcelona: Argos Vergara, 1978.

8 Vid. T. Zeldin, *Histoire des passions françaises 1848-1945*. Paris: Seuil, 1980-1981. 5 vols. Vid. *Histoire de la vie privée*, dirigida por Ph. Aries y G. Duby. Paris, 1982-1987. 5 vols.

9 La bibliografía en este campo es creciente desde mediados de los años setenta, los nombres de Gordon, Friedan, Michel, Delphy, Kelly, Gadol, Nicholson o Flax...por solo citar algunos, jalonan esta pujante expansión.

10 H. Vidal, *Sentido y práctica de la crítica literaria socio-histórica: panfleto para la proposición de una arqueología acotada*. Minneapolis: Institute for the Study of Ideologies and Literature, 1984.

11 Entiendo por socialización, el proceso encaminado a promover las condiciones que favorecen en los seres humanos el desarrollo de su persona.

12 Recordemos que se trata de una literatura realista y naturalista que apela al análisis y a la observación de la realidad como instrumentos de la propia creación.

13 A. Hauser, *Sociología del Arte*. Madrid: Guadarrama, 1975. pp. 11 ss.

14 J. I. Ferreras, *Introducción a una sociología de la novela española del siglo XIX*. Madrid: Edicusa, 1973. p. 102.

15 Utilizo aquí el término discurso en el sentido que le da el profesor Jover, "conjunto de segmentos narrativos relativos a un mismo tema, en la medida que tal tema comparece en la narración como proyección inmediata de una experiencia histórica o biográfica", vid. J. M. Jover, *Edición, introducción y notas a "Mister Witt en el cantón" de Ramón J. Sender*. Madrid: Castalia, 1987. p. 53.

[16] Hay que recordar, sin embargo, la obra de Ma. Pilar Oñate, *El feminismo en la literatura española* Madrid: Espasa Calpe, 1938.

[17] Tras el Sexenio Democrático prosigue en España el desarrollo puesto en marcha durante la era isabelina, continúa la expansión de la burguesía y la organización del mundo obrero, se consiguen unas libertades democráticas y se inicia con pujanza una fase ascendente de la cultura española. Vid. J. M. Jover , "La época de la Restauración: panorama político social, (1875-1902)", en *Historia de España*, dirigida por M. Tuñón de Lara. Barcelona: Labor, 1981. Vol VIII. pp. 271-406.

[18] En los años ochenta tiene lugar un Congreso Nacional Pedagógico en Madrid (1882) , y otro en Barcelona (1888) , en los que se reconoce el derecho femenino a la educación. En el Congreso Pedagógico Hispano-Americano celebrado en Madrid en 1892 se plantea la igualdad educativa y profesional entre los sexos. Vid. R. Ma. Capel, "La apertura del horizonte cultural femenino: Fernando de Castro y los Congresos pedagógicos del siglo XIX", en AAVV., *Mujer y sociedad en España (1700-1975)*. Madrid: Min. de Cultura, 1986. 2a. ed. pp. 112-145. Vid. *Actas de los Congresos*. Madrid 1882, Barcelona 1888, Madrid 1892.

[19] M. Nash, —en *Mujer y trabajo 1875-1936*. Barcelona: Anthropos, 1983. pp. 13-14—, se refiere a la persistencia de la desconfianza en la sociedad española, respecto a la igualdad intelectual. Vid. G. Scanlon, *La polémica feminista en la España contemporánea (1868-1974)*. Madrid: Siglo XXI, 1976. Cap. I.

[20] Respecto a *Flora* y a *Escenas de familia*, por no tener catalogadas todas las ediciones ni en la Biblioteca Nacional, ni en el Instituto de San José de Calasanz del CSIC, ni en la Escuela Universitaria Pablo Montesinos de Madrid, depositaria de los fondos mas antiguos de las Escuelas Normales, no puedo tener la seguridad de que aparezcan consignadas todas las ediciones. Pero en todo caso *Flora* se reedita en 1885, 1889, 1895, 1897, 1898, 1926, 1927, 1928, 1935, 1940, 1943, 1954-1955. Y *Escenas de familia* se reedita en 1895, 1898, 1899, 1921, 1927. En cuanto a la obra de M. Carderera, *La ciencia de la mujer al alcance de las niñas*, se publica en 1875, no puedo precisar tampoco el número de veces que se reedita, pero sí quiero señalar que en 1909 figura todavía en el *Catálogo de las Obras de Primera Enseñanza y libros de consulta y utilidad para las maestras*. Madrid: Imp. Perlado, Páea Companía, 1909. La obra de Carderera aparece en el apartado D, "Literatura especial para niñas", y va seguido de la siguiente glosa: "Este librito interesa a las niñas porque en él se obtiene el más completo conocimiento del gobierno y dirección de una casa en el seno de la familia".

[21] M. Carderera, *La ciencia...*, op. cit. p.7. He analizado este texto en "El trabajo doméstico en los manuales escolares (Contribución al

conocimiento de la mentalidad de las clases medias)", en *El trabajo de las mujeres siglo XVI-XX. Actas de las VI Jornadas de Investigación interdisciplinaria sobre la mujer.* Madrid: Universidad Autónoma, 1987.

[22] M. Carderera, *La ciencia.....*, op. cit. p. 35.

[23] El texto de *Flora* por el que voy a citar es el editado en 1928 por la Imprenta Elzeviriana y Lib. Camí, S. A. Vid. pp. 365 -366.

[24] P. Pascual, *Flora*, p. 357; M Carderera, *La ciencia...*, op. cit. p. 23.

[25] He analizado el contenido de las dos obras citadas por P. Pascual en un artículo titulado "La mujer de la clase media en el proceso de modernización de la sociedad española". Vid. *Actas del Primer Colloqui d'historia de la dona,* celebrado en Barcelona el 22-24 de octubre 1986.

[26] P. Pascual, *Escenas...*, op. cit. p. 218. Cito por el texto publicado en Barcelona por el Hijo de Paluzie en 1922.

[27] P. Pascual, *Escenas...*, op. cit. pp. 224-225.

[28] M. Carderera, *La ciencia...*, op. cit. p. 25.

[29] Idem., p. 61.

[30] Idem., p. 54.

[31] J. M. Jover, "España en la transición del siglo XVIII al XIX", en *Política, Diplomacia y Humanismo popular.* Madrid: Turner, 1976. p. 158.

[32] En todo caso la que se alfabetizaba lo hacía generalmente mediante unos textos llamados "Manuscritos".

[33] Vengo trabajando desde hace muchos años sobre la novela de la Restauración con objeto de hacer un estudio sobre las mentalidades y la vida cotidiana de la época. Vid. entre otros, "La imagen de la mujer en la novela de la Restauración: a) ocio social y trabajo doméstico; b) hacia el mundo del trabajo" en AAVV. *Mujer y...*, op. cit. pp.148-205. ; *Palacio Valdés y el mundo social de la Restauración.* Oviedo. IDEA, 1982. p.459; "Literatura y sociedad: reflejos y actitudes sociales en el mundo de la Restauración", en *Homenaje a José Antonio Maravall,* Madrid: Centro de Investigaciones Sociológicas, 1985. pp.199-213; "La clase dirigente madrileña en dos novelas de 1890", en AAVV. *Madrid en la sociedad del siglo XIX.* Madrid, 1986. pp.533-556; "Fin de siglo: la proyección literaria de la situación de la mujer", publicaciones de la Fundación

Ortega y Gasset. Madrid, (en prensa); Edición crítica de *La espuma* de Armando Palacio Valdés. Madrid: Castalia, (en prensa).

[34] La bibliografía en torno al tema es muy abundante, para una definición, vid. A. Steinman, "Veinte años de investigación sobre la misión de los sexos", en AAVV. *Mujeres, sexismo y sociedades*. Madrid: Espejo, 1980. p.142.

[35] Recogido de una carta inédita de Palacio Valdés a Clarín de 29 de agosto de 1883.

[36] Encarnada en María Elorza, en *Marta y María*.

[37] A este tipo responde Ventura Belinchón, personaje de *El cuarto poder*.

[38] Vid. espec. *Marta y María*, caps. IV y VI; *Riverita*, caps. XXII y XXV; *Maximina*, cap. XXV; *El cuarto poder*, cap. VI.

[39] Vid. *Riverita*, cap. XVII.

[40] Idem., cap. I.

[41] Idem., cap II.

[42] Vid. *Maximina*, cap. I.

[43] Palacio Valdés encarna este tipo en una de las protagonistas de *Marta y María*; Benito Pérez Galdós en el personaje central de *Doña Perfecta* (1876) y en María Egipcíaca, protagonista de *La familia de León Roch* (1878).

[44] Vid. *La hermana San Sulpicio*, Cap. XV.

[45] Vid. *Maximina*, cap. VII.

[46] B. Pérez Galdós, *El amigo Manso*, en O.C. Madrid: Aguilar, 1964. espec. pp.1206. vol. IV.

[47] Entiendo por emancipación una concepción igualitaria de los sexos en sus tres ámbitos: doméstico, económico y político.

[48] Vid. *El amigo manso*, pp. 1238, 1208, 1275-1276.

[49] Idem., p. 1273.

50 Idem., p. 1196.

51 Idem., p. 1288.

52 Idem., p. 1209.

53 Vid. *Tormento*, en O.C. op. cit. pp. 1567-1568.

54 J. F. Montesinos, *Edición, introducción y notas a"Lo prohibido"* de B. Pérez Galdós. Madrid: Castalia, 1980. p. 34.

55 El Código Civil de 1889 deja bien claras las limitaciones de la mujer Vid. J. Abella, *Código Civil vigente en la península y ultramar. Reformado conforme a lo dispuesto en la ley del 26 de mayo y Real decreto del 24 de julio de 1889.* espec. arts. 22, 42, 45, 55-56, 83, 327, 294, 1336-1391.

56 Vid. *La alegría del capitán Ribot*, cap. VI.

57 Vid. *El maestrante* (1893).

58 Vid. *Tristana*, en O.C. Madrid: Aguilar, 1963. vol. V. p.1610.

59 E. Pardo Bazán, *Una cristiana*, in O.C. Madrid: Aguilar, 1947. vol. I.

60 Vid. *Un viaje de novios*, en O.C., op. cit. p. 95.

61 Vid. *Insolación*, en O.C., op. cit. pp. 524-525.

62 También el convento aparece en la obra de doña Emilia como una solución decorosa para la muchacha, y tranquilizadora para la misma familia. Vid. *Memorias de un solterón*, en O.C. Madrid: Aguilar, 1947.

63 Vid. *Doña Milagros*, en O.C.II , op. cit. p. 451.

64 Vid. *Memorias.....*, op. cit., pp. 527-528; 544-547.

65 E. Pardo Bazán, "La mujer española", en *La España Moderna*, marzo 1890, p. 106.

66 *Una cristiana*, op. cit., p. 713.

67 Vid. *La prueba*, en O.C. I, p. 744.

68 Vid. *Doña Milagros*, op. cit. p.476.

[69] Doña Emilia, que ha tomado parte en el debate feminista de la época, y conoce bien los prejuicios sociales que limitan y condicionan la vida de la mujer, crea en las dos primeras y únicas novelas del interrumpido ciclo "Adán y Eva" —*Doña Milagros* y *Memorias de un solterón*—, un personaje, Feíta, que es la encarnación de su propio ideal femenino.

[70] Vid. *Memorias...*, pp. 560 ss.

[71] Idem. pp. 572-573.

[72] Vid *Doña Milagros*, op. cit. p. 495-496.

[73] Su obra, sus artículos y su participación en distintos congresos, conferencias, etc., dan fe de ello.

[74] Recordemos que los últimos años del siglo XIX coinciden con la crisis económica de la Gran Depresión, con la presencia en la calle del mundo obrero, con la crisis del positivismo —filosofía de la burguesía—, y con una serie de guerras coloniales que terminaron en el Desastre del 98.

EN-GENDERING STRATEGIES OF AUTHORITY:
EMILIA PARDO BAZAN AND THE NOVEL

Maryellen Bieder
Indiana University

...si la señora duquesa levantase la cabeza
había de alegrarse de ver a una joven marinedina tan instruida y tan amiga de libros como
lo era la señora. *Memorias de un solterón*

When my interest in the dynamics of female authorship first lead me to reread Emilia Pardo Bazán a decade
ago, I sought to discover how a female author constructs
in her writing the female role models which her own life
seems to embody. I saw Pardo Bazán's fiction as a supple-
ment to her essays, the projection in textual form of contemporary debates over social reforms in opportunities
and roles for women. But as I read her novels I came to
the conclusion that the textual construction of female experience seemed to reinforce existing patterns for women,
rather than to challenge them. Although Pardo Bazán
clearly incorporates into her fiction social questions of
immediate concern to her contemporaries, she appeared
ultimately to retreat from social change and to reaffirm the
authority of a patriarchal society (see Bieder, "Marriage").

In the decade since I first began formulating my reading
of Pardo Bazán's novels, two major factors have reshaped
the context of our reading of female authors. On the one
hand, the development of an extraordinary fertile feminist
criticism, especially rich in studies of English and American women writers, has posed new questions of texts and
made imperative the rethinking of traditional parameters
of reading. On the other hand, a growing awareness of the
scope and nature of the female literary tradition has given
us a new context in which to read women writers. Emilia
Pardo Bazán herself appears to contextualize her own fic-

tion largely within the contemporary male literary tradition, and we have continued to read her within that tradition. At the same time, in her essays she identifies a female literary tradition in Spain.[1] Her rereading of these female precursors serves to naturalize her own writing within a tradition of talented writing women.

As long as the model of reading remains male-defined, the relationship of a woman author to her text constitutes an anomaly, a deviation from the normative author-reader relationship. To a greater extent than when reading male authors, readers have sought signs of the woman author's presence, that is to say her "difference," in her fiction. Perhaps in response to this imposition of the woman author onto her texts, "women's fiction," fiction written by women for women, specifically proliferates with signs of its female authorship and its female reader. If not by linking textual events with the author's own life, then by identifying female sentiments, emotions and experiences at all levels with those of the author, readers have projected a definition of female authorship onto the text itself. The problem as I perceive it is to read the woman author in her text, that is, to read a woman-authored text, without merging the biographical author with her characters' experiences or sentiments. We need, in Nancy K. Miller's phrase, to "discover the embodiment in writing of a gendered subjectivity; to recover within representation the emblems of its construction" ("Arachnologies" 272).

Pardo Bazán necessarily writes as a woman, but she also consciously situates her texts within established generic conventions, writing within realist, naturalist, or *costumbrista* modes, for example, and drawing on the discourses of science, art, literature and hagiography, among others. In short, she interweaves multiple discursive and generic strategies in a single text, as I have argued elsewhere (see "Female Voice"). What sets Pardo Bazán apart from her contemporary female writers in this regard is her ability to manipulate the conventions of generic traditions to produce in the reader different and at times competing effects. The importance of identifying the weight of genre and the pull of gender enters feminist critical discourse with Elaine Showalter's *A Literature of Their Own* and expands dynamically throughout Gilbert and Gubar's discussion in *The Madwoman in the Attic*. In Hispanic criticism, Susan Kirkpatrick has shown the significance of assessing gender and genre in reading *La gaviota*.

Following quite different patterns from those employed by the majority of her contemporary women writers in Spain, Pardo Bazán seeks to write within the reigning currents of male narrative and to address the same broad readership as do her male contemporaries. To some extent one could argue that Pardo Bazán's ideal readers are male. Like her contemporary male authors, she writes within and for a patriarchal society and she builds her fiction on analogous patriarchal structures and institutions (even on closed and intensely patriarchal worlds, as in *Los pazos de Ulloa*). She employs male-voiced strategies at both the (implied) authorial and narrative levels to shape her fictional world. By adopting male-voicing, Pardo Bazán creates no disruption for her readers on the surface. She does not create an identifiably female voice, either in focalized narration or through a dramatized female narrator. Nor is the undramatized narrative voice in her novels overtly female.[2] Instead, Pardo Bazán gives shape to female experience within her novels through a male narrator or focalizer writing from within a male-centered society and circumscribed by a predominantly male-defined authorial voice.[3]

Writing during the same period which produced the great woman-centered novels in European fiction, Emilia Pardo Bazán in contrast de-centers female experience in her fiction. Through her manipulation of genre traditions, she opens up a space at the confluence of competing conventions which allows her to deflect recognized narrative strategies to fulfill unexpected functions. In so doing, she is exploiting the potential which the novel offers for reshaping and rewriting existing models. In discussing Pardo Bazán's novels, Maurice Hemingway argues convincingly that "the conflict between Romanticism and Realism...is one of the major concerns of her fiction" (47). As Noël M.

Valis persuasively demonstrates in her reading of *El Cisne de Vilamorta*, the novel is essentially a cannibalistic form which ritually, relentlessly devours other forms whole and then transforms them" (322).

Within the generic conventions which she so effectively deploys and displays, Pardo Bazán elaborates a disruptive vision in her fiction. Without appearing to reject conventional techniques of plotting, structure and narrative, at a deeper level she subverts their function. The works I wish to privilege in this discussion of authority are precisely those in which Pardo Bazán appears to distance her female characters from the centers of institutional, social and narrative authority in her textual world. I draw on the Gilbert and Gubar discussion of authority for my treatment of the strategies of authority in Pardo Bazán's fiction. Like the authors they examine, Pardo Bazán inscribes in her fiction the conflict between male authority and the "monstrous" embodiment of female autonomy (28). But authority in textual terms does not limit itself to male-female, or author-character conflicts. Edward Said cogently observes that in most literary texts "the unity or integrity of the text is maintained by a series of genealogical connections: author-text, beginning-middle-end, text-meaning, reader-interpretation, and so on" (cited by Gilbert and Gubar, 5). These connections reveal hierarchical assumptions which embody the layers of authority implicit in the narrative, structural (plot), and reader response levels of textual construction and communication. In examining the relationship of female experience to "authority" in Pardo Bazán's fictional worlds, I am applying the term to at least four levels of textual communication.

External to the text is the authority evoked by the writer herself, authority which Susan S. Lanser formulates in the following terms: "In all forms of verbal activity, whatever is known about the identity of a speaker affects the degree and manner in which the audience is disposed to receive, interpret, and evaluate the message s/he communicates" (87). The genre whose conventions shape the reading process at any given point in the text imposes the second level of authority on the reader. Thirdly, the narrative voice, whether dramatized or not, communicates the world of the text to the reader with varying degrees of authority. Within the textual world itself, of course, some characters embody greater authority than others; male characters traditionally convey the authority of their sex, as well as their social, economic, and moral positions. Only a few specially situated female characters attain a similar authority. The problem of embodying authority in the female may explain in part the continued presence of aristocratic female characters in late 19th-century fiction as models of social and moral authority.

The authority communicated by the author of a text is external to that text, being grounded in social identity, biography, cultural and historical circumstances, whereas the other levels of authority take shape within the text itself. The question of the authority of a woman writer is always problematic. Women authors in the 19th century, both contemporaries of Emilia Pardo Bazán and women of earlier generations, adopt two primary strategies for dealing with the problem of authority. The use of a male pseudonym serves as an erasure of difference, a surface masking of the problematic relationship of female authors to their texts. By altering reader expectations, pseudonymous women authors open up the restricted space of female narrative and ease the boundaries of genre. (The manner and extent to which women writers exploit the potential of this strategy is not at issue here.) In her short novel, "La corruptora y la buena maestra," Cecilia Böhl de Faber demonstrates that the inverse strategy fulfills an analogous function for male writers. Her female character rails against the attack on Andalucía and on another author by a novelist, an "autor (que se firmaba *autora*, pero que a nadie engañó, y el que lo quiso saber supo quién lo había escrito)" (218). Shielding himself behind a female identity, the disguised male author creates a different narrative space for himself, one which apparently exempts him from responsibility for his novel.

The opposite strategy from pseudonymous authorship serves other women writers contemporaneous with Pardo

Bazán precisely as a way of affirming the strictures of female narrative space and confirming reader expectations. By underscoring their female identity and the female-linked genres within which they write, women maintain the stability and authority of their relationship with their readers.

In contrast to these two dominant strategies, Pardo Bazán locates the authority of authorship in her own name. While many contemporaneous women writers foreground the social status of marriage in their literary signature (for example, María del Pilar Sinués de Marco, Concepción Gimeno de Flaquer), Pardo Bazán retains her own constant writing identity. In so doing she marks the separation of her social identity from her writing self.[4]

Until recently, however, critics have denied the authority embodied in Pardo Bazán's name and attempted to displace her writing self by representing the author as "la Condesa," "doña Emilia," or simply "Emilia." In privileging her gender and her social identity, critics subordinate her individual creative voice to patriarchal authority. The use of an undifferentiated first name implies a personal bond between critic and author that subordinates the author to the critic. As "doña Emilia," the writer is always daughter, never the male writer's equal. These strategies of subordination serve to denature the threat the female writer poses to the male writer's exclusive claim to creative expression. (Although the presence of the feminine marker corresponds to the gender imperative of the Spanish language, the gendered designation "la Pardo Bazán" similarly serves to mark her subordination to the dominant male discourse. The presence of the article marks the woman author as the "other," as not male.) It is significant that recent feminist critics break this pattern by suppressing the grammatical (la Pardo Bazán) or social (la Condesa, doña Emilia) signifiers that mediate the authority of the writer.[5] The elimination of markers represents a challenge to and rejection of the dominant critical discourse. In wresting the writing self away from her assimilation and denaturalization by patriarchal literary culture, critics are now challenging the very processes that made possible her incorporation into the canon. In addition to locating the authority of her texts in her own name, Pardo Bazán adopts another highly significant strategy for aligning authority with female authorship: she shapes the conventions of different generic traditions to her own purposes. She thus diminishes the authority of genre on reading and keeps the reader in flux under the pressure of competing responses. Maneuvering within alternative genre conventions, rather than writing from within the authority of one established genre and confirming its reader expectations, Pardo Bazán writes for a male or mixed readership rather than for the predominantly female readership of her contemporary women authors. Other women writers frequently address their *lectoras* directly, shaping an image of their ideal reader and guiding the response to their text. Although Pardo Bazán adheres to the realist conventions of narration, her dramatized male narrators employ the conventions of direct reader address. Within her novels, then, a male narrator may ingenuously abuse the reader address of a male author to his male audience which Pardo Bazán herself avoids. By not addressing a reader directly, she avoids reducing the limits of her authority by circumscribing the boundaries of her readership. She offers instead an open challenge to the reader to read without overt signposts to mark the route.

In her novels Pardo Bazán creates a text world in which authority at all levels is exercised by men: social authority, narrative authority and the authority of reading. The female presence in this world is thus projected through the multiple layers of male authority. By definition, female characters do not inhabit the space of authority. In her play *Cuesta abajo*, for example, Pardo Bazán resolves this problem by locating female authority in the matriarchal figure of the grandmother who reclaims moral and economic authority when her son and grandson no longer exercise them. Apart from the elderly matriarch, a figure associated primarily with rural Galician aristocracy in Pardo Bazán as in Valle-Inclán, female authority figures are rare. The strong-willed female, for example Ilduara in *Memorias de un solterón*, embodies a monstrous challenge to male authority in her reversal of normative gender attributes. Ilduara's strong will dominates her husband's weak one; at the same time his generative capacity results in the 28 pregnancies of her astonishingly fertile, and ultimately self-destructive, reproductivity. Each spouse embodies the grotesque and complementary exaggeration of gender norms. Hence the strong female is traditionally a comic figure, especially in male-authored texts. In female-authored texts the exericise of authority may carry a cautionary message; Ilduara's unceasing responsiveness to her husband drains her of her own life.

Having invoked the layers of authority which constrict her female characters, Pardo Bazán has then to de-authorize these strictures in order to rewrite the boundaries of female experience. The weight of male-centered social institutions and the counterweight of female experience constitute the dual and contradictory impulses which dominate her texts. The mechanism which makes possible the space for the expression of female experience within a world which denies this very experience is the narrator (in a first-person narrative) or focalizer (in a third-person narrative). By incorporating the perception of female experience as difference and by giving expression to female experience on the same plane as male experience, the narrator integrates female experience into the male world. In short, while Pardo Bazán does not give the dominant discourse to the female voice in her text, she nevertheless writes the experience of being female in a patriarchal society into that text. In Pardo Bazán's novels to be a woman is to exist from a male perspective, to be seen and judged by men. Her central female characters are viewed objects, women perceived and written by individual men and, by extension, by the norms of the male community.

In order to open a space within the text for the representation of female experience, Pardo Bazán faces the double task of establishing the norms of the textual world and simultaneously subverting them to allow for female authority. The difficulty arises in granting authority to a female since her experiences, perceptions and knowledge, being those of a female, are inherently unreliable. This problem, of course, does not arise with male figures unless the text explicitly problematizes their reliability. The parameters of reliability and conformity within which a male narrator or focalizer operates are flexible. Pardo Bazán explores this flexibility in novels written between 1886 and 1896 by utilizing male focalizers, from Julián in *Los pazos de Ulloa* to Gabriel Pardo in *La madre naturaleza*, or male narrators, from Salustio in *Una cristiana* and *La prueba* to Benicio Neira in *Doña Milagros* and Mauro Pareja in *Memorias de un solterón*. In the tension between the prescribed male role and the self-projection of her narrators, Pardo Bazán begins to undermine the normative vision of society which those very narrators, focalizers and centers of consciousness convey. My contention here is that Pardo Bazán specifically adopts a male narrator to shape and transmit female experience in her fiction, but the male center of narrative consciousness himself occupies an ambiguous position with regard to the normative structure which he conveys and within which he functions.

Critics have condemned Pardo Bazán's failure to mask her own voice as she projects her novelistic vision through a male narrative voice, arguing that she continues to write as a woman even when the narrator/writer is male. Hemingway, for example, detects the overlay of Pardo Bazán's voice onto that of her narrator Salustio in *Una cristiana* and *La prueba*, observing that Salustio "notices and comments on things which one would expect to interest only a woman" (72). One might argue, of course, that Pardo Bazán constructs her narrative on what she perceives as a distinctly *male*, as opposed to female, voice and that the critic mistakenly reads this as exclusively female. It is quite possible that Pardo Bazán draws the boundaries of male and female knowledge and experience differently from where we contemporary readers expect. In these novels she does not account for male experience and knowledge; she assumes their existence for the male, whereas elsewhere she must account for female knowledge and make possible female experience.

In other novels Pardo Bazán consciously deconstructs the rigid boundaries of male and female social and sexual roles. Her use of the male narrative voice explores the possibilites of the dramatized male narrator to project female experience from within the male-centered society. By making her male narrators receptive to the female perspective and experience, she opens up the way for double-voiced narration within the controling male-voiced narrative. In two of her novels the narrators convey normative definitions of male and female while consciously or effectively violating them in their own lives. Pardo Bazán exploits the fusion of female consciousness and male gender to great effect in *Los pazos de Ulloa* and *La madre naturaleza*.

By again exploiting gender role ambiguity and strong maternal models in *Doña Milagros*, Pardo Bazán constructs a narrator whose ambivalent modeling of male sexuality and failure to exercise authority (except in the strict sense of paternity where his authorship manifests itself in excess) result from a close identification with female suffering. This makes the narrator sympathetic to Doña Milagros's ambiguous status as a childless wife and, on the level of narrative, an emotional, unperceptive and unreliable witness and narrator. In *Memorias de un solterón* Pardo Bazán most visibly deconstructs gender boundaries and foregrounds female experience within the male-voiced narrative of Mauro Pareja. As in two earlier novels, *Una cristiana* and *La prueba*, she also problematizes gender through incorporating contemporary debates over female emancipation and gender identity. Her characters discuss Ibsen's Nora and English suffragettes, for example, as they explore possible models for rewriting gender identity.

To a greater extent than in her earlier novels, *Doña Milagros* and *Memorias de un solterón* raise questions of gender definitions and social roles. In the words of an early reviewer of the novel, the 11 daughters of Benicio Neira give "motivo a la Sra. Pardo Bazán para pintar...las múltiples fases del carácter femenino; en la casa de D. Benicio hay de todo: la niña mística, en cuyo corazón se mezclan el amor divino y el humano; la entontecida señorita, que no piensa más que en trapos y moños; la muchacha indiferente y linfática; la joven exaltada y nerviosa; la avinagrada solterona y la chicuela diablejo, avispada y marisabidilla como ella sola" ("Lecturas").

Through the daughters Pardo Bazán represents a range of female responses to the diminished economic and social expectations and the stiffling reality of the gender proscriptions of their provincial society. In confronting directly the "binding of female energy" on which, as Naomi Schor shows for the French novel, "the production of realist fiction depends to an unsuspected degree," Pardo Bazán again challenges the gender conventions of the dominant genre (142).

The female is both disembodied ideal and immediate experience for Pardo Bazán's focalizers and narrators. The embodied (sexual) female subverts the narrator's image of the female coded since childhood in the image of the widowed, abandoned or martyred mother. The insistence on the moral authority of the idealized female becomes untenable in the face of the social, sexual and emotional reality of woman, forcing the son/man to choose between the female ideal and the flesh-and-blood individual onto whom he has projected this scripted role. If in the first two novels, Julián and Gabriel's projection of the ideal woman meshes uneasily with the living figure, in Salustio adoration of the unattainable woman coexists with the desire for possession. In the last two novels the narrators' textual projection of the female, the rewriting of the female into a recognizable text, founders on the active experience on the female herself. Neither Doña Milagros nor Feíta Neira is reducible to pre-scripted text nor submerged into the self-effacing mother. In these novels especially the female embodies a physical, sexual reality which the narrator cannot displace and distance from himself.

Once the authority from within which the narrator writes is established—this is not in itself a problem when the narrator is male, as I have already argued—the narrator's degree of reliability may vary without eroding the underlying authority of his narrative. The act of narrating retains its authority even as the narrator loses his reliability for the reader. Especially in matters which regard the fickle and inherently unreliable sex, the reader does not expect the male narrator to model consistent authority or reliability. This is precisely the situation from which Mauro Pareja narrates in *Memorias de un solterón*. As an educated, cultured, professional gentleman, but above all as a man, Mauro voices the authority of the social order which he represents, even as he proclaims his own distance from it as a non-participating observer. At the same time, his carefully circumscribed attentions to women and his protestations of confirmed bachelorhood underscore his deviation from the normative patterns he communicates.

More effectively than in any other novel, Pardo Bazán employs a male narrator in *Memorias de un solterón* to construct a reading of female experience at odds with the dominant social norms from within which he narrates. As in any narrative, her vision requires the complicity of her readers to realize its subversion. The normative authority established within the text by the male narrator is displaced by growing dis-authorization in the face of the subversion of authority by the previously distanced and silenced female voice. This displacement of authority initially occurs within a limited domestic context, but the marriage of Mauro and Feíta brings her challenge to masculine authority into the social sphere. In the novels discussed earlier, marriage silences or subjugates the subversive potential of the female, whereas in *Memorias de un solterón* marriage reinforces female authority within the social structure.

As narrator, Mauro has authority grounded in the access to the institutional and social norms conferred by his sexual identity and confirmed and enhanced by the strategies of reader control exercised in the narrative. At the same time, Pardo Bazán problematizes and subverts each of these factors. The narrator's androgyny blurs normative male and female gender identification and suggests an overt rejection of sexuality. If society dismisses Feíta as the unwomanly woman, it also labels Mauro, the chaste don Juan, as the unmanly man. Both Mauro and Feíta construct their own gender boundaries at odds with the dominant social construction of gender identity, but while Mauro's definition is largely proscriptive, Feíta's is inherently expansive. The self Mauro's narrative projects is not the self he sees, nor is the female he condemns the Feíta the reader perceives. As distance and irony reveal the humorous unreliability of the narrator, they free the reader from seconding the narrator's disapproval of the comically marginal female, Feíta. The narrator's control over his narratee weakens and reverses as the narrator's unreliability in matters of human psychology reveals itself. Authorial irony distances reader and narrator in the face of the narrator's increasing falibility. The humor which marks the reader's disengagement from the narrator's inability to read competently his own situation serves to shift the reader further away from the narrator towards the reading he rejects. The implicit reader, like the narratee, is male, and hence he distances himself from Mauro without breaking the shared bond of identification with male experience and the male-center world. The reader reads against the narrator's protestations of disinterest and a commitment to bachelorhood, until reader and narrator come full circle and merge again in the resolution of marriage. The comic role reversals of two gender misfits, "el Abad" and "la mujer nueva," the narcissistic bachelor and the liberated young woman, restore balance through imbalance. By leading the reader away from the attitudes and experiences she appears to espouse, Pardo Bazán imposes a subversive vision on an unsuspecting public through the timeless strategies of comic devaluation and ironic reversal.[6]

I am suggesting here two contrasting movements in reader control, engagement and distancing, both categories explored by Robin Warhol in her recent study of the narrators in 19th-century English and American novels by women. On one level, Mauro Pareja's narrative strategies are directed towards engaging his narratee, whom he addresses frequently and eloquently. Even here distance is a factor and Mauro seeks to close the gap between them by allying his socially-bound narratee to his rejection of marriage. At another level, the implied author, by shaping the narrator's unreliability and constructing irony, projects an implied reader who reads *against* the narratee. The implied author thus employs a distancing narrative strategy to undermine the identification of narrator and narratee. Warhol queries at the close of her study whether "the engaging narrator [is] a historical phenomenon, reflecting certain nineteenth-century women's impulses to speak—if not from a pulpit then from a text—directly, personally, and influentially in the only public forum open to them" (817). Pardo Bazán certainly finds a forum in fiction and exercises through it the control of reader expectations and responses. But more than through direct reader address she conveys her voice in the subversion of patterns of social and sexual identity and thus, by extension, in the subversion of strategies of authority at the narrative and experiential levels.

In *Memorias de un solterón,* Feíta moves within the space of the male-voiced narrative from ex-centric, antisocial margination towards the attainment of authority within society. This movement towards authority is triple-pronged, shaped by three privileged spaces outside the social norm: Mauro Pareja's library, Doctor Moragas's scientific knowledge, and Primo Cova's silence (that is, his suspension of verbal damnation in forgoing gossip about Feíta). In another dual and contradictory movement, the protection afforded Feíta by the town gossip allows the subversion of the male prerogative of knowledge to proceed. A library constitutes exclusionary space sealed off from women, for whom reading is a controlled activity. Feíta's access to the library represents her entrée into the rights and privileges of the male sphere through access to the inherited knowledge on which male authority resides. To Mauro, Feíta's uncontrolled appetite for reading constitutes an essential dimension of her lack of femininity. Having violated the strictures of female experience by reading mysticism, physiology and medicine, novels by

Ortega y Frías, and "hasta las poesías de Verlaine que le facilitó secretamente un empleado en la biblioteca del Puerto" (469), Feíta is unfit for womanhood. She has crossed the barrier into the sphere of male knowledge and male-voiced experience and at its most deadly points. But by meeting in the library, Feíta and Mauro center their acquaintance outside the normative social sphere and trace a shared if unsanctioned space on which to build their relationship.

The source of transmission of the library collection which Mauro controls and Feíta invades is, perhaps not surprisingly, female. A female guardian, Mauro's landlady, safeguards the collection and at the same time converts it into an object devoid of intrinsic value, possessed as an icon. From its owner, a liberal bibliophile, to his friend, the Duchess, to her companion in exile, Mauro's landlady, the library passes intact and inviolate. The forbidden fruit of knowledge guarded in the sanctum sanctorum by women like Doña Consola, who never enters except to dust (and who, not coincidentally, has delivered the key to the only reader, Mauro), makes an intellectual meal for Feíta in her ravenous appetite for education. Women may serve as the keepers of culture, but men are its active producers and consumers.[7]

Pardo Bazán's irony comes clear in the inviolate transmission of the library from female to female in between male readers. At the same time, Pardo Bazán suggests a female precursor for Feíta in the Duchess, a model of independence and liberalism revered by Doña Consola and rejected by Mauro as a product of her English exile. Devoted to the memory of her mistress, Doña Consola makes Feíta the Duchess's heir: "si la señora duquesa levantase la cabeza había de alegrarse de ver a una joven marinedina tan instruida y tan amiga de libros como lo era la señora" (479). Feíta is no longer alone and anomalous in her desire for education and independence, even if an earlier Marineda woman who attained a degree of both lived abroad as the wife of an exiled liberal. Pardo Bazán offers an unassailable model to counterbalance Mauro's negative judgment of Feíta, an aristocratic lady with unimpeachably

charitable credentials, the Duquesa de la Piedad. In delin-
eating a female precursor for Feíta, Pardo Bazán suggests a
diachronic female community to compensate for the lack
of a synchronic female community. Outside the home and
its competitive, and normatively temporary, community
of unmarried sisters, female communities rarely exist in
Pardo Bazán's fiction.[8]

Mauro initially labels Feíta unfeminine and unladylike
in physical as well as moral and social terms. As with others of Pardo Bazán's "flawed" female characters, Fe Neira
reveals, among her other imperfections which distort the
female ideal, "indicios de bozo" (468). The androgyny implicit in her unfettered movements and behavior is confirmed in a slight but ominous moustache. And yet Pardo
Bazán undermines Mauro's reading of Feíta by making
him the vehicle for conveying contradictory readings of
the same text in an interpretive act which replicates the
reader's role throughout the novel. As text, Feíta embodies hidden meaning beneath the facile surface reading. After first enumerating her flaws, Mauro finds a model for
Feíta in the female figure in a Florentine bronze and recognizes the contradiction in these dual readings: "Sólo que
para adivinar esta que, sin duda alguna, es perfección y
gracia del cuerpo de Feíta, hay que ser, más que lince, za-
horí" (469). Damnation, an excess fringe of hair, and
salvation, an analogue in Renaissance art, coexist in
Mauro's narrative as Pardo Bazán uses him both to convey his immediate, flawed reading of Feíta and to ground
his long-range reversal of this misperception. The submerged reading sets in motion the process of undermin-
ing Mauro's authority in matters feminine and amorous
and reversing Feíta's distance from the model of female
beauty.

Pardo Bazán utilizes the convention of marriage to effect reversal and impose textual closure in *Memorias de
un solterón*. For both male and female, marriage represents a change of status and the end of a trajectory. Since
marriage defines the woman's future role, it marks the
working out of the plot of the marriageable young woman
and exhausts her potential as novelizable material (Hinz,

903-04; Boone, "Modernist Maneuverings" 376). In this case, closure through marriage completes the reversal of the socially disruptive identities of bachelor and independent woman. Of course, marriage itself also becomes novelizable, with an inward-focused tension (woman-man) not a socially-focused tension (woman-society), but the novel-culminating-in-marriage and the novel-of-marriage remain two largely differentiated structures. Pardo Bazán herself utilizes both these plot structures, writing the story of a marriage in *Un viaje de novios, Los pazos de Ulloa* and *Doña Milagros*, while closing *La madre naturaleza* and *Memorias de un solterón*, for example, with a decision about marriage.[9] In the latter case, Pardo Bazán blurs the boundary between the two plot structures by leaving the ending open to the possibility of a further volume of "memorias de un casado."

In her novels Pardo Bazán not only invokes but also problematizes the function of marriage as textual closure. If in social terms, marriage integrates both male and female into the social fabric, beneath the surface of this strategy of closure Pardo Bazán constructs a text which carries its subversion of gender identity into the social definition of marriage. In his study of marriage in the 19th-century Anglo-American novel, Joseph A. Boone reaches a similar conclusion, arguing that "the perpetuation of conventional marriage (as theme) and narrative closure (as form) have reinforced each other, and that novels that have subverted the conventional marriage theme have done so through analogous subversions of formal conventions" (*Tradition Counter Tradition*). While utilizing marriage as a device for structuring plot, Pardo Bazán subverts it as a confirmation of the male-female gender assumptions on which it rests. The multiple marriages in *Doña Milagros* and *Memorias de un solterón* share a constant feature: the inability of the individual to model his or her ideal gender role in marriage. Avoided or sought, within or between classes, childless or hyperproductive, no marriage fulfills the social expectations of both partners. Rather than the synthesis of opposites or the harmonious equality it represents in the fiction of many of her contemporary women writers, marriage in Pardo Bazán's fiction inscribes a permanent imbalance. Strong-willed female/weak-willed male, childless wife/manly but sterile male, the non-normative gender modeling of each partner defies resolution. In *Memorias de un solterón* even the seduced-and-abandoned plot of an earlier novel, *La tribuna*, is rewritten through a belated marriage, but the new ending does not erase the original plot or its tensions. Surface conformity belies hidden disruption in these novels, because marriage does not free the individual from either the self-imposed or the externally-imposed tyranny of gender definition.[10]

At the level of plotting, then, Pardo Bazán does not so much model alternative roles for women as subvert the existing boundaries of gender definition which circumscribe social patterns, spheres of movement, and socially-defined marriage roles. In her novel the marriage plot may function to impose closure on the narrative, but marriage itself projects an open-ended, conflictive process rather than stasis. In defying social norms through their self-projected gender definitions, Feíta and Mauro differ from other couples in Pardo Bazán's novels for whom the need to model the social norms makes marriage an experience of deception. Indeed, one could argue, adapting Nancy K. Miller's argument, that Pardo Bazán has inscribed "the sign of both-and, concretized by [Feíta's] final dual residence": in gendered society *and* in marriage (Miller, "Emphasis Added," 43).

Feíta gains authority over her own life as Mauro Pareja loses authority over his and thus over the material of his own narrative. At the close of *Memorias de un solterón* Feíta already exercises her new authority (in itself a usurpation of male authority) to impose a verbal shape on the lives of her siblings. In upholding the moral norms of the patriarchal community, she enacts male authority on a female community.[11] At the same time she uses her authority to enunciate previously unspoken alternatives not sanctioned by social norms. Feíta shares the central space of authority with Mauro, but within the family the patriarchal voice is hers. In marriage the authority attained by

Feíta through her own experiences gains social sanction and a social forum. In the subversion of rigid gender identity and the association of gender and authority, Pardo Bazán rewrites the conventional closure of marriage and creates a socially-sanctioned space (which displaces the library) within which both male and female enact their gender difference (difference from each other and from the community). Through her male narrator Pardo Bazán has communicated the trajectory of female experience from a position of ex-centricity to one of socially-sanctioned centrality in the male world of her novel. With *Memorias de un solterón* she opens a new space within which a woman embodies and voices authority.

NOTES

[1] References to Spanish women writers occur throughout Pardo Bazán's essays. Among the women of her century she cites Concepción Arenal, Gertrudis Gómez de Avellaneda, Cecilia Böhl de Faber, Carolina Coronado and Teresa Arróniz. Pardo Bazán conceived and edited the Biblioteca de la Mujer, which includes works by la Venerable de Agreda and María de Zayas, in an attempt to give women a parallel cultural formation and forge a shared female culture among middle class women. As she asserts in an article in *La Época* in 1896, "El número de mujeres verdaderamente superiores, sin que por esto sean célebres, sería incalculable; la mujer española es inteligente y la instrucción hacía aquí maravillas."

[2] While identifying the narrative voice in *Los pazos de Ulloa* as feminine, Carlos Feal remarks on Pardo Bazán's use of male-voicing at both levels, observing that "hay momentos en que la voz narradora, lejos de expresarse en términos femeninos o de fundirse con la voz del sacerdote, coincide extrañamente con la de la sociedad masculina reflejada en la novela" ("La voz femenina" 215).

[3] In an article on irony and the representation of female characters in Pardo Bazán, Galdós and Clarín, Biruté Ciplijauskaité makes in passing a similar observation which she applies to *Los pazos de Ulloa*: "otra observación curiosa: estas novelas aparentemente dedicadas a la mujer son en realidad novelas de hombres" (132). Elsewhere I have ar-

gued that within the male-voiced narrative of *La madre naturaleza* a female voice is discernible (Bieder, "The Female Voice.")

4 Carmen Bravo-Villasante records the opposite phenomenon in Pardo Bazán's private life. As a young married woman she romantically intertwines the "J" of her husband's name (José) with her own, signing her correspondence "J. Emilia" or "J. Emilia Pardo Bazán." Bravo-Villasante identifies this practice as "siguiendo la costumbre aristocrática." Pardo Bazán drops this symbolic subordination in the aftermath of the *La cuestión palpitante* controversy which led to her separation from her husband. Pp. 94-95.

5 The use of female markers still prevailed when Ruth A. Schmidt published her feminist reading of *Insolación* in 1974. Some earlier critics referred to the author consistently by her full name; see, for example, Gregorio (and María?) Martínez Sierra's article on "La feminidad de Emilia Pardo Bazán."

6 Feíta's first, silent suitor is a masculine male of ambiguous social identity. Although on the surface their alliance would challenge the social order, the putative social rebel upholds and indeed enforces the social model of the (incompatible) marriage. Despite appearances, he models conformity to gender definitions. Thus they only appear to share the project of challenging social and/or gender strictures. The comic reversal lies in his rewriting the past rather than engendering a new future.

7 In contrast, of course, the library of that masculine world, *Los pazos de Ulloa*, lies abandoned and decaying, reclaimed by nature like the degenerate patriarchal culture which it records. The library is thus a potent representation of historical decline and the ruin of patriarchal culture.

8 One of Feíta's sisters exchanges the impecunious sororal community of the family for its genteel counterpart, the female community of the Benedictinas in Santiago. In contrast to the solitude in which middle-class females live, the community of women who congregate around Sabel and María la Sabia in *Los pazos de Ulloa* convert the netherworld of the kitchen into female space, in an inverted image of the patriarchal world of the *pazo* itself.

9 As Carlos Feal Deibe observes, Pardo Bazán "formula una crítica contra el matrimonio" as early as *Un viaje de novios* ("Religión y feminismo" 193).

10 I apply here the argument developed by Joseph A. Boone in his illuminating study of *The Golden Bowl*. Like James, Pardo Bazán inscribes "gender-related schisms of marital unhappiness into the text itself"; p. 377.

11 Feíta exercises authority in the absence of a male figure: her father is dead, her brother is unresponsive to the demands of the family, and she has as yet no husband. On the one hand, Pardo Bazán contradicts Schor's thesis that "representation in its paradigmatic nineteenth-century form depends on the bondage of woman" (142). Through Mauro Pareja's narrative of male experience, Pardo Bazán "unbinds" Feíta Neira's intellectual, sexual and creative energy. At the same time, in assuming the position of authority within the family and within marriage, Feíta herself binds her sisters to the patriarchal canons of morality and duty. Nevertheless, by defining the social and economic circumstances of her siblings, she reverses her father's inability to come to terms with these circumstances.

WORKS CITED

Bieder, Maryellen. "Capitulation: Marriage, Not Freedom. A Study of *Memorias de un solterón* and *Tristana*." *Symposium* 30 (1976): 97-113.

—. "The Female Voice: Gender and Genre in *La madre naturaleza*." *Anales Galdosianos* 22 (1987): in press.

Böhl de Faber, Cecilia. "La corruptora y la buena maestra." In *El alcázar de Sevilla, Simón Verde y otras relaciones*. Sevilla: Editoriales Andaluzas Unidas, 1985, pp. 189-227.

Boone, Joseph A. "Modernist Maneuverings in the Marriage Plot: Breaking Ideologies of Gender and Genre in James's *The Golden Bowl*." *PMLA* 101 (1986): 374-88.

—. *Tradition Counter Tradition: Love and the Form of Fiction*. Chicago: University of Chicago Press, 1987.

Bravo-Villasante, Carmen. *Vida y obra de Emilia Pardo Bazán*. Madrid: Novelas y Cuentos, 1973.

Ciplijauskaité, Biruté. "El narrador, la ironía, la mujer: perspectivas del xix y del xx." In *Homenaje a Juan López-Morillas: De Cadalso a*

Aleixandre. Ed. José Amor y Vásquez and A. David Kossoff. Madrid: Castalia, 1982, pp.129-49.

Feal Deibe, Carlos. "Religión y feminismo en la obra de Emilia Pardo Bazán." In *Homenaje a Juan López-Morillas: De Cadalso a Aleixandre.* Ed. José Amor y Vásquez and A. David Kossoff. Madrid: Castalia, 1982, pp. 191-207.

—. "La voz femenina en *Los pazos de Ulloa.*" *Hispania* 70 (1987): 215-21.

Gilbert, Sandra M., and Susan Gubar. *The Madwoman in the Attic: The Woman Writer and the Nineteenth-Century Literary Imagination.* New Haven: Yale Univ. Press, 1979.

Hemingway, Maurice. *Emilia Pardo Bazán: The Making of a Novelist.* Cambridge: Cambridge Univ. Press, 1983.

Hinz, Evelyn J. "Hierogamy versus Wedlock: Types of Marriage Plots and Their Relationship to Genres of Prose Fiction." *PMLA* 91 (1976): 900-13.

Kirkpatrick, Susan. "On the Threshold of the Realist Novel: Gender and Genre in *La gaviota.*" *PMLA* 98 (1983): 323-40.

Lanser, Susan S. *The Narrative Act: Point of View in Prose Fiction.* Princeton: Princeton Univ. Press, 1981.

"Lecturas: La última novela de la Sra. Pardo Bazán." *La Epoca,* 7 May 1894.

Martínez Sierra, Gregorio. "La feminidad de Emilia Pardo Bazán." In *Motivos.* Madrid: Calleja, 1920, pp. 131-43.

Miller, Nancy K. "Arachnologies: The Woman, the Text, and the Critic." In *The Poetics of Gender.* Ed. Nancy K. Miller. New York: Columbia Univ. Press, 1986.

—. "Emphasis Added: Plots and Plausibilities in Women's Fiction." *PMLA* 96 (1981): 36-48.

Pardo Bazán, Emilia. "Un artículo de Doña Emilia Pardo Bazán: La mujer española." *La Epoca,* 6 February 1896, p. 1.

—. *Obras completas.* 3 vols. Madrid: Aguilar, 1973.

Schmidt, Ruth A. "A Woman's Place in the Sun: Feminism in *Insolación.*" *Revista de Estudios Hispánicos* 8 (1974): 69-81.

Schor, Naomi. *Breaking the Chain: Women, Theory, and French Realist Fiction.* New York: Columbia University Press, 1985.

Showalter, Elaine. *A Literature of Their Own: British Women Novelists from Brontë to Lessing.* Princeton: Princeton Univ. Press, 1977.

Valis, Noël M. "Pardo Bazán's *El Cisne de Vilamorta* and the Romantic Reader." *MLN* 100 (1986): 298-324.

Warhol, Robyn R. "Toward a Theory of the Engaging Narrator: Earnest Interventions in Gaskell, Stowe, and Eliot." *PMLA* 101 (1986): 811-18.

IMAGEN FEMENINA, HEGEMONIA Y DISCURSO LITERARIO

Cristina Dupláa
Universidad de Barcelona

La institucionalización de una cultura nacional, a partir de un modelo económico, social y político en un determinado espacio geográfico, al que denominamos nacionalidad —con o sin Estado jurídico—, permite al analista realizar un trabajo interdisciplinario donde se combinen metodologías que abarcan materias distintas. Así, la historia intelectual, la crítica literaria y, algo más importante para este trabajo: la necesidad de una nueva lectura de la Historia bajo parámetros de interpretación feminista, permitirán conocer hasta qué punto la utilización de la mujer como *objeto* sirve para legitimar un proyecto colectivo. Es en este preciso instante cuando el discurso literario servirá para "autentificar" los intereses nacionales de ese proyecto globalizador: de ese proyecto que se transmite bajo la retórica de un lenguaje interclasista, aunque en realidad es demostrable que son intereses de clase lo que, en verdad, está en juego.

La Cataluña finisecular, como otras nacionalidades europeas en el mismo momento (Bohemia, etc.) recuperan aquel romanticismo de principios del siglo XIX, adaptándolo a las nuevas necesidades del momento. Así, los sentimientos de libertad individual y de libertad de los pueblos del ideal romántico pueden llegar a armonizarse con los propósitos regeneracionistas de una intelectualidad y las aspiraciones modernizadoras de uno o varios grupos sociales. El resultado es ambiguo y contradictorio, pero ofrece muchas posibilidades analíticas por la diversidad de códigos que se entrecruzan para, finalmente, elaborar aquél que sea más reconocido por amplias capas de la población.

El trabajo ideológico que se lleva a cabo en todo el proceso no está, únicamente, condicionado por intereses de clase, sino también, de género. El discurso político y filosófico está hecho por hombres; las mujeres no participan en la elaboración de ideologías[1], pero su imagen es utilizada para legitimarlas. Pocas veces son sujetos literarios —en el período de fin de siglo hay pocas mujeres autoras— pero es indudable que son objetos de ese mundo ficticio y receptoras de las ideologías que lo sustentan. A veces el papel del receptor es activo y puede llegar a participar en la propia producción del discurso/mensaje[2], pero tampoco aquí las mujeres —salvo notables excepciones— han podido corresponder a las exigencias de un emisor masculino. Por lo tanto, su rol en la recepción también ha sido pasivo. Nos encontramos, pues, que la ideología dominante elabora un discurso patriarcal que aspirará a ser hegemónico dentro de una sociedad marcadamente clasista. Las mujeres reciben todo este código de actuación dentro de la doble perspectiva de género y clase. Una aproximación metodológica feminista hará énfasis en el primer concepto diferenciador citado, entendiéndolo, no como una diferencia biológica con contenidos genéticos y de especie humana, sino como una "diferencia adquirida". Es decir, a partir de una realidad social determinada de una cierta manera —arquetipo viril—[3] se ha modelado el comportamiento de los géneros masculino y femenino.[4]

LA BUSQUEDA DE UN PROYECTO HEGEMONICO

La crisis finisecular en España

La crisis de fin de siglo se vive en el Estado español como la crisis de un modelo económico que fracasa cuando se pierden las últimas colonias de ultramar; como la crisis de un modelo social que es ineficaz para la industrialización del país; como la crisis de un modelo político que funciona gracias a la concepción caciquil del sistema parlamentario; y como la crisis de un modelo ideológico de corte liberal que parte de una concepción jacobino-centralista de la estructura del Estado. El período de la Restauración, al tiempo que institucionaliza esta manera de entender España, la cuestiona y, a la vez, ofrece alternativas. Dos van a ser, principalmente, los focos de ese cuestionamiento. Uno, muy unido a los valores estéticos de la cultura castellana; y, otro, a los de la catalana. Alrededor del primero se sitúa la denominada Generación del 98, y, del segundo, los modernistas. Cada grupo de artistas (escritores, pintores) entenderá la solución de los males de España a partir de un conocimiento de las necesidades sociales que viven en su momento. Esta realidad social va a ser diferente según se viva en Barcelona o en Madrid; ambas ciudades se constituyen en capitales autónomas de cultura dentro de un universo latino, cuya metrópoli indiscutible es París.[5]

El nacionalismo catalán y el liberalismo español[6] van a cuestionar el modelo de la Restauración y a proponer alternativas regeneracionistas que van mucho más allá de los intentos noventayochistas y modernistas. Eugeni d'Ors (1881-1954) y José Ortega y Gasset (1883-1955) van a ser los líderes del pensamiento novecentista en sus respectivas culturas.

El novecientos se inicia con el objetivo de marcar distancias con la centuria anterior y sanear el país a partir de una propuesta nueva. D'Ors y Ortega renuncian a aquella juventud de lamentos al lado de los escritores del 98 y de los modernistas catalanes y emprenden toda una labor filosófica que acabará por proclamar la necesidad de conseguir una parcela de poder político. Por lo tanto, el salto dado en las intenciones doctrinales es considerable: ya no se habla de artistas, sino de intelectuales. Y esos intelectuales van a crear un cosmos ideológico donde se presenta como necesaria su participación en el nuevo proyecto colectivo. Ya no aceptan la idea del erudito marginado, sino que postulan la de guía de los ciudadanos; en definitiva, la de "seres escogidos" para marcar las directrices "científicas" a seguir por la gran masa.

La contraposición Cataluña-España

La modernización de la sociedad catalana se lleva a cabo a partir de una síntesis ideológica que une pasado, presente y futuro. En efecto, el discurso regeneracionista del modelo cultural de la nueva centuria, conocido por Noucentisme, cuenta con todo un trabajo doctrinal que pretende integrar aquellas corrientes de pensamiento que han configurado las aspiraciones nacionalistas de Cataluña. Así, los positivismos de la Restauración, ya sea el de corte cristiano-católico, liderado por el canónigo Jaume Collell (1846-1932) y el obispo de Vic Josep Torras i Bages (1846-1916) —y sintetizado en la frase:"Catalunya serà cristiana o no serà"— y el laico-federal con Valentí Almirall (1841- 1904) a la cabeza —resumido con ésta otra: "Catalunya serà moderna o no existirà"—, quedan sintetizados en una única doctrina.

La nacionalitat catalana (1906) de Enric Prat de la Riba (1870-1917) inaugura una nueva etapa en la historia intelectual. El siglo XX se inicia, pues, con un gran trabajo teórico —con bastantes elementos retóricos neo-románticos— que tiene como principal misión conseguir un modelo ideológico y cultural hegemónico. Es decir, la recuperación de la identidad catalana debe llevarse a cabo a partir de un esfuerzo colectivo donde queden fuera las tensiones sociales y las injusticias derivadas de unas relaciones económicas marcadamente clasistas. Por lo tanto, el discurso emitido para tal fin se caracterizará por su lenguaje interclasista. La aparición de conceptos románticos de la escuela historicista alemana, tales como el "volkgeist" o "espíritu nacional", junto a la influencia de la doctrina social de la Iglesia —especialmente de la Rerum Novarum—, desarrollada a raíz de los desequilibrios humanos derivados de la industrialización, van a ser pilares discursivos sobre los que se asentará el proyecto intelectual de los novecentistas catalanes. Ante tal situación la pregunta aparece de inmediato: ¿es posible compaginar estas aspiraciones ideológicas, fuertemente enraizadas en la tradición, con un planteamiento modernizador basado en el desarrollo de una industria nacional? No cabe duda de que es posible si hay una clase social poderosa capaz de hacer suyo ese discurso y esas necesidades sociales.

Haciendo un breve repaso histórico, vemos que en el último tercio del siglo XVIII se inicia en Cataluña el fenómeno industrializador, basado en el desarrollo de una industria textil, que entrado ya el siglo XIX, provocará una lucha ideológica de largas y duras consecuencias. La Cataluña industrial entrará en conflicto con la España agraria, chocará con su mentalidad no modernizadora y, especialmente, con su Estado, su burocracia y su ejército.[7] Este bienestar económico, basado en el desarrollo del sector secundario, dará pie a la aparición de una nueva clase hegemónica: la burguesía industrial, que unida a un sector medio integrado por comerciantes y artesanos independientes, y al proletariado de origen catalán, desembocará en una mentalidad moderna y, por encima de todo, urbana. Las necesidades económicas de esta población encuentran sus mayores obstáculos en la política llevada a cabo en Madrid, más sensible a los intereses de las oligarquías financieras y latifundistas que a la burguesía industrial. Los años finiseculares en Cataluña se caracterizarán por las campañas a favor del arancel proteccionista frente a las iniciativas librecambistas de los sectores que ostentan el poder central. Cuando la polémica se plantea abiertamente el propio discurso traiciona a ambas tendencias. A los industrialistas, basados en cierta medida en una argumentación realista, la retórica proteccionista los convierte en mentes limitadas y provincianas. A los segundos, la defensa del librecambismo los hace universalistas y liberales, sin tener en cuenta que España necesita la articulación de un mercado nacional fuerte que facilite la rápida acumulación de capital para invertirlo en el desarrollo de unos medios de comunicación y transporte modernos.

Las contradicciones ideológicas de esta polémica llegan a alcanzar su grado máximo cuando en aras a defender el proteccionismo como política de desarrollo, la burguesía industrial llega a pactar con los cerealistas castellanos, enemigos eternos en la lucha por reformar y modernizar el país en beneficio de una política proindustrial. A los librecambistas, tan desesperados como los demás ante la pérdida del mercado colonial en el 98, prefieren caer en ac-

titudes victimistas que buscar soluciones a la realidad latifundista del campo castellano y andaluz, principal obstáculo para la articulación de una sociedad avanzada con
pretensiones cosmopolitas.

Es evidente que tal estado de la cuestión ayuda a la contraposición Cataluña-España. Esa burguesía industrial se
siente como grupo social con características propias fuera y
dentro del territorio catalán y poco a poco consigue que sus
intereses no sean únicamente los de su clase, sino los de
toda la población catalana. Su hegemonía se basa precisamente en ese dato: empezar una reivindicación de clase y
acabar con una reivindicación nacional[8] (léase "nacional"
como sinónimo de "catalana").

El paso político se dará en 1901 con la creación de la
Lliga Regionalista, primer partido político que rompe el
tándem bipartidista del parlamentarismo de la Restauración; y, el ideológico, con la doctrina pratiana y los intelectuales capaces de asumirla y darle protagonismo en el proceso de institucionalización de la cultura catalana.

LAS MUJERES EN EL PENSAMIENTO OCCIDENTAL CONTEMPORANEO

A lo largo del siglo XIX el pensamiento occidental, o
mejor dicho, el discurso patriarcal de Occidente, elabora
una modelo de mujer en el ámbito de las ideas, en función
de las coyunturas ideológicas. Básicamente, serán tres las
figuras femeninas que el discurso literario recogerá y tras-
ladará al receptor/a como parte de un "todo" ideológico.

Hace escasamente un mes, la historiadora Michelle Perrot[9] ha sintetizado muy bien estas tres figuras en las Jornadas de Investigación Interdisciplinaria, organizadas por
el Seminario de Estudios de la Mujer de la Universidad
Autónoma de Madrid.

Siguiendo su esquema encontramos:

> *La mujer negra*, considerada como un ser histérico y enfermo,
> demasiado dominado por la naturaleza.
> *La mujer blanca*:
> —la "virgen" para los católicos. A lo largo del siglo XIX hay
> un renacimiento del culto a la Virgen.

—el "ángel del hogar" para los protestantes.
—la "musa laica" para los poetas, quienes la simbolizan con imágenes del mundo clásico. Vemos, pues, cómo las mujeres no son autoras,no son emisoras, pero sí son fuente de inspiración: es decir "medio" para la comunicación.
La mujer roja. El color de la sangre la asocia a la maternidad. En otras palabras: al nacionalismo biológico.
Tres funciones:
1—madre de la familia.
2—madre de la sociedad.
A través de esta doble misión consigue redimir su pecado original y educar a los futuros hombres/hijos. No hemos de extrañarnos por la utilización del género masculino porque las dos figuras femeninas más representativas del catolicismo tienen su procedencia en él: la Virgen es "madre de lo masculino" y Eva es "hija de lo masculino".[10]
3—madre de la Historia.

Los conceptos abstractos son representados por una imagen femenina: la patria, la nación, la justicia, la libertad, la constitución, etc.; mientras que el Estado, es masculino: es la representación jurídica del Dios-Padre, claramente definido en los tiempos del absolutismo por el Dios-Rey. Algunas de estas imágenes femeninas, como sería el caso de la que simboliza la República Francesa, aparecen con un seno descubierto, porque su objetivo y misión fundamental es la de MADRE; en este caso, madre de todos los franceses: Madre de la Historia de Francia.

Como señala la socióloga, Carmen Elejabeitia, en el pensamiento burgués hay un desvío de la vida individual hacia la Historia que se apoya, una vez más, "en situar a las mujeres en la función de reproducción, no en los estrictos términos biológicos de reproducción de la especie, sino en los más sofisticados —de ahí el desvío— de reproducción material del proyecto. (...) La institución familiar socialmente producida como unidad básica de la historia (...) *necesita* a la mujer/madre, y en tanto que la necesita, *la sujeta.*[11]

*Mujer/madre, Mujer/patria en el discurso nacionalista
catalán*

El discurso nacionalista que inaugura el período
romántico en Cataluña, cuya repercusión en la vida cultural se conoce historiográficamente por "Renaixença",
marca las primeras pautas de esa tradición en el discurso y
en la función social que el Noucentisme otorga a las
mujeres. Es a partir de la necesidad intelectual de recuperar una identidad para elaborar una cultura nacional que
la mujer, como figura, será el símbolo de la patria; y la familia, como institución, la metaforización del ser catalán.[12]
En una publicación de este período del renacimiento de la
lengua y cultura catalanas, aparecida en New York y titulada, *La Llumanera de Nova York*, se deja constancia del
papel/misión de las mujeres en esta nueva etapa histórica:
"...perque en la dona s'amotllan las generacions, perque la
dona es la anella de la cadena que uneix lo present ab lo
pervindra; perque la dona d'avuy es la encarregada de
formar la posteritat (sic)".[13]

Este modelo de reproductora se proyecta en el positivismo de corte cristiano. Así, tanto Jaume Collell como
Torras i Bages harán mención expresa de esta función social de las mujeres catalanas. Para Collell "la casa peyral"
—la casa familiar— es el lugar donde se nutre el espíritu
de las enseñanzas que generación tras generación se
transmiten por vía oral de padres a hijos. La metáfora de la
"casa" como sinónimo de "región" comporta que los
miembros de la familia sean los miembros de la regionali-
dad y, por tanto, los defensores de la catalanidad entendida
como concepción de vida.

De esta forma, Torras i Bages, fijando las bases de lo que
será el nacionalismo católico neo-romántico, afirma que:
"L'antigua casa catalana és un admirable exemplar de pur,
fecund i dolcíssim esperit de família". Se trata de mantener esta "casa" para transmitir a las futuras generaciones
este "espíritu de familia" —léase como sinónimo de
"espíritu nacional"— y, sin duda, las "transmisoras" de
todo el proceso son las mujeres. La mujer/madre dentro
de la casa acaba siendo la mujer/patria dentro de la nación,
y, por lo tanto, el símbolo de la continuidad y de la tradi-

ción. El propio obispo de Vic señala en la introducción de su libro, *La tradició catalana* (1892), que "patria" y "tradición" son sinónimos; con palabras suyas: "Pàtria i tradició" són una mateixa cosa pel ser racional (sic)". Por su parte, el positivismo laico de los federales evita hacer mención expresa del papel que han de ocupar las mujeres en la sociedad catalana que ellos propugnan. Almirall en su obra, *Lo Catalanisme* (1886), busca la realidad social y cultural del Estado español desde el punto de vista del "particularismo castellano" y del "particularismo catalán". Dada su renuncia, de forma explícita, a cualquier sistema filosófico de corte idealista no es fácil llegar a encontrar elementos retóricos que otorguen un lugar concreto a las mujeres. Almirall no habla de "familia", sino de "carácter", y el término "región" lo convierte en "pueblo", pero a ellas no las menciona.

Este período de fin de siglo marca de forma muy clara y definida las pautas ideológicas del pensamiento contemporáneo en Cataluña. Las dos propuestas citadas plantean la necesidad de una regeneración de la sociedad catalana a partir de la recuperación de unas señas de identidad. Los positivistas cristianos modernizarán, gracias al "discurso regionalista" —como ellos lo denominan—, los esquemas integristas que caracterizan a sectores del clero popular — muy vinculados al carlismo— y a la jerarquía —siempre reticiente a los cambios que comporta el pensamiento liberal. A los federales, el positivismo les sirve como instrumento para la denuncia objetiva de los males de la Restauración, al tiempo que frena el radicalismo verbal a favor de la Razón y la Libertad, que tanto los desprestigia después del fracaso de la I República. Los nuevos tiempos exigen la adaptación de la Tradición y la Monarquía a las necesidades de una sociedad moderna e industrial.

El Modernismo —en términos generales podría considerarse como la expresión cultural del positivismo laico— muestra, precisamente en las figuras femeninas que modela, las contradicciones del momento histórico. Utilizando el esquema de Michelle Perrot, me atrevería a señalar que la imagen de mujer que proyecta es una mezcla de la "mujer negra" y de la "mujer blanca", pero con un saldo favorable a la primera. La blanca o virginal aparecerá en la última etapa con la penetración en Cataluña del discurso neo-romántico del nacionalismo integral francés —concretamente de Maurice Barrès y su *Le jardin de Bérénice*—, desarrollando aquella figura finisecular de "mujer-frágil".[15]

Volviendo a las contradicciones ideológicas que sufren los artistas modernistas, encontramos que la mujer que aparece en sus textos, o bien está unida a la naturaleza[16], en el sentido más salvaje del término, o bien es un ser enfermizo y decadente muy unido a las imágenes de "mujer-demonio" y "mujer-carne" como sinónimos del "mal" y del "vicio". La mujer modernista no puede vencer las condiciones ambientales de su entorno y por esto es seductora y sensual. Más irreal que real y más objeto que sujeto se la utiliza de forma ambivalente: para ilustrar el mal espiritual y también la belleza del eterno femenino —recuérdese aquellas imágenes de mujeres con vestidos volátiles y cabellos largos. Los modelos literarios más conocidos son la Roda-soques de la novela de Raimon Casellas, *Els sots ferèstecs* (1901), y el de la Adelaisa de *El Comte Arnau* de Joan Maragall.[17]

El nuevo siglo, o mejor dicho la fecha de 1906, inicia con *La nacionalitat catalana* de Prat de la Riba otro período en el discurso nacionalista, cuyo propósito fundamental es unir esfuerzos y llegar a síntesis ideológicas para alcanzar el poder político en Cataluña, institucionalizar la cultura catalana y "catalanizar" al resto del Estado español. Se parte de que el modelo económico, social, político e ideológico que se está gestando en Cataluña es el más avanzado de la geografía peninsular, por tanto hay que modernizar España a partir de la experiencia catalana. Prat de la Riba no duda en calificar este proceso de: "etapa imperialista".

Quedan fuera aquellas contradicciones que desembocan en modelos femeninos débiles y sinónimos de maldad. Ahora hay que defender dos únicas imágenes: la de pureza espiritual, simbolizada por la mujer blanca o virginal y la de la belleza racial, hegemonizada a través de la mujer roja o madre de familia, de la sociedad: de la Historia de Cataluña. Es importante entender el término "historia" en su doble significado: el de pasado/tradición y el de futuro/transformación.

Una nueva mujer y una nueva estética

La mujer moderna[18] que el Noucentisme se propone modelar simbolizará en la vida real y en la ficción literaria las ansias del nacionalismo y del reformismo burgués. Precisamente su modernidad se eregirá en torno a la simbiosis: conservadurismo-nacionalismo. La sociedad precisa de una mujer instruida, culta, pero mantenedora de la esencia de la tradición. Los valores doctrinales del catolicismo social[19], junto a una participación en el nuevo proyecto ideológico-cultural —como elemento reproductor y como elemento estético— son los pilares sobre los que se sustentará la mujer novecentista.

A continuación intentaré analizar cuál es la imagen femenina y, en consecuencia, el modelo de mujer que Eugeni d'Ors propone para la Cataluña novecentista. Los textos escogidos corresponden a una serie de glosas publicadas en el periódico que hace de medio de difusión del proyecto nacionalista del catalanismo político de la LLiga Regionalista, *La Veu de Catalunya*. Desde 1906 hasta 1920 Eugeni d'Ors contará con una columna diaria, titulada "Glosari", en la que bajo el seudónimo de "Xènius", irá codificando la vida cotidiana del receptor, a través de un comentario, entre irónico, ingenuo, alagador o despreciativo —depende del tema— sobre aconteceres de la actualidad noticiable o bien ideológica. Es decir, no sólo se comentan sucesos y hechos aparecidos en la prensa, sino que cualquier dato puede utilizarse para bombardearlo de doctrina pratiana. A lo largo de estos años aparecen distintas glosas dedicadas a "temas femeninos". Debido a la insistencia del propio autor sobre la necesidad de crear una estética de mujer nacional catalana, hemos escogido las glosas que dedica a este tema.

Como ya he señalado anteriormente la mujer novecentista no puede ofrecer una imagen ligada a los desórdenes de la naturaleza ni a los conceptos de fragilidad y fatalidad. La cultura nacional que se institucionaliza con la nueva centuria crea un modelo femenino anclado en un mundo urbano, en un proyecto civilista —en el que la existencia de una ciudad como Barcelona monopoliza el discurso—, dentro del cual debe ejercer una labor estética e ideológica a fin a la idiosincrasia mediterránea y al papel metafórico de mujer/patria (Cataluña), y una labor social en consonancia con su misión de mujer/madre (Barcelona). En este ambiente ordenado, sincrónico y laborioso nace la necesidad de crear una mujer nacional que deje constancia de su existencia a las futuras generaciones. A través de sus glosas diarias, d'Ors propone en 1906 la creación de una galería de catalanas "formoses" y en 1911, tras la superación del descrédito del catalanismo burgués después de los sucesos de la Semana Trágica, inventa el personaje literario que mitificará al discurso nacionalista hegemónico. Dejando aparte a su "Ben Plantada", señalaré en este apartado los aspectos argumentales más destacables en su propuesta por conseguir una estética nacional en el terreno pictórico.

El 26 de marzo de 1906 d'Ors —a través de su interlocutor "Xènius"— escribe una glosa titulada "Bellesa Regina", en la que tras comentar las fiestas de la Mi-Carême de París, donde se elige a una reina por criterios de belleza, apunta ya la idea de perpetuar —por medio, también, de la belleza— a las mujeres catalanas. Tal propuesta la sostiene, defiende y justifica en días sucesivos en las glosas del 6, 7, 9, 10, 16 y 17 de abril, 9 de mayo, 26 de julio, 10 de octubre y 20 de mayo de 1907.[20] Concretamente el 6 de abril de 1906 propone bajo el título: "La galeria de catalanes formoses", la creación de un concurso anual de pintura en el que se ofreciese un premio al mejor retrato femenino. Así, cada año la galería contaría con una nueva adquisición, lo que con el tiempo alcanzaría ser un museo de las mujeres catalanas.

¿Por qué hay que llevar a cabo este proyecto? En primer lugar, por razones metafísicas centradas en el deseo y derecho a la inmortalidad: la belleza de un retrato para la posteridad. En segundo lugar, por razones sociales donde se estableciera el siguiente intercambio: belleza femenina, ingenio masculino (el del pintor, se entiende). En tercer lugar, por razones artísticas con el fin de contribuir a la "mediterraneización" del arte y de la perfección social. En cuarto lugar, por razones patrióticas porque la estética femenina, junto a la ciudad como proyección nacional, armonizarían con la obra civilizadora de los novecentistas. En quinto lugar, por razones orgullosas, ya que sería producto de un momento muy concreto del resurgir nacional; es decir, quedaría como prueba más del esfuerzo por institucionalizar una cultura autóctona. Y, por último, para que ninguna mujer catalana tenga que verse simbolizada por la Maja de Goya.

Biologismo y espiritualidad

En el último apartado de este trabajo pretendo presentar una aproximación de crítica literaria feminista a dos textos que sintetizan de forma muy clara la imagen femenina que propugna el Noucentisme: *La Ben Plantada* de Eugeni d'Ors y *D'espiritualitat femenina* de Jaume Bofill i Mates. A fin de que el método de análisis[21] quede estructurado de forma cómoda para el/la lector/a, centraré mis comentarios en función de los siguientes puntos:

1.- Representación artística de las mujeres.
2.- Examen de los prejuicios a partir de la diferencia social que se da a los géneros.
3.- Las imágenes y los símbolos que se atribuyen a la estética femenina.
4.- El contenido de clase social inherente al modelo de mujer propuesto.

Las glosas dedicadas a "La Ben Plantada" suman un total de treinta y aparecen en *La Veu de Catalunya* entre los días 23 de agosto y 5 de octubre de 1911.[22] Por su parte, "D'espiritualitat femenina" es el título de una conferencia dada por Bofill i Mates en la Sala Mozart de Barcelona en diciembre de 1916.[23]
Empezando por el primer punto, encontramos que tanto el texto de d'Ors como el de Bofill sitúan la estética femenina dentro de aquellas imágenes-musas, —citadas,ya, en el planteamiento de la historiadora Perrot— representadas bajo las formas estilísticas del mundo clásico: es decir, de la esencia de la cultura mediterránea y de la formación del pensamiento occidental. Van a ser, por

tanto, imágenes esbeltas, generalmente con el pelo recogido y con un cuerpo que transmite energía y salud. Las
ropas,cuando aparecen descritas, serán de color blanco —
símbolo de la pureza y virginidad— y los senos, generosos
—símbolo de fecundidad y garantía de reproducción de la
raza—. Xènius describe así a su Ben Plantada (nótese que el
propio título de las glosas es ya de por si significativo):

> "El tronch, donchs, generós y del tot
> helènich (...) s'escau d'acord plenament
> ab les modes blanes, folgades, clàssiques,
> harmoniosíssimes de 1911 (sic)".

. y Guerau de Liost (seudónimo literario de Jaume Bofill i Mates) añade:

> "El vestit ha de respectar, en el ordre
> estètic, allò que ès essencial, allò
> que ès ideal en les dònes, més que l'encant
> dels ulls, i la finor del somriure i el
> suau voleiar dels cabells: l'estructura
> del còs".

En lo que respecta a un examen de los prejuicios a partir
de la formación social del género ,podemos indicar que la
mujer novecentista debe traspasar la esfera doméstica para
alcanzar la pública porque tiene que estar a la altura de las
nuevas circunstancias. Como acompañante del esposo, es
decir, del que tiene el deber de comulgar con el espíritu del
proyecto colectivo y, por tanto, de ser un elemento activo
en él, las mujeres deben ser cultas y deportistas. Han de
instruirse y leer, pero no dramas folletinescos, sino literatura educativa, formativa, y han de estar fisícamente sa-
nas. No olvidemos que su misión principal es la de
transmisora, biológica y espiritual, de la "tradición moder-
nizada y regenerada" a los jóvenes y futuras generaciones.
En el único párrafo de la obra de d'Ors en el que la voz la
tiene la protagonista, dice textualmente: "M'agradaria tant,
tenir criatures que fossin meves!". La misión maternal la
redondea el texto de Bofill, pero no para darle ternura,
sino todo lo contrario: fortaleza. La mujer es fuerte por su
condición de reproductora, ya que en esa tarea se dan "les

dues majors dèus d'energia moral que són la capacitat de dolor i la capacitat d'amor".

Referente a los símbolos atribuidos a esta "nueva mujer" nos encontramos con el más característico de los discursos nacionalistas: el árbol:[24] "Per les arrels baixes l'arbre es ben plantat en la terra. Per les arrels altes es ben plantat en l'aire y el cel (sic)". Es el elemento afín a un planteamiento ideológico que arranca de la tradición/suelo y se eleva a la divinidad/cielo. Esa verticalidad es la máxima representación del discurso del poder y, a la vez, del sufrimiento. Arbol y cruz forman un "todo" en el pensamiento cristiano.[25]

Otro símbolo que también nos sitúa hacia lo divino es el nacimiento de la Ben Plantada en Asunción. Si hacemos una lectura histórica podemos pensar que d'Ors quiere reconocer el ligamen económico que existió hasta 1898 entre Cataluña y las colonias de ultramar. Si la lectura es autobiográfica podemos entender que al ser el propio autor hijo de catalán y cubana ha creado una figura literaria a su imagen y semejanza. Pero, si la lectura es más bien retórico-literaria quizás habrá que buscar el significado de la palabra asunción. Para los críticos literarios expertos en la estructura y vocabulario sermonístico[26], este término lo interpretan como la recepción que se ofrece en el cielo a la Virgen después de su ascensión. No olvidemos que el libro termina con la ascensión de la Ben Plantada a los cielos, que su figura es equiparada a la de la Madre de Dios y que d'Ors cita expresamente en su obra las exquiseces de la Historia Universal del sermonista francés, Bossuet. Para Bofill el modelo ideológico es sin duda el de las mujeres de la Biblia. Las Esther, Judit... y, por supuesto, la Virgen son las que simbolizarán a esta mujer fuerte biológica y espiritualmente.

Por último, quisiera añadir un pequeño comentario en lo que concierne a la recepción: ¿A quién va dirigido este mensaje?. Sin lugar a dudas, a todo el mundo. Los discursos nacionalistas tienen la retórica interclasista, en el sentido de que utilizan el lenguaje aglutinador de la primera persona del plural: del "nosostros". Frente a este "nosostros" están los "otros", de alguna manera, los enemigos. Ahora bien, no debemos dejarnos engañar por las formas: este mensaje iba dirigido a las mujeres de la clase social media y pequeña burguesía. El catalanismo político representa, entre otras cosas, el mantenimiento o mejora de unas condiciones sociales, políticas y económicas de unos sectores de la población. De aquéllos que perdieron el mercado de ultramar cuando se perdieron las colonias y miraron al resto de España, dándose cuenta de que el país estaba atrasado y que en ningún momento les ofrecía beneficios a corto plazo. La política que se hacía desde Madrid no les interesaba porque la dirigían los sectores vinculados a la oligarquía latifundista y financiera con intereses librecambistas y no proteccionistas para los tejidos catalanes. La política nacionalista que desde 1898 monopolizaba a la sociedad catalana era la política de la burguesía industrial y capas medias, no era la política que interesaba al momiento obrero. Las mujeres de la clase trabajadora no podían sentirse representadas por las mujeres novecentistas, por tanto, quedaban discriminadas como mujeres y como obreras.

Pero, y esto que también quede claro: esta mujer novecentista va a ser una avanzada a nivel de Estado. Los sectores conservadores de la geografía española, incluidos los del nacionalismo vasco —mitificado en un mundo rural— no ofrecieron ningún modelo de mujer burguesa. La aristocracia ilustrada del liberalismo madrileño no propicia una imagen para las clases medias, sino para la alta burguesía. Las mujeres de las tertulias —cuando podían participar— eran marquesas, condesas, no eran las esposas de los fabricantes y de los sectores productivos de la sociedad. Ahora bien, hay que señalar que el liberalismo, cuando intentó dar un mensaje a las mujeres —Ortega y su grupo— lo hizo desde posiciones más laicas que el nacionalismo catalán. Pero esto también tiene una explicación después de ver el papel jugado por la iglesia catalana dentro del desarrollo de la ideología nacionalista. No se quedó al margen del proceso, sino que, ya fuese para mantener a sus feligreses o por convicciones culturales e ideológicas, participó en el proyecto que se iba gestando en el período de la Restauración. Por tanto, pierde el integrismo característico del carlismo y moderniza sus planteamientos sociales y religiosos por medio, precisamente, del propio pensamiento nacionalista. Si pensamos un poco en la estética de "La Ben Plantada", del catolicismo social, del catalanismo político veremos que sigue estando presente en los modelos culturales del nacionalismo catalán del presente momento. Los novecentistas dejaron —como lo hicieron los modernistas de una manera más escandalosa— unas directrices de comportamiento que todavían hoy funcionan. El franquismo supuso una ruptura con todo un proceso estético e ideológico que hizo que cuando se tuvo que buscar un modelo cultural para recuperar la identidad nacional, se partiera del que se elabora en el cambio de siglo. Con todas las contradicciones apuntadas, los recelos y objetividad que, al transcurrir de los años, comporta la crítica histórica y literaria, la generación que vivió y protagonizó la política, la economía, la cultura, etc. de aquel período ha dejado unas señas muy marcadas en la Cataluña actual. De todas formas, habrá que buscar modelos que representen a todas las mujeres y ¿por qué no? que sean ellas mismas las que los creen. Así dejaremos de ser receptor pasivo para pasar a emisor activo.

NOTAS

[1] María Angeles Durán, prólogo a *Literatura y vida cotidiana*. (Actas de las IV Jornadas de Investigación Interdisciplinaria. Seminario de Estudios de la Mujer. Universidad de Zaragoza y Autónoma de Madrid, 1987).

[2] Jane P. Tompkins, *Reader-Response Criticism. from Formalism to Post-Structuralism* (Baltimore and London: Johns Hopkins University Press, 1980).

[3] Amparo Moreno, "El arquetipo viril y el yo cognoscente del saber". Comunicación presentada en las VII Jornadas de Investigación Interdisciplinaria del Seminario de Estudios de la Mujer de la Universidad Autónoma de Madrid. Madrid 10 y 11 de marzo de 1988. En breve aparecerán publicadas las Actas.

[4] Joan W. Scott, "Gender: A Useful Category of Historical Analysis", *The American Historical Review*, Vol. 91, Nº 5, december, 1986. Pilar Domínguez et al., "Interacción entre pensamiento feminista e historiografía en España". Comunicación presentada en las VII Jornadas ... cit. Marisa Navarro, "El androcentismo en la historia: la mujer como sujeto invisible". Comunicación presentada en el II Congreso Mundial Vasco en la sesión sobre: Mujer y realidad social. Donostia 5-8 de octubre de 1987.

[5] Vicente Cacho Viu, "Modernismo catalán y nacionalismo cultural". Ponencia presentada en el Encuentro: La Literatura Comparada: la Crisis de la Institucionalización de la Literatura en el siglo XIX. Segovia 5- 7 de diciembre de 1985.

[6] Para el regeneracionismo liderado por los liberales vinculados a la intelectualidad madrileña, el término "español" contiene las connotaciones "nacionalistas" que para los novecentistas catalanes tiene el de "catalanismo". Por tanto, respetemos el término en cuestión, pero en el nivel cultural lo utilizaremos como sinónimo de "castellano". Así, "cultura española" y "cultura castellana" serán una misma cosa, en tanto en cuanto se entiende al Estado español únicamente en su expresión castellana.

[7] Josep Termes, "El despertar nacional en Cataluña", *Historia 16*, extra V, abril 1978.

[8] Jordi Solé-Tura, *Catalanismo y revolución burguesa* (Madrid: Edicusa, 1974).

[9] Este año las VII Jornadas de Investigación Interdisciplinaria ..cit. han centrado sus debates en humanidades y ciencias sociales en torno al tema: "Mujeres y hombres en la formación del pensamiento occidental". Michelle Perrot del C.N.R.S. de la Universidad de París presentó una ponencia sobre: "Representación y pensamiento sobre la mujer durante el siglo XIX en Europa occidental".

[10] Maribel Aler Gay, "La mujer y el discurso ideológico del catolicismo", *Nuevas perspectivas sobre la mujer I* (Madrid: Actas de las I Jornadas de Investigación Interdisciplinaria. Seminario de Estudios de la Mujer. Universidad Autónoma de Madrid, 1982).

[11] Carmen Elejabeitia, *Liberalismo, marxismo y feminismo* (Barcelona: Anthropos, 1987) 96.

[12] Cristina Dupláa, "Les dones i el pensament conservador català contemporani", *Més enllà del silenci: la veu de les dones a la Història de*

Catalunya. Nash, Mary, ed. (Barcelona: Generalitat de Catalunya, 1988).

[13] *La Llumanera de Nova York*, nº 49, mayo 1879. Este número está dedicado a las mujeres que participaron en la Renaixença. La cita corresponde al editorial.

[14] Jaume Collell, "Catalanisme. Lo que és i lo que deuria ser" (Barcelona: Estampa Peninsular, 1879) 141-156. Josep Torras i Bages, *La tradició catalana* (Barcelona: Edicions 62 i "la Caixa", 1981).

[15] Sobre las figuras finiseculares en el discurso literario es interesante el libro de Hans Hinterhäuser, *Fin de siglo. Figuras y mitos* (Madrid: Taurus, 1980).

[16] En Cataluña al naturalismo literario se lo tradujo por "ruralismo" o "naturaleza".

[17] Es muy interesante el capítulo de Laia Martín Marty, "Modernisme i Noucentisme", *Aproximació a la imatge de la dona al Noucentisme català* (Barcelona: Ed. R. Dalmau, Fundació Salvador Vives Casajuana, 1984) 15- 33.

[18] Mary Nash et al. "La dona moderna a Catalunya", *L'Avenç*, nº 112, febrero 1988, 7-29.

[19] Vicente Cacho Viu, "Catalanismo y catolicismo en el ambiente intelectual finisecular", *Aproximación a la Historia Social de la Iglesia Española Contemporánea* (Real Monasterio de El Escorial: Biblioteca "La Ciudad de Dios", 1978. Teresa Camps, "Una aproximació al contingut moral del noucentisme artístic", *Ateneu*, nº 8, 1986.

[20] Las glosas de Eugeni d'Ors comprendidas entre 1906 y 1910 se hallan recopiladas en, *Obra Catalana Completa* (Barcelona: Ed. Selecta, 1950).

[21] Gabriela Mora, "Crítica feminista: apuntes sobre definiciones y problemas", *Theory and Practice of Feminist Literary Criticism*, Mora and Van Hooft, eds. (Ypsilanti, Mich.: Bilingual Press/Editorial Bilingüe, 1982) 2-13.

[22] La segunda edición de *La Ben Plantada* aparece en formato de libro el 31 de diciembre de 1911 en una edición de Alvar Verdaguer. En lengua catalana existen siete ediciones más entre 1911 y 1958, a las que hay que añadir la de la Editorial Selecta de 1976 y la de Edicions 62, "la Caixa" de 1980. En lengua castellana hay cinco ediciones entre 1914 y 1954.

23 La conferencia de Bofill i Mates está publicada en Barcelona por Bloy y Gay editores en 1916. También aparece este texto en *Obra Poética Completa* (Barcelona: Selecta, 1948).

24 Para Taine: "le platane"; para los vascos: el árbol de Guernika; y para la comunidad catalano-parlante: "El pi de les tres branques" (Catalunya, País Valencià, Illes).

25 Mircea Eliade, *Imágenes y símbolos* (Madrid: Taurus, 1986).

26 Esta contribución analítica se la debo a Gwendolyn Barnes, autora de la tesis doctoral "Sermons and the Discourse of Power: The Rhetoric of Religious Oratory in Spain (1550-1900)." Departamento de Español y Portugués de la Universidad de Minnesota.

BETWEEN CIVILIZATION AND BARBARISM: WOMEN, FAMILY AND LITERARY CULTURE IN MID-NINETEENTH-CENTURY ARGENTINA

Francine Masiello
University of California, Berkeley

In 1836, Juan Ignacio Gorriti, an Argentine in exile, wrote an essay in which he reflected upon the internal order of the newly independent nations of Latin America. Civil society, he argued, finds its origins in the family, whose structures serve as the basis for understanding political and social life:

> Basta leer con atención la historia del nacimiento y propagación del género humano, para advertir que es en un orden semejante que han venido a formarse los pueblos, las naciones, las ciudades mercantiles, en una palabra, las sociedades políticas. Podemos pues presentar la escala de estas asociaciones en el orden siguiente—1o. la sociedad conyugal; 2o. la de los padres con sus hijos; 3o. la de los hijos entre sí, y con el padre común; 4o. la de los descendientes en línea recta o transversa; 5o. la reunión de personas de diferentes familias, de diferentes países, en un local donde la conveniencia particular aconsejaba a cada uno establecerse (p. 41)

Gorriti's essay expresses a commonly held belief about the organization of society in Latin America; working in contrast to a Rousseauian concept of social contract, which circulated in Europe at the time, he argued that American societies were born from a family-like interdependence that links individuals in harmony within the fledgling nation.

As a metaphor for the state, the family unit was invoked to protect national interests in a post-colonial age. Nestled together with blood relations who shared a host of common sympathies, the members of the family were called upon to protect their home and to defend the do-

mestic space from invasion. This microcosm for govern-
mental order was also construed as a policing function so
that parents who brought order to the family ultimately
served the larger designs of the nation. Richard Morse and
other historians have recently commented on the importance of this hierarchical model for national organization,
explaining it as a tool for articulating the peculiar course of
Latin American democracy in the nineteenth century.
Both those who favored monarchy and those who defended republican democracy relied on the language of
family exchanges to serve the debate on nation building.

The representation of the unified family thus served
the stability of the emerging nation.[1] As a metaphorical
model, it was used as an instrument for the reproduction
of national values and for the advancement of state ideology. It provided an equilibrated version of domestic life in
the newly independent society and challenged any evidence of a nation plagued by anarchy or chaos. Thus, as the
colonies broke free from the Spanish fatherland, and the
image of orphaned nations circulated in the aftermath of
the independence wars, the nuclear family was used to
represent a normalized America. Domestic order was designed to show the basis of national prosperity.

But the family unit was more than a metaphor during
the early years of Latin American independence. In fact,
the powerful Latin American families of the last century
exercised vast power in matters of state authority, often
drawing clear alliances between family and national interests. Studying this phenomenon, Kuzneszof and Oppenheimer, for example, signal various phases of family participation in Latin American government in the colonial
period, in which the family passes from a corporate model,
essentially self-contained, to a form of compadrazgo, in
which the family patriarch comes to exercise leadership
over a wider community of citizens.[2] Through these extended family branches, an almost feudal control was dictated over natural resources and human relations in the
emerging society.

In the Argentine case, where the paradigm of civilization versus barbarism defined nineteenth century political

tensions, the family was thought to cast a semblance of order upon the new society, mediating the extremes of chaos and autoritarian rule. As a programmatic objective, tied to ideals of liberal governance, family coherence was significant in the meditations of Argentine intellectuals, as the earlier citation of Juan Ignacio Gorriti surely indicates. But the conservatives in power during the years following independence equally used the family metaphor to secure their positions in government, claiming the unified family as a reflection of civic and religious values. While both sides claimed an exacting definition of the responsibilities of the family, gender assignments paradoxically became less stable, resulting in a reversal of masculine and feminine roles. Often the center of family authority—found in the husband or father—became highly feminized in representation, while traditionally feminine roles of wife and mother became invested with patriarchal power. Less fixed in their roles as mothers and teachers of the young, women in nineteenth century Argentina are described in a variety of masculinized poses so that even the institution of marriage is put into question. At the same time, masculine authority becomes a topic of active inquiry, with the effect of testing the positions of power commonly ascribed to men. These positions are, of course, unstable, varying according to historical moments and periods of crisis in national history. In addition, the representation of gender and family in the literary writings of the nineteenth century is subject to political allegiances and the sexual identity of the author. While the masculine version of Argentine history posits certain forms of gender structuration, women writers will turn these principles around, investigating the seemingly naturalized boundaries of self, family, and society. In the pages that follow, I investigate these conflicts in nineteenth century Argentina in the hope of expanding a debate on women's roles in social and political formations. What is striking here is not only the diffused images of femininity utilized by men in their struggles for power, but also the ways in which women writers engage in debates about their self-representation, offering an indictment of the abuses of marriage and the limited

access to formal education through which men have restricted women's choices and denied them a voice in
political action.

1. TYRANNY AND GENDER: LITERATURE OF THE ROSAS PERIOD

> ...según el estado de nuestra sociedad y en la indigencia int-
> electual en que por mas de veinte años el tirano ha querido
> tenerla;...las mugeres no hemos salido de aquella esfera en que
> un envegecido costumbre nos tiene prefijado.
> —Rosa Guerra (1852b)

In the period of the Rosas dictatorship (1829-1852), a host
of symbols was invented to give meaning to the leader
and his adversaries. The federalists, representing Rosas,
brandished crimson ribbons as a sign of endorsement, and
denounced their unitarian counterparts as savage desert-
ers of the nation. The unitarians, defined as the liberal
group who opposed Rosas's program for consolidation,
created a legend about "civilization and barbarism" in
which their opponents were identified with destructive,
primitive forces, while the liberals claimed allegiance to
all that represented a civilized Europe. Within both
camps, woman and the family came to stand as symbols of
state power. Thus, the Rosas government, within its pa-
ternalist designs, enforced severe strictures on female behavior; women's activities were designed to support state
functions and uphold the morality of the Church. Even
within the Rosas family, women became the watchdogs of
government unity. Rosas's wife, doña Encarnación, and
his sister María Josefa, were reportedly in unofficial command of the networks of secret agents who spied on behalf
of the tyrant. His daughter, Manuelita, about whom leg-
endary tales proliferated, served as Rosas's amanuensis for
twelve years, until the end of his rule. Clearly, women
covered for Rosas's affairs of state, implementing activities
of espionage and surveillance that kept the tyrant's gov-
ernmental house intact. Within the unitarian fold, however, women were perceived as agents of resistance. They
became identified as experts in feelings, refusing the tren-

chant rigor of male domination; they brought values of virtue and family ethics to a land ravaged by fratricidal war. This reception of woman was also part of a feminization of discourse, a liberal, bourgeois way of pacifying the barbarism of Rosas. Thus, if the masculine were identified with the dictator's reign, as a chartable, marked rhetoric and behavior located within the public sphere, the feminine was seen as strategically private, evasive and less formally determined. In this context, women inserted multiplicity in the official discursive system, refusing to conform to a single strategy of interpretation and control; the feminine, in liberal works of art and literature, eluded domination by any one political program.

In the years of the Rosas's dictatorship, described by José Luis Romero as a time of immobilizing ideologies, the multiple, plural positions occupied by the feminine offered a disturbing yet attractive advantage. Liberal men and women cultivated the idea of the feminine as an elusive challenge to tyranny. Despite the obscurity to which the dictatorship had condemned them, women became emblems of resistance, responsible for devising potential subversions of the Rosas regime, or at least, for denouncing the silence that had been imposed upon the citizens of the nation.[3]

Women, through their special skills, through cleverness of speech and strategies of subversion, were thought to manage a more effective protest against the paternalism of Rosas than even the most talented men. The generation of 1837, called by some the feminine generation, utilized metaphors of femininity to recast its battle for power within history (Little, 236). Perceiving women as a source of resistance, this generation especially appreciated in the feminine the possibility of control and subversion. Women thus acquired a new symbolic value in the building of the nation.

In the manner of the Saint-Simonian romantics, with their strongly feminine inflections, the Argentine generation of 1837 turned to the example of woman to build a case for liberty. Not only through their educational programs which they equated with training for freedom and

patriotic discipline, but also through the metaphors and
images which brought order to their creative writings, the
generation of 1837 opened the possibiities of feminine discourse as a way to structure the space of the imagination.
Esteban Echeverría's literary texts, *La cautiva* (1837) and *El
matadero* (1839), indicate the strategies for gender structuration that inform liberal intellectuals of the time. *El
matadero* best exemplifies the perceived status of weakened masculinity and its gross inefficiencies during the
Rosas years. The short story is organized around a series of
binarisms, governed by the principal antithesis of civilization and barbarism. Divided in two sections, the first part
of the story ends with the slaughter of the bull, symbol of
masculinity defeated by the knife of "rosistas"; the second
part of the narrative offers a mirror reflection of this image in the unitarian hero, whose ferocious struggle for
survival is likened to that of the bull who refuses to be
tamed. Despite his efforts, he too is defeated and ultimately killed by the merciless slaughterhouse crowd.
Echeverría leaves no doubt about the masculine failures of
his literary figures; clearly, in the age of Rosas, where the
masculine triumph is reserved for the dictator, all other
men will be reduced in stature, and deprived of power
identified with their sex. Echeverría's poetic text, *La cautiva*, corroborates this statement, positing a weakened
Brian as a victim of barbarism. Interestingly, Echeverría
turns to María, the heroine of the poem, to demonstrate
the strength and resourcefulness necessary for survival in
the desert. The woman carries the debilitated Brian in her
arms and, using only the boldness of her gaze, wards off
threats by a tiger in the desert. She thus absorbs the weight
of masculine responsibility in an era when real men are
all but defeated. Only when María reverts to feminized
mode, upon learning of the death of her son, does her
masculine dignity collapse; she then dies from loss of love.
Echeverría thus posits a curious paradox in his poem: in
an age when opposition to Rosas can only spell certain defeat for men, women carry the burden of responsibility
and survive in masculine pose; they only succumb to ex-

ternal threats when they revert to traditional role of mother.

Jose Mármol, another leading thinker of the romantic generation, expands the thesis of Echeverría with respect to gender assignments. Engaged in struggle with federalist thinkers over meaning, values, and morals, Mármol defines the terms for debate through his representations of men and women. In particular, he examines the ideology of the couple and the metaphor of the unified family, structuring a critique of Rosas and the possibility of an organized resistance. To this end, he is especially concerned with producing a new male subject, who exists in androgynous pose in order to defeat the regime. Like Echeverría's men, Mármol's male characters are resourceful in conceptual and lingusitic skills and weak in physical power. Yielding the site of masculinity to the federalists, the unitarian men of Mármol's fiction assume a feminized pose. Yet despite this apparent gesture toward feminization, the catch lies in Mármol's final proposal, by which men find new sources of bonding with each other and eliminate the need for women entirely.

Mármol's major opus, *Amalia* (1851-55), considered the paradigm of romantic prose fiction in Argentina, exposes the conflicts around family and gender that guide the intellectuals of his time. As a standard discourse belonging to men, *Amalia* is the normative text against which later models will deviate; it articulates the liberal version of women and gender circulating in the years of dictatorship. For our purposes, the novel also sets the stage for appreciating the contibutions by liberal women writers of Mármol's era.

Amalia uses the gender system in flux as a metaphor for dissent in the nation. Mármol manipulates an unstable gender situation, as perceived within the unitarian camp, using it to dramatize the conflicts among federalists and unitarians while also providing a tool for understanding the debates among unitarians themselves.[4] Accordingly, he also raises questions about the uses of feminine discourse in the domination of others.

Amalia is a novel about spies and counterspies in Argentina of 1840, in the period surrounding Lavalle's advance on the capital and his subsequent retreat. Two couples in love position the major gendered exchanges in the novel: Daniel Bello, the unitarian masking as a federalist, is engaged to Florencia, who later leaves Buenos Aires for a life in exile in Montevideo. Daniel's cousin Amalia loves and eventually marries his best friend, Eduardo. This unconsummated union is short-lived, however, since federalist agents burst in moments after the marriage ceremony, killing Eduardo and bringing the novel to a close. In any event, the preoccupation with marriage is a major topic of discussion in the book, standing as a metaphor for failed political unity and bringing the novel to an end.[5] Despite the title of Mármol's work, which refers to a female protagonist, the prime mover in *Amalia* is clearly Daniel Bello. He moves the narrative along with the oratory of unitarian doublespeak, pretending to support Rosas while constantly plotting against the state. Amalia functions as his alter-ego, offering her home as a safe haven to shelter unitarians in need (especially Eduardo); she also relies on her feminine powers of transformation to act, like Daniel, as a double agent and secure information for the unitarian cause. In other ways, too, Amalia echoes Daniel's designs and emotions. When she falls in love with her cousin's best friend, the surrogate bonding between the two men is strengthened. As the intermediary between the male characters of the novel, she also serves as the agency of transformation that is supposed to bring success to the rebel endeavor.

Mármol uses these gender distinctions to play with the oppositions of civilization and barbarism, in which the feminine, or invisibility of spirit, is identified in the sphere of the unitarians, while the masculine, or paternal authority, is equated with the crass materialism of the federalists. Mármol's neat binary model in nonetheless torn asunder as the gross confusions of male and female are announced early in the novel, especially with reference to the body. In *Amalia*, symbolic systems are in flux. Daniel and Eduardo are described as effeminate while Amalia is masculinized; cross-dressing is noted in the some of the characters and becomes the object of narrative jokes. In fact, in one episode Amalia is advised, "Digo que en ese matrimonio están invertidos los sexos, ella es él, y él es ella" (i, 248). These observations, along with the unconsummated love of the protagonists, cause us to doubt the future of the unified family model which the narrator appears to defend. Mármol also indicates that the power of speech is a feminine trait, although masterfully controlled by intellectuals like Bello, who earns distinction for his skills as an orator. Allied with beauty and good taste, metaphor belongs to women while the visible body pertains to man. Thus Bello, when in the process of delivering his forceful lectures or engaged in clever doublespeak, is often described as one who assumes the blush of a romantic woman (i, 237); Amalia and Florencia gather information with similar charm and eloquence. A feminine aura surrounds those who gracefully manage language, yet in the mouths of rosistas, linguistic virtuosity is consistently degraded. Thus, when Mercedes Rosas de Rivera is introduced in the novel as a writer, she is ridiculed for her inability to seize control of rhetoric. Similarly, Marcelina, whose speech is perforated with classical quotations, is depicted as the foolish woman who cannot measure the weight of her words; and Doña María Josefa, as the vulgar gossip and spy in the service of Rosas, is described as a woman who exchanges words for money.[6]

In Mármol's novel, unitarian men usurp the voice of the feminine. In the equation of civilization and barbarism, the abstract ideas found in the feminine mode are appropriated by Daniel Bello. This dubious tribute to feminine skills is echoed in another feature of the novel, specifically in the redefinition of the family and the bonding among unitarian men. The ending of *Amalia*, as already noted, bodes ill for the future of marriage. The heroine, after a valiant defense of the unitarian underground, is relegated to silence at the close of the novel; her marriage is quickly curtailed. But Mármol, at the same time, promises another solution for the unitarian cause found in allegiances among men.

Consonant with the program of the generation of 1837, Mármol, in *Amalia*, proposes an association of anti-Rosas intellectuals. He restructures the political body in a loosely defined unity, organized by a family of men, without the service of women. His project is utopian—literally, without a place, and most likely outside of Argentina—, where he dreams of an association of men who can serve as the basis of resistance, metaphorically fathering a nation without the intervention of a mother. Like Echeverria, who in the *Dogma socialista* (1846) saw that the family in Argentina was in desperate need of rebuilding,[7] Mármol looked to a fraternity among men to give order to his novel. Thus, the family that was not destined to emerge from the unity of Eduardo and Amalia finds its realization in male community (i, 237; ii, 219-220). Mármol's vision is reinforced at the close of the novel, when Daniel's father, unheard of throughout, suddenly appears to save his son. Amalia is pushed aside, her fate unknown to readers. Since the partnership of men and women in union cannot survive, it is now left to men—in the alliance of father and son— to determine the course of the nation. In this way, Mármol tells us that marriage, under the force of tyranny, cannot be fruitful; the only course of resistance is found in the association of men who appropriate feminine virtue as their own. It remained for the unitarian women to prove Mármol wrong.

2. A VOICE OF THEIR OWN: WOMEN'S JOURNALISM IN ARGENTINA

> "la civilización no existe sino en el matrimonio"
> —La Camelia (1852)

Following the prescriptive material of the generation of 1837, women of unitarian persuasion were instructed to cultivate the domestic sphere to offer a safe haven from tyranny. By guiding her family in moral issues and maintaining the household economy, the modern woman was thus allowed to contribute to affairs of state. This coincides with what Linda Kerber has defined as "republican motherhood," in which women could exercise their patriotic mission by dint of their services in the home. It assumes that women's lives were shaped primarily by family obligation and, in turn, that women could bring virtue to the nation through their domestic advantage as mothers. In other words, through domestic restraint, woman was considered to have made her mark in society. Clearly excluded from public activity, she cultivated the space of the home as her contribution to the nation. This obligation was reinforced in the post-Rosas years in important publications such as the *Revista de Buenos Aires*, where editor Vicente Quesada insisted, "es en el seno materno que reposa la civilización del mundo" (1863: 186). This kind of mythology circulated actively among Argentine intellectuals in the years of the dictatorship and after, but women seized upon these legends of domesticity to create a productive space of their own. The home became a site for education and reflection, publicized by women as a space that might be shared by a community of fellow travelers in search of ethical and democratic ideals. In this way, women of mid-nineteenth century Argentina utilized the domestic sphere allowed them to develop new codes of learning and enhanced their limited opportunities for public circulation by building intra-domestic networks of dialogue. These were marked by conversations sustained in cultural journals and cookbooks, fashion magazines and tutorial programs designed to increase women's knowledge of science and philosophy. Finally, through this expanded community of authors and readers, women revealed their broad dissatisfaction with their assigned roles in the household.

Indeed, while it is claimed that the task of nation building lay in the hands of literate men, the public record reveals a number of fissures in these seemingly rigorous discourses. With censorship lifted in the aftermath of Rosas's defeat at Caseros, women began to participate actively in contemporary debates on state reconstruction. The daily newspapers of the post-Rosas period indicate an increase in the number of literate women and also signal the female presence as a significant proportion of the readership. In one issue of *La tribuna* for example, a daily devoted to commerce and trade, a survey conducted among a sample of Argentine citizens born in Buenos Aires indicated 11,111 illiterate men and 17,312 illiterate women; by contrast, 10,212 men and 14,667 women were literate (10 April 1856: 2) Despite the probable inefficiencies in the survey, the early study provides modern readers with remarkable information: women exceeded men in literacy skills in mid-nineteenth century Argentina. With roughly half the female population literate, and in equal proportion to men, the female presence certainly determined the character of print culture. This fact was carried over even in minor details of commercial journalism: in the classified columns of *La tribuna*, for example, the services of mid-wives, gynecologists, and governesses were offered directly to women readers. These posted announcements in a commercial daily indicate an active female audience, one which was devoted to informing itself about national life while securing medical treatment and domestic assistance.[8]

The considerable female readership in Argentina in mid-nineteenth century prompted a contestatory response by women to the restrictions imposed upon them. In fact, they engaged in systems of writing that portrayed new ideas on womanhood, revising concepts of domestic obligation, education, and public life for the female in society. The forum for this discussion was found in the expanding number of women's journals set against the abundant publications authored by men, appealing to the "bello secso", which often projected an image of women devoted exclusively to domesticity and fashion.[9] Frequently anonymous, of short duration, the journalistic production by women is as dramatic as it is revealing. These journals not only pass review of the domestic slot allocated to women, but they also revise concepts of women's beauty and patriotic mission. Rather than serve as surrogates of men in the struggle for national identity, a preoccupation observable in the writings of the generation of 1837, women organized a platform of their own in which they ardently demanded autonomy. Three areas of discussion are frequently identified in women's journalism: the home as a safe haven from tyranny and the importance of family obligations; the body as a debatable site for meaning in the public sphere; and the insistence on women's right to receive education and to engage in creative activities.

As part of this publication history, *La Camelia* offers an attractive example of emerging feminine concerns within the arena of literary journalism. *La Camelia* appeared in April 1852, two months after Rosas's defeat, and was published anonymously by three women editors, taking as its masthead the following claim: "Libertad, no licencia; igualdad entre ambos secsos."[10] In its first issue, *La Camelia* took stock of the plight of Argentine women:

> Nuestra existencia es una cadena de sinsabores y cuidados, a que la sociedad nos ha sometido, nuestra vida es aborrecible, si la prudencia no nos guiase" (11 April 1852: 4).

The asperities of women's existence, sketched by the hard realism of social life in nineteenth century Argentina, are relieved by women's intelligence and by her active pursuit of a scientific rationale to comprehend her position in society.

In this respect, the contributors to *La Camelia*, like so many other women of this period, defend and insist upon differences between the sexes, rather than abolish them, in order to demand equality under law and claim an enhanced appreciation of their uniqueness. Accordingly, they reject their status as the "weaker sex" in the social order, explaining that woman's mode of perception and her structures of intelligibility separate her from men and in fact make her stronger. (9 May 1852: 1). This will open the path for a strident demand for increased training of woman, the feminine cultivation of wit and verbal dexterity, and her enhanced moral strengths. In addition, this rationalization clears the way for the major proposals of *La Camelia* in which the editors first reconsider the female body as object within the public sphere, and then demand a program of education for women commensurate with that of men.

In the manifesto of *La Camelia*, the editors present themselves as anonymous figures: "Sin ser niñas ni bonitas, no somos ni viejas ni feas" (11 April 1852: l). Self-portraiture follows a Victorian mode of representation, designed to to conceal one's physical presence, diminishing the importance of the female body. But this statement is also to be read as a sign of feminine protest. The editors refuse to participate in the circulating discourses on fashion in which beauty or youthfulness determines individual merits and condemns women to the judgments of others. Accordingly, they insist on a privatized language of the body that can be shared only among women. Clearly invested in debate with the fashion magazines of the period, most of which were organized by men, the editors of *La Camelia* propose an appropriation of the discourse on dress, taking charge of the world of style and cosmetics to invent a language of their own. Thus, through descriptions of wigs, evening gowns, and accessories, a social subject dominated by men is reformulated in the language of women. Women now assert their right to defend sexual difference based on a uniquely feminized language that they propagate and control. But it is also way of clouding the distinctions between the public and private spheres so that the private conversations among women come to occupy the space of the journal.[11]

At the same time, by reversing the semiotic markers available in the discourse on beauty, women use the advantage of cosmetics and dress to protect themselves from the immodesty of the public sphere. Using the disguise or false persona created by fashionability, the women are able to create a mobile, elusive subject, which in its peculiar ways inverts the icon-fixing patterns belonging to the idiom of style. These discussions are situated within a general awareness of commerce in nineteenth century Argentina; clearly part of a recent modernization, style and fashion become part of the Argentine debut in modernity. And, in fact, journals like *El Album de Hogar*, a fashion magazine for women published by men, the message on commercial aspects of beauty is remarkably similar. Yet the distinguishing factor separating men and women's editorial positions depends on the perceived use of the body, cloaked as it is by fashion. The male authored journal creates the image of a coquette; the women's journal avoids fixed definitions for females and creates a private identity for women that assures both self-insulation and safety. In that way, the editors of *La Camelia* refuse to serve a masculine debate; rather, they reserve the female body from injuries or aggressions by others, and create a feminine lexicon to serve a dialogue among women.

The true conquest of the physical differences separating women and men is to be achieved by training the intellect through education and morality, or as the editors put it: "Donde falta la fuerza fisica, suple la moral" (13 April 1852: 2). In this respect, *La Camelia* directs its attention to formal instruction for women, linking education to the service of the new republic.[12] The editorial appeals of *La Camelia* consistently reiterate this concern:

> Dotadas nosotras como los hombres, con las mismas facultades que la naturaleza les ha concedido, con las mismas obligaciones para con la sociedad, con el mismo fin de civilizar y engrandecer los pueblos y el Universo todo: ¿por que pues, se niega el cultivo a una mitad de los seres de la tierra? ....La Patria precisa que se hagan universal el conocimiento de las ciencias en ambos secsos, por que así puede esperar, que la nueva generación de ciudadanos útiles, y capaces de sostituir a los que hoy presiden los altos destinos de la República. (29 abril 1852: 1)

The authors proceed in their claims on knowledge, insisting on a scientific model of learning to refine their powers of abstraction. In one issue, this plea was issued clearly:

> No sabemos porque a nuestro secso, siendo más perspicaz y persuasivo, así como, más dispuesto a los grandes progresos que los hombres ambicionan, les esté prohibido los conocimientos de varias ciencias, y circunscripto a una enseñanza mezquina (27 April 1852: 1)

The editors go on to protest the limited arena reserved for women: since they are only allowed to read novels and poetry, or view theatrical spectacles, they lack a theoretical framework for the contemplation of beauty. Thus, they recommend that educational models be drawn from the example of Europe, which harbors a long tradition of illustrious women devoted to scientific resarch and writing. Although it is doubtful that this or any contemporary publication in Argentina recognized the writings of such European feminists as Mary Wollstonecraft or Catherine Macaulay, the editors nonetheless acknowledge the advantage of European women in the debate on eduation. More importantly, invidious comparisons with Europe on the point of women's education also carry the paradoxical effect of renewing the debate on civilization and barbarism. Indeed, in the split between Europe and America, between established tradition and the new society, the women's question sets the tone in separating the civilized from the savage. Accordingly, civilization is to barbarism, as female freedom is to her slavery.

> Los hombres que no respetan la Religion, que no tienen moral, no pueden jamas llamarse civilizados.—Esos criminales que han vejado nuestro secso, nuestra Religion, y hasta el mismo Dios, no son otra cosa, que una tribu de salvages, y a las puertas de nuestros Templos (20 April 1852: 1).

Even in the relation between husband and wife, the gentility of exchanges among European couples is claimed as a paradigm from which Americans might learn, especially since New World partnerships are marked by disrespect and brutality (27 April 1852: 2).[13] Within these terms, the scientific spirit is clearly allied with European thought, while the emphasis on crass materialism is viewed as an exclusively Americanist concern. As part of a widely used metaphoric distinction to identify the ills of the nation, the civilization and barbarism antimony serves to rally a demand for education for women; Argentina, the editors claim, will languish on the fringes of civilization until its traditions of education for women are altered.

La Camelia's proposal for educational reform is replete with conflicts about women's role in the public sphere. Thus, in a particularly revealing essay, the editors link national welfare to women's education, but clearly express reticence about aspiring to positions of power. Their case for public education is based on the following arguments:

> 1. Well educated women make better wives and mothers, allowing them to defend the men of their family with intelligence and verbal sophistication.
> 2. Education for women does not imply an abrogation of feminine roles; in fact, the defensive editors claim, women have no plans to threaten state power, but only care to educate their children and train future citizens.
> 3. Young girls need to know more than music, fine arts, and needlework, since these skills are essentially useless.
> 4. The illustrious mother is needed for the social good. (6 May 1852: 1-3).

In the broad discussion of educational reform, *La Camelia* constructs contradictory arguments about social roles for women. On the one hand, the idea of republican motherhood, described earlier in this essay, surfaces clearly in the programmatic objectives of the editors of *La Camelia*. As if in anticipation of a hostile response by readers, the editors advocate education for women designed only to enhance the family. *La Camelia* thus endorses a relational feminism, described by sociologist Karen Offen as a situation in which women take their political positions as supporters of their husbands and children. Offen argues coherently, I believe, that the public understanding of the word "feminism" varies in historical periods so that a women's discourse tied to concepts of marriage and motherhood, as in the case of the program of *La Camelia*, is not to be misconstrued as evidence of nineteenth century conservatism. Rather, it proves more fruitful to trace these early representations of domesticity insofar as they challenge our modern assumptions about the narrowness of activities in the home.[14] Indeed, through their tasks as homemakers and mothers, the Argentine women claimed a role for themselves within the projects of the nation. At the same time, the home provided a new space for concepts of female independence, allowing women the right to authorship and a voice of their own.

3. THE STRUGGLE FOR PUBLIC SPACE: THE WOMAN WRITER IN THE NATION

"Qué fatalidad es el ser muger!"—Rosa Guerra (1852a)

The considerations raised in *La Camelia* are reiterated in the course of Argentina's struggles for democracy, expanded by a generation of women determined to claim their rights as authors. Rosa Guerra, Juana Manuela Gorriti, Juana Manso, and Mercedes Rosas de Rivera form part of a constellation of figures who take their identities through writing. Though disparate in their projects, they are joined by a common wish to link women's perspective to a new national discourse in formation and to enter the public arena through the privileges of authorship.

The women writers who rise to prominence during and after the government of Rosas unseat the authority vested in masculine traditions and challenge the repressive practices of years of dictatorship. From their earliest writings of the mid-1840s through the democratic period following Rosas, they cover a span of strategies to deal with observable shifts in the state, while also marking the confusion of masculine culture and the contradictions of official discourse. At the same time, these women are also concerned with narrowing the presumed gap between civilization and barbarism, using marriage and domesticity as a site of meaning where these oppositions might converge. Mercedes Rosas de Rivera, sister of the tyrant, challenges the institution of marriage as a felicitous space for women. Rosa Guerra and Juana Manuela Gorriti return to the legends of the conquest, investigating those ambiguous sites of meaning which belong to feminine experience insofar as they straddle the boundaries between civilization and barbarism. Categories of intelligibility, drawn frequently through a female voice in fiction, underscore the irrational qualities of the colonizing endeavors. As such, even the validity of the unitarians' mission is called into question, and their European-focused project is met with guarded faith. These women also engage in debate on the formulation of a national language, using their fictions as vehicles to test the Spanish idiom in formation. Far from seeking a pure, "castizo" language in the style of some unitarians, the women writers insisted on a gleeful heterogeneity of expressions to repudiate official meaning.[15] At the same time, they also found unrestricted pleasure in the transformative power of women's words. Despite the occasional dangers that this kind of double agency provokes, the ambiguity in language most often serves to attack the policies of the state, targeting in particular the brittleness of official discourse. This multiplicity is seen in the semantic representations of the family, which, in the imaginative writings of nineteenth century women, is perceived to be under siege, capable of affecting the contemplative space of readers and writers alike.

The urge to heterogeneity is reflected in the writings of women as if to defy the linguistic authority of the state and advance a voice of their own. Juana Manso displays the ambiguities of language as a syntactic and semantic complication belonging to the mysterious age of Rosas. The period, as Mármol had also noted, is characterized by confusion and double speak, but Manso will take advantage of the chaos to advance the agenda of women. Rosa Guerra brings into question the transformational powers of language when used as a mediator between different cultures. Like Guerra, Juana Manuela Gorriti also insists on linguistic ambiguity as a way to confuse hegemonic, masculine culture in a newly independent America. In her early stories, Gorriti is concerned with the retaliations of the Rosas regime; but she is also obsessed with Indian language and the secrets it guards from the white man. The double messages of cross cultural insemination, the clash of oral and print expression, and the confusion of Indian and white discourses (in which the woman is identified invariably with the concerns of Indians) are brought to bear on the question of dominant and oppressed groups, using the role of women as mediators of these struggles.

When they addressed questions of gender, the women writers of mid-nineteenth century Argentina echoed a preoccupation for the multiplicity of meanings that circulated in society. Through plural interpretive strategies and an insistence on ambiguity, they also challenged the fixed position from which any individual might be heard. In this way, they made an incursion into the institutions of gender and the family insofar as they mediated conflicting symbolic realms and public and private spaces. The economy of nineteenth century women's fiction thus decentered official discourse and multiplied the possible positions from which women might speak.

4. MERCEDES ROSAS DE RIVERA. RETHINKING MARRIAGE IN THE NATION

An appropriate starting point for a discussion of the feminine resistance to tyranny is found in the fiction of Mercedes Rosas de Rivera, sister of the Argentine strongman. Writing at a time when the restrictions upon women were severe, Mercedes Rosas described the image of the silenced woman, excluded from the public sphere, whose only identity was formed by her alliances through the convent or marriage. This problem surfaces in her widely neglected novel, *Maria de Montiel,* a text most likely written in the 1830s, but published in 1861, after the fall of Rosas.[16] Outside of a few derisive statements made by Mármol of her literary talents in his novel *Amalia,* and a hasty reference by Lily Sosa de Newton in her history of Argentine women, little is known about the literary life of the younger sister of the Argentine strongman. The position of characters in her novel, however, gives us a clue to her personal concerns as she describes the meager possibilities available to intelligent women. Marriage and children or convent life are set in opposition in the novel as the only choices available to women in periods of civil strife.

The Argentine heroine, María de Montiel, trained for the domestic paradise of the family, is promised in marriage to her father's elderly friend, a benevolent warrior hero. Thus, in a tactic used in traditional novels to preserve the stability of the established classes, marriage between surrogate father and daughter is planned. But war intervenes to call the groom away, and in his absence, a second, younger suitor appears, committed not to military engagements, but to commercial negotiations between Europe and America. Failing to court María with success, this second suitor then travels to Spain, where a countess of considerable intelligence catches his attentions. A triangular tension in narrative is thus established: commercial and martial activity divide the attentions of María while old and new courtship rituals are also placed in opposition. Finally, when María's warrior groom is killed in battle, Jorge abandons the Spanish countess who loves him and returns to Argentina to take a dazed María for his bride.

The marriage of María to her commercially minded suitor represents the rise of a new entrepreneurial class to replace the generation of warrior heroes and, indeed, as Mercedes Rosas announces, the dawn of a new society. But Rosas also provides a sub-text of equal interest to us here, for she demonstrates the lack of free will of her women characters. María accepts marriage without a commitment to love while her counterpart, relegated to a life of solitude, chooses to enter the convent to pursue her intellectual interests. One form of incarceration is thus set against another in a society that offers limited choices to the modern woman.

Mercedes Rosas's statement dramatically illuminates the dilemma of women in nineteenth century Argentina. An object for the attentions of men, the protagonist is used as a pawn in a war of competing ideologies while the countess, as a woman of intellect, is shown to survive only in the convent. From her position within the federalist camp, Mercedes Rosas identified the restricted roles available to women at a time when devotion to the nation was the sine qua non for Argentine progress. It depended upon the unitarian women to expand their resistance to tyranny, taking into account the mobility of the modern woman.[17]

5. ROSA GUERRA. WOMEN AMONG THE SAVAGES

The expansion of women's voice as a programmatic objective of nineteenth century female intellectuals becomes especially clear in the statements of Rosa Guerra (d. 1864), a normal school teacher and defender of the Society of Beneficence, a friend of Juan María Gutiérrez and Vicente Fidel López and the major figures who emerged in Argentina in the aftermath of Caseros. Although she conscientiously addressed the need for education for women, her most impassioned essays are devoted to a defense of the woman as writer. In one of the many journals she directed, *La Educacion* (1852), Guerra published a letter addressed to the director of *El Progreso*, the newspaper in which Sarmiento wrote, upholding her right as a woman to engage in creative activities of the pen. Although clearly within the conventions of the period by which she and other women exalted the merits of republican motherhood, she adamantly expanded the definition of family roles—those of mother, daughter, and sister—to allow women to pursue commitments to writing:

> Comunmente se cree que una muger que se ocupa de una contraccion de esta especie pierde el precioso tiempo que la madre de familia, la hija, y la hermana deben dedicar a los que-haceres domésticos. Esto es un error! Una madre puede escribir en ausencia de su esposo y al lado de la cuna de su niño, pensamientos llenos de interés y de ternura que dejará olvidada sobre el lecho de la infancia....
> Diez o doce renglones escritos al pie de la cuna de su hijo que mese al mismo tiempo que escribe, bajo aquella divina influencia de madre, en uno de aquellos raptos tan frecuentes de amor maternal, no hacen perder el tiempo a una señora de su casa, ni la distraen de las sagradas obligaciones en que está comprendida la madre de familia. La hija y la hermana del mismo modo. Despues de concluidas todas sus tareas y obligaciones del dia que en toda su estension deben llenar; que hacen de pre-

ciosos ocios? de esos ratos perdidos y de aburrimiento....? fas-
tidiarse! No seria mejor que para distraerse abriesen sus
portafolios y ya con pluma o con lápiz escribiesen unas cuantas
líneas, y que cuando su padre o hermanos se acercasen a su mesa
y abrieran sus cuadernos conocieran los primeros en el corazon y
en el pensamiento de su hija y de su hermano? (1852b, 3-4).

This remarkable text is rich in suggestions about the
role of women as creators of literary art. Clearly situated
within the terms of a relational feminism that did not ob-
struct the traditional family, Guerra's argument nonetheless exposed the tedium of woman's day at home. Despite
the fact that women's privacy (the much lauded "room of
one's own") seemed not to be an issue, Guerra claimed the
authority of the pen as woman's inalienable right and as
an avenue of salvation for woman locked in the domestic
sphere.[18] The militancy of Rosa Guerra's position is only
fully appreciated when these demands are read in conjunction with her editorials in *La Educacion*, in which she
denounced the domestic enslavement of women:

> Pero, quienes son las mugeres para hacer un discurso particular
> sobre su educacion? Esos seres desgraciados son considerados
> entre los salvages como esclavas, entre los orientales como flo-
> res destinadas para su regalo y placeres teniéndolas no obs-
> tante entre cadenas; y entre los pueblos cultos a pesar de la
> libertad de costumbres, se las cree unicamente capaces de
> govierno de la familia, materiales quehaceres de casa, y
> sometidas en un todo al absoluto imperio de la opinion. Qué
> fatalidad es el ser muger! si tiene entendimiento es preciso que
> lo oculte, que deje sin cultivo su talento y que siga una rutina que
> no la permita salir de la esfera que una envegecida costumbre
> la ha prefijado (1852a, 1).

Notably isolated at the time in which her denunciations
were issued, Rosa Guerra's defense of the female writer
was not to be echoed again publicly until some twenty five
years later.[19] Her missions, however, were supported by
her endeavors in the field of the fiction.

In her journalistic essays, Rosa Guerra describes the
abuse of women as evidence of the sustained conflicts between the ideologies of civilization and barbarism. While

modern nation states exhibit generous treatment of the female population, the barbaric primitives, by contrast, show heedless disregard for women subjects. Domestic enslavement is therefore a sign of the degree to which the modern woman is abused in barbaric societies. The tension between civilization and barbarism is also the subject of her novel, *Lucía Miranda* (1860), a fictional reconstruction of one of the well known legends of the Spanish conquest of the River Plate region.

The story of Lucía Miranda, part of the mythical explanation of the trials of the Spanish settlers of Argentina, engages questions of conquest and racial difference with perspectives on the function of gender. Included in the earliest chronicles of the discovery of the River Plate region, and also in the Jesuit records, the tale emerged again as a literary topic shortly after the defeat of Rosas when Argentines set themselves to the task of nation building and to the restoration of national mythologies.[20] Guerra and Eduarda Mansilla both addressed the topic in 1860; Miguel Ortega wrote a drama about Lucía in 1864. In the twentieth century, the theme again gained importance in the popular fictions and *folletines* of nationalist inspiration, in the school children's tales written by Ada Elphein, and the pulp novels of Hugo Wast.

Lucía Miranda, the beautiful wife of a Spanish captain, travels to the Paraná River where her husband sets up a fortress. There, she occupies herself with acts of charity, guiding the Indians in a Christianizing mission. The "cacique," Mangora, falls in love with Lucía and, when she rejects his advances, he, in an act of jealous revenge, sets fire to the fortress and destroys almost all of its inhabitants, except of course for Lucía. In his dying moments, Mangora repents and asks to convert to catholicism, assisted by Lucía, who performs the baptismal rites. Siripo, Mangora's successor and the new cacique of the tribe, then tries to possess Lucía, who, consistent with her virtuous principles, refuses his advances. Both Lucía and her husband are then burned at the stake, represented as martyrs of the conquest and models of conjugal devotion.

Rosa Guerra takes advantage of this tale not only to claim a voice for herself within patriotic discourses, but also to show the ways in which the presence of women can alter the destiny of a nation. The arena of fiction is thus redefined by Guerra to serve as a forum for didacticism, teaching about the ways in which women mediate the conflict between civilization and barbarism, and then offering counsel to women on the importance of discipline and self-control.

In Guerra's version of this story, Lucía is carved out as an individual who resists female stereotypes. Defying the model of the heroine of the *folletín*, who engaged the attention of Argentine audiences of the period, Lucía is represented as a more complicated character, not of common fold:

> no tenía quince años, ni labios de coral, ni dientes de perlas, ni ojos color del cielo...Lucía Miranda era más bien una de las mujeres de Balzac (p. 19)

Literature, here, is played against itself; refusing to trade with a fictional heroine of high predictability, Guerra moves to a Balzacian model for a contrapuntal strategy. Less codified or maudlin, the new heroine, in Guerra's mind, will attract by her volatility. In this way, Guerra also moves against her unitarian colleagues, the emerging statesmen-writers of the post-Rosas era, who sought to describe in the their prolific fictions the perfect woman in the service of the nation. Although not allowed to share the political podium with Juan María Gutiérrez, Vicente Fidel López, Bartolomé Mitre, or Miguel Cané, she certainly undercut the stable fictional heroines invented by these men.[21] With her not-so-conventional heroine, Guerra was able to expand the possibilities for women as subjects in Argentine fiction, while she also took advantage of the forum of the novel to offer counsel to female readers, teaching them of their civilizing mission in society and of the authority of verbal discourse.

In the novel, Lucía acts according to principles of Christian charity, sermonizing about Christian values before her Indian audience. Not only is it surprising that the heroine seizes the power of the word, delivering addresses in public before the indigenous masses, but she also speaks with eloquence and intended verisimilitude. Thus, Lucía effectively moves from the private domain reserved for women into public view, accomplishing through her humanizing (and linguistic) virtues what the Spanish men failed to do. But Guerra is quick to remind us of the dangers of this activity if women lack adequate training in the consequences of verbal expression. This becomes the principal didactic point addressed to readers.

When Lucía communicates with the Indian Mangora, she describes the beauty of conjugal love; her story is so convincing, the power of her words so effective, that the Indian's imagination is stirred and he is inspired to passion. Guerra demonstrates that Lucía has effectively seized her authority as a teller of tales, but she fails to recognize the transformational powers of her own verbal expression. Without an awareness of the ideational effect of words, she stimulates the passions of the Indian, awakening his desire. The equation of word and desire is clearly set forth in the novel and is repeated to show the uncontrollable effect of verbal discourse by the uninitiated. Thus, when Mangora asks Lucía to proclaim that she loves him, she answers affirmatively as if to convey the authenticity of fraternal affection. This ambiguity prompts chaos; her error in self-expression generates a series of misunderstandings; the imprecision of the "as if" construction spells disaster for the Spaniards.

The linguistic error signals a cultural clash between whites and Indians; as an example of slippage in language, it shows points of non-communication, and the imposition of a dominant discourse over those of minority cultures. Even the interception of a letter written by Lucía to her husband exacerbates this point, furthering the enmity and misunderstanding between settlers and Indians; once again, Lucía engages in a verbal discourse she cannot control and the Indians find themselves victimized by the white woman's caprices. In this respect, Guerra throws her sympathies to the Indian and initiates a discussion of the shortcomings of the colonialist engagement in America. She points to the opposition of civilization and barbarism, between the varieties of print and oral cultures, all of which are mediated in the novel by the presence of Lucía. When the Spaniards are murdered and the protagonists burned at the stake, the narrator of Guerra's novel speculates on the unnerving denouement: "Es de presumir si la causa de la humanidad hubiera entrado en el proyecto de estas empresas, hubiesan sido menos desgraciados" (p. 77). The colonial mission is denounced, not because the Spaniards had no business in America, but, more importantly, because they lacked a humanizing plan for the Indians. But Guerra, not given to facile solutions, also exposes the faulty preparation of her heroine who is unable to manage the heterogeniety of cross cultural messages. In this way, Rosa Guerra indicates that, despite the speaking role acquired by her heroine, the larger discursive system shared by Indians and whites is still in need of repair in order to accommodate subalterns struggling for communication.

6. JUANA MANUELA GORRITI: ON GENDER, RACE AND MARRIAGE

Juana Manuela Gorriti (1819-1892), popularized recently in the novel of Marta Mercader, is indeed worthy of mythmaking. An ambitious women who directed literary salons in Peru and Argentina, she wrote prolifically in exile and then again in her native country. She left Argentina at twelve to take refuge in Bolivia, where later she married a military officer who was to become president of Bolivia. His ongoing infidelities led Gorriti to move with her children to Lima, where she hosted an important literary coterie and earned a living through teaching. Traveling though countries dominated by eminently masculine struggles for power in the aftermath of independence, Gorriti chose to address questions of feminine rights, and initiate a dialogue among women and men of international scope.[22] The agenda of her literary salon in

Lima (1876-1877) is indicative of this commitment to women's issues. There, she drew upon the distinguished intellectuals of her time to exchange poetry and prose and share ideas about women's issues, ranging from public education to legal emancipation for women.[23] Eminently active in women's publications and feminine circles throughout Spanish America, Gorriti had a clear vision about women's rights and progress and earned a public following from Latin American women of her time. Her journals, her published cook book, *La cocina ecléctica*,— an anthology of recipes drawn from women throughout Latin America—, and the wide diffusion of her essays in the mid-nineteenth century attest to her strength as a writer and an organizer of women in the Americas. Perhaps the consequence of this internationalism, in addition to the instability of exile, her prolific writings were fragmented and only rarely recuperated in books.[24] Like Mercedes Rosas and Rosa Guerra, whose extant fictions are scarse, Gorriti poses an enigma to literary scholars; her popularity in her time was enormous, yet by the middle of the twentieth century she slipped into near oblivion. Gorriti's feminism is evidenced in her journalistic contributions, in her organization of some of the most prestigious literary salons in nineteenth century Spanish America, in her notes on marriage and the family, and even in the legends that survived her, suggesting at least two natural children, countless extramarital encounters, and even attempts at cross-dressing, which earned her comparison with George Sand.[25] Nevertheless, her perspective on women is most clearly articulated in the folds of her literary texts. In her early writings (those stories published in periodical presses and later joined in *Sueños y realidades*, in 1865), she addresses two principal literary and historical problems; first, the question of family discord as a key to understanding social organization under the Rosas regime and, with it, the opposition to Rosas set in motion by women; and second, the unity of subaltern groups drawn by issues of race and gender. Perhaps drawn from autobiographical elements of Gorriti's life—her father and uncle were drawn to the unitarian cause and took up life in exile, while another uncle joined the federalists, taking his cue from the heroism of Dorrego—, she returns consistently to the family unit to represent national political conflict. Civilization against barbarism is now recast as a struggle within the family.

Gorriti emphasizes these political discontinuities by hinging her narrative logic on a series of wayward women; the errant daughter and the non-conformist wife are literary subjects who refuse to collaborate with authority. In addition, she prevails upon the cross-cultural metaphor of miscegenation in which women are allied with Indians in order to oppose the cultural hegemony of criollos in America. Thus, if the civilization versus barbarism theme is attractive to many of the members of the generation of 1837, Gorriti takes these elements to display other features of the same dichotomy: the language barriers that isolate the members of oppressed groups, the marginal status of those who fail to comply with official laws, and the heterogeneity that challenges any single authority all come forward as part of a conflict between dominant and subaltern sectors in society. At the same time, she also issues a critique of the unitarian program while simultaneously appearing to support its basic paradigms. The unitarian project was designed to impose an official language on the Argentine people, suppressing alternative modes of expression that circulated in the mid-nineteenth century. But Gorriti, in the first phase of her writing, formulated a counter-program to this plan, perceiving the need to defend linguistic variation as a principle of alterity in modern Spanish American society. Accordingly, she challenged the project of the unitarians insofar as they conceived of language as an instrument of domination over others. Taking language as a tool for social change, she urged a voice for subalterns to be integrated with different sectors to form a new, composite society. This is not to say that Gorriti's political program opposed the innovations of the generation of 1837; rather, she inserted a uniquely subaltern response within their possibilities for political action, and also revealed the flaws that rippled through shared unitarian wisdom.

In all cases, Gorriti's interest in cultural pluralism centers on a defense of women and Indians as actors allied in social theater. Her recognition of indigenous and feminine traditions in America not only stands at odds with the European models defended by Argentine thinkers; more importantly, it clears a space for the hybridization of all cultural models represented in her texts. Accordingly, the great binarisms that separate body and spirit, materialism and abstract ideals, and even federalists and unitarians, are collapsed in Gorriti's categories for understanding gender and racial differences. Beyond emphasizing "otherness" as a position in civil society, Gorriti gives attention to the alliances established among subalterns.

In the first page of this essay, I quoted from Juan Ignacio Gorriti, who defended the unity of the family as a metaphor for political stability. His niece Juana Manuela, however, upsets this decisive metaphor, by insisting on family discord as an example of modern chaos. In fact, she tells us that the family can never be unified in America, owing to the competing beliefs and opinions circulating in a post-independence age. Equally important, the modern family in America refuses strict organization because of the absence of hierarchies and traditional categories of rank and difference.

In "El pozo de Yocci," a story included in *Panoramas de la vida* (1872), Gorriti exposes the reasons behind the loss of the unified family. In the conflict between Spain and America, we witness the rebellion of adolescent youth against the father; the family is irremediably torn in the growing pains of independence. Equally tragic, brother is set against brother in a series of fratricidal wars that have plagued the homeland of the young:

> Los héroes de la independencia, una vez coronada con el triunfo de su generosa idea; conquistada la libertad, antes que penar en cimentarla, uniendo sus esfuerzos, extraviáronse en celosas querellas; y arrastrando a la joven generación en pos de sus errores, devastaron con guerras fratricidas la patria que remieran con su sangre. Olvidados de su antigua enseña: unión y fraternidad, divididos por ruines intereses, volviéronse odio por odio, exterminio por exterminio. Un nombre, un título, el

> color de una bandera pusieron muchas veces en sus manos el
> arma de Caín, que ellos ensangrentaron sin remordimiento,
> oscureciendo con días luctuosos la hermosa alborada de la
> libertad (p. 368).

In the new post-independence life, fratricidal wars an-
nulled the missions of the revolution against Spain. This
message was aimed, of course, at describing the Argentine
situation, where families had been destroyed by conflicting
versions of how to construct the state.

Gorriti's stories are replete with images of this kind, in
which federalist fathers kill their children in moments of
blind rage, and where the personal and the political become hopelessly entwined. In "El lucero del manantial"
(1860), included in *Sueños y realidades*, a young girl living
in a desert outpost dreams she is violated by a soldier and,
months later, gives birth to his child. Years pass and she
marries an anti-Rosas statesman who cares for her and her
adolescent son. When the legislator pronounces a criticism of Rosas, he is assassinated by federalist agents; the
boy, protecting his stepfather and denouncing the fatal
crime, is detained, soon to be killed by the strong man,
Rosas. At this point, the boy's mother intervenes and begs
the tyrant to save his life since now it is revealed that
Rosas is the child's natural father. Callously, the tyrant rejects the woman's pleas; the boy is killed and the woman
returns to the desert outpost. She is later reported to be in-
sane, roaming among the Indians on the frontier between
civilization and barbarism. Stories of this kind show the
folly of male ambition, set on destroying the family for the
vanity of political gain. At the same time, defiance of male
authority surges from the courage of the mother, who, in
defeat, takes refuge on the borders of civilization, joining
the Indians as her only recourse against the atrocities of
civil society.

This activity upsets the conventional unitarian understanding of woman in defense of the nation. Far from engaging in political struggle, Gorriti's heroine withdraws to
the primitive desert as if to escape contamination from a
corrupt and impenetrable society devoid of reason. Mar-

mol had already defined a course for the ideal woman who aided the unitarian cause, but in Gorriti's hands, the benign intelligence and charity of woman are converted into a source of resistance; the feminine is in a clearly adversarial position, voicing opposition to the violence of the state.

Though the federalists are consistently degraded for their barbaric acts, the unitarians rarely escape unscathed in the fictions of Gorriti. Male identity is upset, the missions of the family confused, as Gorriti insists upon women's right to reverse political allegiances for love. Thus, in "Una noche de agonia" (1862), also from *Sueños y realidades*, while men fight on the side of federalists, their women shift roles and narrative perspectives, turning to the unitarian camp; charity and good will are the agents of their transformation. Similarly, from the same volume, in "La hija del Mashorquero", a thinly disguised tale about Manuela Rosas and her father, the girl supports the victims of her father's regime while he behaves like a bloodthirsty tyrant. In both cases, the counter-revolutionary mission is set in motion by women in defiance of family order. While daughters and wives are seen in constant throes of rebellion against the irrational programs of partisan politics, Gorriti also positions her female characters squarely in the Indian camp. In her first story, "La Quena," dating from 1845, she addresses the problem of transculturation between women and Indian groups (*Sueños y realidades*). In this story, Rosa is promised in marriage to Ramírez, a criollo in America. Her true love, however, is Hernán, the bastard son of an Inca princess and a Spaniard. After much intrigue and digressive material, a jealous Ramírez first kills Hernán and then Rosa. The last chapter of the novella describes the transformation of the dead Rosa's skeleton into a melodious quena, destined to haunt the spirits of men who suffer from love. Woman is the source of musical harmony and textual unity as well, but Rosa's transformation into a quena is also her incorporation as an instrument of Inca culture; against the viciousness of the Spaniard, her body becomes the servant of indigenous expression. Thus, Gorriti situates women and Indians in a joined denunciation of Spaniards; the girl's body becomes allied with Inca culture to resonate an enduring melody of protest. Against the option of the convent for women, which Gorriti clearly detested, alliance with the Indian promises women the chance of historical redemption. In death, Gorriti's heroine comes to occupy a position in circulating public discourses.[26]

Efraín Kristal has situated the emergence of *indigenista* fiction within the context of modernization projects in Peru and treats the ideological shifts in the perspective on the Indian as part of an ongoing political debate. While I am not questioning the political origins of the *indigenista* tradition in letters, it is nonetheless important to use these examples to draw attention to the interweaving of the discourses on gender and race. The Indian stands as a repository for all subaltern cultures, offering a blank space in literary texts upon which issues of gender may be imprinted. Thus, the confusion of bicultural exchanges or the double-edged social conflicts among dominant and subalterns are also instrumental for Gorriti's formulations on the role of women in society.

In the split between nature and culture, so frequently described by anthropologists and more recently by femininst scholars such as Sherry Ortner, women are positioned in the natural sphere while the arena of cultural transformation is assigned to the masculine domain. During the nineteenth century, these worlds stood in clear opposition, to be mediated in literary texts by the intervention of the fantastic. In Gorriti's stories, women are in fact synonymous with the super-real. Ghosts, phantoms, and dream-like scenarios are engendered by female characters, who then provide a space for the recodification of disparate realms of experience. Of more immediate political importance, through Gorriti's women characters, unitarian and federalist discourses are confused, regionalist-urban conflicts are upset, and the authority of print culture is undermined. Moreover, a community of women in fiction sustains secret continuities, prevailing upon intuition to rectify the failures of partisan politics.

By giving voice to marginal groups who have little authority or power, Gorriti managed to insert doubt in the structuration of official history. Showing the co-existence of independent languages and cultures at a crucial moment of nation building in Latin America, she not only offered a critique of the dominant unitarian project to which she subscribed, but she also exposed the problematic issues that the major statesmen-writers had been reluctant to address.[27]

7. JUANA MANSO: THE CRITIQUE OF THE UNITARIAN FAMILY

Juana Manso de Noronha (1819-1875), perhaps the most interesting figure among nineteenth century women intellectuals, corroborates the efforts of Rosa Guerra and Juana Manuela Gorriti by emphasizing the rigidity of a brittle disursive system that fails to accommodate the "others." She lived her adult years in exile, in Montevideo, Rio de Janeiro, Havana, and New York, and when her Brazilian husband abandoned her in 1853, she returned to Argentina to work on Sarmiento's school projects. The founder of feminist magazines in Argentina and Brazil, the author of an anti-slavery novel and of numerous plays and travelogues—an opus almost lost in its entirety—, Juana Manso was singularly devoted to the emancipation of women.[28] In a statement that reads more like a manifesto than an essay on contemporary realities, she called attention to the desperate situation of women of her time:

> La emancipación moral de la muger, es considerada por la vulgaridad como el apócalipsis del si[g]lo; los primeros corren al diccionario. y ciñiéndose al espíritu de la letra exclaman:
> Ya no hay autoridad paterna!
> Adiós al despotismo marital!
> Emancipar la muger! Cómo! Pues ese trasto de salón (o de cocina), esa máquina procreativa, ese cero dorado, ese frívolo juguete, esa muñeca de las modas, será un ser racional?
> Emancipar la muger! y qué viene a ser eso?

Concederle el libre ejercicio del libre arbitrio? Pero si recono-
cemos en ella que Dios le dio una voluntad, que la hizo libre
como a nosotros hombres; que le dio una alma compuesta de las
mismas facultades morales e intelectuales que a nosotros,
hombres, entonces la habremos hecho bonita! De ese modo la
muger se tornará un ente racional, que dejará de ser un valor
nulo! y que trastorno social! qué caos!!

Al desaparecer el prestigio de la supremacía no sería necesario recurrir a calidades morales cuya influencia es irre-
sistible?

Cómo! (dicen los empecinados) después de tratar a la muger
como nuestra propiedad tendríamos que reconocer en ella
nuestro igual! habíamos de ser justos, respetuosos y comedidos
con ellas!

No puede ser!

Y con todo llegará un día en que el código de los pueblos
garantirá a la muger los derechos de su libertad y de su inteligencia.

....

Su inteligencia cultivada, mejora sus facultades morales, y le
hará egercer la inevitable influencia que le da la naturaleza
en los destinos de la humanidad: sí, porque la misión de la
muger es seria y grandiosa. Angel del hogar doméstico, incumbida por Dios de imprimir a la infancia el primer
movimiento del bien en su hermoso titulo de Madre, parece que
la misma Eterna Sabiduria del Creador ha impreso en la
misión de la Madre, el empleo de las facultades del alma de la
muger.

....

Nunca hemos querido apartar a la muger de su misión de
madre de familia, jamás le hemos deseado otro campo, para
egercer su influencia, que el hogar doméstico, es ese el verdadero pedestal de su gloria, el apogeo de su grandeza, y el
centro de su felicidad.

El amor es la vida de la muger, así como tambien es la necesidad que domina la existencia borrascosa del hombre....

Esta nuestra digresión es destinada a probar que no entendemos por emancipación de la muger su divorcio del hombre, y la
ilustración de su espíritu, lejos de perjudicarle, la ennoblece, la
eleva y da al matrimonio un fin mas moral aun del que tiene, y
que lo dignifica en el sentido moral.

No creemos nosotros que puede existir algo de mas santo que la
familia, ni fuera del domestico, una felicidad mas pura, mas
verdadera, ni mas legitima, pero tambien estamos seguros que
no ha de ser en la union de una muger ignorante y de un marido
brutal y despota, que se podrán ir a contemplar los idilios de la
poesía simple y primitiva de esos cuadros de la familia, que

tan suaves y profundos recuerdos nos dejan de la infancia y que
son al corazón ulcerado como el blando aroma que trae brisa al
verano, al enfermo y gime en el lecho de agonía.
—"Emancipación moral de la mujer," (1853, pp. 5, 17-18)

Like her colleague Rosa Guerra, Manso stands in defense of motherhood and marriage, but issues a strong in-
vective against the domestic abuse of women. Even the
few extant literary pieces that belong to Juana Manso confirm her defense of a marriage partnership that is based on
compatibility of the intellects and mutual respect. This is
especially clear in *Los misterios del Plata: episodios his-
toricos de la epoca de Rosas* (1846), Manso's unfinished
historical novel about the Rosas regime in which Antonia
Maza de Alsina is staged as devoted wife and heroine. *Los
misterios del Plata*, whose title acknowledges an indebted-
ness to the work of Eugene Sue, is among the first denunciations of the Rosas regime to appear in form of the
novel. The mysteries indicated in Manso's title are not
about intrigues in the cosmopolitan city, but about the age
of tyranny that enshrouds political subjects in a cloud of
darkness.[29] Embedded in this structure is a major critique
of the mysteries of marriage and love, which have been
abused not only by Rosas's men, but by the unitarians as
well. To expose these terrible secrets about politics and
amor, Manso relies on two parallel but complementary
strategies: first, she turns to a narrative structure of cross-
overs and contradiction to frame problems of narration;
and, second, she situates her narrative intrigue around a
defense of the unified family. It is her female protagonist,
Adelaida, lightly disguised as Antonia Maza de Alsina,
who manages to save her husband from prison and invents a course of resistance to Rosas. But these tales are
never directly narrated: rather, a serpentine course of de-
ceptions confuses the order of narration; secret is added to
secret to conceal the truth of history. Finally, the oppositions of mystery and clarity, light and darkness, and
tyranny and democracy are brought to the center of the
novel through a discussion of matrimony.

Reading *Los misterios del Plata* as a companion text to
Amalia (the two were almost contemporaneous and the

authors were acknowledged friends) reveals not only the strategies of the unitarians in their organization of fictional discourse, but also allows us to refine our appreciation of the emerging debates on women. Unlike Mármol, who sacrifices the image of the married couple for an association among men, Manso proposes a course of narrative action that demands marital commitment and partnership. The anti-Rosas couple, with their child, gives rise to the narrative action of *Los misterios del Plata*, as they attempt to flee their country by boat. When Avellaneda, the hero, is captured, Adelaida, his wife, uses her feminine wiles to sabotage the Rosas regime and plan an escape for her husband. While both novelists concentrate their narrative on the disappearing body, here Adelaida is charged with the sphere of the visible. As if by magic of the wit and tongue, she produces her imprisoned husband, persuading prison guards and agents of the regime to secure his release. Manso's heroine is clearly part of the public scenario. Not one to guard the domestic order and use her house as a space for security, like Mármol's heroine Amalia, she participates in political debates and shares the consequences of public life.

But despite the liberated position of Adelaida as heroine, and her unambiguous devotion to her husband, Manso emphasizes the ruinous state of marital union in general by describing the lives of other unitarian couples. Thus, *Los misterios del Plata*, while focusing on the disappearance of the hero and the aggravated hostilities toward citizens during years of the Rosas regime, also reviews the success and failure of marriage as an institution during the period. Manso, of course, calls attention to the failure of domesticity in the presidential household; Rosas's house, she explains, is in a shambles, and bereft of integrity or love:

> no debemos buscar allí la armonía pacífica de la familia, la santa poesía del hogar doméstico, el todo que representa y caracteriza las gentes de vida laboriosa y tranquilas de conciencia pura y alma virtuosa (107)
> .... El mismo desorden que reina en las instituciones, reina en la sociedad, y despues en el interior de la familia. Rosas es el

amo del pueblo, por consiguiente es también el amo de la familia (108)

As such, Rosas's amoral household serves as a model for institutions in society; as *pater familias*, the leader spreads discord throughout the nation. Manuelita is described as an amazon, driving along the federalist cause without grace or eloquence, and every bit as perverse as her father. It is of significance that Manuela,"la amazona vestida con traje de los gauchos y enormes espuelas teniendo por montura el mulato Biguán enfrenado y ensillado" (p. 167), is dressed like a man; authoritative and ferocious, she lacks the feminine charms that Mármol had ascribed to her in his fictions. Adelaida, on the other hand, because of her unitarian devotion, distinguishes herself by her verbal expression and her quick wit. Manso forms distinctions among women clearly based on political allegiance; as such, she also reshapes gender categories, using physical appearance and verbal skill to corroborate their intellect and political allegiances. Unlike Mármol or other unitarians who sought to defend the daughter of the tyrant, Manso squarely and without apology situates Manuela within the sphere of the monstrous.

While women are separated in the novel by their political persuasions, the men are universally affected by the loss of values brought about by Rosas. Even the unitarian opposition is subject to federalist ruin; family harmony is absent from even the most prestigious homes. In this novel, Manso points to the unitarian officer accused of murdering his wife out of jealousy, to Victor Maza, the highly ranked dissident, who brought his natural child born by his lover to be raised at home by his wife, to the go-between who serviced the sexual appetites of Dorrego. Manso's thesis, drawn from these frequently grotesque examples, is that a good marriage is hard to maintain, a good man hard to find. Yet another mystery of modern life is shown in the affairs of the heart; both the enemy and the allies are confused when it comes to matters of love.

Manso adds these scenes of family discord (which she calls mysteries of the heart) to the list of confusing episodes that emerge in the age of the tyrant. In search of an adequate language to make sense of the confusion, she emphasizes the conflicts of oral and print cultures, she refers to the ambiguous innuendos that organize official discourse, and she displays the falsifications that deprive us of basic truths. This heterogeneity of forms, described by some as a conflict of cultures or as an intersection of many languages in a single text, perhaps best marks the work of early women writers like Juana Manso, who integrates the unitarian strategies of opposition to Rosas with her unique brand of social observation, acutely critical of the sources with which women find themselves identified. In Manso's novel, two languages intersect, the official and the subaltern.[30] On the one hand, she modifies her story by altering the formal appearance of the narrative; she appends footnotes throughout the text, as if to add an historical truth that federalist narration could not provide. In the same vein, as if to correct the limitations of verbal expression, she inserts visual prompters. One character is described as the number "5" for the posture he assumes while sitting; another character looks like the number "4" for the way he crosses his legs. The visual and verbal thus compete for space in the novel as the characters become artefacts in the larger play of discourses. On the other hand, Manso mixes the formal language of literature with a series of translations and foreign dialects so that Italian, Gallician, English, and provincial gaucho idiolects are consciously placed in relief in the novel, showing the fluidity of oral culture in mid-nineteenth century Argentina.[31] In this way, she emphasizes the competition between history and invention, confusing the realms of experience that have been engendered through verbal expression. But Manso also shows the insignificance of language as a way to sustain rationality, as evidenced by the encounter of Avellaneda with unitarian agents. Initially, neither Avellaneda nor his wife can succeed in securing his release; the federalist agent, by contrast, silences all opposition, reducing all attempts at rhetorical persuasion to an inefficient display of words. At the same time, the author finds herself immersed in contradiction, for while her feminine character, Adelaida, struggles to find a language of her own, Manso as novelist also becomes the subject of enforced silence. Manso's concerns about dominant and suppressed languages meet their own ironic destiny in this novel, and provide a certain *trompe l'oeil* for readers of a feminist perspective. The final twenty pages offer a striking reversal of plot, when a male editor intervenes and claims the conclusion as his own invention. Not only do we witness an appropriation of a feminine text, but we also observe a reversal of narrative expositions and anticipated denouements. Yet through this masculine imposition, we come to understand the masculine version of marriage destined for women in nineteenth century literature.

Ricardo Isidro López Muñiz, in an edition of *Los misterios del Plata* published in 1924, admits that Juana Manso presented a partially completed manuscript of the novel and takes to task the completion of the tale in a style coherent with the author's intention. Thus, in the final twenty pages, Adelaida, described throughout as the patient and quick witted wife, suddenly takes on the task of saving her husband through tricks of disguise and verbal deception. She dresses like a man, enters combat with federalist guards and uses the resources of double agency with slaves, wet nurses, and prison officials to secure the release of her husband. The behavior of Adelaida is thus described by the narrator as a gesture of "singular anarquía" and is designed to show the subversion of women to advance the unitarian cause. The male editor's version of woman is, interestingly enough, not consonant with the pacificist course demonstrated in the earlier sections of Manso's novel; rather, the heroine of these final pages looks more like the women of Amalia, while the examples of double agency coincide with Mármol's plan as well. Taking liberty with the original text, López Muñiz insists on the heroine's double identity to bring resolution to the novel. This shift from one discursive system to another, redefining feminine roles, is indeed a curiosity item for readers of

Juana Manso. From evidence available, Manso sought to confuse the subaltern population represented in the novel; she inserted heterogeneity in the fiction by crossing verbal and visual discourse, and by playing with dates and pseudonyms to organize the historical figures of her story. Her female characters, however, are consistent in their devotion to the unified family, not given to the excesses of adventure or to cross-dressing of any sort. Nevertheless, in the appropriation of Manso's text, the editor confirms a common vision of women held by men in the nineteenth century, with which women were seen as agents of deception, engendering transformations of nature and man. Like Mármol's Amalia, who is charged with reform through acts of apparent magic, the character offered by López Muñiz is similarly empowered. This image is indeed derived from the sense of woman as Medusa, capable of transforming destiny and discursive order as well. In this way Adelaida assumes the belligerance of a warrior, inspiring a discursive rebellion that exceeds the limits of the feminine. Her marriage, too, is stained with elements of sedition; even in the felicitous arrangement of the couple, the honest woman is shown to slip from dignity and honor. In effect, she engages in a civilizing mission through recourse to the practices of barbarism. Like Mercedes Rosas, Juana Manuela Gorriti, and Rosa Guerra, whose writings have been lost in large part, Manso is also the subject of repression, appropriated by men of letters in positions of editorial authority. By the terms of this uncanny editorial situation we are reminded of a curious situation, which would seem to allow women to fight for democratic freedom while depriving them of the privilege of authorship.

A reading of these nineteenth century texts from the perspective of feminism allows us to rethink the uses of marriage as a symbolic institution that is transformed in moments of crisis. It is not sufficient to dismiss these women writers for their entrapment in the bourgeois ideology of the couple; more productive, I believe, is to examine the literary treatment of the family in the writings of both men and women, to trace the subtle ways in which the official meaning of marriage and gender is expanded, accommodating principles of nation building while also testing the philosophies of state. Thus, while promienent men of letters—Mármol, Cané, or Gutiérrez—masked the conflicts of weakened masculinity behind the powerful screen of feminine discourse, women writers broke open the narrative principles which ordered the masculine ideational space. In this respect, marriage in the nineteenth century was seen by women as a mediating zone between civilization and barbarism, a site in which national conflicts were called into question or challenged completely. Love thus provided the pretext for conflating the oppositions that defined liberal projects of state while offering the possibilities of forging new alliances among women readers and writers.

NOTES

[1] Ricardo Rodríguez Molas explains that market demands after 1810 had resulted in reductions in the size of the Argentine family; it is especially provocative, in view of this, to think about the extensive mythmaking accorded the nuclear family especially at a time when when its very core was threatened in size.

[2] The alliances among great families of nineteenth century Latin America and their role in state formation is also addressed by the contributors to Asunción Lavrin's anthology.

[3] This is apparent in the women's journalism of the early Rosas period, such as La aljaba (1830) or the Miscelánea de damas of 1833, in which women protested the obscurity to which they had been condemned. Historians have noted the increased numbers of rapes, violations of minors and assaults on women at home in the late Rosas period along with more stringent legal sanctions against them. See Calvera, Guy, Wainerman and Navarro.

[4] Just as many historian as such as José Luis Romero have explored the divisions among unitarians of the period, Hernán Vidal sees the intra-bourgeois struggles as central to the argument of Amalia.

5 Doris Sommer argues a different point from mine, claiming that the marriage of Amalia and Eduardo signifies the desired unification of Argentina, a joining of the urban elite with the rural oligarchy (since Eduardo represents the interests of Buenos Aires and Amalia, the Tucumán landowners).

6 From a different perspective, it may also be speculated that Mármol, in claiming feminine discourse for his male protagonists, must silence the federalist women who compete for the public space.

7 Echeverría shares this vision in the *Dogma socialista* when he describes the spirit of the Rosas era: "La humanidad o la concordia de la familia humana...no existía. Los tiranos...pusieron, para reinar, en lucha al padre con el hijo, al hermano con el hermano, la familia con la familia" (p. 144).

8 I am indebted to Efraín Barradas for his observations about this section of my essay, inquiring if the posted advertisements might not be indicative of a more repressive mode in which men, as the readers of dailies and uniquely in touch with public sphere activities, might not have made choices for their wives in matters of midwifery and gynecological services. Although his point is useful, it still remains to be explored whether the large number of literate females was excluded from newspaper readership.

9 I have benefitted from the wisdom of Janet Greenberg in the field of feminist journalism in nineteenth century Latin America. For a detailed list of women's publications in that century, her forthcoming essay will be of immense value.

10 Lily Sosa de Newton has attributed editorial directorship to Rosa Guerra, but in No. 12 of *La Camelia*, Rosa Guerra announced her non-participation on the editorial staff and adamantly denied any ties to the journal. Greenberg indicates co-editorship by Rosa Guerra and Juana Manso based on evidence from journal articles that I was unable to see.

11 Another way of bringing private conversation and domestic topics into the public sphere was through the publication of the book of recipes. See, for example, Juana Manuela Gorriti's *Cocina ecléctica*, a cookbook drawn from contributions of women throughout Latin America.

12 During the Rosas period, when education for women was limited to the privileged sectors who could afford the services of a governess or other private school training, the schoolgirl's curriculum was extremely limited, as indicated from the following advertisement, taken from the

Gaceta mercantil of 1851: "En la calle Corrientes No. 50 se ha puesto un establecimiento de educación para niñas con el supremo permiso, donde se enseña a leer, escribir, coser, bordar, la doctrina cristiana, gramática castellana y el idioma ynglés, así como muchas otras cosas que sería largo detallar todos bajo el mejor sistema y según el método español" (No. 8418, 28 November 1851).

[13] It is interesting to compare the use of the civilization and barbarism metaphor to describe domesticity by both men and women. Eugenio Mata, for example, explains that although the fall from Paradise is attributable to women, man, precisely because he is not of the savages, still has an obligation to respect the opposite sex: "La muger, no hay duda, que ella es la causa de nuestra perdición, como consta en las sagradas escrituras, pero ¿habremos por eso de abandonarla como sucede entre la mayor parte de los salvajes que pueblan la endurecida costra de la tierra?".

[14] Offen notes that prior to the 1890s, the history of European women cannot be clarified by using distinctions between "feminism" and "women's rights". Indeed, these terms tend to confuse rather than clarify the rich debates generated by women in that earlier period, often suppressing the dense networks of resistance developed by women who would hardly be called feminists by today's standards.

[15] The women's project is closer to that of Juan María Gutiérrez, who advocated a heterogeneous display of American languages to defy the "castizo" doctrine defended in Spain. On this topic, see his *Cartas de un porteño*, in which he devalues the search for linguistic purity in Spanish.

[16] The novel was published with an anagrammatic pseudonym, that of "M. Sasor." The political activities described in the text along with the author's favorable treatment of Lavalle leave me to suspect that the novel was written before 1840, prior to Lavalle's fall from Rosas's favor.

[17] An interesting contrast to Mercedes Rosas's text is found in Juan María Gutiérrez's "El capitán de los patricios" (1843) in which he organizes assignments for women within unitarian political programs. In Gutiérrez's tale, María, a woman of superior intellect, trained in classical literature and herself the author of eclogues, falls in love with a member of the patriotic fighting unit known as the "patricios" and deliberately places herself in his service. The hero, of course, dies in battle and the girl joins a religious order. Unlike Mercedes Rosas, who shows that women's free will in matters of love is limited and that the woman of letters has no alternative but to enter the convent, Gutiérrez claims that devotion to the warrior through convent life is unequivocally the choice

for a woman of culture and uses this example to show the ways in which female intellect should be bound to the service of the nation.

18 See also "Correspondencias," *La Camelia*, 1, No. 7 (25 April 1852): 2, in which women are defended as "capaces de saber, en todos los ramos que cursaron los hombres que se llaman sabios."

19 Other writers will take up Rosa Guerra's position in the following decades. See, for example, Josefina Pelliza de Sagasta, who defended those women devoted both to literature and to their families: "La muger literata sin pretenciones ridículas—puede ser madre y esposa ejemplar sin que por ello olvide su amor a las letras, y sin que esta pasión noble e inocente, menoscabe en lo más mínimo los deberes y atenciones sagradas del hogar."

20 Cristina Iglesia discusses the early legends of Lucía Miranda as part of a discursive play in justification of the conquest. Explaining the impropriety of the Indian's aggressions against the Spaniards, and Lucía in particular, the sixteenth century chronicler Ruy Díaz de Guzmán could then defend the Crown's retaliations and eventual domination of the indigenous population.

21 These authors produced a number of fictions in the nineteenth century in which women were represented as idealized mistresses to their husbands and servants to the nation. See, most notably, Miguel Cané's *Esther* (1851); Juan María Gutiérrez's *El capitán de los patricios* (1843); Vicente Fidel López's *La novia del hereje* (1854); and Bartolomé Mitre's *Soledad* (1847).

22 Gorriti enjoyed the following of some of the more distinguished men of her generation, among them Bartolomé Mitre, Ricardo Palma, Pastor Obligado, and J. M. Torres Caicedo, but she also expanded a dialogue among prominent Latin American women.

23 The proceedings of this literary salon are recorded in Gorriti's *Las veladas literarias de Lima*.

24 On the fragmentation of Gorriti's oeuvre, see the comments of Vicente Quesada in his review of *Sueños y realidades*. (1864: 414).

25 See Thomas Meehan's recent essay for an account of these details.

26 A curious paradox emerges from Gorriti's stories. On the one hand, she expresses an alliance with marginals in which white women are linked to the fate of the indigenous masses. On the other hand, some of

Gorriti's stories show a clear contempt for Indians and ethnic minorities as a menace to white society. We can interpret this in two ways: first, owing to the debates about the Indian in vogue in Lima in her day, Gorriti might have been unable to formulate a non-conflictual discourse on the Indian (see Kristal); second, these ambiguities may be attributable to Gorriti's conflicts about the public/private sphere dichotomies that organized her life. In other words, her private experience of marginality was expressed through alliance with marginals; but her public sphere persona, in which she saw herself part of the empowered liberal elite, allowed her to perceive the marginals as a threat to civil society. This dual vision may explain the shifts in her narrative fiction with respect to the discourse on the Indian.

[27] Contrast Gorriti's defense of the Indian on linguistic terms to the writings of her contemporary, Lucio Mansilla, who in the book *Rozas*, assumes that Indians have no history because their language is impoverished and limited in metaphoric possibilities; the more signs in the linguistic system, the better the civilization, Mansilla claims. Gorriti reaches the conclusion that the Indian presence contributes to that desire for heterogeneity and, therefore, should be welcomed by modern civilizing forces.

[28] Among Manso's more distinguished periodicals, the *Album de señoritas* (1854) and the *Anales de educación común* (1867-75) clearly reflect her devotion to feminist issues. Jim Levy also lists her Brazilian periodical, the *Jornal das senhoras*, which I have not seen.

[29] Manso insists in her prologue to this novel on the mysteries of Argentina under Rosas: "Misterios negros como el absimo, casi increíbles en esta época y que es necesario que aparezcan a la luz de la verdad " (p. 7)

[30] Elaine Showalter has usefully indicated the ways in which we might understand the intersection in a single discursive situation of two oppositional discourses. Describing women's literary tradition, she explains the common tendencies of the woman author to borrow from two discursive systems at once—the dominant or masculine traditions, and the subaltern version of literary history belonging exclusively to women; from this, the writer forges a language uniquely her own. See also Joanna O'Connell, who has developed a very intelligent analysis of double voiced discourse with respect to race and class conflict in the writings of Rosario Castellanos and Nadine Gordimer.

[31] On this point, Manso is not without her contradictions. In the prologue to her novel, Manso explains in a note": El lenguaje empleado en esta obra es casi semejante al que se usa en el país, y si alguna diferencia tiene es en ventaja; es decir, menos grotesco" (p. 8). Manso

thus represents the different social classes in strife during the age of Rosas, profitably generating a gleeful pluralism that decenters her narrative, but her introductory statement reveals a clear allegiance with a world of privilege in which she treats subalterns with contempt.

WORKS CITED

Calvera, Leonor. *Camilia O'Gorman o el amor y el poder*. Buenos Aires: Leviatán, 1986.

Cané, Miguel. *Esther*. Buenos Aires: Universidad de Buenos Aires-Instituto de Literatura Argentina, 1929. Sección de documentos. 1:7. 271-322.

Echeverría, Esteban. *La cautiva/ El matadero*. Buenos Aires: Sopena, 1940.

—. *Dogma socialista*. Buenos Aires: Librería Juan Roldán, 1915.

Gorriti, Juan Ignacio. *Reflexiones sobre las causa morales de las convulsiones internas en los nuevos estados americanos y examen de los medios eficaces para reprimirlas*. Buenos Aires: La Cultura Argentina, 1916.

Gorriti, Juana Manuela. *Sueños y realidades*. 2 vols. Buenos Aires: Casavalle, 1865.

—. *Panoramas de la vida*. 2 vols. Buenos Aires: Imprenta y Librerías de Mayo, 1876.

—. *Veladas literarias de Lima. 1876-1877*. Buenos Aires: Imprenta Europea, 1892.

—. *Cocina ecléctica*. Buenos Aires: Librería Sarmiento, 1977.

Greenberg, Janet. "Toward a History of Women's Periodicals in Latin America: 18th-20th Centuries." Unpublished MS. Forthcoming in Berkeley-Stanford Seminar on Feminism and Latin American Culture. *Women, Culture and Politics in Latin America*.

Guerra, Rosa. "La Educación." *La Educación*. 1, Nº 1 , 24 July (1852a): 1-4.

—. "Correspondencia." *La Educación*. 1, Nº 2 , 7 August (1852b): 3-5.

—. *Lucía Miranda*. Buenos Aires: Universidad de Buenos Aires, 1956.

Gutiérrez, Juan María. "El capitán de los patricios." In *Crítica y narraciones*. Buenos Aires: El Ateneo, 1928. 199-265.

—. *Cartas de un porteño*. Ed. Ernesto Morales. Buenos Aires: Americana, 1942.

Guy, Donna. "Women, Peonage, and Industrialization: Argentina, 1810-1914." *Latin American Research Review*. 16, N° 3 (1981) : 65-89.

Iglesia, Cristina and Julio Schvartzman. *Cautivas y misioneros: Mitos blancos de la conquista*. Buenos Aires: Catálogos, 1987.

Kerber, Linda. *Women of the Republic*. New York: Norton, 1986.

Kristal, Efraín. *The Andes Viewed from the City: Literary and Political Discourse on the Indian in Peru, 1848-1930*. New York: Peter Lang, 1987.

Kuznesof, Elizabeth and Robert Oppenheimer. "The Family in Nineteenth-Century Latin America: An Historiographical Introduction." *Journal of Family History*. 10, N° 3 , Autumn (1985) : 215-34.

Lavrín, Asunción, ed. *Latin American Women: Historical Perspectives*. Westport, Conn.: Greenwood Press, 1978.

Levy, Jim. *Juana Manso, Argentine Feminist*. La Trobe University Institute of Latin America Studies, Occasional Papers No. 1. Boondora: La Trobe University Press, 1977.

Little, Cynthia. "Education, Philanthropy, and Feminism: Components of Argentine Womanhood, 1860-1926." (1978) In Lavrín, 235-53.

López, Vicente Fidel. *La novia del hereje o la inquisición de Lima*. Buenos Aires: A.V. López, n.d.

Mansilla, Lucio. *Rozas. Ensayo histórico-psicólogico*. Paris: Garnier, 1899.

Mansilla de García, Eduarda. *Lucía Miranda*. Buenos Aires: Juan A. Alsina, 1882.

Manso, Juana. "Emancipación moral de la mujer." *La ilustración argentina*. 2a. época, 18 December (1853) : 5-18.

—. *Los misterios del Plata.* Ed. Ricardo Isidro López Muñiz. Buenos Aires: Jesús Menéndez, 1924.

Mármol, José. *Amalia.* 2 vols. Buenos Aires: Centro Editor, 1979.

Mata, Eugenio. "La muger." *El alba.* 1, Nº 11, 27 December (1868): 84.

Meehan, Thomas. "Una olvidada precursora de la literatura fantástica argentina: Juana Manuela Gorriti." *Chasqui.* 10, Nº 2-3 (1981): 3-19.

Mercader, Marta. *Juana Manuela, mucha mujer.* Buenos Aires: Sudamericana, 1980.

Mitre, Bartolomé. *Soledad.* Buenos Aires: Universidad de Buenos Aires-Instituto de Literatura Argentina, Sección de documentos 1, Nº 4 (1928): 91-168.

Morse, Richard. *El espejo de Próspero.* México: Siglo XXI, 1982.

O'Connell, Joanna. "Prospero's Daughters: Language and Allegiance in the Novels of Rosario Castellanos and Nadine Gordimer." Unpublished MS. Diss. University of California, 1988.

Offen, Karen. "Defining Feminism: A Comparative Historical Approach." Unpublished MS. Forthcoming in SIGNS.

Ortega, Miguel. *Lucía Miranda.* Buenos Aires: Universidad de Buenos Aires-Instituto de Literatura Argentina, Sección de documentos 4, Nº 5 (1926): 251-360.

Pelliza de Sagasta, Josefina. 1878. "La muger literata en la república argentina." *El álbum del hogar.* 1:26 , 29 December (1878): 201.

Quesada, Vicente. "Fundación del Colegio de Huérfanas en Buenos Aires." *Revista de Buenos Aires.* 1, Nº 6, October (1863):185-199.

—. "Sueños y realidades." *Revista de Buenos Aires.* 2, Nº 13, July (1864): 407-416.

Rodríguez Molas, Ricardo. "Sexo y matrimonio en la sociedad tradicional." *Todo es historia.* Nº 186, November (1982) : 8-43.

Romero, José Luis. *Las ideologías de la cultura nacional y otros ensayos.* Buenos Aires: Centro Editor, 1982.

Rosas de Rivera, Mercedes. *Maria de Montiel*. Buenos Aires: Imprenta "La Revista", 1861.

Showalter, Elaine. "Feminist Criticism in the Wilderness." In Elizabeth Abel, Ed. *Writing and Sexual Diference*. Chicago: University of Chicago Press. 9-36.

Sommer, Doris. "Not Just Any Narrative: How Romance Can Love Us to Death." In Daniel Balderston, Ed. *The Historical Novel in Latin America*. Gaithersburg, Maryland: Hispamérica, 1986. 47-73.

Sosa de Newton, Lily. *Las argentinas de ayer a hoy*. Buenos Aires: L.V. Zanetti, 1967.

Vidal, Hernán. "*Amalia*: Melodrama y dependencia." *Ideologies and Literatures*. 1, Nº 2 (1977): 41-69.

Wainerman, Catalina and Marysa Navarro. "El trabajo de la mujer en la Argentina: un análisis preliminar de las ideas dominantes en las primeras décadas del siglo XX." *Cuadernos de CENEP*, Nº 7, Buenos Aires: Centro de Estudios de Población, 1979.

Wast, Hugo. *Lucía Miranda*. Buenos Aires: Editores Hugo Wast, 1929.

MUITA SERVENTIA

Roberto Reis
University of Minnesota, Minneapolis

"Mulher tem muita serventia, o senhor nem imagina. Ajuda até na política. Dá filhos pra gente,
impõe respeito. Pro resto, tem as raparigas..."
— Jorge Amado,
Gabriela, Cravo e Canela.

Sérgio Buarque de Holanda, em livro hoje clássico, es-
creveu que a família era modelo obrigatório de qualquer
composição social no Brasil (106). Antes de aprofundar tal
registro, convém prestar atenção à advertência de Dante
Moreira Leite: o conceito de família patriarcal se aplica a
uma pequena parcela da sociedade e deve ser visto como
unidade de poder (282) e não como passível de explicar a
organização social como um todo — erro em que incorre-
ram ideólogos do porte de um Gilberto Freyre, cuja obra,
ainda segundo Moreira Leite, é "escrita e interpretada do
ponto de vista da classe dominante" (281).
Feita a ressalva, vale a pena explorar o termo e desen-
tranhar algumas de suas implicações. No mesmo *Raízes
do Brasil*, Sérgio Buarque salienta que a própria palavra
'família' deriva de *famulus*, trazendo no bojo de sua eti-
mologia a idéia de servidão (49). Com efeito, a família patriarcal era, no final das contas, uma forma de organização
do poder, estruturada hierarquicamente e cujo desenho
último poderia ser figurado em uma série de círculos
concêntricos: no centro, todo-poderoso, o senhor de terras
(prevalência de uma ordem senhorial), que acumula os
papéis de pai (prevalência de uma ordem patriarcal) e de
homem (prevalência de uma ordem masculina). No âmbito da casa-grande, diretamente sob o mando do senhor, a
esposa e os filhos; quanto mais afastado deste núcleo
emanador de poder, goza de menos prestígio a posição so-

cial do indivíduo, o que esclarece por que todos queriam agasalhar-se sob as asas do ocupante do centro. A presença de uma pessoa neste centro é fundamental para que se definam os demais lugares sociais. E, no mais externo dos círculos, no patamar da pirâmide social, o escravo (prevalência de uma ordem escravocrata).

Com efeito, a organização patriarcal da família encontra a sua contrapartida, na esfera econômica, na escravidão, ocasionando uma extrema polaridade na estratificação social brasileira, estruturada basicamente em torno da relação senhor-escravo. Ao redor deste setor organizado, oscilam dispersos os chamados "homens livres", aspeados porque no fundo são dependentes de um grande, com quem interagem mediante o mecanismo do favor.

Tal configuração do senhoriato estamental brasileiro perdura até as vésperas da Revolução de 30: o patriarca — dono absoluto de sua propriedade, de sua família, de seus servos — se transforma, depois da libertação dos escravos, no coronel e, em seguida, no chefe político que decide as questões através de suas preferências pessoais e suas relações de família e amizade (Leite 283). Com a urbanização do país, a "aristocracia" rural passa a ocupar novos cargos, para os quais carrega a mentalidade familiar. Mas a estrutura senhorial estava abalada e a família patriarcal ia aos poucos se decompondo: 1930 representa a ruptura de um tipo de articulação da sociedade brasileira, resultando no fim da hegemonia dos proprietários de terras ligados à exportação de produtos como o café; significa ainda a fratura de uma forma de relação entre centro e periferia e da ideologia elitista e liberal, que irrigava todo o sistema, já minada desde os anos 20. Mas a relevância da família se arraigou no inconsciente social, legando marcas como o paternalismo e o filhotismo protecionista, que ainda hoje têm trânsito em larga escala e deterioram as relações políticas no país.

* * *

O desenho da organização social brasileira — estruturada, no âmbito das elites dominantes, em cima da família

— propicia um enfrentamento da situação da mulher, ainda dentro dos mesmos estamentos senhoriais. Como regra geral, a mulher de classe superior era submissa ao marido. Dentro de casa e com relação à parentela, desenvolvia intensa atividade, sendo raras a indolência e a passividade (Queiroz 193) — mas, seguramente, dando ordens às escravas que, estas sim, executavam de fato o grosso dos serviços domésticos. Antonio Candido, estudando a instituição da família, procura corrigir a imagem lendária que alguns escritores pintaram da mulher, mostrando que ela estava incumbida de uma função ativa e distinta daquela que competia ao homem: ela dirigia o trabalho dos escravos, a confecção de roupas, providenciava a comida, tomava conta dos filhos (296).

O que está me importando ressaltar agora é este hiato lacunoso entre o que supostamente era a realidade e sua representação no universo simbólico, seja em textos ficcionais, seja no próprio discurso cultural. Preciso transcrever as seguintes palavras de Maria Inácia D'Avila Neto:

> o significado da "autoridade patriarcal" pode se resumir aqui muito esquematicamente: nosso sistema patriarcal apresentou diferentes modos de dominação na relação homem-mulher, variando conforme a cor da pele ou a camada social da mulher, ou seja sua "classe-cor". Nosso sistema patriarcal foi ambíguo, se considerarmos que, enquanto o patriarca era senhor absoluto de sua mulher, prole, escravos, inclusive com direito de morte sobre eles, a mulher era glorificada através de modelos ideais. Essa idealização esteve aí estreitamente ligada à perpetuação dos tabus sexuais. O Culto à Virgem foi uma rica fonte de preconceitos ainda bastante tenazes entre nós. A *Virgem*, freqüentemente associada à mulher branca, idealizada como imagem de mulher pura, jamais tocada em seu sexo, juntou-se à crença nos "poderes mágicos" e "afrodisíacos" das mestiças, mito, aliás, até hoje explorado pelo nosso espetáculo de exportação turística. Foi exatamente através da "sexualidade exaltada" da mulata, de seus "feitiços, dengues e quindins", como chamaram alguns expositores da cultura brasileira, ou, em contraposição, a negação do sexo, no caso da mulher branca, que nasceram os aspectos de idealização mística/e ou mágica das mulheres no sistema patriarcal. O patriarca que tinha, além da mulher legítima, as escravas, que lhe prestavam também serviços sexuais, constituía muitas vezes famílias paralelas. Esse estado de coisas serviu para cristalizar preconceitos em torno da *natureza polígama do homem* (em oposição à *mulher talhada para um só amor*) e o

princípio da dupla moral, que caracterizam o que chamou E. Willens de o "complexo de virilidade" do homem brasileiro (6).

Ora, interessa-me destacar a ambigüidade no tratamento da mulher no discurso cultural brasileiro: de um lado é tida como submissa ao homem; de outro, cria-se o mito da mulher pura, merecedora de um amor espiritualizado, quando pertencente às frações superiores, cujo oposto é a atração carnal pelas mulheres de cor, decantada em sua sexualidade, que invariavelmente pertencem a grupos sociais menos privilegiados. Isto inclusive pode ser fisgado em textos literários, nos quais a senhora desperta um desejo que é recalcado (e que se desloca, metafórica ou metonimicamente — e os exemplos seriam abundantes), enquanto a mulata e a negra, mesmo pelo fato de serem escravas ou de baixa condição social, relacionadas de alguma maneira à propriedade, quando focalizadas franqueiam a manifestação franca do desejo e são submetidas à posse pelo senhor e patriarca ou pelos nhonhôs brancos. Esta bifurcação com referência à mulher subsiste até os nossos dias no comportamento da sociedade e na literatura brasileira e se vislumbra, no último caso, mesmo num poeta da envergadura de um Drummond.

Em outras palavras e explicitando minha tese — o romance brasileiro do século passado, de um modo geral, como que desenha, no que tange às práticas amorosas, um quadro ideal, que muito pouco corresponde de fato ao cotidiano social que lhe era contemporâneo (é sabido como os grandes proprietários rurais, e mesmo seus filhos, mantinham relações com escravas e geravam uma infinidade de filhos bastardos, a ponto de muitas senhoras não consentirem negras belas como escravas). Tal retrato é "puritano", pintando a família como um espaço santo, purificado, para o qual convergem os cônjuges, desde que nivelados socialmente, e no qual vivem afastados, com conotações bucólicas, do convívio social, em contacto com a natureza. Ou seja: a narrativa se trai e há uma captação enviesada da realidade, fornecendo um *auto-retrato* do senhoriato patriarcal nesse gesto mesmo de mascarar o cotidiano oitocentista. E se inscrevendo, desse modo, dentro de um projeto ideológico global: trata-se de uma literatura que, através de noções como a de nacionalismo, acaba armando uma justificativa para a hegemonia da elite senhorial que estava no poder.

* * *

O encobrimento já é flagrado na tática de evitar a tematização ficcional da questão candente do século XIX no Brasil: a escravidão. Como já tratei em detalhe o problema em outra parte (Reis 19-51), limito-me a retomá-lo em termos bastante sumários, apenas para dar seqüência à reflexão objeto deste trabalho.

O romance brasileiro oitocentista como que evita tratar a escravatura. Seria, em derradeira instância, colocar a sociedade senhorial face a face com suas próprias mazelas. Embora não disponhamos de dados conclusivos a este respeito, é bastante razoável supor que os leitores da época (minguado público, composto sobremodo de mulheres e estudantes) pertencessem ou quisessem pertencer às elites dominantes; de igual modo, os escritores utilizaram seu talento como forma de ascensão, buscando o aconchego do senhoriato ou mesmo do Estado monárquico; e, para situar esta literatura no estreito círculo senhorial, assinalo que ela se debruça sobre estes mesmos setores (caso, em particular, dos romances urbanos) ou, quando aborda os segmentos periféricos (como nos romances sertanistas ou indianistas), o faz desde um enfoque centrado, que apreende o outro, não localizado no centro de poder, a partir de uma ótica masculina, patriarcal, senhorial.

O fato de a escravidão, que salta aos olhos ao problematizarmos o século passado brasileiro, não estar presente não quer dizer que ela não se revestisse de importância. Devemos deduzir justamente o contrário: seu escamoteamento, ao se branquear personagens como Isaura (de *A Escrava Isaura*, de Bernardo Guimarães) ou a ausência de escravos em um Alencar, por exemplo, indicam que o assunto inquietava a *mauvaise conscience* dos estamentos senhoriais. Concordando mais uma vez com Dante Moreira Leite, a questão do escravismo, sustentáculo da vida social e econômica, "não poderia ser discutida pela classe dominante, enquanto que a classe dominada não tinha acesso à cultura" (Leite 289). Seu debate pelas camadas mais populares, em vista disso, teria que ser vasculhado em outras manifestações culturais, sendo a literatura uma forma elitista no Brasil.

Ao recalque ao nível da antecena do texto — onde, via de regra, se narra uma intriga sentimental — corresponderá um deslocamento do assunto para a esfera das relações amorosas, provocando a emergência das contradições sociais nos bastidores inconscientes do fundo de cena romanesco e contradizendo o projeto contestador da narrativa, que se revela, afinal, uma mera reduplicadora dos valores em voga. Daí o *amor tirano* (a metáfora está em *Senhora*, de Alencar), que escraviza e implica em submissão e domínio, mas no inocente âmbito das relações entre enamorados, nunca entre verdadeiros senhores ou escravos.

Tendo-se em mente que a condição de escravo implica em inferioridade social, caberia examinar quais os personagens que são dados como "escravos" na relação amorosa. Tal análise conclui que "senhor" é o homem branco e "escravos" do amor são o sertanejo (o homem interiorano), o índio, a mulher. Esta, se for de situação social superior ao homem (o que ocorre quando este é índio ou sertanejo), será a "senhora"; se estiverem no mesmo plano, socialmente falando, ela será a "escrava", sujeita aos postulados masculinos e patriarcais, do amor tirano.

Idêntico tipo de enviesamento, que camufla na antecena o tropeço ideológico do fundo de cena, se detectaria nos textos indianistas. O índio comparece para preencher a necessidade de forjar uma origem heróica, lendária, nobre e etnicamente pura para a "aristocracia" mestiça do país recém-independente e se inscreve no projeto de edificação de uma mitologia nacional. O selvagem ficcionalizado pelos românticos será um cavaleiro medieval de tanga (vestido para não escandalizar a moral vitoriana dos grupos senhoriais) e tacape, que preza valores como a honra e que não representava, ao contrário do negro, qualquer ameaça à ordem escravocrata vigente. O índio contemporâneo, entretanto — o que vivia na miséria, escorraçado para os confins das florestas ou degradado e aculturado nas cidades em crescimento —, não consistia um tema literário (Leite 172).

* * *

Nas seções anteriores trabalhei a coincidência, em termos de um desacordo entre a realidade cotidiana do século XIX e sua representação simbólica, pinçável tanto no discurso cultural quanto ao nível do discurso ficcional brasileiro. Vale frisar que é esta flutuação entre ideário e realidade que dita o tom da vida ideológica do tempo, causando a sensação de as idéias estarem *fora do lugar*, para evocar arguto ensaio de Roberto Schwarz. Importando o liberalismo para um contexto escravocrata, o Romantismo para uma sociedade que não conhecera nada análogo à Revolução Francesa ou à Revolução Industrial, o oitocentos brasileiro se assemelha a um *torcicolo* (a expressão é de novo de Schwarz), ensejando uma vida cultural o mais das vezes escapista, ornamental e mascaradora.

Estou em condições de voltar as minhas atenções para o tratamento da figura da mulher no romance brasileiro do século XIX. Foge aos meus propósitos fazê-lo de modo exaustivo, mesmo porque, salvo eventuais exceções (como *Dona Guidinha do Poço*, de Manuel de Oliveira Paiva) e com pequenas variantes (como a exacerbação naturalista e patológica da sexualidade, em *A Carne*, de Júlio Ribeiro, ou a sutileza psicológica e a ambigüidade moral dos personagens femininos machadianos), o padrão detectado é recorrente: a mulher de certa posição social é pura e casta, despertando um amor espiritualizado (apenas alma, corpo sublimado e recalcado), submissa e "escrava" do homem, seu "senhor", se este for da mesma condição social que ela, ocasião em que estará destinada a ser a esposa, no espaço santificado e recolhido da família. Em caso contrário, como ficou mencionado, ela será a "senhora". Se for de um grupo socialmente inferior, em especial se for de cor, aguçará desejos lascivos e será objeto de um amor físico e carnal (veja-se o caso de Rita Baiana, de *O Cortiço*, de Aluísio Azevedo, ou de Margarida, de *O*

Seminarista, de Bernardo Guimarães). A mulher está para
servir ao homem, o qual, muitas vezes, ascende graças a
ela, a quem é negada a mobilidade social. Em *O Garim-
peiro*, também de Bernardo Guimarães, Elias e o Major (o
primeiro em vias de ser homem da "boa sociedade" e o
segundo um fazendeiro em apuros financeiros) são os fa-
vorecidos com o casamento, em que Lúcia representa um
valor de troca, e com o trabalho de Simão, o criado.
Convém ainda sublinhar que tal situação transcende o oitocentos brasileiro, chegando até nossos dias: em Jorge
Amado a mulher branca e melhor situada econômica e
socialmente é chata e insôssa, ao passo que a mulata é
apimentada (boa de cama e mesa), sensual e entra em cena
para abrir as pernas, como acontece em *Capitães da Areia*.
Ou seja: teríamos que esperar por autores como Clarice
Lispector ou Lygia Fagundes Telles, por exemplo, para
presenciar um equacionamento realmente diverso da
questão da mulher. Embora se possa escrever que é o homem quem dá a identidade da protagonista em *Uma
Aprendizagem*, ou que a falta da figura paterna é um em-
pecilho para que Raíssa se descubra a si mesma, em *Verão
no Aquário*, penso que as escritoras mulheres lograrão
mais êxito em capturar o magma feminino na literatura
brasileira contemporânea.

Meu intento aqui, portanto, se resume em percorrer
um dos "perfis de mulher" de José de Alencar para, por
fim, ensaiar algumas conclusões.

* * *

Em *Lucíola* (1862), Paulo e a narrativa que narra tentam
conciliar a antitética imagem que se desprende de Lúcia. O
narrador não consegue compreender que a menina casta e
pura seja uma mulher, cortesã e necessita resolver o para-
doxo. No primeiro caso, terá que reprimir o seu desejo; no
segundo, poderá dar livre vasão ao gozo e ao prazer.

Lúcia paulatinamente se metamorfoseia, alimentada
pelo amor de Paulo, na purificada e angelical Maria da
Glória. Tendo internalizado as marcas dos grupos sociais
dirigentes, ela fica obcecada pela ambição de pureza. En-

quanto Maria da Glória, ela adere a uma vida recatada, nega o corpo ao ex-amante que, persistindo seu desejo, só pode externá-lo dando "um beijo na ponta da botina que aparecia sob a orla do vestido" de Lúcia (Alencar 187). Porque a Lúcia que interessa a Paulo é a dos "bons dias", que o engolfava "num mar de voluptuosidades" (148). Vale dizer: a Lúcia sexo, corpo. Seu desejo nunca desaparece, ao passo que o de Lúcia, bem mais reprimido, se extravasa na cena do "último beijo" (213) ou se transfere, deslocado primeiro para o ser chamada de Maria da Glória e, em seguida, para a "suprema delícia" que coloca em cena sua irmã, Ana, que ela oferece a Paulo: "não acharás alma tão pura, nem mais casto amor" (220).

Lúcia pinta o amor como "coesão de almas" (217), amor sem interesse que despreza o corpo e que ela associa à "felicidade dos que têm uma família" (40). Lúcia, apesar de transformada em anjo, carrega o estigma do passado de cortesã. Ela almeja ser pura, uma senhora e não uma mulher (a distinção é feita pelo texto), pois a senhora pode pertencer à "boa sociedade", anseio também de Paulo. No contexto patriarcal, a esposa é a reprodutora de filhos, mulher de respeito e de família. Nesta esfera puritana, da camada senhorial, a relação física está recalcada e o amor sexual, liberador do prazer, está reservado para as mulheres, em espaço outro que não o núcleo familiar.

Lúcia, ao propor a Paulo que se case com Ana, insinua que ele precisa "criar uma família e gozar das santas afeições domésticas" (219), que ela não se sente capaz de lhe proporcionar. A família se delineia como o lugar edênico, sublime, para o qual converge a máxima felicidade. O anseio de se recolher em contacto com a natureza e levar uma existência pacata e retirada da sociedade recorre em Alencar. Não raro os rapazes que povoam seus textos urbanos despendem a mocidade em "loucuras", que procuram esquecer ao se casarem, refugiando-se na família.

Lúcia estaria na iminência de ingressar neste espaço sacralizado. Entretanto, Maria da Glória, tendo a "alma virgem", sendo um anjo, ainda percebe em si uma nódoa de culpa e não se acha gabaritada para desposar Paulo e oferecer-lhe os "castos prazeres". Só na morte, que implica na destruição total do corpo e que enseja o "santo consórcio" das duas almas, ela poderá se redimir por completo, expiando o pecado de se ter vendido. Pagando pela ousadia de, tendo sido "mulher", querer ter a vã pretensão de ser "senhora".

Paulo, que anseia ascender socialmente, não pode denegrir sua imagem de homem de bem, permitindo que sua honra seja manchada com a fama de que está envolvido com uma cortesã. Iniciando uma "vida séria" (169), necessitando de aprovação social, a morte de Lúcia é imprescindível para que ele prossiga em seu caminho. A Lúcia, ainda que transfigurada na santa e pura Maria da Glória, apesar de ter uma pequena fortuna (notória credencial para o prestígio) é vetada a salvação. Tendo transgredido com o corpo o contexto puritano e moralista, não pode se tornar uma dama. Lúcia quis trocar de posição e para tal buscou abraçar novos valores. Na verdade, perdeu o seu lugar social, pois deixou de ser cortesã; mas não lhe consentem, pelo fato de tê-lo sido, pertencer à "boa sociedade" e aproximar-se do núcleo senhorial. Querer sair do lugar que lhe estava previamente estipulado, lugar em que sua presença ganhava sentido, seria subverter a cerimônia santa do casamento. Não é facultado, no entanto, violar a fronteira que separa o espaço da castidade (a família) do espaço do prazer (pré ou extra-conjugal), a alma do corpo, as senhoras das mulheres, limite que decreta as posições e os papéis sociais a serem desempenhados pelos indivíduos. Papéis que, como ficou escrito mais atrás, na sociedade brasileira, no seio dos estamentos dominantes, eram designados a partir da figura do patriarca.

Enfatizemos a contradição do texto. À primeira vista, *Lucíola* critica a sociedade do tempo, que produzia "Lúcias". Inocentar a protagonista e condenar esta sociedade parece ser, ao que tudo indica, o intento primeiro desta narrativa de José de Alencar. Todavia, embora imponha a "musa cristã", mártir da sociedade, o romance a imola, por assim dizer, não a perdoa, repisando os mesmos valores que parecia atacar. Couto, Cunha, Sá, o próprio Paulo (a não ser pelo fato de querer exumar, pela escritura, a "Lúcia dos bons dias") saem incólumes.

A intriga amorosa que se declara na antecena textual na verdade oblitera estes aspectos sociais. A ótica que preside o texto é duplamente masculina: a do narrador Paulo e, mais significativo, a da sociedade aí retratada. Consente-se aos homens a realização de seus desejos (desde que com cortesãs) e se lhes reserva as meninas inocentes para os "santos gozos" do amor conjugal. A sociedade, que se mostra tão complacente com a prática amorosa dos mancebos, tende a discriminar as mulheres — basta estarem desacompanhadas para não serem olhadas como "senhoras" (30). Só com as cortesãs é que se abrem as portas da "mansão do prazer" — mas para a saciedade masculina. Para a mulher da "boa sociedade", que tem que manter a compostura, está sublimado o gozo, o amor carnal, entendido como prazer. Visão romântica, sem dúvida. Muito mais interessante é relevar seu vínculo com a sociedade brasileira do Segundo Império. Sociedade, já o sabemos, patriarcal, senhorial, masculina e escravagista.

O desejo carnal e o prazer são tolerados no âmbito masculino, desde que com cortesãs (ou escravas), visto ser o espaço familiar puro e casto, cerceador do prazer. Às personagens femininas socialmente instaladas no centro dos círculos concêntricos é reservado o culto do amor idealizado, espiritual, carregado de conotações religiosas. Há, pois, um duplo recalque: do amor físico, marcado negativamente, e da mulher. Esta, por seu turno, é forçada a decidir em qual polo se situa: no da família, lugar das senhoras e meninas inocentes, da castidade; ou no do gozo, protagonizado por cortesãs ou mulheres de condição social inferior ou de cor. À mulher é vedado o trânsito social e a ambigüidade de acumular os dois extremos. Ao homem, contudo, se faculta circular de um para o outro, já que a organização social se estrutura de modo a beneficiar a ordem masculina.

A abordagem de *Lucíola* nos aponta o caráter hierárquico (repressor e autoritário) da sociedade aí abarcada. E nos ilustra a questão da mulher neste mesmo contexto. O romance de Alencar como que elabora um panorama ideal: implicitamente enaltece a família e coloca a cortesã *em seu lugar*, afastando-a do senhoriato que ocupa o centro do poder. Como que purificando o cotidiano sexual do oitocentos brasileiro, por um lado, mas deixando entrever sua face última por trás da máscara urdida pela narrativa.

Lúcia, heroína no fundo inferiorizada, é comparada em várias passagens a uma escrava. Senhor é Paulo. Lucíola é um "lampiro noturno" — um inseto social.

* * *

Evidentemente, de forma alguma estas páginas reivindicam o adjetivo feminista para seu gesto crítico. Suponho que as feministas mais perspicazes e o feminismo menos epidérmico já percebeu que de nada adianta clamar por um maior espaço para a mulher se a sociedade como um todo não se vergar a uma prática mais justa e respeitadora da *diferença*. Neste sentido, claro está que, segundo entendo, o feminismo estaria em condições de se aliar a outras posturas teóricas e políticas uma vez que, resguardadas suas especificidades e peculiaridades, seus assédios mantêm bastante em comum. Não quero, porém, enveredar por uma discussão mais abrangente e muito menos receitar caminhos.

No que tange ao Brasil, muito ainda há que ser feito a fim de que a mulher encontre um lugar digno na sociedade e esta luta se inscreve na causa de diversas minorias que pleiteiam uma democracia plural no país, entendida não necessariamente como vontade da maioria, mas, ao invés, como convívio dos contrários. Acredito, por outra parte, ser importante tentar compreender o estatuto da mulher desde uma arqueologia que esteja plantada fundo na história da formação social brasileira. Apesar deste ensaio ter operado preferencialmente na órbita dos estamentos senhoriais, as implicações nele avançadas permitiriam desde logo indagar qual seria a situação feminina fora do estreito círculo masculino e patriarcal. A despeito de me haver cingido ao tratamento da mulher em obras ficcionais, fique explicitada a necessidade de se vascular a problemática feminina em outras facetas do discurso cultural brasileiro. E, mesmo se quiséssemos nos ater ao campo da literatura, um sem número de questões restam em aberto: para ficar num único exemplo, a historiografia literária tradicional não consigna, salvo um ou outro nome citado de passagem, até o segundo momento modernista (isto é, nos anos 30), nenhuma escritora mulher — não existiram ou a própria canonização se encarregou de deixá-las de fora?

Em outras palavras e sem querer com isso descartar o feminismo, penso que uma crítica realmente desconstrutora, ancorada no social e na história e que se revista de um caráter eminentemente político, prescinde de adjetivos. Porque, afinal, o que o passado e o presente da América Latina têm mostrado é que o nó da questão não se resume ao confronto entre feminismo e machismo, que a feição autoritária afeta a ambos, homens e mulheres. E que, valha a utopia ao menos como estratégia provisória, no horizonte para o qual aponta uma prática crítica lúcida cintila uma sociedade cujos indivíduos, homens ou mulheres, não terão, enquanto necessidade, uma *serventia*. Serão tão somente pessoas, na integridade e plenitude de sua diferença e de dignos seres humanos, desfrutando, de acordo com um verso de Drummond, da "insuspeitada alegria de conviver".

BIBLIOGRAFIA

Alencar, José de. *Lucíola*. Rio de Janeiro: Ouro, s/d.

Candido, Antonio. "The Brazilian Family". *Brazil, Portrait of Half a Continent*. Ed. T. Lynn Smith. New York: Drysden, 1951. 291-312.

D'Avila Neto, Maria Inácia. "O Autoritarismo e a Mulher Brasileira". *Jornal do Brasil* [Rio de Janeiro] 7 Set. 1980, Caderno Especial: 6.

Freyre, Gilberto. *Casa-Grande & Senzala*. 19 ed. Rio de Janeiro: José Olympio, 1978.

Hahner, June. *A Mulher no Brasil*. Rio de Janeiro: Civilização Brasileira, 1978.

Holanda, Sérgio Buarque de. *Raízes do Brasil*. 12 ed. Rio de Janeiro: José Olympio, 1978.

Leite, Dante Moreira. *O Caráter Nacional Brasileiro*. 2 ed. São Paulo: Pioneira, 1969.

Queiroz, Maria Isaura Pereira de. *O Mandonismo Local na Vida Política Brasileira*. São Paulo: Alfa-Omega, 1976.

Reis, Roberto. *A Permanência do Círculo — Hierarquia no Romance Brasileiro*. Niterói/Brasília: EDUFF/INL, 1987.

Samara, Eni de Mesquita. *A Família Brasileira*. São Paulo: Brasiliense, 1983.

Schwarz, Roberto. *Ao Vencedor, as Batatas*. São Paulo: Duas Cidades, 1977.

TERCERA PARTE

REACCIONES

Elena Sánchez-Mora
University of Minnesota, Minneapolis

La convocatoria de Hernán Vidal para la conferencia intitulada *International Conference on Cultural-Historical Grounding for Hispanic and Luso-Brazilian Feminist Literary Criticism* lanzaba el desafío de emprender una crítica de la crítica literaria feminista hispánica. Esto llevó a los participantes a reflexionar acerca del proceso teórico propio y el del feminismo en general. A riesgo de generalizar demasiado, creo que los trabajos presentados se basaron en su mayoría en el análisis de un texto o un grupo de textos literarios a los que la teoría se fue incorporando de acuerdo con las necesidades de interpretación. Hubo un grupo de trabajos que englobó aspectos teóricos diversos sin centrarse en un texto específico, sino haciendo referencia a diversos textos: los de Lucía Guerra, Rosario Ferré, Sara Castro Klarén, Gabriela Mora. No es casual que sean los trabajos de las latinoamericanas los que entraron en esa categoría. Pero todos los trabajos con excepción del de Hernán Vidal se referían a ejemplos concretos. Creo que ello obedece a que la teoría literaria feminista se ha ido haciendo sobre la marcha. De cualquier forma, esta conferencia ha iniciado lo que podría convertirse —usando el afortunado título del trabajo de Rosario Ferré—, en un coloquio de las perras permanente. De allí que haya que agradecer a Vidal haber lanzado el reto y haber hecho posible el diálogo al hacerse cargo de la coordinación. Sin embargo, hay que reconocer que fue la respuesta entusiasta de las participantes de diversas universidades la que contribuyó a la gran riqueza y diversidad de enfoques, temáticas y opiniones. Entre paréntesis, agradezco a las participantes la valiosa información contenida en los trabajos, la cual desde ahora pienso incorporar en mi trabajo. Como estudiante de posgrado, esta conferencia representó también para mí la oportunidad de asociar los nombres de las autoras de artículos que han sido de gran valor en mi propio desarrollo, con las caras de varias participantes; debo agregar que me sorprendió gratamente que se tratara de mujeres tan jóvenes con un entusiasmo inacabable y con un compromiso personal hacia el feminismo. El saber que estas mujeres se están colocando en lugares clave dentro del medio académico, me hizo sentir un gran optimismo hacia el futuro de la crítica literaria feminista

Acerca del desarrollo de la conferencia, a mi parecer se notó un contraste muy marcado entre las discusiones del jueves y las del viernes. El jueves me quedé con la impresión de una gran dispersión. Quizá ello tenga que ver, por una parte, con mis propias expectativas en relación a otros congresos feministas a los que he asistido y que me llevan a exigir un alto nivel de placer instantáneo. Por otra parte, es fácil olvidar que es necesario pasar por un primer momento en el que se definen el estilo de la discusión y las personalidades de los participantes. El viernes en cambio me pareció mucho más productivo, y creo que se debió a que la discusión se centró más en los trabajos. El último día constituyó la culminación del encuentro, en el que quedaron establecidos lazos permanentes de trabajo y amistad entre los participantes.

En general se dejó sentir un ambiente de camaradería y apoyo en el que no se trataba de monopolizar el discurso, sino de facilitar el intercambio. Debo agregar que si en otros congresos organizados por el Departamento de Español de la Universidad de Minnesota me ha parecido poco menos que imposible expresar mis puntos de vista desde mi posición de estudiante, en este me he encontrado participando casi sin querer, llevada por la dinámica colectiva.

A continuación menciono ciertos temas que sobresalieron por haber generado vivas polémicas.

La categorización de la mujer negra, blanca y roja, que surgió concretamente del trabajo de Cristina Duplaá en relación a la imagen de la mujer creada por la burguesía nacionalista catalana, despertó marcada oposición. A mi juicio, en cierto momento de la discusión se perdió de vista la necesidad de historizar constantemente las formas como se ha conceptualizado a la mujer en el discurso oficial. Es decir, que si en el momento histórico actual cuestionamos como feministas este tipo de arquetipificación porque nos parece limitante, hay que tomar en cuenta que dichas categorías funcionan en el contexto del siglo XIX para explicar las preconcepciones de la sociedad patriarcal en cuanto al papel social de la mujer.

La polémica en torno al concepto de género resultó en una discusión aparte durante el tiempo dedicado a reacciones generales y comentarios en el último día de la conferencia. En esa discusión se pudo ver la urgencia que existe dentro de la teoría feminista de redefinir términos que se habían usado por largo tiempo en las ciencias sociales. En este caso, se trató de buscar un término alternativo al de género, que en castellano posee varias connotaciones, pero que carece de la carga social actual de la palabra inglesa "gender" en contraposición a "sex", que tiene una connotación biológica (no hay que olvidar, sin embargo, que el término "gender" hasta hace poco poseía la misma connotación de función natural de acuerdo a los atributos físicos de cada sexo, tal como la usó Talcott Parsons en los años cincuenta). Se sugirió, entre otras cosas, agregar calificativos que aclararan el uso de género en cuanto a sistema social de división del trabajo de acuerdo al sexo biológico. Se propusieron "género social", "género cultural", "sistema genérico". Como era de esperarse, no se llegó a ningún acuerdo específico. Por otro lado, la polémica en torno a Freud que se suscitó a raíz de la presentación de Teresa Vilarós, demostró que también es necesaria una constante revisión de teorías masculinistas que si bien pueden tener algún valor, deben utilizarse con mucho tiento.

El tema del lesbianismo, surgido a partir del trabajo presentado por Amy Kaminsky sobre Silvia Molloy, comprobó una vez más que el debate sigue en pie, y que está relacionado con un cuestionamiento más amplio de los límites impuestos por el orden patriarcal. En el momento más álgido de la polémica se pudo percibir una división entre aquellos que aceptaban que aclarar que una escritora era lesbiana era reconocer un atributo que caracterizaba a su obra de manera fundamental, y aquellos que pensaban que equivalía a etiquetarla. En mi opinión, el segundo grupo no acertaba a distinguir entre una situación ideal en la que la preferencia sexual no fuera un estigma, y la realidad, en la que el ser lesbiana produce respuestas concretas de expresión de una preferencia sexual que la sociedad considera desviada. En cierta forma, ello se relaciona con el uso del término "persona" que planteaba Hernán Vidal en su trabajo, y en el cual veo el peligro de que se desvanezcan las diferencias genéricas que ahora mismo nos definen, en pos de un universalismo deseable pero utópico.

Para terminar, menciono algunos temas que quedaron pendientes, ya sea porque se tocaron poco o porque no se tocaron en absoluto.

Como el título mismo de la conferencia lo indicaba, la relación literatura/historia no se puede soslayar al discutir la problemática teórica de la crítica literaria feminista hispánica. En este sentido, particularmente los trabajos del siglo XIX hicieron patente esta relación, y resultó especialmente interesante contar con la visión de la historiadora Guadalupe Gómez-Ferrer en cuanto al uso de textos literarios. Sin embargo, convendría tratar dicha relación de manera más explícita. Por ello, secundo la propuesta de Amy Kaminsky de "la convergencia de feminismo, historia y literatura" como tema de una próxima conferencia. Dentro de la misma línea, la ansiedad masculina hacia la invasión femenina del terreno literario a fines del siglo XIX y principios del XX, es un tema que ha sido tratado en el caso de la crítica literaria de habla inglesa, y que hace falta aplicar sistemáticamente al caso de la crítica de habla española.

En mi opinión, un tema que ameritaba atención es la tendencia a rechazar la crítica literaria feminista de textos de autores masculinos a favor de la de autoras. Concretamente, me refiero a la oposición establecida por Elaine Showalter entre "Feminist Critique" y "Gynocritics". Aunque a fin de cuentas Showalter termina por declararse a favor de la integración de ambas, es imprescindible cuestionar, por un lado, que la motivación para emprender la primera sea el mero deseo de estudiar obras reconocidas dentro del canon, y por otro, que se pueda identificar una "cultura femenina" aislada de la cultura global de signo masculino. Una ramificación de este tema que quedó insinuada por Rosario Ferré en su trabajo es si en verdad las autoras latinoamericanas crean personajes femeninos más profundos que los que hasta ahora han producido los escritores. Teniendo en cuenta que las obras latinoamericanas que más influencia han tenido en el exterior han sido las escritas por hombres, creo que debe recalcarse la importancia de continuar su análisis.

En varios de los trabajos se sugirió la necesidad de combinar factores de clase y categoría sexual como variables que van íntimamente entrelazadas, en particular en lo que respecta a la situación de las culturas hispánicas. El ejemplo más claro aparece en el trabajo de Cynthia Steele, donde se analiza la problemática de la escritora de clase media que se propone dar expresión a las vivencias de la mujer de la clase proletaria en México.

La validez del uso de teorías extranjeras para la interpretación del contexto hispánico, que estaba planteada como problemática en la primera convocatoria de la conferencia, se trató someramente. Al respecto, el trabajo de Sara Castro Klarén dejó clara su desconfianza hacia obras de críticas norteamericanas que a mi modo de ver han sentado precedentes fundamentales para el estudio de las escritoras del siglo XIX de habla inglesa, que se pueden aplicar al caso de España y al de Latinoamérica. De hecho, creo que si la crítica feminista hispánica se cierra a esquemas universalizantes, puede caer en una de las formas como la crítica ha tratado de suprimir la escritura de mujeres, que Joanna Russ ha llamado "Anomalousness". De ello es ejemplo la más reciente crítica feminista a Rosalía de Castro hecha desde Galicia, que todavía se niega a ver a esta escritora como perteneciente a una tradición de escritoras dentro de España misma. Derivado del mismo tema, hubo algunas referencias a la posibilidad de aplicación de la crítica literaria feminista de la literatura negra norteamericana al contexto latinoamericano.

Otras ramificaciones del tema son, por un lado, la utilidad de un ejercicio de cuestionamiento de la influencia de teorías específicas, como por ejemplo las francesas, en la crítica hecha desde España, Latinoamérica y los Estados Unidos. El trabajo de Elizabeth Ordóñez realizaba este ejercicio en el caso de su propia trayectoria como crítica literaria en los Estados Unidos. Por otro lado, está el tema de la correlación enseñanza-investigación, que para el femi-

586   ELENA SANCHEZ-MORA

nismo tiene especial importancia. Concretamente, quiero
recalcar la posibilidad de incorporar textos alternativos en
los programas de literatura a nivel universitario. Esta preocupación personal surgió de mi lectura del trabajo de
Francine Masiello—que desgraciadamente no estuvo presente—, en donde se analizaban textos escritos por mujeres
en la Argentina del siglo XIX, que presentaban alternativas
a aquellos escritos por autores liberales que no eran capaces
de ver la problemática de la mujer.

La crítica literaria feminista hispanista o latinoamericanista que se hace desde los Estados Unidos crea el problema
de la necesidad de comunicación entre los críticos feministas que trabajan en este país y los que están establecidos en
aquellas áreas geográficas. En el caso de España, el intercambio con las representantes españolas Cristina Dupláa y
Guadalupe Gómez-Ferrer, hizo patente su productividad, y
la deseabilidad de su establecimiento en el caso de Latinoamérica. Sin embargo, en mi caso particular, como crítica
literaria feminista latinoamericana radicada en Estados
Unidos encontré sumamente fecundo el intercambio con
críticas tanto norteamericanas como latinoamericanas
provenientes de diversas universidades de Estados Unidos.

Finalmente, dentro de los problemas de la crítica feminista en el medio académico, se mencionó la tendencia a la
trivialización del feminismo. Específicamente, se habló del
peligro de que el feminismo se convierta en una moda a la
que cualquiera puede adherirse mediante el uso de ciertas
fórmulas predeterminadas y la aspiración de ciertos críticos
ambiciosos a monopolizar el discurso feminista.

Como conclusión, quiero insistir que tanto los temas que
se discutieron con alguna amplitud como aquellos que tan
sólo se mencionaron someramente, o incluso los que quedaron fuera, apuntaron hacia la posibilidad de continuar el
fructífero diálogo iniciado durante la conferencia. De allí
que surgiera una propuesta para futuras conferencias y una
red permanente de intercambio informal de trabajos.

EDIPO, AUTOGESTION Y PRODUCCION TEXTUAL:
NOTAS SOBRE CRITICA LITERARIA FEMINISTA

Kemy Oyarzún
University of California, Riverside

> "Amarillas flores abrieron la corola: es nuestra
> Madre, la del rostro con máscara. La Diosa está
> sobre el redondo cacto: ¡Es nuestra Madre, la Reina
> de la Tierra! Oh, con greda nueva, con pluma
> nueva está embadurnada."
> —Himno Náhuatl a la diosa madre, Teteoinnan

Incluí no hace mucho, dentro de una variedad de fragmentos poemáticos, la estrofa náhuatl arriba citada sobre la diosa Teteoinnan para que unas estudiantes la identificaran y analizaran en un examen. Dos estudiantes supusieron que se trataba de un texto de transición a la Vanguardia. No era la primera vez que se hacía esta asociación, pero esta vez tomé en serio el desafío de tal "con-fusión" y como resultado, he optado por organizar esta presentación en torno al ideologema de la madre, uno de los ejes más problemáticos del discurso feminista en general y de la crítica literaria feminista en particular. Coincidió que mientras leía las supuestas justificaciones que convertían el poema precolombino en un texto de transición a la Vanguardia, también leía las ponencias del congreso sobre teoría literaria feminista de Minnesota, de modo que se entablaron lazos comunicantes muy seminales entre el "error" de las estudiantes y algunos de los problemas planteados por gran parte de los trabajos del congreso.

Gayatri Spivak, que como muchas feministas desconfía de Freud, trabajó durante un tiempo el concepto de "envidia de vientre" como contrapartida de la supuesta "envidia de pene" que el fundador del psicoanálisis asignó a la mujer en su desarrollo ontogenético como sujeto genérico-sexuado.[1] No me interesa tanto discutir aquí la validez o no de esta suerte de competencia que suele darse entre los términos hombre/mujer con respecto a una supuesta carencia metafísica, situada en la genitalia masculina o en la femenina. Me interesa rescatar un sólo aspecto de la discusión de Spivak con respecto al ideologema del vientre, su acento en la *productividad*: "I am only placing [womb-envy] beside the definition of the physical womb as a lack. I speculate that the womb has always been defined as a lack *by* man in order to cover over a lack *in* man, the lack, precisely, of a tangible place of production [...] The womb is not an emptiness or a mystery, it is a place of production" (p. 45).

Mientras más leo sobre feminismo más me convenzo de la necesidad de volver sobre la problemática relación entre producción y generidad-sexual. Se ha criticado al marxismo el haber descuidado problemas ideológicos en torno a la opresión femenina en función de una atención casi exclusivamente "económica".[2] Por otra parte, en respuesta a este economicismo—sospecho que más atribuíble a ciertos marxistas que a los propios clásicos—durante las décadas de los 60 a los 80 la escuela francesa acusa una tendencia a descuidar a tal grado las cuestiones económicas que se desemboca en la construcción de un concepto "esencialista" de la mujer, vaciado de particularidad histórico-social, "idéntico a sí mismo".[3] El número especial que *Latin American Perspectives* dedicó a este problema constituye una excepción que confirma la regla.[4] Allí se avanza muchísimo en dos direcciones que me interesa subrayar aquí, la última de las cuales aparece planteada por muchas de las participantes del congreso de Minnesotta: a) la crítica a Levi-Strauss y b) la difícil cuestión de la "sororidad" femenina por sobre las diferencias de clase, etnia o raza. Este último aspecto ha sido destacado implícita o explícitamente por una gran mayoría de las ponentes del congreso: Sara Castro Klarén, Cristina Duplá, Lucía Guerra-Cunningham, Rosaura Sánchez, Cynthia Steele y, por supuesto, Hernán Vidal, y las anónimas voces del diálogo informal sobre feminismo latinoamericano.

La crítica a Lévi-Strauss es más problemática. La discusión afecta las bases de los postulados "esencialistas" de di-

versas maneras, pero sobre todo con respecto al semantema de la madre. A partir de Juliet Mitchell, lo más generalizado entre las críticas feministas, tanto de la escuela
francesa como de la anglosajona, es la negación de la existencia de un matriarcado; se afirma, en base a las recientes
investigaciones antropológicas, lo obsoleto de las observaciones que Engels—apoyándose en Morgan—hiciera al
respecto. Pese a la constatación de la organización matrilí-
nea en ciertas comunidades antiguas, el consenso general
apunta en la dirección de una universalización del
patriarcado puesto que aún en casos de transmisión ma-
trilínea, Lévi-Strauss demuestra que lo intercambiado fueron siempre las mujeres sin importar si la línea de transmisión fuera materna o paterna.[5] Esto lleva a Hernán Vidal a afirmar que ver "a la mujer como objeto transhistórico, transcultural y transnacional de opresión corresponde
a la información y evidencia antropológica de que disponemos" (Vidal, p. 288).

Por su parte, Rosaura Sánchez advierte contra los peligros ideológicos de un fetichismo de la madre,[6] en tanto
que Lucía Guerra-Cunningham insiste en que "los recientes estudios antropológicos han puesto de manifiesto el
carácter generalizante de la estructura patriarcal" (Guerra,
pp. 130-131). Curiosamente, es común que hasta la crítica
que trabaja con un instrumental poroso a las
contradicciones de género, clase y etnia, oriente su análisis
en la dirección de un cierto esencialismo antropológico a
la hora de intentar establecer la genealogía de la opresión
femenina. Ese esencialismo antropológico revela en
algunos casos un repliegue biologista en función al nexo
que se establece entre patriarcado y maternidad al ser esta
última concebida dentro de un marco teórico que funde las
categorías de lo ontogénico (pertinente a lo psicológico), lo
filogenético (pertinente a la especie) y lo histórico
(articulación de ambos en en el desarrollo de los modos
productivos). Para Lucía Guerra, "el rol materno de la
mujer posee un efecto profundo tanto en los patrones
sexuales e ideológicos como en la organización misma del
trabajo" (p. 131). De modo que "es en el cuerpo femenino
como *locus* de la reproducción de la especie donde se

encuentran los orígenes mismos de una problemática de la
subordinación que se hace evidente en la organización
económica y las construcciones culturales de un grupo" (p.
131).

Me parece importante hacer dos distinciones en torno a
la polémica génesis de la subordinación femenina. En
primer lugar, creo que no es operativo subsumir en una
sola categoría el problema de la línea de transmisión
ma/pa/terna y el problema de la hegemonía. En segundo
lugar, me parece que la tendencia a centrar el análisis en
las relaciones de mercado (circulación) y no en las de producción, dificulta la posibilidad de ver los cambios que las
funciones genérico-sexuales han manifestado a través de
la historia. Este acento en la circulación emparenta a
análisis tan variados como los del estructuralismo, el pos-
testructuralismo y algunas vertientes de la teoría de la
marginalidad, incluídos ciertos dependentistas. Sería importante ver si el hecho aparentemente universal del intercambio de las mujeres indica en todo momento que las
relaciones genéricas se inscriban en el circuito de la coerción y el dominio. Aún en el caso en que la diferencia
genérica—al ubicar a la mujer como signo intercambiado—implicara desde los orígenes un cierto tipo de dominio de la mujer por parte del hombre, la necesidad de
operar con una metodología histórica se hace inevitable si
hemos de comprender la *especificidad* de esas relaciones
de dominio de acuerdo a las modalidades productivas y
sus articulaciones étnico-culturales.

Al parecer, Engels evitó usar el concepto de matriarcado;
introduce la noción de patriarcado precisamente para
indicar que el advenimiento de la división coercitiva de
los géneros sexuales coincide no meramente con el paso de
lo matrilíneo a lo patrilíneo, sino con la articulación de lo
patrilíneo, el origen de la propiedad privada y del Estado.
Aun cuando Lévi-Strauss haya constatado que no hay una
relación cronológica entre una y otra línea de transmisión
(se dan simultáneamente en la "prehistoria" sociedades
matrilíneas y patrilíneas), el problema sigue asociado a la
génesis del Estado. El origen de la socialización coercitiva
de los géneros está vinculado al paso de una economía de

subsistencia a una economía de excedente y cultivo inten-
sivo. Engels indicó que "todo el excedente que desarrolló la
adquisición de nuevas necesidades recayó sobre el hombre:
las mujeres compartían su disfrute, pero no tuvieron parte
en la propiedad". En consecuencia, los hombres adquirie-
ron control de los medios productivos y con ello, de las
instituciones sociales.[7]

Para Engels, se trataba de determinar si existía alguna
relación entre el origen de una estructuración coercitiva de
los géneros y las clases y el modo patrilíneo y patrilocal de
transmisión. Ese interrogante revela hasta qué grado lo
que a él le preocupaba no era meramente un asunto económico, sino la posibilidad de demostrar que el someti-
miento de unos por otros no era esencial a la "naturaleza"
del *homo sapiens*, de ahí que situara el problema de la división social de los géneros sexuales no sólo en los
umbrales de la propiedad privada, sino también y sobre
todo en los de la constitución del aparato estatal. Pese a la
insistencia de los estudios antropológicos contemporáneos, sospecho demasiado de las categorías
"transculturales" o "transhistóricas" como para no considerar que por lo menos la "universalidad" del patriarcado
queda aun por demostrarse. No obstante, el hecho de que
fueran las mujeres los signos (objetos) intercambiados
constituye un factor perturbador que la ciencia antropológica debe intentar resolver con criterios más históricos, incorporando las dimensiones de la circulación y la producción en el análisis económico y, a su vez, articulando esas
dimensiones con el análisis de las relaciones de poder. Es
aquí donde el trabajo crítico feminista se topa con uno de
esos nudos difíciles de desembrollar; núcleos seminales,
perturbadores, desafiantes y sobre todo reveladores de la
inestabilidad de la relación entre las "palabras y las cosas".

A medida que releo los versos náhuatl y pienso en lo
que revela el hecho de que fuesen considerados proto-
vanguardistas más me detengo a pensar en el problema de
la semantización, la desemantización y la resemantización. Es obvio que el semantema "madre" no significa hoy
lo que significaba en la época precolombina. De tan distante en tiempo y episteme, el poema se ha convertido casi

en ícono o jeroglífico. Me sitúo frente a ella, la *figura* de esa diosa madre (no la imagen, ni la representación) y lo que esta contemplación me devuelve es la constatación de *mi propia incapacidad para llenarla de sentido.* Es una marca de lo que no retorna. Neruda lo sintió frente a Macchu Picchu. Queda la figura, pero no queda el sentido que la comunidad le daba. El fue capaz de rescatar por lo menos las huellas de la dominación al constatar que las inmensas moles habían sido "producidas", re-elaboradas por el "trabajo vivo" de miles de seres humanos esclavizados. Cardenal vuelve sobre este tema en su texto sobre Tohil y sobre las "Economías de Tahuantinsuyu". En su poema a los indígenas nicaragüenses, Cardenal insiste: "Son de extremo ligeros y veloces para correr/tanto los hombres como las mujeres./Nadan maravillosamente en el agua, como peces,/ y las mujeres mejor que los hombres./[...] No tienen jefes ni capitanes de guerra/sino que andan sin orden, cada uno libremente./Esta gente vive en libertad, no obedece a nadie/no tiene ley ni señor. No riñen entre sí./[...]Sus riquezas son plumas de aves de varios colores/o cuentas que hacen de los huesos de los peces/o piedrecitas verdes y blancas./Pero desprecian el oro y las piedras preciosas".[8]

Arguedas se pasa media vida produciendo una escritura que se desgarra ante la inevitable erosión del modo de producción vital-social (es decir imaginativo, es decir simbólico, es decir económico) precapitalista. Asturias le da vueltas y vueltas a la figura de Tohil (el déspota con que se "inicia" la cadena metafórica del Estado guatemalteco en particular y latinoamericano en general). Luego yuxtapone la figura precolombina de la "Manzana-Rosa", máscara femenina partida en dos mitades: una "de verdad" y la otra de "mentira". Indudablemente tienen razón quienes insisten en la importancia de realizar una relectura feminista de la Colonia y de las civilizaciones precolombinas, sobre todo si tenemos en cuenta la vigencia de los problemas en torno a la función materna y a la genealogía de la socialización coercitiva de los géneros sexuales en América Latina.

Concuerdo con Jean Franco cuando advierte contra el reduccionismo de "fundir la teoría feminista en una teoría general del colonialismo"[9]; pero al mismo tiempo, creo que es inevitable que—sin fundir los dos problemas—en los países neocolonizados la subyugación de la mujer sea estudiada en términos de relaciones globales de poder que incluyan por cierto el dominio y la superexplotación de los recursos humanos, simbólicos, económicos y sociales de amplios sectores nacionales, raciales y étnicos. En este sentido, creo que es importante tener en cuenta dos instancias del trabajo crítico feminista: a) la necesidad de aislar nuestro objeto a fin de avanzar en el conocimiento de la *especificidad* de lo femenino y b) la importancia de ahondar en las *zonas relacionales*, tanto sincrónicas (clases, etnias) como diacrónicas (distintos momentos de la historia de los modos productivos). Estas dos instancias teóricas deberían ser articuladas a la hora del análisis. De lo contrario, se corre el riesgo de caer en el esencialismo de lo femenino (privilegio del enfoque ontológico) o en la dispersión de nuestro objeto de estudio en categorías que, por importantes que sean, *no* pueden ni deben subsumir la esfera específica de lo genérico-sexual (privilegio del enfoque *exclusivamente* etnicista o de clase).

Debemos rescatar aquí la larga y tortuosa trayectoria del feminismo tanto en los países occidentales como tercermundistas, trayectoria que ha significado que en la década actual, los movimientos por la emancipación de la mujer hayan adquirido estatuto propio, independientemente de la participación que un número de sus integrantes tengan en partidos políticos de izquierda. En Chile, para dar un ejemplo, la reorganización de MEMCH (Movimiento de Emancipacipación de la Mujer Chilena) en 1983—con claros objetivos feministas a largo plazo—ha significado no sólo una lección al interior del movimiento, sino para el conjunto de las fuerzas de la población. El movimiento—cuyos orígenes se confunden con los primeros experimentos de los frentes populares de los años '30—optó por autodisolverse luego de logradas las metas sufragistas para la mujer en Chile. Al reorganizarse unas décadas más tarde en plena dictadura pinochetista el movimiento ha debido

superar por una parte la tendencia a reducir los objetivos
de la lucha femenina dentro de un reivindicacionismo exclusivamente "femenino" y por otra, la tendencia a disol-
ver las luchas femeninas en las consignas y metas
"populares". De ahí que MEMCH '83 se plantee la emancipación femenina dentro del marco de la *persona-mujer*,
proponiendo así la articulación (y no la disolución) de las
demandas específicas de la mujer con las demandas del
movimiento global por los derechos humanos, pero sin
perder de vista esta vez su objetivo de luchar a corto y
largo plazo por la "eliminación de todas las formas de discriminación que se ejercen sobre la mujer".[10] Es notable en
este sentido el grado de coincidencia que existe entre estos
planteamientos y las propuestas de Hernán Vidal para la
constitución de una crítica feminista que opere en torno a
una arquetipificación más universalista de persona (Vidal,
p. 273).

MA/PA/DRE: SEMANTEMAS E IDEOLOGEMAS

¿Qué entendemos hoy por los semantemas madre y padre? ¿Cuánto de lo que hoy asignamos a los términos es
proyectado por nosotros y superimpuesto a otros momentos de la historia? Si este es un problema dentro de la historia, ¿qué podemos decir de la prehistoria? ¿Cuánto de lo
que hoy asignamos a esos semantemas es proyectado
cuando tratamos de imaginar las relaciones genérico-
sexuales que vendrán en un futuro hipotético? ¿qué grado
de dependencia existe entre la resemantización de los términos ma/pa/dre y las estrategias de poder? ¿Qué intereses, deseos y voluntades hemos invertido para que nuestros artefactos culturales populares, literarios, artísticos o
crítico-científicos se filtren por la grilla imaginativo-sim-
bólica de la familia nuclear?
    Desde esta perspectiva, es importante recordar que *no
siempre la diferencia implicó una subordinación*. De los
2.500.000 de años que en la actualidad se atribuyen a los
homínidos, el 99% de este período se vivió en torno a las
tareas de subsistencia (caza y recolección), en condiciones

que la caza no constituía una actividad exclusivamente masculina, sino altamente cooperativa entre los sexos[11]. Son innumerables los ejemplos en los que se demuestra que aun cuando existiera una división social de los géneros, ambos sexos compartían el trabajo, el respeto mutuo y la dirección política en las sociedades preesclavistas y en algunas de las comunidades de modo productivo híbrido que tánto abundan en América Latina. Ello no sólo en un pasado remoto e irrecuperable, sino en la Guatemala de Rigoberta Menchú.[12] No obstante, creo que uno de los peores encubrimientos sobre la condición de la mujer en el pasado tiene que ver con su productividad. Cuesta imaginar un hecho que es todavía vigente hoy en día en América Latina y otras sociedades tercermundistas: la productividad económico-social del quehacer doméstico y de otras labores "invisibles". Se ha revelado que hasta en los Estados Unidos, la mujer colonial desempeñaba labores altamente productivas.[13] Obviamente, el grado de productividad varía en función del modo de producción que prevalezca en la sociedad, y sobre todo según la ubicación de clase de la mujer en cuestión. En otro trabajo, me he referido a este problema cuya vigencia en la actualidad latinoamericana dictamina el que con creciente frecuencia más amplios y vastos sectores del pueblo—y no solamente la mujer— vayan quedando "marginados" de la producción. Hoy en día, la subordinación política oculta el hecho fundamental de que la acumulación capitalista cuenta con la "invisibilidad" (abaratamiento) del trabajo de las grandes mayorías latinoamericanas y tercermundistas.

Es posible que cueste imaginar la "improductividad" (capitalista) del trabajo doméstico como una productividad (trabajo real, transformación social y cultural de lo natural en un para-nosotros) porque se ha llegado a internalizar la reificación del capital. Como no se trata de una mercancía, el quehacer simplemente "no existe". El paso siguiente, es negar la realidad cultural (y por lo tanto histórica y social) de lo que ocurre en el recinto *privado* de la familia nuclear. Aquello no sólo es invisible sino privado: dos categorías mediante las cuales si algo se produce es una mujer esencializada, "noble salvaje" de la era moderna, vientre reproductor cuya productividad remite al registro "intraducible" de lo molecular, biológico, parasocial.

Pero lo biológico no se da de forma inmediata en las esferas de lo humano. El feminismo de raza negra ha estado discutiendo este problema durante años ya que la doble articulación de racismo y clasismo en Estados Unidos ha implicado la arquetipificación del hombre y la mujer afronorteamericanos como reproductores ("stud" y "breeder" respectivamente).[14] No obstante, Angela Davis demuestra lúcidamente que la nodriza o la reproductora femenina de la esclavitud guarda escasa relación con la arquetipificación de la madre africana; la madre ha sido reinventada, convertida en pieza productiva de la gran maquinaria del capital del trabajo humano: "Thus a premium was placed on the slave woman's reproductive capacity. During the decades preceding the Civil War, Black women came to be increasingly appraised for their fertility (or for the lack of it): she who was potentially the mother of ten, twelve, fourteen or more became a coveted treasure indeed. This did not mean, however, that as mothers, Black women enjoyed a more respected status than they enjoyed as workers. Ideological exaltation of motherhood...did not extend to slaves. In fact, in the eyes of slaveholders, slave women were not mothers at all; *they were simply instruments guaranteeing the growth of the slave labor force*" (Davis, p. 7).

Es fácil constatar la socialización de las funciones ma/pa/ternas (la "aculturación" de lo biológico) en el seno de la familia nuclear de hoy; allí donde se produce el hijo-objeto a imagen y semejanza de la producción de mercancías (objeto de posesión, rivalidad y fascinación), reproduciéndose el ciclo de relaciones objetales que luego entrampan a la "sagrada familia" en la estructura edípica de todos conocida. Nada escapa a dos procesamientos fundamentales: el que se lleva a cabo en todo momento de la vida social (la transformación de la primera en segunda naturaleza) y el que se efectúa a nivel histórico sobre la articulación del modo productivo prevaleciente y predominante en la sociedad. Esos dos procesamientos ocurren simultáneamente dentro de sus ámbitos específicos. En todo caso, se trata de un procesamiento del que "no se salvan" ni los dioses de la antigüedad.

La diosa madre, he ahí el último umbral del mito de lo no socializado en la civilización. "Amarillas flores abrieron la corola:/ es nuestra Madre, la del rostro con máscara", dice el verso náhuatl significando dos movimientos: el de la naturaleza (plural, fértil, productivo) expresado por las "amarillas flores" en apertura y el de la sociedad, expresado por el "rostro con máscara". Sintácticamente, la figura de Teteoinnan abarca lo múltiple y lo uno, lo femenino ("nuestra Madre") y lo masculino ("Tamoanchan"). Lo social y lo estético—la marca sobre el rostro—son también productivos: "con greda nueva, con pluma nueva/está embadurnada". Embadurnada y enmascarada, la Diosa Madre es una producción secundaria, ornamentada para nosotros y por nosotros, humanizada y reelaborada.

Naturaleza y sociedad: dos registros productivos, aunque sus modalidades sean diferentes. Nuevamente, la diferencia no implica *en sí* ni dominación, ni subyugación. Sólo productividad. Luego, es a nivel histórico que hay que situar de qué modo y en qué instancias se produce la dominación. Lo cierto es que la coerción—jerarquización subyugante—es un efecto de producción y no al revés. Es aquí que empieza el lento trabajo desconstructivo. La diosa madre está *"sobre el redondo cacto"*; aparece al abrirse las "amarillas corolas". Jamás la imaginación edípica del siglo 20 hubiera podido concebir a la diosa como producto de una producción que le antecede. Tal vez ello empezaría a ser posible, a insinuarse acaso, en cierta Vanguardia, en aquélla que empieza por desmantelar el teatro clásico del Edipo.[15] Hay estudios que revelan coincidencias entre cierta pintura vanguardista y la vivencia del esquizo, tal vez porque "lo que el esquizofrénico vive de un modo específico, genérico [...] es la propia naturaleza como proceso de producción", hecho que *en las sociedades precapitalistas no tiene nada de "esquizoide"*.[16] Es posible visualizar el "en-sí" no sólo "afuera" sino en nosotros ("inconsciente"), un cuerpo "sin órganos", fragmentos atravesados "por ejes y umbrales, latitudes, longitudes, geodésicas, gradientes.

Aquí nada es representativo; la emoción vivida en los senos no se parece a los senos, no los representa, del mismo modo como una zona predestinada en el huevo no se parece al órgano que de allí va a surgir. Solo bandas de intensidad, potenciales, umbrales y gradientes. Experiencia desgarradora, demasiado conmovedora, mediante la cual el esquizo es el que está más cerca de la materia, de un centro intenso y vivo de la materia" (D-G, p. 27).

En el principio, no el verbo. No el Padre. Tampoco la Madre. En el principio, como en todo momento, producción deseante, deseo productivo, es decir, real, es decir, material. No hay carencia metafísica que llenar ni a nivel ontogenético ni a nivel filogenético. Ontogenia: *lactante (niño/niña)*, fragmentos anedípicos o "huérfanos", ni envidia de pene, ni envidia de vientre; deseo de seno-boca como deseo de flujo (el seno cubista no pertenece a nadie, no es imagen de nada ni intenta representar a una persona; es fragmento lleno). No deseo de mamá/papá, sino de lo que está inmediatamente en frente, presencia sin pasado, ni memoria, ni futuro. Flujo, corte de flujo (objetos, catexis); continuidad y discontinuidad; máquinas conectadas a máquinas y a megamáquinas. De lo molecular (en sí) a lo molar (para nosotros), máquinas de distintos registros.

En un segundo momento de la ontogenia, el estadio del espejo lacaniano: acceso al Orden Simbólico (el para-nosotros), horizonte del padre totémico y la madre fálica; la memoria construye un sujeto petrificado que hace coincidir el deseo con lo que ya está muerto y el ordenamiento social con la castración. El niño y la niña completan la pareja fragmentaria seno-boca en un personaje aculturado: la madre, a su vez, objeto deseado por el Otro (el padre). El deseo es reinventado como carencia; toma el todo por las partes y se petrifica entre la culpa y el pánico de castración. Sobre el horizonte de una filogenia anedípica, la madre diosa de la antigüedad se perfila como una muerte/vida; su figura no es excluyente. Las partes y el todo que la configuran aparecen como intensidades laterales, no como capas concéntricas: ella *al lado* de los dioses masculinos.

Edipo se encargará de asignar valores y límites interiores a los bordes entre lo uno y lo otro, aunque para el deseo inconsciente esta diferenciación sea irrelevante: "Edipo es el viraje idealista...la producción ya no es más que producción de fantasma, producción de expresión. El inconsciente deja de ser lo que es, una fábrica, un taller, para convertirse en un teatro, escena y puesta en escena. Y no en un teatro de Vanguardia, que ya los había en tiempos de Freud, sino en el teatro clásico, el orden clásico de la representación" (D-G, pp. 60-61). Teme el paranoico hijo de papá: "¿estoy muerto o estoy vivo?". Nadie mejor que Freud para describir el filtraje edípico del deseo en el patriarcado, precisamente porque Freud—como lamentablemente lo hace gran parte de la teoría feminista de hoy—confunde todos los horizontes humanos con el Nombre del Padre.

No obstante, los trabajos de Freud y Lacan sobre la constitución del sujeto sexuado en el patriarcado sirven en la medida en que seamos capaces de descentralizar teóricamente el sistema patriarcal, esto es, ampliando los horizontes sincrónicos (el Padre y su Otra constituyen una construcción cultural, secundaria) y diacrónicos (la historia desantropomorfizada y anedípica de las organizaciones sociales precapitalistas y pre-estatales y la capacidad de generar una organización contrahegemónica en el futuro). Más importante aún. La mayor contribución de Freud para el feminismo no radica en sus contenidos (a la misoginia se le suma una especial y reveladora fobia por la esquizofrenia), sino el haber descubierto las "maquinaciones" de la libido: el verdadero taller productivo del inconsciente, la *economía* del deseo, su trabajo obstinado, material, real, persistente.[17] Empezar a descubrir la proyectora (una verdadera máquina) tras los bastidores de los escenarios del psicoanálisis, intentar desmantelar las imágenes para llegar a la labor de los surtidores, he aquí una de las tareas del feminismo en el terreno de las ciencias sociales y humanas. Incidentalmente, esa labor tiene un antecedente en el trabajo de Marx por desconstruir el fetichismo de la mercancía al volver sobre la base que el objeto reificado oculta, abstrae y niega (en un sentido freudiano); esa base es la es-

tructura binaria "Capital/Trabajo" puesta en movimiento
en virtud de la instancia de la producción.

En el estimulante ensayo alegórico, "El coloquio de perras", las autoras se preguntan por qué tánta crítica femenina se aboca a trabajar más textos de hombres que de mujeres. Al entrar a analizar algunas inconsecuencias, las autoras del ensayo mencionan particularlmente el caso del
asesinato de la Queca en *La vida breve*, cuyo análisis semiótico no llega a abarcar, en la lectura de Josefina Ludmer, las implicaciones que tiene para la problemática de la
mujer. El marricidio tiene—en muchísimos textos de
Vanguardia—valor liberador, transgresor. ¿Por qué—se
preguntan las autoras del "coloquio"—la liberación tiene
que pasar por el asesinato de una mujer? ¿Por qué esta re-
currente simbología marricida y misógina no queda cues-
tionada por gran parte de la crítica feminista latinoamericana?[18]

La pregunta merece atención a varios niveles, y aquí
sólo puedo esbozar alguna respuesta en la dirección siguiente: a diferencia de sus orígenes ilustrados, la novela
latinoamericana de Vanguardia empieza a distanciarse del
orden del padre. Este hecho, que habría que trazar histöri-
camente dentro del desarrollo del taller de la novela latinoamericana está estrechamente vinculado al problema
fundamentalmente ontogenético de la biografía narrativa.
El escritor se plantea negar la *bildungsroman* decimonónica a partir de un cuestionamiento del narcisismo primario, tradicionalmente asociado al género femenino (madre,
mujer/dique, pasaporte metafísico). Se propone el desmantelamiento de la identidad mitopoética de la Romantik porque se presupone que aquélla reproduce la inauten-
ticidad al gestar una cadena objetal de sustitutos de la madre; esa cadena debe ser desconstruída si la escritura va a
inscribirse en la "soledad problemática" y autentificadora
que postulan muchas de las novelas de Vanguardia.

Luego, es hacia la madre y hacia el "hijo de mamá" que
va dirigida la negatividad de ese tipo de novela. La
"traición" es de Rita Hayworth; la Maga desaparece, la
Queca es asesinada, Castel mata a María (*El túnel*), la esposa tullida muere (*Al filo del agua*); también muere Ro-

camadour; uno de los protagonistas de *La vida breve* se tajea el cuerpo; Oliveira salta por la ventana en un posible suicidio. Curiosamente—y esto es seminal dados los cambios que se efectúan en el Estado al pasar del liberalismo al neoliberalismo—el padre raramente es violentado; está misteriosamente *ausente*, interpelando desde su no-presencia los hilos patriarcales de textos que, por muy vanguardistas que sean, son narrados desde la perspectiva del hijo huérfano del liberalismo en crisis. En estos casos se narra un *bildungsroman* en el que se trata de sentar las bases para la autodeterminación de los protagonistas hombres despojándolos de sus objetos/fetiches (madres/amantes), para lanzarlos de lleno en situaciones límites. La violencia en contra de la mujer se convierte en el sacrificio "necesario" (corte umbilical y destete) para la liberación del hijo de la bohemia de Buenos Aires o París.

Creo que lo más revelador es que toda esta secuela de marricidios y filicidios expresa la obsesión edípica de la novela con la imagen de la familia nuclear; desde Onetti a Cortázar, la novela tiende a privilegiar la asociación madre/desorden, dislocación, subversión. Después de todo, el peor fantasma que Oliveira trata de exorcizar en su momento de crisis existencial no es tanto Heráclito (el descenso a la cloaca de París) sino *ella*, la figura de la madre dislocada del surrealismo, desplazada desde la Maga a Berthe Trepas, y de ésta a la Clocharde. Es como si ante el derrumbe de todos los dioses de occidente, la última barrera para el deicidio total tuviese que dirigirse hacia la diosa madre.

¿Qué es esta obsesión literaria con el histeriocentrismo de la familia nuclear? ¿Es solamente una obsesión masculina? ¿Qué relación guarda la literatura con la generidad sexual tal y como ésta se reproduce en la familia nuclear? ¿Qué grado de dependencia existe en el discurso literario entre el Edipo y el acceso al logos? ¿Es posible imaginar una literatura que vaya más allá del campo semántico-semiótico de la familia nuclear y del monoteísmo del Edipo? Elizabeth Ordóñez, apoyándose en el trabajo de Empar Pineda y Jane Gallop deja establecida, en una aguda adver-

tencia, la estrecha relación que existe entre la institución
de la maternidad y el patriarcado.[19]

Mal que nos pese, la asociación esencialista ma-
dre=mujer permea gran parte de nuestra crítica literaria.
Ruth El Saffar descubre la riqueza de *La Celestina* precisamente a partir de la asociación con lo pre-edípico, que ella
identifica con la madre, y por ende, con la mujer.[20] Lucía
Guerra-Cunningham asocia a tal grado los términos mujer
y madre que insiste en que "ha sido el cuerpo femenino en
su dimensión reproductiva el verdadero eje de la
dominación" (Guerra, p. 133). Constance A. Sullivan le
critica a las feministas socialistas, tanto hispánicas como
anglosajonas, la tendencia a "implicar que el capitalismo
es la causa del dominio masculino y del control de la vida,
trabajo y discurso femeninos, en lugar de concentrarse en
el problema más doloroso de la cuasi-universalidad del
patriarcado a pesar de las distintas circunstancias
sociopolíticas, económicas y culturales".[21] No obstante, la
maternidad no ha sido nunca más desvalorada que bajo el
capitalismo, único sistema capaz de privatizar el vientre y
reducirlo a instrumento reproductor no de seres
humanos, ("species beings") sino de objetos de
rendimiento (fuerza de trabajo). Tampoco se había visto
anteriormente una dislocación entre producción
(taller/fábrica) y reproducción (ámbito doméstico) en
términos de la división genérico-sexual, tal y como se la
representa el capitalismo, con la consiguiente devaluación
del trabajo doméstico y de la mujer. El trabajo de Teresa
Vilarós dilucida nítidamente estas conexiones.[22]

En cuanto al cuerpo femenino en su dimensión sexual,
Michel Foucault demuestra en qué medida las nuevas estrategias del poder en la era del consumismo constituyen
la más insidiosa vejación de la mujer al darse el paso del
victorianismo puritano a la incitación a los placeres. Del
Estado victoriano que decía "no" a la sexualidad, al Estado
corporativo que incita a lo polimórfico sexual
(pseudohedonismo objetal), he ahí los resortes retorcidos
de la nueva coerción. Este último neutraliza las transgresiones precisamente al interceptar la sexualidad, el placer y
sobre todo el cuerpo-objeto femenino mediante una com-

pleja red de estratagemas de poder.[23] Todo cuerpo que pasa
por la grilla social (como objeto sexual o reproductivo)
deja de convertirse en mero objeto biológico. Así, el
cuerpo atravesado por la microfísica hegemónica difícil-
mente podría ser concebido como un "eje" de dominación,
puesto que son las relaciones sociales, económicas, simbólicas y políticas las que constituyen al cuerpo como una
entidad "para-nosotros".

Con notables excepciones, el feminismo ha acusado una
tendencia a optar por dos actitudes a ultranza frente al
semantema de la madre, actitudes muy reveladoras de
todo   fenómeno   de   endiosamiento: rechazo
(rivalidad/odio/fobia) o fascinación. Creo que la primera
actitud—más prevaleciente en ciertos sectores radicales—
surge del reconocimiento de la estrecha relación existente
entre las funciones de la madre y las del padre en el sistema patriarcal y constituye un cierto desengaño ante la
ilusión romántica que alimentaba la imagen de la madre
como un *estado* de perfección original. La tendencia actual
a negar a la madre sería la otra cara del fetichismo de la
Romantik; una distopía más desencantada que crítica. A
niveles prácticos, esta actitud condujo a dos salidas falsas:
en primer lugar, la salida economicista característica de las
prácticas feministas de occidente (fuga del ámbito doméstico y empleo=emancipación), y, en segundo lugar, la falta
de comprensión de las funciones de la mujer de América
Latina y el Tercer Mundo, en donde no sólo las mujeres
sino amplios sectores de la población han quedado relega-
dos a funciones y quehaceres domésticos, "improductivos"
y marginales. A un paso del siglo 21, la realidad ha demostrado que—lejos de conducir a una progresiva autonomía
e igualdad de la mujer—la salida economicista ha retar-
dado las posibilidades reales de una contrahegemonía
fundada en solidaridades y proyectos globales de subversión para las grandes mayorías femeninas; esto precisamente porque el economicismo no permite a las mujeres
que trabajan fuera del hogar entender con justeza y respeto
el quehacer de las mujeres cuyo trabajo doméstico es invisible. La propia intelligentsia femenina ha llegado a internalizar la devaluación del trabajo "privado" de la "ama de

casa". Además, el economicismo se funda justamente en el *ethos* protestante ("self-made man"), de modo que hasta la posibilidad de solidaridad entre las propias mujeres trabajadoras se dificulta.

Por otra parte, existe una notoria tendencia al fetichismo materno en las sociedades precapitalistas o sociedades en donde el capitalismo no se ha desarrollado plenamente, como es el caso latinoamericano hoy. Esto ha quedado revelado en algunos estudios sobre el marianismo español, en los trabajos de Kristeva sobre las madonas medievales, en el prolífero repertorio de la cultura popular latinoamericana (¿dónde está el bolero, corrido, tango o valsesito criollo que no encubra o descubra el "altarcito de mamá"?). Para Kristeva, "vivimos una civilización en que la representación consagrada (religiosa o laica) de la feminidad se reabsorbe en la maternidad. Sin embargo, esa maternidad, mirada de cerca, es el fantasma que nutre al adulto, hombre o mujer, con la idea de un continente perdido; *es menos una madre arcaica idealizada que una idealización de la relación que nos une a ella*".24

Kristeva se mueve vacilantemente en el terreno de una ambivalencia: esencialismo estructuralista del semantema de la madre o desplazamiento postestructuralista del signo en el seno de la sociedad histórica. Aquí se llega al núcleo de la fusión y confusión de la crítica feminista entre lo onto, filogenético e histórico. Kristeva da un paso desesencialista al declarar que el ideologema materno es "menos una madre arcaica idealizada que una idealización de la relación que nos une a ella". El culto materno es orientado no a la figura, sino a la relación. A lo largo de su análisis, la crítica revela importantes aspectos de la relación, tanto frente a lo genérico sexual como frente a la articulación de lo filogenético y lo histórico. En su opinión, la cristiandad traduce erróneamente los términos "muchacha soltera" y "virgen" debido a una fascinación indo-europea con la "diosa madre y [el] matriarcado subyacente, tan debatido en la cultura griega" (p. 69); el inconsciente filogenético (creencias paganas) vence así al monoteísmo (cristianismo) surrepticiamente. Una vez en la cristiandad—explica Kristeva—la mística se da a quien asume el *locus* maternal; los místicos "se adaptan al rol de vírgenes esposas del Padre" (Kristeva, p. 69). A nivel histórico, la crítica traza entonces las transformaciones del ideologema materno en los distintos hitos que van desde la genealogía de la función virginal asignada al término en los horizontes originales del cristianismo, pasando por la universalización de María ("virgen" desde siempre a partir de 461; de madre del hombre a "Madre de Dios"), su "Asunción" (celebrada a partir del siglo IV, pero recién dogmatizada por el Vaticano en 1950); sus posteriores resemantizaciones hegemónicas ("María Regina", a partir del siglo VI; "Nuestra Señora" durante el feudalismo; la Dama del amor cortés a partir de Blanca de Castilla, fallecida en 1252; Mater Ecclesiae oficialmente a partir de 1964).

El lector de este tipo de análisis no puede menos que convencerse de las transformaciones que el semantema ha sufrido en la historia. No obstante, la interrogante que surge ante el estudio es la siguiente: ¿se trata de auténticas transformaciones o meros desplazamientos? La crítica albana tiende a subsumir las diferencias diacrónicas en una magna estructura latente, de manera que las transformaciones se convierten en simples desplazamientos. Más que en su análisis, Kristeva realiza una pirueta esencialista a nivel teórico. Repliega las dimensiones históricas y filogenéticas en la universalización ontogenética del semantema materno al hace coincidir la *relación* consagrada de la madre en "nuestra civilización" (sic) con un "imposible de localizar—idealización del *narcisismo primario*" (Kristeva, p. 68).

A imagen y semejanza del estadio lacaniano del espejo, la crítica propone que la propia constitución del sujeto simbólico (narcisismo femenino o masculino) se represente a partir de la "consagración" individual de la imagen materna, hueco que el imaginario rellena con el cuerpo entero de la madre y el simbólico con el pánico castrante de la ley del padre ("Vellón de animal—ardilla, caballo, y la felicidad de una cabeza sin rostro, narciso del tacto sin ojos, la mirada fundida en músculos, pelos, colores densos, lisos, apacibles. Mamá: anamnesis", Kristeva, p. 70). A pesar del lúcido esfuerzo por historizar el signo, la crítica postestructuralista parece incapaz de ir más allá del universo que el Orden Simbólico ha reinventado para lo lactante (¿qué tienen que ver las ardillitas y caballos de Disneylandia con el mapa fragmentado del *infans*? ¿por qué hemos de hacer coincidir el deseo infantil con Mickey? ¿no es la *memoria* del adulto la que ha quedado petrificada en el "cofrecito" de mamá? ¿qué mejor canción de cuna para un adulto que ciertos boleros, tangos o balsesitos criollos?). La productividad deseante (material y no fantasmática) niega tanto el monopolio mascultista de la sexualidad falocrático/genital como la des-sublimación represiva de las consagraciones maternas ("mantelito blanco", histeriocentrismo del "milagro de amor")

¿ES POSIBLE UNA CRITICA FEMINISTA MAS ALLA DE LA MA/PA/TERNIDAD?

> "Edipo nos dice: si no sigues las líneas de diferenciación papá-mamá-yo y las exclusivas que las jalonan, caerás en la noche negra de lo indiferenciado"
> Deleuze-Guattari, *El Anti-Edipo*

Creo que es importante distinguir claramente entre funciones, agentes e instituciones al hablar de la división social de los géneros, de su constitución y de las posibilidades de subversión. Las funciones maternas, precisamente porque son *socialmente biológicas,* pueden y deben ser distinguidas de la categoría del género femenino no sólo en el análisis sino sobre todo en las prácticas. Por muy imbricadas que estén, es fundamental separar a nivel teórico-metodológico las funciones tradicionalmente consideradas "biológicas" de las categorías ontológicas de generidad sexual. Es preciso constituir una crítica feminista "culturalista" (y por tanto social e histórica) si hemos de exigir la relativización histórica de las determinaciones genérico-sexuales. Se entiende que un hombre no se refiera a su constitución biológica porque dentro del patriarcado esas funciones no han quedado asociadas a su propia definición como ser social. Se entiende también que la mujer—definida por el patriarcado casi exclusivamente en términos biologistas—haya partido precisamente por contemplarse desde esa perspectiva. Pero no se justifica a estas alturas el esencialismo sexual o reproductivo que ha permeado tánta de nuestra crítica.

Toda diferencia es diferida y desplazada; ¿por qué va a ser la genérica una excepción?[25] Dentro de los marcos específicos del género, ¿por qué ha de ser la función reproductiva inmutable y no traducible al registro de de las clases sociales, las culturas, los medios de producción, la historia? Sara Castro Klarén es explícita y firme en este aspecto: "si no hay tal cosa como la naturaleza humana, ¿cómo es posible plantear la esencia de la mujer (*woomanhood*)?". La crítica peruana insiste en la necesidad de considerar a la mujer como el *locus* de relaciones contradictorias, y a los géneros como "categorías contingentes", "situaciones sartreanas", textos múltiples cuya "lectura abarque no sólo la diferencia, sino la contradicción" (Castro-Klarén, pp. 103-104; traducción mía). El vasto recorrido auto-cognoscitivo de la mujer en las últimas décadas muestra un importante espectro de amplificaciones del marco teórico que van desde lo biológico a lo familiar (psicoanálisis, antropología) y de ahí a lo social y político. Nuestro propio objeto de estudio es más exigente que el de gran parte de la intelligentsia mascultista en la actualidad. Exige tal desespecialización de las disciplinas que implica subvertir la institución académica y las condiciones en las que se inscriben nuestras prácticas.

En mi opinión, entender la situación actual de la mujer en América Latina implica tener que enfrentarse al fenómeno del capitalismo dependiente. Aunque estoy consciente de la generalización de la opresión femenina a nivel global, creo que a la hora del análisis lo concreto, contingente y relacional impone su propio peso específico. Una vez que se deja momentáneamente de lado el problema irresuelto de la genealogía de la opresión de la mujer, se hace inminente la necesidad de orientar la crítica no ya hacia la especificidad genérico-sexual en abstracto, sino a las condiciones específicas en las cuales se inscribe la división coercitiva de los géneros en América Latina. No se trata de imponer una serie de determinaciones o sobredeterminaciones a la categoría de la opresión femenina. Intuimos que entre las clases, las etnias y los géneros se establecen puntos de contacto, pero no coincidencias genealógicas.

Pese a que su análisis presupone un grado tal vez demasiado alto de asimilación de lo genérico en favor de una hipótesis global de la pauperización humana a niveles imaginativo, simbólico y económico bajo el patriarcado capitalista ("Edipo", Estado corporativo), hay algunos elementos del trabajo de Deleuze-Guattari que quisiera rescatar para los propósitos de este estudio. Hasta ahora, el análisis que realizaron en torno a la relación entre capitalismo y esquizofrenia me parece insuperable para apreciar las ricas relaciones entre deseo, Estado y producción. Se perfila allí en qué medida: a) el patriarcado es una estructura reincidente, hegemónicamente asimilable por distintos modos productivos, pero cuya esfera de influencia alcanza niveles nunca antes imaginados al llegar al capitalismo (Nombre del Padre, falocracia, monoteísmo, plusvalía), b) la tendencia monopolista del Edipo se manifiesta en la neocolonización del Tercer Mundo a partir de una superposición de formas patriarcales arcaicas (personalistas, más abiertamente coercitivas) sobre las más fetichistas, veladas, insidiosas y neutralizantes estratagemas del patriarcado capitalista.

Para Deleuze-Guattari, el Edipo no es posible en pleno feudalismo; los cuerpos están aún enganchados a la tierra. Se debe pasar por el fetichismo del capitalismo dependiente en América Latina y el Tercer Mundo para entrar al gran teatro clásico del Edipo, cuyo origen no radica en la familia, sino en el anexamiento de ésta a la nueva modalidad productiva. La familia nuclear y los personajes privilegiados por el psicoanálisis y la novela decimonónica (hijo incestuoso, madre histérica, homosexual "latente", bohemios "perversos") son creados por el Edipo (Estado y producción capitalistas) y no viceversa. El sujeto sexuado no es producido por la familia, sino que ambos son generados por el modo productivo. Luego, no es el padre totémico de las comunidades mal llamadas primitivas (agregar a la lista de críticas a Freud su eurocentrismo) quien se desplaza como figura para ocupar el sitio simbólico del poder. Es que ha aparecido otro ordenamiento (sistémico, productivo) que crea, imagina y representa una nueva figura más abstracta y ubicua (Nombre del Padre), desplazando a la familia de las comunidades primitivas y precapitalistas, y con ellas al cuerpo, al deseo y su productividad para inscribirlos en un registro abstracto y generalizador: falo/capital/monoteísmo. Paradoja del proceso: la familia nuclear, privilegiada en la representación estatal del nuevo modo productivo, oculta el desplazamiento real de la familia en la producción.

La estrecha conexión entre Edipo y colonización es evidente. La cultura Ndembu, por ejemplo, no volcaba todo sobre el nombre del padre o del abuelo materno; antes bien, "este se abría a todos los nombres de la historia". Para Sara Castro-Klarén, "la madre terrible pre-edípica no es una formación universal sino propia de la familia nuclear capitalista" (pp. 101-102). Es la lógica excluyente y formal de la máquina colonizadora la que dice: "tu padre es tu padre y *nada más que esto, o el abuelo materno, no vayas a tomarlos por jefes...tu familia es tu familia y nada más*, la reproducción social ya no pasa por ella, aunque se tenga necesidad de tu familia para proporcionar un material que será sometido al nuevo régimen de la producción...Entonces sí, un marco edípico se esboza para los salvajes desposeídos: Edipo de chabolas" (D-G, p. 175). Pronto esta figura reificada ha de ser superpuesta metafóricamente a "sustitutos" de otras instituciones jerárquicas (Dios, padre, autor, psicoanalista), instituciones que ocultan al mismo tiempo que revelan las reales condiciones de producción y la compleja microfísica del poder. Se podría criticar a Deleuze-Guattari el acento en el patriarcado burgués a expensas del problema de la genealogía de la división coercitiva de los géneros sexuales. No obstante, existen pocos estudios que trabajen el problema de la formación filogenética e histórica del patriarcado en el capitalismo (y consiguientemente en los países dependientes) con el grado de complejidad y descentralización de *El Anti-Edipo*. Edipo sería la última "territorialidad sometida y privada del *hombre europeo*" (D-G, p. 108).

HACIA UNA CRITICA FEMINISTA AUTOGESTIONADORA

Siempre ha sido más fácil imaginar una respuesta que proponer un planteamiento (la pregunta y su respuesta) enteramente diferente. Cuando Marta Traba insiste en la importancia de reconocer la especificidad de la escritura femenina,[26] lo hace distinguiendo dos instancias: a) las estrategias "contradiscursivas", es decir, contestatarias y b) aquéllas "planeadas *desde otro lugar*", es decir, estratagemas y prácticas "contrahegemónicas" (Traba, p. ll; Vidal, p. 265). La escritura y la crítica feminista de la actualidad parecen indicar que estamos en proceso de transición hacia planteamientos contrahegemónicos. Hernán Vidal apunta que una de las limitaciones de todo movimiento (en oposición a partidos y los partidos feministas han fracasado históricamente[27]) es que la necesidad de mantener la cohesión de tan plurales intereses y objetivos impone cierta tendencia a la auto-censura frente a la posibilidad de ejercer la crítica y la autocrítica (Ver Vidal).

Aunque como movimiento no es posible tener un referente político cohesionante, la actividad reflexiva y autoreflexiva (urgente y necesaria) del movimiento feminista exige para su ulterior desarrollo superar algunas de las tendencias del pasado, hecho que sólo será realizable en la medida en que se siga trabajando en la dirección de *prácticas discursivas y no discursivas autogestionadoras*.[28] Creo que el concepto de autogestión es fundamental a varios niveles: a) es anti-edípico por definición, pero va más allá de lo contestatario insertándose en el campo hegemónico de manera frontal, crítica y autocrítica; b) es productivo; acentúa la necesidad que señalaba Marta Traba de ir más allá del "dejarse hablar" (Traba, p. 10) para producir la diferencia a partir del propio "generolecto"[29], c) está orientado hacia las transformaciones radicales y sistémicas, d) opera a partir de la diferencia pero en términos relacionales, afirmando la heterogeneidad de intereses, deseos y voluntades sin pretender homogeneizar o verticalizar; antes bien, promueve las solidaridades precisamente a partir de las diferencias, e) es un "modelo" que se ha venido perfilando a partir de las prácticas transformadoras latinoamericanas y tercermundistas (Cuba, Paulo Freire, la teología de la liberación, Nicaragua).[30]

Helena Araújo se pregunta: "En la escritura de la mujer, el lenguaje parece ser visto desde un terreno ajeno, ¿es tal vez contemplado desde el punto de vista de un cuerpo asimbólico y espasmódico?"[31] Por su parte, Lucía Guerra-Cunningham sostiene que la mujer "dispersa en todos los estratos sociales, tradicionalmente no ha poseído una conciencia de clase ni de cultura pues su Hacer doméstico y maternal ha sido relegado al espacio de la No-Cultura" (Guerra-Cunningham, p. 133). Hay una tendencia crítica del feminismo que sitúa la especificidad de lo femenino fuera de lo cultural-simbólico, interpelada por una noción un tanto lacaniana de que la transgresión al Nombre del Padre es prácticamente imposible dentro del laberinto lingüístico-cultural.

En otro ensayo, Helena Araújo se pregunta: "¿Podrá algún día concebirse una lógica por fuera de la coherencia discursiva? [...] ¿Reconocerse a lo femenino una relación con el lenguaje?"[32] Cixous llegó a plantear la especificidad de la escritura femenina en lo sintomático (lenguaje *glífico*), es decir, en aquellos cortocircuitos de la lógica excluyente que la histérica realiza (tal vez inconscientemente).[33] Buxó Rey plantea la importancia de una antropología lingüística capaz de dar cuenta de las diferencias genéricas en el propio lenguaje (conceptos de "sexoglosia", "feminolecto" y "masculinolecto", p. 135). No obstante, ella misma enfatiza que la sexoglosia refiere a "situaciones de *contacto e intercambio cultural*", aun cuando esas situaciones estén asociadas a "comportamientos aculturativos o subaculturativos" (Buxó Rey, p. 137; subrayado mío). De forma que una de las primeras precisiones que debemos hacer frente a la existencia de una escritura diferente es que inevitablemente ella *pasa y ha pasado* (aun en condiciones de asimetría y subordinación) por el reticulado de la cultura. Las prácticas femeninas no sólo se inscriben en la cultura, sino que son interceptadas por relaciones de poder precisamente en el propio campo conflictivo de la sociedad; es importante tener presente que "el elemento natural ha sido siempre invocado para justificar el dominio".[34]

Pese a que Juliet Mitchell niega la posibilidad de una escritura femenina[35], las críticas latinoamericanas y latinoamericanistas concuerdan mayoritariamente en asignar a la diferencia genérica una especificidad escriptural. Elizabeth Ordóñez insiste no sólo en la existencia de una escritura, sino de una imaginación femenina (Ordóñez, p. 82). Para Jean Franco, "la identificación sexual es en tal grado determinada socialmente que las escritoras tienden a constituir la subjetividad y a postular las relaciones de poder de modos diferentes que los de los hombres" (Franco, pp. 33-35). Cynthia Steele opina que la escritura femenina desafía las categorías canónicas de lo literario (Steele, p. 2). Los debates en torno a la mera existencia de una escritura generoglósica han quedado atrás. No obstante, la polémica se centra actualmente en torno al problema de la *modalidad* escriptural de la mujer y de la perspectiva que la crítica debería adoptar ante ella. Rosaura Sánchez, Sara Castro-Klarén (vía Baym) y Hernán Vidal proponen la superación de la tendencia de ciertas escritoras y críticas a definir la modalidad generoglósica femenina desde una perspectiva dominada por la negación freudiana. Se refieren a la asociación de lo femenino con la histeria y la locura, brujas y figuras demoníacas, así como diversos desplazamientos de la carencia (*manque*) lacaniana y derridiana: "ausencia", "silencio", "lo reprimido". En términos generales, esos autores critican la tendencia que asocia lo femenino a la metáfora *espacial* con lo Otro, lo ajeno y marginal, tendencia que guarda estrecha relación con la escuela francesa ("ginesis").[36]

Pienso que esa escuela ha cumplido una importante misión, y que, en este sentido, concuerda con algunos objetivos de las vanguardias literarias; me refiero a la labor resemantizadora y sobre todo revaloradora que esa crítica ha realizado frente a las tácticas excluyentes del discurso hegemónico. A un nivel hermenéutico, no es coincidencia que haya sido en gran medida el trabajo feminista ginético el que haya creado mayor problematización frente al lenguaje como proceso de producción en el que a) el sentido es comunicado tanto por lo que se dice como por lo que se calla; b) el sentido opera no sólo en función de estructuras conscientes, sino inconscientes (impacto indudable de Freud y del psicoanálisis); c) el sujeto es descentralizado; d) lo "extra" lingüístico es vector de la comunicación (intencionalidad, estimación, valor y no sólo aspecto constructivos del sentido).

Por otra parte, la desconstrucción del poder como estructura reificada y ahistórica ("eje", "centro", "objeto") cuenta entre sus mejores exponentes con críticos de la escuela francesa, tales como Michel Foucault y Deleuze-Guattari, sin los cuales la relativización de los criterios de norma, valor, saber y desear hubiese sido más lenta y menos difundida. Si se asume que la aversión a las "desviaciones" constituye aún un serio problema tanto en las sociedades avanzadas como en el Tercer Mundo, se verá en qué medida una crítica dirigida a desmantelar las bases del dogmatismo en el saber y en el valorar tiene todavía mucho terreno por desbrozar.[37] Después de todo, las bases *reales* (objetivas y subjetivas) para la histerización de la mujer y la satanización de las diferencias están dolorosamente presentes y son a diario producidas y reproducidas por las prácticas hegemónicas discursivas y no discursivas.

Una crítica feminista autogestionadora puede rescatar lo avanzado hasta ahora por la escuela francesa en torno al poder y seguir problematizando las implicaciones que pueda tener un concepto más desreificado del Estado para la mujer-persona dentro de un contexto culturalista (histórico y social) que en el caso latinoamericano dé cuenta del colonialismo y del neocolonialismo. Se dice que Freud realizó la "revolución copérnica" de destronizar al yo. De las corrientes autogestionadoras de la actualidad podría decirse que intentan realizar la "revolución copér-

nica" de destronizar el concepto reificado del Estado (Edipo
en el lenguaje de Deleuze-Guattari), último dios de occidente. Uno de los más serios aportes de esta escuela es haber modelado un concepto de poder tan fluído que ya no es
posible volver a concebir al Estado como algo que "está allá
afuera". Asumir que *todos* constituímos una red macro y
microfísica de *relaciones* hegemónicas de la cual no "se
salva" ni la mujer, ni el indígena ni el poblador de las fa-
velas o chabolas, es empezar a trabajar *desde ese otro lado*
que proponía Marta Traba. Ni centro ni márgenes: cuerpos
sociales, funciones, agentes, instituciones, todos atravesados por deseos, voluntades e intereses de poder.

Es común que lo contestatario preceda a los planteamientos contrahegemónicos necesarios para los grandes
momentos de transformación. La constitución de todo un
objeto de estudio (escritura femenina) implica para nosotras pasar por la instancia necesaria del diálogo, cuyos
desafíos exigen refinar los propios métodos de análisis. En
el saber, el peor problema no es errar sino callar (o mono-
logar que es lo mismo). Los errores son productivos y necesarios, sobre todo en la medida en que, expuestos al dialogismo de la sociedad civil, estos se vean convertidos en
material de futura y colectiva productividad. La instancia
de la ontologización de lo femenino ha sido quizás el desvío necesario precisamente para la etapa constitutiva del
objeto de nuestro quehacer crítico. Actualmente, se abren
posibilidades interpretativas más históricas, dirección en la
que parecen apuntar la ginocrítica y varios estudios de esta
colección de ensayos, en especial los análisis de Cristina
Dupláa, Susan Kirkpatrick, Francine Masiello, Cynthia
Steele, Doris Sommer y Constance A. Sullivan.[38] Se puede
aplicar un criterio histórico para entender el momento de
la crítica que estuvo dominado por el discurso de la represión. A nivel de la propia escritura femenina, he tratado
de demostrar en otros estudios que la textualización de la
histeria, tan común a la etapa sufragista en el Cono Sur
implica una internalización del espacio asignado a la mujer en el psicoanálisis. Imposible exigirle a las escritoras de
los años 30 que propusieran alternativas contrahegemónicas y autogestionadoras como las que surgirán posterior-

mente con Amparo Dávila, Rosario Castellanos, Nancy
Morejón, Marta Traba, Silvia Molloy, Diamela Eltit, Isabel
Allende, Elena Poniatowska, Violeta Parra, Rigoberta
Menchú o Domitila Barrios.

En términos generales, podría decirse que la crítica feminista de la "carencia" y la negación freudiana ha quedado interpelada muy de cerca por la concepción un tanto
unilateral del poder como *res* bi-unívoca y excluyente,
descuidándose dos aspectos importantes: a) que el Patriarcado burgués no sólo excluye o margina, sino que simultáneamente crea estratagemas neutralizadores y asimila-
dores; b) que históricamente, el Estado burgués ha pasado
por tácticas represivo-victorianas frente a la sexualidad
femenina (estadio del "no"), pero que a partir de los 60, ha
promovido la era de la incitación a lo polimórfico-sexual,
con lo cual el cuerpo de la mujer ha tendido a convertirse
en objeto de *consumo* de placeres (estadio del "sí").[39] El
poder no sólo actúa como una red de prohibiciones, sino
también con estratagemas seductores. Esto último se ha
descuidado mucho al hacer una lectura eurocentrista de la
situación de la mujer en América Latina. Se llega a suponer que la poca tendencia a emplear tácticas "permisivas"
por parte de los estados latinoamericanos constituye un
marcador del menor grado de liberación de la mujer. Una
tarea importante de la crítica feminista latinoamericana es
entender la relación sexualidad-trabajo fuera de los marcos
objetalistas de las sociedades de consumo.

Leer las prácticas femeninas (literarias o no) más allá de
lo sintomático es empezar a trabajar con la mujer como
sujeto plural y autogestionador (mujer-persona). Ver solamente sus vacíos, interrupciones, ausencias y carencias
es ver aún con los ojos de Edipo, para quien la mujer será
siempre Echo (reproductora de las voces de Narciso).
Cuando Virginia Woolf insistía en el "espacio" femenino,
ya se ponía en marcha el marco productivo que he intentado configurar en este ensayo. Crear "cuartos" para la
mujer es asumir la capacidad generadora y transformadora
que como personas tenemos; sobre todo si por "cuartos"
entendemos también signos, discursos, prácticas,
instituciones. Frente a lo hegemónico, una actitud

productiva: resemantizar los textos usurpados, reapropiarse de los espacios allanados. Sobre todo no internalizar la marginalización.

Francine Masiello lleva a cabo una arqueología de las operaciones dislocadoras de algunas escritoras frente al liberalismo argentino del siglo 19.[40] Para realizar esa labor, la crítica ha debido ir más allá de los límites que el propio liberalismo ha impuesto a los términos nación/pueblo, civilización/barbarie, y sobre todo al binarismo entre esfera privada/esfera pública. Para Masiello, es precisamente dentro del marco de restricciones domésticas que la mujer "ha dejado su marca en la sociedad. Claramente excluída de la actividad pública, ella cultivó el espacio del hogar [...] Las mujeres *se tomaron* estas leyendas de la domesticidad para *crear un espacio productivo propio*" (Masiello, p. 527; traducción y subrayado míos). Las afirmaciones auto-gestionadoras se multiplican. Se redescubre el pluralismo cultural de Gorriti (Masiello, p. 550), se escucha el "aire polifónico" de Teresa de la Parra[41], se comprueba que "la Avellaneda [compartió] con el esclavo al borde de la rebelión una *función productiva*" (Sommer, "No hay", p. 21); se relee dentro del positivismo, un desconocido "juego de [...] *combinaciones creativas*" mediante el cual la escritora del pasado llevaba a cabo su propia labor de poner "en tela de juicio la noción de auto-ridad" (Sommer, "No hay", p. 18); se redefinen y reorganiman los cánones literarios[42].

Marta Traba alcanzó a ver con mucha lucidez que los aportes de la mujer a la escritura implicaban seriamente el cuestionamiento de los postulados de la escritura fetichista de occidente. Insistió en la comunidad de valores que existía entre su propia escritura (*Homérica Latina y Conversación al Sur*) y la de los textos testimoniales frente a: a) la importancia de lo metonímico sobre lo metafórico, b) el recurso de la explicación y la autoexplicación más que el de la interpretación o la representación clásica, c) la "continua intromisión de la esfera de la realidad en el plano de las ficciones, lo cual tiende a empobrecer y a eliminar la metáfora y acortar notablemente la distancia entre significante y significado" d) la deuda del relato femenino al "relato popular" y las "estructuras de la oralidad"; característica "expansiva" que orienta la escritura hacia "afuera" (historia y público receptor) y que la dota de una tendencia a las "repeticiones, los remates precisos, los cortes aclaratorios", la "memorización" (Traba, p. 11). Por otra parte, Doris Sommer demuestra la validez crítica de un modelo heterogéneo de lo literario al revelar en qué medida no es sólo la autor-idad y la escritura fetiche lo que los testimonios cuestionan, sino el propio concepto del sujeto singular de la autobiografía, pilar de la construcción subjetiva de occidente (Sommer, "Not Just...", p. 1-13).

A pesar que en la práctica los estudios como los que acabo de citar involucran una nueva modalidad analítica que incorpora el estudio de las literaturas femeninas dentro de los marcos generales de las literaturas heterogéneas y del modelo bajtiniano del dialogismo, se hace cada vez más urgente una elaboración teórica que plantee las conexiones entre la heteroglosia, la generoglosia y el dialogismo de forma sistemática y rigurosa.[43] Al mismo tiempo, dada la diversidad de condiciones en las que la mujer actúa, escribe e imagina en América Latina y en los países occidentales, parecería más adecuado operar con un concepto pluralista de *literaturas femeninas* que con el modelo esencialista de *escritura femenina*, heredado de la escuela francesa.

Al parecer, la realidad latinoamericana sorprendió una vez más a la crítica al ofrecer el vasto mapa de textos testimoniales que conocemos hoy en día. La escritura femenina ha venido produciendo mucho más de lo que la propia crítica ha sido capaz de abarcar. No obstante, a la importante tarea de salir a rescatar la producción femenina del pasado tal vez debamos sumar la labor de constituir una crítica feminista de la literatura capaz de aceptar el desafío de desfetichizarse. Sólo un quehacer orientado hacia los problemas reales y surgido al calor del debate intelectual que de ellos emana puede aspirar a convertirse en práctica mínimamente autentificadora y transformadora. Responder a la creciente literatura de mujeres latinoamericanas implica una labor igualmente autogestionadora de parte de la crítica: cuestionar y

modificar sustancialmente sus bases para conocer y
valorar, sus artefactos interpretativos, su modo de
insertarse en la realidad social. Atravesadas como están
nuestras prácticas por el reticulado de fuerzas conflictivas
de poder, nuestra crítica más eficaz será aquélla capaz de
orientar la producción femenina imaginativa y simbólica
no meramente hacia otra orilla, tampoco solamente hacia
la ardua labor dislocadora, sino en la dirección de otro
juego de fuerzas, otra organización cultural, otra
modalidad estatal.

NOTAS

[1] Gayatri Chakravorty Spivak, *In Other Worlds. Essays in Cultural
Politics* (New York y Londres: Methuen, 1987), pp. 45 y ss; 80 y ss. Las
citas incluídas en el texto provienen de esta edición.

[2] Lucía Guerra es una de las portavoces de esta crítica. Ver, "Las sombras
de la escritura: hacia una teoría de la producción literaria de la mujer
latinoamericana", en esta colección. Ver, Enrique Dussel, *La producción
teórica de Marx* (México: Siglo XXI). Sobre la importancia de la
categoría de la producción y su relación con el Edipo, la ideología, el
deseo y la escritura, ver Deleuze-Guattari, *El Anti-Edipo. Capitalismo
y Esquizofrenia* (Barcelona: Seix Barral, 1974).

[3] Sara Castro Karén, "La crítica literaria feminista y la escritora en
América Latina", en *La sartén por el mango*, ... Citada por Hernán
Vidal en "La crítica literaria feminista hispanoamericana como
problemática de defensa de los derechos humanos. Argumento en apoyo
de una arquetipificación universalista", en esta colección.

[4] *Women in Latin America: An Anthology from Latin American
Perspectives* (Riverside, California: Latin American Perspectives,
1979).

[5] Lévi-Strauss, *Elementary Structures of Kinship* (Boston:Beacon Press,
1969, p. 116).

[6] Rosaura Sánchez, "Feminine Discourse in Chicano Literature", en esta
colección.

[7] Engels, F., *El origen de la familia, la propiedad privada y el Estado*, en C. Marx y F. Engels, *Obras escogidas* (Moscú: Editorial Progreso, t. III, 1972), p. 221. El debate en torno a Engels tiene una extensísima bibliografía. Consultar, entre otros, Gayle Rubin, "The traffic in women: notes on the 'political economy' of sex", en Rayna R. Reiter, comp., *Toward an Anthropology of Women* (N.Y.: Monthly Review Press, 1975); Karen Sacks, "Engels revisitado: las mujeres, la organización de la producción y la propiedad privada", en Olivia Harris y Kate Young, comps., *Antropología y feminismo* (Barcelona: Anagrama, 1979); Wally Seccombe, "El trabajo doméstico en el modo de producción capitalista", en *El ama de casa bajo el capitalismo* (Barcelona: Anagrama, 1975); Heidi Hartmann, "Un matrimonio mal avenido: hacia una unión más progresiva entre marxismo y feminismo", *Zona abierta*, 24 (1980); Ludolfo Paramio, "Lo que todo marxista vulgar debe saber sobre feminismo" en *Nuevas perspectivas sobre la mujer. Actas de las primeras jornadas de investigación interdisciplinaria* (Madrid: Jornadas de Investigación Interdisciplinaria, vol. 2, 1982), pp. 171-179.

[8] Ernesto Cardenal, "el estrecho dudoso", *Poesía* (La Habana: Casa de las Américas, 1979), pp. 127-128; citado por Margaret Randall, "Introducción" en *Todas estamos despiertas. Testimonios de la mujer nicaragüense hoy* (México: Siglo XXI, 1980), pp. 11-12.

[9] Jean Franco, "Apuntes sobre la crítica feminista y la literatura hispanoamericana", *Hispamérica* 15, 45 (1986), p.35.

[10] Elena Caffarena, Olga Poblete, et al, comps., MEMCH: *Antología para una historia del movimiento femenino en Chile* (Santiago: Ediciones Minga, 1984; segunda edición), pp. 1-12.

[11] Lee, R.B. y Devore I, *Man, the Hunter* (Chicago: Aldine Publishing Company, 1969), p. 33. Ver además, Goodale, J. "Tiwi Wives: a Study of the Women of Melville Island, North Australia", *American Ethnological Society*, 51 (1971), p. 72.

[12] Rigoberta Menchú, *Me llamo Rigoberta Menchú y así me nació la conciencia*, Elizabeth Burgos, comp., (Barcelona: Argos Vergara, 1983).

[13] Barbara Wertheimer, *We Were There: The Story of Working Women in America* (New York: Pantheon Books, 1977).

[14] Gerda Lerner, editor, *Black Women in White America: A Documentary History* (New York: Pantheon Books, 1972); E. Franklin Frazier, *The Negro Family in the United States* (Chicago: University of Chicago Press, 1969); Herbert Gutman, *The Black Family in Slavery and*

Freedom, 1750-1925 (New York: Pantheon Books, 1976); Angela Davis, *Women, Race and Class* (New York: Vintage Books, 1983).

[15] Sara Castro-Klarén advierte contra las fusiones del feminismo y el vanguardismo en la crítica desconstruccionista. Aun cuando creo en la importancia de aislar el objeto de estudio en una instancia del proceso de desarrollo de la ciencia feminista de la literatura, cabe notar que es precisamente durante este movimiento que se empiezan a sentar las bases de una imaginación contestataria de la cultura hegemónica de occidente, tanto en lo que respecta al eurocentrismo como al falologocentrismo. Al mismo tiempo, Castro-Klarén cita el rechazo que Baym expresa por la misoginia de la teoría a partir de la asociación mujer=locura. Si tomamos la sin-razón como un indicador de los límites internos del saber, se hace útil discutir la constitución que cada episteme hace de de la "locura" a fin de apreciar la ideología en su productividad y anti-productividad, en sus locuciones y silencios, en la correlación entre estrategias asimiladoras y excluyentes. Desconstruir un aparato ideológico como el patriarcado implica entonces desmantelar, entre otras, la relación entre cordura y locura, puesto que está estrechamente relacionada a la relación genérico-sexual. Ver Michel Foucault, *Historia de la locura en la época clásica* (México: Fondo de Cultura Económica, 2 vols., primera edición en español, 1967); *Vigilar y castigar* (México: Siglo XXI, 1975).

[16] Deleuze-Guattari, *op. cit.*, p.13.

[17] Una crítica tan severa del freudismo como lo es Nancy Chodorow reconoce que "Psychoanalitic theory remains the most coherent, convincing theory of personality development available for an understanding of fundamental aspects of the psychology of women in our society, in spite of its biases", *The Reproduction of Mothering, Psychoanalysis and the Sociology of Gender* (Berkeley, Los Angeles, London: University of California Press, 1978), p. 142.

[18] Rosario Ferré, "El coloquio de las perras". Trabajo presentado en la conferencia de Minneapolis pero no incluído en esta colección.

[19] Elizabeth Ordóñez, "The Problematical Permutations of Feminist Theory", p. 89, en esta colección.

[20] El Saffar, Ruth. *The Evolution of Psyche Under Empire: Literary Reflections of Spain in the Sixteenth Century*, en esta colección.

[21] Constance A. Sullivan, "Constructing, Deconstructing, and Reaffirming Concepts of Gender: Three Gendered Discourses of Pre-Capitalist

Spain", p. 2; traducción mía. Trabajo presentado en la conferencia de Minneapolis pero no incluído en esta colección.

22 Teresa Vilarós, "Maternidad, economía y poder en el matrimonio burgués del siglo XIX: el ejemplo de *Fortunata y Jacinta*", en esta colección.

23 Michel Foucault, *History of Sexuality*, Robert Hurley, transl. (New York: Vintage Books, vol. I, 1980).

24 Julia Kristeva, *Desire in Language. A Semiotic Approach to Literature and Art;* trad. Thomas Gora, Alice Jadine, Leon S. Roudiez (Oxford: Basil Blackwell, 1980). Ver también, Julia Kristeva, "Herética del amor", *Escandalar* 6, 1-2 (1983), pp. 68-79; p. 68. Las citas incluídas en el texto refieren a "Herética del amor".

25 Sheila Rowbotham, "The trouble with 'patriarchy'," en *People's History and Socialist Theory*, compilado por Raphael Samuel (Londres: Routledge y Kegan Paul Ltd., 1981), pp. 364-369; citado por Rosaura Sánchez, "Feminine Discourse in Chicano Literature", p. 3.

26 Marta Traba, "Hipótesis sobre una escritura diferente", *Quimera* 13, 9-11 (1981), pp. 9-11.

27 Una de las más connotadas exponentes de esta corriente es Lidia Falcón, *Mujer y sociedad* (Barcelona: Editorial Fontanella, 1969).

28 El concepto de autogestión surge en América Latina a partir del acento en la organización masiva desde la base. Creo que es un concepto profundamente arraigado a los lineamientos de Paulo Freire. Ver, Paulo Freire, *La educación como práctica de la libertad* (México: Siglo XXI, 29a edición, 1982).

29 Refiero sobre este tema al excelente libro que editó Margaret Randall, *Todas estamos despiertas. Testimonios de la mujer nicaragüense hoy* (México: Siglo XXI, pra. edición, 1980). Ver allí la introducción de la crítica en las páginas 11-38.

30 Lucía Guerra-Cunningham trata el problema de la mujer y el lenguaje incorporando las tesis de María Jesús Buxó Rey, *Antropología de la mujer. Cognición, Lengua e Ideología Cultural* (Barcelona: Promoción Cultural S.A., 1978).

31 Helena Araújo, "Narrativa femenina latinoamericana", *Hispamérica* año XI, 32 (1982), pp. 23-24. Citado por Lucía Guerra-Cunningham.

32 "¿Escritura femenina?", *Escandalar* 4, 3 (1981), pp. 32-36, p. 35.

33 C. Clément y H. Cixous, *La jeune née* (Paris: INEDIT, 1975), pp. 22 y ss.

34 Dora Kanoussi, *Mujer, locura y sociedad* (Puebla, México: Universidad Autónoma de Puebla, 1985), p. 18.

35 Juliet Mitchell, "Femininity, Narrative and Psychoanalysis", en *Feminist Literary Theory. A Reader*, Mary Eagleton, comp. (Oxford, UK: Basil Blackwell, 1986) p. 103.

36 Ver en esta colección: Sara Castro-Klarén, Rosaura Sánchez, Hernán Vidal.

37 Ver en esta colección: Amy Kaminsky, "Lesbian Cartographies: Body, Text, and Geography".

38 La ginocrítica—de orientación histórica—trabaja con la escritura femenina tal como ésta se da en la práctica, intentando definir su especificidad lingüística, generoglósica y literaria dentro de los marcos de raza, nacionalidad y clase. Ver: Elaine Showalter, "Woman's Time, Woman's Space; Writing the History of Feminist Criticism," en *Feminist Issues in Literary Scholarship*, Shari Benstock, comp., (Bloomington, Indiana: Indiana University Press, 1987), p. 37. Citado por Sara Castro-Klarén, p. 3.

39 Michel Foucault, *History of Sexuality, op. cit.*

40 Francine Masiello, "Between Civilization and Barbarism: Women, Family, and Literary Culture in Mid-Nineteenth Century Argentina", en esta colección.

41 Doris Sommer, "'No hay que tener razón': Mamá Blanca y el lenguaje femenino". Trabajo presentado en la conferencia de Minneapolis pero no incluído en esta colección.

42 Imposible entrar aquí en detalle en las seminales implicaciones que la literatura testimonial tiene para una definición autogestionadora de la escritura femenina. Refiero al lector a los trabajos de Doris Sommer, "'Not Just a Personal Story': Women's *Testimonios* and the Plural Self" y Cynthia Steele, "Committed Feminism and Feminist Commitment in the Criticism of Latin American Literature" (ambos presentados en la conferencia de Minneapolis pero no incluídos en esta colección) y a un nú-

mero entero que *Latin American Perspectives* ha dedicado a la literatura testimonial y que está actualmente en prensa.

[43] Sobre las literaturas heterogéneas, ver: Mario Cornejo Polar, *Sobre literatura y crítica latinoamericana* (Caracas: Universidad Central de Venezuela, 1982); César Fernández Moreno (ed.): *América Latina en su literatura* (México: Unesco-Siglo XXI, 1972), pp. 367 y ss.; Carlos Rincón, "Para un plano de batalla por una nueva crítica en Latinoamérica", Casa de las Américas, No. 67 (1971) y "Sobre crítica e historia de la literatura hoy en Latinoamérica", *Casa de las Américas*, No. 80 (1973), del mismo autor; Roberto Fernández Retamar, "Para una teoría de la literatura hispanoamericana", *Casa de las Américas*, No. 80 (1973) y "Algunos problemas teóricos de la literatura hispanoamericana", *Revista de Crítica Literaria Latinoamericana*, No. 1 (Lima, 1975); Noé Jitrik, *Producción literaria y producción social* (Buenos Aires: Sudamericana, 1975); Angel Rama, "Sistema literario y sistema social en Hispanoamérica, *Literatura y praxis social en América Latina* (Caracas: Monte Avila, 1974); Nelson Osorio, "Las ideologías y los estudios de la literatura hispanoamericana", *Casa de las Américas*, No. 94 (1976).

Notes After Words: Looking Forward Retrospectively at Translation and (Hispanic and Luso-Brazilian) Feminist Criticism

Carol Maier
Bradley University

I

> Diversity in cultural and political backround guaranteed that there would be moments of tension or discomfort at Sisterfire.... participants were reminded now and then that coalition-building is a process, not a safely accomplished fact.
>
> Rina Ycount, "Diverse Artists Play with 'Fire' "

Ever following the words of another, her work often acknowledged as an afterthought, the translator seems to be always a step behind, a shadow or perhaps a reflection—faithful only when she is clever enough to turn an inevitable infidelity to her advantage. At times I am even convinced that the very verb of her activity announces (determines?) her position of perpetual tardiness and compromise, makes her something of a Janus whose work progresses just to the extent that she captures an experience already lived and repeated. Not only does she look forward by looking back, she looks back in advance, aware that a certain nostalgia will accompany the rush of satisfaction occasioned by even the greatest of her successes, since to wrest one translation from the many possible (even correct) ones is to turn others into resonances, echoes. On the other hand—and hence the allure of her flip, ever flipping side—, so much delay also implies that although she may never be on time, immersed *in* time she can only be fully present: as she runs to bring up the rear, she thinks avidly and articulately of the future, of a restatement soon to be verbalized.

Clearly a slippery, complex state of exhilaration and discomfort, that state of belated foresight is also the one that comes to mind when I look back to the three days in Minneapolis and reflect on the importance translation might have for the "cultural-historical grounding" of work in Hispanic and Luso-Brazilian feminist literary criticism. Translation was scarcely mentioned in the sessions, but it was in my thoughts throughout the conference, and I was acutely aware of its absence. No doubt this owed to both my work as a translator and my place in the conference. I had agreed to serve as a discussant for one session, and as chance would have it, that session was the final one. This and the fact that two of the three papers were not available before the conference meant that I would spend a good part of the time looking ahead to what would, hopefully, be a session in which the discussion returned to the preceding days and entertained them in terms of the future.

Even though I knew they would most likely prove inappropriate when the time came, I had written some contents about the paper I did have, Rosaura Sánchez's "Feminine Discourse in Chicana Literature." This was an attempt to be prepared and "on time", but it was also an effort to make certain that if work by Latina writers had not been addressed before, it would at least be discussed with respect to Sánchez's essay. It troubled me that even at a feminist conference Latinas seemed to suffer what, following the Sara Castro-Klarén ("La crítica literaria" 43) might be called a triple (or perhaps even a quadruple) negativity—as women, as mestizas or Latin Americans, as Latinas, and then again as members of the individual ethnic groups within that term. Sánchez's comments about the multiplicity of Chicana "voices and subjectivities" as represented in the stories of Helena María Viramontes (8) warn against this kind of conflation and against an *abrazo* that welcomes the Other only by refusing difference, through fusion rather than coalition. She is not, of course, the first feminist to issue such a warning,[1] but her comments struck me as particularly apt for the conference, where I felt sure the Latinas were included implicitly, but where they were none the less virtually invisible in their "different strategies of acquiescence and rebellion." [2]

When I wrote my remarks before the conference, my intention was to question that invisibility and some of the implications for feminists, taking as point of departure my work as critic and translator of the poetry of Ana Castillo. That work—based as it has been of necessity—on a very careful reading,[3] had led me to experience in terms of language itself some of the difficulties inherent in what might be read as the challenge of Sánchez's essay: to join with the Chicana in "her struggle to be heard" without reducing either *Chicana* or *struggle*, and to bear in mind constantly that comprised in both words is a "network of interacting signifying practices" (339-340). I had planned to note several instances in Viramontes's stories where as a reader I tripped on what impressed me as some unintentional inconsistencies or breaks in her use of written language and to move from those instances to a consideration of that role of a sympathetic, highly "literate" critic with respect to published work that reveals uncertainty about or even unfamiliarity with writing.[4] My translation of Ana's poems and the scrutiny of her language it demanded had given rise to considerable correspondence between us about precisely this issue, and I remembered that repeatedly—and at times painfully— my effort to understand Ana's poetry and make it available in English (an effort she welcomed) was also a violation. In other words, for me to catch (up to) her poems, it was necessary to work in her place. I did that within a mutual respect, even perhaps a certain affection, but both Ana and I were constantly aware that when I spoke as Ana I was clearly assuming her "I" (her disguise or subjectivity) as a disguise.[5] Affinity was challenged continually by the fact that my very efforts to get that poetic subjectivity down "right" were a wronging, for they exposed (even threatened to unravel) its seams and revealed my own determination to pen an independent poem in English—a "good" translation.

Although prior to reading the conference papers I had not verbalized my work with Ana in those terms and it had been some time since I completed the translations of her poems, as I read the papers and listened to the discussions, I returned to my interaction with her. In particular, I thought about the informal pact we established for the purpose of giving voice in English to the part of her work she wrote in Spanish (not so much, of course, a pact between Carol and Ana as between poet and translator or between speaking subjects). I recalled the pact as a friendly, yet cautious strategy, a coalition of two. In its space, Ana's place, which was now also mine, I worked with her, instead of her, despite her, not because we were fused but because—for the task of translation—we agreed that one voice would speak for us both. As this sense of coalition became clearer, or, rather as I was able to speculate about translation as a possibly noncombative struggle occurring within a compact (agreement, small container), a construction analogous to the familiar attempt at a tantalizing present, I wondered if it would not also be possible to see it as analogous to "la metáfora de una organización alternativa" proposed in the essay by Lucía Guerra Cunningham, the "space for struggle between centripetal and centrifugal forces" Castro-Klarén suggests when, referring to Foucault and Bakhtin, she calls for the opening of "unified, closed concepts" (105), or even something of Gloria Anzaldúa's border strategies. Finally, I began to think of ways in which translation as a site of transformation might participate in the analogies that formed under my ballpoint during a long exchange (involving, if I remember correctly, the papers of Teresa Vilarós, Guadalupe Gómez Ferrer, Susan Kirkpatrick, and Alda Blanco) about women assuming new, radically different identities as they trade the needle for the pen, or wield both at the same time. I could not but think of that trade as an accession to a complex, even dangerous space where the possibility of creating new guises[6] is concomitant in either Spanish or English with the risks and limits of representation itself. For example, both pens and *plumas* are also held by men, who—in what is often considered a less than masculine occupation—are also free to reconstruct themselves however they wish. In the margin of my notebook the situation took shape as follows:

needle: pen: :pen: sword   aguja: pluma: :pluma: espada

As I made those drawings and mentally superimposed, so to speak, various spaces, I realized that I was running the risk of oversimplification and neutralization being dicussed at the conference. I also realized that my representation of spaces of coalition as spaces of translation and writing engaged words to a degree that many of the conversations seemed to resist. It was as if all the participants were aware that attention to language would unleash the *puma* or *púa* hidden in the plumage that offered the way out of a trap; it would pen us up, tangle, paralyze us, perhaps, in some tricky twist of the tongue. We (work, coalition) would be held back, slowed down, late. Or, in words more reminiscent of the conference, the waters would be muddied.

Seen from the perspective of progress, such a derailment is exactly what occurred in the final session, when the most heated and lengthy discussion was not about space and strategies but about the need for a critic (or translator) to learn to read a foreign literature (in this case Chicana literature) on its own terms without unthinkingly imposing the values and expectations of her own culture. That conversation, pursued to its limits, might have led to a discussion about translation and its links to writing and literary criticism. Because of time constraints, however, issues like the following, which are crucial for Hispanic and Luso-Brazilian studies, as well as integral to issues of feminism, were left unexplored or even unmentioned: the need for translation of work by women; the role of women in publication, marketing, and reviewing of work in translation;[7] the ways in which history and culture bear (or do not bear) on the practice of translation; the integration of both translation (as practice) and of translation into language and literature classes, especially, perhaps, in women's studies classes; the relation between translation and gender, in particular with respect to Hispanic, Luso-Brazilian, and North American cultures.[8]

My initial response, when I reviewed that last discussion and thought of translation and of literature by Latinas, was one of disappointment because it seemed that little had been accomplished. As I thought about it further, however, I realized that the conversation had been a provocative one and that, albeit indirectly, there had been consideration of the fact that, as a penned activity, translation both gives and silences voice. The other issues, while of no less importance, are readily accessible. That bond of double voicing, however, is often not seen at all, for the translator's gesture of generosity, her enthusiastic embrace, tends to mask—despite the continual representation translation as a struggle, a conquest, or even a murder—that gesture's inherently rapacious nature.[9]   Although a generalized acknowledgement is often made of something "lost", the appearance of an author in translation is received by and large as a reasonable likeness, which resembles only faintly a nearly invisible translator, and does not seriously compromise the integrity of the translated work. Curiously enough, then, at least to judge from conversation at the conference and elsewhere, even the increased and widely disseminated assertions of the originality of translations as copies have not occasioned much discussion about the substantive alteration of an "original" when it undergoes translation. What is stressed, even by "progressive" readers, is increased availability, no matter that for many works, translation involves passage to a culture, a language, even a relation to language and literacy so different that only in the most general of ways can it be said that translation makes their world "available". In such situations, where the disjuncture between cultures is extreme, to ignore the phenomenon of translation and the dual presence of translator and author is not to acknowledge the alterations a translator makes to get a work to fit into her language. It is also to deny the poet a distinctiveness that resists absorption by another culture.

The paradox is even more stubborn, and it bears restatement in this context despite the familiarity of the translator's struggle with faithful infidelity; to try for a duplication that resembles the original poet is, most likely, to have an awkward, naïve version rather than a vital new work; to recreate the aesthetic "sense" of the original is to risk resemblance, i.e. the "identity" of the original. In the case of the Chicana writer, to continue with my example, who both aspires to recognition within the North American literary tradition and affirms her ties to an essentially oral culture, the dilemma for the translator may be even greater: does she strive for an English that matches hers, one that reflects the Spanish of the original (even if that Spanish is "unlettered" and may result in a halting English less fluent than the poet's own—the Chicana poet is indeed likely to speak English even though she prefers to write in Spanish, the language in which she works instinctively—)[10], or a compromise English that sounds like the poet but has been edited, standardized? And what to make of the possibility that once the initial difficulties of translation are surmounted, the translated work might seem to be out of step with or even contradictory to the world into which it has been inserted? Is the translation complete if no one stops, risks lateness long enough to listen, to build further on the coalition it represents?

None of those questions is "rhetorical," and to answer them in practice as a translator is to engage in the issues of evaluation and cultural sensitivity discussed at the conference. It is also to realize that to refuse to entertain the complexities of translation, either by subsuming the poet in the translator's voice (arrogance or excess aggression) or by giving her too strong a voice of her own (excess compassion) is to render her speechless and invisible in the new language. Finally, it is to evade what might be the greatest challenge of translation: the struggle with the paradoxes of verbal identity, the acknowledgement of translation's double drive to welcome and wipe out, and the singular, dynamic way in which it can contain two worlds.

II

El Sueño

Ana Castillo, *My Father Was a Toltec*

Lucía
mi traje zapoteco
un huipil
rojo
rojo
color de sangre
brillante
alumbrante
del sol
oaxqueño
más suave
que los pétalos
de la flor
macizo
como los nopales viejos
que adornan
la sierra
dulce
como el maguey
caliente como el
mezcal.

Lucía mi huipil colorado
por las calles
de una ciudad
tan orgullosa
tan fuerte
que no sentí
el primer golpe
del rechazo.

The Dream

1	2
I was radiant	i was radiant
wearing my Zapotecan	wearing my Zapotecan
dress	dress
a red	a red
red	red
huipil	*huipil*
color of Zapotecan	color of Zapotecan
blood	blood
sparkling	sparkling
gleaming	gleaming
with sun	with sun
from Oaxaca	from Oaxcaca
softer	softer
than petals	than petals
on a flower	on a flower
sturdy	sturdy
like the old nopals	like the old nopals
that adorn	that adorn
the sierra	the sierra
sweet	sweet
like the maguey	like the maguey
fiery like	fiery like
mescal.	mescal.
I was radiant	i was radiant
wearing my scarlet *huipil*	wearing my scarlet *huipil*
through the streets	through the streets
of a city	of a city
too proud	too proud
too strong	too strong
to feel	to feel
the first slap	the first slap
of rejection.	of rejection.

3

i was radiant
wearing my Zapotecan
  dress
a red
red
huipil
color of Zapotecan
blood
sparkling
gleaming
with sun
from Oaxaca
softer
than petals
on a flower
sturdy
like the old nopals
that adorn
the sierra
sweet
like the maguey
fiery like
mescal.

I was radiant
wearing my scarlet *huipil*
through the streets
of a city
too proud
too strong
to feel
the first slap
of rejection.

4

I was radiant
wearing my Zapotecan
  dress
a red
red
huipil
color of Zapotecan
blood
sparkling
gleaming
with sun
from Oaxaca
softer
than petals
on a flower
sturdy
like the old nopals
that adorn
the sierra
sweet
like the maguey
fiery like
mescal.

i was radiant
wearing my scarlet *huipil*
through the streets
of a city
too proud
too strong
to feel
the first slap
of rejection.

5
Radiant,
wearing my Zapotecan
    dress
a red
red
huipil
color of Zapotecan
blood
sparkling
gleaming
with sun
from Oaxaca
softer
than petals
on a flower
sturdy
like the old nopals
that adorn
the sierra
sweet
like the maguey
fiery like
mescal.

Radiant, wearing
my scarlet *huipil*
through the streets
of a city
too proud
too strong
to feel
the first slap
of rejection.

III

...para el indígena es bastante doloroso que un ladino
use la ropa indígena.

Rigoberta Menchú, *Me llamo Rigoberta Menchú y así
me nació la conciencia*

At about the same time as the conference in Minneapolis I read Rigoberta Menchú's book for an inter-
disciplinary course about Central America taught with a
colleague in history. Because some of the students were
working in English, we spent considerable time discussing
both the translation and the role of Elizabeth Burgos as
Menchú's first translator and editor. The discussions were
arresting for me; as a translator who has worked primarily
with texts written by men, I was accustomed to thinking of
the space (or time) of the translation as one in which I
often wished to recover voices excised by the original
speaker, one in which I felt uncomfortable or even
unwilling as a reader. To consider the rapport between
Burgos and Menchú was a challenge, because it led me to
question what I had more or less accepted as a paradigm
for translation and to see its reverse as I recognized rather
suddenly how without intending to do so Burgos
threatened Menchú. Not only did she identify herself as
the author of the book,[11]   she eliminated the dialogue
between the two women, preferring instead a first person
narrative. Although it is totally clear to the reader that the
speaker is Menchú and not Burgos, Burgos also makes it
clear that Menchú's Spanish has been corrected so as to
keep it from seeming "folklórico" (18). What is more, and
this is where I began to question the nature of the
collaboration between "translator" and writer, she
assumed Menchú's "I." As she smelled and ate the
tortillas and beans Menchú prepared during their work
together, she was returned to her childhood in Venezuela
(13), and she recovered a lost self: "Ella me ha permitido
descubrir ese otro yo-misma. Gracias a ella mi yo
americano ha dejado de ser 'una extrañeza inquietante'"
(18). In the next paragraph, and in the way Burgos closes

her introduction, she quotes several lines of a poem by Miguel Angel Asturias, which *she* dedicates to *Menchú.*

The problems of translation could hardly be more patent: in order for Menchú to tell her story and have Burgos translate it into appropriate Spanish, the two agree to share the space of the pen. Closed up together for eight days, they eat the same food and apparently wear some of the same plumage (the cover of the English edition has a photograph of Burgos in a shawl—not a *huipil* like Menchú's, but definitely an indigenous-looking wrap). That Menchú feels both endangered by and grateful to Burgos is evident; she refers repeatedly to secrets she will not reveal, yet after they separate she sends Burgos a tape of some important information they did not discuss. In fact, as John Beverley explains in a discussion that recognizes thoroughly the contradiction inherent in the relationship between the two women (14-15), Menchú seems to view her work with Burgos as a strategy, employed as apart of a larger, collective struggle (shared by Burgos only indirectly). This use of Burgos may not be "callous," but neither is it naïve, for she knows that her will to survive is matched (or even surpassed) by Burgos's determination to get her story into written Spanish and— not incidentally—to save herself.[12]

Quite similar, I could not but think, to my work with Ana Castillo and my speculation about translation, tardiness, and coalition. Our project, which comprised some dozen poems, had been far less extensive and it involved only written—as opposed to oral and written—material, but we grappled with the same issues of language and culture faced by Burgos and Menchú. As if to remind me of those issues and of my numerous conversations with other Anglo critics about our work with Latina writers, a small indigenous doll sits on my shelf, a present Ana sent me after one of her trips to Mexico. I have always liked it because it suggests for me Ana's ambivalent relationship to Mexico and to Spanish and my own thoughts about why I—and other Anglo women—have been so attracted to the work of Latinas. [13] In fact, even as I write that, I think unexpectedly of the winter afternoon about ten years ago when I first saw Ana. After several phone calls and letters, we had agreed to meet in downtown Chicago, in a rather neutral space, on the corner of Randolph and Michigan. No *huipil*, but so I could identify her, Ana had described herself as a woman with an indigenous face. We went for coffee and began, cautiously, to talk about her work and the possibility of doing some work together. [14]

Although I did not plan it as a new meeting with Ana, after the conference in Minneapolis and the class discussions about Burgos and Mechú, I returned to my translations of Ana's poems, several of which had been published not long before in *The Renewal of the Vision: Voices of Latin American Women Poets 1940–1980* , an anthology edited by Marjorie Agosin and Cola Franzen. Several years had elapsed between submission of the poems and their appearance in print, and although I had looked at them on various occasions, I had not given them a truly fresh reading for some time. It was a surprise to me, then, to see the process of translation as coalition-building operative (and perhaps less operative than I would have liked) in my own work. That "seeing" occurred with the first word of "The Dream," the first of six poems in the anthology. It was the word "I", and when I read it, I stopped short. It was capitalized, something that seemed impossible because ever since I have known Ana she has referred to herself in English using the lower case "i." I finished reading the poem. There were other changes I wanted to make, especially a word or two that seemed weak or incorrect, but they were changes of the kind one expects to want after a good amount of time has passed. The "I" was different, however, and it struck me as either an important error or a misjudgment—unless for this poem, Ana and I had decided to make an exception and I had forgotten. A look back through our correspondence showed me that we had not even discussed "El sueño," except for a note on my part about my thoughts on the verb *lucir* and how I felt it could be best conveyed in English. Nothing about the "I" or the effect that its capitalization might have on the poem, since the pronoun is not used or needed in Spanish.

After reading "The Dream" and "El sueño" several times, I quickly roughed out a new translation, making some changes in word choice and arrangement and using the small "i." At first it seemed more appropriate, but the more I read it, the more it also looked quaint or gimmicky, an impression that was confirmed when I reread the other poems in which I had used the "i." I felt they were more faithful translations, but I also found them to be less "successful" poems in English, and I suspected they would be received with the tolerant smile awarded to Ana by even one Chicano critic who declared the "i" trivial.[15]   I thought of Burgos's efforts to keep Menchú from seeming "folklórico," and I wondered if that was the reason I had decided to use the upper case letter in "The Dream." I also thought of what I have referred to as our coalition and of how Ana, or her poem, is inevitably a compromise in either version, of how that first person pronoun—even when added sensitively—*is* an addition, and as such, an intrusion, a violation. Despite my affection for Ana or my admiration for her poem, then, I cannot effect a thorough disguise by slipping into her *huipil*; it may be a perfect fit, but I will still be visible, my well-intentioned first person silencing her expression of anonymous confidence, her pronoun-less activity. A "bind" for us both that the poem itself seems to anticipate, a situation in which even a gesture of affection amounts to a slap of rejection.

I also thought of the ways in which choices and paradoxes faced by an individual translator when she works with one poem are magnified in the case of an entire volume and how well they are exemplified in *The Renewal of a Vision*. To my way of thinking, the anthology makes an important contribution because, confronted by severe page limitations, Agosin and Franzen managed to assemble a collection of poems that is truly "Latin American." Not only did they include work from Central and South America originally written in Spanish, the book also offers poems from Brazil and from the United States written in Spanish and English. It is a broad spectrum, and it hints at a plurality of which most North Americans are unaware. Unfortunately, however, at the same time it also smothers plurality because the book is not bilingual and the poems are totally dependent on their English versions. This omission could certainly be defended,[16] especially in the context of constraints of budget and space, but the trade–off remains for both poets and editors. Moreover, and this is important to mention here although it deals only indirectly with the translation of the poems, in the case of the latter, the trade–off is part of a much larger "work space" in which poets are selected (to chose some is to refuse others) and books are published. This is a space governed by both taste and history—or by their interaction—, one in which insofar as most anthologists (and among them I would include Agosin and Franzen in spite of their many very good choices and their will to honest eclecticism) seem to work more naïvely than guardedly or defiantly. With respect to publication and distribution, anthologists may or may not have more perspective, but in this arena choices are likely to be fewer. Although Spivak is not doubt correct about a "ravenous hunger for Third World literary texts in English translation" that exists at present ("A Literary Representation" 253), publishers' willingness to take risks with writing by Latin American women can hardly be described with such superlatives. [17] With few exceptions, translation projects of women writers are undertaken with low budgets, printed in limited editions, reviewed for and accessible to a limited number of readers. All in all, hardly a warm welcome for a work coming into English, perhaps even a complex "rejection" not unlike that in Ana's poem.

Which returns me to "The Dream" and my own determination to write an acceptable poem in English that will also convey its strong experience of identity with a non–specified subject. Well aware, at this point, that the task is "impossible," since English offers no equivalent for such a relation between verb and subject, I determine that there are five possible versions,[18] each of which provides both English and Spanish with some degree of satisfaction. The first, to translate the entire poem using and upper case "I," is to opt for the most "natural" version in English, to write an easily recognizable poem and one that will enable readers to identify with the speaker (quite a few readers of my published version have in fact "liked" this poem). The feeling of "smallness" that gave rise to the use of the "i" is sacrificed, but even if it had been used, many readers might not have read the poem. Indeed they might have refused to read the poem precisely because of the "i"—a refusal that makes my second version far less likely to prove successful.

The third and fourth versions no doubt also lessen the poem's ability to "speak" to an English reader because they both depend on an interpretation—if not a full acceptance— of the lower case "i." Of the two, it is hard to know which is more appropriate. If the poem is read as an experience of awakening that can give rise to the formation of an identity (whether the city in the dream is in Mexico or the United States),[19] the better translation would suggest the move from "i" to "I," thereby suggesting as well the "mestiza way toward a new consciousness" described by Anzaldúa: "She [the mestiza] learns to transform the small "I" into the total self" (83). I cannot but think as I read Anzaldúa's sentence, however, that Ana might represent the same transformation with a reverse movement of the pronouns, since for her the lower case has always indicated a collective use of the first person. She uses the upper case when she does not use the persona, in other words when she speaks only as an individual.[20] Following this explanation, it seems to me that the speaker in "El sueño" moves from a feeling of individual confidence and pleasure to an awareness of collectivity: her "I" is shaken as she is forced to assume the "i." This expanded use of the small letter, despite its correspondence to the resiliant plurality called for by Anzaldúa, is one I do not believe Ana would capitalize: better to risk charges of triviality than an inflated sense of self.

What of the fifth translation, where the self is removed entirely from the poem so it can be read in English without a nominative first person? My first reaction is that I have finally managed to convey the Spanish; the possessive "my" makes it clear that the speaker is referring to herself. Several readings, however, convince me that this version may in fact be the least satisfactory, for it eliminates the action from the poem, the wearing—which is itself a verb less strong than *lucir*—, and it lessens the impact of the rejection because nothing can "happen" in such a largely descriptive context. What is more, and perhaps more importantly, to translate without the pronouns is to distort their "absence" in Spanish, rendering something that is present in the verb as something missing—and thereby removing not only the pronoun but diminishing the verb as well.

That fifth translation, then, is less acceptable than the others, and if I were forced to choose just one (a choice I strongly prefer to resist), it would have to be one of the first four. Which of the other four, is of course the dilemma, although at this moment I believe I would have to revise my comments above and state that version two is—arguably— the closest to "El sueño" for two reasons: (1) I am not certain that the transformation suggested in versions three and four is actually suggested in the Spanish, at least not to the degree indicated by either combination of pronouns; (2) Ana seems to be using her persona here. The fact that the lower case will jeopardize the poem's reading in English troubles me, but not overly, because I know Ana is willing to take that risk when she writes in English herself. To translate her work so as to protect her from criticism might gain more readers, but I suspect it would also sidestep the challenge of coalition and lateness that has concerned me in these notes.

Why do I say that? Because I suspect that for me as an Anglo to translate Ana's poems and be as fair as possible to both languages is to accept a "lateness" in English that includes more than the time involved in thinking through numerous versions and perspectives. This second delay is a real one, and I do not wish to minimize the importance for either the intensity of the experience or the speed of my work. On the other hand, I also believe that the first lateness is even more crucial because it involves a compromise on the part of the English speaker in the poem who, if she is willing to accept the same pen or *pluma* as the Chicana (and not just hide in the exotic plumage of the Other), may well have to assume a lower case as part of the collaboration. In the most immediate sense, this refers to a specific instance, but I suspect it also involves a willingness to consider the *use* of the small "i" as a practice that is not trivial and *ingenua*. In other words, it involves the recognition of a "lower case" poetics as a serious strategy that consciously employs "triviality," even though it is a form that the translator herself would not otherwise use—as either writer or translator. The "i" was not, for example, my first choice for "The Dream," and I know it will probably not result in the best English if that English is judged by conventional standards. On the other hand, I believe it may well be the best translation of the poem's—and the poet's—poetics if I am willing to accept the poet a a women whose word is capable of orienting its own (and my) translation.[21]

That is a strong, potentially polemical statement for the translator, and as I write it and think about concluding this essay, I realize that it was made with both conviction and questioning. I wonder what its implications will be for further work, and I think of several comments I have read recently by women who are willing to jeopardize what might be considered "correctness" in an effort to have a translation truly contain two worlds.[22] I think of Chamberlain's call for a new paradigm that might offer a less combative but no less problematic practice (472), and I suspect, as she does, that such a paradigm cannot be offered as "feminist" without its being utopic or essentialist. I also suspect, and I have not found this confronted thoroughly, that (like the "lateness" noted above) the formulation of such a paradigm will involve much more of a delay than the time required to articulate it. The actual work of translation has not traditionally been either discussed or carried out as a cooperative activity, and an exploration of it as "double–edged" (Chamberlain 470) may give some feminists unwelcome pause. My thought, however, is that practice is not necessarily undermined by consideration or even revision (as several feminist critics have recently pointed out in somewhat different—and quite varied—contexts).[23] With respect to translation, it seems too soon for conclusions.[24] What the suggestion of coalitions or multiple versions and of a lateness that spans past and future does indicate clearly, however, is that a willingness to slow down, to look at the lower case from altered perspectives and attempt a more inclusive translation will not retard feminist activity but expand and develop it more fully.

NOTES

[1] See, for example, Mohanty and Lazreg.

[2] It is only fair to note here my participation in this omission, since I had not been able to prepare a paper and had therefore not acted before the conference to insure discussion of translation and writing by Latinas. It should also be noted that in her spoken comments for the final session (given in lieu of a paper and titled "Gender and Social Formations: Feminist Frontiers"), Kathleen Newman spoke at some length about Gloria Anzaldúa's *Borderlands/La Frontera*.

[3] As Diana Vélez has recently pointed out so well, the work of translation "involves change, increased subtlety of understanding, and an awareness of the dialogue in which we are engaged whenever we enter into that intimate relationship called reading. For translation is *the act of reading taken one step beyond*, to that space where two languages, two cultures and various subjectivities intersect and play" (20). (Emphasis mine)

[4] I am thinking here, not without irony, of Ong's discussion of literacy and the relation of what he refers to as the "Chicano subculture" (160) to an increasingly literate society. I am also thinking of Cherríe Moraga's comments to Mirtha Quintanales about what Quintanales terms Moraga's struggle "around Spanish," and I am taking Moraga's comments literally—which is no way to detract from her published work. (Quite the contrary, as Ana Castillo also suggests in her review of Moraga's *Loving in the War Years*.)

[5] For a discussion of the "I-slot" following Foucault, see Gayatri Chakravorty Spivak ("A Literary Representation..." 242–34). Although Patai is not working with translation per se, I find her comments relevant here (both articles), and I believe they can be

helpful in the formation of the altered paradigm for translation discussed below.

6 *Guise* as in *garb*, but in addition as (historically) in *manner* or *way*. Hence, the possible suggestion of the genres and genders that are also constructed in the space of writing.

7 With respect to writing by Hispanic and Luso–Brazilian women, this role is being recognized and filled increasingly by presses like Cleis (Pittsburgh), Spinsters/Aunt Lute (San Francisco), and Seal (Seattle).

8 As explained below, that "relation" is more one of question than definition. See Lori Chamberlain and Jill Levine. I also find pertinent here Zöe Anglesey's suggestion of a specific linking between gender and the practice of translation, in her introduction to *Ixok Amar.Go* : "I sought poets to translate because I trusted their willingness to recreate poems and knowing also they would be sensitive to obsolete masculinized language that excludes rather than includes. They did not translate generic 'hombre' into 'men' or 'hijos' into 'sons' when the terms meant people and children" (xxix). This topic needs much further discussion; Anglesey's decision, for example (and her trust of poets), could be challenged—as well as defended—by feminists, although Frank Graziano's concern with gender as he translated poems by Alejandra Pizarnik (5) would seem to bear her out.

9 In addition to Chamberlain, who discusses this representation fully, see Paul Mann's trenchant comments about the "darker current of intercultural betrayals that flows through all translation practice" (7) and Myriam Díaz Diocaretz's detailed description of her translations of Adrienne Rich's poems into Spanish (especially chapter 3, "Translation of a Women's Poetic Discourse").

10 As indicated above (note 4), Chicanas have spoken and written poignantly and eloquently about this phenomenon. In addition to Moraga's comments, see, for example, Ana Castillo's "Everywhere I go," "Daddy With Chesterfields in a Rolled Up Sleeve," and "A Christmas Gift for the President of the United States, Chicano Poets, and a Marxist or Two I've Known in my Time" (*My Father was a Toltec*) and Lorna Dee Cervantes's "Refugee Ship" and "Oaxaca, 1974" (*Emplumada*).

11 This "erasure" is also noted by Rosemary Feal (and I am grateful to her for the opportunity to read her paper) in her discussion of the genre of *Me llamo Rigoberta Menchú*...(2). As Feal points out, in the English version Menchú is credited as the book's author.

12 Feal is also aware of what she terms a "tension" between "ethnobiographer" and "interlocutor"(3–4). In "'Not just...," Doris Sommer, on the other hand (114-115), accepts Burgos's version as an "apparently more direct transcription" (in comparison with Elena Poniatowska's *Hasta no verte Jesús mío* and Miguel Barnet's *Biografía de un cimarrón*), although she acknowledges both the need for "socially responsible writers in Latin America have had to come to terms with their unrepresentativeness" (113) and a "tension in the testimonial 'I'" (123). In "Can the Subaltern Speak?," Spivak write extensively about the assimilation of the Other by the "investigating subject" that is able to "disguise itself in transparency" (394). Indeed, what she refers to as a "masculine radicalism that renders the place of the invesigator transparent" (395) seems very close to the dangers of the pen described above. See also her "Imperialism and Sexual Difference."

13 Daphne Patai ("Ethical Problems") discusses some of the painful contradictions of intercultural work. Anglos are not, of course, the only readers to ask that question, as Tey Diana Rebolledo's article demonstrates.

14 Ana's distrust of academics glimpsed in "Not Just Because My Husband Said" *(Women Are Not Roses)* and "In My Country" *(My Father Was a Toltec)* arose, as she explains in her interview with Binder, in "discouragement I received from my white instructors" in the Chicago Public School System (20). That discouragement was in art; it led Ana to write poetry but also to refrain from seeking direction from any "structured source."

15 See Paredes 127. I am indebted to Rebolledo's article for referring me to Paredes's review.

16 Borges, for example spoke emphatically against bilingual editions because they "work against the translator," who is led "to a more literal version" by a fear of the inevitable comparison between original and translation (51).

17 As recently as 26 June 1987, for example, Herbert Bailey, Jr., director emeritus of the Princeton University Press was quoted as saying that in the future University Presses "may steer almost entirely away from books on topics for which markets are especially small—Latin American studies, for example" ("Footnotes"). One can only imagine what such a trend would mean for work by Latin American women writers. For a discussion of the historical and political ups and downs of

Latin American literature in translation, see Castro–Klarén and Campos.

18 Needless to say, five is a somewhat arbitrary number, which I have purposely limited because of constraints of time and space. If, to cite just one instance—but one pertinent to the first person pronoun—, the last stanza is translated differently and the pronoun is used to translate *sentí*, additional variants of the "I" are possible. All of the versions reflect several small changes Ana made in the poem for its publication in *My Father Was a Toltec*.

19 This absence of a specified place enriches the poem. Although the dream could well occur in Chicago ("the 'belly' of the shark," according to Ana [Binder 34] and where she lived for a long time), the speaker could also have a similar experience in Mexico. Thinking of that possibility, it is interesting to read Cervantes's "Oaxaca, 1974".

20 I am surprised that Binder did not ask Ana about the "i" in his interview, which is quite thorough and provides a good introduction to Ana's work. She and I have discussed this in person and in writing, and I base my statements on those discussions and on my readings of her poems.

21 Here I am alluding to the collection of Evangelina Vigil. Needless to say, this acceptance does not necessarily mean agreement. On the contrary, a translator—like a critic—may have serious reservations about a particular strategy, but—accepting it as a strategy—, she will take issue with it, rather than dismiss it outright or "overlook" it (a patronizing response that is perhaps more offensive than dismissal).

22 I am thinking here of Díaz–Diocaretz's discussion of her work with Adrienne Rich's poems and of Margaret Sayers Peden's explanation of George Steiner's "backward reach" demanded of a translator who, Peden believes, must translate the poetry of Sor Juana Inés de la Cruz using meter and verse: "The baroque cannot come to us. We must go to the baroque; we must attempt to recreate it by means of that backward reach... While I am obviously not capable of perfectly recreating Sor Juana's verse, I believe that the greater service is to make the attempt *within the conceptual framework of her art*" (9). (Emphasis added.)

23 See, to cite just several examples (whose authors are drawn into this "coalition" by my pen), the recent work by Alcoff, Patai ("Ethical Problems"), Schweickart, Scott, and Weedon. Also: any discussion of lateness and translation will benefit from a reading of Caw's article.

24 The "unfinished" nature of these notes is apparent. Perhaps the biggest question or issue they raise is whether or not (or to what extent) the victory of a "good" or a complete translation requires a defeat—the conquest or death of the original. In other words, can translation occur without mortal combat, or does the word *coalition* harbor some inevitably unsatisfying limbo between languages that is not clearly located in one tongue or another—nor in an appropriate, tantalizing way on the border between them? See, for example, J. David Danielson's accurate but awkward attempt to provoke a "bilingual encounter" in his recent translation of Horacio Quiroga's stories.

Also of interest here: Monique Bosco's comments in the "Roundtable on Translation" included in Jacques Derrida's *The Ear and the Other* (and the way in which they were not fully addressed); Spivak's "Displacement and the Discourse of Women"; the articles by Maggie Humm and Nicole Ward Jouve; and Levine's comments on "Traduttora Traditora," her work with Guillermo Cabrera Infante and Severo Sarduy, and subversion as an integral element of translation.

WORKS CITED

Agosin, Marjorie and Cola Franzen, ed. *The Renewal of the Vision: Voices of Latin American Women Poets 1940–1980.* Cambridge, UK: Spectacular Diseases, 1987.

Alcoff, Linda. "Cultural Feminism Versus Post-Structuralism: The Identity Crisis in Feminist Theory". *Signs* 13 (1988): 405-36.

Anglesey, Zöe, ed. *Ixok Amar.Go: Central American Women's Poetry for Peace.* Penobscot, MA: Granite Press, 1987.

Anzaldúa, Gloria. *Borderlands/La Frontera.* San Francisco: Spinsters/Aunt Lute, 1987.

Beverley, John. "Anatomía del testimonio". *Revista de Crítica Literaria Latino–americana* 25 (1987): 7–16.

Binder, Wolfgang, ed. *Partial Autobiographies: Interviews with Twenty Chicano Poets.* Erlangen: Verlag Palm and Enke Erlangen, 1985.

Blanco, Alda. "Domesticity, Education and the Woman Writer: Spain 1850–1880," included in this collection.

Borges, Jorge Luis. *Twenty-Four Conversations With Borges: Interviews by Roberto Alifano 1981–1983. Including a Selection of Poems.* Ed. Roberto Alifano. Trans. Nicomedes Suárez Araúz, Willis Barnstone, Jorge Luis Borges, Noemí Escandell. Housatonic, MA: Lascaux Publishers, 1984.

Burgos, Elizabeth. *Me llamo Rigoberta Menchú y así me nació la conciencia.* 2ª ed. Mexico: Siglo Veintiuno, 1986.

Castillo, Ana. *My Father Was a Toltec.* Novato, CA: West End Press, 1988.

—. "Rev. of *Loving in the War Years: lo que nunca pasó por sus labios,*" by Cherríe Moraga". *Third Woman* 3.1+2 (1986): 137–38.

—. *Women Are Not Roses.* Houston, TX: Arte Público Press, 1984.

Castro Klarén, Sara. "The Novelness of a Possible Poetics for Women," included in this collection.

—. "La crítica literaria feminista y la escritora en America Latina". *La sartén por el mango: Encuentro de escritoras latinoamericanas.* Ed.

Patricia Elena González y Elena Ortega. San Juan, PR: Ediciones Huracán, 1984. 27–46.

Castro–Klarén y Hector Campos. "Traducciones, tirajes, ventas, estrellas: El 'Boom'". *Ideologies and Literature*, 4 (1983): 319–38.

Caws, Mary Ann. "Literal or Liberal: Translating Perception." *Critical Inquiry* 13 (1986): 49–63.

Cervantes, Lorna Dee. *Emplumada.* Pittsburgh: U Pittsburgh Press, 1981.

Chamberlain, Lori. "Gender and the Metaphorics of Translation." *Signs* 13 (1988):454–72.

Derrida, Jacques. *The Ear and the Other: Otobiography, Transference, Translation.* Ed. Christie V. McDonald. Trans. Peggy Kamuf. New York: Schocken Books, 1985.

Díaz–Diocaretz, Myriam. *Translating Poetic Discourse: Questions On Feminist Strategies in Adrienne Rich.* Philadelphia: John Benjamins, 1985.

Feal, Rosemary Geisdorfer. *Spanish American Ethnography and the Slave Narrative Tradition: Biografía de un cimarrón and Me llamo Rigoberta Menchú.* Feministas Unidas. MLA Convention. San Francisco, 28 December 1987. Forthcoming in *Modern Language Studies* (1989).

—."Footnotes". *The Chronicle of Higher Education.* 26 June, 1987: 4.

Gómez–Ferrer, Guadalupe. "Mentalidad, vida cotidiana y literatura. Las actitudes femeninas socializadas en la novela española de la restauración," included in this collection.

Graziano, Frank. "Editor's Note". *Alejandra Pizarnik: A Profile.* Ed. Frank Graziano. Trans. Maria Rosa Fort and Frank Graziano, with additional trans. by Suzanne Jill Levine. Durango, CO: Logbridge-Rhodes, 1987.

Guerra-Cunningham, Lucía. "Las sombras de la escritura: Hacia una teoría de la producción literaria de la mujer latinoamericana," included in this collection.

Humm, Maggie. "Translation as Survival: Zora Neale Hurston and *La Malinche.* " *Fiction International,* 17.2 (1987): 120–29.

Kirkpatrick, Susan. "The Female Tradition in Nineteenth–Century Spanish Literature," included in this collection.

Lazreg, Marnia. "Feminism And Difference: The Perils of Writing as a Woman on Women in Algeria," *Feminist Studies* 14.1 (1988): 81–107.

Levine, Suzanne Jill. "Translation as (Sub)version: On Translating Infante's *Inferno.* " *Substance* 42 (1983): 85–94.

Mann, Paul. "Translating Zukovsky's Catullus." *Translation Review* 21–22 (1986): 3–9.

Menchú, Rigoberta. *I, Rigoberta Menchú: An Indian Woman in Guatemala.* Ed. Elizabeth Burgos. Trans. Ann Wright. London: New Left–Verso, 1984.

Mohanty, Chandra Talpade. "Feminist Encounters: Locating the Politics of Experience." *Copyright* 1 (1987): 30–44.

—. "Under Western Eyes: Feminist Scholarship and Colonial Discourses." *boundry* 2 12+13 (1984):333–59.

Ong, Walter J. *Orality and Literacy: The Technologizing of the Word.* 1982. New York: Methuen, 1985.

Paredes, Raymund A. "Review Essay: Recent Chicano Writing." *Rocky Mountain Review of Language and Literature* 41.1+2 (1987): 124–28.

Patai, Daphne. "Constructing a Self: A Brazilian Life Story." *Feminist Studies* 14.1 (1988): 143–66.

—. "Ethical Problems of Personal Narratives." *International Journal of Oral History* 8.1 (1987): 5–27.

Peden, Margaret Sayers. "Introduction." *Sor Juana Inés de la Cruz: Poems.* Trans. Margaret Sayers Peden. Binghamton, NY: Bilingual Press/Editorial Bilingüe, 1985. 1–9.

Poovey, Mary. "Feminism and Deconstruction." *Feminist Studies* 14.1 (1988): 51–65.

Quintanales, Mirtha. "Loving in the War Years: An Interview with Cherrié Moraga." *off our backs,* January 1985:12–13.

Quiroga, Horacio. *The Exiles and other Stories.* Ed. and trans. J. David Danielson, with Elsa K. Gambarini. Austin, TX: U Texas Press, 1987.

Rebolledo, Tey Diana. *The Politics of Poetics: Or, What Am I, A Critic, Doing in This Text Anyhow?* Chicana Creativity and Criticism: Charting New Frontiers in American Literature. Ed. María Hererra–Sobek and Helena María Viramontes. Spec. issue The Americas Review 15.3+4 (1987): 129–38.

Sánchez, Rosaura. "Feminine Discourse in Chicano Literature," included in this collection.

Schweickart, Patrocinio P. "Reading Ourselves: Toward a Feminist Theory of Reading." *Gender and Reading: Essays on Readers, Texts, and Contexts* Ed. Elizabeth A. Flynn and Patrocinio P. Schweickart. Baltimore, MD: Johns Hopkins U Press, 1986. 31–62.

Scott, Joan W. "Deconstructing Equality–Versus–Difference: Or, the Uses of Poststructuralist Theory of Feminism." *Feminist Studies* 14.1 (1988): 33–50.

Sommer, Doris. "'Not Just a Personal Story': Women's Testimonios and the Plural Self." *Life/Lines: Theorizing Women's Autobiography.* Ed. Bella Brodzki and Celeste Schenck. Ithaca, NY: Cornell U Press, 1988. 107-30.

Spivak, Gayatri Chakravorty. "Can the Subaltern Speak?" *Marxism and the Interpretation of Culture.* Ed. Cary Nelson and Lawrence Grossberg. Urbana and Chicago: U Illinois Press, 1988. 271–313.

—. "Displacement and the Discourse of Women." *Displacement: Derrida and After.* Ed. Mark Krupnick, 1983. 169–95.

—. "Imperialism and Sexual Difference." *The Current in Criticism: Essays on the Present and Future of Literary Criticism.* Ed. Clayton Koelb and Virgil Lokke. West Lafayette, IN: Purdue U Press, 1987. 319–37.

—. "A Literary Representation of the Subaltern." *In Other Worlds: Essays in Cultural Politics.* New York: Methuen, 1987. 240–68.

Vélez, Diana, ed. and trans. *Reclaiming Medusa: Short Stories by Contemporary Puerto Rican Women.* San Francisco: Spinsters/Aunt Lute, 1988.

Vigil, Evangelina, ed. "Woman and her Word: Hispanic Women Write." Spec. issue *Revista Chicano–Riqueña* 11.3+4 (1983).

Vilarós, Teresa. "Maternidad, economía y poder en el matrimonio burgués del siglo XIX: el ejemplo de *Fortunata y Jacinta*," included in this collection.

Viramontes, Helena María. *The Moths and Other Stories*. Houston, TX: Arte Público, 1985.

Ward Jouve, Nicole. "'Her Legs Bestrid the Channel': Writing in Two Languages." *Women's Writing: A Challenge to Theory*. Ed. Moira Monteith . New York: St. Martin's, 1986. 34–53.

Weedon, Chris. *Feminist Practice and Poststructuralist Theory*. Oxford: Basil Blackwell, 1987.

Yount, Rena. "Diverse Artists Play with 'Fire'." *The Guardian*. 20 July 1988: 24.